COMPREHENSIVE SRIMAD BHAGAVAD GEETA

(A Critique in Sociology of Religion)

COMPREHENSIVE SRIMAD BHAGAVAD GEETA

(A Critique in Sociology of Religion)

J P SINGH

Professor of Sociology (Retd.)

Patna University, Patna

KALPAZ

ISBN : 978-93-532-4048-6

First Published, 2019

Published by

Kalpaz Publications
C-30, Satyawati Nagar,
Delhi – 110052
Ph.: 011-47034999, 9811692060
www.kalpazpublications.com
E-mail: kalpaz@hotmail.com

Printed at: G. Print Process, Delhi

Dedicated to

Peace, Prosperity and Brotherhood of Mankind

CONTENTS

PART- I
THE INTRODUCTION

PART- II
TEXT, TRANSLATION AND COMMENTS

PART- III
APPENDICES, REFERENCES AND GLOSSARY

Preface and Acknowledgements

The Srimad Bhagavad Geeta has drawn the attention of a wide range of scholars across the world. But different scholars have presented same facts in different ways because of obvious differences in their perspective. Most commentators have gone beyond the usual meaning of the given verse in the praise of Lord Krishna. Some have treated the Geeta as a piece of pure Bhakti literature, while others have written on it to express and propagate their own views for their own reasons. Yet others have tried to be too abstract and pedantic, as if the Geeta is a compendium of philosophical lectures meant for a class-room discussion in the Department of Philosophy and Religion. The verses of the Geeta need not to be disentangled from its literal, surface meaning even when read symbolically. Personalized interpretations by many of them have led to diverse commentaries on the Geeta. There are some who have treated the incidence of the Mahabharat as a kind of pure fiction and have argued that the incidence of the Mahabharat takes place within human body. It was not exterior to human mind. Such scholars have treated the Mahabharat as an epic based on fictional facts. Most social scientists have, however, no problem in recognizing the Mahabharat as a historical event, forming a part of India's history. Despite containing certain fictional facts and concocted stories it is not a book of pure imaginary narratives.

The commentators should not lose sight of the situation or the context in which the Geeta was created. Readers must bear in mind that Krishna's precepts were meant for ordinary disciple or devout like Arjun to help him win the war against falsehood and the crafty people. It should be taken as a simple book of spiritualism based on hard realities of life, suggesting what is right or wrong or what is moral or immoral. This great book of Geeta has been created purely in the interests of entire humanity for purposeful, peaceful and righteous living. It is not to be treated as a pure religious scripture or book of fiction. It is a book of righteous life, cutting across the boundaries of all cults and systems of belief. A great work like the Geeta comes into being only when an enlightened person exhorts a worldly person like Arjun who is inclined to learn about the meaning and purpose of life. The Bhagavad Geeta is really a timeless treatise. It does not require any great scholarship to understand it. It requires no more than mere heart-felt devotion to Sri Krishna. Here my effort has been simply to help out the common men and women to understand the precepts of the Geeta enthusiastically. It is not easy, but not impossible either.

The Geeta, in the words of Lars Martin Fosse (**The Bhagavada Gita,** 2007), "is not only a spiritual monument– an essential scripture of Hinduism, recited daily for two millennia and to this very day, whose teachings have spread throughout Asia and around the globe– it is also a literary masterpiece, the linchpin of a great epic of war and peace, honour and disgrace, loyalty and betrayal. It is a book people everywhere in the world return to again and again throughout their lives for insight into the nature of reality." As a work of literature, the epic was immensely important to the cultural life of India and even beyond her shores. The Geeta is, however, not to be treated as a religious treatise. It is the magnum opus of secular philosophy of life, as it neither champions the cause of Hindu religion, nor does it downgrade or relegate any religion or religious philosophy. It has not been composed to eulogize any system of belief. It is a matchless work of its own kind. It is an anthology of spiritual wisdom which guides the individual into the mysteries of self-realization and God-realization. A person who strongly believes in the precept of Sri Krishna or one who has fully understood the teachings of the Geeta is bound to be free from the narrow confines of all religions. Sadly enough, not many people know the distinction between spiritualism and religion. Spiritualism is not ritualism either. A truly spiritual person can never be a sectarian. A man observing the precepts of Geeta is bound to be a human being of very extraordinary kind with stunning success in every walk of life. It is the first book of humanity that has taught us to fight for righteousness. However, it does not mean that it teaches us violence in life. Perform ance of moral duty is no violence. The Geeta is a compendium of spiritual wisdom and the most appropriate guide for living a harmonious life in all respects.

Introducing the Bhagavad Geeta

Over 5,000 years ago Krishna instructed his fickle-minded friend Arjun on the philosophy of human life– its purpose, goal and its attainment. Known as the Bhagavad Geeta, the Song Celestial, it is accepted as the quintessence of all the Vedas. The Geeta is unique because, unlike any other religious scripture, it is believed to be spoken by God (Krishna) Himself.

The Lord speaks the philosophy in the midst of the opposing armies of two closely related families ready to fight a fratricidal war. When Arjun is reluctant to fight against his kith and kin, whom he may have to kill, Krishna tells Arjun that he should not shirk from or ordained duty which, as a Kshatriya, is to fight. While most religions advocate compassion, mercy, forgiveness, and exhort to abjure war and killing, here God Himself urges Arjun to fight and finish the unjust people.

Krishna convinces Arjun of where his duty lies, and the same Arjun who in the beginning refuses to fight now promises to Krishna's bidding. In no other scripture does God so unabashedly glorify Himself. To convince Arjun that He is the master and controller of all that be, Krishna recounts His innumerable *vibhutis* or glories, opulences and powers and shows His *Virat swaroop* or universal form in a brazen display of His majesty and powers. The Geeta jolts us into contemplation when it tells us that we are not the body and mind that we believe we are, and that, in fact, we are pure spirit, soul or *Atman*, a tiny part of God, the Supreme Spirit, and we are eternal, indestructible and immutable. The realization of this basic truth is a pre-requisite to any spiritual progress. This is the Vedantic philosophy of great Adi Shankar.

The Geeta does not propose attainment of heaven and its sense pleasures as the goal of life. Krishna warns that gratification of the senses cannot bring happiness. The Geeta describes the material world as *dukhalayam*, a place full of miseries, wherein birth and death take place in a continuous cyclical fashion. It urges us to liberate ourselves from worldly life and reunite with the Lord and thereby attain to His nature of *Satta-Chitta-Anand*, the state of being eternally existent– completely knowledgeable– full of bliss, which is the goal of human life and which alone can bring real peace and happiness.

To achieve that goal the Geeta elucidates four different paths: *Rajayog* or meditation, *Karmayog* or work, *Gyanayog* or knowledge and *Bhaktiyog* or devotion– from which the aspirant may choose according to his temperament, capacity and inclination. In *Bhaktiyog,* the Geeta makes available to us an easy and effective means to reach the Lord. *Bhaktiyog* requires neither elaborate paraphernalia nor cumbersome rituals, for Krishna says: "If a *bhakta* offers Me with love and devotion, a leaf, a flower, a fruit or a little water, I will wholeheartedly accept it".

The essence of the Geeta is summed up in verses 65 and 66 of Discourse 18 wherein Krishna asks Arjun to abandon all religious practices and simply pay homage to Him, adore Him, worship Him and unconditionally surrender unto Him, after which Arjun need not have fear, for Krishna would absolve him of all his sins and take complete care of him.

The Song of God or the Bhagavad Geeta is unique because it is free from dogma. After explaining the most confidential spiritual knowledge, Lord Krishna tells Arjun that as he has heard everything by now, he should feel free to do whatever he thinks fit and proper in the given situation. In essence, the Geeta recognizes the individual's liberty and leaves the ultimate choice in the hands of the seeker. Liberal and without prejudice, the Bhagavad Geeta is Lord Krishna's gift to humankind, to help us deal with the turbulence of life in as rational a manner as is humanly possible. In a brief discourse, later turned into seven hundred Sanskrit verses by the sage called Vyas, Krishna outlined to Arjun the way to live an entire life so as to gain perfect self-knowledge and self-mastery.

All those born are necessarily human beings, but that does not mean that all human beings are exactly the same. They cannot be the carbon copy of others. But some people can definitely be more special than others. God is never born. Sri Krishna was definitely very special, possibly a super human. The Almighty God could have a special human appearance with some elements of divinity in extraordinary circumstances for exceptional purposes. One must keep this fact in mind, while analysing the Geeta or any other religious scriptures. Similarly the Vedas also are not divine creation. In fact, no scripture is so. They are pure human creation by some people with divine genius.

Let me say a few words on the concept of *Yog* also. The word '*Yog'* in various forms occurs almost one hundred and fifty times in the Geeta. It is a complex term, and allows for a number of different interpretations, all dependent upon the context. In the colophons, Yog means a reflection or meditation upon a given subject. Same as the word *'Guna'*, there is no English equivalent for the word *'Yog'*. The basic meaning is yoke– *Yog* is in fact etymologically related to the English word yoke– but through various metaphorical processes the word came to envelop a much wider semantic field. In the Geeta the word *'Yog'* has a wide range of meanings: path, practice, meditation depending on the context, while a *Yogi* is a master of such path or discipline. It also refers to more specific forms of discipline, such as *Karmayog* (translated as the discipline of action) and *Bhaktiyog* (translated as the discipline of devotion), and to creative or magical power.

The Message— The Geeta had been spoken on a battlefield because life itself is a battle, where evil perpetually attacks good things and our sacred ideals are destined to be tested. We would all be confronted by grave dangers and fearsome demons within and without. There was much to be gained from facing these aggressors with integrity and faith. A serious reader of the Geeta is likely to be struck by the fact as to how powerfully the Geeta reveals the science of self-realization beyond sectarian or historical boundaries. It elucidates such intricacies as, how the soul is related to God, how that changeless soul is affected by the material nature, how *Karma* (the natural law of action and reaction) affects all of us and how the imperceptible influence of time acts on creation. As a lonesome wanderer seeking truth, where danger, temptation and fear could pounce a person at any moment, one finds solace and direction in words of the Geeta. But what is truth is not defined in the Mahabharat anywhere.

Why did Krishna prefer a battlefield to enlighten Arjun? In addition to being a historical fact, the setting of Geeta signifies a deeper conflict within our consciousness. Within every human psyche is a lower self, represented by the Kauravas, who fought against Arjun and his brothers, the Pandavas. There is also a higher self, represented by Arjun and the other Pandavas. The war thus represents a conflict between virtue and vice within our hearts. Arjun's breakdown in the battlefield of Kurukshetra signifies our own bewilderment about right and wrong in the face of intractable perplexity and Krishna's instruction illuminates for us the path of the highest morality based on selfless devotion to God. Arjun's eventual victory after enlightenment represents the potency of the divine wisdom of the Bhagavad Geeta to empower us to ultimately triumph over our lower nature and achieve inner fulfilment in this life and eternal joyful life thereafter.

Although the Bhagavad Geeta is sacred for Indians in general and Hindus in particular, the appreciation of Bhagavad Geeta is not limited to Vedic circles. Many Western scholars have found the Bhagavad Geeta to be amazingly coherent and cogent. Ralph Waldo Emerson's remark is a sample, "It was the first of books; it was as if an empire spake to us, nothing small or unworthy but large, serene, consistent, the voice of an old intelligence in which in another age and climate had pondered and thus disposed of the questions which exercise us."

Commentaries— There are more than 250 commentaries in existence on the Geeta by now. The main commentaries have, however, come from a few devotional genius of ancient and medieval India- Adi Shankaracharya (788-820), a reformer of Hinduism, Ramanujacharya (1017-1137), a Hindu theologian and philosopher, Nimbark (or Nimbaditya) (1130-1200), Madhvacharya (1238-1317) and Vallabhacharya (1479-1531). They were men of very strong views to cast the Geeta in their own ways to suit their religious belief and convictions. Since the Geeta largely conveys the Vedantic philosophy, it is strongly believed that the great Vedantic philosophers like Adi Shankaracharya and Ramanujacharya must have made substantial interpolations into the Geeta to uphold their philosophy. Those days it was not difficult to do so either. Adi Shankar was one of the greatest thinkers of his time so much so that none could ever beat him in any extempore debate and discourse. But Sri Krishna must have conveyed His message to Arjun in pure unambiguous terms in response to his usual worries, questions and queries to dispel the state of crisis and confusion with a view to helping Arjun to behave in a righteous manner. But then why are there so many commentaries on the Geeta? It is unfortunate for the humanity at large that we do not or cannot know which commentary of the Geeta is the most authentic one. It is indeed a million dollar question. In their commentary the most modern day authors have gone far beyond the standard or commonsense meaning of the verses to demonstrate their sky-scraping scholarship of Hindu religion and philosophy.

As several works of translation of the Sanskrit hymns into English by renowned scholars of Sanskrit, English, philosophy and religion are already available, there is no need to make fresh attempt on this subject here. Among numerous others the following books were found to be quite useful– **The Bhagavad Gita: The Lord's Song** by Annie Besant**, Srimad-Bhagavad-Gita** by Swami Swarupananda, **Bhagvadgita** by S. Radhakrishnan, **Bhagavad Gita** by M. W. Burway**, The Song Celestial**: **Srimad Bhagavad**

Gita by Edwin Arnold, **The Bhagavad Gita** by Franklin Edgerton, **The Bhagavad Gita** by Richard Gotshalk, **Bhagavad Gita** by Sri Swami Sivananda,**The Bhagavad-Gita: As It Is** by A. C. Bhaktivedanta Swami Prabhupad, **Gita: The Song Extraordinary** by Damodar Thakur, **Bhagavad Gita: A New Translation** by Stephen Mitchell, **The Bhagavad Gita** by Lars Martin Fosse, **The Bhagavad-gita: The Sacred Song** by Ramananda Prasad and **The Legacy of Yoga in Bhagawad Geeta** by Prabha Duneja. I have heavily depended upon these translations with some modifications. But I have been inclined somewhat more towards the translations by Western scholars, as there appears to be greater objectivity in their translation work. At many places the Indian scholars appear to have been guided by their orthodox Hindu view of life in their translation. However, it is also simultaneously true that many Western scholars have no approval or admiration for Indian philosophy because of their age-old bias Hinduism. Many of them have presented Sri Krishna as an ordinary character of some literary work. Striking a balance between the Western and Indian scholarship here translation has been done verse by verse with the Sanskrit text of the Bhandarkar Oriental Research Institute's critical edition. This makes a handy reference for the Sanskrit scholar. The Bhandarkar Oriental Research Institute's critical edition is considered to be the most authentic work on the Mahabharat. For this reason at some places verses in this book may not closely match with those of other such books on the Geeta.

There are numerous Sanskrit words which have been used as they are in Sanskrit, since their exact English equivalents are not available; for instance, *Yog, Guna, Om, Prakriti, Purush, Sankhya, Sattva, Rajas, Tamas, Dharma, Karma, Sthitapragya, Gyan, Atman*, etc. But my commentary has been developed with little reliance upon other translators and commentators. To be fair, objective and unbiased in interpretation I have not followed anyone of them. I have tried to give primacy to the commonplace or usual meaning of each verse in a coherent manner. At places I have depended on my intuitive perception as a practitioner of social science and Indology. I have always kept historical condition, society and culture of India of that time in mind while translating and analysing the verses. If any word or verse has got two diverse meanings, I have accepted the interpretation which is in harmony with everything else in the Gita, especially with its overall messages as I understand it. Hence, at several places my commentaries tend to differ from those of others. Anyway, the basic text should be read as a guide on how to lead one's life. Additional commentaries, wherever needed, provide practical answers to many of life's concerns. They may satisfy the more ardent spiritual seekers' curiosity regarding the text's more difficult points. For the benefit of readers all the 18 discourses have been preceded by a short summary giving the substance of those discourses in a nutshell.

Some have suggested that one should try to keep in mind the commentaries of certain great philosophers of ancient times like Adi Shankaracharya whose commentary came about in the early 8th century- about 3000 to 3500 years after the Mahabharat war possibly took place. But how can one accept authenticity or originality of interpretation offered by Adi Shankar? He was succeeded by another great commentator like Sri Ramanujacharya. But again there is a gap of about three hundred years between Sri Shankar and Sri Ramanuj and similarly there is a gap of over two centuries between Sri Ramanujacharya and Sri Madhavacharya. Sectarian views of commentators must have influenced the interpretation of the original message of the Geeta. In fact, the Geeta does not exist in its original form. Precisely speaking, the available Geeta is possibly more than the original, as it comprises original plus something else too. Hence, what is indeed important is the gospel of Srimad Bhagavad Geeta.

The Geeta and the West— Quite often the *British* are subjected to criticisms for being colonialists with vested interests, but it is seldom recognized that they have brought India into world focus through the discovery of India's ancient history and heritage. It was during the British Raj that the Geeta first achieved worldwide acclaim. Many educated Indians were struggling to defend Hinduism against the onslaught of the western culture, and gradually the Geeta was found to embody the essential spirit and deepest truths of Hinduism. The Hindu reformer Raja Ram Mohun Roy referred to the Geeta as 'the essence of all *Shastras,*' or the essence of all scriptures. By 1912, C. F. Andrews could claim that the Geeta had become a common and well-read scripture for the whole of educated India.

The Geeta has found a rapt audience in various parts of the West also, and a fascinating global cross-fertilization has followed. It has appealed both to the German Romantics, notably Schlegel, Humboldt and Goethe, and to the American Transcendentalists, a group in New England, who thought that insights which transcended logic and experience would reveal the deepest truths. Ever since the teachings of the Geeta have become known to the people in Europe and America, it has won interests and admiration of millions. Many philosophical and religious groups in foreign countries hold the same respect for the people in India.

The Bhagavad Geeta was first translated into English in the year 1785, by Charles Wilkins, on the orders of the Court of Directors of the East India Company, with special interest shown by Warren Hastings, the then Governor-General of India. This edition had an Introduction to the Geeta by Warren Hastings. Soon the work was translated into other European languages such as German, French and Russian. In the Introduction Lord Warren Hastings prophetically wrote: "The writers of the Indian philosophies will survive when the British Dominion in India shall long have ceased to exist, and when the sources which it yielded of wealth and power are lost to remembrance." He further wrote, "I hesitate not to pronounce the Geeta's performance of great originality, of sublimity of conception, reasoning and diction almost unequalled and a single exception amongst all the known religions of mankind". Now the Geeta is available in all major languages of the world. According to Richard H. Davis, the Bhagavad Geeta has been translated into more than 75 languages worldwide, though the Hindus have not gone outside India to propagate their religion like the Christian missionaries. In English alone over 300 translations have been published. The Geeta is found in every household in India. Literally billions of copies have been handwritten and printed.

Today, the Srimad Bhagavad Geeta is firmly established around the world as a true classic, but not a dusty old classic. It is astonishingly fresh and inspiring, even to readers who do not share the underlying assumptions of the text. Knowledge and self discipline are still virtues. Selflessness is as sound today as it was then. Doing one's duty regardless of consequences is needed now more than ever before. We may not share the Geeta's views on *Varna* system or endorse the social system it once supported, but we don't have to. We are free to choose, and the Geeta offers a number of choices. Its core of universal values and its poetic grandeur makes the Geeta a living classic for all time to come.

A true follower of the Geeta can never be bad tempered or even talkative, let alone be criminal. It teaches us selfless Karma or duty, tolerance, humility and a sense of love and compassion for all. Since some scholars have tried to interpret the verses of the Geeta as if it was a book of mysticism, here every effort is made to give the simplest interpretation of verses to demystify the messages of the Geeta in the larger interest of the readers. It is a book of applied philosophy of life. This has always been kept in mind that Sri Krishna is giving sermons to Arjun to fight for a just cause in a just manner so that darkness may not envelop the earth.

This book has been authored keeping all these facts in view, more particularly the circumstances in which the kind of discourse went on between Lord Krishna and Arjun. I have tried to brush aside the fictional facts, interpolated interpretations and highly abstract or philosophical connotation of verses. The fact which has to be kept in mind that the circumstances in which the Geeta was created was very mundane relating to everyday life in ancient days.

It is pertinent to add here that my prime job herein lies in the plain analysis of different verses of the Bhagavad Geeta for the good of humanity rather than in giving any fresh publicity to Geeta's discourses on spiritualism or religion. Enough has been done through the publication of countless commentaries on the subject. Furthermore, it also does not bother me whether those ideas were really conveyed by Lord Krishna to Arjun which came to Dhritrashtra through Sanjay and then to the people at large through Vyas, the so-called writer or compiler of the Bhagavad Geeta. It is indeed an uphill task for ordinary mortals to ascertain the veracity of who said what to whom or what really transpired between Arjun and Sri Krishna. What is really relevant for us is the essence and implications of all the 18 Discourses.

Significance of Bhagavad Geeta in Modern Life— One may ask what is the use of studying Bhagavad Geeta in the present day? How is it relevant to modern life? And what value does it add to one's life? Here I wish to throw light on how the learning of Geeta is necessary for us to live our life more fruitfully. The Geeta is an incredible book because of its intrinsic value in solving the basic human problems. It shows us a way to live our life effectively. It will continue to bless people of the past, present and posterity, the only thing is that, one has to choose to expose oneself to it. I, therefore, request people of all ages to learn this book of amazing wisdom. Mahatma Gandhi once observed, "When doubts haunt me, when disappointments stare me in the face, and I see not one ray of hope on the horizon, I turn to Bhagavad-gita and find a verse to comfort me; and I immediately begin to smile in the midst of overwhelming sorrow. Those who meditate on the Gita will derive fresh joy and new meanings from it every day."

The perspective followed in this discussion on the Bhagavad Geeta is that it is universal and belongs to all mankind. The Bhagavad Geeta is one of the central teachings of the *Sanatan Dharma*, today often called Hinduism. It has its setting in Indian history, culture and religion of a particular era and with ongoing influences of Indian religious history. While not ignoring these, I see its meaning as being evolutionary beyond the borders of its country of origin. Its applicability has since gone beyond the era in which it was conceived to modern times and has travelled outside of India around the world and through time and place, it has been incorporated into different cultures.

The Bhagavad Geeta was a timeless, universal devotional text that looked beyond all differences and which was understandable and easily practised by the simplest, every common person. As long as individuals do not take the responsibility to make changes in their behaviours, and make better choices, things will not change significantly at a global level. Mahatma Gandhi very rightly said, "Be the change you want to see in others". This point we seem to miss often in responding to many challenges in the world. Bhagavad Geeta enables you to realize your potential to be that person who is mature and responsible, so please don't wait till you are old to study this book that has timeless wisdom.

Caution

A word of caution is necessary here with regard to the use of spelling of certain Indian words, especially of Sanskrit origin. It may here be pointed out that herein all proper nouns have been written in English the way they are pronounced in Sanskrit or Hindi to avoid erroneous pronunciation of Indian words. Unlike English or other European languages we tend to pronounce each letter of a word quite distinctly in Sanskrit as well as in Hindi. It is often noticed that words like Bhim, Mahabharat, Ved, etc., which are written as Bhima, Mahabharata and Veda, are also pronounced as such by the English knowing people. This sounds very ludicrous and comical to the Indian audience. Such pronunciations have developed because the letter 'a' is suffixed at the end of these words, while it was done for making accurate pronunciation of Hindi or Sanskrit words. But in course of time this practice has done more harm than good to pronunciation or spelling of Sanskrit or Hindi words. Blind replication of the English style sounds more like a caricature. Same thing has happened with numerous Hindi words, but as this principle was not followed in the case of Urdu words, Akbar could not become Akbara, Babar could not become Babara or Taj Mahal could not become Taja Mahala so and so forth. In order to get rid of funny pronunciation, letter 'a' at the end of all proper nouns, wherever not necessary for the purpose of proper pronunciation, is dropped so that the readers may pronounce all such Indian words correctly. Similarly for the convenience of general readers words like *'Jnana', 'Yajna' and 'Ahimsa'* have been spelled as *'Gyan', 'Yagya'* and *'Ahinsa'* respectively.

The use of diacritical marks, as often used in philosophical and historical writings, has been consciously avoided for the convenience of general readers. One should also keep in mind a little difference in spelling between 'Brahm' (ब्रह्म) and 'Brahma' (ब्रह्मा). These two words do not mean the same thing, as the former spelling is used to signify the 'Ultimate Reality', while the latter stands for one of the Vedic gods, the originator of all beings. The word 'Gita' has been spelled as 'Geeta' in this book, as this is how this should be written correctly in view of its spelling in Devanagari script (गीता). However, wherever it forms a part of the title of any published work or wherever the word is within quotation marks, the original spelling of 'Gita' has been retained as it was.

Yet another point worth noting here is that most translators or commentators of the Geeta have used such social science terminology as *varna*, caste, family, race, clan, scion, descent, dynasty, kins, self, spirit, tradition, norms, values, rites and rituals as equivalents of certain Sanskrit words liberally, while they have got a very restricted or standardised meaning in social sciences. Liberal use of these words have made rendering of Sanskrit *Shlokas* into English very faulty and confusing. In Sociology and Anthropology these words have got a very precise and specific meaning. They must be used very carefully to appreciate and express the message of the Geeta in a proper perspective across varied kinds of readers. The knowledge of English language alone is not enough for translation of such a literary work, having pure social and cultural contexts. The contextual background of a given word has its own importance in translation work from one language to another, especially when the two languages represent two diverse socio-cultural set-ups. In order to make the Geeta easily comprehensible by the general readers, verses have been translated following the prose style. I, however, have taken care to preserve the literary flavour of the epic. No effort has been made to attach any fresh connotation to any of the verse. I have offered a very simple and readily understandable translation into English, keeping the interests of various kinds of readers in mind. It simply contains an objective translation and interpretation of the verses of Srimad Bhagavad Geeta. In fact, there already exist several translations of this kind and yet it must look different and somewhat special because of concerns for objectivity.

At several places two-three verses and so also their meanings have been put together to offer their coherent and meaningful interpretation because some verses independently do not mean much, especially when each one is read separately. The original poets have not composed couplets keeping their complete meaning in view; rather, one verse contains merely six to ten words without conveying any clear meaning and the meaning of such a verse becomes apparent only when it is read in conjunction with the preceding or succeeding ones. Some of the verses are repetitive and incongruous in nature also, which means several scholarly people had tried to incorporate or insert their own views before the Geeta took its final form. Ever since the book was made available in the printed form for general public, the room for any such addition and alteration has been closed. Under the situation, the commentators have tried to offer their mystical interpretation to sound scholarly or stress their individual views or ideology. This has widened the gap between the general readers and the Geeta. While one must remember that the Geeta was created for the ordinary people for a great cause of the humanity.

Let me reiterate in the words of Lars Martin Fosse, "Finally, casting aside for a moment the historical conundrums, the scholarly debates, and the technical minutia, just know one thing: You are about to read one of the world's truly great books. It is essential reading for a nontrivial understanding of Hinduism, of India, and indeed of life itself. The Bhagavad Geeta still speaks to people everywhere– across the oceans, across the millennia, and across the boundaries of language, religion, and culture." Sri Krishna's Geeta is the most unique philosophical gem of this world.

Though the book is primarily concerned with the study of this philosophical gem– the Geeta, effort has been made to view it against the backdrop of other religions, Islam, since India has been a country where several cults and religions have flourished since the ancient times under the patronage of different rulers showing a strong sense of likes and dislikes for the mainstream Hinduism. Both Islam and Christianity were established and promoted as a parallel religion or better alternative of Hinduism, leading to sporadic sectarian hostility and violence both in medieval and modern times, in particular. And yet the Hindu religion has survived all through, facing all sorts of ordeals and turmoil spanning over a millennia. India comprises the largest Muslim population in the world and hence the ideological conflicts or strains between Hindus and Muslims have come to the fore in a violent form now, though India happens to be a secular state. It is for this reason that Chapters 2 to 4 have specifically focussed on the Geeta *vis-a-vis* other religious ideology with a bit greater emphasis on Christianity and Islam with a view to enhancing a better understanding among people of differing religious faiths and persuasions, keeping the perspectives of Anthropology, History, Philosophy and Sociology in mind.

No religion should be taken as a personal possession of any individual, a group of individuals or the community as a whole. Religious ideologies have always stood for a system of shared values of society evolved over a long period of time through the processes of social interaction and acculturation. Thus all the knowledge relating to religion, same as any branch of human knowledge, comes under the public domain. Keeping this fact in mind, here the subject of religion is dealt with on a brooder canvass in the larger interest of society. Moreover, once a person is allowed to share any branch of knowledge freely, he is as well allowed to hold his own opinion or views on the subject of religion. Everyone must have a freedom to exercise his own free-will about the system of belief and dogmas or any kind of knowledge in the public domain. Being a practitioner of social science I have tried to pursue this approach towards religion in the book as objectively as possible– possibly more or less on a nearly similar line pursued by a great Indian saint like Kabirdas. However, I am partly in agreement with Damodar Thakur's (**Gita: The Song Extraordinary**, 2005) observation that in the case of the Geeta 'pure objectivity is a myth'.

Simultaneously my professional background of Sociology and Anthropology has also come into play while working on this book. As the story of Mahabharat is concerned with family feud, anthropological and sociological perspectives, in particular, are more relevant than any other perspective to understand the teachings of the Geeta. So far the philosophical perspective has heavily overshadowed the sociological and psychological aspects of the Geeta and hence all the earlier commentaries appear to be pure philosophical pieces of writing. Anyway, I owe a deep sense of gratitude to Sri Krishna without whose blessings I could not have understood, whatever little I could do, His teachings. Sri Krishna is doubtlessly all the time the greatest teacher or instructor for one and all both in peace and in crisis.

The book in hand is only a modest addition to the work which has been accomplished by the earlier Geeta scholars and commentators. This work combines the ancient wisdom of the Vedic philosophy with the contemporary thoughts and ideas of the West. It has also shed light on the problems of present-day society relating to religion. It is a systematic guide which can help out the individual, both believer and non-believer, to enhance his experiences of contentment, creativity, peace and fulfilment. This has been one of most challenging, enlightening and satisfying experience of my life. I have tried to communicate with the English knowing modern readers of the Geeta. I hope this work will initiate people into the subtle understanding of the Geeta and also direct them into the practice of the science of Yog, as discussed in this book. The sum total of this work is to share my own views and awakening with others to help the posterity.

Finally it may also be noted that my approach to the Geeta has been both reverential and analytical. The interpretation of Srimad Bhagavad Geeta is a radical departure from many of the dogmas and theories associated with it. It may not find approval among some orthodox devotees of Hinduism. But then truth is no one's grandchild. I have tried to present the Geeta as a student of social science. One of the goals of this book is to bring to the general public the true intent, spirit and wisdom in the Srimad

Bhagavad Geeta. The Geeta should be understood and interpreted primarily in the context in which it was created. This would keep restraint on multiple interpretations of verses of the Geeta.

I must make it known that this has been the toughest piece of writing of my life because of the intricacy of philosophy involved in the Geeta. I had to struggle a lot for a fairly long time to come to an end. Maybe I had undertaken to do this work because I had some indirect blessings of the Supreme Being, as my mother inadvertently named me Janardan after one of the names of Sri Krishna. For this I am ever indebted to Him. I must express a sense of gratitude to some of my old colleagues and friends such as Professors R. C. Sinha, A. DasGupta and Samir Kumar Sharma (all Patna University) who could find time to go through some chapters of the book and benefited me through their helpful comments. Last but not the least, I owe a deep sense of thankfulness to my old friend Shree Niwas Sharma, formerly Head of the Department of English of the K. S. S. College, Lakhisarai (Bihar) for taking exceptional pains to go through some parts of the manuscript to help me make further improvements in the quality of presentation. Finally, it is pertinent to add here that I am alone accountable for all the shortcomings and limitations which may be inherent in the book.

Where there is Lord Krishna, *Dharma* or righteousness is there; and where there is righteousness, victory is predestined.

J. P. Singh

Aphorisms of the Srimad Bhagavad Geeta

The Srimad Bhagavad Geeta is regarded as the greatest poetical and spiritual discourse ever given to the mankind. It is in the form of a dialogue between Lord Krishna and Arjun, narrated in the *Bhishma Parva* of the Mahabharat. It is a book with sublime thoughts and practical instructions on *Yog,* Devotion, *Vedant* and *Karma*. It comprises 700 Sanskrit verses spread over eighteen discourses developed over a long period of time. It is said that on the battlefield of Kurukshetra, Sri Krishna, during the course of His most instructive and interesting talk or conversation with Arjun, revealed profound, sublime and soul-stirring spiritual truths, and expounded the rare secrets of *Yog, Vedant, Bhakti, Karma* and *Gyan*. All the teachings of Lord Krishna were subsequently compiled as the Song Celestial or Srimad Bhagavad Geeta by sages or scholars popularly designated as Vyas for the benefit of humanity at large.

Among all the spiritual literatures of the world, there is no book so elevating and inspiring as the Geeta. It expounds very lucidly the cardinal principles or the fundamentals of the Hindu religion or *Santan Dharma*. It is the source of all wisdom. It is our great guide. It is our supreme teacher. It is an inexhaustible spiritual treasure. It is a fountainhead of bliss. It is an ocean of knowledge. It is full of divine splendour and grandeur. The Geeta is the cream of the Vedas. It is the essence of the soul-elevating Upanishads. It is a universal scripture applicable to people of all temperaments and for all times. It is a marvellous book, profound in thought and sublime in heights of vision. It is a book for eternity. The Geeta is a boundless ocean of nectar.

According to Swami Tyagisananda the philosophy of the Geeta is intensely practical and affects all aspects of life. A thorough understanding of this philosophy can be had only by a study of the lives of some great personalities who were associated with the Mahabharat. They come from all walks and stages of life, from all classes of society, from both sexes, and from all age-groups. But the greatest amongst them all is Sri Krishna, who, according to Swami Vivekananda, is the first great teacher in the history of the world to discover and proclaim the grand truths of love for love's sake and duty for duty's sake. Born in a prison, brought up by cowherds, subjected to all kinds of tyranny by the most despotic monarch of the day, and derided by the orthodox, Krishna still rose to be the greatest saint, philosopher and reformer of his age. All the greatest sages and the most immaculate saints of his time pay him divine honours; they consider him the best and most perfect among the spiritual men of the age, and with one voice acclaim him as divinity manifest on the earth, looking up to him for light and guidance. To them, he is not only a *Vibhuti* (an especial divine manifestation), *vyuha* (the fourfold expression of *Purushottam*), *Bhagavatam* or *Avatar* (incarnation), but also the personal God and even absolute Reality. In him we find the ideal householder and the ideal *Sannyasin*, the hero of a thousand battles who knew no defeat, the terror of despots, sycophants, hypocrites, sophists, pretenders, the master statesman, the uncrowned monarch, the king-maker who had no ambition for himself. He was a friend of the poor, the weak, the distressed, the champion of the rights of women and of the social and spiritual enfranchisement of the Shudra and even of the untouchables, and the perfect ideal of detachment. In him, again, we find the perfect harmony of *Gyan, Bhakti* and *Karma*—of head, heart and hand.

In this unique book one easily finds an unbiased exposition of the philosophy of action, devotion and knowledge, together with a wonderfully woven synthesis of these three. The Geeta is a rare and splendid flower that wafts its sweet aroma throughout the world. If all the Upanishads should represent cows, Sri Krishna is their milker. Arjun is the calf who first tasted that milk of wisdom of the Self, milked by the divine Cowherd for the benefit of entire humanity. This milk is the Bhagavad Geeta. It solves not only Arjun's problems and doubts, but also the world's problems and those of every individual. Just as the dark unfathomed depths of the ocean contain most precious pearls, so also the Bhagavad Geeta contains spiritual gems of incalculable value. You will have to dive deeper into its depths with a sincere attitude of reverence and faith. Only then will you be able to collect its spiritual pearls and comprehend its infinitely profound and subtle teachings. The following are the most remarkable observations of the holy Geeta:

Find time to read the Geeta and ask yourself: Why do you worry without cause? Whom do you fear without reason? Who can kill you? The soul is neither born, nor does it die.

Whatever happened, happened for the good; whatever is happening, is happening for the good; whatever will happen, will also happen for the good only. You need not have any regrets for the past. You need not worry for the future. The present is happening...

What did you lose that you cry about? What did you bring with you, which you think you have lost? What did you produce, which you think got destroyed? You did not bring anything– whatever you have, you received from here. Whatever you have given, you have given only here. Whatever you took, you took from God. Whatever you gave, you gave to Him. You came empty handed, you will leave empty handed. What is yours today, belonged to someone else yesterday, and will belong to someone else the day after tomorrow. You are mistakenly enjoying the thought that this is yours. It is this false happiness that is the cause of your sorrows. So, whatever you do, do it as a dedication to God!

Change is the law of the universe. What you think of as death, is indeed life. In one instance you can be a millionaire, and in the other you can be steeped in abject poverty. Yours and mine, big and small– wipe out these ideas from your mind. Then everything is yours and you belong to everyone.

This body is not yours, neither are you of the body. The body is made of fire, water, air, earth and ether, and will disappear into these elements. But the soul is permanent– so who are you?

Dedicate your being to God. He is the one to be ultimately relied upon. Those who know of his support are forever free from fear, worry and sorrow.

Whatever you do, do it as a dedication to God. This will bring you the tremendous experience of joy and life-freedom forever. In the words of Karen Armstrong, "In our troubled times, humanity needs the message of this sacred scripture as never before."

The Bhagavad Geeta is a message addressed to each and every human being to help him or her to solve the vexing problems of life for a better future. It is not merely a book of 'religious teachings', nor even a Hindu holy book. It transcends the bounds of any particular religion or race, and is actually divine wisdom addressed to the mankind for all times in order to help human beings face and solve the ever-present problems of life. The *Geeta* again and again emphasizes that one should cultivate an attitude of non-attachment or detachment. It urges repeatedly that an individual should live in the world like a lotus leaf on water. Attachment is due to infatuation.

The Bhagavad Geeta is a unique book for all ages. It is one of the most authoritative books of the Hindu religion. It is the immortal song of the Soul, which bespeaks of the glory of life. The instructions given by Sri Krishna are for the whole world. The teachings of the Geeta are broad, universal and sublime. They do not belong to any cult, sect, creed, age or country. They are meant for the people of the whole world. Based on the soul-elevating Upanishads– the ancient wisdom of seers and saints– the Geeta prescribes methods which are within the reach of all. All your miseries will come to an end and you will attain the highest goal of life– immortality and eternal peace.

Select Aphorisms of the Geeta

1. Neither in this world nor elsewhere is there any happiness in store for him (human being) who always doubts.
2. Delusion arises from anger. The mind is bewildered by delusion. Reasoning is destroyed when the mind is bewildered. One falls down when reasoning is destroyed.
3. The power of God is with you all the time; through the activities of mind, senses, breathing and emotions; and is constantly doing all the work using you as a mere instrument.
4. The wise see knowledge and action as one; they see truly.
5. The mind acts like an enemy for those who do not control it.
6. Perform your obligatory duties because action is indeed better than inaction.
7. Sever the ignorant doubt in your heart with the sword of self-knowledge. Observe your discipline. Arise.
8. Man is made by his belief. As he believes, so he is.
9. Hell has three gates: lust, anger and greed.
10. There is nothing lost or wasted in this life.
11. The mind is restless and difficult to restrain, but it is subdued by practice.
12. People will talk about your disgrace forever. To the honoured, dishonour is worse than death.
13. To the illumined man or woman, a clod of dirt, a stone and a piece of gold are the same.
14. Creation is only the projection into form of that which already exists.

15. One can become whatever one wants to be if one constantly contemplates on the object of desire with faith. Fear not what is not real, never was and never will be. What is real, always was and cannot be destroyed.
16. The wise should not unsettle the mind of the ignorant who are attached to the fruits of work.
17. The faith of each is in accordance with one's own nature.
18. Death is as sure for that which is born, as birth is for that which is dead. Therefore, grieve not for what is inevitable.
19. Unnatural work produces too much stress.
20. Setting aside all deeds even though noble, just surrender completely to the will of God. He shall liberate you from all sins. Do not grieve.
21. Much better to do one's own work even though imperfectly than to do somebody else's work perfectly.
22. I give the knowledge to those who are ever united with Me and lovingly adore Me.
23. I look upon all the creatures equally; none are less dear to Me and none dearer. But those who worship Me with love live in Me, and I come to life in them.
24. A Self-realized person does not depend on anybody except God for anything.
25. One attains the eternal imperishable abode by My grace, even while doing all duties, just by taking refuge in Me.
26. Only the fortunate warriors, O Arjun, get such an opportunity for an unsought war that is like an open door to heaven.
27. God is in everything as well as above everything.
28. The wise do not rejoice in sensual pleasures.
29. Neither do I see the beginning nor the middle nor the end of Your Cosmic Form.
30. The one who sees inaction in action, and action in inaction is a wise person.
31. I am the sweet fragrance in the earth. I am the heat in the fire, the life in all living beings, and the austerity in the ascetics.
32. You grieve for those who are not worthy of grief, and yet speak the words of wisdom. The wise grieve neither for the living nor

for the dead.

33. There was never a time when I, you, or these kings did not exist; nor shall we ever cease to exist in the future.
34. Work does not bind Me, because I have no desire for the fruits of work.
35. Both you and I have taken many births. I remember them all, O Arjun, but you do not remember.
36. The one, who truly understands My transcendental birth and activities, is not born again after leaving this body and attains My abode.
37. To those ever steadfast devotees, who always remember or worship Me with single-minded contemplation, I personally take responsibility for their welfare.
38. *Karma-yog* is a supreme secret indeed.
39. Karma does not bind one who has renounced work.
40. The wise should work without attachment for the welfare of the society.
41. For those who wish to climb the mountain of spiritual awareness, the path is selfless work. For those who have attained the summit of union with the Lord, the path is stillness and peace.
42. Though I am the Author of this system, one should know that I do nothing and I am eternal.
43. They all attain perfection when they find joy in their work.
44. One who abandons all desires and becomes free from longing and the feeling of 'I' and 'my' attains eternal peace.
45. There is no one hateful or dear to Me. But, those who worship Me with devotion, they are with Me and I am also with them.
46. Those who long for success in their work here [on the earth] worship the demigods.
47. I give heat, I send as well as withhold the rain, I am immortality as well as death.
48. The evil doers, the ignorant, the lowest persons who are attached to demonic nature, and whose intellect has been taken away by *Maya* do not worship or seek Me.
49. Whosoever desires to worship whatever deity with faith, I make their faith steady in that very deity.

50. I know, O Arjun, the beings of the past, of the present, and those of the future, but no one really knows Me.
51. The unsuccessful *Yogi* is reborn, after attaining heaven and living there for many years, in the house of the pure and prosperous.
52. The mind alone is one's friend as well as one's enemy.
53. I am seated in the hearts of all beings.
54. There is nothing, animate or inanimate, that can exist without Me.
55. The one who leaves the body, at the hour of death, remembering Me attains My abode. There is no doubt about this.
56. Those who have no faith in this knowledge follow the cycle of birth and death without attaining Me.

OM TAT SAT

Select Popular Verses of the Srimad Bhagavad Geeta

न त्वेवाहं जातु नासं न त्वं नेमे जनाधिपाः।
न चैव न भविष्यामः सर्वे वयमतः परम् ॥ 2.12 ॥

Never was there a time when I (Sri Krisnhna) did not exist, nor you, nor all these rulers of men, nor shall any of us ever cease to exist hereafter.

नैनं छिन्दन्ति शस्त्राणि नैनं दहति पावकः ।
न चैनं क्लेदयन्त्यापो न शोषयति मारुतः ॥ 2.23 ॥

No weapon can cut this *Atman*, no fire can burn it, no water can wet it, no air can dry it.

कर्मण्येवाधिकारस्ते मा फलेषु कदाचन ।
मा कर्मफलहेतुर्भूर्मा ते सङ्गोऽस्त्वकर्मणि ॥ 2.47 ॥

On action alone let thy interest be fixed, never on its result; getting too much attached to the idea of the fruit will lead you to inaction.

ध्यायतो विषयान्पुंसः सङ्गस्तेषूपजायते ।
सङ्गात्संजायते कामः कामात्क्रोधोऽभिजायते ॥ 2.62 ॥

When a man thinks of sense objects, attachment for them arises. From attachment arises desire; from desire arises anger.

क्रोधाद्भवति सम्मोहः सम्मोहात्स्मृतिविभ्रमः ।
स्मृतिभ्रंशाद् बुद्धिनाशो बुद्धिनाशात्प्रणश्यति ॥ 2.63 ॥

From anger arises bewilderment, bewilderment causes loss of memory, from loss of memory comes the destruction of the capacity for taking intelligent decisions and because of the destruction of this capacity for intelligent decisions, a man perishes.

विहाय कामान्यः सर्वान् पुमांश्चरति निःस्पृहः ।
निर्ममो निरहंकारः स शान्तिमधिगच्छति ॥ 2.71 ॥

One who abandons all desires and becomes free from longing and the feeling of 'I' and 'my', he attains the peace.

तस्मादसक्तः सततं कार्यं कर्म समाचर ।
असक्तो ह्याचरन्कर्म परमाप्नोति पुरुषः ॥ 3.19 ॥

Therefore, always perform your duty to the best of your abilities without any attachment to the results, because by performing action without attachment, one reaches the supreme goal of life.

यद्यदाचरति श्रेष्ठस्तत्तदेवेतरो जनः ।
स यत्प्रमाणं कुरुते लोकस्तदनुवर्तते ॥ 3.21 ॥

Because whatever noble persons do, others follow. Whatever standard they set up, the world follows.

यदा यदा हि धर्मस्य ग्लानिर्भवति भारत ।
अभ्युत्थानमधर्मस्य तदात्मानं सृजाम्यहम् ॥ 4.7 ॥

Whenever there is a decline of *Dharma* (righteousness) and a rise of *Adharma* (lawlessness), then I send forth Myself.

परित्राणाय साधूनां विनाशाय च दुष्कृताम् ।
धर्मसंस्थापनार्थाय सम्भवामि युगे युगे ॥ 4.8 ॥

For the protection of the good, for the destruction of the wicked and for the establishment of righteousness, I come into being from age to age.

न कर्तृत्वं न कर्माणि लोकस्य सृजति प्रभुः ।
न कर्मफलसंयोगं स्वभावस्तु प्रवर्तते ॥ 5.14 ॥

The Lord of the world does not act on our behalf, nor does He create actions or the conjunction of an action with its fruit; it is only the innate nature that operates.

न प्रहृष्येत्प्रियं प्राप्य नोद्विजेत्प्राप्य चाप्रियम् ।
स्थिरबुद्धिरसंमूढो ब्रह्मविद् ब्रह्मणि स्थितः ॥ 5.20 ॥

Whatever pleasures are born of worldly contact are sources of sorrow, they have a beginning and an end and no wise man delights in them.

उद्धरेदात्मनात्मानं नात्मानमवसादयेत् ।
आत्मैव ह्यात्मनो बन्धुरात्मैव रिपुरात्मनः ॥ 6.5 ॥

Let a man uplift himself by himself; let him not degrade himself. He himself is his friend and foe.

सुहृन्मित्रार्युदासीनमध्यस्थद्वेष्यबन्धुषु ।
साधुष्वपि च पापेषु समबुद्धिर्विशिष्यते ॥ 6.9 ॥

He is esteemed, who is of the same mind to the well-wishers, friends, foes, the indifferent, the neutral, the hateful, relatives, saints and sinners.

अव्यक्तं व्यक्तिमापन्नं मन्यन्ते मामबुद्धयः ।
परं भावमजानन्तो ममाव्ययमनुत्तमम् ॥ 7.24 ॥

The foolish regard Me, as the unmanifested, as come into manifestation, not knowing My supreme state- immutable and transcendental.

नाहं प्रकाशः सर्वस्य योगमायासमावृतः ।
मूढोऽयं नाभिजानाति लोको मामजमव्ययम् ॥ 7.25 ॥

I am not manifest to all, veiled (as I am) by Yog-Maya. This deluded world knows Mc not the unborn, the immutable.

वेदाहं समतीतानि वर्तमानानि चार्जुन ।
भविष्याणि च भूतानि मां तु वेद न कश्चन ॥ 7.26 ॥

I know, O Arjun, the beings of the whole past, and the present, and the future, but no one really knows Me.

अवजानन्ति मां मूढा मानुषीं तनुमाश्रितम् ।
परं भावमजानन्तो मम भूतमहेश्वरम् ॥ 9.11 ॥

The fools disregard me, dwelling in human form. They do not know my transcendental nature, as the great Lord of all beings.

येऽप्यन्यदेवता भक्ता यजन्ते श्रद्धयान्विताः ।
तेऽपि मामेव कौन्तेय यजन्त्यविधिपूर्वकम् ॥ 9.23 ॥

Even those devotees who, endowed with faith, worship other gods, worship Me only, O Arjun, but by the wrong method.

समोऽहं सर्वभूतेषु न मे द्वेष्योऽस्ति न प्रियः ।
ये भजन्ति तु मां भक्त्या मयि ते तेषु चाप्यहम् ॥ 9.29 ॥

I am the same to all beings: to Me there is none-hateful or dear. But those who worship Me with devotion, are in me, and I too am in them.

न मे विदुः सुरगणाः प्रभवं न महर्षयः ।
अहमादिर्हि देवानां महर्षीणां च सर्वशः ॥ 10.2 ॥

Neither the hosts of the Gods nor the Great *rishis* know my origin; for I am the source of all the Gods and the great *rishis*.

अहं सर्वस्य प्रभवो मत्तः सर्वं प्रवर्तते ।
इति मत्वा भजन्ते मां बुधा भावसमन्विताः ॥ 10.8 ॥

I am the origin of all. Everything evolves from Me. Knowing this, the wise worship Me with devotion and reverence.

सर्वधर्मान्परित्यज्य मामेकं शरणं व्रज ।
अहं त्वा सर्वपापेभ्यो मोक्षयिष्यामि मा शुचः ॥ 18.66 ॥

Abandoning all duties, come to Me alone for shelter. Be not grieved, for I shall release you from all evils.

OM TAT SAT

PART- I

THE INTRODUCTION

Chapter - 1

The Perspective

Some scholars have observed that the war of Mahabharat occurred only in the minds of people. The human body is taken as the battlefield of Kurukshetra. For instance, Swami Nikhilanand considers Arjun as an allegory of *Atman,* Krishna as an allegory of Brahm, Arjun's chariot as the body, and Dhritarashtra as the ignorance filled mind. Mohandas Karamchand Gandhi, in his commentary on the Geeta, interprets the battle as an allegory in which the battlefield is the soul and Arjun, man's higher impulses struggling against evil. Swami Vivekananda also emphasized that the first discourse in the Geeta related to the war could be taken allegorically. Vivekananda further remarked that this Kurukshetra War is only an allegory. When we sum up its esoteric significance, it means the war which is constantly going on within human mind between the tendencies of good and evil. In a way they seem to have negated the historical base of the Mahabharat.In Aurobindo's view, Krishna was a historical figure. He clearly rejected the interpretation that the Geeta, and the Mahabharat by extension, is 'an allegory of the inner life, and has nothing to do with our outward human life and actions' (Sri Aurobindo, ***Essays on the Gita,*** 2000). One must bear in mind that Vyas did not create Mahabharat from nothing. Something cannot be created out of nothing. Nothing creates only nothing. Existence of Vyas is a proof for the existence of Mahabharat. The Ramayan and the Mahabharat are '*Itihasam*'– *iti iha asam*– which means, it happened like that. Unlike the *Puranas*, which were stories, the former are historical. Characters in *Itihasa* lived and walked on this earth. But most of the characters in Puranas are, however, imaginary.

All the places mentioned in the Mahabharat still exist with the same name or similar other names. There are many other stories from various places which mention about the Mahabharat and the places and incidents. Recently the Archaeological Survey of India has excavated the cities of Dwarka, Indraprastha, Kurukshetra, etc. which still exist with the same name. The description of all the *Akshaunis*, weapons used, where it happened, when it happened is available in some form and is proved through scientific evidence.

Some Western scholars, especially those unacquainted with Indian spiritualism, have described the Mahabharat and so also Sri Krishna together with other characters as a part of Indian mythology. Many of the Indian scholars have also expressed similar views on the Western line. They tend to endorse the views of Western scholars, especially because the Westerners are often taken as men of great scientific outlook and partly also because they are considered superior to us, especially with respect to economic development. In order to ascertain the truth, in the recent past some Indian scholars, with special expertise in the field of astronomy and computer science, had conducted intensive high-tech excavations on the historicity of the Indus River Valley Civilization and the Mahabharat. Their study was based on the astronomical and scientific facts and phenomena like the conjunctions, eclipses, earthquakes, meteor showers and comet sightings as noted in the Mahabharat. They have come to the conclusion that the Mahabharat is a part of India's history and it is older than commonly believed to be by historians. This has really dismayed archaeologists and historians of both India and abroad.

Historicity of the Mahabharat War

The determination of the period of the Mahabharat war has been an indeed very contentious issue. There has always been total lack of unanimity among scholars of varied subjects. Since the powerful PCs with very accurate astronomical programmes like Planetarium have become available, it is possible to construct the sky map of any day and time in the distant past and review the positions of the planets and other astronomical events. A whole new science called 'Archaeoastronomy' has now evolved. Eclipses have become very predictable and are very precise events to date the past events. There may be no written or archaeological evidence of the ancient past, but the sun, the moon and stars are still the same and move according to the same natural or physical laws. With the intensive research into the past astronomical phenomena, as described in the Mahabharat, it has been established that the epic is not a pure fiction rather a part of history. It is very much possible that lots of legends, fables and anecdotes have been added to the main event, but the incidence of Mahabharat war is not a fiction or concocted story.

It has been argued by some scholars using the Planetarium computer package that the great war of Mahabharat took place in 3139 B.C. A practitioner of social science may not readily own up the view that the Mahabharat war took place in 3139 B.C., as this period overlaps a part of the commonly acknowledged period of the Indus River Valley Civilization. However, the fresh date regarding the incidence of Mahabharat may be true because the latest view about the period of the Indus River Valley Civilization itself has questioned the generally accepted view about the historicity of this Civilization. But this much is almost certain that the war of Mahabharat was not a fairy tale rather a historical reality. Usually the most acceptable view is that the period of the Mahabharat war followed the Rigvedic period which was subsequent to the Indus River Valley Civilization. This suggests that the period of the Rigved goes much beyond 3100 BC.

A fresh debate about the historicity of the Indus River Valley Civilization based on a very recent scientific research conducted by the scientists from IIT, Kharagpur and the Archaeological Survey of India has appeared in a famous journal called **Nature** (25 May, 2016). They have uncovered evidence that the Indus River Valley Civilization is around 8,000 years old, which means it is about 5,000 years older than generally believed by the most historians of the world based on the past excavations done by the British archaeologists during the early 20th century. The scientific authenticity of the earlier research was relatively much poorer compared with the present one, as it is based on more advanced technology. The Indus Civilization actually spread across large swathes of India covering parts of Rajasthan, Gujarat, Jammu & Kashmir, Punjab, Haryana and Western Uttar Pradesh. What we know today from the history books is purely based on the old British excavations of very limited nature.

The language of the Mahabharat was Sanskrit and there is no evidence of Sanskrit as a language in use before and during the Indus River Valley civilization. A complete linguistic divergence between the people of Indus Valley and that of the post-Indus Valley period is noted by historians. It is for this reason that the available inscriptions of the Mohenjo-daro and Harappa civilizations are not yet deciphered, as they are completely different from Sanskrit. The people of Indus River Valley Civilization possibly used to communicate through signs and symbols and other unknown languages, but not Sanskrit. There is no evidence of the use of such a grammatically sophisticated language as Sanskrit during the Indus River Valley Civilization. Even now the literary standard, traditions or the potential of coining new words for the purpose of communication and grammar of Sanskrit is indisputably far superior to most Indo-European languages. The Mahabharat, as said before, is an epic of Sanskrit literature. Yet another notable fact is that the place like Kurukshetra (presently located in the State of Haryana) or character like Lord Krishna or any other character of the Mahabharat has not figured in the Rigved. Historians have almost unanimously suggested that the Rigvedic civilization followed the Indus River Valley Civilization by which it is obvious that the story of Mahabharat originated subsequent to the Rigvedic period. Archaeologists are not able to find any firm cultural connection between the Indus Valley Civilization and the Vedic Civilization despite the fact that both of them flourished in more less the same geographical region.

Sanskrit, which was the prime language of the Mahabharat, originated sometimes during ca. 2nd millennium BC–600 BC. With regard to the language in use, there is some sort of hiatus between the pre-Rigvedic and the Rigvedic society. The above dates are taken as the least controversial by most historians and archaeologists. Despite controversy with regard to the historicity of the Kurukshetra war, most historians estimate the date of the Kurukshetra war to Iron Age of India of the 10th century B.C. Based on excavations after India's independence, archaeologists suggested a date of 900 B.C. This view was supported by several eminent historians and archaeologists like K. P. Jayaswal, A. S. Altekar, Frederick Eden Pargiter, H.C. Raychaudhury and B. B. Lal. But now the latest view about the historicity of the Mahabharat war, stated as above, is that it dated back to about 3100 B.C. The conventional view about the historicity of the Mahabharat is outright rejected in favour of the new findings, stated as above.

As the period of the Mahabharat can be stretched back to 3100 B.C., the Vedic era too can be thrown back still further in a similar fashion. The Geeta is definitely a post-Vedic creation, since it incorporates the Vedantic philosophy of life. The actual incidence of the Mahabharat war took place much before the compilation of the great epic of Mahabharat, as the writing work was not going on side by side as we see in the modern age. The verses of the Mahabharat existed in the form of oral tradition for a fairly long time in certain sections of the Indian society. Worship of Krishna, either in the form of deity Krishna or in the form of Vasudev, Bal Krishna or Gopal can be traced back to as early as the 4th century B.C. The Mahabharat, the Harivansa, the Bhagavat Puran and the Vishnu Puran happen to be the principal scriptures discussing Krishna's story. At the same time it is also true that the most Pauranic stories are pure fiction or imaginary tales, going far beyond the commonsense knowledge.

Composition/Compilation of Mahabharat and Geeta

Next to periodization of the onset of the war of Mahabharat, the authorship of the greatest epic of India, the Mahabharat, which is called the Fifth Ved, too is a contentious issue. Who would have written such a complicated book in a poetic manner, incorporating numerous myths and anecdotes with sufficient literary flavour? Before this question is taken up, one must bear in mind that the Mahabharat before being written was in an oral form for thousand years. The art or science of writing developed much later. People are commonly made to believe that the entire Mahabharat was written by a single person named Ved

Vyas, and many traditional pundits continue to hold this view. Modern scholarship has arrived at a more complex answer. There is no single author or single date of composition, and it began as an oral poetry. A reciter would have had to know the story, but his reputation depended upon his skill in bringing the traditional material to life. Then as now, a first-class narrator was much in demand. We know from other oral-poetry traditions that the same bard would present the same story in different versions, longer or shorter, as it suited the occasion. Thus, in its oral form, the epic had a reasonably fixed core, but its performance was highly flexible, with additions, embellishments, and digressions made on the spot to please the audience. In addition, the oral poets had at their disposal a large number of formulaic expressions that could be easily fitted into the epic's sixteen-syllable meter in which the length of only a few syllables was fixed. The original nucleus of the epic may have been the creation of a single bard, or possibly a small group of bards, but it is now irrecoverable.

Those days there was hardly any necessity of writting everything what was heard or spoken. In school and college textbooks the authorship of the Mahabharat is often attributed to Ved Vyas, while it was not created and finished in the lifetime of any single individual since the Mahabharat existed in the oral form (*Shruti*) or as folk tales for a fairly long time, at least much longer than the lifetime of an individual one can imagine. When the Mahabharat was revised or re-narrated time and again, it was but natural that it had multiple authors or contributors over a period of about one thousand years. It is because of the multiplicity of authors that lots of verses are paradoxical, repetitive or incongruous. Some have endorsed the Vedic philosophy while others decry the significance of the Vedic rituals. At some places Sri Krishna is described as Absolute Reality or Supreme Godhead and at others one of the ten incarnations of Vishnu.

It is also contended by some scholars that there has been more than one Vyas. Despite being the name of a single saint or sage, Vyas was also the name of a profession dealing with religious or moral preaching and writing or compiling of scriptures those days. In fact, Vyas also means a compiler. The Vedas also are said to be the creation or compilation of Ved Vyas, while single Vyas would not have survived for so long. Reply to all these questions or doubts can be seen in the Vishnu Puran where it is stated that 'Ved Vyas' is a title applied to the compilers of the Vedas who are *Avatars* of Vishnu; 28 people with this title have appeared so far. Hence, persons compiling the Vedas and the Mahabharat were two different Vyas. One such Vyas was the grandfather of the Kauravas and Pandavas. It is generally agreed that it was the 28th Vyas, whose actual name was Krishna Dvaipan who actually put down the earliest version of the Mahabharat in the written form only somewhere between 300 BCE to 300 CE. A significant portion of the epic was only added in later centuries, which then came to be known as Bharat and then as Mahabharat. The word Krishna was added as prefix before Dvaipan because he was a dark complexioned person. This period is, however, not acceptable to some of the Geeta scholars. They have argued that the origin of the Mahabharat lies sometime during the eighth or ninth centuries B.C., although some scholars consider the roots of the epic to be much older still.

The title of the epic Mahabharat may be translated as 'the great tale of the Bharat clan/descent'. According to the Mahabharat itself, the tale is extended from a shortest version of 8,800 verses, called the ***Jaya*** and later it was expanded to 24,000 verses called simply ***Bharat.*** Now it has got more than 100,000 verses. All this expansion happened over a long period of time extending up to the Gupt period in the 4th century A. D. and each verse or *Shlok* is a couplet finally known as the Mahabharat. Enlargement of the Mahabharat from originally 8,800 verses to one lakh verses suggests nothing but additions and alterations in the main story and so also in the verses of the Geeta over the years. As the Mahabharat developed in three phases it is hard to determine which portion of the existing Mahabharat is the real or the original one. Anyway, the Mahabharat is the longest known epic and has been described as 'the longest poem ever written'. With about 1.8 million words in total, the Mahabharat is roughly ten times the length of the ***Iliad*** and the ***Odyssey*** combined, or about four times the length of the ***Ramayan.*** It is unimaginable to believe single Vyas survived for centuries to give a finishing touch to even Bharat, leave aside the question of complete treatise of Mahabharat. In terms of contents the

Mahabharat appears to be a book more of mythology than of history. It contains a good amalgam of myths and facts.

As said before, the Mahabharat was originally composed or compiled by 28th Ved Vyas as a poetic narrative of the Kurukshetra War between the Pandavas and Kauravas and it was then known as Jaya. The work was later expanded by two of Ved Vyas's disciples, with Ugrasrava producing the Mahabharat as we know it today. We don't know exactly when the Mahabharat in its present form was finally written down. It was certainly a gradual process, where parts of the epic were put into manuscripts, whereas other parts were still transmitted orally. Whenever the process started, there were only two possibilities: in the north, birch bark was used; and in the south, palm leaves. These are brittle materials, and frequent recopying was required if the text wasn't to be lost. The earliest surviving manuscript is from the ninth century A.D. An owner of a manuscript could do with it as he pleased, and books consisting of leaves bound together with string allow other leaves to be easily inserted. The quality of the copying varied with the scribe– a bad scribe might make errors, and a better scribe might subsequently improve the text. Among the specialists, there is now a general agreement that the oldest portions of the epic that have been preserved are not likely to be older than 400 B.C. On the other end, it is difficult to fix an upper limit for the Mahabharat's composition. The didactic portions of the twelfth book in particular seem to have been added very late, perhaps in the fourth century AD.

It should be remembered that the epic Mahabharat was not meant to be a history book, despite the fact the war of Mahabharat was a historical realty. It is an epic (*prabandha-kavya*) and the poet enjoyed absolute liberty to let his imagination fly high. Thus, one cannot question his use of superlatives while describing the palaces or the strength of the armies on the battlefield or the supernatural weapons used by them. Yet another problem with the literary work of religious importance is that it comprises a huge body of fictional facts. Reasonable doubts are raised whether the war of Mahabharat was truly fought by the members of a kin group of four generations concurrently? The following names evidently suggest the involvement of people of four successive generations of the same kin group: Bhism (son of Shantnu)—a General of the Kaurav army. 2. The blind king Dhritrashtra (son of Vichitravirya— the youngest step brother of Bhism) who preferred to listen the running commentary of the war while sitting in his palace. Dhritrashtra was well represented by his brother-in-law Shakuni. 3. Duryodhan (the eldest son of Dhritrashtra) along with his 100 brothers and his cousins Pandav brothers (sons of Pandu— a step brother of Dhritrashtra). Bhism happened to be the eldest of grandfathers of both Duryodhan and Pandu brothers— the chief belligerents, and (4) Abhimanyu (the son of Arjun) who fought valiantly in the war of Kurukshetra. Abhimanyu was already married and his wife Uttara was pregnant at the time of war. The people of all these age groups were accompanied and escorted by their friends, kinsmen, well-wishers, teachers of military science together with their sons. Here the matter of disquiet is the fact when the Pandav brothers themselves were men of very advanced age, their grandfather Bhism was certainly too old to take an active part in the war. If Bhism in reality took part in the war, he must have been in a very fragile health state, as the conservative estimate of his age works out to be around 130 years at the occurrence of the war. In fact, we fail to grasp as to how the people of even more than two generations could fight such a deadly war for 18 days. Senility or poor health condition could not come in their way of fight is really mindboggling. Such an illustration bears out that there is a fair amount of fictional or make-believe facts inherent in the story of Mahabharat.

Since the story of Mahabharat was transmitted from one generation to another in an oral form (*Shruti*) and even when it took the form of a crudely written document, it was modified or recomposed by numerous saints and sages with numerous inclusions and exclusions of certain parts due to memory loss over the years, the texts have become quite unstructured and chaotic and there is nothing like original Mahabharat. This is nothing unusual about it, as it happens with all great events or legendary personalities. In course of time new anecdotes were inadvertently added or old ones modified, as there is no system of check and balance with the rise and development of any literary work or historical event. Same thing has happened with the Ramayan also. There are many versions of the story of the Ramayan in different languages. Furthermore, the Ramayan of Valmiki and the

Ramcharitamanas of Tulsidas, despite the former being the basis of the latter, is not or need not be exactly the same. It is, however, generally agreed that unlike the Vedas, which have to be preserved letter-perfect to a great extent, the epic was a popular work whose reciters would inevitably conform to changes in language and style. Same as the Ramayan there are several versions of the Mahabharat as well.

As a matter of fact, there have been many attempts to unravel the historical growth and compositional layers of the Mahabharat. Some scholars have argued that the Mahabharat is the oldest epic which has been added to over a large period of time right from the Vedic times to 400 BCE. in the Gupt period. The poetic fantasies and exaggerations, combined with several Brahminical accretions, have made it very difficult for the historians to agree on a small range of time for the epic. Historians have contended that the epic Ramayan came into being sometime during 5th century BCE to first century BCE, but it was a work of a single person, consisting of 50,000 lines. Even though it talks about a time (*Treta Yug*) earlier than Mahabharat (*Dwapar Yug*), it is newer in chronological order. Indeed, historically Ram is a much later addition to the Hindu pantheon as compared to Krishna. It can be seen clearly in Valmiki's Ramayan where Ram is treated as a mighty and just man and not as almighty God. Based on the skin colour both Ram and Krishna can be regarded as non-Aryan gods and that could be one of the possible reasons why they did not find reference in the Vedic literature.

It may further be added in connection with the historicity of Mahabharat and the Ramayan that the Ramayan (***Ramayanam*** in Sanskrit), which is attributed to the poet Valmiki, appeared quite late. Here one should not ignore that the name of Gautam Buddha was mentioned in the Ramayan. Ram addresses Jabali and refers to Buddha as a cheat and the Buddhist religion as a non-Vedic religion– *'yatha hi chorah sa tatha hi Buddha'*. It suggests that the Ramayanam was written after the death of Buddha who belonged to the 6th century B.C. Historian R. C. Dutt has rightly observed that "the Ramayan, like the Mahabharat, is a growth of centuries, but the main story is more distinctly the creation of one mind." Questions are often raised whether the first to the last chapters of Ramayan were composed by the same original author. The Ramayan text has got several regional renderings, recensions and subrecensions.

The treatise of Mahabharat comprises myths and anecdotes relating to several lines and generations of the Kuru clan stretching over a fairly long period of time before and after the actual war of Mahabharat. Those days it was not humanly possible for any single Vyas to cover the complete the story of more than two to three generations, which simply means that the Vyas of more than one generation was involved in completing this work. Since the story of the Mahabharat was alive in its oral form for more than a thousand years, it is evidently obvious that the completion of the work must have taken the services of more than one Vyas. It is also obvious that the work could be complete in a minimum of three phases—Jaya, Bharat and Mahabharat. Even on the final completion of the Mahabharat we actually do not know how many times it was subjected to addition, alteration and improvement before it was printed at the press. Hence, the debate concerning the determination of date of completion of the present treatise of Mahabharat remains an inconclusive issue for the Indologists till this date.

A Brief Outline of the Mahabharat

Now let us briefly understand the background story of Mahabharat to understand the context of the Geeta. The central story of the Mahabharat is a conflict over succession to the throne of Hastinapur, a kingdom just north of modern Delhi that was the ancestral region of a lineage or tribe most commonly known as the *Bharatas*. (India was at that time divided amongst many small, and often warring, kingdoms.) The struggle was between two groups of cousins, the Pandavas, or sons of Pandu, and the Kauravas, or sons of Dhritarashtra. Because of his blindness, Dhritarashtra, the elder brother of Pandu, was passed over as king, the throne going instead to Pandu. Once, while hunting in the forest, King Pandu was cursed by a sage that he would die if he would ever establish intimate relationship with a woman. Since he was childless at the time, he handed over the control of his kingdom to his elder brother (Dhritrashtra) and went into the forest with his wives to perform penance to get rid of the curse.

In the forest, Kunti and Madri were said to have invoked various gods to beget sons. It sounds like a concocted story to cover up extra- or intra-marital relationships. Kunti was blessed with Yudhishthir, Bhim and Arjun and Madri was blessed with twin sons named Nakul and Sahadev. They are all known as the Pandavas. Pandu died very shortly because he was cursed to face death in case he established sex with any woman. So the intimate relationship of Pandu with Madri or maybe Kunti as well, cost him dearly. In a state of agony Madri preferred to be a *sati* by burning herself on Pandu's pyre and Kunti returned to Hastinapur as a widow with all the five sons, the capital of the Kuru clan. Although the Pandavas were the rightful heirs to the throne of Hastinapur, this was deeply resented by the sons of Dhritarashtra, the Kauravas, especially Duryodhan, who was the eldest of them.

The sons of Dhritrashtra, especially Duryodhan, hated and envied Pandavas. And the blind and selfish Dhritrashtra wanted his sons, not those of Pandu, to inherit the kingdom. Because of intense hatred against his cousins (Pandavas), Duryodhan continuously tried and wished instantaneous death for them. In fact, his hatred was encouraged and orchestrated by his crafty maternal uncle, Shakuni. An idea of Shakuni's character can be had from this advice to Duryodhan: 'Duryodhan, God gave speech to man not to express himself, but to hide what is in his mind.' Aided by Shakuni, Duryodhan with the consent of Dhritrastra executed various plots to finish the Pandavas, but thanks to their luck or the careful protection of their uncle Vidur and Lord Krishna as well that the Pandavas escaped numerous attempts against their life.

While hatred and animosity between them was already there, the Pandavas and the Kauravas grew up in Hastinapur and learnt various kinds of martial art from their teacher Dron. Karn, the illegitimate eldest son of Kunti who was born to and abandoned by her when he was an infant, also entered the story. Though an exemplary archer, everyone believed him to be the son of the charioteer who picked up the discarded baby Karn and raised him as his own son. No one, except for Kunti, knew the hard truth about the identity of Karn. In fact, Karn was in a way the rightful heir to the throne, though no one knew it except Kunti. Karn was befriended by Duryodhan, who noticed his archery skills as a valuable counter to Arjun's archery.

As the story progresses, the Pandavas were forced to go into hiding in the forest to escape the Kauravas' assassination attempts. During their time in the forest, Arjun won the hand of Draupadi, the daughter of Drupad, the powerful king of Panchal by being victorious in a matrimonial episode known as a marriage by trial in anthropological literature. On return from that event Arjun told her mother vaguely about the prize or reward he received at the hand of the king. As usual the mother blessed and advised him to have equal shares in the prize among all the brothers. Thus Draupadi became the common wife of all the Pandavas, which is referred to as the system of polyandry. This is how the practice of polyandry has been vindicated or justified. Guided by Krishna the Pandavas escaped many traps laid by Duryodhan and finally returned to claim one half of the kingdom. But Yudhisthir, the eldest Pandav, had a weakness for gambling, and Shakuni, a master of the dice game, tricked him into gambling, winning away his wealth, kingdom and even his wife Draupadi, whom the Kauravas attempted to strip her naked before the entire assembly of princes and kings, for causing insult to the Pandavas. She could be saved only by a divine intervention of Sri Krishna. In shame for allowing such a thing to happen to a woman's honour, the elders of the court cancelled the entire rigged game and returned everything to the Pandavas, but forced them into thirteen years of exile.

Bereft of their wealth and honour, the five brothers and their wife together with mother had to go into an exile for twelve years, plus one year in disguise (during which they narrowly escaped detection). Upon returning from the exile Pandavas rightfully requested for the return of their kingdom, but Duryodhan bluntly refused to concede this. Then Pandavas reduced their requests to merely five villages. But Duryodhan arrogantly replied that he would not give land even as much as the tip of a needle to the Pandavas.

The Mahabharat epic is primarily about a Great War between two sets of cousin princes over the inheritance of their ancestral kingdom of Kuru in northwest India. These cousin princes of the Kuru family at war were collectively known as the Bharatas, being the descendants of the great legendary king Bharat who lived several generations earlier.

Sri Krishna tried to act as a reconciliator or adjudicator, but that too did not work either. This inevitably led to the war of Kurukshetra, the 'mother of all battles', where every king had to choose his sides. This verily offers a loud message to the deprived or downtrodden for waging war against discrimination or deprivation. One should not harbour cowardly attitude towards life, for death is imminent for all today or tomorrow. Sri Krishna is always present in the form of consciousness. He does not have to reincarnate in human form for every crisis-ridden person. One should be merely a true devout for His blessings without being a Hindu or a religious person. Sheer complete faith in Him is adequate, as it has been exhorted time and again in the Geeta. Anyway, it was just before the beginning of the Great War that Krishna imparted the preachings or sermons to Arjun as contained in the Geeta and gave him the *Vishwaroop Darshan*, a glimpse of the divinity. Before this Arjun, surprisingly enough did not have any occasion to know that Krishna was a Supreme Being. Perhaps this was crucial to reassure a devout like Arjun of his victory in the Great War.

The war of Mahabharat went on for eighteen days; each day was filled with incessant bloodshed. The Kaurav's army had 11 *Akshaunis* or divisions of soldiers and the Pandavas had only 7, making a total of 18 (one *Akshaunis* consisted of 21,870 chariots (Sanskrit *ratha*); 21,870 elephants; 65,610 horses and 109,350 infantry). There also happened to be 18 chapters or discourses in the epic. Doubts have been raised by some Geeta scholars that the original Geeta comprised all the 18 discourses. Genuine doubts have been raised about the last six discourses. This issue has been raised once again at the relevant place in the book.

The presence of a huge army on the side of the Kauravas suggests that the fraudulent are relatively more organised and tend to outnumber the honest or righteous people– no matter what happens to them at the end. Here some readers might pose a question as to where did the huge army of people go for camping after the sunset or during the night. Was the night really peaceful and secure enough for the retiring soldiers? Since the Kauravas were the rulers, a part of their huge army might be returning home or large make-shift camps after the sun set for rest and respite. On the Pandava's side there was no room for camping anywhere but to stay overnight in the battlefield. Making arrangement of food and water and medical care of the injured at one place for 18 days appears to be a very herculean or unimaginable task. It is really unbelievable as to how the people fought for eighteen days when the stinking dead bodies of innumerable fighters could be piling up every day. If cremation was going on everyday on both sides, how could the grief-stricken people be fighting under the mournful scenario. Under this scenario combating for 18 consecutive days prima facie seems to be unconvincing. Alternatively, it was not a fierce battle, but of sporadic nature spread over 18 days, as the people were fighting with free-style low or crude level of warfare technology like the bow and arrow and the nature of casualty was either minor or grievous. Sometimes it also involved face-to-face physical fight like wrestling and boxing. The Mahabharat has recorded the war as the deadliest one.

Anyway, the first day belonged to the Kauravas, while the second belonged to the Pandavas. The third day belonged to the Kauravas again as Bhishm (Vichitravirya's brother), the Kaurav's commander and the eldest of the Kuru clan, finished many Pandav soldiers. On the fourth day, Bhim killed eight of the Kauravas. Arjun's son Iravan was killed on day eight. On the ninth day, Krishna, who had promised not to take up arms and would stay merely as Arjun's charioteer, lost his cool with Bhishm for using powerful divine weapons against common soldiers of Pandav. Only then Krishna took out his *sudarshan chakra* to slay Bhishm, but Arjun refrained Him from doing so. The Pandavas hatched a plot to remove Bhishm from the war since his prowess was wrecking havoc on the Pandav army. As Bhishm had taken the vow that he would never raise a weapon when faced with a woman, so Arjun hid behind Shikhandi and attacked Bhishm with a devastating volley of arrows on the tenth day and ultimately Bhishm was grounded in a helpless manner, but remained alive in a state of intense pain because of numerous arrows into his body.

On the thirteenth day, Abhimanyu, Arjun's son was killed in an unfair manner, as he was attacked by many warriors simultaneously. It was a ploy that was against the rules of conduct of war those days. Thus both sides started to deviate from all codes of conduct and the war turned increasingly brutal and unethical. Such thing is not unusual, as a holy war becomes increasingly unholy with the lapse of time. On day fourteen, Arjun took a vow that he would kill Jayadrath– one of those responsible for Abhimanyu's unfair killing– before the sun sets, or else take his own life. Knowing this the Kauravas rallied around Jayadrath and prevented Arjun from coming anywhere near him. As the day was going to end, Krishna created an illusion of sunset with the help of His *Sudarshan Chakra* in order to mask the sun and create an illusion of sunset, misleading the Kauravas into believing that they had managed to protect Jayadrath. However, the sun was still up, and while the Kauravas were busy rejoicing and thus Arjun soon took Jayadrath's head off. On the day fifteen, Dron revengefully devastated the Pandav army, and so Yudhisthir, the ever-truthful, was forced to make a false statement that Ashwathama (Dron's son) was killed. Dron dropped his arms in grief and sat in meditation, and Drishtadyumna (Draupadi's brother and son of Dron's sworn enemy Drupad) beheaded him.

While Bhishm was lying on a bed of arrows, Dushasan, the second eldest among the Kauravas and the one most involved in trying to disrobe Draupadi, was killed by Bhim. On the penultimate day Karn was killed by Arjun. On the final or the eighteenth day, Yudhisthir killed Shalya and Shakuni was killed by Sahadev. Bhim broke Duryodhan's thighs and left him for dead. The war was thus won by the Pandavas but it was not much of a victory. Many of their family and friends lost their life; in fact none of their sons survived the war. The Pandavas' army was no match to that of Kauravas, but the latter lost the war because Sri Krishna was indirectly fighting against Kauravas. Arjun was merely an instrument in the hands of Lord Krishna, the Absolute Truth, Almighty or the Supreme Authority. Truth always prevails over falsity. Anyway, the story ended with all odd consequences and the beginning of kingship of Yudhisthir who became undisputed ruler of India for 36 years. The Pandavas along with Draupadi went on pilgrimage up the heights of the Himalayas to the abode of the Lord, and into the true being God, into true immortality.

The Mahabharat war shattered the economy and abolished many localized or regional civilizations of the then India. Thousands of kings and millions of people were said to have lost their life in that battle. As the incidence of mortality was quite high, loss of population those days was a big thing, and as a consequence of the battle, big patches of uninhabited land lay stretched across the subcontinent. One may be astonished to learn as to how everybody who took part in the war died, except for 12 warriors— 7 from the Pandav camp and 5 from the Kaurav camp. In the case of Sri Krishna it is understandable, but it is a matter of great surprise in the case of the Pandavas. Was the Mahabharat war a complete holocaust? If yes, did really the throne of Hastinapur carry any sense for the Pandavas when it became a ghost like deserted kingdom. Such scenario, however, can be imagined only in the case of a literary work like the epic of Mahabharat.

During the Mahabharat period society was highly patriarchal and the position of women was relatively lower compared to that of men. The practice of polygyny, betting of wife in gambling by husband or effort to disrobe Draupadi in public can be cited as glaring evidence of low status of women in society. There existed a system of polygamy– a combination of both polygyny (a practice of having more than one living wife at the same time) and polyandry (a practice of having more than one living husband at the same time). The system of concubine also existed those days. People tended to have a largely liberal views about sex. It is evident from the fact that the marriage of Dhritrashtra could be possible through the system of marriage by capture and he had hundred sons and one daughter which was biologically impossible for Gandhari (a highly imbalanced sex ratio of children ever born is also not true from the angle of both medical science and demography). It is also possible that Dhritrashtra had many secondary wives. The father of Yudhishthir, Bhim and Arjun is not precisely known and their mother Kunti got married after she gave birth to Karn who is the son of a fictional Sun God. There are several such characters in the Mahabharat whose biological fathers are missing. In fact, the Mahabharat is replete with such instances.

The story of Mahabharat suggests active participation of characters like Bhism, grandfather of the Pandavas and the Kauravas, and Abhimanyu, the eldest son of Arjun, in the battle of Kurukshetra as warriors. Bhism happened to be the great grandfather of Abhimanyu who was already a young and capable warrior at the time of war and whose posthumous son Parikshit later succeeded the throne of Hastinapur after Duryodhan. The story suggests simultaneous involvement of members of families of four successive generations in the war. Furthermore, when the war took place the Pandav brothers were themselves quite old and Sri Krishna was still older than them. Here one may pose questions whether the longevity of people was really so high those days and the people really strong enough to fight war at the age of 100 and above? Demographers or medical scientists have a serious difficulty in accepting such a fact about the longevity of people those days.

Collating the Bhagavad Geeta— Looking more specifically at the Geeta, most scholars reckon the oldest parts may go back to the third century B.C., whereas the theistic portions could have developed in the middle or towards the end of the second century B.C. Discourse twelve through fifteen may date from the first century A.D., whereas Discourse seventeen is possibly even younger. The Geeta was possibly composed somewhere in north-central India, perhaps in modern Haryana or western undivided Uttar Pradesh. These conclusions would probably hold good whether we believe that the Geeta was originally composed independent of the Mahabharat, as some claim, or that it was originally a part of the great epic. Even if the Geeta was not originally a part of the epic, it has by now been handed down and read that way for many centuries. This, however, should not be taken to mean that even the shorter version of the Geeta did not originate from the war of Kurukshetra.

It is estimated that the Geeta probably reached something of a 'final form' by the early Gupt period (about the 4th century AD). Since the Geeta contains the Upanishadic philosophy, it becomes obvious that the present Geeta was certainly developed much after the formulation of the Upanishads irrespective of the fact that the Mahabharat period was much earlier than that of the formulation of the earliest Upanishads collated probably between c. 800 BCE and c. 500 BCE. The actual dates of composition of the original Geeta, however, remain unresolved. Theories on the date of composition of the Geeta vary considerably, although it is an integral part of the Mahabharat now. Hindu traditionalists assert that the Geeta came into existence in the third or fourth millennium B.C., around the beginning of *Kali Yug*. Historians accept dates from the fifth century to the second century B.C. as the probable range. Professor Jeaneane Fowler, in her commentary on the Geeta, considers second century B.C. to be the likely date of composition. Kashi Nath Upadhyay, a Geeta scholar, on the basis of the estimated dates of Mahabharat, *Brahma Sutras*, and other independent sources, concludes that the Srimad Bhagavad Geeta was composed in the fifth or fourth century B.C. All these facts clearly suggest that all the verses of the Geeta were not the part of the original conversation between Krishna and Arjun. Anyway, the treatise of Mahabharat, and so also the Geeta, is not to be regarded as a Brahminical literature, but in the course of the subsequent purposeful interventions by Brahmins by way of addition, alteration or interpolation of certain verses or fresh commentary on the Geeta, the Geeta has got fervour of a Brahminical literature.

Anyway, the Geeta in its present form first rolled off a printing press before there were complete editions of the Mahabharat itself. As noted earlier, it was translated into English for the first time in 1785 by Charles Wilkins. The first Sanskrit edition came out in 1806 under the supervision of Sir William Jones. In 1823, the German scholar August Wilhelm von Schlegel produced a first rate edition of the Geeta and added a Latin translation. The first printed edition of the Mahabharat was the so-called Calcutta edition, completed in 1839, which was based on the Bengali recensions of the text. The next attempt was the Bombay edition, largely based on the recensions in Devanagari script and completed in 1863. The Kumbhakonam edition of 1910 incorporated the southern recensions.

This situation was clearly less than satisfactory, so one of the greatest scholarly undertakings of the twentieth century was started in 1919 at the Bhandarkar Oriental Research Institute in Poona (now spelled Pune). No less than ten distinguished editors, initially led by V. S. Sukthankar, and a host of assistants laboured for forty-seven years to produce the definitive edition of the Mahabharat. The objective was to reconstruct the oldest possible form of the text on the basis of hundreds of manuscripts collected from all over the Indian subcontinent and Indonesia. The resulting set of nineteen volumes, containing thirteen thousand pages, was completed in 1966.

It is noticed that some of the Western scholars who have translated the Geeta into foreign languages had a hatchet job to portray the Hindu faith in a less than a stellar light to prove superiority of Christianity over the Hindu religion. A similar was the intention of a German Scholar, Max Muller, who was first to translate the Rigved into English. This veiled agenda was disclosed in a letter dated December 9, 1867 of Max Muller addressed to his wife residing at Oxford. To quote a part of that letter, "The translations of theVeda will hereafter tell to a great extent on the fate of India and on the growth of millions of souls in that country. It is the root of their religion, and to show them what the root is, I feel sure, is the only way of uprooting all that has sprung from it during the last 3000 years." Hazaribagh based (the State of Jharkhand) Father Camille Bulcke S. J. (1909-1982), a Belgian Jesuit missionary in India, wrote his doctoral thesis on ***Ram Katha Ka Vikas*** in Hindi with a similar objective in mind. But Indians, who do not really understand their perspective, take pride in quoting their work to convey a message glorifying their past or to assert that the Indian epics and scriptures are the best in the world. The Indians who do not understand such scholars or Indologists tend to eulogize their work and they are often favourably quoted in their write-up or speech. Many a people fail to understand that the purpose of translating the Hindu scriptures by the Western scholars was not so much an academic exercise to learn what these scriptures intended to convey, but in reality to show the world that all that was reprehensible in India was directly attributed to them. The **Bhagavad Gita: A New Translation** (2002) by Stephen Mitchell, among many others, is one of the latest examples wherein lots of endnotes in poor taste have been appended. Such thing, however, does happen with all those who have got a poor appreciation for the Hindu religion. One can easily understand how India once looked like from the following excerpt from a long speech of Lord T. B. Macaulay in the British Parliament on 2 February, 1835:

> "I have travelled across the length and breadth of India and I have not seen one person who is a beggar, who is a thief. Such wealth I have seen in this country, such high moral values, people of such calibre, that I do not think we would ever conquer this country, unless we break the very backbone of this nation, which is her spiritual and cultural heritage,

and, therefore, I propose that we replace her old and ancient education system, her culture, for if the Indians think that all that is foreign and English is good and greater than their own, they will lose their self-esteem, their native self-culture and they will become what we want them, a truly dominated nation."

Sri Krishna as Godhead

Who was Lord Krishna by the way? Neither the Geeta deals with any Vedic god and goddesses nor do the Vedas incorporate God named Sri Krishna. One can always react stating that Lord Krishna was a later day incarnation of Divine Being, especially Vishnu, but then the question emerges as to why are the most Vedic Gods and goddesses missing from the story of Mahabharat. A God is always a God after all. Yet another point of contemplation is that all the Vedic gods and goddesses were of Brahminical origin and later God namely Lord Ram was of Kshatriya origin, while the last one Lord Krishna alone belonged to either Vaishya Varna or some local ethnic group, which is evident from the fact that Krishna always pursued the cattle-raising occupation throughout his adulthood. At many places Sri Krishna has been addressed as Yadav in the Geeta. Sociologically speaking, Sri Krishna was never a man of the Kshatriya origin, as many Rajputs often tend to argue these days in order to glorify their caste identity. In his article on Vaishnavism R. N. Dandekar ***(The Encyclopedia of Religion)*** has clearly observed that Krishna was the deified tribal hero and religious leader of the Yadavas. Most importantly, it is not necessary that Krishna had the same name or origin whenever he came to this world. Variations in name due to variation in time, place and language are but natural, as Lord Krishna has himself told Arjun that he has come to the earth so many times in the past: "Never was there a time when I did not exist, nor you, nor all these rulers of men, nor shall any of us ever cease to exist in the future." (2.12) All the ancient sages and great Acharyas have rightly regarded Sri Krishna as the Supreme Personality of Godhead (**Krishna** by A. C. Bhaktivedanta Swami Prabhupada, ISKCON, Mumbai, 1996). No one is equal to Him, no one is greater than Him.

Countless are the people who distrust the greatness of God, because there is no concrete evidence to corroborate His existence. But it must be borne in mind that everything cannot happen in this universe in the lifetime of an ordinary mortal for his or her satisfaction and approval. For all such modern men with scientific temper one of the easiest and most reliable ways to understand Him is to find time to go through the available literature relating to the real life story of Sai Baba of Shirdi in Maharashtra, an Indian spiritual master who was regarded by his devotees as a saint, a *fakir*, a *Satguru* and an incarnation of God. He lived a full life of a normal human being about 100 years ago. Those who are knowledgeable about him revere him as a true manifestation of God. Now millions of people throng the Shirdi temple throughout the year as an important centre of pilgrimage from varying parts of the country. The available literature on the life and works of Shirdi Sai Baba offers merely a fraction of the idea of greatness of divinity present in a human being like Sai Baba of Shirdi. This ordinary case in point can unquestionably be a reliable source or basis to imagine or form a firm opinion about the greatness of Lord Krishna— the true Supreme Being? We all recognise the difference between a divine person and Supreme Being is unfathomable. Everybody cannot be equally divine, for divinity is a matter of degree, and Sri Krishna was immeasurably more divine than all other saints and *Devas*.

Now let us come to the discussion relating to the use of such expressions as Absolute Reality, Ultimate Reality, Supreme Being, Supreme Self, Supreme Spirit, Spirit, Super Soul, Super Self, Lord, Divine Being, Incarnation (*Avatar*), Cosmic Being, God, Eternal Being, and Eternal Lord in different books on the Geeta, causing substantial confusion both among commentators themselves and also among the the common readers. The problem with these terms is that they do not have a very precise or standardized meaning same as scientific terminology. All these words do not connote the same thing to everybody even within a discipline like religion and philosophy and hence they need to be defined very firmly. Different English commentators have used or operationalized these terms very loosely or arbitrarily. This has happened also because different commentators are not much clear or unanimous about the true identity of Sri Krishna in the Geeta. Some have taken Sri Krishna as God, Supreme Being or Self, some as incarnation of God, while some have treated him as Deity or Divine Being and yet others have recognized him merely as an enlightened person. If we go by what Sri Krishna has stated about Himself in response to Arjun's questions, it is explicit that he is no other than Absolute Reality, Ultimate Reality, Supreme Being, Supreme Self, Supreme Spirit, Super Soul, Super Self, God, Eternal Being or Eternal Lord. All mean the same thing. There are numerous verses to support this, including Discourse 15, Shlokas 15.16-19 in particular. Discourse 11, dealing with the *Yog of the Vision of the Universal Form,* is a clear testimony to the fact He was the Lord Himself. Arjun could have a rare occasion to behold the cosmic form of the Lord. Let us have no iota of doubt that such an occurrence is possible only in the case of the Supreme Being. In view of this He is not to be described as Divine Being or merely as Spirit, Self or Incarnation of God, since these expressions stand for further expansions of the Supreme Being in the material world. Since nobody has got enough knowledge, wisdom or spiritual attainments of a very high order to ascertain the final truth in the realm of metaphysics, one should trust what has been stated concerning Sri Krishna in the holy Geeta. Further difference of opinion on all such matters is always inconclusive because of the elements of subjectivity in religion for obvious reasons.

Let us discuss one more fact about Sri Krishna, that is, we should not think of Krishna or any Hindu God in terms of *Varn* or caste like a lay Indian. Anyway, what is emphasized here is that the Geeta was created for an entirely different purpose. At several places the Vedic philosophy and rituals have been subjected to criticisms in the Geeta. In contrast with the Vedic philosophy, there is a heavy emphasis on the theistic philosophy centred on the Lord Krishna to transform the Brahminism that had developed with the Vedas and which in the sixth century B.C., was being challenged in many directions. However, over the years scholars supporting the Vedic philosophy or Brahminical ideology made patchy additions and alterations in the verses of the Geeta in support of the Brahmanism. At times, it seems that the Geeta was created to re-establish the Upanishadic philosophy through the creation of new God, Lord Krishna, as the excessively ritualistic Vedic philosophy was getting increasingly obsolete and overtly countered by some ancient saints and thinkers. The Geeta was crafted in furtherance of the secular and devotional perspective of a new class of non-Brahminical elites of those days. The development of unorthodox systems of philosophy like Charvakism, Jainism and Buddhism are the obvious examples.

There is some debate with regard to the identity of Krishna because different religious scriptures offer differing information. A scholar like Franklin Edgerton in his book ***The Bhagavad Gita*** (1964: 133) has made an interesting comment on the identity of Sri Krishna: "In the Gita he is still both god and man; an incarnation of the Deity in human form. We know nothing of the process by which he attained divine honours, nor of his earlier history as a god before the Bhagavad Gita, which is probably the earliest work preserved to us in which he appears as such. In this work he as we shall see, the attributes of the Upanishadic Absolute. In other words, the popular God is philosophized into a figure who can appeal to both the higher and the lower circles of the population." Questions or doubts raised here are quite normal when one does not understand the Upanishadic philosophy or the hymns of the Geeta. Some knowledge of Indian spiritualism is a pre-requisite for a proper understanding of the Geeta. The Westerners have got a different cast of mind because their cultural heritage and *Sanskars* are different from ours. The Geeta should always be read with faith, self-confidence and poise.

Some may be astonished to learn a very outlandish argument that Krishna was the king of Jerusalem according to Gene D. Matlock. Melchizedek of New Testament was none other than Lord Krishna, and that Jesus was an incarnation of Krishna (Melchizedek) as Paul has himself explained. Krishna was father of Abraham– the king of Salem. Some historians have struggled for hundreds of years to find out how and why the stories about Jesus and Krishna, who were born about 3,000 years apart, are nearly so identical. Some of the identical facts, which do not match with the historical evidence, as many of them are imaginary, but captivating, may be noted thus:

- The future births of both messiahs were predicted ahead of time.

•Christ descended from Abraham

•Krishna was the father of Abraham (Brahma). (This is a highly concocted fact.)

•Christ was at once a Koresh, a Hebrew, and a Yehudi. Krishna was at once a Kurus, an Abhira and a Yadav.

•Christ was an incarnation of Yah-Veh

•Krishna was at once an incarnation of Vishnu and Shiv (highly debatable)

•Christ's first name, Jesus, was Yeshua

•Krishna did not have an earthly father as such, but a protector, named Vasudev

•Jesus did not have an earthly father as such, but a mortal protector named Joseph

•An evil king tried to kill Christ and Krishna both when they were infants

•To protect the infant Jesus, Joseph and Mary took him to Maturai, Egypt

•To protect the infant Krishna, his father, Vasudev, took him to Gokul in Mathura.

•Christ was crucified in Jerusalem and then resurrected. (This is said to be concoction- See Holger Kersten, **Jesus Lived in India: His Unknown Life Before and After the Crucifixion**, Penguin Books India, 2001).

•Krishna was killed by a hunter's arrow and impaled on a tree. Later, he returned to life.

Some Western scholars believe that Krishna died in Jerusalem, having gone there when his coastal city of Dwarka sank under the sea. Others say he went to Iraq, following the natural catastrophe in the coastal city of Dwarka. Christ appeared after his 'death' same as Krishna appeared after his 'death.' Some scholars say Christ was not crucified. He came to Kashmir where he had his last breath at the age of 80 and was buried in the Rozabal shrine. Literature also exists where it has been said that between ages 12 and 30 Jesus lived in Kashmir to learn Hindu and Buddhist philosophy. It is altogether a different matter that many fundamentalist Christians may not recognize this fact because of their sense of religious superiority over the Hindusism.

The Hindu equivalent of the Old Testament story of Abraham is very relevant here. The story begins with Abraham or Brahma as the Hindus called him. His father was Lord Krishna; his brother was Mahesh or Moses (Heb: *Moshe*). The Hindu triad consists of the Gods like Brahma, Vishnu and Shiv or Mahesh. Actually Shiv and Vishnu are believed to be one and the same. Together, they are Brahm (God). The Bible tells us that Jesus was both Shiv and Vishnu, for Jesus' biblical names are *Isa/Isha* (Shiv), *Yeshua* (*Ishwar*, pronounced in Sanskrit as Yeshwar), Kristos and Yesu, another name of Krishna. These names prove to us that Jesus was both Shiv and Vishnu, thus making Jesus the begotten son of the Un-begotten-Brahm. Since Krishna was not born of man, he was not actually the earthly father of Brahma and Mahesh. Therefore, he himself was the protector (*Tara, Trayeti*) of Brahma. In Sanskrit, *Tara* means 'saviour or protector.' It is a term generally used with the gods Rudra, Shiv, Vishnu and Brahma.

Even the Old Testament says that the father (protector) of Abraham was *Terah* (*Genesis* 11:26.). The Bible tells us that Abraham and Sarah were half-siblings (*Genesis* 12:19-20.). The Hindu holy books also tell us that a blood relationship existed between them. The Puranas relate Saraswati to Brahma and Vishnu. Most frequently, she is associated with Brahma. Her connection with him dates earlier than to any other God. She is portrayed mostly as his wife and occasionally as his daughter. Abraham or Brahma's home was the land of Haran (Genesis 1:4). Haran was the coastal principality governed by Krishna. It was even named after him because Hara (Sun God) is another name of Krishna.

There is also another 'Haran' in India today's State of Haryana. It is the region where Abraham decided to stop making idols and worship only one God. Brahmavart, a region in North-eastern Haryana, is said to be the place where mankind was first created. (Varta=dwelling.) Brahmavart was the site of the Kurukshetra War between the Kauravas and Pandavas, in which Lord Krishna distinguished Himself. An ancient and holy river, now dried up, the

Saraswati, once flowed through Brahmavart. The Hakra (the Biblical Haggar) was a tributary of the Saraswati.

Lord Krishna, the Divine Father (Terah/T'ra) of Brahma/Abraham, was the king of Haran, with the sea port of Dwarka as its capital. It has been argued that in about 1900 BC, hundreds of thousands of native Indians emptied Northern and Central India and fled to the Middle East after Krishna's Dwarka sank under the water. It is also argued that Krishna along with his family fled either to the Middle East or to what is now Iraq. Only some gigantic natural disasters, such as earthquakes and floods could have caused such an exodus. It was at this time that the Saraswati and the Indus rivers changed their proper beds. All such arguments put forward by the Catholics of the Western world indirectly suggesting that Jesus was out of a Hindu parentage.

Paramesh Choudhury has claimed in his book, **The India We Have Lost,** that Krishna and his family probably fled to Iraq. But some say that they went to Jerusalem. The word Jerusalem is derived from Sanskrit: Yadu-Ishalayam, meaning 'The Holy Rock of the Yadu Tribe.' Lord Krishna was a Yadu. The Moslems still revere this huge rock under the Dome of the Rock on Jerusalem Temple Mount. It has been amply demonstrated that all of us, irrespective of our faith, religions and nationalities, are grandchildren of India. Will this knowledge help keep us away from tearing ourselves and the world apart?

Some religiously oriented scholars have tried to calculate dates for the birth of Krishna, some believing that Krishna, under the name of 'Vasudev Govind Krishna Shauri', flourished as the ruler of Shuraseni and Vrishni tribes on the now-submerged island of Dwarka (off coast Gujarat) sometime between 3200-3100 BC. Worship of the deity Krishna, either in the form of deity Krishna or in the form of Vasudev, Baal Krishna or Gopal can be traced to as early as the 4th century BC. Worship of Krishna as the Supreme Being or God arose in the Middle Ages in the context of the Bhakti movement in India. From the 10th century AD, Krishna became a favourite subject in performing arts and regional traditions of devotion developed for forms of Krishna such as Jagannath in Odisha, Vithoba in Maharashtra and Shrinathji in Rajasthan. Since the 1960s the worship of Krishna has also spread in the Western world and in Africa largely due to the effort of the

International Society for Krishna Consciousness (ISKCON).

Here it may be important to point out that not many people know or would really accept the view that there was possibly more than one Krishna in Hindu religion. Similarly there was more than one Arjun also. The earliest mention of Arjun can be seen in the Rigved who was a contemporary of Indra. Krishna of Puranas (or Vrindaban) and Krishna of the Mahabharat do not appear to be the same person. Prima facie, they might look similar in many respects, but not exactly the same person. There was a time gap of over one thousand years between the two. It is interesting to note that Sri Krishna of the Mahabharat held no flute in his hand; was rather a bare handed person or holding a conch in the battlefield and was a great statesman, diplomat and Commander-in-Chief and served as a charioteer on the side of the Pandavas in Kurukshetra. He chose to help Arjun, as he was his brother-in-law, while Krishna of Puranas was a cattle raiser who always held a flute in his hand and was a pure romantic personality in the concert of Radha, least interested in giving sermon to others or encouraging others for warfare. Besides being a prankster in the concert of Radha, he was in the role of an enchanter and protector of people as well as cows. He never claimed to be a supernatural being despite possessing some divine power. Lots of Indologists and mythologists have mixed up both the Krishnas knowingly or unknowingly without any deeper understanding of the history of Hindu mythology or religious scriptures. Both may be regarded as a great deity of the Hindus because of possessing supernatural power, but they possibly belonged to two different epochs of the Indian history. It was during the Gupt period that Krishna was worshipped as God based on myths, legends and fictional stories as compiled with substantial borrowings from the Vedic and post-Vedic literature in *The Bhagavat Puran* (Devanagari: **भागवतपुराण**), also known as Srimad Bhagavad Mahapuran, Srimad Bhagvadam or Bhagavad. Krishna of the Mahabharat proved himself as a Supreme Being, while talking to Arjun in the battlefield (see Discourse 11). On the other hand, Krishna of Vrindavan never tried to prove himself as Supreme Being despite being a killer of demons like Putna, Kansa, Shishupal and others. There is yet another scriptural evidence of being more than one Krishna. In the Braj region of India, Krishna used to celebrate holi (a festival of colour) with much gaiety and fanfare and the common people continue to celebrate holi as a commemoration of the celestial love of Radha for Krishna. But during the Mahabharat period there was no evidence of celebrating holi festival. This suggests that Krishna of the Mahabharat could be different from the later day Krishna of Puranas. Anyway here no effort is made to prove that they were not cosmic. Islam has also acknowledged the existence of Krishna. Bahá'ís believed that Krishna was a 'Manifestation of God. Members of the Ahmadiya Community believe Krishna to be a great prophet of God as described by their founder, Mirza Ghulam Ahmad. Undoubtedly both the Krishnas were full of divinity, a friend of virtue and an enemy of evil.

A large number of Hindu scholars have reckoned and argued that Krishna is neither mythological nor historical, but transcendental. He is the Supreme Being who lives eternally in His transcendental abode and He descended five thousand years ago to this world to re-establish a cosmic order. The activities He performed during His descent can be called historical, though, accurately speaking, they are eternal, manifesting to human vision through history.

The Geeta— a Post Mahabharat Composition

By now it is obvious that the actual occurrence of war took place a long time before the so-called Vyas composed or prepared the whole epic of Mahabharat. So the Geeta, same as the Mahabharat, is definitely a post-facto composition of great ideas for the people of that time. This definitely appears to be more logical or reasonable, as the Mahabharat grew very slowly over a long period of time, covering the story of several generations of the Bharat lineage. There emerges another moot question here– were the precepts of the Geeta really passed on to Arjun by Krishna in the battlefield of Kurukshetra itself? Was it the right place or the right moment for a question-answer discussion? Great philosophy of life cannot be conveyed on the spur of the moment. All the thoughtful ideas of the Geeta were either discussed with Arjun by Krishna much before the onset of the actual war while the preparation of the war was underway or the verses were composed and inserted later by different authors of the Mahabharat in the larger interests of society. The battlefield, where everybody is angered enough to kill everybody, cannot be the right place for teaching the great philosophy of life. All great ideas were said to have been conveyed to Arjun through Krishna to make the people believe readily or accept the preachings of the Geeta with good grace. Despite being related to a special kind of battle, the 700 *Shlokas* of Geeta were never conveyed or recited in the battlefield. Furthermore, while the Geeta in its written form is quite difficult to grasp even by well-educated people, it is hard to believe that Krishna conveyed such a complex piece of Vedantic philosophy in a poetic form to an archer like Arjun in the battlefield. Though the Geeta is useful for every one of us now, it was, sociologically speaking, originally written for priests and warriors and hence women and ex-untouchables have been marginalised which is obvious from Discourses 9 and 18. It was, however, in consonance with the cultural ethos of that period.

In all likelihood the Geeta was a post-war composition, keeping the story of the war of Mahabharat in mind, and it was inserted at a later stage into the Mahabharat. The epic Mahabharat itself came into being in its present form several centuries after the actual war of Mahabharat took place. In multiple verses Arjun has been addressed as 'O son of Kunti', 'O descendant of Bharat' or similar other expressions by Sri Krishna instead of being addressed merely as Arjun. Such an indirect way of addressing is very unusual in the case of a face-to-face situation. Since the Geeta was composed by several scholars or philosophers, both Sri Krishna and Arjun have been addressed by so many adjectives in different verses. The war of Mahabharat and the composition of the epic Mahabharat did not belong to the same era. The literary work always takes its own time and it develops very slowly and that too after the actual incidence is over. In brief, the existing Geeta is a narration of stories about the war between Sanjay and Dhritrashtra. It is highly unlikely that on making queries by Dhritrashtra, his charioteer-cum-secretary Sanjay would reply in the form of a poem or celestial song. Had the Geeta really contained on-the-spot-narrative of war between the Kauravas and the Pandavas in the battlefield of Kurukshetra stretched over a period of 18 days, it would have been in the form of pure dialogues containing a series of questions and answers in a conversational style. It is not easily understandable as to how and why Lord Krishna and Arjun made highly thoughtful conversations in the battlefield in the form of verse or songs. The battlefield is not meant for reciting songs having poetic diction or giving sermons on the high philosophy of life. Arjun, unlike Lord Krishna, is an ordinary warrior. Arjun is not an enlightened being either.

To those who consider that the Geeta, in its present form, comprises original and highly philosophical messages conveyed by Sri Krishna to Arjun right in the battleground of Kurukshetra, there are many queries and questions in the mind of the inquisitive? Should one readily admit the fact that the Geeta was composed or recited while the war of Kurukshetra was under progress, stretching over a period of 18 days? Was Sanjay a great poet to recite all the *Shlokas* in a poetic manner before his master, king Dhritrashtra? How and why did the conversation, as recorded in the Geeta, was confined to two persons only— Sri Krishna and Arjun, while all the close and distant kinsmen of both Kauravas and Pandavas were present in the battlefield with a do and die motive? Why is there no conversation recorded between Lord Krishna on the one hand and the brothers of Arjun, including highly respected eldest brother Yudhishthir or other members of Arjun's family on the other? After all, the Pandavas were fighting collectively against the Kauravas. Was there no worthwhile conversation or dialogue between Arjun and Sri Krishna before and after such a decisive battle of Kurukshetra? As the Geeta is a rare piece of thoughtful creation developed in a very systematic and coherent manner, one is likely to pose another legitimate question: Was it really created in the battlefield or developed and inserted into the Mahabharat subsequent to the Great War, installing Sri Krishna as Godhead? The latter part is definitely much more straightforwardly acceptable than the former. As a matter of fact, additions were done even within the Geeta itself. This fact has been dealt with at many places while commenting on different verses in the subsequent chapters. "There is general scholarly consensus that in its original form it was an independent poem, which was later inserted into the present context, Book Six of India's national epic, the Mahabharat" (Stephen Mitchell, **Bhagavad Gita**, 2002).

Due to its presence in the Mahabharat, the Srimad Bhagavad Geeta is classified as a Smriti text or 'that which is remembered'. The Smriti texts of the period between 200 B.C.-100 A.D. belong to the emerging 'Hindu synthesis', proclaiming the authority of the Vedas while integrating various Indian traditions and religions. Acceptance of the Vedas became a central criterion for defining Hinduism over and against the heterodoxies, which rejected the Vedas. Some scholars have rightly argued that the Mahabharat is much older than the Geeta. The Geeta, as said before, was inserted into the Mahabharat at a much later stage which is highly likely. The sermons of the Geeta neither seem to emanate from the social order of the Mahabharat period, one might imagine, nor does it match with the life style of any character of the Mahabharat including that of Sri Krishna as described in the Bhagavadam.The Geeta contains very lofty and at times impractical philosophy of life, originating and developing steadily outside the battlefield of Kurukshetra. Addition, deletion, alteration or improvement in the contents of the Geeta at the subsequent stage was inevitable, as there existed neither any system of audio recording nor was any Vyas, the so-called poet of Mahabharat, or writer present to scribble down the on-going conversation between Krishna and Arjun in the battlefield or between Sanjay and Dhritrashtra in the palace. The early great *Acharyas* like Adi Shankar, Ramanuj, Madhav, Vallabh and others, who have offered fresh commentaries on the Geeta, must have made substantial alterations and additions in the verses of the Geeta to further their own views, as the Geeta is heavily loaded with the philosophy of Advait Vedant. Those days the Geeta was not available in a fixed printed form for obvious reasons. These scholars were men of great ideas and strong views. Adi Shankracharya, in particular, was a great spiritual genius of his time who, besides writing a commentary on the Srimad Bhagavad Geeta at the age of mere 15, he wrote extensively on the Vedas, Upanishads and Brahma Sutras and propounded the philosophy of Advait Vedant in a very limited span of 32 years of his life.

Context and Contents of the Geeta— Besides poetic narration of the Kurukshetra war and the fates of the Kaurav and the Pandav princes, the Mahabharat contains philosophical and devotional material, such as a discussion of the four 'goals of life' or *Purusharthas*. Among the principal works and stories in the Mahabharat are Srimad Bhagavad Geeta, the story of Damayanti, an abbreviated version of the Ramayan, and the Rishyasringa, often considered as works in their own right. This part is definitely a later addition as the story of Ramayan surfaced during the post-Mahabharat period. The Mahabharat consists of 18 *Parvas* and from *Parva* 5 (*Udyog Parva*) to *Parva* 12 (*Shanti Parva*) is a part of the Geeta which is the essence of lofty philosophy of life (the Geeta comprises chapters 23-40 of the 6th book of Mahabharat, which is called *Bhishm Parva*). The central part of this poetic work is that of a family feud culminating into inevitability of war for the throne of Hastinapur, a kingdom ruled by the Kuru clan. The two collateral branches of the same family participated in the struggle are the Kaurav and the Pandav. The war produced complex conflicts of kinship and friendship, instances of family loyalty and duty taking precedence over what is right, as well as the converse. Because of the prevalence of the system of primogeniture those days, the crown should have been offered to Yudhisthir- the eldest son of the family, but it was not acceptable to Duryodhan, the eldest son of Dhritrashtra (but younger than Yudhisthir or even all the Pandav princes) maybe because only the eldest son of the king should have been the real successor. The blind king Dhritrashtra was certainly the eldest of all and hence his eldest son Duryodhan was considered the rightful claimant of the throne from the Kaurav's point of view.

The Geeta opens with Dhritrashtra's query to Sanjay about the course of the battle. It may be important to point out that the Geeta is a conversation within a conversation. Dhritarashtra begins it by asking a question, and that is the last we hear from him. He is answered by Sanjay, who narrates what is happening on the battlefield. Dhritarashtra is blind. Vyas, Dhritrashtra's uncle, offers to restore his sight so that he could follow the course of the battle. But Dhritarashtra declines this boon, feeling that seeing the carnage of his kindred would be more than he could bear. So instead, Vyas bestows clairvoyance and clairaudience upon Sanjay, Dhritrashtra's minister and charioteer. Great Rishi Vyas said that the occurrences in connection with the war would be reflected in the mind of Sanjay and he would faithfully report them to Dhritrashtra. As they sit in their palace, Sanjay relates what he sees and hears on the distant battlefield. Sanjay pops up now and again throughout the book as he relates to Dhritarashtra the conversation between Krishna and Arjun. This second conversation is a bit one-sided, as Krishna does almost all of the talking. Thus, Sanjay describes the situation, Arjun asks the questions, and Krishna gives the answers.

Here one may question how Sanjay was able to give an audio-visual running commentary on the sequence of events to the king despite not being directly involved in the war. How could Sanjay be able to listen to the personal conversation going on between Krishna and Arjun in the battlefield is not really comprehensible. If this telepathic power was because of some blessings of Vyas Rishi, then why were the events, as narrated in the Geeta, first reflected in the mind of Sanjay? Should one really trust clairvoyance and clairaudience as reliable means of communication? Why did Vyas himself not narrate the entire story to the king? Why did Vyas choose Sanjay- a charioteer of Dhritrashtra for this purpose? Where was Vyas then? It seems that the so-called author himself watched the events of war from some safe place for eighteen days; otherwise, he would not have offered such a poignant description of the events of the Mahabharat war. It also seems that Vyas was a neutral character as he happened to be grandfather of both Duryodhan and Arjun. The alleged poet used character like Sanjay to convey his thoughtful ideas through him. This is after all a great literary work. These are the likely queries or issues which agitate the mind of modern men perusing the Mahabharat with some seriousness. For there exists absolutely no clue in the Mahabharat about the copying of the Geeta while it was being recited by poet Sanjay before the blind king Dhritrashtra, it becomes clear that it was documented much after the actual war of Kurukshetra was finally over. In addition, it is also a fact that not many people survived the war to prepare the manuscript of the Geeta immediately following the great war.

The theme of the Geeta does not comprise even one percent of the Mahabharat and yet it commands a greater admiration of readers than the Mahabharat. The Geeta happens to be the kernel of the Mahabharat. The main subject of the Geeta is as follows: The Kauravas and Pandavas assemble in the battlefield of Kurukshetra for the great war of Mahabharat. The greatest hero of the Pandavas, Arjun, has come in his chariot and is stationed in the middle of the battlefield between the two opposing armies. He is making serious conversation with Sri Krishna who accompanies him as his charioteer. In a fit of despondency, Arjun throws down his bow and refuses to fight, deploring the immorality of the coming war. It is a moment of supreme drama: time stands still, the armies are frozen in place, and Sri Krishna speaks. The situation is extremely grave. A great kingdom is about to face self-destruction in internecine warfare, making a mockery of Dharma, the eternal moral laws and customs that govern the universe. Arjun's objections are well founded: He is the victim of a moral paradox. On the one hand, he is facing persons who, according to Dharma, deserve his respect and veneration. On the other hand, his duty as a warrior demands that he should kill them.

Yet no fruits of victory would seem to justify such a heinous action. It is, seemingly, a dilemma without solution. It is this state of moral confusion that the Geeta sets out to mend. When Arjun refuses to fight, Krishna has no patience with him. Only when he realizes the extent of Arjun's despondency does Krishna change his attitude and start teaching the mysteries of Dharmic action in this world. He introduces Arjun to the structure of the universe, the concepts of Self, *Prakriti*, primordial nature, and the three *Gunas,* the properties that are active in *Prakriti.* Then he takes Arjun on a tour of philosophical ideas and the ways of salvation. He discusses the nature of theory and action, the importance of ritual, the ultimate principle, Brahm, all the while gradually disclosing his own nature as the highest God. This part of the Geeta culminates in an overwhelming vision: Krishna allows Arjun to have a glimpse of his supernatural form, the *Vishwaroop*, which has a terrifying effect on Arjun's heart. The rest of the Geeta deepens and supplements the ideas presented before the epiphany– the importance of self-control and faith, of equanimity and unselfishness, but above all, of *Bhakti*, or devotion. Krishna explains to Arjun how he can obtain immortality by transcending the properties which qualify not only primordial matter, but also human character and behaviour. Krishna also emphasizes the importance of doing one's duty, declaring that it is better to do one's own duty without distinction than to do another's duty well. In the end, Arjun is convinced. He picks up his bow and is ready to fight.

Geeta's Discourse— The Bhagavad Geeta is far from being an unproblematic text. The message of the Geeta seems to mean different things from different directions. Brief though, it is being generally considered an interpolation into the sixth book of the great epic: it is thus an autonomous text from one viewpoint, but a text-within-a-text from another. It takes the form of a dialogue between Krishna and Arjun, but that dialogue is itself embedded in another dialogue of the Mahabharat, that between Sanjay and Dhritarashtra. It prepares the triumph of Arjun and his fellow Pandavas, yet it is framed within a dialogue between two on the losing Kauravas side; it is full of blazing imagery, yet, again in the frame-narrative, it is a tale being told to a blind man, Dhritarashtra.

Krishna appears– here as elsewhere in the Mahabharat– in a very different guise from how he is presented in the other canonical representations of his godhood, the Puranas. The Krishna of the Geeta is a warrior and philosopher, he of the Puranas is the lover of Radha, the playful youth who robs the Gopis of their clothes, and reconciling the two Krishnas has been the task across time of the many manifestations of the devotional cult of the godhead– including, in our day, the International Society for Krishna Consciousness, better known as the Hare Krishna. Nor can Krishna be viewed as a purely self-contained character even within the Geeta: he is not merely himself, but an incarnation of another deity, Vishnu. But interestingly enough in Discourse 11 Lord Krishna appears as the Supreme Being and thus placed at the highest pedestal of cosmic reality, even higher than Vishnu.

The Geeta begins with the preparation of a battle between the two opposing sides: on the left stands the collected armies of the one hundred sons of Dhritrashtra and on the right lie the soldiers of the Pandav brothers. Warring relatives feuding over the right to govern the land of Kurukshetra, both forces stand poised and ready to slaughter one another. The warrior Arjun, leader of the Pandav armies, readies himself as his charioteer, Lord Krishna, steers toward the opposition when the armies are ready to attack. Arjun stops Krishna short before the two sides clash together. Before Krishna begins his teachings, Arjun analyzes his emotions and describes to Krishna the way his heart feels.

'Krishna, I seek no victory, or kingship or pleasures'. Arjun admits that he stands to gain nothing of real worth from the war. He knows he cannot consciously triumph over family for his own wealth and glory. "We (the Pandav brothers) sought kingship, delights, and pleasures for the sake of those assembled to abandon their lives and fortunes in battle." Arjun continues on to state that once the family is destroyed and family duty is lost, only chaos is left to overcome what remains. Arjun goes so far as to describe how chaos leads to corruption in the life of women at the familial level through imbalance in sex ratio, creating disorder in society. Arjun tells Krishna that the punishments for men who undermine the duties of the family are destined for a place in hell. Finally, Arjun asks Krishna which is right: the tie to sacred duty or reason?

Krishna begins his explanation by stating the supreme philosophy of life: that is, life on this earth is indestructible. "Never have I not existed, nor you, nor these kings; and never in the future shall we cease to exist". Because life has always been, reasons Krishna, then how can a man kill or be killed when there is no end to the self? Also, Krishna tells Arjun that his emotions of sorrow and pity are fleeting, and that endurance is all that is necessary to outlast the temporary thoughts. "If you fail to wage this war of sacred duty, you will abandon your own duty and fame only to gain evil". Krishna reinforces the idea of *Dharma*, reminding Arjun of the consequences faced when one does not fulfil the duty set before him. "Your own duty done imperfectly is better than another man's done well. It is better to die in one's own duty, another man's duty is perilous". A job done well by others is preferable to one done poorly by oneself. Even if talents lie in a different area, the duty one is assigned to is the responsibility of the individual. Failure of Arjun to abide by his duty would have a profound effect on his worldly life as well. Enemies would slander Arjun and companions would lose faith and respect in the man they once held in such high esteem. If Arjun loses his life, then he gains heaven and if he wins then he gains the earth; thus there is no need for Arjun to fear for his own fate.

To complete his sacred duty, Arjun must perform the necessary actions. "Be intent on action, not on the fruits of action; avoid attractions to the fruits and attachment to inaction!" In the third teaching, the abstinence from action fails because one cannot merely reject one's actions and find success. Inaction threatens the well-being of the physical body, warns Krishna. Discovered through techniques like Yog and inner reflection, action allows the freedom of the self to be found and attained.

Once Arjun drops desire in the consequences of his actions, a new kind of discipline can be realized. Understanding, rated superior to action by Lord Krishna, provides the necessary tools to perform the skills needed to execute the action. Krishna warns Arjun that this understanding can be lost once a man begins a downward process by lusting after pleasurable objects which create desire, and from desire anger is born, from anger arises confusion, from confusion comes memory loss, and from this the loss of understanding, signalling the ruin of man. Krishna blames Arjun's current emotions on worldly desires, and encourages him to seek a detachment from these worldly attachments, so that the duty be performed and Arjun will achieve his release from human suffering.

In order to understand the cosmos and the self, Arjun tries to learn about Krishna Himself. Krishna describes Himself as having eight aspects: earth, fire, water, wind, space, mind, understanding and individuality. These are His worldly aspects labelled as His lower nature. His upper nature is Krishna's ability to sustain the universe, and be the source of all in existence. The three qualities of nature (*Gunas*) arise from Him, as well as the beneficial aspects of strength without desire and desire without imposing on the duty all men must possess.

"The disciplined man of knowledge is set apart by his singular devotion; I am dear to the man of knowledge, and he is dear to Me". To Krishna, the man of wisdom and knowledge goes hand in hand with the man who has complete devotion to the Lord. Krishna likens the man of knowledge to Himself, saying '...self-disciplined, he holds Me to be the highest way', once again establishing the need for complete submission. Knowledge, while seen as a way to achieve freedom, requires enough discipline to be able to fully devote oneself to Lord Krishna.

It is through devotion, Sri Krishna reveals, that man can truly achieve freedom from life and death. "By devotion alone can I, as I really am, be known and seen and entered into, Arjun". In His teaching on devotion, Krishna tells Arjun to renounce all actions to Him.

In the fifth teaching, Krishna calls for the release from attachment and the fruit of the action, saying that once this occurs, then joy is found in the detached individual. Yet, freedom cannot be achieved through renunciation alone; it is action with discipline that is essential for the success of the enlightened.

As Krishna continues His discourse, He begins to talk about the divine and demonic qualities inherent in all men. 'All creatures in the world are either divine or demonic'. Apparently, all creatures are naturally good or evil. "...do not despair, Arjun, you were born with the divine". Born with the quality of good or evil, the individual is fated to be what is in his nature. If it is his duty to be evil, then it is at evil that the man will succeed. Krishna states that living in evil leads to the bondage of the self into worldly things. Unable to free himself, the demonic man is forced to repeat the cycle of life and death in an everlasting manner, as Krishna casts each evil man back into demonic wombs. Krishna also identifies the evil man as a slave to his own desires. Controlled and dictated by futile efforts, 'they hoard wealth in stealthy ways to satisfy their desires'. The Lord also warns against three gates of hell: desire, anger and greed. The renunciation of these allows for the release of the self.

In the seventeenth teaching, Krishna discusses the differences in the nature of man. As stated before, these three aspects (also thought of as aspects of faith) are *Sattvic, Rajsic* and *Tamsic*. The *Sattvic* person sacrifices to the gods, eats simple and vegetarian foods. The *Rajsic*, the man of passion, sacrifices to the spirits and demons, eats harsh and bitter food that causes suffering, and sacrifices only to gain. The *Tamsic* or the sluggish sacrifices to the dead and ghosts, eats food that has long spoiled, and sacrifices void of faith or any real emotion. Into one of these three types of *Gunas* fits every human being on the earth. Krishna praises the *Sattvic* while warning the passionate and the sluggish.

The discussion comes to a close when Krishna begins to summarize and conclude the points He has already mentioned. He specifies the difference between 'renunciation' and 'relinquishment'. Renunciation is the refusal of action grounded in desire, while relinquishment is the rejection of the fruit of action. In death, the relinquishing of the fruits allows the self to lose all ties to the body and the desires that go with it. Krishna reminds him that resistance to his duty, that is, refusal to go into battle is futile because Arjun's nature compels him to it. Krishna spurns Arjun to go against his will and do what his heart forbids. Arjun learns to take refuge in Krishna and to commit fully to Him. Krishna vows that Arjun will be received by Him in good time. Sri Krishna asks,

"Arjun, have you listened with your full powers of reason? Has the delusion of ignorance now been finished?"

"Krishna, my delusion is destroyed, and by Your grace I have regained memory; I stand here, my doubt dispelled, ready to act on Your words," so replied Arjun. Thus Arjun, through his discourse with Lord Krishna, accepted his duty with devotion and learned how to overcome his desire, while freeing himself from all the worldly sufferings.

Let us briefly come back to the word 'renunciation', as it has appeared so many times in the Geeta, but most of us have misinterpreted it. As it is often misunderstood, some light needs be thrown on this concept for a proper understanding of the Geeta. It is often taken to mean giving up the good things of life and lead a life of deprivation and misery like a recluse. Renunciation is not giving up things you enjoy. It is moving up to far more fulfilling avenues. Renunciation is not dispossession. It is all possession. Renunciation is not giving up action. It is performing dynamic action in a spirit of renunciation. Action and renunciation go together. They are not mutually exclusive. Renunciation is shedding weaknesses for strength. Renunciation is abandoning of attachments for worldly things even while living in the midst of worldly things. It is asserting oneness and rising above differences, exuding warmth and shunning bitterness, creating goodwill and giving up ill-will. Renunciation is giving up the residue of grudges, prejudices and hatred to live a life of freedom and happiness.

In the context of the Mahabharat, Sri Krishna is confirming Arjun in his role as a warrior and asking Arjun as a Pandav to go forth and kill his immediate kinsmen, the Kauravas; and yet this book, with its apparently warlike message, has been interpreted time and again as embodying philosophical calm and detachment from everything. The Geeta should not be read as a manual for warriors but as an extended metaphor of the journey towards enlightenment. The Geeta was intended not to exhort Arjun to do well in the battle of the Mahabharat but to tell every one of us how we can give a good account of ourselves in the journey of life. The philosophy of the Geeta is ultimately summed up in a single notion: the classic text presents life as an endless journey from being to becoming.

Numerous Geeta scholars have stated that it was on the battlefield of Kurukshetra that the immortal and perennially inspiring teachings of the Bhagavad Geeta poured forth from Krishna's lips. Arjun and Sri Krishna were remarkable personalities. The former was a great disciple while the latter was a divine teacher. Krishna as teacher was a man full of compassion, and endowed with universal vision. The Geeta is thus a heroic message from a heroic teacher to a heroic pupil. Its universality makes it applicable to any human being anywhere in the world, to make him or her realize one's fullest human possibilities. The Upanishads or the Vedant expounded the science of human possibilities a thousand years earlier, and the Geeta expounds the practical application of that science. Hence, Swami Vivekananda considered the Geeta as the best book of practical Vedant.

Krishna's teachings are for everyone—as much for the beginner in spiritual life as for the most advanced *Sadhak*. Whether one is inclined towards *Karma, Bhakti or Gyan*—one can benefit greatly by studying the Geeta. It has the essence of all Vedic and Upanishadic knowledge. As the colophon at the end of each chapter of the Geeta announces, the text is both *Brahm Vidya*, an exposition on the knowledge of Brahm, as well as Yog Shastra, a compendium of the science of Yog. 'Its message is universal, practical, strengthening, and purifying'

The Geeta provides spiritual food for seekers of every shade. In the very second chapter, Krishna teaches Arjun about the immortality of the soul that in its real nature the Atman is one with the absolute Brahm. In later chapters, He explicates the means to realization of the Divine. These include cultivation of the *Daivi sampad,* divine attributes of character, avoidance of such opposites as attachment and hatred, and practice of various spiritual disciplines harmonizing them in one's life. He reminds Arjun of the impermanence of the world and advises him to practise non-attachment assiduously and perform his duties without hankering for results. He emphasizes that cultivating real devotion and dependence on God is the key to happiness in life.

Krishna is Himself the embodiment of the teachings of the Geeta. A cursory look at His life is enough to convince us that from His very birth difficulties and problems kept pounding Him like waves, one after the other; but He faced them all with perfect equanimity—with a smile on His lips. His numerous victories did not affect His poise, nor was He dejected on having to flee in the face of Jarasandh's threats. He performed the duties of every station of life to perfection, but remained unattached all the same. He was strongly committed to the welfare of the inhabitants of Vrindavan, who were not only deeply attached to Him but also loved Him with all their hearts. However, this did not prevent Him from moving to Mathura and then to Dwaraka in response to the call of duty. In fact, He never looked back at Vrindavan, the playground of His childhood, even though He ensured the well-being of its residents. He was equally at ease on the throne of Dwaraka and the seat of the charioteer. He is the perfect master of Yog, the Yogeshwar; in His person are harmonized all the Yogas.

Rationale Behind the Geeta

The Geeta is called Upanishad, because it contains the essence of Self-knowledge, and because its teachings, like those of the Vedas, are sub-divided into three parts- *Karma* (work), *Upasana* (devotion) and *Gyan* (knowledge). The Geeta is indeed not a book of religious preaching or creed; rather, it contains the philosophy of life which has traversed beyond the confines of all religions. It is purely meant for the well-being of entire humanity for all time to come. The central teaching of the Geeta is the attainment of freedom by the performance of one's *Swadharma* or duty in life. Always perform the duty without having any worry about the consequences thereof. No social or religious philosophy has ever matched the philosophy of the Geeta in any respect. It is indisputably the highest philosophy of human life. No knowledge of religion can ever be complete without having good understanding of the Geeta no matter how great scholar a particular person is. It is the only Holy book which has got very high regard for the people of all faith, belief, cult or sect; for instance, Sri Krishna said, "Whosoever desires to worship whatever deity– using any name, form and method– with *Shraddha* (faith), I make their *Shraddha* steady in that very deity. Endowed with steady faith, they worship that deity and obtain their wishes through that deity. Those wishes are, indeed, granted by Me alone" (Shlokas 7.21-22).

Everyone who is familiar with Srimad Bhagavad Geeta knows its Mahabharat context, as said above. However, there is another context of Srimad Bhagavad Geeta, that is, historical. This context consists of decadence of excessively rituals based Vedic Dharma, commonly known as Brahminism, and the rise of various heterodox Dharmas during the post-Vedic period in opposition to it. The original Geeta was probably composed in defence of the class system known as *Varnashram Dharma*, one of four pillars of Brahminism. In a sense it was a kind of 'Policy Paper' on the Brahminic doctrines of the *Gunas* and *Karma* on which *Varnashram Dharma* rested. There are 64 shlokas of the original Geeta in the current text of Srimad Bhagavad Geeta. Various later interpolations into its text were made by the Upanishadic and Bhagavad seers in an attempt to overthrow Brahminism and by Brahminic seers to re-establish it. Owing to the addition of fresh verses or modification of the old ones, lots of verses are of repetitive nature with respect to contents or messages. Anyway, the Srimad Bhagavad Geeta is not just a dry and esoteric document elucidating the ancient Indian philosophy. It is a dynamic text which brims with conflict, energy and practical wisdom. One can discern a battle of wits between two groups holding diametrically opposite views about the cultural ethos of India.

In broad terms the Geeta addresses three fundamental issues of life which were raised by Arjun in the battlefield of Kurukshetra just as the Great War was about to begin: *Shokum* (grief), *Dwandwam* (fickleness or unsteadiness of mind as a result of loss of wisdom, engendered by mind's attachment to sense objects) and *Karmaphalam* (good and bad consequences of action). As a result of these three issues, Arjun suffers from a paralyzing emotional crisis resulting in a massive panic attack (1.28-30). Anticipating death of his own people, Arjun suffers from *Shokum* (1.47). His attachment to his own people causes him to suffer *Dwandwam* (1.35-37): Should I fight for the restoration of my kingdom or should I just walk away? Should I kill them or should I die in their hands unarmed and unresisting? Arjun fears incurring sin– bad *Karmaphalam* (1.36)– in the act of killing his own people, and consequently going to hell. The apparent agenda of Srimad Bhagavad Geeta are as follows: How to overcome *Shokum, Dwandwam* and *Karmaphalam* consequent to desire for, attachment to and possessiveness of sense objects (people, power and wealth) and desire-driven action by means of knowledge of Atman/Brahm/ Lord and *Buddhiyog.*

In the Bhagavad Geeta, Krishna explains to Arjun his duties as a warrior and prince and elaborates on different Yogic and Vedantic philosophies, with examples and analogies. This has led to the Geeta often being described as a concise guide to Hindu philosophy and a practical, self-contained guide to life. But there are question marks against certain ideas, as the modern men are rational enough not to be gullible like the people of the Mahabharat age.

A Critique— Verses of the Geeta often contradict each other. For example, in 2.37, Lord Krishna tells Arjun that if he died fighting, he would attain heaven; if he won, he would enjoy the earth. Therefore, he must fight. Till this point it seems alright, but in the very next verse, Krishna tells Arjun to fight without worrying about any gain or loss, victory or defeat, pleasure or pain like a *Karmayogi* or *Sthitpragya* (steadfast). There are numerous such contradictions. At times Arjun is reminded of some great gains of war while at others he is encouraged to fight without any kind of interest in the war like a *Sthitpragya*. Such a contradiction is noticeable because the Srimad Bhagavad Geeta, as contended by numerous commentators, was not composed by one person. As a result of interpolations into its text by various later composers or compilers, we can find embedded in the Srimad Bhagavad Geeta three distinct Geetas promoting three pairs of distinct doctrines. They are:

1. The Brahminic Geeta promoting the doctrines of the *Gunas* and *Karma* (3.5, 27, 33; 18.59-60).

2. The Upanishadic Geeta promoting the doctrines of knowledge of Atman and *Buddhiyog* (2.39-40).
3. Srimad Bhagavad Geeta promoting the doctrines of Lord Krishna as the *Avatar* of Lord Vishnu or Supreme Being and *Bhaktiyog* (Discourses 11, 12 and 18.64-66).

The prime agenda of the Srimad Bhagavad Geeta is that it is the manifesto of a great socio-religious revolution to overthrow the decaying orthodox Vedic *Dharma* (*Brahminism*) and to establish in its place a New *Dharma* centred on Lord Krishna. The New *Dharma*, successively engineered by the Upanishadic and Bhagavad seers, rested on the doctrines of Lord Krishna as the manifestation of the Supreme Lord and *Bhaktiyog*. The two pillars of this *Dharma* were the two aspects of the Upanishadic doctrine of *Buddhiyog: Sannyas* (detachment from sense objects 5.1) and *Tyag* (renunciation of fruits of action 2.51). He offers Himself as the power greater than the *Gunas* (7.14; 14.19). Taking refuge in Him alone would help one to overcome the force of the *Gunas.* Surrendering to Him alone in *Bhaktiyog* one would overcome the doctrine of *Karma* and attain *Moksha* (18.66). He goes on to downgrade or condemn Vedic ritualists (2.41-44); the Vedas (2.46, 52-53); Kamya Karma (2.47-51) and the *Varnashram Dharma* (5.18-19; 6.29). The true spirit of Lord Krishna's *Dharma* in Srimad Bhagavad Geeta is exactly opposite of Brahminism: to establish a New *Dharma* centred on One God; worship of that God by *Bhaktiyog* (Bhakti combined with *Sannyas* and *Tyag*); equality of all people regardless of their birth, class, caste or family; simplicity of life based on detachment from sense objects and selfless service to God and humanity.

The Upanishadic scholars have tried to address the three issues of life raised by Arjun on the battlefield such as *Shokum, Dwandwam and Karmaphalam* are as follows. They have blamed the doctrine of the Gunas as the cause of *Shokum* and *Dwandwam*, and the doctrine of *Karma* as the cause of *Karmaphalam*, resulting in *Sansar*- the cycle of birth, death and rebirth. They said that desire (*Kama*) for, attachment (*Sangas*) to and possessiveness (*Moh*) of sense objects are the functions of the Gunas, and one must cross over them by taking refuge in Brahm or the Lord in order to get over *Shokum* and

Dwandwam. They said that desire for fruits of action (*Sankalp*) causes one to earn *Karmaphalam*, and therefore one must give it up from all *Yagyas* in order to overcome the doctrine of *Karma*. Lord Krishna advises Arjun to abandon all *Dharmas* (Brahminical rituals and all its sub-Dharmas such as *Varnashram Dharma, Jati Dharma* and *Kul Dharma*; and also all heterodox Dharmas: Buddhism, Jainism and *Ajeevika*) and surrender unto Me alone (not to the doctrines of the *Gunas* and *Karma*; or other gods, such as Indra and Agni), because now I am the Eternal *Dharma* (14.27); I shall liberate you from all evils (*Shokum, Dwandwam* and *Karmaphalam* engendered by the doctrines of the *Gunas* and *Karma*); do not grieve (18.66). With this one *shloka*, Lord Krishna ended the decaying Brahminism and all other Dharmas of the land and launched a new *Dharma of Krishna Bhakti*.

OM TAT SAT

Chapter - 2

Soul, Salvation and Spiritualism

As the notions of God, soul, rebirth, incarnation, salvation and spiritualism happen to be the core subject matter of Hindu religion, we should try to understand them at the outset. We should also try to understand them vis-a-vis their conceptualization outside Hinduism. A comparative overview would help us understand discern these highly abstract, complex and at times puzzling concepts holistically. This is crucial for a deeper understanding of the philosophy or messages of the Geeta.

The Supreme Being, also termed as God, *Bhagwan, Prabhu, Parmatman, Brahma, Khuda, Allah, Hari* and *Brahm,* is a pure celestial power— the combined power of all purified *Atmans* (souls) in the Cosmos at a given point of time. These names of God are not to be used as synonyms, since *Brahm* is placed above God in the Geeta. Sometimes confusion arises mainly because some Geeta scholars have treated Sri Krishna as God, while others as *Brahm.* The might of Supreme Being is exercised the moment collapse of the entire Cosmos occurs. The existence of God is not like a property in dispute. Those who firmly believe in God, they believe in the existence of God. The existence of God can only be felt or realized by reaching the stage of enlightenment (*Moksha*). Similar as the metal within an ore requires requisite machinery for its separation, the soul also requires manifesting a body to work out its *Karma* cleanse itself of the impurities within. No human being ever sees or meets God. Only when our soul within gains absolute purity, the enlightened one interacts with the Supreme Being. In simpler terms it is only our soul that interacts with the Supreme Being and not the human form or the physical manifest form.

In connection with Supreme Being or God two questions are often raised by some people: what came before the *Parmatman*? Who created the Supreme Being?' The answer is that it is something that is ever-present and everlasting; it has neither beginning nor end; it is infinite. When something is born, it has to die. This applies to planets, stars, humans, animals and all other things which have a beginning. But the Supreme Being is all-pervasive. He can be experienced or accessed through the spiritual path only as explained in the Geeta.

The moment a human being reaches the stage of enlightenment, he becomes a god-like in a human form same as Mahavir, Gautam Buddha, Jesus Christ or Prophet Mohammed. All these gods in a human form reached the stage of enlightenment in their lifetime. If a single purified soul is an independent piece of puzzle, the Supreme Being is the biggest puzzle. If a single grain of sand is an independent soul, the whole mound being Supreme Being. Supreme Being is always present within us in a minuscule form as our soul. Regaining our true inner self purifying our soul is the ultimate goal of life for every human being. Who knows what we shall be in the next manifestation, so why not travel the spiritual path now. Supreme Being ordained a journey of 12.4 million earthly years in the human form to reach the stage of enlightenment and salvation. There is absolutely no hurry about it, the prime reason why the gist of the sacred scriptures does not become clear so soon. Understanding the Bhagavad Geeta is the ultimate crux of life. The Bhagavad Geeta has got the panacea of all problems of this as well as afterlife. It offers the key to the threshold of the abode of Supreme Reality.

According to the Nyaya Darshan, God is the efficient cause of creation, maintenance and destruction of the universe. God does not create the world out of nothing or out of himself, out of eternal atoms of space, time, mind and soul. The creation of the universe refers to the ordering of these central entities, which are in coexistence with God, into a mortal world. Thus, God as the first efficient cause of the universal forces is the creator of the world. And God is also the preserver, as he causes the atoms to hold together and continue their existence in a particular order that maintains the physical universe. God is also called the destroyer, because he lets loose the forces of destruction when the energies of the mortal world require it. God is one, infinite and eternal, and the universe of space, time, of mind and soul, does not limit Him. God is believed to possess six elements or traits of perfections– infinite glory, absolute sovereignty, unqualified virtue, supreme beauty, perfect knowledge and complete detachment.

Nyaya provides a few arguments to establish the theory of God. The first is the causal argument. According to this line of reasoning, the entire universe is formed by the combination of atoms. Mountains, fields, rivers, etc. must have a cause, for they are made up of parts, have limited dimensions and are not intelligent. This being so, they cannot be the cause themselves and require the guidance of an intelligent cause. That cause must have direct knowledge of all matter and of the atoms that underline all matter. He must be omnipresent and omniscient. This entity cannot be the soul because it does not have the knowledge of other souls. Therefore, there must be an ultimate intelligent entity, which is termed as God.

The second argument is based on *Adrasta* that means 'the unseen or the unknown' and may be translated as providence or fate. The Nyaya system inquires as to why some people are happy while others are not. It is the law of *Karma*, which governs the life of every individual soul, requires that every human being must reap the fruits of his own actions. There is often a long interval of time between an action and its effect, however, and many pleasures cannot be traced to any action performed in this life. Likewise many actions performed in this life do not produce fruits immediately. The sum total of all the *Punya* (good deeds) and *Paap* (bad deeds) collected in the soul is called *Adrasta* or fate and this produces present pain and pleasure. *Adrasta* is not an intelligent principle and must be guided by some intelligent agent to the proper consequences. That intelligent agent, who guides, directs *Adrasta* through proper channels to produce proper consequences is called God.

A third argument for God is based on scriptural testimony. According to this reasoning, the Vedas, Upanishads and all other authoritative scriptures state the existence of God. These scriptures were written by great sages who had experienced the truth within. Thus, the authority of testimony depends on direct experience, which is the only source of knowledge about any and all facts. The Vedas are the expressions of such direct experiences of God. Therefore, God exists.

Now let us discuss the notion of God in the context of Sri Krishna in greater detail. As the word *Bhagwan* (God) is prefixed before the name of Krishna in the Geeta everywhere, some light needs to be shed on the use of the word 'God' here. In a common parlance this word is used so freely that Ram or Krishna is generally addressed or described as God by Hindus. They are described as *Avatar* (incarnation) of God. Agreeing with Swami Dayanand Saraswati (**Satyarth Prakash**) one may pose a question as to what is the necessity before God to take one birth after another or to descend in the form of a lower order creature who is subject to all sorts of problems of worldly life. Furthermore, a human being can be godly or holy, but God Himself cannot be a human being. A human being can have many births, but not God. God is always God. He is free from birth and death. God needs no incarnation to act like a cine star to perform different roles in different movies. When God is greater than infinite universe and is all pervasive and almighty, He in human form is bound to be extremely smaller than even neutron and proton in the universe. The necessity before God to take such a miniature form for a life as long as that of a human being is not really understandable to many. When God is almighty, omnipresent, timeless, and free from birth and death, He could always run the universe the way He liked. He need not take birth as a small creature like a human being who is bound to be mortal. The notion of reincarnation of God is a pure myth or religious concoction created by Brahmins. God does not reincarnate, but only manifests (incarnate). In the case of God 'manifestation' in some form is more appropriate than 'reincarnation'. Incarnation (*Avatar*) of God simply means manifestation of God because he is free from birth and death. There is no room for incarnation or rebirth in other religions such as Christianity, Islam and Buddhism. This topic is further dealt with more exhaustively in the following discussion.

It is also worthwhile to note that those who preach or soothe the people suggesting that God is great, all merciful or kind and can wash away or pardon all sins committed by human beings are bluffing their way out of troble to safeguard their vested interestss. God does not do any good or bad things because He is not like a living being with any sensory organ. How can a human being state whether a particular act of God, if any, is either good or bad? God is completely above the thinking process.

Sri Krishna has clearly explained the reason why He sometimes manifests in the human form in Discourse 9. But that is not to be branded as reincarnation, as He remains present everywhere in the form of Supreme Being. His appearance or disappearance is not like any material object or like a human being. God can remain present in both *Vyakta* (manifest) and *Avyakta* (unmanifest) form all the time simultaneously. God is Supreme Being– a kind of Absolute Consciousness. He is above both the states of manifest and unmanifest. Absolute Consciousness does not incarnate, but manifests using His own celestial potencies. His birth, activities and form are transcendental or out of this world. Lord Krishna had shown his *Vishwaroop* in Mahabharat thrice: first, when He visited the court of Hastinapur as the peace messenger, secondly when He gave the divine knowledge of Bhagavad Geeta to Arjun. And finally when He met Utanka after the Mahabharata battle. Some commentators have taken Sri Krishna as reincarnation of Vishnu. Verses equating Sri Krishna with Vishnu or suggesting Sri Krishna as reincarnation of Vishnu are later day insertions, as the Geeta has grown over a long period of time. Ramanujacharya, an exponent of *Visishtadvait* Vedantic philosophy and subsequently the 13th century scholar Madhavacharya, have also believed in the supremacy of Vishnu, they have described Sri Krishna as incarnation of Vishnu. On the other hand, for many scholars Vishnu is a fictional God. Hymns relating to Vishnu were added in dramatically appropriate places in the main epic story of the Mahabharat by the end of the second century B. C, as W. Douglas P. Hill has rightly argued in his book, **The Bhagavadgita** (1966). Vishnu is a Divine Being, not Absolute Reality. Only Sri Krishna is considered Absolute Reality or Supreme Being. **Srimad Bhagavadam,** the greatest of all Puranas, declares Krishna as the original Supreme Personality of Godhead. The Geeta is not an extension of the Vedic view of Hindu Gods and Goddesses. Both directly and indirectly, the Geeta has noted in numerous verses that all Gods and Goddesses are a mere reflection of Sri Krishna, as Sri Krishna is nothing but Absolute Consciousness. The Almighty does not need to incarnate in a miniature form or a lower level living being. A critical study of the Geeta, hopefully enough, endorses this conception of Sri Krishna. To most Hindus He is the God Himself, the Supreme Being or the *Purna Purushottam*. Also the exponents of *Shuddhadvait* regarded Sri Krishna as the Supreme Lord. It is a very puzzling problem of the Hindu religion or the Indian philosophy that the name of God is Sri Krishna or Vishnu, while God is not identified by any semantic name. This problem has arisen chiefly because most of the early scholars were not much clear about the notion of God. Different philosophers were so confused that they had different conceptions of God.

Considering the Bhagavad Geeta, the reincarnation theory is a totally flawed concept something beyond comprehension of most human beings. Every soul never takes rebirth nor is reincarnated. It only manifests in bodies one after another after the occurrence of death of mortal body. The manifestation of next body is directly related to the residual balance of *Karma* of present life.

The authors of religious books always try to convey the message that whatever is said in the name of God is to be trusted blindly as the ideas are not from this world. Most Hindus tend to hold a very bizarre view about the notion of God as it is evident from various Puranas. They have humanised or personified God in such a manner that the identity of God is at times reduced to an ordinary human being. It is constantly noticed on the devotional TV channels saying that God is just like a human being who speaks like common people, marries with women and procreates children and performs all sorts of humanly activities. God, like humans, also eats, drinks, dances, gets sick, hates others and tends to clash for personal interests, kills adversaries and at times shows compassion for others. Such traits of God are called anthropomorphism by social scientists. This is a kind of failing of ordinary human beings that they are not able to understand anything beyond their own appearance and understanding because of their poor use of mental faculty.

Krishna was in the form of a super human being, but at the same time He was a Supreme Being. The notion of God is so abstract or supernatural that He is not to be defined like a concrete object which has got some sort of shape and feature. God has neither any beginning nor end. There is no portrait of Lord Krishna available; all are man-drawn and hence based on a picture of a random man. It is generally agreed that God is Supreme Being conceived as perfect, omnipotent, omniscient originator and ruler of the universe. God is beyond words, as all languages are pure human creation. God cannot be subjected to any semantic definition, as nobody knows the traits of God. In fact, He is always above all human traits and attributes. Conceptualization of God in a human form was not acceptable to Gautam Buddh, Jain saint Mahavir, Charvak, Nanak and many such great saints and thinkers. Even the great illiterate saintly poet like Kabirdas or other such *Bhakti* poets never accepted Hindu Gods and Goddesses in a human form. They are creations of orthodox Brahmins to serve their vested interests.

With respect to the number and volume of religious scriptures Hindu religion is the richest of all religions put together, besides being the oldest one. No religion has been more wide open for diverse views and commentaries by so many saints, sages, philosophers with diverse perspectives than the Hindu religion. Hindu religion is so vast, varied, and complex that important characteristics of all the religions can be easily discerned here. Hindu religion is so varied that it comprises numerous cults, sects, faiths and philosophies with incompatible conceptions of God. All of them can never be equally truthful at the same time. Some of them are, in fact, highly contradictory, inconsistent and paradoxical. In Hindu scriptures the concept of God has been so variously defined that the notion of God continues to be shrouded in mystery. Hindus have conceived countless number of gods and goddesses in their religious scriptures and legendary tales. At the same time there have also been thinkers, commonly called agnostic or sceptics, who have even questioned or negated the existence of God. Answering the volley of questions the Vedantic philosophy suggests that God is infinite existence, infinite consciousness and infinite bliss and yet God can be personal as well, assuming human form in every age. The second part of the argument has been often subjected to criticisms by a host of philosophers and religious leaders.

Some scholars have tried to question the divinity of Krishna. Only agnostic or sceptic can subscribe their views. As an arch believer in Indian spiritualism, we always consider the supremacy of the Cosmic Being like Krishna. One need not harbour misunderstanding of any kind in this regard, as Krishna has neither a beginning nor an end. He is limitless and Almighty. Sri Krishna of the Mahabharat is a mere symbolic of that Lord Krishna. He was a creation or manifestation of none other than the Lord Himself known by so many names in different languages. He is immortal and free from the incidence of birth and death, because He is Supreme Being. God does not have a rigid form. Everything begins and ends with Him. A cosmic person is not necessarily an incarnation of God.

The word 'Lord' has been used as a prefix before the name of Krishna in the Geeta to distinguish him from other characters, as Krishna was definitely in an extraordinary role dissimilar from all other characters of the Mahabharat. The word 'Lord' is prefixed before Krishna in this book treating it as a part of his respectful name (i.e. Bhagwan Krishna). Krishna is in the role of Godhead in the Geeta. Furthermore, one should not be bogged down by the legends or the story of Mahabharat, what is really important is the gospel of Lord Krishna in the Geeta. The Geeta was conceptualized when the level of development of society as a whole was in its primordial phase. It simply suggests that even in ancient days, there were some genius with a very high level of intellectual development. At times I wonder whether a modern man who considers himself very knowledgeable, wise, rational or scientific can really imagine creating a work of the Geeta's order, cutting across all sorts of narrow considerations, barriers or systems of belief. One may dispute certain messages, but one cannot create their substitute. The Geeta may be a creation of the Hindus, but it is not a book of or for the Hindu religion. It does not contain even the word 'Hindu'. As it is the greatest work on spiritualism, it encompasses all religions. In a plain language it teaches complete surrender to the Lord without any ifs and buts, and expects performance of all duties of life in a righteous manner. Sri

Krishna has stated that He does not dwell in anything, though everything is His manifestation only. Hence it is needless to clash over the construction, demolition or possession of a temple, mosque or a church or other such places of worship, especially when everything belongs to the same God. The ownership of everything rests with the Supreme Being only.

In modern times some of the saints or preachers on the devotional channels of the TV all the time talk about Krishna, Ram, Shiv, Durga, Hanuman and a host of other gods, goddess and deities in such a lively manner as if they have really met them and listened to their conversations in person. In a plain language all such preachers are bamboozlers and in the name of religion they tend to befool the masses to earn their living. Many such people have made good use of God, goddesses or even religion as a gainful enterprise with intent to serve their vested interests. Some have actually succeeded to amass huge wealth in millions which cannot be normally achieved in the lifetime of an individual through any other secular occupation or profession. Many such preachers, *Guru, Baba* or even the so-called *Bhagwan,* enjoying a lavish life, were found involved in such criminal activities as money laundering, sex racket, corruption, fraud, rape and were either put behind the bars or are still facing criminal charges to be finally imprisoned. Persons like Satya Sai Baba, Chandraswami, Bhagwan Shree Rajneesh and Swami Premananda are no more with us now, while others like Swami Nithyananda, Asharam Bapu and Sant Rampal are struggling for their respectable face both in the eyes of law and the people in general. Some phony spiritual leaders like Virender Dev Dikshit of the *Adhyatmik Ishwariya Vishwa Vidyalaya* and many more are waiting in wings to be put behind the bars. Such people have thrived in India because most Indians, especially the barely literate or the poorly educated ones, are generally very traditional, credulous, superstitious and fatalist. This is clearly evident from one of the very recent facts that a fake Indian Guru named Gurmeet Ram Rahim Singh *Insan*, the Chief of Dera Sachcha Sauda in Haryana, who was convicted of rape by a special court of the Central Bureau of Investigation and was sentenced to 20 years in jail on 25 August 2017, had millions of hysteric following both within Hindu and Sikh communities. This is not a matter of any great surprise that such an immoral or illegitimate incidence in the name of religion pervades more or less all communities. One more such recent shocking incidence, for instance, relates to the Madarsa Jamia Khadeejtul Qubra Lilabnat in Yasinganj area under Saadatganj police station of Lucknow City. On 30th December 2017, 51 school girls, who were subjected to sexual harassment by the Madarsa Manager, were rescued by the Lucknow police. For alleged sexual harassment the Madarsa Manager was arrested and sent to 14 days' judicial custody. Most recently in June 2018 a woman had filed a rape complaint against a self-proclaimed godman called Daati Maharaj for being raped by him at his Ashram in Delhi on January 9, 2016, and then again on March 26, 27 and 28 at his Ashram in Rajasthan. The fake godman had to appear before the Delhi Police Crime Branch for the investigation into the rape charges levelled against him. He was booked under sections 376, 377, 354 and 34 of the Indian Penal Code (IPC).

God: One, Multiple or None

Whether God is one or many, this leads to a never ending debate on the subject. Hindus, Buddhists and Islam tend to differ quite widely with respect to number of God– from none to multiple. Abrahamanic religions are dominated by the notion that One is better than many: One God, One Book, One Son, One Church, One Nation of God. In Hinduism, the more the better: many gods, many books, many sages, and many insights.

In this ever-growing community of endless gods and goddesses, the roles of the gods and even their hierarchy are somehow diffuse. Some gods get more attention than others and different accounts suggest different hierarchies. Olympian gods, who had a clear hierarchy, may look greedy and envious compared with the tolerant gods of Hinduism. Agni, Indra, Shiv, Brahma, Vishnu, Durga and Ganesh are just a few examples of very important Hindu gods and deities that were regarded at different times and by different sects as the most important gods. Shiv, Vishnu and Brahma were parts of a holy Hindu trinity (*Trimurti*). Shiv is sometimes associated with the destruction process and Vishnu as the creator who takes the remains destroyed by Shiv in order to regenerate what has been destroyed. For the Ganapatya Hindu sect,

Ganesh is the most important deity. Ganesh is highly recognizable with his elephant head and human body, representing the soul (*Atman)* and the physical body (*Maya*) respectively. He is also the patron of writers, travellers, students, commerce, and new projects (for which he removes obstacles from one's path) and is rather fond of sweets, as various legends suggest.

The Supreme Being (Brahm) is often described in Indian philosophy in negative terms, i.e. *na-yeti* or *neti-neti*. It is not this, and not this also. One may go to the extent of becoming a nihilist. It is, however, to be remembered that *neti-neti* negates the super-imposed characteristics/qualities of Brahm and not the Brahm itself. It proves the indescribability of Brahm and not the being of Brahm. It is so-stated in order to understand the notion of God. It tends to describe the one who cannot be described. Literal meanings may confine the Brahm in the perception and not in the being. Literally Brahm means the largest and yet ever enlarging, 'that which contains all but is not contained by anything.' Because of this, Brahm is taken to be as space. **The Vrihadaranyak, Chandogya** and **Taittariya Upanishads** indicate that Brahm is space or (Akash). **Isavasya Upanishad** states that Brahm is the inside of all and the outside of all. The Brahm, at best, can be felt and realised rather than be described. *Moksha* is the realization of Brahm. The essence of whole argument is that God is one.

All major religions, except for Buddhism, have supported the existence of God. But nobody knows what truth is. Frankly speaking, most people do not worry much whether God is one or many. Even if God is too many, they are similar and mean same thing. The fact of the matter is that if anything is based on some system of belief, there is not much room left for logic and discussion. If we accept there exists God, whether one or many, we should have a close look at the following verses which would dispel the confusion whether there is only one God or more than one:

"We believe in that which has been revealed unto us and revealed unto you; our God and your God is One, and unto Him we surrender." (Koran 29:46)

"There exists nothing whatsoever higher than Me, O Dhananjay! All that is here is strung on Me, as a row of gems on a string." (Bhagavad

Geeta 7.7) 'And whatever is the seed of all beings, that also am I, O Arjun. There is nothing, animate or inanimate, that can exist without Me.' (Bhagavad Geeta 10.39) "I am the origin of all. Everything evolves from Me. The wise who understand this worship Me with love and devotion." (Bhagavad Geeta 10.8). Thus both in the Koran and the Geeta there is only one God.

Both Christians and Muslims criticize Hindu religion on the ground of multiplicity of God in Hinduism. In Hinduism the people have many demigods like Indra, Shiv, Brahma, etc. and these are not one with Krishna. God is one, as said before. Many of the 'gods' accepted by the Hindus are not gods at all; they are just like us, Jeev or souls. They are merely far more elevated than us. In fact, Hindus are a divided house, as some believe in one God, others believe in multiple gods, goddesses and demigods and yet some believe in none. They are themselves at loggerheads about the notion of God. Some have treated certain deities as gods. It is impossible to say conclusively whether God is one or many. Both are based on some sort of argument or logic. Can we really understand God logically? Certainly not. God is not a product of some logic. They are all far from truth. Nobody knows the final truth. Truth about God is a pure mystery. When we do not know how many earth, sun, moon, star or universe exists, how can we say that there is only one God. There have been lots of thinkers, philosophers, saints or sages who do not believe in any God. When human beings actually do not know what is God, how can they count the number of God? If any, where is He? Who counted Him or Them and where and when? Hindu religion as such does have diverse opinions about the number and notion of God, but not the Geeta in particular. The notion of God is crystal clear in the Srimad Bhagavad Geeta, but again that is meant for a spiritual or enlightened person.

A genuine question is raised here: why do we have so many gods and goddesses in Hinduism? As stated in the holy Bhagavad Geeta the creator of whole cosmos is one termed as Brahm in Hinduism. The Supreme Being is known by so many names in Hinduism such as Bhagavan, Ishwar, Karta, Sanatan Purush, Parmatman and Prabhu. In the nascent stages of life when spirituality had not yet evolved mankind survived rigors of day-to-day life by praying to Supreme Being all the time. As many human beings, as many different forms of Supreme Being existed in their thinking. If one was suffering from drought one prayed to Indra Devta (God of rain) so that the grace of Indra Devta brought rains in plenty. As per Hindu mythology there exist a total of 330 million gods in all (This myth is based on distorted interpretation of some hymn of the Rigved. Actually that hymn means merely 33 high class gods.). Going by religion such a number carried some meaning as people prayed to different forms of gods and goddesses all the time, depending on individual circumstances. But from the spirituality point of view there was only one God termed Brahm in Hinduism— the one and only one. The Advait Vedant theory of Hinduism confirms this point of view. It was only by undertaking the path of *Gyan Yog* that human beings could finally realize their true inner self reaching the stage of self realization or God realization called enlightenment. For a true seeker of spirituality hordes of Hindu gods carry no meaning.

Lord Krishna is the source of everything and being the proven God has appeared so many times and each time He proved He was the one true God. Lord Krishna revealed his identity to Arjun as the Absolute Truth. Krishna clearly explained to us the concept of one God. He is the origin, the creator and proprietor of everything. He has given us options, not mandates to choose various religious paths. Krishna also introduced true secularism which may not exist in other religions. Krishna clearly stated in the Bhagavad Geeta that all gods and goddesses depended on Him. Despite that He did not force us to worship Him only. Krishna said as many rivers ultimately reach the same ocean, similarly the people of all religious backgrounds ultimately reach Me. Such a thought is certainly missing from the Bible as well as the Koran. In the following verses Lord Krishna has taught us to have the same regard for all religious faiths, as all are same to Him. He did not favour any discrimination based on the faith and yet people of other religious faiths dislike or hate Hinduism because of their religious bigotry. "Whosoever desires to worship whatever deity– using any name, form, and method– with *Shraddha* (faith), I make their *Shraddha* steady in that very deity. Endowed with steady faith, they worship that deity and attain their wishes through that deity. Those wishes are, indeed, granted by Me alone." (Geeta 7. 21-22).

If there is only one God, God remains definitely the same for all the people of all the faiths. Why are the people fighting against each other in the name of God then? Is it because everybody has got separate name for the same God? But this difference is on account of linguistic variations, not on account of differences in understanding of God. God has become very helpless here. He is not able to tell the believers that they worship the same God in different ways. Srimad Bhagavad Geeta is an exception to this. It seems religious fanatics are not fighting for the sake of God but for themselves. Religious conversions too do not serve any purpose of God because God is the same for one and all. Thus all persons engaged in religious conversion are pure religious fraud.

Concepts of Soul and Rebirth

The subject of re-incarnation or rebirth has always evoked tremendous fascination and curiosity both outside and inside Hinduism. Rebirth removes finality from death, reaffirms the imperishable nature of the spirit and affords a second chance. It is believed that rebirth does not occur at a future date but is co-extensive and simultaneous. It is here and now. The originator of the *Karma* takes over the unfinished task through his progeny. Hindu religion regards rebirth as a compelling tool for emancipation of soul from the *karmic* fetters.

The word 'reincarnation' derived from Latin literally means 'entering the flesh again'. An alternate term is transmigration implying migration of soul from one life (body) to another. Although reincarnation and rebirth prima facie appear to mean same thing, they are not to be used synonymously. They are to be used in two different contexts. The reincarnation refers to rebirth of a divine being, while the rebirth refers to transmigration or rebirth of an ordinary soul after death. The word 'incarnation' is not to be used in the context of rebirth of an individual soul and so also reincarnation. This subtle difference should be kept in mind to avoid unnecessary confusion. In fact, it has already been stated that reincarnation even in the context of God is not sustainable.

Rebirth refers to the belief that an aspect of every human being (or all living beings in some cultures) continues to exist after death, this aspect may be the soul or mind or consciousness or something transcendent which is reborn in an interconnected cycle of existence.

Rebirth is a central tenet of all major Indian religions, namely Buddhism, Hinduism, Jainism and Sikhism. Although the majority of denominations within the Abrahamic religions of Judaism, Christianity and Islam do not believe that individuals take rebirth, particular groups within these religions do believe in rebirth. Etymologically speaking, the origin of the notions of incarnation, rebirth or reincarnation is obscure. Discussion on the subject is seen in the philosophical traditions of India only. The ideas associated with incarnation and rebirth may have arisen independently in different regions, or they might have spread as a result of acculturation.

The idea of rebirth and incarnation has early roots in the Vedic period, predating the Buddha and the Mahavir. The concepts of the cycle of birth and death, *Sansar* and liberation partly were derived from ascetic traditions that arose in India around the middle of the first millennium BCE. The Rigved has made references of incarnation and rebirth. Though these early textual layers of the Vedas, from 2nd millennium BCE, mention and anticipate the doctrine of Karma and rebirth, the idea is not fully developed there. It is in the early Upanishads, which are pre-Buddha and pre-Mahavir, where these ideas are more explicitly developed in a general way. Detailed descriptions first appear around the mid 1st millennium BCE in diverse traditions, including Buddhism, Jainism and various schools of Hindu philosophy, each of which gave unique expression to the general principle.

Indian religions consider the release from the cycle of rebirth as the ultimate spiritual goal, and call the liberation by terms such as *Moksha, Nirvan, Mukti* and *Kaivalya*. However, the Hindu, Buddhist and Jain traditions have differed since ancient times in their assumptions and in their details on what takes rebirth, how rebirth occurs and what leads to liberation. In the following discussion we present the major beliefs associated with the subject of rebirth within Hinduism and other religions.

Hinduism—According to Hindu scriptures, individual souls pass through many cycles of births and deaths, and live upon earth as humans, animals and other living beings until they are liberated from the bonds of Nature. Rebirth facilitates the gradual progression of souls from ignorance to knowledge, untruth to truth, darkness to light, and death to immortality. It gives an opportunity to the souls to start anew on the path of liberation to use the lessons learned in the past lives and work for their liberation. The earliest layers of Vedic text incorporate the concept of life, followed by an afterlife in heaven and hell based on cumulative virtues (merit) or vices (demerit). However, the ancient Vedic Rishis challenged this idea of afterlife as simplistic, because people do not live an equally moral or immoral life. Between generally virtuous lives, some are more virtuous than others; while evil too has degrees, and the texts assert that it would be unfair for people, with varying degrees of virtue or vices, to end up in heaven or hell, in 'either or' and disproportionate manner irrespective of how virtuous or vicious their lives were. They introduced the idea of an afterlife in heaven or hell in proportion to one's merit, and when this runs out, one returns and is reborn. This idea appears in ancient and medieval texts, as the cycle of life, death, rebirth and redeath. With the lapse of time the notion of hail and heaven has become highly archaic and obsolete and the notion of rebirth more dominant in Hinduism. In a plain and straight forward language the conception of permanent hail and heaven as the ultimate abode for impious and pious souls respectively is a kind of huge religious bluff to the innocent people by clever and crafty Brahmins and their henchmen.

According to Hindu beliefs the material world is a personification of the Lord of Death, known as *Kala* (Time). Death devours everything in this world. Every living being and object in this world is food to Death. Beings are caught in between the grinding teeth of this great devourer and none can escape his hungry jaws. Death touches and destroys everything in the objective world when its time comes. However, it cannot touch the individual selves (*Atman*) which are immortal and indestructible. Death is for the physical body. The soul remains intact and escapes from the body to take birth again. It goes on and on until the soul is liberated.

Each soul is enveloped inside a field (body) made up of the components (*Tattvas*) of Nature and permeated with the influence of *Gunas,* namely *Sattva, Rajas* and *Tamas*. These three qualities are responsible for our thinking and actions. In the body, the soul remains the witness consciousness. It does not undergo any change, but it is enveloped by the impurities of the mind and body. The soul's reflection in the qualities is the ego. It assumes the soul's identity and acts according to its predominant desires, which are caused by the predominant *Gunas* present in the body. Under their influence the ego or the being (*Jeev*) becomes attached to the objects of the world and experiences attraction and aversion. Here comes the notion of *Karma*.

According to the Hindu traditions, the body dies, asserts, but not the soul. The soul is taken as the eternal reality, indestructible and bliss. Everything and all existence is believed to be connected and cyclical in Hinduism, all living beings are composed of two things, the soul and the body or matter. *Atman* does not change and cannot change by its innate nature in the Hindu belief. In contrast, the body and personality constantly change. They are born and hence they die. Current Karma impacts the future circumstances in life as well as the future forms and realms of lives. Good intent and actions lead to good future, bad intent and actions lead to bad future, impacting how one takes re-birth. This is the Hindu view of existence. Hindus believe the self or soul (*Atman*) repeatedly takes on a physical body, until it attains *Moksha*.

There is no permanent heaven or hell in Hinduism. In the afterlife, based on one's *Karma,* the soul is reborn as another being in heaven, hell, or a living being on earth (human, animal). It is believed that gods too die once their past *karmic* merit runs out, as do those in hell, and they return getting another chance on the earth. The rebirth continues, endlessly in cycles, until one embarks on a spiritual pursuit, realizes self-knowledge, and thereby gains *Moksha*, the final release out of the rebirth cycles. The Upanishads primarily focus on the liberation from rebirth. The Bhagavad Gita discusses various paths to liberation. It states:

Just as the soul passes from childhood to youth, from youth to old age, similarly it passes from one body to another. A wise man is not confused about this.– (2.13)

Just as we abandon our worn-out garments and put on new ones, so the spirit abandons an old body and enters a new one.– (2.22)

When the soul transcends these three *Gunas* arising out of the body, it is liberated from birth, death, old age and pain and attains deathlessness.– (14.20)

The Hindu philosophers have not been unanimous about the interpretation of rebirth and liberation; rather, there are huge differences within Hindu traditions on rebirth and the state of *Moksha*. For example, the dualistic devotional traditions such as Madhvacharya's Dvait Vedant champions a theistic premise and asserts that human soul and Brahm are different, loving devotion to Brahm (Lord Vishnu in Madhvacharya theology) is the means to release from *Sansar*, it is the grace of God which leads to liberation and spiritual liberation is achievable only in afterlife (*Videhamukti*). The nondualistic traditions, such as Adi Shankara's Advait Vedant, champion a monistic premise, asserting that the individual human soul and Brahm are identical. Only ignorance, impulsiveness and inertia lead to suffering through *Sanskar.* In reality they are no dualities. Meditation and self-knowledge is the path to liberation, the realization that one's soul is identical to Brahm is *Moksha,* and spiritual liberation is achievable in this life (*Jeevanmukti*).

The souls are bound to the cycle of births and deaths mainly because of desires and desire-ridden actions. The scriptures identify three main reasons for the rebirth and suffering of the souls in the mortal world, namely egoism (*anava*), attachments (*pasas*) and delusion (*Maya*). *Anava* means atomicity or the feeling of being small, distinct and separate from the rest of creation. It stands for egoism, beingness or individuality, which is responsible for selfishness, duality, and desire-ridden actions. Attachments are the bonds we form with the objects and people in the world. They hold us down and prevent us from achieving complete freedom from the hold of Nature. Delusion or Maya is mistaking the unreal for real and real for unreal. One example is believing that the mind and body are the self, and the objective world is real. In reality, both are impermanent and unreal. The delusion prevents us from knowing the truth and finding the truth. These three impurities produce *Karma* and bind the souls to the cycle of births and deaths.

In order to understand the dynamics of birth and death one has to understand the doctrine of *Karma*. As summarized in the Bhagavad Geeta the doctrine of karma and the theory of evolution played a pivotal role in the life cycle of every soul. In the absence of *Karma* or in the absence of process of evolution the entire cosmos carries no meaning.

Ever since souls started their cosmic journey the doctrine of *Karma* and the process of evolution become governing. At the time of death of mortal body, if the residual balance of *Karma* demands a soul manifesting next form as a manual labourer, one cannot be born as a king. In the domain of Supreme Being there is nothing like a free lunch, nor can we expect mangoes to grow on a guava tree. Everything results from inscrutable laws of *Karma*. As we sow, so shall we reap, nothing less or more. As stated in the Bhagavad Geeta *Karma* acts as accountant general of the cosmic system keeping record of the minutest action indulged by human beings. Every single thought, positive or negative, precipitates into an act of *Karma*. For gaining enlightenment or for reaching Supreme Being one has to cut across shackles of *Karma* forever. There is no other alternative.

Rebirth— Now let us briefly understand the doctrine of rebirth. In a plain language it is a kind of migration of soul from one manifestation to another or from one body to the next and thus the journey of a soul continues uninterrupted, unbroken. In Hinduism the entire lifespan of 8.4 million manifestations covers an earthly life cycle of 96.4 million years which is one single span of life for a soul. As the soul can neither be created nor destroyed, it cannot have rebirth. Rebirth only means our soul manifesting body is after another body until it reaches the last leg of cosmic life through 8.4 millionth manifestations before the human being finally attains salvation. Travel in the human form is the most pleasant experience for a soul. It is only in human form that a soul is finally released from the cycle of birth and death forever. Human being is the highest manifest stage in the cosmic life cycle and hence it becomes our sacrosanct duty to assist our soul in completing its cosmic life cycle at the earliest. It is only by taking the spiritual path that we can reach our true inner self or the spirit within. So why not travel the spiritual path now and complete the cosmic journey at the earliest?

As per the Bhagavad Geeta when nothing dies, how can something take rebirth? As revealed in the Bhagavad Geeta every soul is indestructible. It can neither be created nor destroyed. In the circumstances the rebirth theory that people often talk of is an absolute farce. A soul never takes rebirth in a new body, it only manifests new body after the death of present body.

Now another question emerges, that is, is there any chance of liberation from rebirth? The answer to this question is in affirmative. It is possible to escape the cycle of births and achieve liberation through self-realization. For that one has to practise renunciation, cultivate virtues, perform obligatory duties selflessly, surrender to God and lead exemplary lives pursuing the highest knowledge, fixing their minds completely upon the Self or the Supreme Self. Those who fill the minds and bodies with purity (*Sattva*) qualify to achieve liberation. The Upanishad describes the path by which these immortal souls travel the path of the gods (Devayan) or the northern path. People who achieve liberation are forever freed from mortality. They may become future gods, but do not return to the earth.

Now let us understand the difference between incarnation and reincarnation. Incarnation (*Avatar*) means a manifestation of God (Isvara) upon earth in a physical form as a living being, human or animal. Reincarnation means the rebirth of divine souls upon earth. According to Hinduism, the purpose of incarnation of God is preservation of Dharma and continuation of the worlds and their order and regularity. The purpose of rebirth is also continuation of obligatory duties (Dharma) and preservation of the social, moral and world order. An incarnation is a self-willed divine act. The rebirth of a soul happens because of *Karma* and past life impressions. It is not a wilful act but a consequence of previous desire-ridden action. It is believed that only Vishnu, the preserver, incarnates upon earth. However, some of the incarnations ascribed to Vishnu now were originally attributed to Brahma. The Puranas describe nine incarnations of Vishnu so far. Sri Krishna has been described as one of the incarnations of Vishnu which has been contested in the book at several places. The tenth one will happen in future at the end of Kaliyug, when Vishnu manifests as Kalki and destroys all evil beings.

Buddhism— According to various Buddhist scriptures, Gautam Buddha believed in the existence of an afterlife in another world and in rebirth. The early Buddhist texts discuss rebirth as a part of the doctrine of *Sanskar*. This asserts that the nature of existence is a 'suffering-laden cycle of life, death and rebirth, without beginning or end'. Liberation from this cycle of existence, Nirvana, is the foundation and the most important purpose of Buddhism. Buddhist texts also assert that an enlightened person knows his previous births, a knowledge achieved through high levels of meditative concentration.

The Buddha also asserted that *Karma* influences rebirth, and that the cycles of repeated births and deaths are endless. Before the birth of Buddha, ancient Indian scholars had developed competing theories of afterlife, including the materialistic school such as Charvak, which posited that death is the end, there is no afterlife, no soul, no rebirth, no *Karma*, and they described death to be a state where a living being is completely annihilated, dissolved. The Buddha rejected this theory, adopted the alternate existing theories of rebirth, criticizing the materialistic schools that denied rebirth and *Karma*. According to Buddha, such beliefs are inappropriate and dangerous, because such annihilationist views encourage moral irresponsibility and material hedonism; he tied moral responsibility to rebirth.

The Buddha introduced the concept that there is no permanent self (soul), and this central concept in Buddhism is called *Anatta.* The major contemporary Buddhist traditions such as Theravada, Mahayan and Vajrayan accept the teachings of Buddha. These teachings assert there is rebirth, there is no permanent self and no irreducible atman (soul) moving from one life to another and tying these lives together. According to the Buddha, soul is temporary. All living beings are aggregates which tend to dissolve at death, but they take rebirth. The rebirth cycles continue endlessly and it is a source of *Dukkha* (suffering, pain), but this rebirth and *Dukkha* cycle can be stopped through *Nirvana.* The *Anatta* doctrine of Buddhism in a contrast to Hinduism, the latter asserting that 'soul exists, it is involved in rebirth, and it is through this soul that everything is connected'.

Different traditions within Buddhism have offered different theories on what takes rebirth and how rebirth happens. One theory suggests that it occurs through consciousness or stream of consciousness upon death, which reincarnates into a new aggregation. This process is similar to the flame of a dying candle lighting up another. The consciousness in the newly born being is neither identical to nor entirely different from that in the deceased but the two form a causal continuum or stream in this Buddhist theory. Transmigration is influenced by a being's past

Karma. The root cause of rebirth, states Buddhism, is the abiding of consciousness in ignorance (*Avidya*) about the nature of reality, and when this ignorance is uprooted, rebirth ceases. The 14th Dalai Lama has stated emphatically that it would be difficult for science to disprove rcbirth.

Jainism— The Jain philosophy assumes that the soul (*Jeev* in Jainism) exists and is eternal, passing through the cycles of transmigration and rebirth. After death, rebirth of soul into a new body is instantaneous in the early Jain texts. In Jainism, the rebirth doctrine, along with its theories of *Sanskar* and *Karma*, are central to its theological foundations, as evidenced by the extensive literature on it in the major sects of Jainism, and their pioneering ideas on these topics from the earliest times of the Jain tradition. Rebirth in the contemporary Jainism traditions is the belief that the worldly life is characterized by continuous rebirths and suffering in various realms of existence.

Karma forms a central and fundamental part of the Jain faith, being intricately connected to other of its philosophical concepts like transmigration, rebirth, liberation, non-violence (*Ahinsa*) and non-attachment, among others. Actions are seen to have consequences: some immediate, some delayed, even into future incarnations. So the doctrine of *Karma* is not considered simply in relation to one life-time, but also in relation to both future rebirths and past lives. The *Jeev* or the soul is sometimes born in the world of gods, sometimes in hell. Sometimes it acquires the body of a demon; all this happens on account of its *karma*.. This *Jeev* sometimes takes birth as a worm, as an insect or as an ant. The text further states that *Karma* is the root of birth and death. The souls bound by *Karma* go round and round in the cycle of existcncc.

Actions and emotions in the current lifetime affect future rebirths depending on the nature of the particular *Karma*. For example, a good and virtuous life indicates a latent desire to experience good and virtuous thing in life. Therefore, such a person attracts *Karma* that ensures that his future births will allow him to experience and manifest his virtues and good aspects of life unhindered. In this case, he may take birth in heaven or in a prosperous and virtuous family of human beings. On the other hand, a person who has indulged in immoral deeds, or with a cruel disposition, indicates a latent desire to experience cruel thing in life. As a natural consequence, he will attract *Karma* which will ensure that he is reborn in hell, or in lower forms of life to enable his soul to experience the cruel aspects of life.

There is no retribution, judgement or reward involved but natural consequences of the choices in life made either knowingly or unknowingly. Hence, whatever suffering or pleasure that a soul may be experiencing in its present life is on account of choices that it has made in the past. In view of this doctrine, Jainism attributes supreme importance to pure thinking and moral behaviour.

In all, the Jain texts speak of a cycle of 8.4 million birth destinies in which souls find themselves again and again as they cycle within *Sansar*. In Jainism God has no role to play in an individual's destiny; one's personal destiny is not seen as a consequence of any system of reward or punishment, but rather as a result of its own personal *Karma*. Violent deeds, killing of creatures having five sense organs, eating fish, and so on, lead to rebirth in hell. Deception, fraud and falsehood lead to rebirth in the animal and vegetable world. Kindness, compassion and humble character results in human birth; while austerities and the making and keeping of vows lead to rebirth in heaven. This clearly means that quality of life in the text birth depends upon the quality of life in the present life. God has no role to play in such matters. Hence one should try to be a decent human being. He alone is the maker of his destiny.

Each soul is thus responsible for its own predicament, as well as its own salvation. Accumulated *Karma* represents a sum total of all unfulfilled desires, attachments and aspirations of a soul. It enables the soul to experience the various themes of the lives that it desires to experience. Hence a soul may transmigrate from one life form to another for countless number of years, taking with it the *Karma* that it has earned, until it finds conditions that bring about the required fruits. In certain philosophies, heavens and hells are often viewed as places for eternal salvation or eternal damnation for good and bad deeds. But according to Jainism, such places, including the earth are simply the places which allow the soul to experience its unfulfilled *Karma* .

The early texts of Buddhism, Hinduism and Jainism share the concepts and terminology related to rebirth, but they disagree in their assumptions and theories about rebirth. Hinduism relies on its foundational assumption that 'soul, Self exists' (*Atman, Atta*), in contrast to the Buddhist assumption that there is 'no soul, no Self' (*Anatta, Anatman*). Hindu traditions consider soul to be the unchanging eternal essence of a living being, and what journeys across rebirths until it attains self-knowledge. Buddhism, in contrast, asserts a rebirth theory without a Self, and considers realization of non-Self or Emptiness as *Nirvan (Nibbana*). Thus Buddhism and Hinduism have a very different view on whether a self or soul exists, which impacts the details of their respective rebirth theories.

The rebirth doctrine of Jainism is different from that of Buddhism, even though both are non-theistic *Sramana* traditions. Jainism, in contrast to Buddhism, accepts the foundational assumption that soul exists (*Jeev*) and asserts that this soul is involved in the rebirth mechanism. Further, Jainism considers asceticism as an important means to spiritual liberation. It marks the end of rebirth, while Buddhism does believe in it.

Judaism—The belief in rebirth had first existed amongst the Jewish mystics in the ancient world, among whom differing explanations were given concerning afterlife, although with a universal belief in an immortal soul. Today rebirth is an esoteric belief within many streams of modern Judaism. The Kabbalah (Jewish mysticism) teaches a belief in *Gilgul*, transmigration of souls, and hence the belief in rebirth is universal in Hasidic Judaism, which regards the Kabbalah as sacred and authoritative, and is also held as an esoteric belief within modern Orthodox Judaism.

Christianity—Though the major Christian denominations reject the concept of rebirth, a large number of Christians profess the belief. During recent decades, many people in the West have developed an interest in rebirth. Recent studies have indicated that some Westerners accept the idea of rebirth including certain contemporary people who were from Catholic families. To many western scholars both spiritualism and spiritism appear same thing, though both are not the same thing. Spiritism is concerned with spirit in a very limited manner. Spiritism teaches rebirth into human life after death, while spiritualism is much more than that.

Islam— The Islamic scriptures reject any idea of rebirth of human beings or God. It teaches a linear concept of life, wherein a human being has only one life and upon death he or she is judged by God, then rewarded in heaven or punished in hell. Islam teaches final resurrection and Judgement Day, but there is no prospect for the rebirth of a human being into a different body or being. During the early history of Islam, some of the Caliphs persecuted all rebirth-believing people to the point of their extinction (Manichaeism) in Mesopotamia and Persia (modern day Iraq and Iran). However, some Muslim minority sects such as those found among the Sufis, and some Muslims in South Asia and Indonesia have retained their pre-Islamic Hindu and Buddhist beliefs in rebirth. The idea of rebirth is accepted by a few Muslim sects, particularly of the Ghulat and by other sects in the Islamic world.

Doctrine of *Atman* and *Moksha (*Salvation)

In many religious, philosophical and mythological traditions, there is a belief in the incorporeal essence of a living being called the soul. Depending on the philosophical system, a soul can either be mortal or immortal. In Judeo-Christianity, only human beings have immortal souls. Other religions (most notably Hinduism and Jainism) hold that all biological organisms have souls (*Atman, Jeev*). Different philosophical systems of India have shown different views about the notion of soul. The Charvak system states that the soul consists of the living physical body and its attributes. According to the Buddhists, there is no soul. Buddhism teaches that the stream of ever changing thoughts and feelings is the ultimate reality. This may be termed as soul, but it is not considered to be a permanent entity, as is maintained by other philosophies.

According to the Nyaya and Vaisheshik systems, the soul is a non-material substance, of which all desires, aversions, pleasures, pains and cognitions are constituent qualities. The soul is indestructible and its attribute is consciousness. Because it is not limited by time and space, the soul is also seen as infinite or pervading. The concept of soul is comparable to that of the self or *Atman*. The Nyaya system considers consciousnesses an accidental property. In other words, when the soul associates itself with the body, only then it acquires consciousness. Thus, consciousness is not considered an essential quality of the soul. The mind (*Manas*) is accepted as atomic but indivisible and eternal substance. The mind helps to establish the contact of the self to the external world objects. The soul develops attachment to the body owing to ignorance. The soul identifies itself with the body and mind. The soul is trapped in the bondage of *Karma*, as a consequence of actions results from countless desires and passions. It can be free from the bondage only if it becomes free from actions.

Nyaya gave various arguments to prove the existence of soul. It first argues that the body is not soul because immaterial consciousness cannot be said to be an attribute of the material body, which in itself is unconscious and unintelligent. Neither can the functioning of the senses explain the process of imagination, memory and ideation. The mind cannot be the soul because the mind is considered to be an imperceptible substance. Nor can the soul, as the Buddhists maintain, be identified as the ever-changing series of cognitions. In sum, the soul is not consciousness, but is a non-material substance having consciousness as its attribute.

The soul, as said before, experiences the external world through the mind and the senses. All the cognitions and conscious states arise in the soul, when the soul is related to the mind, the mind to the senses, and the senses to the external objects. It is because of this sequential contact that the whole process actuates. How can one know whether there is such a thing as an individual soul? The Nyaya system answers that the soul is not known by sensory perception but by inference or testimony. The existence of the soul is inferred from the functions of desire, aversion and volition, from the sensations of pain and pleasure, and from memories of these. These memories cannot be explained unless one admits a permanent soul that has experienced pain and pleasure in relation to certain objects in the past. One's own soul can be known through mental perception, but someone's soul in another body can only be inferred.

Like other systems of the Indian philosophy, the Nyaya system maintains that the ultimate goal of human life is to attain *Moksha* (liberation) which means 'absolute freedom from all pain and misery'. This means a state where the soul is completely released from all bondage and from its connection with the body.

To attain the state of liberation, one has to acquire true knowledge of the soul and of all the objects of experience. This knowledge is called '*Tattvagyan*', that means 'to know reality as completely distinct from unreality'. The Nyaya system prescribes a three-fold path for reaching the goal of liberation: the study of scriptures, *Sravan* and contemplation. The *Satsang* has been the good source of *Sravan*. Besides studying the scriptures one has to listen authoritative persons and saints. Following this, one must use one's own reasoning power to ponder over what has been learnt. This process of rumination is called *Manan*. Finally, one must contemplate on the soul, confirm his knowledge and practice that truth in life. This is called *Nididhyasan*. Through this a person realizes that the true nature of the soul is totally different from the body, mind, senses and all other objects of the world. The truth realized within dispels the darkness of self-identification and misunderstanding considering 'I-ness' and 'Thy-ness'. When this happens a person begins to perform his duties selflessly without having any desire to reap the fruits of action. The fire of knowledge, figuratively speaking, roasts the seeds of one's past *Karmas*, making them unable to germinate. Thus, true knowledge leads a person to the state where there is no cycle of birth and death. This state is called liberation.

Related to the notion of liberation is the doctrine of *Moksha* (salvation). Salvation has been defined differently in different religions. There are several views and connotations applied to the word 'salvation'. According to the Jain and Buddhist religions, Moksha is *Kaivalya* and/or *Nirvan*. But within Hinduism definition varies from school to school and sometimes even within the same school it varies from one sub-school to another. Broadly speaking, salvation is synonymous or near-synonyms with *Nirvan* of Buddhism, *Kaivalya* of Jainism, *Mukti* of Hinduism, etc. Salvation in Hinduism stands for an evolved state which cannot be fully described. It is to be self-realised; it is a kind of *sva-anubhutigamya* and *Aparokshyanubhutigamya*. According to Sankhya School, *Moksha* (*Kaivalya or Apavarg*) is the only end of (or freedom from) pains. It believes that *Moksha* is beyond 'pain' or 'pleasure' and no state of bliss can, therefore, be associated with it.

The Hindu scriptures tell us about the four proper goals or aims of human life which are known as *Purusharth*. The four *Purusharthas* are *Dharma* (righteousness, moral values), *Artha* (prosperity, economic values), *Kama* (pleasure, love, psychological values) and *Moksha* (liberation, spiritual values). The fourth objective, *Moksha*, cannot be accurately comprehended because it relates to *Atma-anubhav*— an intensely personal experience. So only the one who experiences *Moksha* will know what it is like. Adi Shankar said that one should rise above the first three and get liberated from them via *Moksha.* The *Moksha* experience cannot be described. For instance, try describing the sweet taste of *Misri* (sugar candy) to someone who has never tasted it— and you'll find that the best way to make him understand its taste is to let him try it. Similarly *Moksha* can be understood only with direct experience only. *Moksha* is an intensely personal experience. It can be attained during one's lifetime and not necessarily after death. As stated in Upanishads, Brahm can be achieved here on this earth and in this birth. Hence, (1) *Moksha* is being free from nescience; (2) *Moksha* is feeling and being Brahm; and (3) *Moksha* is a state of perpetual bodylessness. The Vedant regards it as a state of pure existence (*Satta*), pure knowledge (*Chitta*) and pure bliss (*Anand*) i.e. *Satta-chitta-anand* which is reached after attaining freedom from nescience.

In this regard let us face a couple of strange questions here. Can one transcend even the desire for *Moksha*? Once *Moksha* has been achieved, can we seek '*Moksha* from *Moksha*'? No, because that would be a contradiction. This is an absurd question because in Hinduism *Moksha* refers to the simultaneous end of suffering and the experience of *anand* or bliss— what we call *Satta-Chitta-Anand*. It is the experience of the eternal and unchanging truth, revealing the universal limitlessness and our nature as the source of infinite peace and joy. So there is nothing beyond this state. This is the ultimate, when the *Atman* unites with the *Parmatman*, when the individual energy merges with the Supreme energy. Why should one seek release from such a state? *Moksha* is not something to be attained but that it is a state to be experienced, a natural state. *Moksha* is not a ritual like bathing or offering flowers. That is why the ***Bhaj Govindam*** says don't look for *Moksha* outside but search within.

The Geeta contains a lot of sermons relating to *Moksha* or liberation from this worldly life, which have raised a volley of exciting and thoughtful questions. It is often said that this life is full of miseries and worries. There is nothing to rejoice in this life. Hence, one need not aspire to take another birth and experience all sorts of miseries of this world. Rebirth is taken as a kind of God-ordained retribution. Hence one should surrender to God in this life completely and try to be one with the Supreme Being same as a drop of water mingles with the ocean. That should be the ultimate stage of blissful life. But how is it possible when the soul and Supreme Being may not be the exactly same thing necessary for a proper mingling? Who really knows what happens to the soul after death? None knows indeed, as God does not make any open or apparent conversation with humans. The Sankhya philosophers did not believe in transmigration of soul, as the proponent of this school, Sage Kapil, did not believe in God. According to him Nature is the source of all creation, but the Bhagavad Geeta identifies Brahm as the first cause of creation and Nature as a dependent reality. The notion of *Moksha* appears to be a pure intellectual nonsense, as none knows firmly about the fate of soul after death. Many of us even do not trust the idea of self and Super Self. Madhavacharya, a proponent of the dualistic philosophy, has long back emphasized the distinction between God and individual soul (*Jeev*). This school differentiates God from matter as well as the soul from matter. It has argued that the God, *Jeev* and the *Jagat* are three separate and everlasting entities. Relationship between God and soul has been a highly contentious topic in the Indian philosophy. Both exponents and opponents of relationships between God and soul have not been able to conclusively hold up or throw it out once for all. The subject is so abstract that it goes beyond our intellectual ability and hence one has to either accept it blindly or reject it rationally. This is not the subject of human intelligence. To the practitioners of social or natural science, this subject leads to an everlasting debate defying all logical conclusions.

If the notion of salvation as the ultimate aim of life is taken for granted, birth of great souls like Ram, Krishna, Buddha, Mahavir, Jesus Christ and various other prophets, saints and thinkers like Adi Shankar, Sant Gyaneshwar, Kabir, Chaitanya Mahaprabhu, Guru Nanak, Satya

Sai Baba and a host of other great hermits or sages would not have been possible because once a person attains salvation after death, the soul tends to mingle with the Supreme Self and hence there is no question of any rebirth for such great souls. This philosophy of *Moksha* does not seem to be credible or convincing to many of us. So one should better try or at least think of being a better and better human being in every successive birth rather than aspiring for *Moksha* or salvation to get rid of rebirth. Rebirth of everyone has not been so bad throughout the human history. Some people, noted as above, have rendered great services to the mankind without any self interests. To me, it seems the notion of salvation was introduced to ensure order in society. It sounds more like an allurement or phony incentive for the deviants to behave properly in society.

Yet another question is why does a person aspire for eternal pleasure of being with God who is said to have descended Himself on this earth several times in the form of a human being through *Avatar*? One cannot enjoy the pleasure of life all the time unless there is a pain of some kind in one's life. A soul is said to be indestructible and free from life and so also all sorts of pains and pleasures, hence the state of eternal pleasure does not mean much for the soul. In addition, pain or pleasure is experienced by the living body which has got a nervous system with brain. It cannot be felt by the *Atman* or soul devoid of any nervous system or mental faculty. When the soul is indestructible and beyond the control of human mind, it is not possible to control its conduct and future prospect. Then one may pose a hypothetical question why does a person worry about the future prospect of the soul in his physical body? What would really happen to this world or humanity, if the soul in every being finally mingles with God? Obviously complete absence of life on this earth, for it is the soul which makes a distinction between the living and the dead. Rebirth seems to be quite indispensable for the continuation of this world. Hence one need not get bogged down by the notion of *Moksha* of Hindu philosophy. The notion of liberation from pleasure and pain in this life appears to be a religious or philosophical gimmick to most of the thinking people of the modern age.

God Realization or Self Realization

As per the Bhagavad Geeta the notions of self realization and God realization mean the same thing. Reaching self or reaching Supreme Being truly means the same in the field of spirituality. The moment human beings reach their true inner self, the spirit within; the cosmic journey for a soul finally comes to an end. God realization or self realization indicates something that relates to our true inner self, the real self of us. As revealed in the Bhagavad Geeta our real self is the only abstract truth of life. Reaching the source of our soul, the spirit within, is what self realization is all about. The moment we as a soul gains absolute purity in the field of pure spirituality, it is termed reaching the stage of self realization

A soul gaining absolute purity means the absence of need for soul to manifest in another body. Having gained absolute purity, the liberated soul finally enters the abode of Kingdom of God called Vaikunth. As said above, realizing self or realizing God always meant the same, since in both the cases the liberated soul finally enters the Kingdom of God. The ultimate goal of human life is reaching the stage of God realization or self realization. Every form of meditation or every form of spiritual indulgence results in reaching higher stages of spiritual life. Self realization is not something that could be imparted by a master of self realization, a spiritual preceptor. In the journey of life, every spiritual master can only act as a guide.

The path of self realization is always travelled via path of spirituality, never via path of religion or path of the rituals. Unless one indulges in Gyan Yog (the path of absolute wisdom), nothing in field of God realization is ever achieved. Stated in simpler terms, the journey of spirituality is always travelled all alone. The entire wisdom contained in Hindu sacred scriptures is only meant as a guide that helps in negating our *Karma* to zero.

Self realization is termed enlightenment in English. All the three such as enlightenment, God realization and self realization always meant the same. Those who thought that self realization, God realization or enlightenment had different connotations were absolutely in the dark. Such human beings have always failed to travel the spiritual path sincerely and diligently. Final liberation from the cycle of birth and death is what God realization, self realization or enlightenment is all about. The liberated soul is nowhere to go any further and finally reaches the Kingdom of God.

The conceptualization of self realization is simple. We are primarily a soul or the spirit within on its cosmic journey of 8.4 million manifestations that roughly requires an earthly travel of 96.4 million years. Out of 8.4 million manifestations in one life cycle of a soul, the initial 7.3 million manifestations occur in insect, plant and animal life. In the remaining 1.1 million manifestations in human form one is expected to reach the stage of self realization, which simply means that our soul within must gain absolute purity for reaching the stage of salvation. Moksha can never be reached without reaching the stage of enlightenment.

As revealed in the Bhagavad Geeta the present journey of life belongs to our soul and never to the manifest physical form. The human life is but a medium for our soul to purify itself in totality. It is our soul that manifests in the human form to work out its *Karma* , removes dross impurities within. The moment we as a soul gain absolute purity, the need for soul to manifest in another body ceases to exist, because that is the stage of salvation. As per Hindu scriptures the journey of rebirth finally comes to an end, the moment a soul gains absolute purity. The ultimate goal of life for all human beings in the world is reaching the stage of self realization.

Unless we indulge in *Nishkam Karma* way of life we can never proceed ahead on the spiritual path. Offering fruits of *Karma* performed to the Supreme Being all the time is what *Nishkam Karma* is all about. Human beings who pursue materialistic goals of life find it extremely difficult to offer fruits of *Karma* to the Supreme Being. Undertaking spiritual journey means indulging in our real self essence of soul. Our inner being is pure spirit something we cannot see even with the eyes of science. It has always been beyond comprehension of human beings, catch of science. No matter how modified our scientific machinery becomes we as human beings would never be able to identify the structure of a soul.

Furthermore, the field of spirituality starts from the point where science ends. To be able to realize God via the path of science is totally out of question. That is the prime reason why scientists the world over have failed to travel the path of pure spirituality. The path of spirituality is directly governed by our faith in the Supreme Being. Science demands proofs that are never forthcoming in the field of spirituality. Supreme Being can only be reached by ardent seekers of spirituality like Swami Vivekananda. We have to be firm in our decisions rather absolute. We can never leave anything to chance in the field of pure spirituality. Most people pursue the path of spirituality half-heartedly. Supreme Being is never reached that way.

The symptoms of self realization are many and far-fetched. A person immediately becomes knower of almost everything when he attains self realization. The entire wisdom contained in the Bhagavad Geeta looks like ABCD of life for him. The wisdom contained in the Upanishads (independent treatises) also becomes like the ABCD. For a self realized person immediate family carries no meaning. The entire world becomes one large family for a self realized human being. A self realized human being also establishes absolute control over his sleep. Just five to ten minutes of sleep becomes like eight hours of sleep of a normal person. When the entire world sleeps the self realized human being keeps working all the time. For a soul that reaches absolute purity the mundane affairs of life carry no meaning. One practically wins death. Death of body carries no meaning for a self realized soul. The definition of self realization truly becomes clear only after gaining self realization, never before. Once spiritual journey has started in search of the Supreme Being, there is no chance of returning back. The path of spirituality is always one-sided; one can never return to the material fold after lapsing certain period of time.

Many a people in present times have equated self realization to self actualization, self affirmation or self awareness. Terms like self actualization is a creation of religious preachers who indulge in preaching half baked theories to gullible people. Such religious preachers must never be trusted. They have no inkling what spirituality is truly all about. The roots of self realization lay in understanding the structure of our soul. As our soul is pure spirit we have to indulge in spirituality to gain absolute purity as a soul. We have to cut across shackles of *Karma* forever to reach the stage of enlightenment. Self realization is never imparted by one person to another. It was not possible even for Mahavir, Gautam Buddha, Jesus Christ or Prophet Mohammed to impart self realization to anyone in the world. The doctrine of *Karma* plays a central role in the cosmic system of life.

Meditation and Self Realization— Meditation is the path and self realization is the end goal of life. Meditation and self realization are intrinsically interconnected. Without indulgence in different techniques of meditation, self realization is not possible. Unless human beings indulge in contemplation on Supreme Being via the path of *Neti* (not this, not this) one can never reach the stage of self realization.

The path of *Neti* is a form of meditation best practised and preached by Maharishi Raman one who could realize God in his lifetime. The path of *Neti* involves contemplation on Supreme Being all the time. It was only through the path of Gyan Yog, the path of absolute wisdom, human beings finally succeeded in contemplation on Supreme Being. Contemplation on Supreme Being was not that easy as many people the world over think. It is through the path of contemplation that the human beings step-by-step succeeded in finally negating their *Karma* to zero.

It is absolutely true that the stage of self realization can never be reached by literally following sacred texts contained in the holy books of Hinduism. The path of Gyan Yog demands our remaining ever truthful in life. By remaining truthful we can practically hear the sweet, fine inner voice of our soul that seems to come from within our heart. People are often confused about meditation with abstract knowledge contained in the sacred texts. None wants to indulge in true meditation as revealed in the Bhagavad Geeta. Meditation, contemplation or self inquiry, *Neti* all are different modes of reaching God in the present life. Contemplation on Supreme Being is one form of meditation and indulging in self inquiry is another. Practising *Neti* is also a form of meditation.

Pranayam (breathing process) is yet another form of meditation through which one reaches the source of life that resides in our heart. It was only through the process of *Pranayam* human beings finally succeeded in reaching their soul that resides in their heart. *Pranayam* is a pure form of meditation that can always be practised while lying in the *shavasna* pose (death pose) of Yog. The self inquiry path of *Neti* is also best practised in the *shavasna* pose of Yog. The *shavasna* is a very vital form of meditation.

Just as the time taken by different routes to reach a particular destination varies, each path of Yog takes its own time. The shortest and most suitable path ordained in this modern age is *Bhakti Yog.* This form of Yog and all other forms of Yog come under *Astanga Yog* or the eight-fold Yog which comprises the following:

1. *Yam or Ahinsa, Satya, Astey, Brahmacharya* and *Aparigrah*, meaning non-violence, truthfulness, non-stealing, continuous meditation or remembrance by salutation to God and non-accumulation of non-essential things.
2. *Niyam or Saucha, Santos, Tapas, Swadhyay and Ishwar Pranidhan*, meaning cleanliness, both internal as well as external, contentment, rightful penance, self-study and self-surrender to God.
3. *Asan* or body postures in the yogic tradition.
4. *Pranayam* or control of *Pran*.
5. *Pratyahar* or withdrawal of sense organs within.
6. *Dharana* or contemplation.
7. Dhyan or meditation.
8. *Samadhi* or total union with God.

A practical thing to opt for is a practice of the eight-fold Yog with a special stress on *Bhakti Yog.* The importance of *Bhakti* and the resultant cessation of *dukh* or sorrow has been recorded in the scriptures. Saints and also ordinary people who have practised *Bhakti Yog* in their day-to-day life vouch for its efficacy. *Bhakti Yog* stands for intense love of God.

The practitioners of *Bhakti Yog* do not ask for anything in return from God; they believe that God, as the mother and father of all, understands His children. Sometimes God does not fulfil the immediate desires of His *Bhaktas.* However, the *Bhakti Yogi* continues to nurture his devotion and love for God as he is convinced that whatever God gives, He gives for the ultimate good of the devotee.

One may follow any path of meditation for reaching the stage of self realization but assimilation of pearls of wisdom contained in the Bhagavad Geeta is an absolute necessity. In the absence of wisdom contained in 700 verses of the Bhagavad Geeta none can reach God in the present scientific age. Great divine beings like Mahavir, Gautam Buddha, Jesus Christ and Prophet Mohammed finally reached God in their life following the path of spirituality revealed in the Bhagavad Geeta. What matters most is our goal of present life. If we have a fixed goal of reaching the stage of self realization in present life our journey is half done. One can easily duplicate the path undertaken by some masters of self realization like Sri Ramakrishna Paramhansa or Maharishi Raman. The Bhagavad Geeta exhorts that every single human being in the world has the potential to become a Mahavir, Buddha, Jesus Christ or Guru Nanak. In the present scientific age one need not indulge in the study of voluminous Vedas and even Upanishads. Simply by following dictates of the Bhagavad Geeta any human being can easily reach the stage of self realization, but cutting across shackles of *Karma* forever definitely was.

One need not be a Hindu to be a spiritual. The teachings of the Bhagavad Geeta can be followed by any human being the world over without ever converting to Hinduism. Even while following one's religion one can simultaneously follow the teachings contained in the Bhagavad Geeta. The teachings contained in the Bhagavad Geeta have a universal appeal; they have never diluted with time. If one has the will, the Bhagavad Geeta shows the way. How to reach the stage of self realization is clearly revealed in the Bhagavad Geeta, but the most human beings inquire where it is written. Trying to read the Bhagavad Geeta literally none can ever understand it. We must always learn to read in between the lines. Only there lies the true answer.

Spiritualism

As self realization is a part of spiritualism, there is a need to shed some light on the notion of spiritualism here. Clarification is also necessitated because it has been observed before that religion and spiritualism do not mean the same thing. They are neither synonyms nor contradictory in connotation; rather, they are intertwined. The important points of difference between religion and spirituality have been highlighted in the subsequent discussion. As regards the meaning of spiritualism, it is said that it is a metaphysical belief that the world is made up of at least two fundamental substances, matter and spirit. This very broad metaphysical distinction further includes various forms of details about what spiritual entities such as a soul, the afterlife, spirits of the dead, deities and also the nature of the relationship between spirit and matter. It may also cover the philosophy, doctrine, or religion pertaining to a spiritual aspect of existence. The Indians have developed various thoughts of philosophy and spiritualism and have given to the world maximum number of systems of spiritualism in the form of philosophical thoughts such as Nyaya, Vaisheshik, Yog and Vedant. The Vedas provide spiritual orientation to the Indians giving them the basics of spiritual and moral life. Hence, the Vedic *Rishis* should be acclaimed as the earliest spiritual masters on the earth as their *Mantras* resound with the kernel of spiritualism, and the Indian nation as the cradle of spiritualism.

The precepts of the Bhagavad Geeta are beyond the purview of science. Spirituality starts from the point where science ends. Science needs proofs that are not obtainable in the field of spirituality. In the domain of Supreme Being it is absolute faith in the Supreme Being that rules the roost. Unless we trust God in totality we can never take spiritual path sincerely or diligently. In our sufferings we always remember God, but remember nothing when we experience happiness. How many of us remember God in times of happiness? For a serious seeker of spirituality it is the absolute faith in the Supreme Being that matters most. Unless we have faith in the Supreme Being or unless we are truthful to the Supreme Being to the core, we can never gain enlightenment no matter what. Only those people who exhibit will power, as demonstrated by Swami Vivekananda, are fit enough to travel the spiritual path reaching the cosmic end of life of 8.4 millionth manifestations in the cosmic life cycle.

Right from the Vedic times, India has enjoyed a rich spiritual tradition. The Indian spiritualism is termed as a form of philosophy or *Darshan*, and the Upanishads are held as proper sources of Indian spiritualism. As to the question what is spiritualism, the answer would be it is the inner quest; a pathway for reaching the higher truth in life; a composite thinking for enlightening the realities of life, for considering challenges of life, human values and their evaluation. However, under the purview of spiritualism are also included queries regarding the nature of God, about the creation of the world; essential values of a human being and his ethics. The last constituent of spiritualism is ethics reflecting the fine side of Indian culture, which emphasizes unity in diversity, and treating the entire universe as pervaded by one Almighty Brahm. Basically spiritualism, reiterated as before, differs from religion. As the religion affirms a faith or belief about God's supremacy over the beings and the matter, and also enjoins man's faith in the rituals and cultic practices.

Whereas spiritualism exhorts faith in the collective reality of the world and imparts knowledge of oneness of the God with the whole world. Hence, spiritualism should be treated as a theoretical approach to truth; and religion as the practical approach to the same goal. Spiritualism is also defined as the science of soul, or the *Adhyatma Vidya*, the higher knowledge which helps man to rise above the worldly agonies; knowing which everything else of the world is known. It is also believed that a person bereft of spiritual knowledge can never bring any worldly activity to success. Thus, there is great importance of spiritualism in Indian life.

The path of spirituality simply means we have to reach our true inner self, the spirit within. As per the Bhagavad Geeta we are a spirit, a cosmic consciousness that pervades entire cosmos. However, in the absence of a body every soul remains inert, inactive. Enlightened persons like Mahavir, Gautam Buddha, Adi Shankaracharya, Kabir, Guru Nanak, Sri Ramakrishna Paramhansa, Sai Baba of Shirdi, Maharishi Raman all belonged to India. The stage of enlightenment, stage of *Moksha or Nirvikalp samadhi* (also termed absolute nothingness) is not that easily reached. It is the prime reason why during the last about 150 years, amongst 7.6 billion people existing the world over, only two publicly known persons, namely Sri Ramakrishna Paramhansa and Maharishi Raman, are believed to have succeeded in gaining enlightenment. Both these spiritual stalwarts started their pursuit of God via the path of religion, the path of *Bhakti Yog*. But finally both of them switched to the path of *Gyan Yog* (path of absolute wisdom) in their later stages of life. Following the Bhagavad Geeta is a necessity of spiritual path, never religious convictions or the path of rituals.

Spiritual path always has to be taken all alone. In their lifetime Mahavir, Gautam Buddha, Jesus Christ and Prophet Mohammed none of these gods in a human form ever had a spiritual preceptor a spiritual *Guru* to guide them. So was the case with Sri Ramakrishna Paramhansa and Maharishi Raman. The uncharted path of spirituality truly has to be taken all alone.

Subduing Kundalini helps one reach the stage of *Nirvikalp Samadhi* (the stage of absolute nothingness) when not a single thought enters brain uninvoked. One exists in a state of absolute bliss all the time. Remaining in communion with the Supreme Being all the time one can invoke any cosmic power that is. Compared to the path of spirituality people prefer taking religious path, path of rituals that never leads anywhere. One never reaches the Supreme Being via the path of religion, a path of rituals. Spirituality is not to be confused with religion. Before one travels to the spiritual path, one has to be truthful to the core. We must learn to establish control over our five senses and mind. Unless absolute control over five senses and mind is established, *Karma* cannot be negated to zero. Complete annihilation of *Karma* demands the highest level of patience, persistence and perseverance that could ever be practised by the human beings.

The Indians generally prefer spiritual pursuits to other pursuits of human life—*Artha* and *Kama*— which are much subordinate to it, as the same leads them to attain *Moksha*, a state of existence of *Jeevanmukti* or liberated soul. Hence, in India, spiritual wisdom, which has gained an upper hand over material prosperity, inculcates practising such attitudes that man is divine by nature, since the Vedas extol him as the offspring of divine— *Amratasya putra*— that the divine being resides in every being high or low, big or small; that every human being carries within him a divine potentiality.

Spiritualism in India is a complete philosophy of human life, the correct way of living and the right way of thinking. A spiritual man is one who is detached from the dual effects of *Karma* (success and failure); who is devoid of self-interest, egoism and sees God everywhere, permeated in all the beings; who keeps himself in continuous communication with God, and hence is the messenger of God and the benefactor of mankind. Spiritualism, a philosophy of values if adapted at large by people, would usher in civilization that is socially just (*Satyam*); emotionally integral (*Shivam*); and aesthetically beautiful (*Sundaram*).

Religion, Spiritualism and Science

Every religion has three components: rituals, cultural and spiritual. There is a scope for differences only in the first two. But the third, the spiritual element, helps us overcome conflicts arising from differences in the first two. Rituals including ceremonies relating to birth, marriage and death are important constituents of all faiths. Culture springs from the way of life, and its nature hinges a great deal on heritage and environment. The spiritual aspect is free of all differences and so is able to help us direct our mind towards the *Parmatman*. Despite similarity of ideas with respect to spirituality, it is also true that all religions are not equally developed with regard to the doctrine of spiritualism.

Here one can say that spirituality is a subset of religion. Since religion overlaps spirituality, they are not to be taken synonyms. But they are also not contradictory. An effort is made to bring out some differences between religion and spirituality. Religion can be defined as a system of belief in and reverence for a divine power. It can be a personal or institutionalized system grounded in such belief and worship. Institutionalized religion focuses on dogmas and rules whereas spirituality focuses on the soul that dwells within us.

Religion is all about beliefs and worship. In short it can be said that religion refers to a group of people with common faith. Religion focuses more on the outside due to its indulgence in dogmas and rules that are often felt fixed by the people. Religion aims at imbibing faiths in us about certain dogmas pertaining to a group of followers of a particular faith. It helps in shaping our character by giving importance to the adherence of the dogmas and rules. It says once we stick to the rules and dogmas we are sure to emerge out as men of special kind. Religion is in short a character-building concept. Religion leads towards discipline in the life of individual practitioner.

Spirituality is about the soul within matter. The matter corresponds to our body. Soul is different from the body. Anything pertaining to the soul or the spirit is spiritual. Spirituality refers to an individual. Unlike religion, spirituality on the contrary concentrates and focuses more on the 'within.' The term 'within' applies to the individual soul. Spirituality is all about the individual. It is about the realization of the supreme self within oneself. The realization of the innate power within oneself to combat all situations in life is the goal of spirituality. Spirituality aims at building strength of the mind and the spirit. It speaks about the real truth of life. Spirituality aims at making a person strong by mind. It aims at the elimination of what are all untrue. Spirituality is a mind-building concept. It shapes the mind of the individual. It is individual oriented in content. Spirituality leads towards enlightenment. Spirituality builds the individual himself.

Difference between religion and spirituality are as follows: The perfect combination of both is needed in the present days for man to succeed in life. One needs to have a perfect blend of religion and spirituality to succeed in one's life. One needs to be spiritually strong to react to successes and failures of life. One needs to be religiously strong too in order to shape one's character.

- Religion focuses on dogm`as and rules followed by a particular section of people whereas spirituality focuses on the soul that dwells within human beings.
- It can be said that religion focuses on the outside; spirituality focuses on the within.
- Religion comes from outside whereas spirituality comes from within.
- Religion shapes the character of a group of individuals whereas spirituality aims at shaping the individual himself.
- Religion makes a person disciplined outwardly, whereas spirituality makes a person strong by mind.
- Religion aims at building faiths and customs, whereas spirituality aims at building the strength of the soul. It makes the person ready to combat any situation in life.

If one contemplates deeply then one comes to realise that spirituality makes a person very strong and there is no need for any religion for one's survival and success in life. Everything becomes smooth and easy for a spiritual person. We become a very special person once we train ourselves in spirituality.

Now let us finally come to the notion of science in relation to spiritualism. Lots of scholars with scientific thinking have tended to raise volley of questions against the relevance of Indian spiritualism and religion because both are said be based on blind faith. There may be fair amount of truth in it, but everything is not necessarily a matter of blind faith. One does not need scientific temperament all the time to understand spiritualism, as scientific method creates hurdles in our thinking process. Science is always concerned with finite and spiritualism deals with infinite.

True, science is based on reasoning, while spirituality is based on faith and experience. Science, whether we speak of physics, chemistry or biology, deals with matter. It studies its properties and arrives at certain conclusions after making necessary experiments. It is based on empirical evidence, while spiritualism is based on extra-sensory experience. But in a way science too leads to faith in ultimate analysis.

A research scientist works on the cause and effect principle. If he observes a phenomenon occurring with regular frequency, he draws certain conclusions. A stage comes when such a conclusion is described as a law or as a universal principle. But spiritualism goes much beyond such laws or principles.

The scientist picks up matter and studies its origin, and how it attained its existence. Recently it was concluded that the whole universe was a matter of evolution from what was described as a 'sub-atomic particle'. It was claimed to be a discovery consistent with the long sought Higgs boson– popularly known as the 'God Particle'– that explained what gives all the matter in the universe its size and shape. The universe, in this way, was described as a matter of self-evolution. Who created this 'sub-atomic particle' or 'God Particle'? It has been only discovered– not invented or created. This brings us to faith, the cornerstone of spirituality. Here, it is a matter of belief. There is no intention to dispute, deny or disprove it. The spiritual master tells us all about the Creator and Creation along with its purpose and we believe him, trust him. Here the Geeta is a case in point.

The question arises as to when this stage of belief, trust or faith arrives. We describe what is written in scriptures as the outcome of the lifelong experience of the great spiritual masters who wrote them. We trust them simply because we do not want to make any more experiments or apply our own reasoning to arrive at the same conclusions.

True, faith must be based on Truth. And Truth does not admit plurality. It implies that we have exhausted all other concepts, options and alternatives. We may love many but faith can be reposed only in one. Here, all our arguments are at their end. In fact this kind of stage exists in the field of science also. There are certain principles like Newton's Law of Gravitation that nobody would venture to challenge even today. It is accepted as final. In spirituality, too, we are convinced that 'faith' has arrived only after exhausting all the processes of reasoning.

It is said that even if God did not exist, we would have invented one because there is so much happening in Nature and in our own lives that we fail to understand. Spiritual masters, however, have explained enough with due justification about God, His existence and His ways of working.

OM TAT SAT

Chapter - 3

Religions in India at a Glance

Religion is commonly defined as a cultural system of designated behaviours and practices, worldviews, texts, sanctified places, ethics, or organizations that relate humans to the supernatural or transcendental world. Religions relate humanity to what anthropologist Clifford Geertz has referred to as a cosmic 'order of existence'. Different religions may or may not contain various elements ranging from the 'divine', 'sacred things', 'faith', 'a supernatural being or supernatural beings' or 'some sort of supremacy and transcendence that will provide norms and power for the rest of life'. Religious practices may include rituals, sermons, commemoration or veneration (of deities), sacrifices, festivals, feasts, trances, initiations, funerary services, matrimonial services, meditation, prayer, music, art, dance, public service, or other aspects of human culture. Religions have sacred histories and narratives, which may be preserved in sacred scriptures, and symbols and holy places that aim mostly to give a meaning to life. Religions may contain symbolic stories, which are sometimes believed to be true, that have the side purpose of explaining the origin of life, the Universe and other things. Traditionally, faith, in addition to reason, has been considered a source of religious beliefs. According to some estimates, there are roughly 4,300 religions in the world (see, *adherents.com*). About 84 percent of the world's population is covered by the five largest religions, namely Christianity, Islam, Hinduism, Buddhism or forms of folk religion.

Here we are concerned with only those major religious practices which have been popular in India through the ages.

India has been a crucible of various religious faiths and practices since the ancient days. It is one of the most diverse nations of the world in terms of religious practices, it being the birthplace of four major world religions: Hinduism, Jainism, Buddhism and Sikhism. Islam and Christianity also came to India and had a fast expansion with the patronage of state. They have become numerically overriding features of religious faiths of this country. There is need to see the course of rise and expansion of various religions in India. If one is interested to understand the true spirit or nature of Hindu religion, one must try to understand the course of events of the history of Hinduism in a systematic manner. It must be pointed out at the outset that Hinduism is different from all religions. Though it is labelled as a religion, it is actually more than that. It is a vast and complex socio-religious body which, in a way, reflects the complexity of Indian society. A rich geography, multiplicity of languages and dialects, variety of creeds, racial diversity, and all these elements have shaped Hinduism and made it so heterogenic. The lack of unifying overall religious authority and the total absence of a book claiming supreme truth and dogmas have contributed to the diversity of Hinduism as well. It is fair to mention that even the texts we find in Hinduism that claim some sort of divine inspiration do not declare their view to be better than any other and they all exist together in a tolerant fashion. The numerous manifestations of Hinduism go from highly intellectual philosophies concerning variety of puzzling metaphysical concerns, countless rituals, mental and physical exercises such as *Yog* to simple, almost childlike, tales and legends.

The history of Hinduism is unique among the world religions in that it has no founder or date of origin. While most religions are rooted in ideas taught by some charismatic personalities, Hinduism is simply the religion of the people of India, which has gradually evolved over five thousand years. The origin and authors of its sacred texts are largely unknown. The history of Hinduism denotes a wide variety of related Hindu denominations native to the Indian Subcontinent, most of whom live in modern-day Nepal and India. Its history overlaps or coincides with the development of Indian religions since the Iron Age India. It has thus been described as a primitive religion or the 'oldest living religion' of the world. Scholars regard Hinduism as a synthesis of various Indian cultures and traditions, with diverse roots and no single founder or source.

Although today's Hinduism differs significantly from the earlier forms of Indian religion, its roots date back as far as possibly 5500 BC, making it the oldest surviving religion of the world. Because of its age, the early history of Hinduism is blurred. The most ancient writings have yet to be deciphered, so for the earliest periods scholars must rely on educated guesses based on archaeology and contemporary texts.

As said before, unlike other religious traditions, Hinduism did not originate in a single founder, a single book or a single point of time. It contains many different beliefs, philosophies and viewpoints, not always consistent with each other. These apparent contradictions strike only those who are not familiar with this tradition: the Hindu insight claims that the Oneness expresses itself in many different forms.

The foundations of Hinduism can be found in the teachings of anonymous ancient sages or *rishis*, which were originally transmitted orally. We know very little about Hinduism beyond what can be learned from the Vedas, a collection of hymns and other ritual texts composed and compiled over a long period of time. These texts contain a lot of materials including the teachings of the early sages. The oldest evidence of religious practices in India dates back approximately to 5500 BCE. It is a mistake to reduce all early Hinduism to Vedic religion: there were many other non-Vedic religious traditions in early Hinduism which have left no early texts and that can be known to some extent by archaeological evidence.

Just like Zoroastrianism and Judaism (the other two major world religions also coming to us from prehistoric times), Hinduism has received numerous shocks that threatened its foundations and it has resiliently survived all of them. Perhaps no religion has received more jolts and jerks than Hinduism and yet it has moved from strength to strength due to its robust philosophical base. Judaism and Zoroastrianism also survived the many impacts they received, but Judaism failed to absorb Christianity, its all-conquering offspring, which after just a couple of centuries clearly overshadowed it, and there are only around 200,000 Zoroastrian believers left today. The basis of Hinduism has been hit, sometimes even smashed, by many sects, movements and systems of thought: in the worst case scenarios it receded for a while, only to return more powerful than before. Movements challenging the authority of Brahminical orthodoxy, irreligious schools such as the Charvak, atheist traditions like Jainism, the Buddhist agnostic approach, nihilists and sceptics denouncing the cunning behind the sacrificial fees, all of these beliefs weakened Hinduism for some time and were eventually absorbed, recycled and merged into the enormous body of this old Indic faith. In brief, Hinduism is a complex religion and a way of life, with a diversity of ideas on spirituality and traditions. It has no ecclesiastical order, no unquestionable religious authority, no governing body, no prophet(s) nor any binding holy book; Hindus can choose to be polytheistic, pantheistic, monotheistic, monistic, agnostic, atheistic or humanist.

Historicity of Hinduism

The history of Hinduism can be broadly sub-divided into periods of development, with the first period being that of the historical Vedic religion dated from about 5000 BCE to 1500 BCE or maybe even more. The subsequent period, between 1500 BCE and 200 BCE, is 'a turning point between the Vedic religion and Hindu religions', and a formative period for Hinduism, Jainism and Buddhism. The Epic and Early Pauranic period, from c. 200 BCE to 500 AD, saw the classical 'Golden Age' of Hinduism (c. 320-650 AD), which coincides with the Gupt Empire. In this period the six branches of Hindu philosophy evolved, namely *Sankhya, Yog, Nyaya, Vaisheshik, Mimansa and Vedant.* Monotheistic sects like *Shaivism* and *Vaishnavism* developed during this same period through the Bhakti movement. The period from roughly 650 to 1100 AD forms the late Classical period or early Middle Ages, in which classical Pauranic Hinduism is established, and Adi Shankar's *Advait Vedant*, which incorporated Buddhist thought into Vedant, marked a shift from realistic to idealistic thought.

Hinduism underwent profound changes, aided in part by teachers or philosophers like Ramanuj, Madhvacharya and Chaitanya

Mahaprabhu. Followers of the Bhakti movement moved away from the abstract concept of Brahm, which the philosopher Adi Shankar consolidated a few centuries before, with emotional, passionate devotion towards the more accessible *Avatars*, especially Ram and Krishna. According to Nicholson, already between the 12th and the 16th century, "certain thinkers began to treat as a single whole the diverse philosophical teachings of the Upanishads, epics, Puranas, and the schools known retrospectively as the 'six systems' (*Saddarshan*) of mainstream Hindu philosophy." Michaels notes that a historicization emerged which preceded later nationalism, articulating ideas which glorified Hinduism and the past.

Conceptualization of Hinduism is a real problem because it is difficult, if not impossible, to define Hindu religion or even adequately describe it. Unlike other religions in the world, the Hindu religion did not have any one prophet, it does not worship any one god, it does not subscribe to any one dogma, it does not believe in any one philosophic concept, it does not follow any one set of religious rites or performances, in fact, it does not appear to satisfy the narrow traditional features of any religion or creed. It may broadly be described as a way of life and nothing more. The main difficulty in defining 'Hinduism' is that it is a matter of common knowledge that Hinduism embraces within itself so many diverse forms of beliefs, faiths, practices and worships and thus it is difficult to define the term 'Hindu' with precision.

Hinduism, as said before, is one religion which has developed over a long period of human history slowly and steadily in its natural course as a way of life of the people and hence it is a purely people's religion. On the other hand, other religions were created and crafted by some people with specific interests in mind. Hence other religions have been imposed, propagated, protected and defended by certain class of people with vested interests. This has led to numerous instances of crusade and sectarian violence in the world. Such religions are likely to cause intermittent aggression and violence time and again for their dominance in society.

Hinduism under both Hindu and Islamic rulers from c. 1200 to 1750 AD saw the increasing prominence of the Bhakti movement, which remains influential till today. Ram and Krishna became the focus of a strong *Bhakti* tradition, which found expression particularly in the **Bhagavat Puran**. Being based on the doctrine of self-realization and escapism the Bhakti movement made Hinduism a highly individualistic or individual-centric religion, as it tried to disengage the devotees from the worldly life or a sense of collective societal living.

Hindutva

The word Hinduism did not exist before 1830. It was created by the English colonialists. I quote this from the secular Encyclopaedia Britannica, and not from an Indian text, that can be said to be 'Hindutva propaganda', a common but ignorant idiom of attack. There is no mention of the terms 'Hindu' or '*Sanatan Dharma*' in the Vedas, Puranas or any other religious text prior to 1830 AD. Nor are they found in any inscription or in any record of foreign travellers to India before the English rule. The term 'Hindusthan' was first used in the 12th century by Muhammad Ghori, who dubbed his new subjects 'Hindus'.

Throughout India's ancient history, the word Hindu was never meant to denote religion. It was a geographic and cultural term used by the Greeks, Persians and Arabs, derived from the Sanskrit word Sindhu to describe the people living in and around the valley of the river Sindhu. The Greeks modified Sindhu to Indos, and it is said that ancient Persian explorers because of their pronunciation rules dropped the letter 'S' from Sindhu, and called the people living around the Sindhu River as Hindus.

Though initially an outsiders' term, this nomenclature stuck and became a label after the Muslim conquests to distinguish the original inhabitants of the land from the invaders. Then came the first census of India by the British in 1871 that defined 'Hindu' as an omnibus term to encompass several religions that were not Muslim, Christian, Buddhist or Jain. Later, the term Sanatan Dharma was coined to deliberately encompass the English invention of Hinduism. The British, after the mutiny of 1857, had made it a policy to use every possible means– political, administrative and social to accentuate identity differences and promoted conflict between the Muslims and the Hindus and started official use of the term Hindu to connote religious identity. Thus, a term that originated to give a geographical and cultural identity to the people, mutated through usage attributed by the rulers through the turbulent history of India, into a word connoting a religion, and that is how it stands today.

And what according to the British did their newly coined religion 'Hindu' stand for? They couldn't figure out too much, except that it was an extremely lofty philosophy that truth or reality cannot be encapsulated in any dogma or creedal formulation, a perspective expressed in the Hindu prayer 'may good thoughts come to us from all sides, 'translated into multileveled, and pluralistic traditions. Since the term 'Hindu religion' denotes all the religions of India together, Shaivism, Vaishnavism, Tantrism, Shaktism, etc. each with different doctrines, often contrary to one another, it could not refer to any one single religion.

Indeed, **Encyclopaedia Britannica** accepts that 'Hinduism' is a blanket term covering several religions and does not refer to a single religion. ". . . Hinduism is both a civilization and a congregation of religions; it has neither a beginning, nor a founder, nor a central authority, hierarchy nor organization. It is the glorious catholicity of Hinduism that one can be a believer in one God, or multiplicity of Gods or even none at all. Hinduism does not expel much less crucify alleged non-believers. Every attempt at a specific definition of Hinduism has proved unsatisfactory in one way or another.... Hinduism is not a revealed religion and, therefore, has neither a founder nor definite teachings or common system of doctrines... . It has no organization, no dogma or accepted creeds. There is no authority with recognized jurisdiction. A man, therefore, could neglect any one of the prescribed duties of his group and still be regarded as a good Hindu."

Now, what is Hindutva? It is rooted in the word Hindu that historically referred to people beyond the Indus, but was created into a religious denomination by the British. All it means is, 'the way of life of the Indian people and the Indian culture or ethos', and by no means an anti-minority or anti-Muslim potion. "Ordinarily, Hindutva is understood as a way of life or a state of mind and is not to be equated with or understood as religious Hindu fundamentalism... it is a fallacy and an error of law to proceed on the assumption... that the use of words Hindutva or Hinduism per se depicts an attitude hostile to all persons practising any religion other than the Hindu religion... " These are the words of the Supreme Court in a judgement of 1995(1996 SCC (1):130. In no judgement has the apex court even remotely identified Hindutva as the militant or fanatic version of Hinduism. Hindutva never means Hindu extremism, as many so-called secular people have publicly misused this word for pure political reasons in recent years. Hindutva is nothing but a secular way of life.

However, the sectarian propaganda machinery relentlessly disseminates 'Hindutva' as a communal word, something that has also become embedded in the minds and language of opinion leaders, including politicians, media, civil society and the intelligentsia. Such people are advised not to reconsider the true meaning of the word 'Hindutva' as defined in the Supreme Court judgement, before they use it with sectarian overtone, as they have commonly been doing, even in the recent times.

Hindutva is not hostility to any organised religion nor does it proclaim its superiority over any other religion. It is the shield of security and freedom for all people irrespective of their religion or faith. This is the seminal reason why various religions, from moderate to hard core fundamentalists, have flourished in India at times even at the cost of Hindu religion. The Hindu awakening of the late twentieth century will go down as one of the most monumental events in the history of the world. Never before has such a demand for change come from so many people. Never before has Bharat, the ancient word for the motherland of Hindus– India, been confronted with such an impulse for change. This movement, Hindutva, is changing the very foundations of Bharat and Hinduism the world over.

The Hindu society has an unquestionable and proud history of tolerance for other faiths and respect for diversity of spiritual experiences. This is reflected in many different philosophies, religious sects and religious leaders. The very foundation of this lies in the great Hindu heritage that is not based on any one book, teacher, or doctrine. In fact the pedestal of Hindu society stems from the great Vedic teachings *Ekam Sat Viprah Bahudha Vadanti (***Truth is one, sages call it by many names**) and *Vasudhaiv Kutumbakam (the* **whole universe is one family**). It is this philosophy which allowed the people of

Hindusthan (land of the Hindus) to shelter the Jews who faced Roman persecution, the Zoroastrians who fled the Islamic sword and who are the proud Parsi community of India today.

Rise and Spread of Jainism and Buddhism

Jainism is as old as the Vedic religion. Jainism is the outcome of the teachings of twenty four Tirthankaras or prophets. The first twenty two Tirthankaras are, however, unknown to history. They were so legendary in character that doubts may be entertained regarding their existence. But the twenty-third Tirthankar, Parsvanath, had a real existence. He was the son of King Asvasena of Varanasi. He was brought up amid luxury. But at the age of thirty he left home in search of spiritual life. After three months of intense meditation he attained *'Kaivalya'* or '*Keval Gyan*' or perfect knowledge. He spent the rest of his life as a religious teacher till his death. He died at the age of 100 at Sammeda Sikhar Srunga (Mount Parasnath near Gomoh in Jharkhand). This event possibly happened in the eighth century B. C.

Let us briefly understand Jainism. Jain philosophy is the oldest Indian philosophy that separates body (matter) from the soul (consciousness) completely. Jain philosophy deals with reality, cosmology, epistemology (study of knowledge) and Vitalism. The concept of non-injury or ***Ahinsa*** lies at the core of Jain philosophy. Jain philosophy attempts to explain the rationale of being and existence, the nature of the Universe and its constituents, the nature of bondage and the means to achieve liberation. Jain texts expound that in every half-cycle of time, twenty-four Tirthankaras grace this part of the Universe to teach the unchanging doctrine of right faith, right knowledge and right conduct. Jain philosophy means the teachings of a Tirthankar which are recorded in sacred Jain texts. The distinguishing features of Jain philosophy are as follows:

A. Belief in independent existence of soul and matter.
B. Refutation of the idea that a supreme divine creator, owner, preserver or destroyer of the universe exists.
C. Potency of *Karma*, eternal universe.
D. Accent on relativity and multiple facets of truth and
E. Morality and ethics based on liberation of soul.

Jainism strongly upholds the individualistic nature of soul and personal responsibility for one's decisions; and that self-reliance and individual efforts alone can help attain one's liberation. Jainism spread to different parts of India during the life time of Mahavir and also after his death. Several factors are responsible for its rise and spread. Mahavir was the true pioneer of Jainism. He moved from place to place and preached his teachings. His simple way of life, penance and austerity attracted people towards him. Mahavir used common dialect in place of Sanskrit to spread his religion. Vedic scriptures were written in Sanskrit which was the language of the intellectuals. But Mahavir preached his religion through the language of the common people like Magadhi, Prakrit and colloquial languages. So the people were drawn towards it and accepted the religion.

The sixth century B. C. is considered a wonderful century in history, great thinkers like Buddha, Mahavir, Heraclitus, Zoroaster, Confucius and Lao Tse lived and preached their ideas in this century. In India, the republican institutions were strong in the 6th century B. C. This enabled rise of heterodox sects against the orthodox religion dominated by rites and rituals. Among them the most successful were Jainism and Buddhism whose impact on the Indian society was remarkable.

Buddhism— Buddhism is not the same as Jainism. Both are two different philosophies of life. So let us briefly throw light on the Buddhist philosophy now. Buddhism arose in and around the ancient Kingdom of Magadh (now in Bihar), and is based on the teachings of Siddharth Gautam who became 'Buddha' which means 'Awakened One'. Buddhism spread outside the Magadh Empire and it started in the lifetime of Buddha. With the reign of the Buddhist Mauryan Emperor Ashok, it spread throughout India and split into numerous sub-sects. Since it received the patronage of Emperor Ashok in ancient India, the practice of Buddhism and the Buddhist monasteries received laity and royal support through the 12th century, but generally declined in the 1st millennium CE, with many of its practices and ideas absorbed into Hinduism. Except for the Himalayan region and South India, Buddhism almost became extinct in India after the arrival of Islam in the late 12th century.

Lord Buddha expressed his philosophy when he said: "I teach

only two things, O disciples, the nature of suffering and the cessation of suffering."

The Buddha taught the famous 'Four Noble Truths' and 'Eightfold Path', which allow people to achieve enlightenment. Enlightenment (*Nirvan*, awakening, realization, *satori*) is the cessation of suffering, freedom from conditioned existence (*Sansar*). The Buddha taught that every action has a consequence; things are because of previous conditions. If one practices the Four Noble Truths and the Eightfold Path, one will no longer be subject to the cycle of existence in *Sansar*.

"My teaching is not a philosophy. It is the result of direct experience...

My teaching is a means of practice, not something to hold onto or worship.

My teaching is like a raft used to cross the river.

Only a fool would carry the raft around after he had already reached the other shore of liberation."

To his favourite disciple, Anand, the Buddha once said (from: *Old Path, White Clouds* by Thich Nath Hanh):

Three Marks of Existence

Annica- Everything is subject to change.

Dukkh- All pervasive unsatisfactoriness.

Anatta- Everything is empty of a separate self.

Four Noble Truths

Dukkh- Life is unsatisfactory, disjointed, suffering.

Samudaya- There is a cause of suffering, which is attachment or desire (*tanha*).

Nirodh- There is a cessation of suffering, which is to eliminate attachment and desire.

Mar- The path that leads out of suffering is called the Noble Eightfold Path.

The Buddha taught that in order to attain enlightenment a man must free himself from his ego, and give up all desires. He taught that by having so many desires (such as wanting pleasure, wealth, happiness, security, success, long life, etc), a man condemns himself to suffering, and will never escape the cycle of rebirths. Therefore,

Buddhism believes that suffering is a self-creation.

Reasons for the rise of Buddhism— Social and economic factors considerably contributed to the rise of a protestant creed like Buddhism in India. The extensive use of iron implements for felling trees of jungles brought new lands under plough. The use of heavy ploughs drawn by bullocks for tilling the land and the practice of manuring the fields revolutionized agriculture. House-holders mobilized the Shudra labourers for cultivation of extra lands. The traditional system of cultivating small plots by surface digging was replaced by improved method of cultivation. The house-holders or Gahapati class became wealthy due to surplus production in agriculture. They were mostly Vaishyas and in a caste ridden society they had no chance of enjoying higher caste status in spite of their wealth.

In the 6th century B. C. trade and commerce increased due to expansion of Aryan settlements in the Gangetic Valley. Trade was carried by land and river routes and also by sea routes. In short the tribal, self-contained village economy of the Aryans and the tribal social structure was cracking under the impact of changing economy. In such a transitional stage the caste-oriented Vedic religion was out of tune with the changing social and economic life of the people. The Gahapati, Shreshthi class due to their wealth wanted higher status in the society which the hereditary caste system denied them. The artisan class also felt unhappy due to class/*varna* rules which treated them as Shudras. The growth of towns and the increasing contact between different parts of the country broke the barriers of old tribal bonds and economy. The Brahminical religion failed to meet these challenges. Society was ready to embrace a new philosophy and religion.

In addition to the above, the other reason for the rise of Jainism and Buddhism was the religious unrest in India in the 6th century B. C., resulting from the orthodoxy of Vedic religion. The complex rituals and sacrifices advocated in the Later Vedic period were not acceptable to the common people. The sacrificial ceremonies were also found to be too expensive. The superstitious beliefs and *Mantras* confused the people. The teachings of Upanishads, an alternative to the system of sacrifices, were highly philosophical in nature and therefore not easily understood by all. So what was needed in the larger interests of the people was a simple, short and intelligible way to salvation. Such religious teaching should also be in a language known to them. This need was fulfilled by the teachings of Buddha and Mahavir.

Other than the religious orthodoxy, social and economic factors contributed immensely to the rise of these two religions. The rigid caste system prevalent in India generated tensions within the Hindu fold. Higher classes enjoyed certain privileges which were denied to the lower classes. Also, the Kshatriyas resented the domination of the priestly class. It should also to be noted that both Buddha and Mahavir possibly belonged to the Kshatriya origin. The growth of trade led to the improvement in the economic conditions of the Vaishyas. As a result, they also wanted to enhance their social status but the rigidity of the caste system acted as a barrier. Therefore, they began to extend support to Buddhism and Jainism. It was this merchant class that extended the chief support to these new religions.

Though Buddha did not openly deny caste and God, he was not in favour of them. His moral codes free from caste restrictions and complicated forms of worship attracted the low castes and Shudras to his fold. Buddha did not accept the supremacy of the Brahmins and their claim to divinity. He even ascribed the term Kulaputtas or noble Kula or birth to Gahapatis and rich merchants. His religion also satisfied the people of Kshatriya varna who were jealous of the Brahmins.

Since Jainism and Buddhism strongly believe in the philosophy of non-violence, the practice of either religion can ensure permanent peace to the humanity at large, but humanity has been rarely interested in peace. To many, religious crusade is a better option to secure peace. Most people talk of peace only to show their sane and sensible face, but in reality they are tyrants at heart and often in deeds also.

Rise of Islam in India

Now we come to Islam which is numerically the most predominant religion of India after Hinduism. But before we focus upon the rise and spread of Islam in India, let us briefly understand its basic philosophy at the outset. Islamic philosophy is a systematic investigation of problems connected with life, the universe, ethics, society, and so on as conducted in the Islamic world. Islamic philosophy is a generic term that can be defined and used in different ways. In its broadest sense it means the world view of Islam, as derived from the Islamic texts concerning the creation of the universe and the will of the Creator. In another sense it refers to any of the schools of thought that flourished under the Islamic empire or in the shadow of the Arab-Islamic culture and Islamic civilization. In its narrowest sense it is a translation of *Falsafa*, meaning those particular schools of thought that most reflect the influence of Greek systems of philosophy such as Neo-Platonism and Aristotelianism.

It is not necessarily concerned with religious issues, nor exclusively produced by Muslims. Nor do all schools of thought within Islam admit the usefulness or legitimacy of philosophical inquiry. Some argue that there is no indication that the limited knowledge and experience of humans can lead to truth. It is also important to observe that, while 'reason' (*'aql*) is sometimes recognized as a source of Islamic law, this may have a totally different meaning from 'reason' in philosophy.

Early Islamic philosophy began in the 2nd century AH of the Islamic calendar (the early 9th century AD) and lasted until the 6th century AH (late 12th century AD). The period is known as the Islamic Golden Age, and the achievements of this period had a crucial influence on the development of modern philosophy and science; for Renaissance Europe, the influence represented 'one of the largest technology transfers in world history.' This period began with *al-Kindi* in the 9th century and ended with Averroes (Ibn Rushd) at the end of 12th century. The death of Averroes effectively marked the end of a particular discipline of Islamic philosophy usually called the Peripatetic Arabic School, and philosophical activity declined significantly in the Western Islamic countries like Islamic Spain. Philosophy persisted for much longer in the Eastern countries, in particular Persia and India where several schools of philosophy continued to flourish: Avicennism, Illuminationist philosophy, mystical philosophy and transcendent theosophy. Ibn Khaldun, in his **Muqaddimah**, made important contributions to the philosophy of history. Interest in Islamic philosophy revived during the *Nahda* (awakening) movement in the late 19th and early 20th centuries, and continues to the present day.

Islamic philosophers were greatly influenced by Greek philosophy and sought to use it to understand, defend and further their faith. However, their theorizing often led them astray from orthodox Islamic teachings. For example, some of them believed, following Aristotle, that the material world was eternal, though they also affirmed that it existed only because God made it to exist. Others denied physical resurrection, substituting the continued existence of the soul. Still others proposed a replacement body that looked like the original, but actually was not. Most philosophers advocated the idea that God was a Necessary Being (a being who could not exist) and that the world was dependent upon God for its existence.

Islamic philosophy argues for the existence of entities beyond the natural world; affirmation of the existence of God, for example, illustrates that Islam denies naturalism in favour of super-naturalism. Islam also affirms the existence of the human spirit beyond death as well as the existence of angels and *jinns*. In admitting the existence of angels, Abdalati also alludes to the Islamic view of epistemology: not all things may be known through human senses, nor may we limit the field of existence to what our senses perceive.

Fundamental to Islam is the belief in final judgement, necessitating an implied belief in life after death. Muslims further affirm the bodily resurrection of the dead (though they deny that Jesus died and was resurrected). "See thee not that God, Who created the heavens and the earth... is able to give life to the dead? Yea, verily He has power over all things" (Koran 46:33). And he [unbelieving man] makes comparisons for us, and forgets his own (origin and) Creation: He says, "Who can give Life to (dry) bones and decomposed ones (at that)?" Say, "He will give them Life Who created them for the first time! For He is well-versed in every kind of creation" (Koran 36:78–79). The story of Islam begins with Muhammad receiving divine visions and communicating with the angel Gabriel, indicating an acceptance of the supernatural. Indeed, the Koran affirms that prophets performed many miracles.

Many of us wrongly believe that Islam reached India first from North direction, not from South. The truth is that South India was in constant touch with Gulf countries for trading spices before the foreign Muslims established any contact with North India. The Islamic preachers reached the Indian coasts of Kerala long before Gazani or the Mughals came from the north direction. These preachers were mostly like the Sufi saints and they were passive in their mode of conversion in contrast to active conversion done when invaders entered India from north at the later periods of history. Trade relations existed between Arabia and the Indian subcontinent since ancient times. Even in the pre-Islamic era, Arab traders used to visit the Konkan, Gujarat coast and the Malabar region, which linked them with the ports of South East Asia. Newly Islamised Arabs were Islam's first contact with India. The first ship carrying Muslim travellers was seen on the Indian coast as early as 630 AD. The first Arab Muslims settled on the Indian coast in the last part of the 7th century AD. Shaykh Zainuddin Makhdum's '**Tuhfat-al-Mujahidin**' is also a reliable work. It was with the advent of Islam that the Arabs became a prominent cultural force in the world. The Arab merchants and traders became the carriers of the new religion and they propagated it wherever they went.

The first great expansion of Islam into India came during the Umayyad Dynasty of caliphs, who were based in Damascus. In 711, the Umayyads appointed a young 17 year old man from Ta'if (Muhammad bin Qasim) to extend Umayyad control over Sindh. Sindh is the land around the Indus River in the North-western part of the subcontinent in the present-day Pakistan.

Islam came to North India much later in the form of rulers who won wars and settled in India. After that there were various reasons for conversion. Some converted to show loyalty to their king. Some converted because they accepted the message of Islam. Some also converted to flatter their king and so on. As in any kingdom the religion of King is usually considered superior. Conversion to Islam, particularly in North India, was due to sword and *Jizya* too, and to a lesser extent by Sufis in Kerala. Many of them who were converted were upper caste Hindus like Rajputs and Brahmins to avoid *Jizya* and protect their kingdoms. This was least important that Hindus were attracted by the notion of equality preached by Islam. Islam did not derive much benefit from inequality existing in Hinduism. Sufism did bring tolerance and also tried to spread ideas like equality, love and submission to God is a path to enlightenment but these qualities were soon adopted by Hindus through the *Bhakti* movement. Since Muslims in India do have the caste system even though Islam does not believe in it. The caste system is still in existence in India, but no conversion is taking place for the caste reason.

It is often observed that almost all the faiths more or less did spread through violence, created out of individual ambition for 'power'. This is a very controversial viewpoint indeed. Historical evidence suggests that conversion was definitely via sword. Mohammed Bin Qasim, for example, an 18 year old Syrian military general conquered Sindh and ransacked the city and took women as slaves. This is still celebrated in Pakistan as Bin Qasim Day when Islam made its acquaintance in India with sword. This continued over the centuries with other invaders. But somewhere during this period, Islam integrated itself with local traditions and this synthesized into a more tolerant, locally acceptable form with distinctly Indian flavour. Some percentage of conversions took place under the influence of Sufism. The economic incentives and scope for upward mobility for the lower castes and similar other considerations provided fillip to the process of Islamization of Hindus and others. More than missionaries or saints, it was the Emperors who offered great incentives to the natives of the Indian subcontinent to convert to Islam. Incentives were in the form of military protection or tax benefits, for example. The Emperors also brought numerous Muslim soldiers and workers from Afghanistan, etc. who settled on the Indian subcontinent.

In brief, in North India Islam spread primarily by the sword, and in South India it primarily spread through centuries of trade and cultural contacts (e. g. Arab trade with Kerala, the establishment of the Mappila Hindu/Muslim Arab mixed community, the arrival of Yemeni refugees from Hadramut, following a Yemeni tribal civil war), the adoption of Islam as a military/law enforcement ideology by a local zamorin, who decreed that each household in his kingdom would raise one son as a Muslim to serve in his army and police forces), as Alqama Pervez has outlined, though towards the end of Muslim rule in India (and with the onset of the British) bigots like Tipu Sultan of the Sultanate of Mysore began spreading Islam in the South by the sword.

The difference in the spread of Islam between North and South

India probably accounts for why the North Indian Muslims anecdotally seem to have a more predominant 'martial' trait than the South Indian Muslims. Even before the life of Prophet Muhammad in the 600s, Arab traders were in contact with India. Merchants used to sail regularly to the West coast of India to trade goods such as spices, gold and African goods. Naturally, when the Arabs began to convert to Islam, they carried their new religion to the shores of India. The first mosque of India, the Cheraman Juma Masjid, was built in 629 (during the life of Prophet Muhammad) in Kerala, by the first Muslim from India, Cheraman Perumal Bhaskar Ravi Varma. Through continued trade between Arab Muslims and Indians, Islam continued to spread in the coastal cities and towns, both through immigration and conversion. Though Islam came to the Indian subcontinent in the early 7th century with the advent of Arab traders, it started impacting Indian religions after the 10th century, and particularly after the 12th century with the establishment and then expansion of Islamic rule in the northern parts of India.

In the first half of the 10th century, Mahmud of Ghazni added the Punjab to the Ghaznavid Empire and conducted 17 raids on modern-day India. In the 11th century, Ghazi Saiyyad Salar Masud played a significant role in the conversion of locals (Hindus) to Islam. A more successful invasion came at the end of the 12th century by Muhammad Ghori. He is credited with laying the foundation of Muslim rule in South Asia that lasted for several centuries. He reigned over a territory spanning over parts of modern-day Afghanistan, Bangladesh, Iran, India, Pakistan, Tajikistan and Turkmenistan.

It appears from the memoirs of Timur, who destroyed the Delhi Sultanate, that he was the first Islamic dynasty of the Indian subcontinent. He used to refer himself as the Sword of Islam and wanted to restore the rule of Genghis Khan or Chinggis Khan. He was a devout Muslim and by expert estimates got 17 million people killed (5 percent of world's population in his time). His memoirs specifically describe killing of non-Muslims and massacre of 100, 000 captive Hindus when he captured Delhi.

"Hindus were forcibly converted to Islam and were massacred in case they refused to be convert", writes Hasan, a Muslim chronicler.

He has further observed, "And Sikandarpora (a city laid out by Sultan Sikandar) was laid out on the debris of the destroyed temples of the Hindus. In the neighbourhood of the royal palaces in Sikandarpora, the Sultan destroyed the temples of Maha-Shri built by Praversena and another by Tarapida. The material from these was used for constructing a 'Jami' mosque in the middle of the city."

After the conquest of Persia by the Mongol Empire, a regional Turko-Persio-Mongol dynasty was formed. Just as the eastern Mongol dynasties inter-married with locals and adopted the local religion of Buddhism and the Chinese culture, this group adopted the local religion of Islam and the Persian culture; their descendants ruled in India as Mughals.

The official state religion of the Mughal Empire was Islam, with the preference to the jurisprudence of the Hanafi Madhhab (Mazhab). Hinduism remained under strain during Babur and Humanyun's reigns. Sher Shah Suri, the Afghan ruler of North India, was comparatively non-repressive. Hinduism came to fore during the three-year rule of Hindu king 'Hemu' during 1553-56 when he had defeated Akbar at Agra and Delhi and had taken up the reign from Delhi as a Hindu 'Vikramaditya' king after his '*Rajyabhishek*' or coronation at 'Purana Quila' in Delhi. However, during the Mughal history, at times, subjects had freedom to practise any religion of their choice, though non-Muslim able-bodied adult males with income were obliged to pay the *Jizya* (*Jizya* was a kind tax levied by the Muslim rulers on certain permanent non-Muslim residents of the Muslim territory under Islamic law), which signified their status as *Dhimmis* (responsibility of the State, in regard to safety of life and property).

Akbar, the Mughal emperor Humanyun's son and heir from his Sindhi queen Hameeda Banu Begum, had a broad vision of Indian and Islamic traditions, although he was illiterate. One of Emperor Akbar's most unusual ideas regarding religion was Din-i-Ilahi (Faith of God), which was an eclectic mix of Islam, Zoroastrianism, Hinduism, Jainism and Christianity. It was proclaimed to be the state religion until his death. These actions, however, met with stiff opposition from the Muslim clergy, especially the Sufi Shaykh Alf Sani Ahmad Sirhindi. Akbar's son, Jahangir, half Rajput, was also a religious moderate, his mother being Hindu. The influence of his two Hindu queens (the Maharani Manbai and Maharani Jagat) kept religious moderation as a centre-piece of state policy which was extended under his son, Emperor Shah Jahan, who was by blood 75 percent Rajput and less than 25 percent Moghul.

Religious orthodoxy became prominent during the reign of Shah Jahan's son and successor, Aurangzeb, a devout Sunni Muslim. Aurangzeb was comparatively less tolerant of other faiths than his predecessors had been, and his reign saw an increase in the number and importance of Islamic institutions and scholars and he also coerced Hindus to convert them to Islam. He led many military campaigns against the remaining non-Muslim powers of the Indian subcontinent– the Sikh states of the Punjab, the last independent Hindu Rajputs and the Maratha rebels– as also against the Shia Muslim kingdoms of the Deccan. He also virtually stamped out, from his empire, open proselytization of Hindus and Muslims by foreign Christian Missionaries, who remained successfully active, however, in the adjoining regions: the present day Kerala, Tamil Nadu and Goa.

Guru Tegh Bahadur was executed by Aurangzeb because he refused to convert to Islam. The fall of Vijayanagar Empire to Muslim rulers had marked the end of Hindu imperial assertions in the Deccan. But, taking advantage of an over-stretched Mughal Empire (1526–1857), Hinduism once again rose to political prestige under the Maratha Empire from 1674 to 1818.

During 1760–1860, India was once more divided into numerous petty and unstable kingdoms, gradually coming under the paramountacy of the British Empire: the 'lesser Mughals', the Kingdom of Mysore, Hyderabad State, Maratha Confederacy, Rajput Kingdoms, Palaiyakkarar states, North-Eastern states such as Kingdom of Manipur, Himalayan states, etc. From 1799 to 1849 the only major stable kingdom in India was the Sikh Empire, although it had a syncretic character with a large number of Hindu and Muslim subjects living in peace. It too became unstable after the death of Maharaja Ranjit Singh. The entire subcontinent fell under the British rule (partly indirectly, via princely states) following the Indian Rebellion of 1857.

Religious Conversion

Because the pre-Islamic India was entirely based on the caste system in which society was stratified into numerous rigid strata, conversion to Islam happened in a step-by-step process. Often, certain castes tended to convert themselves to Islam at a time. This happened for many different reasons. Often, however, the equality Islam provided was more attractive than the caste system's organized discrimination. Within the caste system, people have no choice to change their pre-ordained position in society. There was no opportunity for upward social mobility or to achieve greater than what their parents achieved. By converting to Islam, people had the opportunity to move up in society, and no longer were subservient to the Brahmin caste. At the same time it is also true that the converts could not be fully free from caste based hierarchy and discrimination. This is the reason why the caste system is found among the Indian Muslims as well. Brahmins, though most of them do not readily admit their guilt even these days, are definitely accountable for playing a havoc with the unity and integrity of the Hindu social order through the introduction of values of caste based discrimination, differentiation and hierarchy. The notion of untouchability or practice of casteism within the Hindu society is the glaring example of supporting and nourishing hatred within the Hindu fold. It is extremely strange that Hindus tend to offer prayer to or have reverence for certain rivers, trees, animals, mountains, stones, sun, moon, planets and other such natural objects, but they have an unprecedented record of hating people of their own kind, based on the notion of untouchability.

Buddhism, which was once very popular in the subcontinent, slowly died out under the Muslim rule. Traditionally, when people wanted to escape the wrath of caste system, they preferred to convert to Buddhism. But when Islam became an option people began to convert to Islam instead of Buddhism to get rid of the tyranny of caste system.

Wandering Muslim teachers also had a major role to play in bringing Islam to the masses. Muslim scholars travelled throughout India, making it their goal to educate people about Islam. Many of them preached Sufi ideas, a more mystical approach to Islam that appealed to the people. These teachers had a major role in bringing Islam to the masses in the countryside, not just to the upper class Hindus around the Muslim rulers.

Indians got real taste of Islam or political Islam only after 1000 AD, and were shocked to know that they were killed just because they were not Muslims, temples were destroyed, Jizya was forced, slavery introduced, universities (such as Nalanda University in Bihar) were destroyed which caused irreparable damage to the Indian civilization. Children from raped women from this period onwards were not accepted back. Jauhar (the Hindu custom of mass self-immolation by women to avoid capture, enslavement and rape by invaders, when facing certain defeat during a war) became popular. Bajirao Mastani was another case.

From 1000 AD to 1750 AD it was a period of great stress, as every possible attempt was made to cause destruction to Hinduism. It was the first time where Hindus were questioned about their faith, belief, secularism, meditation, Yog, language and history. Hindus moved and hid into interiors, and cities which were Muslim ruled became 100 percent Muslim populated cities. That ultimately gave rise to a new religion of Sikhism in India.

According to Muslim historians, Muslims rulers got killed anything between 60 to 80 million Hindus for refusing conversion to Islam. Some historians question those claims and state they are exaggerated. Some of the Hindus got converted because of *Jizya* and wanted to save money (form of forced conversion). *Jizya* was the prime factor behind coersive conversion. Under the system of *Jizya* where taxes went as high as 50 percent, failure to pay resulted in loss of female child or wife or male child. Some people got converted through marriage, and slavery (forced conversion). Very small percentage of Hindus accepted Islam on their own and they were mostly *Dalits.* There are very few Muslims close to 0.1 percent whose ancestry is Arab. Most of the Indian Muslims were originally Hindus. Converted people were never accepted in larger society, as Hindus felt betrayed by those who converted or left their original religion and acceptance of them was disrespect to those who preferred to die rather than convert. Most of the converted Muslims were not allowed to reconvert to the religion of the land and many did not do it because of the simplicity of Islam as a religion compared to the complexity of Hinduism and multiple philosophies of the land. Hinduism connects you to your land only whereas Islam connects you to global *Ummah* or pan-Islam.

Currently Muslims constitute about 33 percent of the total population of the Indian subcontinent, but in 1750 they were only 6 percent of the total population. The percentage of Muslims moved up from 6 percent in 1750 to about one-third of the total population by the time of India's independence due to massive conversion and relatively higher fertility among Muslims.

William James Durant calls the Muslim conquest of India 'probably the bloodiest story in history'. During this period Buddhism declined rapidly, while Hinduism faced military-led and Sultanates-sponsored religious violence. There was a widespread practice of raids, seizure and enslavement of families of Hindus, who were then sold in Sultanate cities or exported to Central Asia. Some texts suggest that a large number of Hindus were forcibly converted to Islam. Starting with 13th century, for a period of some 500 years, very few texts, from the numerous written by Muslim court historians, mention any 'voluntary conversion of Hindus to Islam', suggesting its insignificance and perhaps rarity of such conversions. Typically enslaved Hindus converted to Islam to gain their freedom. There were occasional exceptions to religious violence against Hinduism. Akbar, for example, recognized Hinduism, banned enslavement of the families of Hindu war captives, protected Hindu temples, and abolished discriminatory *Jizya* against Hindus. However, many Muslim rulers of the Delhi Sultanate and Mughal Empire, before and after Akbar, from the 12th to the 18th century, destroyed Hindu temples and persecuted non-Muslims. There is no necessity to dwell any further on this issue, as the detailed description of such historical facts is likely to be labelled as sectarian.

Bhakti Movement

Now let us briefly dwell on the Bhakti movement, as it had a massive impact on cultural values, religious practices and the general system of belief of different communities. The Bhakti movement refers to the theistic devotional trend that emerged in medieval Hinduism and later revolutionised Sikhism. It originated in the seventh-century Tamil

Nadu and Kerala, and then spread northwards. It swept over east and north India from the 15th century onwards, reaching its zenith between the 15th and 17th century AD.

The Bhakti movement regionally developed around different gods and goddesses, such as Vaishnavism (Vishnu), Shaivism (Shiv), Shaktism (Shakti goddesses) and Smartism. The movement was inspired by many poet-saints, who championed a wide range of philosophical positions ranging from theistic dualism of *Dvait* to absolute monism of *Advait Vedant*. The movement has traditionally been considered as an influential social reformation in Hinduism, which provided an individual-focussed alternative path to spirituality regardless of one's caste of birth or gender. Some postmodern scholars have questioned this traditional view and state whether the Bhakti movement ever was a reform or rebellion of any kind. Scriptures of the Bhakti movement include the Bhagavad Geeta, Bhagavat Puran, Padma Puran, Ramayan, etc.

Usually it is accepted that the most characteristic feature of the religious development during the medieval period was the movement which emphasized single-minded intense devotion to God. It was a complete surrender of oneself to God. The movement which emphasized primarily these ideas was the Bhakti movement– devotion to God. Bhakti to God was accepted as salvation. Main features of the Bhakti movement were as follows:

1. Unity of God or one God though known by different names.
2. Bhakti, intense love and devotion, the only way to salvation.
3. Repeated utterances of the True Name.
4. Self-Surrender.
5. Condemnation of rituals, ceremonies and blind faith.
6. Rejection of idol worship by many saints
7. Open- mindedness about deciding religious matters.
8. No distinction based on caste.
9. Need of a *Guru* for guidance advocated by some.
10. Preachings through local or regional languages and travelling from place to place for spreading the religious message.

Many doctrines of the Bhakti cult may be found in the Bhagavad Geeta. The idea of the unity of God is reflected in these words, "Even those devotees who, endowed with faith, worship other gods, worship Me only, but by the wrong method." (9:23). It is not the way of worship but the love of a selfless devotee of pure heart that matters, "I (Sri Krishna) accept the devotional offering of a pious self even if it is only a leaf, a flower, a fruit or water." (9:26). The doctrine of self-surrender is echoed in the words of Lord Krishna, "Abandoning all duties, come to Me alone for shelter. Be not grieved, for I shall release you from all evils." (18:66). "Thus I have imparted you the most secret knowledge of all. After fully reflecting on this in its entirety, you can do what you like." (18:63).

However, the real development of Bhakti took place in South India between the 7th and the 12th centuries through the teachings of poet saints known as Alvars and Nayanar whose hymns were collected and compiled in the 10th century. The Sufi saints of the Muslims also emphasized devotion to Allah (God). The spiritual yearning made Kabir, Guru Nanak, Meerabai, Surdas, Tulsidas, Chaitanya Mahaprabhu and others the great exponents of the Bhakti movement.

Impact of the Bhakti Movement— With intent to understand the impact of the Bhakti movement, we have to consider the background under which the movement gained momentum. Under the impact of the Muslim rule, the Hindus had suffered a lot materially, morally and spiritually. The Muslim rulers in general wanted to enforce the Islamic laws on the Hindus. The Muslim rule had put terror in the hearts of the Hindu masses. They wanted some solace to heal their despairing hearts. The Bhakti movement brought them hope and support and inner strength to save themselves. During the course of time, several evil practices had crept into the Hindu society. There was a lot of caste based animosity. The ruling Muslim class created panic for the Hindus.

There was a good deal of bitterment between the two communities– the Hindus and the Muslims. Some healing touch was needed. Fortunately with the foreign invaders, some Sufi saints also came to India and settled here. They were very liberal minded. They emphasized the virtues of love and devotion, brotherhood and equality. This helped to bring the two communities closer. It also helped to harmonise the conflicting interests of different communities.

The saints of the Bhakti movement rejected the differences based on *Jati* or religion. An important factor which led to the popularity of Bhakti movement was that most of the promoters of this movement attempted to reconcile the differences between the Hindus and the Muslims by stressing that Ram and Rahim were one and the same. They condemned the attitude of the orthodox Pundits and fanatic Mullahs alike.

The Hindus realized that it was difficult to drive away the Muslim rulers and Muslims from India. On the other hand, the Muslims also appreciated that the Hindus were in absolute majority and it was impossible to force all of them to embrace Islam. So under the impact of the new movement both sides started making efforts for coming closer to each other. For the Hindus the effort was initiated by the Hindu saints of the Bhakti movement and for the Muslims by the Sufi Saints.

The Hindu as well as the Muslim saints emphasized religious simplicity. They stressed human qualities and moral attitudes. They stressed that a true religious man is one who is pure in thought and action. The Bhakti saints believed in the notion of equality of men regardless of caste and creed. According to them there was no distinction and consideration of high and low on the basis of birth. Their doors were open to all classes.

The Bhakti saints like Chaitanya, Kabir, Guru Nanak, Dadudayal, Mira Bai, Tulsidas, Surdas and Malukdas tried to generate an environment of good will between the Hindus and the Muslims. The Bhakti saints were social reformers also. They condemned several social evils. The Sufi saints like Khwaja Muinuddin Chisti, Bakhyiya Kaki, Nizamudin Aulia, Nasiruddin Chirag-i-Delhi, etc. attempted to restrain the fanaticism of the Muslims and tried to bring them nearer to the Hindus. Several Hindus became followers of the Sufi saints but without relinquishing their own religion.

The most important social impact of the Bhakti movement was that the followers of the Bhakti movement rejected the caste distinction. They began to mingle and interact with one another on the basis of social equality. They took their meals together from the common kitchen. The movement tried to loosen the age-old bond of caste. A spirit of harmony among different sections of the society and religion received impetus. The evil practice of '*Sati*' received some setback. The status of women received greater attention. The movement aroused awakening among the Hindus and Muslims regarding the futility of ritualism and superstitions. The feeling of appreciation of the difference between the thought and practices of the two religions emerged. The movement encouraged religious tolerance. Guru Granth Sahib, the holiest book of the Sikhs, which was compiled later on included the messages of saints belonging to different sects. This was on account of the spirit of tolerance preached by the Bhakti saints.

The movement attempted to infuse a spirit of piety in the daily life of the people. It emphasized earning of wealth through hard work and honest means. It encouraged the value of social service to the poor and the needy. It developed a humanitarian attitude. It pointed out the virtues of contentment and self control. It drew attention to the evils of anger, greed and vanity.

Rise of Sikhism

The philosophy of Sikhism is covered in great detail in the Guru Granth Sahib, the Sikh holy text. Detailed guidance is given to followers on how to conduct their lives so that peace and salvation can be attained. The holy text outlines the positive actions that one must take to make progress in the evolution of the person. One must remember the Creator at all times– it reminds the follower that the 'soul is, but a part of the whole that is God, who is ever merciful', and that the followers must dedicate their life to all good causes to help make this life more worthwhile.

The Sikhs must believe in the following values relating to the principles of universal equality and brotherhood, right to life, simple living, good deeds, remembrance of God (*Naam Simran, Kirtan*), living a family life, sharing (to give a charity of 10 percent of one's net earnings) and accept God's will, the four fruits of life: truth, contentment, contemplation and *Naam* (in the name of God).

Sikhism was founded by Guru Nanak Dev (1469-1538) at the beginning of the sixteenth century. Guru Nanak was born on April 15, 1469 in the Western Punjab village of Talwandi. Even as a child, he used to have deep thinking with no interest in worldly life. At the age of thirty, he got enlightenment. Thereafter, he travelled almost the whole of the country and went over to Mecca and Baghdad, preaching his message. Guru Nanak sculpted Sikhism on the elevated ideology of Equality. His clarion call to the sea of humanity echoes in the modern-day dream of a global unity- '*na ko Hindu, na ko Musulman*', approximates to 'There is no Hindu, there is no Muslim'. His keen interest in the unexplored mysteries of the world enhanced his spiritual quest. He discovered the paramountcy of the Omnipotent. A true messenger of God, Guru Nanak, went ahead to distribute the precious 'TRUTH' among the ignorant masses. His teachings generated a resurgence of reformation that precipitated into the growth of Sikhism. On his death he was followed by nine other great Gurus in succession.

Guru Angad Dev Ji (1504-1552) was a Guru next to Guru Nanak Dev. He remained Guru for thirteen years (1539-1552). He created a new script Gurumukhi and gave the Sikhs a written language. After his death Guru Amar Das Ji (1479-1574) followed in succession. He showed great devotion and made the *langar* an integral part of Sikhism. Guru Ram Das Ji took over as the fourth Guru, he composed hymns, which were later incorporated in the sacred writings. Guru Arjan Dev Ji became the fifth Guru of Sikhism. He built the world famous Harmandar Sahib, popularly known as the Golden Temple in Amritsar. He also compiled the holy Granth Sahib, a sacred religious book of the Sikhs. Guru Arjan Dev suffered martyrdom in 1606 and was followed by Siri Guru Hargobind, who maintained a standing army and symbolically wore two swords, representing spiritual and temporal power.

Guru Siri Har Rai, the seventh Guru was born in 1630 and spent most of his life in devotional meditation and preaching the teachings of Guru Nanak. He passed away in 1661 and ordained his second son, Harkishan as the Guru. Guru Siri Har Krishan Ji got enlightenment in 1661. He gave his life while serving and healing the epidemic-stricken people in Delhi. The place where he had his last breath is one where the renowned Gurudwara Bangla Sahib stands in Delhi. Siri Guru Tegh Bahadur became Guru in 1664. When the Mughal Governor of Kashmir resorted to forcible conversion of Hindus, Guru Tegh Bahadur decided to fight it out. Gurudwara Sisganj in Delhi stands at the place of Guru

Sahib's martyrdom and Gurudwara Rakabganj at the site of his cremation. The tenth and last *Guru*, Guru Gobind Singh, was born in 1666 in Patna and became *Guru* at the age of nine after the martyrdom of his father Guru Tegh Bahadur. Guru Gobind Singh, at the time of his death vested the **'Guru Granth Sahib'** as the supreme head of the Sikhs, thus bringing the practice of nominating a religious head to a grinding halt.

Banda Bahadur (1670-1716) became the commander of the Sikh army in the post-Guru Gobind Singh period. He cast many raids against the hostile Mughal to stop their pernicious persecutions against the Sikhs. He died a martyr, being assassinated by the Mughal Emperor, Jahandhar Shah. He rejected the disgraceful mercy to change into Islam, which might have spared his life. Hindus owe a lot to the Sikh, as the rise of Sikhism acted as a buffer community between Muslims and Hindus. Sikhs stood like a rock against the terrible onslaught of Muslims on Hindus. Their sacrifice for the cause of Hinduism is unprecedented in the history of this country. Sikhs acted as saviour of Hindu religion.

The decline of the Mughal Empire was marked by the rise of the Sikhs under the outstanding leadership of Maharaja Ranjit Singh on April 12, 1801. Ranjit Singh architectured a pan-Sikh empire which earned for Sikhism, a national identity. However with the death of the monarch, the empire crumbled into dust, owing to the turbulent Anglo-Sikh Wars. British overpowered their land of Punjab.

Sikhs joined the freedom-struggle of the Indian National Congress. The resolute Sikhs cemented their Sikh foundation through the setting up of Shiromani Gurudwara Prabandhak Committee and the Shiromani Akali Dal. The weird Partition of 1947 witnessed a massacre of thousands of Sikhs and forced immigration to West Punjab as destitute refugees. Thereafter the Sikhs have emerged as a dominant enterprising community spread all over the world.

Christianity in India

Lastly let us deal with the spread of Christianity in this country. The Christian philosophy requires faith in Biblical revelation; one might assume that the Christian worldview cannot possibly have a philosophy of its own. According to the secular worldviews, naturalism and materialism are grounded firmly in the modern scientific methodology and enlightened human experience. Christian philosophy represents an entire worldview, a view that is consistent with the Bible throughout. In the end, we must choose between a materialist/naturalist worldview and a supernaturalist worldview– and our choice will create repercussions throughout every aspect of the human life. The Christian philosophy embraces the meaningful, purposeful life, a life in which one shapes one's beliefs according to a coherent, reasonable, truthful worldview.

The philosophy of Christianity involves the reason for human life, why human life was created and sustained by God and nourished by His Spirit, and lastly, to where our human life is destined to lead us to in the future. The word 'life' by which Christianity is denominated is interpreted by its profound and expansive usage as promoted and detailed by the apostle John in his Gospel. He writes: "In the beginning was the Word, and the Word was with God, and the Word was God. He was in the beginning with God. All things came into being through him, and without him not one thing came into being. What has come into being in him was life, and the life was the light of all people. The light shines in the darkness, and the darkness did not overcome it.... [Christ Jesus is] the true light, which enlightens everyone" (John 1:1-9 NRSV). This is the true 'life' that mankind must adopt. Its acceptance by humanity makes Christianity a Philosophy of Life. It is our emulating and living that particular 'life' that enlightens us with unlimited truth and in an inseparable way it unites us with the personality and the bodily presence of Christ Jesus.

Now Christianity constitutes about 2.3 percent of India's total population and its proportion has gradually risen because of the incidence of religious conversion through enticement. It arrived in India almost about the same period as it arrived in Europe, meaning about 2000 years ago. Christianity originated in Israel. The first Christians were Jews and in the beginning Christianity was seen as a Jewish cult. Most of the Apostles of Christians acted in Europe to convert the Europeans to Christianity. But one of the Apostles, St. Judas Thomas, arrived in India and converted Indians to Christianity. St. Thomas was a carpenter and a disciple of Jesus. He was brought to India by a merchant to build a temple. St.Thomas arrived in Kerala in south India in 52 AD. He succeeded in converting local Indians to Christianity. His converts were called Syrian Christians. One assumption says that some of the Syrian Christians were actually Jews converted by St. Judas Thomas to Christianity. The disciples of Jesus at first intended to convince the Jews to adopt the philosophy of Jesus as new Judaism. Later on other Christian saints came to India as missionaries. But most of the Indians were converted to Christianity by the missionaries who arrived in India with the European powers from 15th century.

The European powers came to India for commercial purposes, especially trades in spices. But they also started converting the locals to Christianity. Five European countries sent their representatives to India, Great Britain, France, Denmark, Netherlands and Portugal. Of the five European powers, the Portuguese were most enthusiastic to baptize Indians. The Portuguese were the first European power to arrive in India. Their first ship, under the leadership of Vasco da Gama, arrived in South India in 1498 after it had circled the whole continent of Africa. The Portuguese inspired by the Pope's order to baptize people around the world not only fought wars against the local Indian rulers, but they even tried to enforce their Roman Catholic prayers on the Syrian Christians.

After many wars the Portuguese were defeated by local rulers and they had only one big pocket of control in India, Goa. The Portuguese not only fought against the Indian rulers, but they also against other European powers in India, especially the Dutch and the English. Many Portuguese churches in Kerala were turned into English and Dutch churches after they were captured by these powers.

The English missionaries started acting in India at a much later period. The British, unlike the Portuguese, didn't allow the missionaries to enter their territory in the beginning. The British arrived in India in 1600 and they allowed the missionaries to enter their territory only from 1813 onward. The British allowed different churches to establish missionaries in their territory. The missionaries didn't only spread Christianity, but they also did humanitarian deeds by providing basic necessities of life like food, clothes and shelter. The missionaries also built schools in India and many of them even today have Christian or

European origin names. The British church missionaries succeeded less than the Portuguese in converting Indians to Christianity, but unlike the Portuguese who tried to enforce Christianity, these Protestant converts were voluntary. The Portuguese were also aware of the Indian custom according to which the wife followed her husband's faith and therefore married their men to Indian women.

Christianity is India's third-largest religion according to the census of 2011, with approximately 27.8 million followers, constituting 2.3 percent of India's population. The major centres of this faith in India are Kerala, Tamil Nadu, Goa, Manipur and Mizoram. There is also a big community of Christians in Mumbai. The main division of Christians in India is like in the Christian world, Protestants and Catholic. There are also different denominations among them, Syrian Church, Armenian Church, Anglican Church and others. Most of the India Christians were converted by the Portuguese. There is also an Anglo-Indian community in India.

Mass forced religious conversion in India by Christian missionary groups are not reported in mainstream news, but conversion is vigorously pursued by the Christians, particularly among hill tribes, scheduled castes and population residing in forest regions and other downtrodden or the poorest sections of society. Approximately 3.2 million Indians are being converted every year by Christian missionary groups because of freedom of religion in India is a fundamental right guaranteed under Article 15 and Article 25 of the Constitution of India.

Rate of forced Christian conversions taking place in India is accounting for the rapid rise in Christian population. Most of the increase in the Christian population is coming through conversion of Hindus and other minor religions such as Sikhs, Jains and Buddhists in India. Most of these people are poor and vulnerable sections of society being tempted through money by Christian missionary groups.

The conversion of Hindus to Christianity is being done by missionary groups who propagate that the Hindus and the people of other religions such as the Sikhs, Jains and Buddhists would go to hell unless they follow Christianity. The extent of the forced conversion activity taking place in the country is very alarming. The Christian population in India has grown from 26. 5 million in 2001 to 76.9 million in 2015. This implies that 3.2 million Hindus (and members of other religions) are being converted annually by Christian missionary groups. Simultaneously it is also worth noting that although Christianity came to India much before Islam had a foothold here, Muslims share 6-7 times larger population than that of the Christians because of massive coercive conversions of the Hindus by the Muslims in the past and persistence of high fertility. Regardless of the level of education, development or income, a Muslim woman tends to reproduce on child more than a Hindu woman on an average throughout the country including the State of Kerala which has got the highest level of literacy (94 percent). Such a stupendous rise in Muslim population can be still higher if we consider the total population of pre-undivided or pre-Independent India. On the other hand, Christianity did not follow the path of coercion to boost their numerical strength; rather, they pursued the policy of constant persuasion and humanitarian services to the needy or the depressed. This fact is clearly evident from the studies of prevailing demographic scenario of the country.

Hinduism in Modern India

With the commencement of the British Raj, there started a Hindu renaissance in the 19th century, which profoundly changed the understanding of Hinduism in both India and the West. Indology as an academic discipline of studying Indian culture from a European perspective was established in the 19th century, led by scholars such as Max Müller and John Woodroffe. (Not many people know that Max Muller was interested in Indology because he was too desperate to bring Christianity into India so that the religion of the Hindus be doomed.) They brought Vedic, Puranic and Tantric literature and philosophy to Europe and the United States. Western orientalists searched for the 'essence' of the Indian religions, discerning this in the Vedas, and meanwhile creating the notion of 'Hinduism' as a unified body of religious praxis and the popular picture of 'mystical India'. This idea of a Vedic essence was taken over by Hindu reform movements as the Brahmo Samaj, which was supported for a while by the Unitarian Church, together with the ideas of Universalism and Perennialism, the idea that all religions share a common mystic ground.

The British period saw the emergence of various Hindu reform movements partly inspired by the Western movements, such as Unitarianism and Theosophy. During the 19th century, Hinduism developed a large number of new religious movements, partly inspired by the European Romanticism, nationalism, scientific racism and esotericism (Theosophy) popular at the time (while conversely and contemporaneously, India had a similar effect on European culture with Orientalism, 'Hindoo style' architecture, reception of Buddhism in the West).

These reform movements are summarised under Hindu revivalism and continue into the present.

•Sahajanand Swami established the Swaminarayan Sampraday (sect) around 1800.

•Brahmo Samaj was a social and religious movement founded in Kolkata in 1828 by Raja Ram Mohan Roy. He was one of the first Indians to visit Europe and was influenced by the western thought. He died in Bristol, England. The Brahmo Samaj movement thereafter resulted in the Brahmo religion in 1850 founded by Devendranath Tagore, the father of Rabindranath Tagore.

•Sri Ramakrishna and his disciple Swami Vivekananda led a reform in Hinduism in the late 19th century. Their ideals and sayings have inspired numerous Indians as well as non-Indians, Hindus as well as non-Hindus. Among the prominent figures whose ideals were very much influenced by them were Rabindranath Tagore, Mahatma Gandhi, Subhas Bose, Satyendranath Bose, Meghnad Saha and Sister Nivedita.

•Arya Samaj ('Society of Nobles') is a Hindu reform movement in India that was founded by Swami Dayananda Saraswati in 1875. He was a *Sannyasi* (renouncer) who believed in the infallible authority of the Vedas. Dayananda Saraswati advocated the doctrine of Karma and rebirth, and emphasized the ideals of *Brahmacharya* (celibacy) and *Sannyas* (renunciation). Dayananda outright rejected all non-Vedic beliefs. Hence the Arya Samaj unequivocally condemned idolatry, animal sacrifices, ancestor worship, pilgrimages, priestcraft, offerings made in temples, the caste system, untouchability and child marriages on the grounds that all these lacked Vedic sanction. The Arya Samaj came to be a universal church based on the authority of the Vedas. Dayananda stated that he wanted 'to make the whole world Aryan', i. e. he wanted to develop missionary Hinduism based on the universality of the Vedas. To this end, the Arya Samaj started *Shuddhi Movement* in the early 20th century to bring back to Hindus who converted themselves to Islam and Christianity, set up schools and missionary organizations and extended its activities outside India. It now has branches around the world and has a disproportionate number of adherents among the people of Indian ancestry in Suriname and the Netherlands in comparison with India.

Besides these traditional denominations, movements of Hindu revivalism have also been inspired by great personalities like Swami Vivekananda, Swami Dayananda (Arya Samaj), Rabindranath Tagore, Raman Maharshi, Aurobindo, Shriram Sharma Acharya, Swami Shivananda, Swami Ram Tirtha, Narayana Guru, Paramhansa Yogananda, Swami Chinmayananda, Shri Shri Anandamurti, Pandurang Shastri Athavale (Swadhyay Movement) and others.

In the 20th century, Hinduism gained prominence also as a political force and a source for national identity in India. With origins traced back to the establishment of the Hindu Mahasabha in the 1910s, the movement grew with the formulation and development of the Hindutva ideology in the following decades; the establishment of Rashtriya Swayamsevak Sangh (RSS) in 1925; and the entry, and later success, of RSS offshoots Jan Sangh and Bharatiya Janata Party (BJP) in electoral politics in post-independent India deserve a special mention. Hindu religiosity played an important role in the nationalist movement.

The Partition of India in 1947 was along the religious lines, with the Republic of India emerging with a Hindu majority. In the Republic of India, Hindu nationalism has emerged as a strong political force since the 1980s, the Hindutva Bharatiya Janata Party forming the Government of India from 1999 to 2004, and its first state government in South India in 2006, and also the Narendra Modi led Government at the Centre in 2014.

Rise of Hindutva— The seeds of today's Hindu awakening or *Hindutva* were sown by direct attacks of Muslims on the fabrics of Hindu society which has always been known for religious tolerance.

The vibrancy of Hindu society was noticeable at all times in the sense that despite widespread barbaric acts of the Islamic hordes of Central Asia and Turkey, Hindu rulers never acted or reacted like Muslim invaders. The widespread act of conversion of innocent Hindus pursued by the Christian missionaries has also been accountable for uniting Hindus who have remained divided for so long on the basis of caste, religious practices, language, region and diversity of cults across the country. The Marxist and Muslim intelligentsia, led by Nehruvian ideologues who are never short of distorted history, have been unable to show that any Hindu ruler of India ever matched the cruelty of even a moderate Muslim ruler. Such are the characteristics of Hindu society and the Muslim psyche that describe the Indians today. Hindus never lost their tolerance and willingness to change. However, Muslims, led by the Islamic clergy and Islamic society's innate unwillingness to change, did not notice the scars that the Hindus had in the past. It is admirable that Hindus never took advantage of the debt Muslims owed Hindus for their tolerance and non-vengefulness.

In modern times, Hindu awakening gained momentum when Muslims made the greatest abuse of Hindu tolerance: the demand for a separate state and the partition of India, a nation that had a common history and culture for countless years. Thus the Muslim minority voted for a separate state and the Hindus were forced to sub-divide their own land in 1947. After the partition of India, Muslim superiority was quickly asserted and the non-Muslim minorities suh as Hindus and Sikhs were forced to flee due to the immense discrimination in the political and religious spheres in Pakistan. Again, Hindus did not respond to such an onslaught. The Hindu majority India continued with the Hindu ideals by remaining secular.

India even gave the Muslim minority gifts such as separate personal laws, special status to the only Muslim majority state– Kashmir, and other rights that are even unheard of in the bastion of democracy and freedom, the United States of America. Islamic law was given precedence over the national law in instances that came under the Muslim personal law. The Constitution was changed when the apex court, in the Shah Bano case, ruled that a secular nation must have a common civil code, not separate religious laws. Islamic religious and educational institutions were given a policy of non-interference. The list goes on.

More painful for the Hindus was forced negation of Hindu history and factors that gave pride to this community. Hindu customs and traditions were mocked at as remnants of a non-modern society, things that would have to go if India was to modernize like the West. The self-proclaimed guardians of India, the leaders of the Congress Party who called themselves secularists, forgot that it was the Hindu psyche that believed in secularism, it was the Hindu thought that had inspired the great intellectuals of the world such as Henry David Thoreau, Ralph W. Emerson, Leo Tolstoy, Albert Einstein and others. When Hindus realized that pseudo-secularism had reduced them to the role of an innocent bystander in the game of politics, they demanded a true secularism where every religious group would be treated equally and a government that would not take Hindu sentiments for granted. The ideology of Hindutva awakened the Hindus to the new world order where nations represented the aspirations of people united in history, culture, philosophy and public personalities. Hindutva successfully took the Indian icon of Israel and made Hindus realize that their India could be just as great and could do the same for them.

In a new era of global consciousness, Hindus realized that they had something to offer the world. There was something more than tolerance and universal unity. The ancient wisdom of sages through eternity also offered the systems of thought, politics, music, language, dance and education that could benefit the humanity. With the rise of Islamic fundamentalism resulting in massive sectarian violence and the spread of the media of mass communication in the modern world, the notion of Hindutva has progressively grown stronger. Islamic sectarianism has been the primary source of Hindu sectarianism, if any. Now the educated and politically conscious Hindus are not going to surrender before the terrorists, as they did before the barbarous aggressors of the medieval period. The ascendancy of a political party like the BJP with the massive Hindu followings on the political scene of India is a clear sign of reaction against the upswing of Islamic fundamentalism. In short, the rise of Hinduism is an aftermath of rise in Islamic fundamentalism, as Hinduism has always been imbued with secular and spiritual values. Individualism has always been the characteristic feature of Hinduism, as opposed to strong community sentiment in Abrahamic religions (major Abrahamic faiths are Judaism, Christianity and Islam). A seeker of spiritualism has always tended to become a *Sadhu* or *Sannyasi* since ancient times in Hindu religion. A sense of collectivism has always been a very poor feature of Hindus. The aggressive posture of Islam has politicized Hindu religion.

For pure religious reasons the identification of Indian Muslims continues to be so strong with such Muslim invaders from outside India, who were notorious for their barbaric acts during the medieval period, that they hate their Hindu neighbours or countrymen despite the well-known historical fact that both Hindus and Muslims belong to the same ethnic stock. Both belong to the same race and had a common history and common religious beliefs and practices from time immemorial. Before Islam or Christianity came to India, the ancestors of all Indians were Hindus and worshippers of idols and deities well connected with the Vedas, Upanishads, Ramayan and Geeta. Hence, it is really amazing to see that mere religious difference between the two communities tends to play such a huge role in the life of people, sharing a common land, means of livelihood and destiny, if any, that there prevails a deep seated sense of hatred and mistrust. Further distressing fact of life is that despite development, modernization and spread of education the gap or mistrust between the two communities has widened over the years. The continuing problem of Kashmir, for instance, is a purely religious or sectarian problem by all means.

Hinduism is a religion unlike others, especially the Abrahamic faiths, in that a person can be only a born Hindu. He cannot be converted into one through any ceremony. Hinduism has been a basically closed door religion with wide exits. There is also no fundamental creed or any book or books which every Hindu should know or recite. The basis for the spread of Hinduism across the Indian subcontinent was its pluralism, its acceptance of differences and its catholicity. However, there were Hindus who increasingly believed that their polytheistic faith lacked the wherewithal to face monotheistic faith like Islam. A conservative backlash within Hinduism started which led to the creation of various organizations, some educational and cultural and others political. A Hindu revivalist, Nathuram Godse, who believed that India's founding father Mahatma Gandhi was too sympathetic to Muslims, assassinated him on January 30, 1948. This assassination and the bloody and violent partition left a legacy on Indian nationalism and the definition of citizenship in the Indian constitution. The Indian constitution provides wide-ranging rights to its citizens, including to its large minority populations. India is a secular, pluralistic democracy where citizenship is territorial and all minorities, ethnic and religious, are treated as equals.

Hindutva, or Hindu chauvinism and revivalism, instead defined citizenship differently. Vinayak Damodar Savarkar, the leading ideologue of Hindutva, wrote a pamphlet in 1923 titled 'Who is a Hindu'/'Essentials of Hindutva' where he defines what he refers to as citizenship for any Hindu or person who lives in the Indian subcontinent. Savarkar states that a Hindu is he who considers the land from the Himalayas or the Indus to the Indian Ocean as his Fatherland (*Pitribhumi*) and Holy land (*Punyabhumi*). This meant that only followers of these religions, Hinduism, Sikhism, Jainism and Buddhism can be true citizens. Since all the other faiths in India– Zoroastrianism, Christianity, Islam and Judaism– have their holy lands outside the Indian subcontinent, their followers cannot be seen as true citizens. India's future is tied to its identity as a pluralistic, democratic and secular society that is a pillar of stability in a region and world that is increasingly chaotic.

There have taken place enormous changes in the thinking of the Hindus, unlike that of the Muslims, spearheaded over the course of a century by innumerable groups and leaders who made their own distinct contributions to the Hindu society: Swami Vivekananda, Rabindranath Tagore, Mahatma Gandhiji, Rashatriya Swayamsevak Sangh, Swami Chinmayananda, Maharishi Mahesh Yogi, International Society for Krishna Consciousness, Muni Susheel Kumarji, Vishwa Hindu Parishad, Bharatiya Janata Party and others. Each in their own way increased pride in being a Hindu and simultaneously showed Hindus their greatest strengths and their worst weaknesses. This slowly shook the roots of Hindu society and prompted a rear-guard action by the ingrained interests: the old politicians, the Nehruvian intellectual community, and the appeased Muslim leadership.

The old foundation crumbled in the 1980s and 1990s when Hindus respectfully asked for the return of their most holy religious site, Ayodhya. This demand promptly put the 40-year old apparatus to work, and press releases were churned out that spew the libellous venom which called those who represented the Hindu aspirations 'militant' and 'fundamentalist' stigmas which had heretofore found their proper place in the movements to establish Islamic law. Hindus were humble enough to ask for the restoration of an ancient temple built on the birthplace of Ram, and destroyed by the men of Babur, a foreign invader. Some Hindus were interested in the establishment of a monument for a national hero of ancient times, a legend whose fame and respect stretched far beyond the borders of India into Southeast Asia, and even into Muslim Indonesia. A hero who existed before there was anyone in India who considered himself separate from Hindu society. The 400-year old structure at one of the holiest sites of India had been worshipped as a temple by Hindus even though Mir Baqi, a commander of the Mughal emperor Babur, had partially built a non-functioning mosque on it. It was very important that no Muslims, except for those who were appeased in Indian politics, had ever heard of anything called Babri Masjid before the pseudo-secularist forces started the campaign against the rising Hindu voice. It was also important that no Muslim had ever offered prayers at the site for over 40 years.

Hindutva is here to stay now. It is up to the Muslims whether they should be included in the new nationalistic spirit of Bharat. It is up to the government and the Muslim leadership whether they should have some regard for the Hindu sentiments. The era of one-way compromise of the Hindus is over, far from now on, secularism must mean that all parties must compromise without any fear or favour. Hindutva does not mean any Hindu theocracy or theology. There is no truth behind the Saffron terror/Hindu terrorism in India. It is merely a political tool to counter rising minority communalism in the country. The kind of politics which is being pursued in the contemporary period is one of primary reasons for the rise of Hindutva ideology. Here is one of the recent examples of the kind of politics accountable for the rise of Hindu extremism. When the External Affairs Minister made a confirmation in the Indian Parliament on 20th March 2018 that all the 39 Indian workers, who were kidnapped by the Islamic State in Iraq in June 2014 are declared dead, a few self-styled secular leaders made a big hue and cry against the Modi Government for announcing death in the Parliament instead of collectively criticizing the Islamic terrorists. In turn the Foreign Minister soon made a scathing attack on the Congress Party at a press conference for causing unexpected and unseemly uproar in the Lok Sabha and accused it of 'playing politics over death.'

Unfortunately India is one of the biggest victims of terrorism in the 21st century world. Interestingly, it has become very fashionable over the last one decade to flash Hindutva 'terror' or Saffron 'terror' at the drop of a hat. Hindutva is essentially an ideology which is pro-Hindu, and Saffron is a colour most associated with *Sanatan Dharma*, or Hinduism as the world labels it. Many people bring 'Hindu terror', 'Hindutva terror' or 'Saffron terror' into political and media discussions to score brownie points with the generally Hindu-despising crowd out there– the so-called secular people, socialists and some 'friendly neighbours' who have a big stake in projecting Hindus in bad light.

Since Islamic terror has been so much in news this century, some people felt obligated to bring in an 'equal-equal' balancing act to emphasize their own secular credentials. Of course it would be brainless to say that there are no bad people who are Hindus. They exist. There are criminals, rapists, murderers and much worse people who happen to be from practising Hindu family or just have a Hindu name. But 'Hindutva terror' or 'Hindu terror' is mostly meaningless, as hardly any Hindu would go out and commit terrorism for the glory of the Bhagavad Geeta or for attaining heaven or for the sake of Krishna or Durga, or cite a Vedic *Mantra* before blowing up a group of non-Hindu people. Hindu criminals surely exist, but Hindu 'terror' (of the Islamist variety) is mostly imaginary. Nobody has ever come across an act of Hindutva 'terror' that killed even 10-20 people (that is less than 0.1 percent of the number of global terror victims in 2018) anywhere in the world in one incident.

Now let us go beyond our opinions and claims. Let us get some hard statistics from some credible reports. Beyond the studios of some select media houses, does Hindutva 'terror', so fondly peddled by our neo-intellectuals, even exist? If it exists among 15-18 percent of the world's population, shouldn't it be a very visible form of terror in international reports and news items? That too when India itself features among the 6 most terror-affected countries in the global ranking.

There is one very credible and internationally accepted report on recent statistics on terrorism. I was actually hoping to see a lot of 'Hindutva terror'-related information from this comprehensive world report on terrorism in 2011. To my surprise, there was not even a single mention of 'Hindu', 'RSS', 'Sangh', 'Saffron' and other labels that Indian media regularly feed us. There were 16 mentions of India in this 33-page comprehensive report, but not one mention of the word 'Hindu'!

How come the world's most comprehensive report on terrorism from 2011 does not have a mention of even one terror incident involving 'Hindutva' or 'Hindu' which many politicians and media persons don't seem to stop talking about in India? One can download and read the entire report here from the official National Counter Terrorism Center website of the USA. There were over 10,000 terrorist attacks in 2011, affecting nearly 45,000 victims in 70 countries and resulting in over 12,500 deaths. That's a very large number of people getting affected, even though the number of attacks was fewer compared to 2007. The CNN has reported that between June 2014 and mid February 2017, the self-proclaimed Islamic State had conducted or inspired more than 140 terrorist attacks in 29 countries other than Iraq and Syria, where its carnage has taken a much deadlier toll. Those attacks had killed at least 2,043 people and injured thousands more. It is hard to get precise information about some attacks, but it is clear that the deadly tentacles of the ISIS have spread quickly from the terrorist group's epicentre in Iraq and Syria to several places around the globe.

India features among the six countries most affected by terrorism in 2011. In Afghanistan, 3,353 people died due to terror attacks in 2011. Iraq saw 3,063 deaths, Pakistan saw 2,033, Somalia saw 1,101, Nigeria saw 593 and India saw 479 victims. These are purely terrorism-related deaths, and do not include deaths in religious/sectarian wars like in Syria where more than 20,000 people were killed in 2011 itself. The war-torn Afghanistan, the unstable Iraq, and the very likely imploding Pakistan together account for 64 percent of the terrorist attacks in the world during 2011. India's most volatile neighbour Pakistan, with a long history of exporting terrorism, saw an increase of 8 percent in terror attacks compared to 2010.

Now let us come to religious demographics. I am not sure whether this even deserves mention, but something needs to stand in contrast to all the 'Hindutva' bashing in Indian media:

1. In 2011, 56 percent of the world's terrorist attacks (5,700) were by Sunni Muslims and 70 percent of the worldwide deaths were also of Sunni Muslims.

2. Effectively, out of the 12,533 terror victims in the world in 2011, 8,886 were killed by Sunni Muslim extremists.

3. There were 279 suicide attacks in the world during 2011; Sunni Muslims conducted 93 percent of these attacks.

4. Out of 12,000+ killed by terrorists in 2011, 6,418 were civilians, 755 were children. Nearly 90 percent of terror victims, with their religion identified, were Muslims.

There is not even one mention of the Hindu terror in the world's most comprehensive report. Not to mention the fact that an overwhelming majority of terrorists listed happen to be Muslims, whom these folks hesitate to highlight, thanks to their 'equal-equal' reporting mission. Is it time for them to get back to their 'terrorism has no religion' cliché?

According to the 2011 Global Report, the top non-Muslim terrorist groups in the world were FARC from Columbia (carried out 377 attacks in 2011), CPI-Maoist in India (351 attacks), NPA-CPP of Philippines that struck 102 times and PKK of Turkey (carried out 48 attacks).

Here were the only 3 Indian terror organizations featured:

1. Communist ideology holding Communist Party of India– Maoist.

2. Indian Mujahideen, the terror outfit that is alleged to have links with Students Islamic Movement of India (SIMI), for which the then Foreign Minister of India Salman Khurshid was a legal voice.

3. Harkat ul-Jehad Islami (HUJI).

The summary of the report is pretty clear. It is unfortunate for India that it did figure as the sixth most terror-affected nation on this planet. However, even though Hindus form 15 to 18 percent of the world's population across dozens of countries, with an overwhelming majority in India, they had zero mention in the comprehensive world terror report for 2011. Not only was there no mention of the word 'Hindu' itself, all other related labels like 'Hindutva', 'RSS', etc. were absent as well. Among the three Indian terrorist outfits featured in the global report, two were Islamist and one was Communist. Ironically, it is the advocates of these very same ideologies that have been trying desperately to project to the world the imaginary idea of 'Hindutva terror' and the huge danger it poses to humanity. The so-called 'Hindutva terror' is the non-existent. It is just a political strategy for vote bank politics?

The RSS only teaches people to be proud of India's glorious 5000+ years' culture and tradition. It teaches *Swayamsevakas* (volunteers for the nation), self defence. Every human on this planet has the right to defend himself or herself. The RSS never advocated killing or converting 'non-believers', like Jehadi terrorists or radical evangelicals do. If any person who claims to be associated with the RSS is convicted of any crime, RSS won't play communal or victim card. While Nehru was unable to stop the bloodshed during partition, it was the RSS that organised over 3000 relief camps for the Hindu Refugees from Pakistan after the Partition. In short, every effort to frame the RSS to a fictional 'Hindutva terror' or 'Saffron terror' has miserably failed till date.

Hinduism is a diverse system of thought with beliefs spanning monotheism, polytheism, panentheism, pantheism, pandeism, monism and atheism among others. Hinduism has no traditional ecclesiastical order, no centralized religious authorities, no universally accepted governing body, no prophet(s), no binding holy book nor any mandatory prayer attendance requirements. Hinduism has been described as a way of life. In its diffuse and open structure, numerous schools and sects of Hinduism have developed and spun off in India with help from its ascetic scholars, since the Vedic age. The six *Astik* and two *Nastik* schools of Hindu philosophy, in its history, did not develop a missionary or proselytization methodology, and they co-existed with each other. Most Hindu sub-schools and sects do not actively seek converts. Individuals have had a choice to enter, leave or change their god(s), spiritual convictions, accept or discard any rituals and practices, and pursue spiritual knowledge and liberation (*Moksha*) in different ways. However, various schools of Hinduism do have some core common beliefs, such as the belief that all living beings have *Atman* (soul), a belief in *Karma* theory, spirituality, *Ahinsa* (non-violence) as the greatest *Dharma* or virtue, and others.

Right to Religion in India

Freedom of religion in India is a fundamental right guaranteed under Article 15 and Article 25 of the Constitution of India. Free India came into existence in 1947 and the Indian constitution's preamble was amended in 1976 to state that India is a secular state. Every citizen of India has a right to practise and promote their own religion peacefully. However, there have been a number of incidents of religious intolerance that resulted in riots and violence. Even though Hindus form close to 80 percent of the population, India also has region-specific religious practices: for instance, Jammu and Kashmir has a Muslim majority, Punjab has a Sikh majority, Nagaland, Meghalaya and Mizoram have Christian majorities and the Indian Himalayas such as Sikkim and Darjeeling, Laddakh, Arunachal Pradesh and the state of Maharashtra have large concentrations of Buddhist population. The country has significant Muslim, Sikh, Christian, Buddhist and Jain populations. Islam is the largest minority religion in India, and the Indian Muslims form the third largest Muslim population in the world, accounting for over 14 percent of India's total population.

The Sikh Gurus built freedom of religion in their faith to such an extent that while being a persecuted minority themselves under many Mughal rulers like Aurangzeb, Sikhs felt obliged to fight for the religious freedom of others. The sixth Guru of Sikhs, Guru Hargobind, even had a mosque built for his Muslim disciples, instead of putting them under any pressure to adopt the Sikh faith. The tradition of religious freedom continued under the Sikh Empire and other Sikh Principalities where Sikh rulers commissioned several Gurudwaras, Temples and Mosques for their subjects of various faiths.

India, with its traditional tolerance, has served as a refuge for groups that have encountered persecution elsewhere. Here are the examples of ideology of secularism inherent in Hinduism:

•Jews: Jews in India were granted lands and trading rights. The oldest of the three longest-established Jewish communities in India, traders from Judea and Israel arrived in the city of Cochin, in what is now Kerala, 2,500 years ago and are now known as Cochin Jews. According to recordings by Jews, the date of the first arrival is given at 562 BC. In 68 AD, more Jews fled to Kerala to escape attacks by the Romans on Jerusalem.

•Christians: Christianity is believed to have come to India in the 1st century through St. Thomas who formed the Saint Thomas Christians in Kerala. Later in the 15th and 16th centuries European Missionaries brought in Christianity in places such as Goa and Mangalore. Protestant Missionaries came in 18th and 19th centuries to North-East India.

•Parsi: The Zoroastrians from Greater Persia arrived in India fleeing from religious persecution in their native land in the 9th century. They flourished in India and in 18-19th centuries intervened on behalf of their co-religionists still in Greater Persia. They have produced India's pioneering industrialist house of Tata and one of the only two Indian Field Marshals in S. F. Manekshaw.

•Tibetan Buddhists: India is now home to the Dalai Lama, a high lama of the Gelug school of Tibetan Buddhism.

•Baha'i: India now has world's largest Baha'i population of 4572 Baha'is, who took refuge in India from religious persecution in Iran.

All these developments took place chiefly because India has been a Hindu dominated country known for lenient attitude towards others. Free entries of people of other religious faiths have not been possible in case of any Muslim dominated country so far. But this has never been a problem in the case of India. This simply provides historical evidence to suggest that Hindus have always been broad-minded in accepting people of other religions. Rise of Islamic fundamentalism in India is primarily because of the tolerance of majority Hindus. The Preamble of the Indian Constitution has the word 'secular', thereby implying that the State will not discriminate, patronise or meddle in the profession of any religion. However, it shields individual religions or groups by adding religious rights as fundamental rights. Article 25 says, "All persons are equally entitled to freedom of conscience and the right to freely profess, practice, and propagate religion subject to public order, morality and health." Further, Article 26 says that all denominations can manage their own affairs in matters of religion. All these rights are subject to be regulated by the State.

Article 25 (2b) uses the term 'Hindus' for all classes and sections of Hindus, Jains, Buddhists and Sikhs. Sikhs and Buddhists objected to this wording that makes many Hindu personal laws applicable to them. However, the same article also guarantees the right of members of the Sikh faith to bear a Kirpan. Religions require no registration. The government can ban a religious organization if it disrupts communal harmony, or has involvement in terrorism or sedition or has violated the Foreign Contributions Act. The government limits the entry of any foreign religious institution or missionary and since the 1960s, no new foreign missionaries have been accepted though long term established ones may renew their visas. Many sections of the law prohibit hate speech and provide penalties for writings, illustrations, or speech that insult a particular community or religion.

Some major religious holidays like Christmas (Christian), Eid (Muslim), Guru Nanak's birth anniversary (Sikh) and Holi (Hindu) are considered national holidays. Private schools offering religious instruction are permitted while government schools are non-religious.

The Article 25 of the Indian Constitution is a basic human right guarantee that cannot be subverted or misinterpreted in any manner. It is in this context that the anti-conversion laws in India must be viewed. Anti-conversion laws are promulgated on the premise that forced or induced conversions happen and need to be prevented. Such laws are controversial because they run the risk of being abused by communal forces who may have the tacit approval of the dominant political party in the state or country.

A consolidation of various anti-conversion or so-called 'Freedom of Religion' Laws has been done by the All Indian Christian Council. Several Indian states passed Freedom of Religion Bills primarily to prevent people from converting to Christianity. Orissa was the first state to bring such law named 'Orissa Freedom of Religion Act, 1967'.

It was followed by Madhya Pradesh in 1968 and Arunachal Pradesh in 1978. Catholics protested against this saying that propagation of their faith was an important part of Christianity. Both laws enacted by the Orissa and Madhya Pradesh high courts were challenged stating Article 25 of the Constitution. The Supreme Court supported the laws saying, "What is freedom for one is freedom for the other in equal measure and there can, therefore, be no such thing as a fundamental right to convert any person to one's own religion". This move was criticized because it ignored Article 25 and it did not differentiate between forced conversion and conversion by persuasion.

Chhattisgarh in 2000 and Gujarat State in 2003 passed anti-conversion laws that prohibit forced or money induced conversions. In July 2006, the Madhya Pradesh government passed legislation requiring people who desire to convert to a different religion to provide the government with one month's notice, or face fines and penalties. In August 2006, the Chhattisgarh State Assembly passed similar legislation requiring anyone who desires to convert to another religion to give 30 days' notice to, and seek permission from, the district magistrate. In February 2007, Himachal Pradesh became the first Congress Party-ruled state to adopt legislation banning illegal religious conversions. It was followed by Rajasthan in 2008.

In 2013, the Bharatiya Janata Party General Secretary Venkaiah Naidu declared that his party would bring anti-conversion laws nationwide if his party was elected to power in 2014. The president of party Amit Shah challenged the opposition parties to support it in enacting such a law. Though Mr Naidu has become the Chairman of the Upper House and yet the promise made remains unfulfilled till the date, possibly due to the lack of majority. The US State Department has said that the recent wave of anti-conversion laws in various Indian states passed by some states is seen as gradual increase in ideological Hindu nationalism (*Hindutva*).

Why don't Hindus ever promote and convert others into their religion, when the Christians aggressively do that? Answer lies in the following. You can either believe in Monotheism (one God) or Polytheism (many Gods) or Atheism (no God) or Agnosticism (doubt God's existence) or Paganism (nature worship) or Pantheism (universe as a whole as God) or Idolatry (worship idols) or a combination of some or all of the above and yet be called a Hindu. One need not subscribe either of the above philosophies, believe in Dharma (societal customs) and *Karma* (one's fate is a result of one's actions) and yet be called a Hindu. Hinduism is a truly democratic concept and believes in a pluralistic society. Hinduism breeds liberal thinking and tolerance for varied viewpoints. Hinduism is an all encompassing melting point of varied philosophies and spiritualism. So, why do Hindus need to convert people from other religions into Hinduism? As one can see, the basic foundation of Hinduism is based on the policy of 'Live and Let Live'. Hinduism is perfectly fine with the diversity in ideologies and philosophies and beliefs and customs. From the point of view of a Hindu, there is really no need to convert people from other religions!

Why do Hindus, Buddhists, Sikhs and Jews not go around the world converting the people of other faiths to their religion, while Christians and Muslims are doing their best? Why are Hindus not preaching like Christians and Muslims? Because Hindus are tolerant of others' faiths. Hinduism has never adopted an aggressive posture. Hindus have always been very accommodative. Hindus developed along with their civilization from times so ancient that their knowledge and wisdom has always been very holistic. Christianity and Islam were, on the other hand, at best political movements that sought to exploit some political opportunity by means of religion. Naturally their survival depends on that what forms the basis of the most successful governance system (I am talking about democracy): the people. More the followers, the bigger the empire. What does it take to expand the empire? Only zealous missionaries and gullible people who want to be 'saved'. For once the parents are converted; the children will grow up to be loyal servants of the faith. For once the women have been forcibly taken; they will reproduce and breed children as per the Father's wishes. Hinduism never imagined these methods and even if it did, the wise men in it kept it to themselves and never allowed it to be acceptable or practicable.

Tarek Fatah, an eminent Canada-based senior Pakistani journalist, has plainly stated that Muslims are to be blamed for communal riots in India. He has said, "You end Muslim personal law, the communal riots would end. Muslims want communal riots and blame Hindus." India has been a heaven for Islamic radicalism, as Muslims have taken full advantages of the horizontal and vertical divisions of the Hindu society in terms of caste, cult, language, region and system of belief since long. Hinduism has never been a monolithic religion. Pakistan has originated out of Islamic communalism. In practice Islam has not been a peace loving religion like Hinduism or Buddhism. Most Muslims directly blame Hindus for communal rights with view to finding excuse to justify the Islamic radicalism in the country. Emergence of Pakistan, demolition of the Babri Masjid, emergence of right-wing Modi Government on the political scene of India and the like are some of the notable aftermaths of rise in the Islamic fundamentalism in South Asia. The rise of Hindu nationalism is resented by Muslims and so-called secular Hindus who treat Muslims as their dependable vote bank to grab political power. Islam has been so much radicalised that the secular Muslims are openly hated or criticized by radical Muslims. For instance, the book entitled ***The Satanic Verses*** of Salman Rushdie was banned at the behest of radical Muslims in India and many other Islamic states. It was once reported in the newspaper that a Bareilly-based (Uttar Pradesh) radical Muslim Moeen Siddique, the head of the All-India Faisan-e-Madina Council announced a reward of Rs 10 lakh to behead a Canadian journalist Tarek Fatah. Similarly Burhan Muzaffar Wani, the Pakistan-trained Kashmiri terrorist once declared: "My goal is to establish an Islamic Caliphate, not just in Kashmir or India, but all over the World." His ambition could not materialise because a week later he was shot dead by the Indian security forces on 8 July 2016.

Many Indian Muslims share the following view of a prominent Islamic cleric and former banker Irfan-ul-Haq who was caught on video speaking to a Pakistani audience during a lecture in 2011: "Pakistanis should consider themselves fortunate that Allah has bestowed the honour to wage war against India to them." He further observed, "The genesis of Pakistan was prophesied to defeat India and Hinduism at the hands of Pakistan." The cleric went on to say that Pakistan's creation was done solely to destroy Hinduism and that Pakistan's military and people will swarm India and wipe out, once and for all, the practice of Hinduism from the face of the earth.

In spite of being assaulted and attacked and plundered over a thousand years, India has risen up again because of the rise in Islamic extremism. "India is a republic rooted in 5,000 years of Indus Valley Civilization, the other (Pakistan) is a concoction of hatred. Pakistan is merely a military enterprise for the *Jehadis,"* so opined Tarek Fatah. All the proponents of Pakistan were "Hindu hate mongers", including the celebrated Urdu poet Allama Iqbal. Iqbal's ancestors were Hindus but he was a Hindu hater. He went to the extent of plagiarising his own poetry to attack the Hindus. India is a civilization that has a past and a future. It's the only civilization that has got both.

Historically speaking, Muslim political power in the Indian Sub-continent came to a close with the fall of the Mughal Empire. But the downfall did not descend from the heaven without any reason. Muslims themselves were accountable for this. The great Empire fell, and with that panic seized Muslims. They are still panic-stricken. Formation of Pakistan in 1947 was an expression of that panic. Muslims took part in the freedom struggle of India not because they had a special love for their country; rather, they took part in freedom struggle to take revenge against the British who shattered the Islamic rule in India. During the initial phase of the struggle under the banner of the Indian National Congress, most Muslims were opposed to India's freedom as it would pave a way for a possible Hindu rule through the system of electoral politics. All those stayed back in India at the time of partition are making a fresh effort for political power in Hindu dominated India through the politics of minority communalism and uncontrolled reproductive behaviour. Having mixed up religion with politics the ruling elites among Muslims have been trying to secure power and regain their lost glory through the electoral deals and alliances at the regional or national levels.

The politics of minority communalism is on the rise in India. In fact, the politics of minority communalism has taken a violent form with the support derived from pan-Islamic radical terrorism across the world. This has greatly contributed to the Hindu uprising in the politics of the 21st century India. Hindus who have remained so divided for centuries look so united now. The nationalist Hindus draw indirect political benefits from the politics of Islamic radicalism. The prevailing scenario has shaped new future politics of India for them. Such political development may not augur well for peace, prosperity and cordial living. It is unfortunate that politics has become a captive of religious ideology. Muslims predominantly tend to look the case of India as Hindu India or a Christian West or a godless Russia and China, scheming against their faith. They are hardly prepared to look into the fallacies or shortcomings of their knowledge system or their thinking process based on the Koran and decaying values system. They live in the excitement of their past glory and petro-dollar splendour of the Middle East.

Secularism and Sectarianism in Contemporary India

With the 42nd Amendment of the Constitution of India enacted in 1976, the Preamble to the Constitution states that India is a secular state. However, neither India's constitution nor its laws define secularism or the relationship between religion and state. The well-educated elite refers it to mean equal respect for all religions by the state. Secularism is a type of governance that is not affiliated with any particular religion. It is defined as the idea that religion should not interfere with or be integrated into the public affairs of a society. But the Indian model of secularism does not conform to any of these conceptions. As the term 'secularism' is often used in different contexts in different societies, its precise definition tends to vary from country to country.

A democracy need not necessarily be secular. For example, the United States of America is a democracy but still has 'In God We Trust' printed on its currency. Another example is the Iraqi Constitution which seeks to establish a democratic government but also calls for the Supreme Federal Court to be made up of judges who are experts in Sharia (Islamic Law). There is a variety of secularism all over the world.

India does not have an official state religion. In matters of law, however, the applicable code of law is unequal, and India's personal laws– on matters such as marriage, divorce, inheritance, alimony– vary with individual's religion. Muslims have Sharia-based Muslim Personal Law, while Hindus, Christians, Sikhs and others live under the common law. The attempt to respect varying religious laws has created a number of problems relating to child marriage, polygamy, unequal inheritance rights, extra-judicial unilateral divorce rights favourable to some males.

Secularism as practised in India, with its marked differences with the Western practice of secularism, is a controversial issue. Supporters of the Indian concept of secularism favour special respect for a Muslim person's religious rights, because of his being a minority. Proponents of this form of secularism claim that any attempt to introduce a uniform civil code, that is similar laws for every citizen irrespective of his or her religion, would impose majoritarian Hindu ideals and values, something that is unacceptable to Muslims.

In practice the Government of India and the legal system do not seem to treat all religions equally. There are countless examples, of which some of the most egregious are the separate civil law provisions for Muslims, in which the civil law sections of the Indian Penal code do not apply to Muslims. Laws relating to marriage, divorce and inheritance are not the same for both Hindus and Muslims. Another is the special status of Jammu and Kashmir State because of the fact that it is a Muslim majority state. A third was the special subsidy given to Muslims by the so-called secular political parties to undertake the Haj pilgrimage, but no such subsidy has ever been available for Hindus to visit their places of pilgrimage. Anyway, the Haj pilgrimage subsidy was stopped by the Government of India in January 2018.

While the government maintains a hands-off attitude to the administration of Mosques, it administers Hindu trusts through the appointment of an Administrative Officer (there is no requirement for him or her to be a Hindu) and yet the government does not subsidize the maintenance or repair work of Hindu shrines. But the Muslim Waqf boards are provided subsidy by the government. Minority educational institutions get subsidies that are not available to Hindu educational trusts. The situation became so dire that once the Ramakrishna Math started by Swami Vivekananda himself once filed petition in the court to be classified as a non-Hindu institution so that it too would be eligible for subsidies. Such unequal treatment under the law is becoming intolerable to the Hindu, who is becoming increasingly alienated in the land of his ancestors, which could be one of reasons for the rise of Hindu nationalism.

Considering the given realities of life, secularism of India appears to be paradoxical and phoney to a large extent. Here I am presenting a summary view of the contradictions and ironies of Indian secularism. Hindu sectarianism is considered worse than Islamic and Christian sectarianism. In fact, any sectarianism pursued by groups other than Hindus is rarely considered sectarianism. If any Hindu highlights any act of minority sectarianism that invites widespread condemnation and he is branded as a Hindu fanatic. Dams and factories are the temples of modern India, but if any necessity arises in course of construction to replace any temple, cemetery, churches or mosques that causes obstruction to development project because of secularism. India is not one nation but a multi-nation state. In other words, it is only notionally a nation state. Secularism is the greatest good to which all other goods are subordinated. All morality and ethics can be sidetracked in the defence of secularism. If you are not 'secular', at best you are a 'sectarian' and are most likely to be branded as a right wing Hindutvawadi who is closely connected to the murder of Mahatma Gandhi, even though you may not have been born then. Marx, Mullah and Missionary are considered the triumvirate of secularism in India. Secularism leads to omniscience. Tribals are immediately branded Hindus when they rape nuns propagating Christianity in mountainous and forest clad regions. It is 'progressive' and 'liberal' to eat beef and to oppose it is to be obscurantist.

Conversion out of Hinduism is a fundamental right of human beings or a part of religious freedom. The conversion to Hinduism from Islam and Christianity is sectarianism. All *Jehads*, crusades and pogroms are secular, if directed against Hindus or non-believers. Hindu lives are relatively cheaper. According to Sharia, they are worth 1/16 the life of a Muslim. According to their philosophy, they are worth even less. It is interesting that the number of Hindu lives lost in the subcontinent since independence in wars, riots, terrorists' attacks, etc. is more than 16 times that of Muslim lives lost. Secularists do not like to call themselves Hindus; rather, they prefer to call themselves socialist, leftist, democrat, humanist, liberal, modern, broad-minded persons of Hindu descent. All Hindu acts of self assertion are Hindu fanaticism. All Hindu organizations that do not say 'all religions are equally good' are Hindu Nazis. To assert pride in being a Hindu is an automatic qualifier to be termed a nationalist Hindu.

The *Sanatan Dharma* is genuinely, however, secular in spirit. Hindus should not specifically try to be secular, as they are born secular. The word secular is synonymous with apostasy in many countries which profess Islam as the state religion. We do not feel such countries have anything to teach India about secularism and have no business lecturing India on the virtues of secularism. In countries with communist ideology, secularism is synonymous with atheism and the communist ideology is for all practical purposes a state religion with little tolerance for any other system of belief. China is a typical example where there is very little tolerance for most religions and those that did not originate in China or did not have a substantial Chinese tradition are treated with special suspicion. China can hardly be termed a secular state. But we never hear the Indian left, many of whom are the ardent admirers of China, rarely have a word to say about lack of secularism in China. Since the left parties are generally anti-religious, it is difficult for them to be secular. Secularism demands similar respect for all religious faiths which is ultimately antithetical to the Marxist-Leninist views on religion.

In our view leftists preaching secularism to a Hindu is like Lucrezia Borgia preaching chastity to Mother Teresa. But this is what happens in India. The bulk of the criticism of the Hindu comes from left wing ideologues, both in India and abroad, who while making no secret of their abhorrence for Hinduism, are careful to hide their equally vehement dislike for protecting the freedom of the individual. In fact, a large part of the antagonism towards the Hindu faith in the West stems from the freedoms which are enshrined in the core values of Hinduism. As far as the West is concerned, the Hindu is in an unenviable position of drawing the ire of both the left and the right wing. We all know why the left wing abhors Hinduism.

The Hindu Nationalist movement arose in reaction to the suppression of the Hindu civilization by Islamic invaders in the middle ages, followed by a lengthy British rule of India in the 18th, 19th and a part of 20th century. The Babri-Ramjanmabhoomi incident has been blown up out of all proportion without considering the historical background of the case. There had not been a prayer conducted at this so-called mosque for well over 30 years till the time of independence. The case had been under litigation for well over 100 years and justice delayed is a case of justice denied. The structure had been one of the hundreds built over the centuries over the remnants of temples destroyed by the Muslim invaders. So pervasive is the distorted form of secularism in India today that to mention such destruction happened is to draw the wrath of the secular brigade. In the entire operation of the destruction of the structure not one life was lost. Still, the Islamists say it was an illegal act and the perpetrators should be brought to justice.

The Hindus are faced with a strange situation. While they are theoretically part of a majority, they are so fractured into various ideological groups that they were virtually powerless to influence the politics of the country until the Narendra Modi Government came to power in 2014. His adversaries know this. The entire burden of maintaining a secular state is placed on the hapless Hindu, when the real perpetrators of anti-secular behaviour lie elsewhere in the electorate. The minority consistently plead for the perpetuation of their minority status for special privileges, knowing full well that the Hindus are divided and have in reality no more power than the Muslim. In order to strengthen unity among the Muslims still further, Muslims are being terrified in the name of present BJP Governments in majority Indian States as well as at the Centre. This is how the politics of minority communalism is being pursued in the country for political gains no matter what damage such a politics is going to cause to the unity of this nation. Once I asked a couple of Muslim scholars as to what damages were caused to them by the present Modi Government that they remain terror-stricken as Muslim. They were virtually speechless and yet they kept on arguing laughingly that the Muslims are terrified by the Modi Government. This is how the politics of Hindu hate campaign is systematically pursued and perpetuated in 21st century India.

Till now the Hindus have eschewed by and large violence as a means of achieving their ends, as the Muslims have done repeatedly using riots as a means of expression in most of the country and using ethnic cleansing in Jammu and Kashmir to drive out the Hindu population. However, one constant characteristic of the Hindu, throughout the ages, has been his inability to stay unified even when confronted by blatantly disruptive forces and there seems to be little hope that they will change their behaviour anytime soon. I do not see a practical way out of this impasse. The question facing the Hindu is stark.

The proponents of so-called secularism or minority politics are highly critical of the Rashtriya Swayamsevak Sangh, abbreviated as RSS, which is a right-wing organization of Hindu nationalists. Since it is regarded as the parent organization of the ruling party of India, they are also very critical of the Bharatiya Janata Party. It is criticized on the ground that it promotes the philosophy of Hindutva and Hindu nationalism in India which is not in the interest of secularism in India. The critics tend to argue that those politicians who want to bag Hindu votes to rule this country, mix up sentimental issue of religion with politics. This may not augur well for the secular fabric of India, but the real question is who is the real precursor of the use of religion in politics or in the system of governance? Was it not Muslim in medieval India or was it not the British colonial master in modern India? For both of them religion was so important that they pursued the state sponsored policy of conversion of Hindus on a massive scale and tried their best to develop Islam and Christianity as a parallel religion of Hinduism. The historical fact is that drawing inspiration from fundamentalist Muslims and right-wing European groups and Christian Missionaries Rashtriya Swayamsevak Sangh was founded on 27 September 1925 to safeguard the interests of Hindus. No religious activity of other religions was ever banned in India, but the RSS was banned once during the British rule, and then thrice by the post-independent Indian government– first in 1948 when Mahatma Gandhi was assassinated; then during the emergency (1975-77); and for a third time after the demolition of the Babri Masjid in 1992. Against this and other such historical circumstances Hindus preferred to vote the right-wing party and finally the BJP succeeded to grab power at the centre in 2014 with absolute majority. This does not, however, mean the Hindus have become more sectarian now. Using the name of Mahatma Gandhi, Muslims as well as some Hindu leaders take full opportunity to vehemently criticize BJP and call their leaders fascist. True, Gandhi was a great liberal or humanist leader of the modern world, but he was so because he was a born Hindu. Islam has neither produced nor has ever tolerated a great liberal leader like Gandhi within the Muslim community. Had Gandhi been a Muslim and expressed similar concerns for the Hindus, as he did for the Muslims during the independence struggle, he would not have survived so long (78 years). Hindus had only one Nathuram Godse, while there have always been countless Nathuram Godses in the Muslim community starting from the medieval days. The whole human history, the medieval history of India in particular, is a witness to this fact. Assassination of Gandhi is wrongly described as an act of communalism, as both the assassin and the person assassinated belonged to the same community and thus there did not exist any communal sentiment.

Anyway, how and why is secularism at threat in India? But the reasons are not very far to seek. For thousand years Hindus advocated the idea of brotherhood of mankind. They accepted even aggressors of all religions from different parts of the world and lived with them in harmony and also accepted them as members of family through marriages despite the fact that they were using coercion and inducements for the conversion of the Hindus. There is no community in the world, other than the Hindu, which has ever allowed so much free religious conversions on such a massive scale to increase the number of their followers. Furthermore, belying all the hopes of Gandhi, Pakistan was created to form an independent country purely based on religion and preferred to call it Islamic Republic of Pakistan, while Hindus comprised more than 80 percent of India's population and yet preferred to remain a secular democracy. There are 50 Muslim majority countries in the world and all of them are either theocratic or pseudo-secular states where the life of people are governed by Sharia laws and in all these countries there is no free air to breathe for the moderate masses. Moderate or liberal Muslims are often subjected to violence at the hands of fundamentalists. Islam is highly intolerant of women's education, empowerment, modern clothing, fashion, cosmetics, etc. to assert their separate and superior identity. A *burqa* or *burka*, an outer garment worn by the women to cover their bodies when in public, is compulsory. The Muslim women, though permitted in Mecca and Medina, are not allowed to join mass prayers along with men either at the mosque or at some other places of worship. They are also forbidden to go on pilgrimage alone to their holy places like Kaaba; while in all other religions women are free enough to take part in prayers both individually and together with their husbands at the places of worship. Islam is antithetical to modernity and scientific temperament. The whole civilized world is terrified by radical Islamic terrorists. Terror has gripped not only the people of other faiths, but also level-headed Muslims themselves in Islamic countries. The relationship between Shia and Sunni is full of hostility and moderates or liberals are also terrified by fundamentalist forces and the state seems to be a helpless organization. For instance, at least 41 people were killed and 84 injured in an IS suicide bombing attack on a news agency and a neighbouring Shiite Muslim cultural centre in the Afghan capital on 28th December, 2017. The centre was targeted mainly because it housed the pro-Iranian Afghan voice news agency. This is one among countless other ferocious attacks in the past.

There is very little freedom of expression there. Muslims, for instance, are virtually forbidden to make a public statement like Hindus that they have same respect for all the religions of the world. Respect for others means disrespect for Islam. Since the Sufis are considered to be the moderate, at least 18 people were killed and dozens more injured when a suicide bomber blew himself up at a Sufi shrine packed with devotees at Fatehpur town of Jhal Magsi District in Baluchistan (Pakistan) on 10th October 2017. For his book **The Satanic Verses** (1988) death threats were made against Salman Rushdie, including a ***Fatwa*** calling for his assassination issued by Ayatollah Ruhollah Khomeini, the Supreme Leader of Iran, on 14 February 1989. The British government had to put Rushdie under police protection. Similarly a physician turned author, Taslima Nasrin from Bangladesh, too has got death threat for her essays and novels with feminist views. She advocates freedom of thought and human rights by publishing, lecturing and campaigning. There are numerous such instances which bolster the view that the Islam is less tolerant not only of other faiths but also of liberal faces within Islam itself. Theocratic politics of many Islamic countries, rise of radicalism and politics of minority communalism in India supported by pseudo-secular Hindus for vested electoral purposes indirectly encouraged Indians in general to vote for the right wing party in 2014. But so long as India is a Hindu majority country, secularism is bound to remain the characteristic feature of this country because of certain inherent values system of our society and culture which naturally favours secularism. Hindus always try to be large hearted. See the case of the neighbouring country of Nepal, which was officially a Hindu kingdom for long, adopted secularism as the state policy after the promulgation of the new Constitution of Nepal in 2015, despite the fact that Hindus continue to constitute more than 81 percent of the total population of the country. Hindus are no threat to secularism also because they cannot be united like Muslims, for Hindu religion is not based on single belief, or an organised church, or one book. Hindus constitute 80 percent of India's total population, but the right wing party like the BJP did not secure more than 40 percent of the total votes polled in 2014, when Narendra Bhai Modi came to power at the Centre with absolute majority. The rise of widespread Islamic extremism is the prime factor behind the seeming unity of the Hindus and the recent rise in Hindutva or Hindu nationalism, if at all. Sources of threat to secularism in India are outside Hindu religion. In the State of Karnataka the ruling Congress Party started state-sponsored celebration of Tipu Jayanthi on 10th November in 2015 in the name of a 18th century Muslim ruler of Mysore, Tipu Sultan (1750-1799), who was a religious bigot. This is one of the examples of how the politics of minority communalism is being pursued in the country to appease the Muslim voters. Since Tipu was both anti-Hindu and anti-Christian, it triggered violent protests in various parts of Karnataka in the past, leading to an uprising of Hindu nationalism in South India.This resulted in the debacle of the Congress led Government in the State of Karnakata in the recently concluded Assembly Election in May 2018.

Muslims are usually found arguing that the people of other religious faiths are intolerant of Islam or unreasonably antagonistic to them on the ground of religion. Muslims expect good conduct or secular attitude from others towards them no matter how they themselves behave with others. A series of historical events till the day bear ample testimony to the fact that bloodshed or religious bigotry has been the characteristic feature of Islam since long, but in order to cover up such a conduct the educated Muslims now squabble stating that the Koran does not favour violence and the extremists have no religion. But at the same time it is also concurrently true that the extremists derive inspiration from the holy Koran itself and get socio-economic and political support from the society they belong to– both tacitly and explicitly. One should always keep in mind that good conduct in a day-to-day life in any society is always a two-way traffic. There exists a big hiatus between profession and practice in a real life situation.

Let us have a look at some similar example on the line of above facts. When the Bollywood stars Aamir Khan and Shah Rukh Khan were stripped-searched or detained at the US international airports, a lot of public outcry was made through the Indian media against the US system of security check. A terrorist-stricken country like the US was branded as an anti-Islamic state by slogan raisers. The critics failed to remember how hard was the USA hit by the September 11 attacks (also referred to as 9/11) which were a series of four coordinated terrorist attacks by the Islamic terrorist group al-Qaeda on the morning of Tuesday, September 11, 2001. The attacks killed 2,996 people, injured over 6,000 others, and caused at least $10 billion in infrastructure and property damage. The same supporters of Aamir Khan and Shah Rukh Khan maintained mysterious silence over the outrageous conduct of the Pakistani officials against the Indian women. The incidence briefly runs as follows: when the wife and mother of Kulbhushan Jadhav, who is languishing in the Pakistan jail under unlawful trial, wanted to see him in Islamabad, they were asked to take out their *chappal/* sandals, *mangal-sutra*, bangles, *bindi* on their forehead and change their usual clothes in December 2017. Wife and mothers were not allowed to meet Kulbhushan Jadhav in a face-to-face situation; rather, they were allowed to talk to him only through an intercom device either in English or Hindi only (but not in their mother tongue,

Marathi) and see through a glass screen in the presence of the Pakistani Officials. What kind of regard is this on the part of Pakistani officials for the cultural ethos of Hindu women from India? Pakistan was not then described a communal country by India-based supporters and slogan raisers of cine stars Aamir Khan and Shah Rukh Khan.

OM TAT SAT

Chapter - 4

Manifest and Unmanifest Aspects of Divinity

The modern civilized world expects that everything should be viewed or studied with completely open mind for the advancement of knowledge, well-being of society, and also to ensure peace and prosperity of the humanity at large. The closed-door policy behind any ideology, philosophy or system of belief has generated enough fanaticism, hatred and violence of all kinds in society across the world. Hence, there is a definite need for an overview of important religious and spiritual precepts as enshrined in the Srimad Bhagavad Geeta *vis-a-vis* other holy scriptures as objectively as possible, knowing the fact that the topic is very touchy and sensitive. Islam, in particular, does not like any interpretation and critical evaluation even by the Islamic scholars with forward-thinking or scientific outlook. The Koran, same as the Vedas, is believed to be of completely divine origin and treated as final treatise on religion. But most people reckon that in a way either everything has got divine origin or nothing has got divine origin in this world. Muslims also believe that it contains guidance for all mankind. Since the message of the Koran is believed to be for all times, it should be relevant to every age. In the Islamic world, many believe that modern science was first developed in the Islamic countries rather than in Europe and Western countries, that 'all the wealth of knowledge in the world has actually emanated from Muslim civilization', and what people call 'the scientific method', is actually 'the Islamic method.' Here lies the problem.

Whenever science and religion are discussed in any academic forum in the Western world, people are quite willing to speak on Judaism and Christianity among the religions referred to, but they hardly ever think of focussing upon Islam. They remain so scared of consequences perpetrated by fundamentalists that they prefer to evade to touch upon the subject of Islam. In India or South Asia generally scholars dealing with Islamic questions with critical mind are branded as sectarian/ communal. The Koran is treated as a very much personal belonging of the Muslim clerics, while the Geeta or other Hindu scripture has always been studied, analyzed and criticized freely by the people of all faiths, creeds and persuasions the world over. In fact, the Western intelligentsia has started the Krishna Consciousness movement across the globe in support of the precepts of the Geeta. It has increasingly highlighted the universal relevance of the Geeta in life.

Before we come to the main theme of this section let us briefly dwell on as to how the knowledge relating to religion should be approached in the larger interest of the humanity across the world. One of the most crucial factors behind the rise and development of religious fanaticism, intolerance or extremism has been the fact that religion has always been treated as a personal property or possession of a few individuals, priestly classes, religious clerics or the given community. Since all the known religions have developed through the process of social interaction of countless number of people, sharing a common culture over a long period of time, it should always be treated as a collective knowledge of the entire humanity regardless of the fact whether a particular group of people are believers or non-believers. Religion is not to be reckoned as a private asset of any individual or the community of believers. All the knowledge relating to religion should be allowed to remain in the public domain without any intervention from any corner, same as the knowledge of science, technology, humanities, philosophy, classics, language, art or any such branch of human knowledge. Science or technology is not a personal belonging of any scientist once it is shared freely by others. Once a person shares a set of common knowledge it becomes a part of the public domain for an unrestricted use. This is the reason why a subject like science or technology has been growing so fast on a massive scale helping the entire humanity without generating any conflict or violence over its use. Everyone must have a freedom to exercise his free mind about religious knowledge. Being a practitioner of Sociology I have tried to pursue this perspective about religion in the book. One must recognize that debate is the only means of helping the knowledge to grow. Blind faith or closed mind always tends to hinder the development of human knowledge.

Here we are presenting some aspects of religious ideology as contained in the Koran, the Bible and the Geeta as believed by the devotees of the ISKCON, the Geeta scholars and others without being judgemental. In fact, none can be taken as authority to make final observations on such abstract subject as the system of belief. Actually where the subject is a matter of faith and conviction, nothing can be taken as conclusive. At the most something can be more logical and convincing than others. I have already addressed most of the issues covered here in the preceding section as well as at the relevant places elsewhere. Herein a special attention has been paid to the contents of discourse between certain Islamic intelligentsia and devotees of the Krishna Consciousness movement from the Western world accessible on different websites. They are likely to be more objective than Indian Hindus with regard to the understanding and interpretation of the Srimad Bhagavad Geeta, as being originally Christian they have no reason to have any bias in favour of Hindu religion. In fact, the devotees of the ISKCON do not like to be branded as Hindus.

Notion of God in Different Religions

Who is God and where did He come from? This has been a key inquisitive question ever since the people have heard about God. Since the notion of God has been highly abstract and enigmatic, the reply to this question too has not been so easy or readily comprehensible. No amount of argument can ever prove or disprove anything relating to God. In fact, this marks the end of working of human mind, as reply leads to a series of complex and everlasting supplementary questions and queries. There is no satisfactory reply to questions relating to the origin, identity and act or relevance of God. It is often said that God created the universe but then the question is who created God. When there is always something behind every action, why is there nothing behind the creation of God? The book, ***The Origin of God*** by Laurence Gardner, fails to address the issue satisfactorily. In fact, there are many such books on the subject, but they do not lead us anywhere. What really works at the end is the system of faith in God, as God cannot be defined or really conceptualized semantically. Let us see how different religious scriptures, which have worked as the primary source of knowledge about God, have dealt with this issue.

Buddhism— We commonly use the word 'God' to designate a supreme power, who is the creator of the entire universe and the chief law-giver for the humans. Different religions and sects believe in the notion of God differently and know Him by different names, but as far as Buddhism is concerned, it has a different perception of God. The Buddhist system of religion rejects the notion of an abstract principle of God operating in the universe. They rather believe that the concept of God has grown out of fear and frustration experienced by humans. According to the Buddhist ideology, when the primitive people found themselves in a hazardous and hostile situation, or had the fear of wild animals and of natural phenomena like thunder and lightning, they discovered the idea of God to console themselves. While dealing with the reasons for the origin of religion this view has been endorsed and shared by most sociologists and anthropologists the world over.

Buddhists do not believe in God because there has been no real and concrete evidence to prove the existence of God. Even the research on God for thousands of years has not proved the existence of God. The Buddhists argue that the belief in God is not necessary to have a happy and meaningful life as there are millions of Buddhists, atheists and free thinkers who are happy without having any faith in God.

Almost all the sects of Buddhism do not believe in the notion of God. Indeed some of the early Indian Mahayan philosophers denounced God-worship in terms which are even stronger than those expressed in the Theravada literature. Some later Mahayan schools, which flourished outside India, ascribed some degree of divinity to a transcendent Buddha, considering living Buddhas to be a manifestation of the Adi-Buddha. But even then it cannot be said that the Buddha was converted into a Divinity comparable to the God of the monotheistic religions. Some regard the Buddha as a kind of God figure. In the Theravada tradition the Buddha is regarded as a supremely enlightened human teacher who has come to his last birth in *Sansar* (the Buddhist cycle of existence). But, the Mahayan traditions, which tend to think in terms of transcendental Buddhas, do not directly make a claim for Buddha as God. Thus the Buddha cannot be considered as playing a God-like role in Buddhism. Rather the Buddha is considered as an enlightened father of humanity.

Instead of believing in God, the Buddhists believe in humanity. They believe that each human being is precious and important and all have a potential to develop into a Buddha– a perfect human being by replacing hatred, anger, spite and jealousy with love, patience, generosity and kindness. Buddhism is, therefore, more of a moral philosophy, an ethical way of life. But since Buddha never laid stress upon his concept of divine, Buddhism is left with some of life's deepest questions unanswered. Questions such as the origin of the Universe, the purpose of man's existence and the like are yet to be answered.

Judaism— Judaism is strictly monotheistic. No consensus has been reached by academics on the origin of monotheism in ancient Israel, but Yahweh clearly came out of the world of the gods of the Ancient Near East. The worship of multiple gods (polytheism) and the concept of God having multiple persons (as in the doctrine of Trinity) are unimaginable in Judaism.

Jews believe that there is a single God who not only created the universe, but with whom every Jew can have an individual and personal relationship. God cannot be subdivided into different persons (unlike the Christian or the Hindu view of God). God is Transcendent which means God is above and beyond all earthly things. God doesn't have a body, which means that God is neither female nor male. God created the universe without help. He is everywhere all the time. God is omnipotent. God is beyond time. He has always existed and will always exist. God is just and merciful. God punishes the bad and rewards the good. God is forgiving towards those who mess things up. God is personal and accessible. God is interested in each individual. God listens to each individual. God sometimes speaks to individuals, but in unexpected ways. The Jews brought new ideas about God. Many modern Jewish theologians have argued that God is not omnipotent, however, and have found many biblical and classical sources to support this view. The Jewish idea of God is particularly important to the world because it was the Jews who developed two new ideas about God: There is only one God. God chooses to behave in a way that is both just and fair.

The Jewish theology has no clearly elaborated views on the relationship between body and soul, or on the nature of the soul itself. Whether the soul is capable of living an independent, fully conscious existence away from the body after death is unclear from rabbinic sources.

Christianity— Christianity is a one-man religion. Jesus Christ is the founder. Jesus declared himself as the Son of God, but not God. Jesus was free from sex and violence and he preached peace and non-violence. But he never said who God was. The result of this is that his followers worship and serve him as God and neglect the real God, if any. The Bible states that the man is made in the image of God. This means that God is a person like us with two hands, two legs, two eyes and so on. But the Christians have no idea who that human like person, God is. Most Christians claim that Jesus was God himself, but Jesus never declared nor proved himself as God.

'My Father is greater than I' (John 14:28). One may ask here who the Father of father is then.

'Why do you call me good? No one is good but God alone' (Mark 10.8)

Jesus wanted his followers to follow his way of life and instructions of 'thou shall not kill' (no meat), no adultery (no illicit sex), simple living (no lust and no desires), no bad habits (no gambling) and always be in control of the mind (no intoxication). But the followers of Jesus simply ignore the real gospel of Jesus and concoct their own beliefs. They worship Jesus as God and neglect the real God. So God is unknown here.

In Christianity, God is the eternal being who created and preserves all things. Christians believe God to be both transcendent and immanent. The God that made the world and all things therein, He, being the Lord of heaven and earth and reflects on the relationship between God and

Christians. In Christian theology the name of God has always had much deeper meaning and significance than being just a label or designator. It is not a human invention, but has a divine origin and is based on divine revelation. The Bible usually uses the name of God in the singular (e.g., Ex. 20:7 or Ps. 8:1), generally using the terms in a very general sense rather than referring to any special designation of God.

Two attributes of God that place Him above the world, yet acknowledge His involvement in the world, are transcendence and immanence. Transcendence means that God is eternal and infinite, not controlled by the created world and beyond human events. Immanence means that God is involved in the world, and Christian teachings have long acknowledged His attention to human affairs. However, unlike pantheistic religions, in Christianity God's being is not of the substance of the created universe.

Christians believe that there is only one God, whom they call Father as Jesus Christ taught them. Christians recognize Jesus as the Son of God who was sent to save mankind from death and sin. Jesus Christ taught that he was the Son of God. His teachings can be summarised briefly as the love of God and love of one's neighbour. Jesus said that he had come to fulfil God's law rather than teach it. Christians believe in justification by faith– that through their belief in Jesus as the Son of God, and in his death and resurrection, they can have a right relationship with God whose forgiveness was made once and for all through the death of Jesus Christ. If Jesus was the Son of God, it means God was either male or female and if the word 'son' is symbolic, it does not mean much. Thus the concept of God remains indistinct or undefined.

Unlike Judaism Christians believe in the Trinity, that is, God as Father, Son and Holy Spirit. Some confuse this and think that Christians believe in three separate gods, which they don't. Christians believe that God took the human form as Jesus Christ and that God is present today through the work of the Holy Spirit and evident in the actions of believers. Christians believe that there is a life after death. While the actual nature of this life is not known, Christians believe that many spiritual experiences in this life help to give them some idea of what the eternal life will be like.

Jesus clearly stated that there were many things he wanted to tell his audience but he couldn't because they were not qualified and thus would not understand. There are many other teachings which can be learnt from a Vedic Guru, but again only the qualified will be taught and only the most pious and sincere humans will understand and not everyone. For most humans, God will remain unknown and invisible, because God is not so cheap.

Islam— About 600 years after Jesus, Prophet Muhammad appeared and produced the Koran; he claimed the Koran was a revelation by God in some cave, and thus Islam is a one-man made religion. It also appears that the level of development at that time was near to the ground that the cave culture was the characteristic feature of society in the region. Prophet Muhammad declared himself as the last prophet of God. It is very important to understand the actions of Prophet Muhammad to understand the Islamic mentality. Islam, like Christianity, believes in only one God.

Who exactly is God– simply says Allah his name, but abode, description, and history is mystery? And the Muslims are forbidden to inquire into and hear about God from other non-Muslims. The holy Koran states this is the only life and after this life we are buried and on the Day of Judgement, based on our deeds, Allah sends us to hell or heaven forever. The Koran also says Allah is all-merciful. One may ask how can Allah be described merciful when He forces some people to go to hell forever after only one chance (i.e. one life)? When will Allah be merciful? When is the Day of Judgement? Human beings have absolutely no idea. Allah is invisible/unknown God of Islam. This view is similar to other religions. When the people die they are buried and in the grave and there they have to wait for the Day of Judgement on that very day Allah decides whether those people should go to hell or heaven forever. Thus there is no second chance for the sinners, they are sent to hell forever. The Islamic scriptures do not mention the age of the Universe nor do humans but they accept the authority of Christian scriptures. Thus Adam, Eve, and this world were created by Allah about 6000 years ago.

Muslims believe that the whole universe was created by Allah. There is only one Allah. Allah is so powerful that He can destroy anybody or anything. In course of some personal discussion some Muslim scholars remarked stating that Allah need not come to the earth and fight with the wrong people. A small mosquito is enough to kill us. When we can be finished by the Dingi virus, why should He take trouble to finish us? Muslims tend to argue that Allah is not weak like Hindu gods, who could not kill Ravan, therefore god Ram himself had to come in the form of a baby and grew up and fight with Ravan to kill him. It seems the Hindu gods have no power. Human body seems to be more powerful than so-called gods of Hindus. Posing counter questions Hindus may also ask: Why do Muslims themselves kill each other and non-believers when Allah is so powerful? Is Allah very helpless or so dependent on human beings? In fact, there are many more such questions to be posed: How do you know there is only one Allah? Where did Allah come from? Who created Allah? When was Allah created and what for? Where does He live and what for? Was the creator of Allah not more powerful than Allah himself? What are the constituent elements of such a powerful Allah? Who gave the name Allah to God? Did Allah know only Arabic? Who has seen Allah? Nearly similar questions can be raised about the Christian or the Hindu God also. In fact, no religion has got satisfactory or proper reply to all these questions except for annihilation of all those who raise such questions.

The hard truth is that Prophet Muhammad was illiterate and hence the Koran was not written by him. The messages of Prophet Muhammad were originally available on some makeshift materials, such as palm leaves, fragments of pottery and on the shoulder blades of camel and they were transcribed in written form some forty years after passing away of Muhammad in 632, as observed by Cherif Bassiouni M. in his book entitled **Introduction to Islam**. The Koran has many scripts copied from Hindu, Zoroastrian, Jew, Christian scripts. Addition, alteration or deletion of ideas must have taken place in the Koran over the years. In fact no religious scripture can be said to be in its pure form. No religious ideology has ever developed in a week or in a few months. It has taken its own time. Religious leaders kept it amending in view of their experience and convenience. It is very sad that Islam grew with violence in the form of terror and killing of innocent people in the name of Allah. To quote Rasamandala Das (**Islam and Vedas:**

Lost Harmony), "With the death of Muhammad in 632, there was a need to choose a new leader to guide the Muslim nation. This marks the beginning of the division of Islam into so many religious sects and political factions. Unfortunately, confusion, rivalries, and unsettlement, as well as long civil wars among believers, followed."

The Islam has nothing new to add in the field of religion. Its followers have tended to eliminate people of other faiths so as to survive as a religion. Islam cannot tolerate logical or scientific debate or discussion because of its rigidity in thinking. About 'good things in the Koran' are nothing but a copy paste from various sources, most of them from ancient civilizations and ancient oral wisdoms. The 1400 years old book simply teaches us how to be in world by accepting some illusory and invisible almighty god 'Allah'? Islam was spread by sword. Historical research suggests that about 80 million to 600 million Hindus were killed during the Muslim invasions and rule in South Asia.

God in Bhagavad Geeta— Here are the views of devotees of the ISKCON on the notion of God in the Bhagavad Geeta. Herein Sri Krishna declares that there is no superior to Him. Sri Krishna is the father and God of everybody. What the Geeta contains are the words of God Himself and not of any prophet. Here are the select examples–

"I am the Supreme Spirit (or Super-soul) abiding in the inner psyche of all beings as soul (*Atman*). I am the beginning, the middle, and also the end of all beings." (10:20)

"Whatever forms are produced, O son of Kunti, in all the wombs, the great *Prakriti* is their womb, and I seed-giving father." (14:4)

"And whatever is the seed of all beings, that also am I, O Arjun. There is nothing, animate or inanimate, that can exist without Me." (10:39)

"The fools disregard me, dwelling in human form. They do not know my transcendental nature, as the great Lord of all beings."(9:11)

"Never was there a time when I did not exist, nor you, nor all these rulers of men, nor shall any of us ever cease to exist hereafter. Just as the embodied self passes through childhood, youth, and old age in this body, in the same manner, it will obtain another body. A wise man is not confused about this." (2:12-13)

"Just as a person puts on new clothes after discarding the worn-out ones, similarly the living entity or the individual soul takes on new bodies after casting off the old ones.' (2:22)

"If you think that the physical body takes birth and dies perpetually, even then, O mighty-armed Arjun, you should not grieve like this because death is certain for one who is born, and birth is certain for one who dies. Therefore, you should not lament over the unavoidable." (2:27)

The truth is that which has always existed. For instance, 2+2=4 is true today, it was true 5000 years ago, it was true 5 trillion years ago, and it will be true in 5 trillion years time. Thus that which exists today but did not exist 5000 years ago cannot be the truth. Sanatan Dharma is existing today, it existed 5000 years ago, it existed 5 trillion years ago and it will exist in 5 trillion years time. Sanatan Dharma is the truth. Truth is Srimad Bhagavad Geeta, and the God is Sri Krishna and love is Sri Krishna. Such an argument seems to be based on some kind of belief because science cannot say anything about such an elongated future.

Deities are authentic forms of God and *Sanatan Dharma* is monotheistic. Actually all demi-Gods and female Goddesses (*Shaktis*) are the expansion of His energies. Krishna (Govind) is the *Adi Purush which* means the original person. This is confirmed by the **Brahma-Samhita.**

Krishna is the Master. He is the Supreme Person. In a layman's language He is like the warden of a jail who can do both– come in and get out of jail any time. He is free to do anything. Allah is his impersonal aspect similar to Brahm. God is a personal, not a ghost. He is independent but due to His mercy He appears/incarnates to deliver us. The Spirit or Soul is made of His Original Spiritual energy. Neither Prophet Mohammed nor Jesus Christ described about God's energies because they were not cosmic beings. So in order to avoid confusion they taught only what was needed. Bhagavad Geeta Discourse 7 verse 15 says: "The evil doers, the ignorant, the lowest of men who are attached to demonic nature and whose power of judgement has been taken away by divine illusive power (*Maya*), do not surrender to My Will." Shari'ah of Allah has also asked for complete submission. For example, when a Prophet came to the people and said: 'Worship God alone, God has sent me to teach you religion', and when he explained the words of God directly, people, generation after generation, took him as God and worshipped him instead of worshipping the one who sent him to teach the divine message. Islam in Arabic means (submission/surrender to the Will of God) that requires turning away from demons (devils). The Koran thus has subscribed this view of the Geeta.

The Geeta preaches spiritualism and not any religious system. Spiritualism and religions are totally different. For a spiritual man it does not matter what religion one follows or what his name is. He needs to take a *Sattvic* food and can choose to be a *Karmayogi* or a *Bhaktiyogi*. In *Karmayog* one needs to do work dedicating to the supreme Lord and here one needs to do '*Nishkam Karma*', duty without attachment to the fruit of action, while in *Bhaktiyog* one needs to have '*Chitta sudhi*' (pure thoughts). This will lead to removal of '*Agyan*' and real '*Gyan*' will dawn. The Supreme is 'pure consciousness' or 'cosmic consciousness' in which individuality is lost. This can be said easily and bookish knowledge cannot help to reach that state. Great religious leaders never read all Shastras or books to reach that state. They had the natural *Asana* (trait) to do *Sadhna* (practice/yog) and acquired that exalted position. Then whatever they said became Shastras. This is also revelation. *Sadhana* starts with chanting '*Bhagavad-nam*' and then thinking of him all the time as a sincere devotee. The spiritual life has nothing to do to with '*Lowkik*' life or worldly life. Worldly pleasure or sorrow is as per our '*Karmic* record' and spiritual person does not bother about this and takes both in the same manner (equanimity of mind).

God in Hinduism and Islam

According to the Srimad Bhagavad Geeta, God is Unmanifest, Unborn and Never-Begotten. Discourse 7 and verses 24-25 of the Bhagavad Geeta say: "The foolish regard Me, as the unmanifested, as come into manifestation, not knowing My supreme state– immutable and transcendental. I am not manifest to all, veiled (as I am) by Yog-Maya. This deluded world knows Me not– the unborn, the immutable." The ignorant think that the Lord, too, like an ordinary mortal, comes down from the unmanifested state and assumes a body, impelled by His past

Karma. This belief is due to their ignorance of His real nature, which is unchanging and ever luminous. Thus disregarding the Lord, the foolish worship the minor deities for the fulfilment of their selfish desires. The misunderstood men come to the conclusion that physical glory of an incarnation is all the eternal truth. Although the form of an incarnation can be the focus of concentration, it cannot by itself be the Truth. The forms we impose on the Formless are due to our limitations. We turn away from the contemplation of the Ultimate Reality to concentrate upon imaginative reconstructions. God is not one among many. He is the One behind the ever changing many, who stands beyond all forms, the immutable centre of mobility. The Koran says: "He is Allah, [who is] One, Allah, the Eternal Refuge. He neither begets nor is born, nor is there to Him any equivalent." (Al-Ikhlas 112:1-4)

Some people may argue that if God has manifested as a man or ghostly spirit, then everyone from the creations would have seen Him and known Him. For example, if a person who lives among the people is God, then both righteous and sinners have seen God, both devils and unrighteous could see God and certainly in the Vision of God there is salvation. This is not necessary as everybody cannot understand and see everything. Everyone is not blessed with same kind of insight, intellect and intuition.

Many Islamic scholars have argued that the last revealed scripture is the Koran which means everyone has to follow its message and instructions completely with his whole heart. One must follow the Laws and Commands and perform the good deeds according to the prescribed ways. At least one's 'Intentions' (*niyyah*) must be sincerely for the sake of Only God and in the correct faith as taught by the prophets and sages! When the Koran is considered to be the last and the Rigved the first scripture, it simply means that the Koran has got some exalted and superior position over all religions. When the Koran has borrowed certain ideas from the Vedic philosophy, why do Muslims hate Hindus and forcibly convert them to Islam? No religious scripture contains the original gospel of God. Who really saw or knew the original gospel? Both the human being and God have been in existence for over a millennium, but no religious scripture is in existence for more than 5000 years. Why did God not provide with any such scripture for those who existed for period preceding 5000 years? All scriptures are obviously creation of human beings for specific purposes in the name of some unknown or mysterious God. God did not give language to the people for the purpose of communication. If yes, why God did make discrimination with regard to the use of diverse languages across the world or across different species of the nature? The Koran is in Arabic which neither originated with Allah nor with Islam. The Arabic language is definitely older than Islam, but newer than the Great Allah. In fact, all existing languages are man-made means of communication. God merely gave some capacity to the humans to develop the oral and written means of communication. No language can be branded as a cosmic language.

Nevertheless, Muslims opine that the divine or holy scriptures in other religions of the world include some remnants of the teachings of divine message, but they cannot rely upon them as we can rely on the Koran. This is because the Holy Scriptures in other religions have been mixed up, changed, altered and distorted; also their chain of transmission is broken and unauthentic. This is in fact true of all religious scriptures including the holy Vedas, Geeta, Koran and others.

Many Muslims think that only Islam, Christianity and Judaism are authentic religions since they were all mentioned in the Koran but the Jewish and Christian scriptures had been changed whilst the Koran had stayed the same. All the other religions are based on idol worship. Islam is said to be the last and final religion and that Prophet Muhammad was the last Prophet. There is nothing like last scripture and last religion. God's incarnations and prophets are infinite.... Nobody knows the last stage of human civilization. Sikhism emerged as a much newer religion in South Asia. Since Islam is described as the last religion that does not mean it is the best of all. The issue of idol worship is raised to create a kind of disgust for Hinduism. But what did Muslims worship before the Koran came into being. The answer is definitely idols. What do they worship in the Kaaba now? The hard truth is that they worship Lord Shiv in the form of black stone. Tarek Fatah, a Canada-based Pakistani journalist has rightly observed, "The *tawaf* (circumambulation of the Kaaba during the *Haj*) and the Hindu *phera* are the same thing. And they still kiss the same stone, just like one kisses the *lingam*."

Whether one recognizes it or not Muslims do consciously or unconsciously worship black stone known as *Hajre Aswad* (an oval black stone) in the Kaaba. But the Muslims in general are either ignorant of this fact or outright reject this hard truth because Islam grew out of hatred for idol worshippers. I will be back to this topic a little later to elaborate this fact still further.

In a way hatred against Hinduism is hatred against religion as such. Hindu religion is different from all other man-made/sponsored religions. Muslims hate Buddhists and Christians also despite the fact that they do not believe in idol worship. 'Hinduism' is the oldest, then came Buddhism, Judaism, Christianity, Islam and then came Sikhism in a successive order. Each had its own needs and purposes. But when you compare the scriptures of each you will begin to see that there is a common thread of ideas. Each believes in ONE ultimate God/Reality and each teaches us about the processes of reaching this final goal/ reality.

Muslims worship small pieces of black stone which once constituted an idol of Shiv temple at the Kaaba and yet they believe and claim that they are opposed to idolatry and Hinduism. Islam does not believe in rebirth. Muslims believe that after this life one is judged by God to go into heaven or hell to enjoy or suffer forever onwards. Whereas the Vedic literatures teach us that indeed at the time of death one is judged according to the deeds one has done in that life (i.e. *Karma*) and given appropriate next life in either heavenly or hellish body based on qualifications and desire.

[**The KAABA**— The word Kaaba might have come from the Tamil Language which originated around 1700BC. In Tamil Nadu Kabaalishwaran temple is Lord Shiva's temple and Kabaali refers to Lord Shiva. The black stone at Kaaba is held sacred and holy in Islam and is called "Hajre Aswad" from the Sanskrit word Sanghey Ashweta or Non-white stone. The Shiva Lingam is also called Sanghey Ashweta. So what is in Kaaba could be the same what Hindus worship. The pedestal Maqam-E-Ibrahim at the centre of the Kaaba is octagonal in shape. In Hinduism, the pedestal of Brahma the creator is also octagonal in shape. Muslim pilgrims visiting the Kaaba temple go around it seven times. In no other mosque does the circumambulation prevail. Hindus invariably circumambulate or Pradakshina, around their deities. This is yet another proof that the Kaaba shrine is a pre-Islamic. In Shiva temples Hindus always practice circumambulation or Pradakshina. Just as in Hinduism, the custom of circumambulation by Muslim pilgrims around the entire Kaaba building seven times shows that the claim that in Islam they don't worship stones is not true. Allah was one of the deities in Kaaba long before Islam was founded. It might come as a stunning revelation to many that the word 'ALLAH' itself is Sanskrit. In Sanskrit language Allah, Akka and Amba are synonyms. They signify a goddess or mother. The term 'ALLAH' forms part of Sanskrit chants invoking goddess Durga, also known as Bhavani, Chandi and Mahishasurmardini.

(Source: http://jesussavessooncoming.blogspot.in/2015/05/allah-muslims-god-is-durga-allah.html)]

The above passage suggests that idol worship forms the very basis of Islam; it is altogether a different matter that the most Muslims either do not recognize or readily accept this hard fact to argue that Islam is different from or superior to idol worshipping religions, Hindu in particular.

Idol or Deity Worship

True, Islam does not preach idol worship. It does not believe in the deity worship either. Idol or deity worship is not the same thing. Deities are the authentic forms of God. Just as in the Koran there are many different names of God (for to Him belong all the beautiful names) at least 99 showing His different attributes. Even in the Koran there are references of God's personal features. The Koran mentions that God has eyes, hands, face, etc. When a devotee sees a picture of Krishna the picture acts as a spiritual tool because straight away he is reminded of God. A long time back when Islam or Christianity was not in existence the Geeta had taught no idol or deity worship. The Geeta was already ahead of all religions with respect to the notion of worshipping idols. It has primarily preached surrendering to God. The Geeta was opposed to the Vedic rituals. The Geeta does not teach worshipping of any idol or deity. Sri Krishna has stated in Discourse 10 that He does not dwell in anything. So it is recommended that one should continue to remember God in the best way one can. If this means keeping His names on your lips then this is also very perfect.

There is nothing wrong or immoral in reading Geeta by non-Hindus. One can offer prayer five times a day, go to Masjid and celebrate Eid or Christmas and yet read the Geeta. There is no apparent contradiction between religions. A true religious person loves all religions with same sense of reverence. If one wants to increase one's spiritual life, one should take advantage of the knowledge in the Geeta. After all, Muslim means one who submits to the will of Allah. Remember spiritual life is a process of realization. It may not happen overnight. Allah means Krishna and Krishna means Allah. It means same thing in different languages, as they are different words to mean the same sun or moon. Even though the word for the sun is different in different countries, they are still talking about the same sun.

Why does God give everything to some and nothing to others? Actually of course everything is given by God. But there is *Karma*. The translation of *Karma* is action. So everyone is performing some action. There are different types of action. There is good action and bad action. So there are reactions to action. Those who perform good action, they get good reactions in the future and those who perform bad action, they get bad reactions in the future. So what people get now is dependent on their *Karma,* or the action they had performed in the past. If they have done bad things in the past they will not be fortunate then. Our present sufferings and enjoyments are a result of our past good or bad actions.

The devotees of Krishna Consciousness from the Western world have said thus in course of some personal conversation:

> "God's name 'Krishna' is so powerful that any soul will be attracted to upon hearing it. We all were once separated from the Lord just like a petal separating from a rose flower. In this age, people will be continuously attracted to the holy names although illusion is blindfolding our eyes with all the possible forces, but can it be more powerful than love? The original Big Boss of Everything has made His divine step in our everyday routine life. We are so lucky, nothing will be lifeless now, God is addicted to the love we have for Him, He will never let us down, and He is so merciful and always smiling.

> Nothing will be black and white and boring anymore because colour in person has appeared. Love is in the air, love is a very dangerous disease, trust me the immune system can't fight love, no one will be able to escape once your love is activated again for Krishna and this time there won't be any separation again."

The word 'Hindu is an Arabic name. It means the people who live on the other side of the Sindhu River. Hindu is never mentioned in any Vedic scripture at all. *Sanatan Dharma* is the eternal nature of the soul. It cannot be changed. That is the real religion. And *Sanatan Dharma* is the same for everyone. That is what the Krishna Consciousness devotees are teaching.

> "It is not religion, it is science. It is like mathematics. For instance, 1+1=2 for Hindus, Christians, Muslims, Atheists, everyone, it is not Christian mathematics. It is mathematics. So we are teaching the fundamental spiritual principles that are valid for everyone everywhere... So just read the Geeta and try to understand who you are and what is your relationship with Krishna and act in that relationship as a servant of Krishna. Chant Hare Krishna and be happy... . Krishna consciousness is there in everyone's heart. It is in the Muslim's heart, the Christian's heart, everyone's heart... So we have to first awaken pure love for God in our own hearts and then we will have some potency to help others also awaken love for God in their hearts. It does not matter what external religion people are following. Krishna consciousness is for everyone."

All the main religions are based on the truth. They all have the same basic ideas but have developed a bit differently because of being explained a bit differently by different prophets in different countries and different languages.

All the original ideas relating to religion can be traced back to the Vedas. One cannot think of a religion which does not comprise some ideas of the Vedas, especially the Upanishads. The Vedas are the fountainhead of all religions. Some elements of all religions can be found in the Vedas that is the original source. Those believing in the Mahabharat have argued that about 5000 years ago there was only one king of the whole world and he was situated somewhere near

Delhi in India, from where he ruled the whole world. At that time there was only one culture, the Vedic culture, and spread all over the world. But since then it is all separated and the knowledge is lost to a large extent by now.

Islam forbids idolatry and intermediary which contradicts other religions. God does not have intercessor nor does He have an image (also stated in Christianity and Judaism). If God is divine and unlimited then He cannot be comprehended, so a man's image is not sufficed and Hindus inherently limiting God. 'There is nothing like Him and He is endowed with hearing, seeing.'

Islamic scholars have observed that the great prophet picked up something from every great religion so that all practising Muslims can get blessings from every major God. Since Prophet Muhammad himself was a born idol worshipper, needless to say that Hinduism was closest to his heart. That is the reason he chose Hindu Moon-God as Islamic deity and moon as the universal Islamic symbol. 'Allah' was the name of a Moon-God in pre-Islamic Arabic mythology (see **The Moon-god Allah in the Archaeology of the Middle East** (1994) by Robert Morey). While 'Hindus have been referring their deity moon as goddess since the early period of Hinduism'. In Hinduism, moon or *Chandra* is a lunar god and a *Graha.* The *Chandra* is the lord of plants and vegetation.

Prophet Muhammad also chose Hindu God Lord Shiva's temple 'Kaaba' (built by King Vikramaditya for Moon-God Shiv) as Islam's holiest place and required all Muslims to pray and bow towards it. In addition he picked Hindu pilgrimage Haj as the highest form of worship and the only worship which washes all the sins away. He made black stone (Hajre Aswad, the symbolic lingum (private part) of Lord Shiv, which was made a part of Shiv temple Kaaba by King Vikramaditya), as the most revered stone of Islam, to be touched and kissed by all pilgrims.

King Vikramaditya's inscriptions were found in the Kaaba in Mecca proving beyond doubt that the Arabian Peninsula formed a part of his empire and that he, who highly revered Lord Shiv, built the Shiv temple called Kaaba. The text of the crucial Vikramaditya inscription, found inscribed on a gold dish hung inside the Kaaba shrine in Mecca, is found recorded on page 315 of a volume known as **'Sayar-ul-Okul'** treasured in the Makhtab-e-Sultania library in Istanbul, Turkey. Rendered in free English the inscription says:

> "Fortunate are those who were born (and lived) during king Vikram's reign. He was a noble, generous dutiful ruler, devoted to the welfare of his subjects. But at that time we Arabs, oblivious of God, were lost in sensual pleasures. Plotting and torture were rampant. The darkness of ignorance had enveloped our country. Like the lamb struggling for her life in the cruel paws of a wolf we Arabs were caught up in ignorance. The entire country was enveloped in darkness so intense as on a new moon night. But the present dawn and pleasant sunshine of education is the result of the favour of the noble king Vikramaditya whose benevolent supervision did not lose sight of us- foreigners as we were. He spread his sacred religion amongst us and sent scholars whose brilliance shone like that of the sun from his country to ours. These scholars and preceptors through whose benevolence we were once again made cognisant of the presence of God, introduced to His sacred existence and put on the road of Truth, had come to our country to preach their religion and impart education at king Vikramaditya's behest."
>
> [Source: http://kaabaisnotahindutemple.blogspot.in/2011/10/exposing-reality-of-sayar-ul-okul.html]

SAYAR-UL-OKUL is a poem by Umar-bine-Hassnam (Poetic Title: ABBUL-HIQAM meaning Father of Knowledge). He was an uncle of Prophet Muhammad. He refused to get converted to Islam. He died a martyr at the hands of Muslim fanatics who wanted to wipe out non-Muslims. He was a renowned poet and wrote many verses in the praise of Lord Shiv. A part of his Arabic poem translates as follows in English:

> The man who may spend his life in sin
> and irreligion or waste it in lechery and wrath
> If at least he relent and return to
> righteousness can he be saved?
> If but once he worship Mahadeva with a pure
> heart, he will attain the ultimate in spirituality.
> Oh Lord Shiva exchange my entire life for but
> a day's sojourn in India where one attains salvation.
> But one pilgrimage there secures for one all

merit and company of the truly great.

[Source: http://www.india-forums.com forum_posts.asp? TID=3729093]

Many Kaaba stones have Sanskrit words inscribed from pagan days. The Hajre Aswad is an oval black stone, about seven inches in diameter 2 feet 6 inches long in the shape of a male private part. Kissing and praying to this stone representing Lord Shiva's lingum is for libido and fertility. It was the practice of Arab pagans including Prophet Muhammad to kiss Hajre Aswad, and pray for *shaktis* (Hindi word for strength) to men's sexual strength and women's fertility. (**Sahih Bukhari**, page 396, No. 808)

"Umar (May Allah be pleased with him) came near the Black Stone and kissed it and said, "Had I not seen Allah's Messenger (Peace be upon him) kissing you, I would not have kissed you."

The edifice of Islam was definitely built on the relics of Hinduism. Hindu religion is so vast and cosmic that one cannot imagine developing any other religion negating all the characteristic features of Hinduism. Hinduism happens to be the oldest religion which developed in that very region a long time before Islam came into being. To whom it was dedicated is another question. To make the lead deity Shiv is questionable in the very least. For starters, 360 Gods were worshiped in the Kaaba. Shiv is generally worshiped alone, or with Parfait, certainly not with the whole Pantheon. It is also well documented that in the Kaaba there were three major Gods, the head God (which was Shiv), his wife and daughter. While the wife can understandably be Parvati, what daughter? The only one I could find was Ashoksundari, who is not at all known, except among Vedic scholars. Karen Armstrong in his book **Muhammad: A Biography of the Prophet** has shed enough light on this subject. It is clearly evident from theory and practice of Islam that since inception Islam and its followers, same as Hindus, have been indirectly worshipping idol, but it is all together a different matter that they tend to counteract and abhor idol and idol worshippers for religious reasons.

Another Hindu tradition Prophet Muhammad maintained from his Hindu days is that of the sacred water concept during Hindu pilgrimage and worship. According to the Hindu tradition sacred water (of Ganga) is also inseparable from the Shiv emblem as the crescent moon. Wherever there is a Shiv emblem, sacred water must co-exist. True to that association a sacred fountain exists near the Kaaba. Its water is held sacred because it has been traditionally regarded representing Ganga water since pre-Islamic times (*Zamzam* water). The Muslim pilgrims who go to the Kaaba for Haj regard this *Zamzam* water with reverence and take some bottled water with them as sacred water (same as Hindus take Ganga water home from pilgrimage). Many Muslims soak their shrouds with the sacred *Zamzam* water, a religious tradition from their Hindu ancestry of pouring sacred Ganga water on their dead. Prophet Muhammad also kept the Vedic practice of circumambulation seven times in their religious ceremonies (circumambulation has always been an integral part of Hindu and Buddhist devotional practice known as *Pradakshina* in Sanskrit). It is said that the Prophet ordered Muslims to go around the Kaaba seven times as a part of Haj which was a part of Hindu worship prior to capture of Mecca.

Another great tenet of Islamic Prophet carried forward from Hinduism is the concept of washing of all of one's sins through pilgrimage to Hindu temples at Ganga River and by taking a dip in the Ganga water. Prophet said you wash all your sins by going to pilgrimage to the Kaaba and drinking sacred Zamzam water. This Haj worship concept is a win-win situation for all concerned. Lord Shiv is happy that millions come and circumambulate his temple and kiss his symbolic private part, pilgrims including killers, paedophiles, adulterers, robbers and rapists are happy that their sins of lifetime get washed just by walking seven times around the Kaaba and the local businesses and Muallims (prayer leaders) are happy that they are able to make enough money for their livelihood. Prophet Muhammad also borrowed the word Eid from Hinduism to celebrate the completion of Haj worship at the Shiv temple of Kaaba. Eid in Sanskrit means worship. The Islamic word Eid for festive days, signifying days of worship, is a pure Sanskrit word.

Hindus also practice all night worship of moon-Goddess Durga (Allah is Goddess Durga) on certain nights called 'Jagrata' and believes that by doing that their worship is worth a lot more blessings. Prophet

Muhammad did not want Muslims to lose out on that count and thus included three 'Jagratas' in Islam, Shab-e-Qadar, Shab-e-Barat and Shab-e-Meraj when Muslim salats are worth a lot more than average salat. Practising Muslims pray like crazy during these nights to gain extra blessings (mostly out of shape Muslims can hardly walk next day from all night of sit-ups)

[*see– http://jesussavessooncoming. blogspot.in/2015/05/ allah-muslims-god-is-durga-allah.html*]

According to some Muslim scholars it is said that their great prophet incorporated the following Hindu religious rituals and concepts to ensure that Muslims also get blessed by Hindu God Shiv and Hindu Goddess Allah (Durga) (along with Yahweh, the God of Abraham and Ahuramazda, the God of Zoroastrians whose religious tenets he also incorporated in Al Islam):

1. Adopting Hindu deity Moon-God as Allah in Islam,
2. Making Hindu Moon-God Shiva's temple named Kaaba as the holiest place of Islam,
3. Making the black stone as the most holy stone of Islam and making touching and kissing of it as a blissful act of Sunnah,
5. Adopting the Hindu pilgrimages Haj and Umra as the highest worship in Islam,
6. Shaving the heads as Hindus do for pilgrimages,
7. Circumambulating the Shiv temple Kaaba 7 times as Hindus did,
8. Adopting the Hindu concept of washing all the sins by making the holy pilgrimage,
9. Collecting holy water representing *Ganga Jal* (Zamzam water) as Hindus do to take holy blessings home,
10. Wearing white seamless cloth during pilgrimage as Hindus wear during their religious ceremonies and pilgrimages,
11. Celebrating the completion of worship of Shiv temple Kaaba by giving it the Hindu Sanskrit name of Eid Eid,
12. Including all night worships of moon God Allah (Durga) called Jagrata as a part of Islam.

Thus the archaeological and historical evidence has narrowed down differences between Hinduism and Islam. It may be good for peaceful living, prosperity and brotherhood of mankind, but in practice Islam is not an accommodative religion. It is highly intolerant of other religious system.

Manifestation of God

There is a special emphasis on *Darshan* (visual experience) in Hindu religion. Brahmnas, a group of sacred priestly texts attached to the Vedas, state: "The eye is the truth. If two persons come disputing with each other [...] we should believe him who said 'I have seen it', not him who has said 'I have heard it."

Hinduism attaches a very special significance to the *Darshan* of gurus, leaders, saintly persons and even the holy places and holy images. Hindus believe that *Darshan* is a two-way flow of vision. While the devotee sees the God, so too the God sees the devotee, and the two can make contact through their special eyes. When the images of gods are made, their eyes are the last part to be completed. It is not until the image is consecrated that their eyes are finally opened with either the touch of a paintbrush or using a golden needle. Popular gods like Shiv and Ganesh have a third eye located in their foreheads. The Lord Brahma, the Thousand-eyes, often has four heads and looks in all directions at once. This emphasis on the vision and the image dominates the Hindu's relation to the gods, appearing to be just the opposite of many other religions.

The Koran admits that some will see God someday (Koran 75:22-23). 'Some faces that day will beam looking towards their Lord.' (Koran 75:22-23) Muslims believe that nobody has seen God so far. But it is not acceptable to all. Some people react stating that they should speak for themselves and not for everyone. Just because some people have not seen Japan that does mean that nobody has seen Japan. The Srimad Bhagavad Geeta has observed, "But you are not able to see Me with your physical eye alone; therefore, I give you a divine eye to see My supreme power and glory." (Bhagavad Geeta 11:8) We cannot see God (Lord Krishna) with our physiological eyes, we need special divine vision which Arjun was given and only then he could be able to see Lord Krishna in His cosmic form which was more effulgent than a thousand suns all rising at the same time. "But by single-minded devotion, I can be seen in this form, can be known in essence, and also can be reached, O Arjun." (Bhagavad Geeta 11:54)

We cannot see God by ordering him. One can see Lord Krishna face-to-face only by undivided devotional service. So far countless number of people have seen face-to-face, right here on this planet. By following the blind, one will not see anything. God will remain unseen and unknown by following those who have not seen God. The Srimad Bhagavadam says, "I exist within everything, and I am, therefore, the essence of the atomic constituents of material elements." (Bhagavadam 11.15.12) It is Lord Krishna who is present in every atom and by His potency every single particle is operating. Atoms combine to form molecules by the potency of Lord Krishna who is inside every atom. "Whatever is endowed with glory, brilliance, and power– know that to be a manifestation of a very small fraction of My splendour. What is the need for this detailed knowledge, O Arjun? I continually support the entire universe by a very small fraction of My divine power." (Bhagavad Geeta 10:41-42) From a single spark of Krishna, millions of universes are created and maintained by Him. Can we really imagine how great Krishna (God) is? "The word *'Sat'* or Truth' is used in the sense of reality and goodness. The word *'Sat'* is also used for an auspicious act, O Parth." (Bhagavad Geeta 7:26) It is Lord Krishna who is aware of everything that has happened in the past, all which is happening in the present, and all that will happen in the future.

Lord Krishna: God in Human Form

Lord Krishna was not God in human form, He was Supreme Being manifest in human form. Here we need to differentiate between Supreme Being and gods in a human form. Mahavir, Gautam Buddha, Jesus Christ and Prophet Mohammed all were born normal human beings. At the end of their life all these spiritual stalwarts gained enlightenment (*Moksha*) and finally salvation or liberation.

For all practical purposes they became gods in a human form someone revered by mankind for times to come. Every enlightened being, every human being who gains enlightenment and salvation at the end of the journey, becomes a God in a human form, a liberated soul. Having liberated self from the cycle of birth and death, all gods in a human form find a place in the Kingdom of God (*Aka,* Vaikunth in Hinduism). The Kingdom of God or the abode of God is a place of no return.

Every single soul having liberated itself having regained its original pure pristine form remains in the Kingdom of God, the abode of God until eternity. And what does this mean? This simply means that until the dissolution of the present cosmos occurs all liberated *atmans* (souls) remain in the Kingdom of God forever. Every human being who gains enlightenment realizes self which simply liberates the soul within from the bondage of life and death, the vicious circle of *Sansar* (worldly life). From the first manifestation as an amoeba to the last as an enlightened one, the journey of soul is to reach the end of the journey, the 8.4 millionth manifestations.

In the history of mankind there has only been one *Avatar* that God manifested in a human form that was witnessed by mankind in the form of Lord Krishna, the *Avatar* of Dwapar Yuga. During the times of Lord Krishna life was rife with brutalities of the highest order. No peace to be found. So the Supreme Being manifested in the form of Lord Krishna. It was only Lord Krishna, an *Avatar* of the era, who would end *Adharma* (lawlessness) and re-establish *Dharma* (righteousness).

To cut short, becoming a God in a human form is the end of journey of life. Every human being would one day become a God in a human form like Mahavir, Gautam Buddha, Jesus Christ or Prophet Mohammed, but to incarnate as Lord Krishna is the forte of only a chosen one. Only one amongst millions in about 3500 years manifests the power of a Supreme Being. Such a noble one is finally termed as an incarnation of God practically Supreme Being Himself. When conditions worldwide deteriorate beyond repair, when things seem out of control, when there is gloom world over humanity is in absolute distress, when hope and enthusiasm seems to have died, it is only Supreme Being who brings the humanity out of the present chaos. It is only an *Avatar,* an incarnation of Supreme Being, that helps restore the system in the world. The world is presently passing through the Kali Yuga phase of life (the metal age) when dark forces of nature finally subdue the godly forces. For Supreme Being to take charge again to imbibe within human beings a feeling of hope manifesting a human form becomes a necessity. Upholding Dharma (righteousness) is the call of the day. The power of an enlightened one (like Mahavir, Gautam Buddha, Jesus Christ or Prophet Mohammed) coupled with the powers of Chanakya the upholder of Dharma is the requisite of the day. One who deals with the affairs of mankind with a firm hand re-establishes Dharma against all odds.

The meaning of incarnation is being explained through an example. Suppose we have a lawn tennis ball and we pitch it (throw it) on the ground so that it rebounds again and again in an upward direction. Now what shall we witness, the ball takes the first strike on the ground and again jumps back. The first crest is when Mahavir, the 24th Tirthankar of Jainism, is born. The ball again strikes the ground and again jumps back to form a crest. And now Gautam Buddha, the preceptor of Buddhism, is born. The ball again strikes the ground and jumps back and Jesus Christ is born. In the same manner and sequence Prophet Mohammed is born. As the time passes other enlightened souls like Nanak, Kabir and Sai Baba is born. There comes a phase in the life of mankind when the ball does not have further energy left to take a strike back and goes flat on the ground. What now? In the absence of the flow of spiritual energy the mankind would have a natural and hasty death. Someone, a force that can lift the ball from the ground and throw it again, is necessitated. It is at this point that Supreme Being manifests a human form; an *Avatar* of the era surfaces. It is only an *Avatar* (God manifest in human form) who lifts the ball up and throws it. None other than an incarnation (or manifestation) of Supreme Being can accomplish this feat.

Sakaar and *Nirakaar Brahm*

If one could ever see one's *Atman* (the true self within), it would have been possible for a person to see God in the *Sakaar* form. But the truth is not so. One cannot see God with physiological eyes. One must have special eyes endowed with cosmic vision as given momentarily to Arjun by the Lord and such person must match the character of Arjun to have such a divine blessing. Every atheist wants to see God through his physiological eyes because seeing is believing.

Seeing God in *Sakaar* form is the desire of many. Mere desires or wishes do not affect the working of the Lord, the Almighty Creator. Our destiny is directly controlled by the *Karma* we perform. We reap what we sow, nothing more or less. So is destined the philosophy of *Karma* by Supreme Being. Though it is a different matter that the *Karma* performed by us in our previous lives may not manifest at all in the present life. Imagine the plight of a person born without eye sight or a man with permanently impaired vision by birth. How does such a person lead his life? Is it only through visualizing the *Sakaar* form of things that the impaired one leads his life? No. It is not within the powers of one to imagine the *Sakaar* form of things for one has never seen a *Sakaar* form at any stage of life. Such one leads his life through the *Nirakaar* (formless) mode of life. It is similar to living by the fragrance of a flower even though we have not experienced the bewitching fragrance at any stage of life.

In truth the whole cosmos comprises a cluster of *Atmans* (souls) and ether, the black dark matter that fills the whole of the cosmos. Beyond these there is nothing else in the cosmos we can talk about. Why is it that we do not see or visualize the structure of the soul within our body? The simple reason is that the concept of *Atman* is beyond the comprehension of senses and the mind.

It is only when we gain absolute control of senses and the mind that the concept of *Atman* and *Parmatman* (Supreme Being) becomes clear to us. Never before. Anyone who becomes enlightened can have a direct *Darshan* of Supreme Being. Only after having realized self that we perceive the complete cosmic structure in its entirety including the definition of God.

The description of *Sakaar rupa* (form) of the Supreme Being (having a form) in the scriptures is the prime reason why the humanity always remembers God in times of distress and also in happiness. Most human beings unable to comprehend the Supreme Being in its *Nirakaar* form (without a form) aspire to visualize a form so that they can pray to God and seek His blessings. For a layman it is next to impossible to pray the Supreme Being in His formless state. This is the prime reason why we have develpoed so many statues of God in temples.

Lord Krishna in His manifested form was an embodiment of pure love and power which none other than Krishna Himself has been able to exercise control over through the Yogmaya ever since the humanity has come into being. Instead of trying to see or visualize the *Sakaar* form of Krishna why not we try to indulge in knowing our real self, the soul within. In doing so we shall be able to get nearer to our desired goal, the Lord Krishna Himself. The moment one crosses over the threshold of senses and the mind, one reaches the stage of *Nirvikalp Samadhi.*

Just, Loving and Merciful God

"The eternal individual soul (*Jeev, Jeevatma*) in the body of living beings is, indeed, My integral part. Abiding in material nature or the body, it activates the six senses, including the mind." (Bhagavad Geeta 15:7) Lord Krishna is most loving. He cares for all living beings because we are all His eternal parts. He has an infallible system of justice called the law of Karma. For every action one takes, he/she will be rewarded or punished accordingly and He gives us unlimited chances and not just one (rebirth). We are all eternal, we existed before this life, just as we exist now, and we will continue to exist after this life also. "For the soul there is neither birth nor death at any time. He does not come into being, nor does he cease to exist. He is unborn, eternal, permanent and primeval. The soul is not killed when the body is killed." (Bhagavad Geeta 2.20) Lord Krishna does not rely on middle men for witnessing all our actions. He is the witness Himself to all our activities in person. Eventually every single soul will go back to the spiritual creation where there is no old age, no disease, no death, and no misery.

Everyone in *Vaikunth*, the spiritual creation, lives eternally in the same body which is completely beautiful, full of bliss and love, and full of knowledge. There is no *Jehad*, no hatred, no envyness nor violence in *Vaikunth*. One can qualify to go back to Vaikunth at the end of this short life, simply by loving all living beings (no hatred/envyness), no violence against any living being (vegetarianism) and accepting that Lord Krishna is the real proven God. "The sun does not illumine My Supreme Abode, nor does the moon, nor the fire. Having reached there, people attain permanent liberation (*Moksha*) and do not come back to this temporal world." (Bhagavad Geeta 15.6) The abode of

Lord Krishna is not like this planet, it is spiritual and supreme. There is no need for the sun or electricity, it's self-effulgent. More details can be found in the **Srimad Bhagavadam**.

The people of other faiths often remain scared of the Muslims because they are usually taken not so just, loving and merciful by others, but they consider themselves very just and so they expect others, including God, should be just, loving and merciful to them. The Indian Muslims are, however, somewhat different, as they have always been relatively more understandable and more accommodative than Muslim brothers outside because they are mostly converts and have grown under the common ethos of Indian culture. Hindus have never been known for their offensive or oppressive outlook and style of living. Hindus, same as the Buddhists, have always believed in individual self or welfare rather than in social self. Hindus and Buddhists are highly individualistic people in the sense that they have always bothered for their own salvation rather than for the welfare of the society as a whole. Hindus have always got poor collective interests as a community. On the other hand, Muslims and Christians tend to act collectively. As a matter of routine the Muslims tend to offer *Namaz* on public places collectively every Friday to demonstrate a sense of unity to others. Religion goes beyond individual or personal concern of life. Still further they tend to convey a sense of strong social solidarity, for they are buried at the common place after their death. Since time immemorial they are buried in cemetery to face the Day of Judgement collectively. Islam, same as Christianity, is predominantly characterized by congregational value system and hence a sense of community feeling or brotherhood based on religion is usually very strong. On the other hand, the Hindus are relatively much less united as a community than others because of the presence of strong caste system inherent in the Hindu society.

The Krishna Consciousness and Others

Now let us dwell on the Krishna Consciousness, as its devotees are the real harbingers of the teachings of the Geeta in the modern world. The Krishna consciousness is not a religion. It is not like any religion. The Krishna consciousness is within everyone. It is a kind of original consciousness. It is not something that we learn. It is something that is already within us to be simply awakened. It is *Sanatan Dharma*, our eternal natural constitutional position.

The devotees of the ISKCON have to get off the bodily platform and stop seeing people as Muslims, Christians, Hindus, etc. And just see them as spirit or souls. The Real ISKCON people do not identify themselves as 'Hindus'. They are not 'Hindus'. These are all bodily concepts. The Krishna consciousness is just as relevant to the Hindus as it is to anyone else. It is non-sectarian. It is like gold is gold; there is no Muslim gold and Christian gold. So the Krishna consciousness is the science of God. It is relevant to everyone and it is not Hinduism and it is non-sectarian. They do not care what religion people belong to. They are simply teaching the science of God. And this science of God is relevant for everyone, no matter what religion they may follow.

A Hindu reads the Koran not because it is a Muslims' holy book, but because it comprises sayings and teaching of the Prophet which teach us how to reach God by following the path mentioned in the Koran. But Muslims hate to touch Hindu scriptures. It is a matter of pure exception that A. P. J. Abdul Kalam, 11th President of India, despite being a Muslim, used to read Bhagavad Geeta and recite its mantras. Yet Hindus have a high regard for the Muslims who are understandable and have respect other religions, including their own and do not support the violent ways the religion is linked to.

Some Muslims are mistaken. They do not understand that we all are made to serve. We can do nothing but serve others. We should simply look around and see what we are doing. It would be soon obvious that every one of us is serving someone else. According to the Krishna consciousness devotees our religion is service. We all do it. We all have to do it. The wife serves the husband; the husband serves his boss at the office. The boss serves his superior. Everyone is serving someone else. So this is the 'religion' or *Dharma* of the living entity– service. We are servants. There is no way to get out of this. And that service is our religion.

But all this service in the material world is not satisfying. It is temporary. We are eternal and we can only be satisfied by eternal service. That is called *Sanatan Dharma*, our eternal religion. And that

Sanatan Dharma is serving God. Serving God is our eternal religion. So one cannot escape religion. And we must serve. We have no alternative. We are made to serve. And that is our religion. It becomes perfect when we serve God.

In Buddhism there is no teaching of God, there is only *Nirvana* which is a release from everything, once you die and have reached enlightenment. Also in Christianity there is only one God. Whereas in Hinduism it is taught that there is three major gods. There is no way that all the religions in the world are connected. They all contradict each other's way so much.

Krishna means 'the all-attractive person'. Krishna is the perfect name of God. So Krishna is the same person that the Muslims refer to as Allah. The Krishna consciousness is non-sectarian. It is for everyone. It does not matter what religion one professes, if one wants to go deeply into understanding God then that deep understanding is there in Krishna consciousness.

How were different religions formed? The Lord is universal but the human beings in the universe differ in their attitudes. The same single Lord adopts different procedures in different regions and such different procedures appear as different religions. A few people wrongly criticize the Lord of other religions. They do not criticize the Lord of their own religion. The external behaviour of the Lord differs due to different internal and external behaviours of the human beings in this universe. The external form, dress, language, food habits and culture of human beings differ from one region to the other. Accordingly the external form, dress, food habits, language and culture of the Lord also differ to suit that particular region. The internal Lord and the internal essence of the same Lord is one and the same in His different human incarnations, which have appeared in different regions or religions.

Islam was conceived as a religion of peace and yet it has championed the notion of *Jehad* in real life. The beginnings of *Jehad* are traced back to the words and actions of Prophet Muhammad and the Koran. This encourages the use of *Jehad* against non-Muslims. The Koran, however, never uses the term *Jehad* for fighting and combat in the name of Allah; *qital* is used to mean 'fighting.' *Jehad* in the Koran was originally intended for the nearby neighbours of the Muslims, but as time passed and more enemies arose, the Koranic statements supporting Jehad were updated for the new adversaries. The first documentation of the law of *Jehad* was written by 'Abd al-Rahman al-Awza'i and Muhammad ibn al-Hasan al-Shaybani. The document grew out of debates that had surfaced ever since Muhammad's death. The definition of *Jehad* is to 'struggle in the way of Allah.' A person's daily *Jehad* could be waking up at 3 AM just to complete one of his 5 daily prayers, the morning prayer; *Fajr*.

Criticising the acts of violence in the name of religion and misuse of *Jehad* one Islamic scholar, Jamal Ahmad Khan (**Speaking Tree**, 23 Sept 2001), has made the following observation:

> "*Jehad*, generally translated as religious war, is perhaps one of the most abused and misused terms in the history of Islam. In the past Muslim kings indiscriminately used it while wreaking havoc on their adversaries, Muslims and non-Muslims alike. In recent times Pakistan in its vain attempt to provide a cloak of legitimacy and religiosity to its ongoing proxy war in Jammu and Kashmir has termed it *Jehad*. Terrorists and militant organizations have been re-christened with religious symbols and terminologies. One of them is called Hizbul Mujahideen or the army of religious warriors. Another one is called Jaish-i-Mohammad or the army of the Prophet Mohammad. Al Badr is operating under the false garb of a devoted group of the Prophet's companions who sacrificed their lives at the battle of Badrin several centuries ago. The so-called modern *Jehadis* either do not understand the true meaning of *Jehad* or are bent upon invoking this religious concept for realising their sinister unreligious designs. The inhuman dastardly acts perpetrated by these organizations are contrary to the very spirit of Islam and *Jehad*. The religious duties or Ibadat of the Muslims centre on the five pillars or Arkan of Islam. They are *Kalma* or the recital of the creed, *Salat* or five daily prayers and the Friday prayer; *Roza* or fasting during the holy month of Ramzan; *Zakat* or alms giving and lastly Haj or pilgrimage to Mecca. We, thus, see that *Jehad* is not the obligatory function imposed upon Muslims by the holy Qur'an."

One ideology that plays a key role in terrorism by using the name of Islam is Wahabism. Wahabism and its allies including Salafism (Salafi Jehadism) supports war against anyone and everyone who is not like them. The Islamic State of Iraq and the Levant, al-Qaeda, Al-Shabaab (militant group), Boko Haram, Indonesian Mujahedeen Council, Taliban, Sipah Sahaba, Lashkar-e-Jhangvi and Hizbul Mujahideen follow intolerant Wahabi or Salafi ideology which is opposed by other Muslims. Non-Muslims, Sufis and Shias are attacked by hard-core Wahabism, Deobandis, and Jamaatis in the same way that socialists and other leftist proletarians were assaulted by Mussolini's bandits, Jews and others by the Nazis, and 'bourgeois,' 'kulak,' intellectual, Jewish, 'Menshevik,' and 'Trotskyist' dissenters, often only alleged to be so, by Stalinism. In India Wahabism was spread in the name of Deobandi movement which was opposed by more tolerant Sufi oriented Indian Muslims.

Why are there different religions, especially Islam and Hinduism, in contradiction to each other? Is it that some are really from God and others not? Islam and Hinduism are just two different ways, but the destination is one and the same God. Unless one opts for a particular path, walks on it till he reaches the destination, he cannot make correct decisions about the path or paths in general. Incomplete or superficial knowledge always leads to catastrophic results. One should try to understand and accept that Koran, Bible, Bhagavad Geeta all of them say same thing such as no violence, responsibility towards humanity, surrendering to God, etc. When one speaks of Allah or when one offers *Namaz*, that is one's meditation or surrendering to God. The definition of meditation is sacrifice of yourself to God or Allah what your name or address is that doesn't really matter. We belong to different countries, cities, districts, area, castes, surname and different names just for our identity. Imagine if there were no differences how you would identify someone without address or identity. God is one, God exists, and God is the real superpower. He has a spiritual self illuminated body. If He can give us a form, cannot He be in that form? He can be in any form as per His wish. He can be a bird, tiger, anything… . All the other thoughts are because of ignorance and hatred for others in the name of religion. Therefore, there is no need of forcible religious conversion, as the people of different religions after all preach same thing, maybe in different ways.

The most ISKCON devotees believe that the only way one can

find Krishna is by the mercy of a pure devotee of Krishna. That is the only way Krishna is available. It is not possible to find Krishna on our own terms or strength, by independent study of the Vedas, by meditation or by mastering philosophy. The only way is by getting the mercy of a pure devotee by pleasing him. So one should try to study Geeta, and from that understand what Sri Krishna wants you to do, then you have to surrender to God as a mission in life. That is the only way. Otherwise, it will not be possible for anyone to understand Sri Krishna.

The Muslim scholars say Allah is present at only one place above the 7 heavens. Allah is not present everywhere, thus Allah is not omnipresent. They justify this based on the following verses from the Koran.

'Every good saying goes up to Him.' (Koran 35:10)

'Those who fear their Lord who is above them.' (Koran 16:50)

All the main news in the country goes up to the President. Does this mean the President is situated in some high building? The Vedic knowledge eternally exists and comes from Lord Krishna (Supreme Being) who delivered it in person and also compiled it into scriptures through His devotees. The non-Vedic knowledge is recently created and thus not eternal, and is based on man-made ideologies. This is the main difference between the teachings of age-old *Sanatan-Dharma* (the Eternal Religion) and the recent man-made religions like Christianity and Islam. The founder of Christianity and Islam is a man named Jesus Christ and Muhammad respectively, and thus Christianity and Islam are based on the understandings and ideologies of an individual. Because a man cannot be present at more than one place at a time, their teaching is that God is also limited to being present only at one place, thus God is not omnipresent. Just because we can only be present in one place, does this mean that God is also limited to one place? "That Supreme Purush, O Arjun, is attainable by unswerving devotion to Him alone within whom all beings dwell and by whom all this is pervaded." (Bhagavad Geeta 8:22). Lord Krishna is omnipresent, meaning He is present everywhere. Lord Krishna is always present on His own spiritual planet called *Golok*, which is the top most planet in the spiritual creation called *Vaikunth*. But He is also present everywhere on this and millions of other planets, in millions of universe. Someone who is present everywhere (omnipresent) is greater than someone who is not present everywhere (not omnipresent) and thus if one believes God is great, then one must accept that God is omnipresent and thus Lord Krishna is the one true God.

All the news of the good and bad actions taken by humans everywhere goes up to Lord Krishna, who is God, who can see and hear everything everywhere. "There is nothing like Him, and He is the All-Hearer, the All-Seer" (Koran 42:11) 'So wherever you turn, there is the face of Allah.' (Koran 2:115) It is Lord Krishna who states that He hears and sees everything, with His ears, eyes and faces everywhere. "Shining by the functions of all the senses, yet without the senses; unattached, yet supporting all; devoid of *Gunas*, yet their experiencer." (Bhagavad Geeta 13:14) "He who knows the *Purush* and *Prakriti* together with *Gunas*, is not born again, regardless of their way of life." (Bhagavad Geeta 13:23) Wherever you turn, there is the face of Sri Krishna but only those who are enlightened can see Him.

The Koran and Hadith tell us about certain attributes of God, such as hearing, seeing, having a face, two hands, etc. but they are not like ours. The Muslims cannot describe God, and thus for them God is unseen, unknown and just a name in a book. Only the Vedic scriptures describe God and in complete. This is because only God made scriptures can give knowledge about Him to us and not any man-made scripture. A full description of Lord Krishna (God) can be found in the Vedic scripture called Srimad Bhagavadam. This also gives detailed pastimes of God dating back to billions of years. There is no such thing as the pastimes of God in any non-Vedic scriptures. Lord Krishna says, "The fools disregard me, dwelling in human form. They do not know my transcendental nature, as the great lord of all beings." (Bhagavad Geeta 9:11) The ignorant cannot understand that God is a person with a human like form and He descends to this and other planets to perform His transcendental pastimes. Is there any King who never visits his citizens? Is there any President who never visits his cities/towns? Is there any property owner who never visits his properties? Is there any father who never sees/visits his sons and daughters?

Lord Krishna descends for many reasons including satisfying His devotees' desire to see Him. As mentioned in the Koran and Hadith, God is a person with two hands, face, ears and eyes. Thus God is human like. That Supreme Person is one who has appeared countless number of times in His original form and millions of times in His other forms, and each time He appeared, many demonic people challenged Him, and He very easily defeated them all. They also got liberation, because anyone who is destroyed by Lord Krishna or in the presence of Him, gets liberation. This is how merciful Lord Krishna is.

The devotees of ISKCON have further argued that God is superior to His creations. There is nobody equal to Him or above Him. Only the greatest sportsman can say that there is nobody equivalent to him. Does this mean he is formless, because we are with a form? It just means that he can play sports better than anyone else. Nobody is equivalent to Him in this sense. It is Lord Krishna who has actually appeared millions of times and each time proved that He is the greatest. Lord Krishna is the only proven God. He says: "There exists nothing whatsoever higher than Me, O Dhananjay! All that is here is strung on Me, as a row of gems on a string. O son of Kunti, I am the sapidity in the water, I am the radiance in the sun and the moon, the sacred syllable 'OM' in all the Vedas, the sound in the ether, and potency in human beings. I am the sweet fragrance in the earth. I am the brilliance in the fire, the vitality in all beings, and the austerity in the ascetics. Know Me, O Parth, as the eternal seed of all beings; I am the intelligence of the intelligent, the bravery of the brave." (Bhagavad Geeta 7:7-10). He further says, " I am the origin of all. Everything evolves from Me. Knowing this, the wise worship Me with devotion and reverence." "Whatsoever is the seed of all beings, that also am I, O Arjun. There is no being, whether moving or unmoving, that has come out of any other source." (Bhagavad Geeta 10:39)

The above and other such statements in the Vedic scriptures were made countless number of years ago and endless number of times in this world. The Koran has only been spoken once and only on this planet about 1400 years ago. Lord Krishna has appeared and proved numerous times before Islam that He is the one true God. He also appeared about 500 years ago as Lord Chaitanya and He once again proved that He was the one true God. Lord Krishna claims to be the origin of everything; no other person on the planet existing now or in the past has ever claimed to be the origin of everything. This is because only Lord Krishna is the origin of everything.

The people associated with the Krishna consciousness movement often quote the following statement of Lord Krishna from the Geeta: 'I am the letter 'A' among the alphabets. I am the dual compound among the compound words.' (Bhagavad Geeta 10.33) Of the alphabet letters, Lord Krishna is अ 'A'. The Islamic name of God starts with 'A', this signifies Lord Krishna. The reason why Muslims wear turbans is not due to the weather, but due to the fact that He wears turbans of various colours and decorations. The Muslims have forgotten their Vedic origins, but still follow many Vedic customs in complete ignorance. The reason why Kings wear turbans/crowns is due to the fact that Supreme King, who wears turbans/crowns.

All arguments relating to form or activities of God advanced by some ISKCON devotees based on scriptures are not readily acceptable to many of us because of varying levels of understanding about religion. God in all major religions is above words or language, colour, form, attributes or qualities. Human beings have superimposed their qualities or attributes over God for their own sake. Human beings can never define infinite or limitless God. When God cannot be defined, no description of God can ever be trusted.

Sri Krishna in Manifest Form

Based on the Koran, Hadith and the learned Islamic people, Allah is a person with a human like forms, but He has not been described. Over billions of years the universe has existed, so far only one real person has stepped forward and declared Himself and proved that He is the one and only God, that person is Lord Krishna. Allah is a name in a book (the holy Koran) that is said to have dictated this scripture in a cave over a period of 23 years. The question is when you can hear God what is difficulty in seeing Him? No prophet has ever seen God, so others cannot see God. Krishna is also a name in a book but He has actually been seen by millions. The ISKCON devotees believe that He has appeared more than 18,000 times in His original form and millions of times in His other forms, and each time proved He was the one and only God. Srimad Bhagavad Geeta was believed to have been recited by Lord Krishna in 45 minutes in front of thousands of men. He also spoke the Uddhav Geeta with 937 verses within two hours, and He performed many transcendental pastimes during the 125 years of his appearance in a human form that He appeared about 5000 years ago.

Now the question is why should God reside in a cave and deliver His message. Why should God take years to deliver His message? Why should God appear only once and that also billions of years after creation? Why should God deliver His message to only one illiterate person? Based on the deeds (actions taken) and desires by humans in this life and previous life times, people develop a particular mentality which enables them to know God in different ways. For some, God will be known as a name in a book, and for some God will be known as a real person with historical facts known about Him dating back to billions of years.

"That is Allah, your Lord; there is no deity except Him, the creator of all things, so worship Him. And He is the Disposer of all things." (Koran 6:102) This statement may not make much sense because Allah is just a name in the book and not a real person seen by anyone. The only person who has actually appeared and proved that He is God, is Lord Krishna. The seen and proven God, who has appeared not just once in a book, but He has appeared millions of times in person and each time, He proved himself as the only God. It is common in every Kaliyug, the age of ignorance and irreligion, for people to be very easily be fooled.

If someone declares himself as the greatest swimmer, then that person must appear and swim with other competitors and prove it. If someone states that a character in a particular book is the greatest swimmer, only the most foolish and least intelligent people would have given that character the title of greatest swimmer. If someone declares himself as the fastest runner, then he must appear and compete with other runners and prove it. Only the most foolish and least intelligent type of people would give a character the title of the fastest runner with zero evidence in a book. "Persons who, mediating on Me as non-separate, worship Me in all beings, to them as thus ever zealously engaged, I carry what they lack and preserve and what they already have. Even those devotees who, endowed with faith, worship other gods, worship Me only, O Arjun, but by the wrong method." (Bhagavad Geeta 9.22-23) "Abandoning all duties, come to Me alone for shelter. Be not grieved, for I shall release you from all evils." (Bhagavad Geeta 18.66)

Since the Koran was spoken just once 1400 years ago on this planet only, this is not to be regarded as eternal or universal. On the other hand, the devotees of the Krishna consciousness believe and argue that the Srimad Bhagavad Geeta was last spoken 5000 years ago by Lord Krishna to Arjun, and before that it was spoken by Lord Krishna to Vivasvan, the person who maintains the sun planet, some 120 million 533 thousand years ago. Before that it was spoken by Lord Krishna when He appeared in the previous daytime of Brahma. In this way, Lord Krishna has spoken Srimad Bhagavad Geeta at least 18,000 times right here on this planet and it has also been spoken millions of times in other universes. Thus Srimad Bhagavad Geeta is eternal and universal. Lord Krishna has been known since time immemorial by billions of people on this and numerous other universes. Such an astonishing view held by the Krishna Consciousness followers may not be readily accepted by men with scientific outlook, but that does not matter for the believers. Thus Lord Krishna is eternal and universal, while the word 'Allah' and the Koran never existed before 1400 years ago. This word cannot be found in the original Christian and Jewish scriptures. And this word cannot be found in the Vedic scriptures, which are accepted by historians as the oldest scriptures on the planet. There are more than 810,000 verses in the Vedic scriptures written more than 5000 years ago, and only 6236 verses in the Koran. This very clearly shows that the Vedic knowledge is the words of God and not man-made. Anyone can create a book with a few thousand verses by copying from the Vedic scriptures after making modification. Only God could have created scriptures with more than 810,000 verses, 5000 years ago.

Allah is a concept of God and Krishna is the real person God. Lord Krishna is very eager to take all the souls back to the spiritual creation where everyone lives in the same body that is completely beautiful, full of bliss, full of knowledge, eternal, with no trace of misery. The Muslims are also welcome and can very quickly become qualified to go to the abode of God (Lord Krishna).

Lord Krishna says, "O Arjun, this is the super-conscious state of mind. Attaining this state, one is no longer deluded. Gaining this state, even at the end of one's life, a person attains the very goal of human life by becoming one with God." (Bhagavad Geeta 2.72) He is so merciful that even if one surrenders unto Him in the last hour before death, one will enter into the Kingdom of God. The Koran is full of statements stating Allah is very merciful but Lord Krishna proves it, because Lord Krishna is the one true God. It is hard to pass any conclusive remark here, as it happens to be a matter of belief.

A real devotee of the Lord does not have the feeling of discrimination based on religion. He simply wants to know who is 'God' and how to love Him. That is the reason why a true devotee always searches for these answers from any scripture till he is not satisfied with his questions. The Vedic literature is the oldest scripture in this world and the detailed spiritual information is available in this scripture only, nowhere else. The word 'Ved' means 'knowledge', and this knowledge is unchangeable, eternal. It doesn't mean that other scriptures and religions are valueless or discriminated. No, all the scriptures are connected with the Vedas.

The Biblical and Islamic concept of God is not wrong. It is perfect and flawless for a certain level of intellect. For example, if one has to explain to a child who has created this world, it is perhaps simpler to state that God has made it. And then when the child asks where is God, it is more relieving to say that He is on the top of the sky than explain why he cannot see Him. And when the child asks pointing to sky, where is God in the sky, it is simplest to answer that He is above the 4th or 7th sky and hence we cannot see Him. When someone asks what happens after death, the easiest answer is to tell him to perform good actions so that God would send you paradise.

The devotees belonging to the ISKCON suggest that all the Muslims who can have access to the Srimad Bhagavad Geeta should have the tolerance to read it impartially without any pre-conceived notion against Hinduism. It will definitely turn them into good tolerant human beings. It is distressing that most Muslims believe that it is a sin to even touch the holy books of other religions. All the religious texts are the same. They preach same thing. We pray to God in different ways. Hinduism sees God in a human form, Islam does not see Him in a human form. Remember the supreme master God has taken various forms in this universe and in accordance with the religion to instil one thing– the discipline in life.

The Christianity and Islam claim that only they are the real ones. But actually only *Sanatan Dharma,* also named as Hinduism later, is the true form of worshipping and coming closer to God. '*Sanatan Dharma*' is not a religion indeed, as religions are created only by human beings, not by God Himself. To prove that point it may be noted that only *Sanatan Dharma* is a special form of religion suggesting ways of coming closer to God through the process of rebirth (the doctrine of 'rebirth' implies movement of human beings from imperfection to perfection through rebirths in due course). Both Islam and Christianity do not believe in rebirth and they reject it because their religions are just directed by any man rather than by God himself. The theory of rebirth has been proved now and several cases of rebirth have been reported and it's only *Sanatan Dharma* which has mentioned about rebirth in the Bhagavad Geeta.

Sociologically speaking, no religion is greater or smaller than others. They all are equal. There were many Muslims who spent their entire life in the *Bhakti* of Sri Krishna. One of the examples is the poet Raskhan (born 1548 A.D.), a great devotee of Krishna and in his Bhakti he composed beautiful poems relating to Sri Krishna and he was said to have His *Sakshatkar* also. We should also not forget about Akbar who was a great believer in the teachings of Meerabai and Shri Swami Haridas. There are numerous such examples of Muslim believers in Sri Krishna. Among the Muslims the Sufi preachers had a deep understanding of the value of mysticism and the Krishna Bhakti. Whether one says Allah, Jesus, Krishna or any other names one's prayer reaches to the same personality– the Supreme One.

He also gave the direct path to reach Him and it can be practically seen in the daily lives of Krishna's devotees. They do not eat meat (who would give it up in this world of Kali), no illicit sex, no gambling, no intoxication (not even tea or coffee).The purpose of religion is not mass conversions or distributing identities to people. Its true purpose is to change the consciousness of people. Its purpose is to elevate our thinking so that we may realize things beyond our identities and gross bodies and attain higher consciousness and unite with Him by serving Him.

By the way Krishna was born more than 5000 years ago and Vashnavism is still older than that. Therefore, there is no doubt in my mind that Hinduism has influenced all major religions of this world. Most knowledgeable people accept the fact that Sanskrit has influenced all major languages of the world and Hinduism must have been the reason. The purpose of Krishna coming down on this earth was to teach us how to love Him and reach His Kingdom.

The symptoms of devotion are the same no matter what your religious background is. What are the symptoms: Gopis always absorbed their consciousness in Krishna, they fulfilled their duties and were always happy. Check yourself how devoted are you to your God. If your religion restricts you to learn about God and who He is, it is not doing any good to you. There is no harm to learn from each other when the goal of life is the same.

Lots of misconceptions are on all sides. Those practising intolerance in the name of Islam are the biggest Kafirs, the Prophet (*sallahu alaihi wasallam*) had predicted the rise of these *khawarij* at the end of days. Islam is an open door religion and daily countless people leave it and enter it because this is Allah's wish. We frequently hear of apostasy punishments from places like Pakistan and other Islamic countries, we need to ask are these more caused by our primitive or tribal customs of the Subcontinent/Central-Asia region.

Krishna is the supreme personality of godhead and when He appears on this earth He does not remain an ordinary person, but a person who is ignorant thinks that Krishna is an ordinary person. Within the Hindu system one must remember that there are various levels of *Avatars* and also Rishis who come for various purposes. For example, Buddha preached atheism, but came at a time to do so when Hinduism had become corrupt. But, that is not to say all Hindus today should misinterpret *Ahinsa*, as Krishna himself states we should take up arms to defend Dharma if required (but not unnecessarily kill for food or invade other nations for the sake of it). We also note that Dayanand Saraswati, the founder of Arya Samaj, came when Islam and Christianity were threatening Hinduism through coercive conversion and demolition of temples, and promoted the true Vedic philosophy and thereby restored the Vedic rituals and chanting of Gayatri, etc.

Guru Govind Singh of Sikh religion also created a movement whereby Sikhs gained greater powers of the Kshatriya or warrior caste to fight invaders and plunderers, and wore turban, bangle, beard, etc. ('five k's'), which were relevant at that time in history but not valid today, as Buddha's doctrine and Arya Samaj. Likewise, Muhammad appeared at such a time of decline in human values in the Arab world and likewise preached a doctrine to bring people back to their senses. Unfortunately, the words of such distinguished people are misinterpreted if taken too literally and not in a yogic or metaphoric or symbolic manner at times also. Some verses of the Geeta also favoured war, as it was the necessity of time (like Mahabharat war served a purpose), but it doesn't mean we should invade others.

If all religions have got the same God, then why are there contradictions? Why does God clearly say in one book that there's no image of Him and attributing any image to Him is a major sin, but in the other book He says He is Krishna and He has an image and not only that there are so many authentic forms of Him (deities) each one with a different physical image. Why does God give contradicting messages to His followers? No wonder Hinduism is far older than Islam, but in the Koran God has clearly said that this is my last and final message and with this Islamic religion is complete. Then isn't it necessary that we follow what is written in the Koran? Why should one follow when there are contradictions with earlier scriptures? But remember that the Koran is one of the revised versions of a part of Hindu religion and it was a pure human creation. No religious scripture has been ever handed down by God to human being. Why should almighty God bother to do that?

In which part of the Bhagavad Geeta, the image of Sri Krishna has been described? The image of Sri Krishna that is worshipped by his devotees, from where was that image obtained? And in which scripture and in which verse different forms of God and their appearance have been mentioned? How many such authentic forms are there? Which are all those? Where have they been mentioned? These are the questions often posed by those who do not believe in the Geeta, although it has offered an exhaustive reply to all these and many more such questions for those who study the Geeta with sincerity and understanding.

Islam was preached by Prophet Mohammed during the time when there was a lot of bloodshed, robbery, loot, rape, alcoholism and injustice in the Arab world and so he gave various rules to lead a pious life which were appropriate to those people at that point of time. They were so sinful and aberrant that they couldn't follow any austerities. They couldn't control their sexual desires. So the Prophet favoured polygamy and thus right to have sexual relationships with more than one woman.

The most devotees of the Hare Krishna have read all the Holy books – Koran, Bible, Bhagavad Geeta and everything. They don't say other holy books are wrong. Everything is correct. It's just the level of understanding of God which differs in each. The Vedas and the Srimad Bhagavad Geeta give a greater amount of information about God than any other scriptures because they were spoken by God Himself unlike the messengers or Son of God in other scriptures. Of course the Holy book teaches right things but people go in a wrong way because they do not have complete knowledge. As rightly said, half knowledge is always dangerous.

Religious Tolerance

Hinduism has stood for the philosophy of brotherhood of mankind. It has never gone anywhere for religious conversion. It is the only religion with wide exits. Millions and millions of people have gone to Buddhism, Jainism, Islam, Christianity, Sikhism and many other minor religious faiths over the years and yet it has survived for the longest period of human history because of religious tolerance, dynamism and the notion of brotherhood of mankind. No religion has ever received more jolts and jerks than Hinduism from the external forces and internal contradictions. It has survived because it has developed as a way of life over a thousand years without having any state patronage or sponsorship of any prophet. Hinduism never has been a monolithic religion like others. Whatever the little fanaticism that has cropped up among Hindus in recent years has come solely from other religions as a compulsive reaction to defend themselves for their survival. Following the philosophy of Hindu religion, Swami Vivekananda in his lectures at Chicago starting from 11 September 1893 gave a call for Universal Brotherhood. He said that the man on this earth has continued too long to be fanatic about insisting that his religion alone was true and other religions being false had no right to exist. He also stressed that as long as this situation persists there can be only bloodshed in the name of religion and no brotherhood which, the practice of religion should actually bring about, would be possible.

Economic hardships, among other factors, made a band of people a martial community for their survival. They had to fight for the basic necessities of life, since life in the desert or hilly region was too hard to imagine those days. They struggled in a barbaric manner to secure and safeguard food, water and shelter and thus expanded their empire. All this forced them to lead a collective life with swords in their hands. Thus they had enough success to expand over a large part of the world. A large family size of polygamous nature with dominant patriarchal value system and uncontrolled fertility with a strong sense of community consciousness were the necessities of time. Had there been no development of science and technology in the Western world, especially in the field of warfare technology, Muslims would have succeeded in capturing the whole world by now. The instinct of struggle for existence followed by survival of the fittest over the years has made Muslims combatant for their ideological dominance through terrorism. According to some, Islamic terrorism is linked to the practice of divinely sanctioned warfare against apostates. Now terrorism has become a powerful tool of assertion of their dominance. For a Muslim, religion does not have much individual significance in society same as Hindu or Buddhist. Their worry has always been of pure collective nature. They do not believe in individual meditation like Hindus and Buddhists. Although there is no threat to Islam, terrorists and a section of politicians have become self-appointed guardians or custodians of Islam. Hence, any loss of life for the sake of Islam of their conception is of no consequence. Therefore, Islam and peace are not compatible in the contemporary world. Theocraticism or autocratism commonly happens to be the preferred system of governance in a Muslim dominated society. Religion has always received state patronage. This was the main reason why the mosque was built either on the site of Hindu temple or the near the temple as a parallel religion in India until 19th century.

Muslims hardly ever collectively oppose terrorism and violence in India. Islamophobia is gradually on the rise. At present though it appears that fanaticism and terrorism is engulfing the whole world, actually it is like the flame that flickers the brightest before getting extinguished. On 11 September 1893 at Chicago (USA) in Parliament of religions Swami Vivekananda had said that, "Sectarianism, bigotry, and its horrible descendants, fanaticism, have long possessed this beautiful earth. They have filled this earth with violence, drenched it often and often with human blood, destroyed civilization and sent whole nations to despair. Had it not been for these possible demons, human society would be far more advanced than it is now? But their time has come…".

A long time back the **Bhavishya Puran** made a prophecy that one day Raja Bhoj would take rebirth as a great religious leader and bring forth a clan of terrible people who would do exactly opposite to Dharma. Islam, however, does not believe in the doctrine of rebirth. Some people say that Allah remains the sole deity in a perpetual state of enmity with the false gods of others. This has led to animosity among Muslims for their own non-Islamic period of history and also for the ancient gods which adorned the Kaaba, iconoclasm; animosity towards non-Muslims. What more can be said? One can often hear a Muslim stating the fact that Islam believes in peace, tolerance, etc. One can also say that you have not read or understood the true teachings of the Koran. It can also be said by a Muslim friend that you have been reading anti-Islamic propaganda. Maybe partially true, but what my question is: Why does truth become the first victim when religious emotion is aroused? When religious passions are stirred, truth is the first victim. We are all set up to defend what is wrong because it is a part of our religion. In fact, this happens with all religions.

The study of history suggests that Islam as a faith is said to have given nothing worthwhile to the humanity. Ever since its inception, Islam seems to have bred a creed of fanatics and killers. As a secular person one feels it is one's duty to differentiate between good and evil. While the Koran might have a few good things written in it, on the whole it also comprises hatred for those who don't call themselves Muslims and don't submit to the Islamic faith. Yet it is hard to give support to the view that Islam has ever stood for violence or blood-bath, since Muhammad himself was a very gracious and peace loving person. He was a true Messenger of Peace. What has been wrong with Islam of either yesterday or today is that lots of wrong people have rallied around Islam to further their own interests in the name of religion. Such narrow-minded followers of Islam have done or are doing more harms than good to their religion, definitely more than even non-Islamic people or pagans, tarnishing the image of Islam. At some later stage certain Islamic scholars with some vested interests, same as other religious scriptures, have inserted some hard-headed ideas incompatible with those of Prophet Muhammad into the religious scriptures of Islam.

The sense of intolerance in the present day Islam runs very high. Islam prescribes death penalty for anyone who ceases to be a Muslim. This helps secure observance. Not a day goes without some Islamic terrorists bombing and killing of innocent people or butchering in some part of the world. Pakistan vs. Afghanistan, Iran vs. Iraq, Kuwait vs. Iraq, Syria Shias vs. Syria Sunnis, Syria vs. Iraq, Syria vs. Lebanon, Yemen vs. Saudi, Somalia vs. Sudan, all Islamic countries are against each other, though they follow the same Koran.

Muslims, including those who have turned leftist, have to offer *Namaz or Salat* every day at least once, if not set five times a day. If health permits, they must assemble at some mosque at least once on every Friday, especially near their habitation or workplace. At the mosque they often tend to occupy such public places as lanes, roads, open fields to show off commitment to their religious faith and social solidarity through the acts of mass prayer. There cannot be a Muslim who has not visited mosque in his life. While there are numerous such Hindus or Christians who do not worship everyday as a matter of routine. In fact, most Hindus do not offer puja at home or outside everyday as a part of their daily routine. They worship God or goddess only when they are in a deep distress or on the occasion of marriage ceremonies and *Shraddha* (performance of rituals relating to death) of their kins. There cannot be educated Muslims who have not read Koran, but most educated Hindus are so casual towards their religion that they have not even seen the Vedas or the Geeta, although they might have same reverence for their holy books. Hindus can be openly *Nastik*, but a *Nastik* Muslim is ridiculous and unthinkable. Many Hindus freely visit mosque or tombs (*Dargah* or *Maqbara*) of Muslims for offering puja or getting blessings of some Muslim *Peer Baba* or *Fakirs*, while Muslims do not visit Hindu temples out of reverence for the sacred places of other religions. Rather, they consciously avoid such an act to show untainted loyalty to their religion. The lower caste people or the people lower in hierarchy of social order remain much less committed to their religions. In fact, many lower caste people have developed hatred against the Hindu religion. This has been but natural because the Brahmins have always kept them outside the Hindu fold, for they are treated as untouchables and yet they are Hindus. While in Islam everybody is equal, at least theoretically. Here one can easily understand the reason for Hindus being relatively more liberal in their attitude than others.

Religions in Practice

It is always said very loudly that all religions teach the basic human values of brotherhood of mankind, peace and harmony and special care for the destitute or the deprived. But when we look at different religions in theory and practice in their historical perspective, we come across a huge gap between the precept and practice. In fact, all look more or less the same, but they differ quite substantially with respect to the degree of gaps between theory and practice. For instance, it is said that Islam is a religion of mercy and so it does not permit terrorism. But in practice Islamic cleric like Zakir Naik who has absconded from India to evade legal action, on the other hand, publicly preached umpteen number of times that every Muslim should be terrorist. In fact there are numerous such Zakir Naiks in the Islamic world. In the Koran, God has said: God does not forbid you from showing kindness and dealing justly with those who have not fought you about religion and have not driven you out of your homes. God loves just dealers (Koran, 60:8). Different clerics tend to deduce the meaning of the same verse differently. This is, however, unfortunately true of most religions of the world.

Prophet Muhammad used to prohibit soldiers from killing women and children, and he would advise them: "...Do not betray, do not be excessive, do not kill a newborn child." And he also said: "Whoever has killed a person having a treaty with the Muslims shall not smell the fragrance of Paradise, though its fragrance is found for a span of forty years." Also, Prophet Muhammad has forbidden punishment with fire. He once listed murder as the second of the major sins, and he even warned that on the Day of Judgement (the first cases to be adjudicated between people on the Day of Judgement will be those of bloodshed.)

Muslims are even encouraged to be kind to animals and are forbidden to hurt them. Once Prophet Muhammad said: "A woman was punished because she imprisoned a cat until it died. On account of this, she was doomed to Hell. While she imprisoned it, she did not give the cat food or drink, nor did she free it to eat the insects of the earth." He also said that a man gave a very thirsty dog a drink, so God forgave his sins for this action. He said: "There is a reward for kindness to every living animal or human." Additionally, while taking the life of an animal for food, Muslims are commanded to do so in a manner that causes the least amount of fright and suffering possible. The Prophet said: "When you slaughter an animal, do so in the best way. One should sharpen his knife to reduce the suffering of the animal."

In the light of these and other Islamic texts, the act of inciting terror in the hearts of defenceless civilians, the wholesale destruction of buildings and properties, the bombing and maiming of innocent men, women and children are all forbidden and detestable acts according to the Koran. Muslims follow a religion of peace, mercy and forgiveness, and the vast majority have got nothing to do with the violent acts regardless of the fact that some are associated with Muslims. If an individual Muslim were to commit an act of terrorism, he would be guilty of violating the laws of Islam.

It is rightly said that Islam propagates peace. Islam means submission before the almighty. It is not submission to terrorism. All acts of terror are anti-Islam and anti-Jehad. Islam symbolises the security of life and property, protection of honour and the right to protest against tyranny towards men, women and children. God is most pleased when He sees that humanity is involved in mutual co-operation and harmonious co-existence. But on other hand, a large number of sensible people, who stand for the above views about Islam, remain passive or act as silent spectators, when some members of their community try to be aggressive or violent or coercively try to convert the people of other faiths, destroy shrines and idols of other religions and indulge in mass slaughter in the name of religion. This is the prime reason why Islam is often judged by what their most debased, fanatical and intolerant followers do.

Now the question arises why has there been so much violence in the life of Muslims ever since the inception of this religion without any sign of abatement in the modern world? There seems to be a huge gap between the preachings and practice of the Koran. Those who perpetrate crime or violence against the innocent, defenceless and unarmed, they also quote the same holy Koran to justify their acts. Those who oppose violence, they also quote Koran to plead that Islam is a peace-loving religion. This is a really a kind of enigma not only for the non-Muslims but also for those Muslims who are devout and intelligentsia. The Islamic State is difficult to comprehend. It is false that Jehadism has nothing to do with Islam; but that does not mean that Islam is nothing but Jehadism. The vast majority of Muslims do not favour terrorism.

The Islamic State is 'Islamic'. Jehadists use Islamic rhetoric, symbols and concepts in the construction of their ideology. They endlessly debate fine intricacies of Islamic theology. They direct their arguments at the Muslim audience and seek new recruits from among Muslims. They invoke the Koran, quote the Hadith of Muhammad, and find bases for their beliefs in the jurisprudence of Islamic law. They claim to be Muslims– indeed, the only true Muslims– and they explicitly claim that their religion motivates, inspires and even commands them to commit their horrific acts of violence. They believe that Islam has a great deal to do with their behaviour. Some scholars have argued that the clash between rival interpretations of Islam should be seen as a civil war within the Islamic world– Jehadists, Islamists, traditionalists and reformers all attempting to pull Islam in different directions– in which case Jehadism most certainly has a strong, complicated and important relationship to Islam and its future. Over the years, the Al Qaeda has committed countless terrorist acts killing many innocent men, women and children. It was responsible for the September 11, 2001 suicide terrorist attacks on New York's World Trade Centre and the Pentagon, which murdered close to 3,000 people without any provocation. On August 7, 1998, the Al Qaeda terrorists almost simultaneously set off bombs 150 miles apart at the US Embassies in the East African countries of Kenya and Tanzania. The blasts killed 12 Americans and about 250 Africans, most of them Muslims. On May 12, 2003, the Al Qaeda suicide terrorists set off bombs in three housing compounds in the capital of Saudi Arabia. The bombs killed 35 people, including 12 Americans.

There are other terrorist groups, often linked to the Al Qaeda, have been responsible for attacks around the globe. Bombings in the underground subway in London in 2005 killed 56 people, and shootings and bombings in the Indian city of Mumbai in 2008 resulted in over 160 deaths. A bomber attempted to set off a car bomb in New York City's Times Square in 2010.

In a 1998 interview, Osama bin Laden called Americans "the worst thieves in the world today and the worst terrorists ... ." He went on to say that, "We do not have to differentiate between military or civilian. As far as we are concerned, they are all targets." He justified targeting Americans in the name of Islam. He said: "The terrorism we practice is of the commendable kind for it is directed at the tyrants and the aggressors and the enemies of God . . .".

On 15th April 2015, 150 people were killed in Kenya in a university college by Islamist for not being Muslims! Over 2000 were massacred in Nigeria by Boko Haram in January 2015. In 2014 more than 10,000 were killed by Boko Harem in Nigeria. The Tunisia killing of 41 people in June 2015, Kuwait Mosque bombing killing 45 people on 30th May 2015 and Saudi Mosque bombing killing 21 people are only very few instances. According to the UN, the ISIS has killed 15,000 people in Iraq alone as on 14 July 2015 and on 18/7/2015 on Eid day, the ISIS slaughtered 150 Iraqis' in a bomb blast. These are just a few examples, yet Islam is professed to be a religion of Peace!

The genocide carried out by West Pakistan led to the extermination of close to 3 million (30 Lakh) people, along with the forced rape of a quarter of a million (2.5 Lakh) young girls and women. In most Islamic countries the women do not like to report the incidence of rape because they are jailed and oppressed under a *burqa* inside the four walls of their house. Women are treated worse so they avoid lodging any complaint. Hence the statistics of rape relating to the Islamic world are far from truth.

The militant Muslims consider Hindu dominated India as 'an unfinished chapter of Islamic conquests'. It may be recalled that all other countries conquered by Islam got fully converted to Islam within two decades of the Islamic invasion. India is an exception. Undivided India in 1947 had 75 percent Hindus even after 800 years of brutal Islamic rule. That is jarring for the Islamic fanatics.

Let us remember that every Hindu-Muslim riot in India since 1947 has been ignited by Muslim fanatics– if one goes by all the Commissions of Inquiry set up after every riot. Even the Gujarat riots were triggered by the brutal killing of 56 women and children by setting fire to a rail coach in Godhara.

By today's definition these riots are all terrorist acts. Muslims, though a minority in India, still have extremists who dare to lead violent attacks on Hindus. Other Muslims of India just lump it, sulk or rejoice. That is the history from Babur's time to Aurangzeb. In modern times it has touched all sections of society because of massive spread of education, media of mass communication and grass-roots politicization for electoral purposes. Violence creates a chain of counter violence without any sign of its abetment in near future. Politics of minority communalism is openly pursued by socialist, leftist and so-called secularists to serve the electoral ends of different political parties. If there is anything like majority communalism or Hindu communalism, it is the natural after-effects of minority communalism. Both Muslims and Hindus, especially so-called secular ones, are liable for politics of minority communalism in India. Lots of politicians often speak of words like 'Hindu communalism' to cover up the rise in Islamic terrorism for pure political reasons. Before the emergence of Islam in India there was no trace of communalism or sectarianism of any kind in the Indian Sub-continent.

Numerous religious leaders of the Muslim community openly preach hatred and violence against the *Kafir*, i.e, the Hindu (for example read Chapter 8 verse 12 of the Koran) to keep up the faith of their followers. Taking full advantage of the constitutional right to freedom of religion a well-known preacher of Islamic fundamentalism from India, Zakir Naik, citing the verses of Koran, openly and actively preached violence through his channel called Peace TV until 2016 and suggested that every Muslim should be terrorist for the sake of Islam. The global scenario of violence suggests that Islam is not a 'religion of peace.' The Islamic terrorist outfits, e.g., the SIMI, have already resolved that India is Darul Harab, and they are committed to make it Darul Islam. That makes them free of any moral compunction whatsoever in dealing with Hindus. The fastest growing Muslims who constitute about 23 percent of the total world population and numerically they dominate in 50 countries of the world and in most of these countries Islam is the state religion. India has got the largest number of Muslim population (about 14 percent of the total population, roughly 172 million people) and yet they claim and defend minority status for pure political reasons. In recent years because of hostile religious policy of Islam, terrorism or violence has become an order of the day and urban living so tense and dreadful across the countries. In fact, terrorist attacks have escalated worldwide since the beginning of 21st century. According to a U.S. State Department report, India topped the list of countries most affected by Islamic terrorism. The historic rivalry between Hindus and Muslims in the Indian subcontinent has also often been the primary motive behind some of the most deadly terrorist attacks in India.

Religion powerfully intermixes with politics in all societies of the world, including India– whether it is the religion of Hinduism, Islam or some others. That Islam has become entwined with the politics of countries in which it predominates is unsurprising, and, naturally, has given rise to attempts to construct a coherent political ideology along Islamic lines– what is broadly called '*Islamism.*' (Islamism is the transmutation of Islam into a political ideology. *Jehadism* is a variant of Islamism.) It is the effort to impose Islamist goals– however defined– by force. Jehadists have found or invented theological justifications to attack their enemies. Jehadist ideology ultimately seeks the dominance of its brand of Islam over the world. The religion which was once predominantly controlled by the priestly class has steadily slipped into the hands of people who are the least religious of men. Consequently the same has become true of other religions like Sikhism and Hinduism as well. Both religion and politics have wrongly taken a common cover for their shelter or survival which may prove detrimental for the both of them in the long run.

Can anybody justify the blast on a London underground train at Parsons Green tube station which left many innocent passengers dead and injured on 15th September 2017? Did the English cause any damage to Islam by electing a Muslim, Mr Sadiq Khan, to the post of the Mayor of London? Still more recently on 30 October 2017, 8 innocent people were killed and 12 more injured in a deadliest attack on New York since September 11, 2001 by a person named Sayfullo Saipov with allegiance to the Islamic State. With the help of a truck he smashed into a school bus and jumped out of it and ran up and down the highway waving a pellet gun and paintball gun, shouting a slogan like '*Allahau Akbar*' which means God is great in Arabic. There have occurred numerous such other blasts in Europe, USA, India and many other Islamic countries in the name of religion. Most recently in a neighbouring South Asian country of Afghanistan on 27th January 2018 the Taliban drove an ambulance packed with explosives into a crowded Kabul street near the Indian Embassy, setting off an enormous blast that killed at least 95 people and injured 158 others, adding to the grim toll in what has been one of the most violent stretches of the long war. The attack came days after a 15-hour siege by militants at the Intercontinental Hotel in Kabul that left 22 dead, including 14 foreigners. We cannot imagine how many more such incidences are going to take place for the sake of Islam. What damage has been done to Islam to cause irreparable damages to peace and prosperity of the humanity at large? Why is religion or its so-called redeemers so thirsty of blood? Since nobody knows the correct or appropriate answer, carnage in the name of religion is continuing without any sign of abatement across the globe.

Muslims not only hate Hindus, Sikhs or Christians, they also hate the Buddhists who constitute mere one percent of the total population of India. For example, without any aggravation from the peace-loving local Buddhists a series of ten bombs exploded in and around the Mahabodhi Temple complex, a UNESCO World Heritage Site in Bodh Gaya (Bihar) on 7 July 2013. Five people, including two Buddhist monks, were injured in the blasts. On the basis of confirmed evidence the National Investigation Agency announced that the Indian Mujahideen was responsible for the bombings. It was a pure senseless act of violence targeting innocent pilgrims and monks who had gathered to worship at this temple dedicated to the great apostle of peace—Gautam Buddha.

Islam has been highly intolerant not only of other faiths but also of moderate and forward-looking people of its own society. It is clearly evident from the recent Aasia Bibi (Aasiya Noreen, better known as Aasia Bibi) blasphemy case which involved a 47-year-old Pakistani Christian mother of four who was convicted of blasphemy by a Pakistani court, facing a sentence of death by hanging in 2010. When she was finally acquitted of the charges by the Supreme Court of Pakistan in a landmark verdict on 31 October 2018, thousands of radical Islamist hardliners flocked on the road protesting against her acquittal. The crowd of fanatics was pressing for her hanging, as she reportedly committed an offence of blasphemy by uttering something against Mohammad Prophet. It is good that some foreign countries soon offered her asylum on the humanitarian ground, but according to the deal between the Government and radical Islamist hardliners she is barred to leave the country. So we do not know what would happen to Aasia Bibi and her legal counsel. The case of blasphemy in brief was thus: In June 2009, Noreen was involved in an argument with a group of Muslim women with whom she had been harvesting berries. The argument began after the other Muslim women objected to a non-Muslim touching the bowl in which she fetched water, referencing the caste system in Pakistan. She was subsequently accused of insulting the Islamic prophet Muhammad, a charge she denied; she was arrested and imprisoned. In November 2010, a Sheikhupura judge sentenced her to death by hanging. It is very sad that the system of religious belief tends to swallow up the elements of scholarship, rational thinking, modernity and liberalism even in 21st century world.

None can ever dare to match internationally notorious terrorists, both dead and alive, to name a very few, like Osama bin Laden, Atiyah Abd al-Rahman, Ayman al-Zawahiri and Abu Yahya al-Libi of al-Qaeda; Jehadi Abu Bakr al-Baghdadi, Abu Fatima al-Jaheishi, Abu Saleh al-Obaidi of Islamic State of Iraq and Syria (ISIS); Syed Salahuddin of Hizbul Mujahideen; Taliwani terrorists like Mohammed Omar, Mullah Akhtar Mansour, Hibatullah Akhundzada and Mullah Muhammad Rasul; Mawlawi Jalaluddin Haqqani of the Haqqani network; Jehadist Maulana Masood Azhar of Jaish-e-Mohammed; and Hafiz Muhammad Saeed of Lashkar-e-Taiba. This is a very limited list of top terrorists. It is very hard to ascertain the actual number of terrorists active all over the world because of clandestine nature of their activity. Tariq Yusuf, an American Muslim, made an estimate of active members of some terrorist organizations in 2016 where he had given a rough estimate of about 106,000 individuals. Radical Islamic terrorists have started endless bloody war in the name of Islam, but the question as to what has happened to Islam that it needs their assistance or backing, is not really understandable to many of us, especially when there is no perceptible threat to Islam as a religion from any corner.

Assume that there are one hundred million Muslims worldwide who would count themselves as believers, supporters, fellow-travellers, fund-raisers, or sympathizers with Jehadism, people who would actively give their time, money, and effort to supporting active Jehadists. That still leaves 94 percent of the world's Muslims who neither participate in nor even sympathize with terrorism. Nearly all Muslims aren't Jehadists. According to a survey done in 2013 (poll by the Pew Research Center, USA), 'Muslims around the world strongly reject violence in the name of Islam,' including overwhelming majorities that reject suicide-bombing, a good proxy measure for support for terrorism. By any reasonable measure, Muslims are not terrorists. This view is, however, not readily acceptable to all. Specific passages in the Koran, Hadith attributed to Muhammad, and much of early Islamic history support the idea that Islam is inherently violent, intolerant, hostile, expansionist and aggressive. If 99.5 percent of Muslims in the world are not terrorists, that's because they are bad Muslims. In this view, the Islamic State is the true embodiment of what Islam actually is, and what all Muslims might become if they woke up to the true calling of their faith. I doubt we have the ability to make accurate judgements about the supposed essence of Islam. There is no single thing called 'Islam' captured once and for all time in the Koran. 'Islam' is a lived religion as much as it is a body of theology.The meaning of Islamic theology and Koranic passages changes across time and culture, as it is interpreted and lived by different people in different times and places. How those 1.6 billion Muslims live should be the key to our interpretation of those doctrines and ancient texts. Dreadfulness of the scenario created by the radical Islamic terrorists cannot be fully grasped by those who have not experienced it directly. I have a humble suggestion to make here that a perusal of the Srimad Bhagavad Geeta, even if reviled for some reason, would surely help the people on the war path in the name of religion. It would restore peace and happiness in the life of people of all kind, as it inculcates a sense of morality in the life of people. Whenever in crisis or in a state of confusion Mahatma Gandhi, one of the greatest champions of politics of non-violence of the modern world, has already tried and tested the messages of the Geeta. It worked with him, as he was a man with pious intension.

OM TAT SAT

Chapter - 5

The Systems of Indian Philosophy

If a person intends to understand the Geeta, s/he should have some background of different schools of philosophical thoughts of India. The Geeta is imbued with complex philosophical thoughts. Indian philosophy refers to any of the several traditions of philosophical thought that originated in the Indian subcontinent, including Hindu philosophy, Buddhist philosophy and Jain philosophy. It is considered by Indian thinkers to be a practical discipline, and its goal should always be to improve human life. Situation in which the plot for the Geeta was created was intensely social, more particularly highly familial, but the ideas conveyed were highly abstract and philosophical. Hence, there is a necessity of briefly elaborating the salient characteristics of different schools of Indian philosophy here.

It usually happens that once the basic necessities of life are fulfilled the human being generally starts thinking— what the purpose and meaning of life is? The result of such an inquiry over a long period of time is philosophy. The Indian mystics found the answers to many such questions by undertaking their search within oneself rather than outside. They went to the extent of experiencing such results of their inquiry which gave them an intuitive capability to acquire a clearer and deeper understanding of the meaning and goal of human life. It is because of this special perception that their thoughts are called '*Darshan*' in Sanskrit which actually means direct vision or realization of the self or soul. The word *Darshan* symbolizes the difference between modern Western philosophy and Indian philosophy in English. Western philosophy mainly relies on an intellectual pursuit, while Indian philosophy relies on a direct vision of truth and pure *Buddhi* (reasoning). These illuminating thoughts of the seers came to be popularly known as the systems of Indian philosophy. Indian philosophy is inward looking and aims to help human beings deal with ups and downs of life with the goal of self-realization.

All the *Darshanas* or systems of philosophy discovered that in spite of all the best efforts put in by man; his life has got more miseries than bliss. Hence finding out the means to escape from the clutches of grief and despair of human existence once and for all became the main goal of their endeavours. Here the Geeta becomes the most relevant for the mankind. It is because of the presence of various schools of thought that there is a variety of commentaries on the Geeta. Keeping these facts in view a brief introduction of various Indian philosophies is presented here.

The ageless and dateless Vedas, especially the exalted hymns of the Rigved, have long been esteemed as the direct expression of what gods and divine seers, *rishis* or immortal sages, saw when they peered into the imperishable centre of Being which is also the origin of the entire cosmos. The Upanishads (from *upa, ni* and *sad*, meaning 'to sit down near' a sage or *guru*), included in the Vedas, constitute the highest transmission of the fruits of illumination attained by these *rishis*. Often cast in the form of memorable dialogues between spiritual teachers and disciples, they represent rich glimpses of truth, not pieced together from disparate intellectual insights, but as they are at once revealed to the divine eye, *Divya Chakshu*, which looks into the core of Reality, freely intimated in idioms, metaphors and *Mantras* suited to the awakening, consciousness and spiritual potentials of diverse disciples. However, divergent their modes of expression, they are all addressed to those who are ready to learn, willing to meditate deeply, and seek greater self-knowledge through intensive self-questioning. The Upanishads do not purport to provide discursive knowledge, conceptual clarification or speculative dogmas, rather focus on the fundamental themes which concern the soul as a calm spectator of the temporal succession of states of mind from birth to death, seeking for what is essential amidst the ephemeral, the enduring within the transient, the abiding universals behind the flux of fleeting appearances.

Since the Vedas are the oldest religious scriptures of the world, they are definitely the mother of all major religions of the world. One can always find some elements or attributes of the Vedic philosophy in different religions. One cannot conceive of a religion completely devoid of the tenets of the Vedas. The Hindu philosophy is so vast and varied that it has worked as a fountainhead of all religions through the process of acculturation. Ideas which are similar to those of Hindu religion in the Bible or the Koran were borrowed from the Vedic literature since Hindu religion is the oldest surviving religion. Hinduism developed independently and steadily as a system of thought and practice over a long period of time. Some fundamentalists or obscurantists of other religions may not like this observation because of their age-old hostility against Hindu religion. The Vedas would always remain the earliest work on religion. Had there been no Vedas, Charvakism, Jainism and Buddhism would not have originated. Even secular philosophy or negation of religion itself is in a way a byproduct of the Vedic philosophy.

The Upanishads

Directly or indirectly all the Indian philosophies have developed either in agreement or disagreement, wholly or partly, with the Upanishadic philosophy, so we must make the readers familiar with the Upanishads first. Even chronologically speaking the Upanishads came into being before the development of any system of Indian philosophy. The Upanishads, a part of the Vedas, are ancient Sanskrit texts that contain some of the central philosophical concepts and ideas of Hinduism. They are a collection of texts of religious and philosophical nature, written in India probably between c. 800 BCE and c. 500 BCE, during a time when Indian society started to question the traditional Vedic religious order. A brief discussion on Upanishads is necessary for all those who are not much familiar with the scriptures of Hindu religion and Indian philosophy. Very little is known today about the pre-Vedic literature or human history before 5000 BCE. But that needn't mean that those were the times of stone-age cave dwellers.

The Upanishads are a collection of texts of religious and philosophical nature, collated in India probably between c. 800 BCE and c. 500 BCE, during a time when Indian society started to question the traditional Vedic religious order. They are among the most important literature in the history of Indian religions and culture, that played an important role in the development of spiritual ideas in ancient India and marked a transition from Vedic ritualism to new ideas and institutions. The Upanishads are commonly referred to as Vedant, variously interpreted to mean either the 'last chapters, parts of the Ved' or 'the object, the highest purpose of the Ved'. More than 200 Upanishads are known, of which the first dozen or so are the oldest and most important and are referred to as the principal or main (*mukhya*) Upanishads. The *mukhya* Upanishads are found mostly in the concluding part of the Brahmnas and Aranyakas and were, for centuries, memorized by each generation and passed down orally. The early Upanishads all predate the Common Era, five of them in all likelihood pre-Buddhist (6th century BCE), down to the Maurya period. Of the remainder, some 95 Upanishads are part of the Muktika canon, composed from about the last centuries of 1st-millennium BCE through about 15th-century CE. New Upanishads, beyond the 108 in the Muktika canon, continued to be composed through the early modern and modern era, though often dealing with subjects which are unconnected to the Vedas.

The Upanishads are referred to in the Bhagavad Geeta as 'the yog of knowledge'; their teachings were summarised around 450 AD in a text known as *Brahma Sutra*, sometimes attributed to Vyas and commented on by Adi Shankar around 700 AD, followed by the various other Vedant philosophers, possibly all of them of the Brahmin origin. The Brahmins kept the Vedas to themselves as long it was possible for them to do so. In 1656 the ill-fated Dara Shikoh, who shared the admiration for Hindus culture of his great-grandfather, the Emperor Akbar, had extensive portion of the Upanishads into Persian, believing them to the secret scriptures referred to by the Koran.

The concepts of Brahm (Ultimate Reality) and *Atman* (Soul, Self) are central ideas in all the Upanishads, and 'Know your *Atman*' their thematic focus. The Upanishads are the foundation of Hindu philosophical thought and its diverse traditions. Of the Vedic corpus, they alone are widely known, and the central ideas of the Upanishads are at the spiritual core of Hindus. Upanishads mark the beginning of a reasoned inquiry into a number of perennial philosophical questions concerning the nature of being, the nature of the self, the foundation of life, what happens to the self at the time of death, the good life, and ways of interacting with others. As such, the Upanishads are often considered to be the fountainhead of the subsequent rich and varied philosophical tradition in India. In addition to *Atman* and *Brahm,* the Upanishads contain some of the oldest discussions about key philosophical terms like *Karma, Yog, Sansar* (worldly existence), *Moksha* (enlightenment), *Purush* (person) and *Prakriti* (nature)– all of which would continue to be central to the philosophical vocabulary of later traditions. In addition to contributing to the development of a discursive language, the Upanishads further frame later philosophical debates by their exploration of a number of means of attaining knowledge, including deduction, comparison, introspection and debate.

Religion vs Philosophy

Before we begin our discussion on different kinds of Indian philosophy, it seems relevant to touch upon the basic difference between philosophy and religion briefly here. This is necessitated in the Indian context because the Indian philosophy is highly imbued with religious ideologies. The line between the two is so thin that sometime we do not know whether we are dealing with Indian philosophy or Hindu religion. Religion and philosophy are certainly intertwined and yet religion and philosophy are two different topics. Religion is all about customary practices and the system of belief and dogmas, whereas philosophy is largely about metaphysics. A religion preaches its followers what they should do, what they should not do. Often a religion presents rewards and punishments. An example is the belief that people who do good they go to the heaven, while those who commit sin they go to the hell. On the other hand, a philosophy searches and questions to get a true and logical answer. A philosophy does not accept everything as a religion does unless it has a logical reason behind it.

Religion— Religion is a belief; it has a set of code of conduct, principles, ethics and morals to follow in one's life. There are several religions in the world. It only means that people of the world follow different kinds of religion that frame different sets of principles, ethics, morals and codes of conduct to follow for the people that belong to them. Thus we have Christianity, Hinduism, Islam, Judaism, Sikhism, and Zoroastrianism to mention some of the religions of the world. Each of these religions prescribes a separate set of principles, ethics and morals along with customs to follow by the people of the particular religion. Religion insists on the performance of rituals. On the other hand, if we are religious we cannot do away with the performance of rituals and rites. They become part and parcel of our life.

Philosophy— Philosophy, on the other hand, speaks about the realization of the supreme truth. It deals with the topic of life after death. It speaks about the existence of the soul and life hereafter. Philosophy establishes the divine nature of man. It questions the absolute truth that each soul is potentially divine. This is philosophy associated with religion. Philosophy can also mean, according to the Oxford English dictionary, 'the study of the theoretical basis of a particular branch of knowledge or experience.' An example is the philosophy of science. While religion insists on the performance of rituals, philosophy does not emphasize the ritualistic aspect of life. Philosophy is, in fact, construed to be a way of thinking. This is the reason why philosophers are called as thinkers whereas propagators of religions are called preachers or leaders. If we are philosophical then we need not perform rituals and other rites connected with religion.

The following are the differences between religion and philosophy?

•Religion is a belief in a supreme power and worship of it as the creator and controller of the universe without reasoning, whereas philosophy is a pursuit of wisdom by intellectual search and logical reasoning.

•Philosophy of religion questions the very existence of the supreme power.

•Religions discipline the people through a set of code of conduct, principles and ethics, whereas philosophy relies on the moral self-discipline.

•Religion is all about practices and customs, whereas philosophy is all about metaphysics.

•Philosophers are called as thinkers, whereas propagators of religions are called preachers or leaders.

•Religion insists on the performance of rituals, whereas philosophy does not emphasize the ritualistic aspect of life.

This is the basic difference between religion and philosophy, but it cannot be said that religion and philosophy are mutually exclusive and they cannot co-exist. There is no need to further this discussion any more. Now we come to the brief discussion on *Shad-Darshan* as well as some other relevant philosophies of the Indian origin.

Kinds of Indian Philosophy

The Indian philosophical systems are classified following the fact whether a particular school of thought accepts the authority of the Vedas or not. The systems of Indian philosophy are classified into two major groups:

(1) The orthodox system (*Astik*)

(2) The unorthodox or heterodox system (*Nastik*)

These two divisions normally convey a division of thinkers into 'theist' and 'atheist' respectively. The orthodox systems are those which accept the authority of the Vedas, while the heterodox systems are those which reject it. The orthodox system includes *Vaisheshik, Nyaya, Sankhya, Yog, Poorva Mimansa and Uttar Mimansa*, while the unorthodox systems include *Charvakism, Jainism and Buddhism*. The reason why some schools of Darshan are regarded as 'orthodox' and others not has little or nothing to do with a belief in God. The real point of difference is whether or not a particular system of thought accepts the Vedas as the ultimate source of philosophical authority. Truly speaking, Vaisheshik, Nyaya, Sankhya and Yog are neither orthodox nor unorthodox.

Among the *Astikas*, the two oldest schools— Sankhya and Poorva Mimansa— strongly refute the theory of God. Thus, the source book for Sankhya philosophy, Ishwar Krishna's **Sankhya Karika**, is full of subtle arguments which reject the possibility of there being an all-powerful creator and controller of the world. Vigyan Bhikshu's

Sankhya Pravachan Bhashya makes a case for why a belief in the divine principle is unwarranted. Even Kapil's classic treatise on the subject, which is far less emphatic in its rejection of God, finds it unnecessary to accept any theistic assumption. Truly speaking, Vaisheshik, Nyaya, Sankhya and Yog are neither orthodox nor unorthodox. These four systems at the time of their origin neither accepted nor rejected the Vedas. The Sankhya philosophy together with *Yog, Nyaya, Vaisheshik, Mimansa* and Vedant nominally accepts the Ved as its guide. Jaimini's Mimansa makes no mention of God.

Although scholars have speculated on the sequential emergence of the *darshanas,* and though patterns of interplay can be discerned in their full flowering, their roots lie in the ancient texts and they arise together as distinctive standpoints. It has also been held that the six schools grew out of sixty-two systems of thought lost in the mists of antiquity. At any rate, it is generally agreed that each of the later six schools was inspired by a sage and teacher who struck the keynote which has reverberated throughout its growths refinement and elaboration. As the six schools are complementary to each other, they are traditionally viewed as the six branches of a single tree. All six provide a theoretical explanation of ultimate Reality and a practical means of emancipation. The oldest are Yog and Sankhya, the next being Vaishesika and Nyaya, and the last pair are Poorva Mimansa and Vedant (also called Uttar Mimansa).

The six *Darshan Shastras* are divided in the groups of two each based on their closely related texts, such as Nyaya and Vaisheshik are closely allied to each other. The next two Yog and Sankhaya are closed to each other, and finally the Poorva Mimansa and Uttar Mimansa are allied to each other. In each of the pairs, the first system is concerned with the practice and the second system focuses on the theoretical aspects. Each of these schools of philosophy differs in one way or the other in terms of its concepts, phenomena, laws and beliefs. Each philosophy has developed, systematised and correlated the various parts of the Vedas in its own way. Each system has its *Sutrakar*, i.e. the one great *Rishi* who systematised the doctrines of the school. They were the sages of very high order who devoted their whole life to the study and propagation of specific philosophy. The following are widely acknowledged as proponents of different schools of philosophy: Gautam for Nyaya, Kanad for Vaisheshik, Patanjali for Yog, Kapil for Sankhya, Jaimini for Poorva Mimansa and Vyas for Uttar Mimansa. Each system is called Darshan, thus the Sanskrit word '*Shad-Darshan*' refers to 'the six systems of Indian philosophy'. They generally deal with four topics: 1. Existence and nature of Brahm; 2. Nature of the *Jeev* or the individual soul; 3. Creation of the J*agat* or the world; and 4. *Moksha* or liberation and the disciplines that lead to it.

All of them propounded the tenets of their philosophical systems or schools in the form of short Sutras, whose elucidation required and stimulated elaborate commentaries. Since about 200 C.E., a vast crop of secondary works has emerged which has generated some significant discussions as well as a welter of scholastic disputation and didactic controversies, moving far away from praxis into the forests of theoria, or reducing praxis to rigid codes and theoria to sterile formulas. At the same time, there has remained a remarkable vitality to most of these schools, owing to their transmission by long lineages which have included many extraordinary teachers and exemplars. This cannot be recovered merely through the study of texts, however systematic and rigorous, in a philosophical tradition which is essentially oral, even though exceptional powers of accurate recall have been displayed in regard to the texts.

Indian thought has been concerned with various philosophical problems, significant among which are the nature of the world (cosmology), the nature of reality (metaphysics), logic, the nature of knowledge (epistemology), ethics and the philosophy of religion. Most of the schools of Hindu philosophy have existed side by side. Three basic concepts form the cornerstone of Indian philosophical thought: the self or soul (*Atman*), works (*Karma*) and liberation (*Moksha*). Leaving the Charvakism aside, all Indian philosophies concern themselves with these three concepts and their interrelations, though this is not to say that they accept the objective validity of these concepts in precisely the same manner. Charvakism is named after Charvak who pioneered this philosophy in reaction to the Vedic philosophy.

Despite the fact there are certain differences between different philosophies, there are some common characteristics as well. These are direct experience, acceptance of authority, harmony amongst schools, parallel growth and coexistence of a number of schools, open mindedness, support of logic and reasoning, belief of eternity, law of Karma, moral and ethical teachings, acknowledgement of suffering, thoroughness and practicality. Charvakism remarkably differs from other systems as it overwhelmingly supports materialism. The following characteristics are common to all other systems:

(1) All the schools emphasize that the philosophy must have a positive impact on the life of man. They have a general agreement on the importance of *Purusharth* in life. All the schools agree that the philosophy should help man in realizing the main ends of human life: the *Purusharthas*, i.e. *Arth, Dharma, Kam* and *Moksha*. (2) All the systems reflect that the philosophy should lead a man from darkness and ignorance to light and knowledge. (3) There is a general agreement among various systems of thinking that the truth and reality should be verifiable. They should be substantiated with reasoning and experience. An experience may be sensory, conceptual or intuitional. (4) It is accepted by all the schools that man's suffering results from his ignorance. Man can conquer ignorance and attain *Moksha* (liberation) in this bodily existence. (5) There is a general agreement on man's essential nature of spirituality. (6) The goal of each philosophy is to end human suffering. (7) The individual self acquires physical bodies due to rebirth under the Law of *Karmaic* action. (8) The individual self suffers because of its contact with matter, worldly external bodies.

Indian philosophical schools could not see themselves as exclusive bearers of the total Truth. They emerged together from a long-standing and continuous effort to enhance our common understanding of God, Man and Nature, and they came to be considered as *darshanas* or paradigmatic standpoints shedding light from different angles on noumenal and phenomenal realities. They refrained from claiming that any illumination which can be rendered in words– or even in thoughts– can be either final or complete.

It is repeatedly stated that the presence of numerous cults and philosophies is said to have done more harm than good to the rise of Hindu philosophy as a systematic discipline because of competing and contradictory ideas. There is a problem of 'single term, diverse concepts' and 'diverse concepts, single term'. In defence of variety of philosophical thought I. K. Taimni, a scientist, has rightly observed "that a system of philosophy however lofty and true it may be should not be expected to give us an absolutely correct picture of the transcendent truths as they really exist. Because philosophy works through the medium of the intellect and the intellect has its inherent limitations, it cannot understand or formulate truths which are beyond its scope.... We have to accept these limitations when we use the intellect as an instrument for understanding and discovering these truths in the initial stages. It is no use throwing away this instrument, poor and imperfect though it is, because it gives us at least some help in organizing our effort to know the truth in the only way it can be known– by Self-realization."

Sankhya

Based on the Upanishads, two schools of philosophy developed in India: (1) The realistic (e.g. Sankhya) and (2) The idealistic (e.g.Vedant). The Sankhya philosophy combines the basic doctrines of Sankhya and Yog. However, it should be remembered that the Sankhya represents the theory and Yog represents the application or the practical aspects. This doctrine of Sankhya is similar to the tenets held by the Buddhists whose main doctrine is that the world is full of miseries.

Sankhya is one of the most prominent and one of the oldest of Indian philosophies. Hinduism owes a great deal to the Sankhya philosophy. It deals with the number of realities that are present in existence. The word Sankhya is based upon the Sanskrit word *'Sankhya'* which means counting or numbering. It connotes the 'enumeration' of the categories used by the system to delineate the structure of the universe. The school specifies the number and nature of the ultimate constituents of the universe and thereby imparts knowledge of reality. In addition, the term *'Sankhya'* also means *Samyak Khyan* or *Samyak Gyan* or discriminating knowledge. Hence it is a system of perfect knowledge. According to Richard Garbe, it is 'the most significant system of philosophy that India has produced.' It exerted profound influence on many scholars in ancient India, China and, according to some, even in Greece. Even today, it attracts the attention of many scholars, although it is not a living philosophy and has no active followers.

Sankhya is said to have been mooted by the legendary sage Kapil of antiquity, though we have no extant work left to us by him. Its principles are founded in especially in **Shvetasvatar Upanishad**. His views are recounted in many *Smriti* texts, such as the **Bhagavat Puran** and **Srimad Bhagavad Geeta,** but the Sankhya system appears to stretch back to the end of the Vedic period itself. **Sankhya Pravachan Sutra** is the main book of this school of thought. It is believed to be written by Kapil, although this fact is rightly disputed by some, as the book dates back to around 14th century A.D. only.

Sankhya is an enumerationist philosophy whose epistemology accepted three of six *Pramanas* as the only reliable means of gaining knowledge. These included *Pratyaksha* (perception), *Anuman* (inference) and *Sabda* (*Aptavachan*, word/testimony of reliable sources). The word '*Apta*' means fit or right. It is applied to the Vedas or inspired teachers. Sankhya adopts the theory of evolution (*'Avirbhav'*) and involution (*'Tirobhav'*). It undermines the foundation of supernatural religions by substituting evolution for creation. The theory that the effect really exists beforehand in its cause is one of the central features of the Sankhya system.

Sankhya believes in pluralism of souls (*Jeevatmas*) who possess consciousness, but denies the existence of Ishwar (God). Kapil, the proponent of the Sankhya School, rules out the existence of God. He asserts that the existence of God cannot be proved and hence God does not exist. Sankhya thinkers argue that if God exists and if God is eternal and unchanging as is widely claimed, then He cannot be the cause of the world. A cause has to be active and changing. But a section of Sankhya philosophers later believed in the existence of Supreme Being who guides *Prakriti* independently accordingly to His will. It tells that the entire *mayic* creation is worth discarding and only the Divinity is to be attained because that is the only source of Bliss.

Kapil's theory is strictly a theory of evolution. Sankhya delineates the structure of the world and believes in radical dualism. It sharply distinguishes between Primal Nature/*Prakriti* and all the products that evolve from it, and the Supreme Spirit /'*Purush*'. *Prakriti* is the fundamental or primal substance out of which the world evolves. *Prakriti* itself evolves under the influence of *Purush*. The cause of development or evolution follows a definite law of succession in space, time, mode and causality. The human self is framed on the analogy of cosmic scheme. Man is a microcosm in which all the factors of reality are repeated, as it were, but on a reduced scale.

According to the Sankhya system, the cosmos is the result of the mutual contact of two distinct metaphysical categories: *Prakriti* (Nature) and *Purush* (person). Before we proceed further let us understand the notions of '*Purush*' and '*Prakriti*' first. *Purush* is the Universal Cosmic Male and *Prakriti* is the Mother Nature. *Purush* is the soul, the Self, pure consciousness, and the only source of consciousness. *Prakriti* literally means 'reatrix', the female creative energy. But the word *Purush* refers to simply 'common man', while *Prakriti* means nature in the modern day Sanskrit. *Prakriti* is that which is created. It is nature in all her aspects. According to the Sankhya philosophy, *Prakriti* is composed of three *gunas* or forces/qualities. The three Gunas are called *Sattva* (purity, light, harmony), *Rajas* (passion, activity, motion), and *Tamas* (inertia, inertness, darkness, inactivity).

In Sankhya philosophy, a *Guna* is one of three 'tendencies, qualities': *Sattva, rajas and tamas.* There is no single word in English language for the concept of *Guna*. The usual, but approximate translation is 'quality', 'strand', 'thread' or 'rope', depending upon the context. All of these three *gunas* are present in everyone and everything. As the three *gunas* belong to the primal nature (*Prakriti*), they are called *Aja* or unborn. They are never separated. They support one another and intermingle with one another like the flame, oil and wick of a lamp.

Purush, said as above, has the quality of consciousness. It is eternally distinct from Nature, but it enters into complex configurations of Nature (biological bodies) in order to experience and to have knowledge. According to the Sankhya tradition, mind, mentality, intellect or *Mahat* (the Great one) is not a part of the *Purush*, but the result of the complex organization of matter, or the *gunas*. Mentality is the closest thing in Nature to *Purush*, but it is still a natural entity, rooted in materiality. *Purush*, in contrast, is a pure witness. It lacks the ability to be an agent. Thus according to the Sankhya school, when it seems as though we as persons are making decisions, we are mistaken. It is actually our natural constitution characterized by the *gunas* that make the decision. The *Purush* does nothing but lends consciousness to the situation. The universe is described by this school as one created by *Purush-Prakriti* entities infused with various permutations and combinations of variously enumerated elements, senses, feelings, activity and mind. According to Sankhya scholars, everything, all life forms and human beings, have these three *gunas*, but in different proportions. The interplay of these *gunas* defines the character of someone or something, of nature and determines the progress of life.

Sankhya is a dualistic realism because it advocates two ultimate realities, as said before: (1) *Prakriti*, matter and (2) *Purush*, self (spirit). Sankhya is realism as it considers that both matter and spirit are equally real. According to the dualistic Sankhya system, the self-intelligent *Purush* and the non-intelligent *Prakriti* are two distinct fundamental principles. *Purush* is more than one, but *Prakriti* is one. The nature of *Purush* is consciousness pure and simple and changelessness. *Prakriti* is the origin of all psychical and physical elements, is altogether devoid of consciousness and is subject to change in the proximity of *Purush*.

Sankhya is pluralistic also because of its teaching that *Purush* (soul) is not one but many. For them *Purush* is sufficient to inspire the unconscious *Prakriti* to manifest herself in the form of universe. The *Purush* (souls) are many, conscious and devoid of all qualities. They are the silent spectators of *Prakriti* (matter or nature), which is composed of three *gunas* (dispositions). The state in which the *gunas* are in equilibrium is called *Prakriti* but when disturbed the state is called *Vikriti*. This disturbance is due to the *sanyog* or effective contact between the *Purush* and *Prakriti*. Disturbance of the equilibrium of *Prakriti* produces the material world, including the mind, which is supposed to be the finest form of material energy.

According to Sankhya, the efficient cause of the world is *Purush* and the material cause is the *Prakriti*. *Purush* is neither produced nor does it produce. *Prakriti* is not produced but it produces. *Prakriti* is uncaused. It is eternal. It itself is not produced but it has inherent potential or tendency to produce. *Purush* (like the Brahm of Vedant) is the Transcendental Self. It is absolute, independent, free, imperceptible, unknowable, above any experience and beyond any words or explanation. It remains pure, 'nonattributive consciousness'.

Purush is the self-intelligent subject and changeless. *Prakriti* is the vibrant, non-intelligent, potential cause of the objective universe. *Prakriti* is one, though manifold. Prakriti is *trigunatmak,* i.e. has three basic attributes *Sattva, Rajas* and *Tamas (Prakriti* refers to a state of state of equipoise of *Sattva, Rajas, Tama*— goodness or passivity, passion, energy or activity and darkness). The whole objective universe— both physical and psychical- evolves from Prakriti when it comes in contact with Purush. This contact results in evolution of twenty four categories, including subordinate ones. *Prakriti* is the material cause of the world. *Prakriti* is dynamic. Its dynamism is attributed to its constituent gunas. The gunas are not only constituents, nor are they simply qualities. The *Gunas* are the very essence of *Prakriti.* The relation between *Purush and Prakriti* may be compared to that between a magnet and a piece of iron. *Purush* itself does not come into contact with *Prakriti*. But it influences *Prakriti*. Thus, the *Prakriti* is prompted to produce. As the *gunas* undergo more and more changes, *Prakriti* goes on differentiating into numerous world-objects. Thus it becomes more and more determinate. This is what is termed as evolution.

In evolution, *Prakriti* is transformed and differentiated into multiplicity of objects. Evolution is followed by dissolution. In dissolution the physical existence, all the worldly objects mingle back into *Prakriti*, which now remains as the undifferentiated, primordial substance. This is how the cycles of evolution and dissolution follow each other.

The Sankhya, to a large extent, forms the philosophical basis of Yog as a method of self-realization. The most important difference between Sankhya and Yog is regarding the view of God. Sankhya does not recognize any ever-free, eternal, Creator God because the existence of anything like this cannot be established by logical proof. The only God it admits is '*Kalp-niyamak-Ishvar*' that is a nearly perfect being temporarily in-charge of a cycle of creation. When the association of *Purush* and *Prakriti* is destroyed, the Purush is liberated and the objective universe created for that *Purush* automatically returns to undifferentiated state of inactive *Prakriti*. Only the knowledge brings about liberation. In contrast to Sankhya, Yog admits a Personal God, a special Being untouched by any kind of misery, having infinite knowledge and unlimited by time. Such a God is the teacher of even the earliest teachers.

Moksha in Sankhya is the eventual cessation or the end of pain. It does not take *Moksha* as a state of perpetual bliss. It is considered as a property-less state where both pain and pleasure cease to be. Owing to its belief in dualism, Sankhya was not accepted by the proponents of Vedant. Adi Shankar has identified Sankhya as the major opponent of Vedant.

Yog

Although the Yog philosophy was known even in the Vedic and pre-Vedic periods, it was not formally systematised for a long time. The systematic expression of the Yog philosophy comes to us from Patanjali's **Yog Sutra**, it comes relatively late in the history of philosophy. Almost nothing is known about Patanjali who wrote the **Yog Sutras**. The dating of his life has varied widely between the fourth century B.C. and the sixth century A.D., but the fourth century B.C. is the period noted for the appearance of aphoristic literature. The traditional Indian literature, especially the **Padma Puran**, includes brief references to Patanjali, indicating that he was born in Illavrita Varsh. The Yog philosophy is also expressed in the Bhagavad Geeta. The actual dating of Patanjali's life is somewhat problematic because there would have lived more than person named Patanjali same as Vyas. Yog is closely associated with Sankhya. Yog is largely based on the Sankhya philosophy. They are two sides of the same coin. Sankhya is the theory, Yog is the practice. It should be noted, however, that Sankhya is basically an atheistic system, but Yog is theistic.

The Sankhya system is based on atheism, but Yog believes in God, especially in Personal God. Both Yog and Sankhya schools hold that there are many *Purushas*. Unlike Sankhya, Yog holds that there is one

Supreme *Purush* (God) who is above all *Purushas* and that no other *Purush* can be like that Supreme *Purush*. This Supreme *Purush* does not create the *Prakriti* or other *Purushas*.

While Sankhya uses three terms *Mahat, Ahankar* and *Manas*– to refer to *Antahkaran*, Yog has only one word– *Chitta*. Yog adopts a single term, *Chitta*, to refer to a complex of *Mahat*, *Ahankar* and *Manas*. *Chitta* is considered as being composed of intellect, ego and mind. *Chitta* has a predominance of *Sattva Guna*.

The Yog School of philosophy believes in Primal Nature / Prakriti, and the Supreme Spirit/ Purush as in case of Sankhya, but it adds one more element (*Tattva*) to those enumerated by Sankhya, making a total of 26 elements. The additional element is that of God in form, i.e. Isvara, the Supreme Ruler of the universe. This makes the Yog philosophy theistic in contrast with the non-theistic approach of the Sankhya school. Owing to this reason, the Yog School is often called theistic Sankhya. The Yog system deals with the practical techniques of disintegrating and dissolving the elements to free the Purush from its entanglement. When an individual soul gains release from the fetters of Prakriti, it attains liberation (*Moksha*), the ultimate goal of both Sankhya and Yog.

The sage Maharshi Patanjali has given aphorisms of Yog in his **Yog Sutra.** Now there are a growing number of people who practise 'Yog'. Some believe that 'Yog' has no religious base and followers of all religions can get benefit from it. Literally speaking, the word 'Yog' means re-integration. It deals with the techniques of self-control. It believes that all the powers of the universe are within us and we need to recognise and utilise them in a balanced way for self-emancipation.

Generally, the word 'Yog' is broadly used for several paths of self-realization such as (i) '*Dhyan Yog*' or contemplation/meditation, (ii) '*Gyan Yog*' which is being one with the Brahm through equipoise, equanimity and serenity of mind by the wise and knowledgeable, (iii) '*Karma Yog*', i.e. piety and complete surrender to the Supreme. Strictly speaking, the 'Yog' is of four types, viz.

1. *Mantra Yog*,
2. *Yog* of Concentration,
3. *Hath Yog* or *Yog* of austerity, and

4. *Raja Yog* or *Yog* of kingship.

The Yog Sutra of Patanjali contains 196 aphorisms, which are divided into four sections. Yog studies all aspects of human personality and teaches one how to control the modifications of the mind through the practice of meditation and detachment and surrender to higher consciousness. The Yog system provides a methodology for linking up individual consciousness with the Supreme Being. The Yog system lays down elaborate prescriptions for gradually gaining physical and mental control and mastery over the 'personal self', both body and mind, until one's consciousness has intensified sufficiently to allow for the awareness of one's 'real Self' (the soul, or *Atman*), as distinct from one's feelings, thoughts and actions. By following these prescriptions or Sadhanas one realizes one's essential nature and instantly freed from *Sansar*, the cycle of transmigration, and attains *Kaivalya*. Various schools of the Yog system are: *Bhaktiyog, Gyanayog, Karmayog, Ashtang Yog, Hath Yog* (practical application of Sankhya Philosophy), etc. Realization of this goal of *Yog* is known as *Moksha, Nirvan* and *Samadhi*. This realization of the *Atman* is nothing other than attaining the infinite Brahm.

Patanjali organized the *Yog Sutras* into four Padas or books: *Samadhi Padas*, the first book, deals with concentration of mind (*Samadhi*), without which no serious practice of Yog is possible. Since *Samadhi* is necessarily experiential, this *Pada* explores the hindrances to and the practical steps needed to achieve alert quietude. Both restraints of the senses and of the discursive intellect are essential for samadhi. Having set forth what must be done to attain and maintain meditative absorption, the second book, *Sadhana Padas*, provides the method or means required to establish full concentration. Any effort to subdue the tendency of the mind to become diffuse, fragmented or agitated demands a resolute, consistent and continuous practice of self-imposed, steadfast restraint, tapas, which cannot become stable without a commensurate disinterest in all phenomena. This relaxed disinterestedness, *Vairagya*, has nothing to do with passive indifference, positive disgust, inert apathy or feeble-minded ennui as often experienced in the midst of desperation and tension in daily affairs. *Vairagya* implies a conscious transcendence of the pleasure-pain principle through a radical reappraisal of expectations, memories and habits.

The third book, *Vibhuti Padas,* considers complete meditative absorption, *Sanyam* (restraints), its characteristics and consequences. Once calm, continuous attention is mastered, one can discover an even more transcendent mode of meditation which has no object of cognition whatsoever. Now the Yogi becomes capable of tapping all the *Siddhis* or theurgic powers. These prodigious mental and moral feats are indeed magical, although there is nothing miraculous or even supernatural about them. They represent the refined capacities and exalted abilities of the perfected human being. Just as any person who has achieved proficiency in some specialized skill or knowledge should be careful to use it wisely and precisely, so too the Yogi whose spiritual and mental powers may seem practically unlimited must not waste his energy or misuse his hard-won gifts.

In *Kaivalya Padas*, the fourth book which crowns the *Yog Sutras*, Patanjali conveys the true nature of isolation or supreme spiritual freedom insofar as it is possible to do so in words. Since *Kaivalya* is the term used for the sublime state of consciousness in which the enlightened soul has gone beyond the differentiating sense of 'I am', it cannot be characterized in the conceptual languages that are dependent on the subject-object distinction. Isolation is not nothingness, nor is it a static condition.

Patanjali's text has a universal appeal for all ardent aspirants to *Raja Yog*. He conveys the vast spectrum of consciousness, diagnoses the common predicament of human bondage to mental ailments, and offers practical guidance on the arduous pathway of lifelong contemplation that could lead to the summit of self-mastery and spiritual freedom.

Patanjali shows the way to emancipation by *Ashtang* Y*og*. Yog is a self-disciplining process of concentration and meditation. Such a Yogic practice leads one to higher states of consciousness. This helps one in acquiring direct knowledge and the result is Self–realization. Patanjali lays emphasis on the complete control and mastery of *Chitta*. He proposes the practice of certain physical and mental exercises. They form the basis of *Ashtang Yog*.

The core of the practical import of the Yog philosophy is what it calls the *Astang Yog*. The *Astang Yog* sets out the eight (*asta*) limbs (*anga*) of the practice of Yog (*Yog Sutra* II. 29). Let us briefly cover the system of *Ashtang Yog*. *Ashtanga Yog* comprises eight *anga* (steps): *yam, niyam, asan, pranayam, pratyahar, dharana, dhyan* and *samadhi*.

These eight steps are divided into two parts:

External part of five *anga: yam, niyam, asan, pranayam* and *pratyahar*.

Internal part of three *anga: dharana, dhyan* and *samadhi*.

Yama means restraint. One must turn to ethics by refraining himself from immoral activities. This is the first step towards self–discipline. *Niyam* means observance. It refers to the cultivation of values and virtues in life. These two *anga– Yam and Niyam–* protects the aspirant from irresistible temptations and desires and offer a protection from the distractions.

The next two steps, *asan* and *pranayam*, prepares the physical body for the Yogic practice. *Asan* means posture of the body. A steady but comfortable posture is essential for Yog. *Pranayam* is concerned with the control of breath. The cycles of inspiration, *Kumbhak* and expiration, have to be carefully monitored. Both of these enhance the steadiness of the body and mind.

Pratyahar is concerned with the withdrawal of the senses. The senses, by their inherent nature, remain focused on the external world. Pratyahar helps to detach the sense organs from the objects of the world. The isolation from the world objects facilitates the concentration of the mind on any particular object.

The ultimate three steps are: *Dharana* (concentration), *Dhyan* (meditation) and *Samadhi* (spiritual absorption). *Dharana* is concerned with the concentration. It is concerned with concentrating the *Chitta* on a single object. The subject is focusing on an object. If the mind diverts to some other object, it has to be fixed again on the chosen object of concentration.

Dhyan is concerned with contemplation. In this stage, the aspirant can keep the mind steady on the object chosen for contemplation. The mind is focused without interruptions and there is unidirectional flow of

Chitta. Though the mind is steadfast, yet there is awareness of the mind of the self. There is an observer; there is also the one that is being observed.

Samadhi is the ultimate stage of Yogic practice. Now all self-awareness of the mind disappears. The aspirant (seeker) becomes aware that his attachment to the *Prakriti* was owing to the ignorance (*Avidya*). The illusion is gone. This is the ultimate, *Nirbeej Samadhi*. There is the unification of the subject and the object. Now there is no object at all. The duo, the subject and the object, mingles into unity. They are no separate entities. There is only one, but it is not an object. There is oneness devoid of material existence; it is pure Consciousness.

The steadfast practice of the *Astang Yog* results in counteracting past *Karmas*. This culminates in a milestone-liberating event: *Dharmmeghasamadhi* (or the absorption in the cloud of virtue). In this penultimate state, the aspirant has all their past sins washed away by a cloud of Dharma (virtue or morality). This leads to the ultimate state of liberation for the *Yogi, Kaivalya*. '*Kaivalya*' translates as 'aloneness.' The state of *Kaivalya* is the state characterized by having no peers, owing to the radical shift in perspective that the *Yogi* attains through *Yog*. The *Yogi*, at the point of *Kaivalya*, no longer sees things from the perspective of individuals in society, but from the perspective of the *Purush*. This arguably is the *Yogi*'s loneliness. Like Advait Vedant, the *Yog Darshan* that liberation/freedom in this life is achievable, and this occurs when an individual fully understands and realizes the equivalence of *Atman* (soul, self) and Brahm.

Nyaya

The term '*Nyaya*' traditionally had the meaning of 'formal reasoning,' though in later times it also came to be used for reasoning in general, and by extension, the legal reasoning of traditional Indian law courts. Actually, Nyaya is a school of logic, and all other schools of Indian philosophy use the Nyaya system of logic, in whole or in part, as a foundation for the philosophical reasoning and debate. The word 'Nyaya' suggests a way by which the mind reaches a conclusion. Since the word also means 'right' or 'just', Nyaya is the science of correct thinking. Nyaya is an orthodox school of philosophy. It is also known as Nyaya Vidya or *Tarkashastra*– 'the science of logic and reasoning'. Because Nyaya analyses the nature and source of knowledge, its validity and invalidity, it is also known as *Anviksiki* which means 'the science of critical study'.

This system was founded by a great sage called Gautam, not to be confused with the Gautam Buddha. The Nyaya School is based on the Nyaya Sutras, written by Aksapada Gautam in the 2nd Century B.C. Its methodology is based on a system of logic that has subsequently been adopted by the majority of the Indian schools, in much the same way as Aristotelian logic has influenced Western philosophy. Its followers reckon that obtaining valid knowledge (the four sources of which are perception, inference, comparison and testimony) is the only way to gain release from suffering. Nyaya developed several criteria by which the knowledge thus obtained was to be considered valid or invalid (equivalent in some ways to Western analytic philosophy).

Nyaya accepts the basic philosophy of Vaisheshik system. It can be said that the Vaisheshik system is theory, Nyaya is the practice. This school of thought is a logical quest for God, the absolute Divinity. It tells that the material power 'Maya', with the help of God, becomes the universe. The Nyaya Darshan is based on establishing the fact that only the Divinity (God) is desirable, knowable and attainable, and not this world. The Nyaya philosophy is primarily concerned with the correct knowledge to be acquired in the human life and the means of receiving this knowledge. Nyaya recognizes God but Gautam does not deal with the issue relating to existence of God in any detail.

Nyaya's prehistory is tied to ancient traditions of debate and rules of reasoning (*Vada-Sastra*). Throughout much of Nyaya's formative period the philosophical development of the school took place through commentaries on the Sutras with important exceptions including works of Jayant, c. 875 and the somewhat heterodox Bhasarvagya, c. 875). Leading commentators include Vatsyayan (c. 450), Uddyotakar (c. 600) Vachaspati Misra (c. 900) and Udayan, c. 975. The school would enter its 'new' phase (*Navya-nyaya*) in the work of the eminent epistemologist Gangesh Upadhyaya (c. 1325). Sixteen major topics were discussed in the Nyaya School of thought, the most important of which is *Praman* (evidence or proof), the source of valid knowledge.

Navya-Nyaya or Neologic, a further development of this school, occurred in the 16th century in Bengal and Mithila.

The most important contribution made by the Nyaya School to modern Hindu thought is its methodology. This methodology is based on a system of logic that has subsequently been adopted by most of the other Indian schools. The followers of Nyaya believed that obtaining valid knowledge was the only way to obtain release from suffering. They, therefore, took great pains to identify valid sources of knowledge and to distinguish these from mere false opinions.

Nyaya epistemology accepts four out of six *Pramanas* as reliable means of gaining knowledge– *Pratyaksha* (perception), *Anuman* (inference), *Upaman* (comparison and analogy) and *Sabda* (word, testimony of past or present reliable experts).

It holds that human suffering results from mistakes/defects produced by activity under wrong knowledge (notions and ignorance). *Moksha* (liberation), it states, is gained through right knowledge. This premise led Nyaya to concern itself with epistemology, which is the reliable means to gain correct knowledge and to get rid of wrong notions. False knowledge is not merely ignorance to Naiyayikas, it includes delusion. Correct knowledge is discovering and overcoming one's delusions, and understanding true nature of soul, self and reality. According to Nyaya Sutras soul, body, senses, objects of senses, intellect, mind, activity, fault, transmigration, fruit, suffering and release– are the objects of right knowledge.

The Nyaya philosophy's another important achievement was to prove the existence of God (one Supreme God, called Ishwar), mostly by logic, in answer to repeated attempts by Buddhists to disprove the existence of God.

Like the Vaisheshik, Nyaya holds that the self is an individual substance, eternal and all pervading. Consciousness is not an essential attribute of the self, but it is only an accidental one. According to Nyaya, salvation is the state of absolute freedom. It is freedom from all pains and pleasures. Then there is freedom from the cycle of the birth and death also.

Nyaya asserts that obtaining valid knowledge of the external world and its relationship with the mind and self is the only way to attain liberation. If one masters the logical techniques of reasoning and dutifully applies these to daily life, he will rid himself of all suffering. The ultimate aim of Nyaya philosophy like other systems of Indian philosophy is liberation– the complete cessation of pain and suffering. Although concerned with the study of logic and epistemology Nyaya is a philosophy of life.

Nyaya believes in transmigration of soul and rebirth. Action (Karma) and defects lead to results/fruits. Liberation is the absolute deliverance from pain and is brought about when knowledge is attained and misconceptions are shed off. Nyaya believes that liberation (*Moksha*) is a state in which one does not experience either pleasure or pain. The liberated beings are devoid of all properties and are similar to a block of wood or a piece of rock. This view has been criticized by several scholars.

Vaisheshik

The Vaisheshik School is one of the six Hindu schools of philosophy (Vedic systems) of India. Historically, it has been closely associated with the Hindu school of logic, Nyaya. It was founded by ascetic Kanad Kashyap (Kana-ad, literally means atom-eater) in the 6th Century B.C., and it is atomist and pluralist in nature. On some accounts Kanad got this name because of the pronounced ontological atomism of his philosophy (*Vaisheshik Sutra* VII.1.8), or because he restricted his diet to grains picked from the field. This system is believed to be as old as Jainism and Buddhism. Kanad presented his detailed atomic theory in *Vaisheshik Sutra*. Although the Vaisheshik system developed independently from the Nyaya, the two eventually merged because of their closely related metaphysical theories.

The basis of the school's philosophy is that all objects in the physical universe are reducible to a finite number of *Paramanu* (atom), and Brahm is regarded as the fundamental force that causes consciousness in these atoms. Knowledge and liberation is achievable by complete understanding of the world of experience, according to Vaisheshik School. The Vaisheshik and Nyaya schools eventually merged because of their closely related metaphysical theories (although Vaisheshik only accepted perception and inference as sources of valid knowledge).

The Vaishesika School's emphasis on particulars is reflected in its name, since *Vishesh* means 'particularity', and it is concerned with properly delineating the categories of objects of experience. These objects of experience, *padarthas*, are six: substance (*Dravya*), quality (*Guna*), and Karma or movement and activity (forming the triplicity of objective existence), and generality (*Samanya*), particularity (*Vishesh*) and *Samavayi* or inherence (forming a triad of modes of intellectual discernment which require valid logical inference). A seventh object of experience, non-existence (*Shunya*), was eventually added to the six as a strictly logical necessity. The Vaisheshik point of view recognizes nine irreducible substances: earth, water, air, fire, ether (*Akash*), time, space, self and mind, all of which are distinct from the qualities which inhere in them. The self is necessarily a substance– a substrate of qualities– because consciousness cannot be a property of the physical body, the sense-organs or the brain-mind. Although the self as a substance must be pervasive everywhere, its everyday capacity for feeling, willing and knowing is focussed in the bodily organism.

This school is called Vaisheshik because it considers uniqueness as an aspect of reality and studies as a separate category. Under the topic of substance, it deals with the physics and chemistry of the body and the universe. The theory of atomic structure was established by this school. Its practical teaching emphasizes *Dharma*, the code of conduct that leads man to worldly welfare and to the highest goal of life. Its aim is to attain happiness in this life (by renouncing worldly desires) and finally to attain the ultimate liberation (through the attachment of the true knowledge of the divine). According to this school of philosophy, atoms (not the one we studied in our elementary science curriculum in school) are the smallest particle which exists in the universe and are eternal in nature.

An atom is, according to Vaisheshik scholars, is indestructible (*anitya*), indivisible, and has a special kind of dimension, called 'small' (*anu*). A composite, in this philosophy, is defined to be anything which is divisible into atoms. Whatever human beings perceive is composite, while atoms are invisible. The Vaisheshikas stated that size, form, truths and everything that human beings experience as a whole is a function of atoms, their number and their spatial arrangements, their *Guna* (quality), *Karma* (activity), *Samanya* (commonness), *Vishesh* (particularity) and *Amavaya* (inherence, inseparable connectedness of everything). Vaisheshik believes in an atomic theory of the universe. The formation of the world is supposed to be effected by the aggregation of countless and eternal atoms. An atom is defined as something that is existing, has no cause and is eternal. Atom is less than the least, invisible, indivisible, intangible and imperceptible by the senses. The atoms are eternally aggregated, disaggregated/disintegrated and re-disintegrated by the power that cannot be seen, i.e. the *Adrasta*. Actually, Kanad does not directly refer to God. God is inferred as *Adrasta,* the unseen force of acts (*Karmas*).

Virtue (dharma), the righteous way of living, is the means to achieve cessation of pain or salvation. Vaisheshik holds that the destruction of all the distinctive characteristics of the substances that bind the individual soul is the liberation. The plurality of the souls is inferred from differences in status or the variety of conditions. Even after salvation, each soul maintains its uniqueness, the mind and body, and abides in the resultant state of absolute and eternal unconsciousness. Thus, the freed souls are conceived as externally existing with specific differences. This is different from the Superconsciousness or pure consciousness of the liberated soul as perceived in the Yog and Vedant systems.

It postulates an atomic pluralism in terms of which all objects in the physical universe are reducible to a certain number of finite atoms (*paramanus*). God is regarded as the fundamental force who causes consciousness in these atoms. Being associated with the school of logic, *Vaisheshik* texts use logical arguments to prove that the world is made of finite number of indivisible atoms. Later, Vaisheshik philosophers developed a theory to explain the properties of materials as the interaction of different types of atoms that make up the material. These materials are called *Padarthas*. According to them the functioning of atoms was guided or directed by the will of the Supreme Being. They accept the existence of God called *Ishwar* or *Maheshwar* which is the Supreme Intelligent Being under whose will and guidance this world is created, sustained and dissolved.

Vaisheshik contends that every effect is a fresh creation or a new beginning. Kanad has not discussed much about God. The eternal atoms are the material cause of the world. Vaisheshik recognizes nine ultimate substances: Five material and four non-material substances which are as follows:

The five material substances are: Earth, water, fire, air and *Akash*.

The four non-material substances are: space, time, soul and mind.

Earth, water, fire and air are atomic but *Akash* is non-atomic and infinite.

Space and time are infinite and eternal. The concept of soul is comparable to that of the self or *Atman*. This system considers consciousness as an accidental property. In other words, when the soul associates itself to the body, only then it 'acquires' consciousness. Thus, consciousness is not considered an intrinsic quality of the soul.

The mind (*Manas*) is accepted as atomic but indivisible and eternal substance. The mind helps to establish the contact of the self to the external world objects. The soul develops attachment to the body owing to ignorance. The soul identifies itself with the body and mind. The soul is trapped in the bondage of *Karma*, as a consequence of actions resulted from countless desires and passions. It can be free from the bondage only if it becomes free from actions. Liberation follows the cessation of all the actions.

The starting point of the creation is the Will of God. The first product of the Divine Will is *Brahma* who is the chief architect of creation. *Brahma* proceeds with further creation in accordance with the totality of the unseen merits and demerits of the individual souls by setting in motion the atoms to combine with one another causing the world. The process of dissolution is in the reverse order where Brahma gives up his body and *Ishwar* takes charge of the process of dissolution. The whole world is then reduced to the primary state of *padarthas*.

Therefore, this system is a theistic form of atomism suggesting that creation is not a process of chance but a choice executed by God in a well planned manner according to the Karmas of the individual *Jeevas* for the proper realization of their ultimate perfection. The Vaisheshikas say that the visible universe is created from an original stock of atoms (*janim asatah*).

Over the centuries, the school merged with the Nyaya system of philosophy to form the combined school of *Nyaya Vaisheshik* because of their closely related metaphysical theories. Though Nyaya and Vaisheshik are separate systems, they have more similarities than dissimilarities. Later Nyaya School, *Navya Nyaya*, developed as a result of the blending of the two. Swami Prabhavanand has pointed out that the two systems differ mainly in their approach to the central problems of philosophy. The Vaisheshik begins with the conception of being and develops its ideas from that while Nyaya begins with knowing. Vaisheshik acknowledges two Pramanas– perception (*Pratyaksha*) and inference (*Anuman*), while Nyaya adds two more to these- Verbal testimony (*Shabda*) and comparison (*Upaman*). These two are included in inference by Vaisheshik. Both these systems are realistic and pluralistic. Basic postulates of the two schools are as follows:

1. God is the efficient cause of the universe.
2. Physical objects exist independently of the mind, although their perception depends on the mind aided by the sense organs.
3. Seven categories (padarthas) are ultimately real. These are substance (*Dravya*), quality (*Gun*), activity (*Karma*), generality (*Samanya*), particularity (*Vishesh*), inherence (*Samavaya*) and non-existence (*Abhav*).
4. Only substance (*Dravya*) is independent entity, the rest belong to it.
5. Nine fundamental substances are- earth (*Prithvi*), water (*Jala*), air (*Vayu*), fire (*Agni*), ether (*Akash*), time (*Kala*), space (*Dik*), self (*Atman)* and mind (*Manas*). First seven substances compose the physical universe.
6. Each Earth, water, fire and air are atomic in their original state and four different types of atoms are their basic constituents.
7. Ether, time and space are infinite and pervasive.
8. Self is eternal and pervasive but mind is eternal but infinitesimal.
9. There are innumerable selves ever distinct from one another and consciousness is neither an intrinsic quality of self nor its essence. In its disembodied state, the self will have no knowledge or consciousness.
10. The self is bound being associated with the mind, organs and body through ignorance.
11. Only true knowledge dissociates the self from these adjuncts

and leads to attainment of liberation. It is a state of complete release from all sufferings without any positive attainment.

12. Righteous deeds and contemplation on truth lead to true knowledge.

Poorva Mimansa or Karma Mimansa

The first major orthodox philosophical system to develop was Poorva Mimansa (Poorva Mimansa is based on the earlier (*Poorva* means earlier) parts of the Vedas. The other one to follow was the Uttar Mimansa (Uttar Mimansa is based on the later (*Uttar* means later) parts of the Vedas. Mimansa means devotional thinking or devotional inquisitiveness. The word is also used for investigation into the meaning of ritualistic texts. It systematizes the 'exegesis' or interpretation of Vedic ritual texts. It started with a focus on deducing principles for analysis and interpretation of the sacred texts that eventually got extended to discussing the theory of knowledge, etc. Poorva-Mimansa is also known as *Karma Mimansa* since it deals with the *Karmic* actions of rituals and sacrifices. The main objective of the Poorva Mimansa School is to interpret and establish the authority of the *Vedas*. It requires unquestionable faith in the *Vedas* and the regular performance of the Vedic fire-sacrifices to sustain all the activity of the universe. Although in general the *Mimansa* accepts the logical and philosophical teachings of the other schools, they insist that salvation can only be attained by acting in accordance with the prescriptions of the Vedas.

The word '*Mimansa*' has originated from the root '*Mana*' which refers to 'thinking' or 'investigating'. The word '*Mimansa*' suggests 'probing and acquiring knowledge' or 'critical review and investigation of the Vedas'. The *Poorva Mimansa* school of Hindu philosophy gains its name from the portion of the Vedas that it is primarily concerned with the initial part of the Vedas, i. e. *Karmakand.* In the context of Hinduism, the *Poorva Mimansa* School is one of the most orthodox of the Hindu philosophical schools because of its concern to elaborate and defend the contents of the early, ritually oriented part of the Vedas.

Mimansa is considered close to Vedant. It deals mainly with the Vedic rituals *(Karmakand)*, whereas Vedant addresses Vedic knowledge (*Gyankand*). Their propinquity is evident from the first clause of both which states that Mimansa is the 'inquiry into religion' whereas Vedant is the 'inquiry into the Supreme. The aim of the Mimansa is to examine the nature of religion or dharma.

The Vedas are the most valuable scriptures of the mankind. They present the most exalted form of superhuman knowledge and wisdom. The Vedas are eternal. They are timeless since they might have taken ages to acquire the written form. The four Vedas are: **Rigved, Yajurved, Samaved and Atharvaved.** Each of the Vedas is divided into four parts: The *Samhitas,* the *Brahmnas,* the *Aranyakas* and the *Upanishads*.

Jaimini is credited as the chief proponent of the Mimansa system. His glorious work is **Mimansa Sutra** written around the end of the 2nd century A.D. **Mimansa Sutra** is the largest of all the philosophical *Sutras*. Divided into 12 chapters, it is a collection of nearly 2500 aphorisms which are extremely difficult to comprehend. Earlier scholars wrote commentaries on **Mimansa Sutra**. Unfortunately they are lost with the passage of time.

The **Mimansa Sutra**, like the **Vaisheshik Sutra,** begins with the assertion that its main concern is the elaboration of *Dharma*. Like many other schools of Indian philosophy, *Poorva Mimansa* takes Dharma ('duty' or 'ethics') as its primary focus. Unlike all other schools of Hindu philosophy, *Poorva Mimansa* was not interested in subjects like *moksha*, or liberation. The very topic of liberation is nowhere discussed in the foundational text of this tradition, and is recognized for the first time by the medieval *Poorva Mimansa* author Kumaril (7th cent. A. D.) as a real objective worth pursuing in conjunction with *Dharma*. The main objective of this school of philosophy is to support and reinforce the Vedic rites and rituals in reaction to opposition of the Vedic philosophy by heterodox.

The **Mimansa Sutra** is the largest of all the philosophical Sutras. It has been argued that the Ved is the final authority on all matters. It provides a comprehensive method for interpreting and understanding the underlying meaning of the Ved. It lays great emphasis on rituals, worship and ethical conduct and provides a systematic lifestyle and direction. *Mimansa* offers guidelines for a practical application of the Vedantic theory. This school is foremost in the analysis of sound and *Mantra*.

Earlier scholars wrote commentaries on **Mimansa Sutra.** Unfortunately they are lost with the passage of time. The earliest available commentary is Sabarsvamin's **Sabar-bhasya**, which is still the authoritative basis of all subsequent works on *Mimansa*. Renowned scholars Kumaril Bhatt and Prabhakar independently wrote their commentaries on **Sabar-bhasya.** Prabhakar was a disciple of Kumaril Bhatt. However, they differed, to some degree, on the interpretation of **Sabar-bhasya** and wrote separate commentaries. Mandan Mishra, the erudite scholar, was a follower of Kumaril Bhatt. He also wrote a commentary, but at a later stage he changed his thinking and became a disciple of Shankaracharya. Eventually this school was divided into two groups: the school founded by Prabhakar and the one founded by Kumaril Bhatt. According to the former, there are five sources of valid knowledge: perception, inference, comparison, testimony and postulation. According to the latter there is only one source of knowledge– noncognition.

This system outrightly accepts the Vedas as the eternal source of 'revealed truth'. Thus though it differs from the earlier four philosophical systems (Vaisheshik, Nyaya, Sankhya, Yog which neither accept nor reject the authority of the Vedas), a great chunk of *Mimansa* philosophy is derived from the Vaisheshik-Nyaya duo.

Mimansa adopts the theory of plurality of selves to account for the variety in nature. It believes that all non-living and living forms, whether under bondage or liberated, are true. The universe was neither created nor can be destroyed. It undergoes changes. Mimansa accepts the infallibility of the Vedas, which are emanation of Reality in the form of Cosmic Sound (*Sabda Brahm*) and Vedic hymns are sacred formulae (*Mantras*) with the inherent meaning and power to reveal the truth. Mimansa earlier aimed at heaven through religion. Salvation, according to Mimansa, is the cessation and absence of pain. Mimansa is a polytheistic philosophy believing in the existence of a host of supernatural beings called Devas, popularly known as lesser gods. These lesser gods reside in heaven. As stated above, Mimansa stresses on religion. It lays emphasis on different kinds of ritualistic practices through which one can qualify for ascent to heaven after death. These practices are mainly composed of religious ceremonies such as Yagya.

The main objective of the *Poorva Mimansa* School was to establish the authority of the Vedas. Consequently this school's most valuable contribution to Hinduism was its formulation of the methodology of interpretation with the help of which complicated Vedic injunctions regarding rituals are understood and practised. The **Mimansa Sutras** of Jaimini are the basic text of this system. Its adherents (Mimansakas) believed that–

1. One must have unquestionable faith in the Vedas which are infallible.
2. There is a soul which survives the death of the body and enjoys the fruits of the rituals in heaven.
3. There is a power of potency which preserves the effects of the rituals performed in the soul yielding fruits after death.
4. The world is real.
5. Our life and actions performed here are real and not mere dreams.

They believe in a magical power of the mantras and *Yagya* which sustains all the activity of the universe. In keeping with this belief, they laid great emphasis on *Dharma,* which they understood as the performance of Vedic rituals. Every human being is bound to perform these Vedic duties for duty's sake only because Vedas command them and none has got the choice not to do them or do them in a different way.

Mimansa thinkers have held that all cognition is valid at some level and to some degree. There can be no false knowledge; whatever is known is necessarily true. As a consequence, they saw no reason to prove the truth of any cognition. Rather, they sought to demonstrate its falsity, for if disproofs were successful, it would show that there had been no cognition at all. The promise of gnosis rests upon the sovereign method of falsifiability rather than a vain attempt to seek total verification in a public sense. Mimansa rests upon the presupposition of the supremacy of Divine Wisdom, the sovereignty of the Revealed Word and the possibility of its repeated realization. Even among those who cannot accept the liturgical or revelatory validity and adequacy of the

Vedas, the logic of disproof can find powerful and even rigorous application. As a method, it became important to the philosophers of Vedant.

The Mimansa system attaches considerable importance to the verbal testimony which is essentially the Vedic testimony. Jaimini accepts the 'word' or the '*Shabda*' as the only means of knowledge. The 'word' or the '*Shabda*' is necessarily the Vedic word, according to Jaimini. This system strongly contends that the Vedas are not authored by an individual. Since they are 'self-revealed' or '*Apaurusheya*', they manifest their own validity (this illogical propaganda was made to convey a strong message across the society that nobody should try to question Vedas so that those supporters should enjoy absolute supremacy in society to help safeguard their age-old vested interests).The earlier *Mimansakas* do not give much importance to the deities. Hence they do not endorse God as the creator of the universe. But later *Mimansakas* show a bent towards theism. While *Mimansa* does not receive much scholarly attention these days, its influence can be felt in the life of the practising Hindu in the performance of rites, rituals and observance of religious directions.

Uttar Mimansa or Vedant

Uttar Mimansa is the Vedant, one of the most significant of all Indian philosophies. As compared to other systems, its advent and growth is recent. Still it is the most influential orthodox philosophical system of India. The Vedant school concentrates on the philosophical teachings of the *Upanishads* (mystic or spiritual contemplations within the *Vedas*), rather than on the *Brahmnas* (instructions for ritual and sacrifice).

Vedant literally means 'the end of the Veda.' It comprises the doctrines set forth in the closing chapter of the Vedas, which are called the Upanishads. The views expressed in the Upanishads also constitute the final aim of the Ved or the essence of the Vedas. In a broad sense, the word '*Vedant*' covers not only the Upanishads but all the commentaries and interpretations associated with the Upanishads. All these works constitute the Vedant philosophy. Vedant is the essence of all the four Vedas which are encapsulated in the Upanishads.

The word 'Ved' is derived from the root 'vid' which means 'to know.' There are four Vedas, viz Rigved, Yajurved, Samaved and Atharvaved. Rigved is the oldest. It has hymns in praise of gods. It has 10 mandalas or sections and 10552 mantras or hymns. Yajurved has 40 sections and 1975 mantras mostly dealing with Yagya. Samaved has 1875 mantras; most of the hymns being those derived from Rigved. The hymns are melodious and are relatively easy to understand. Atharvaved has 20 sections and 5987 mantras, many of which are derived from the Rigved. The four Vedas totally contain 20389 mantras. The Vedas have generally three parts and each dealing with (i) action which gives details of how to perform a Yagya, (ii) knowledge which explains Atman and Parmatman and related aspects, and (iii) devotion which gives details as to how to worship the God. The Vedas have two main sections, viz Samhita or the Ved proper and Brahman scriptures. Brahman scriptures have three parts, viz Brahman, Aranyak, and Upanishads. Brahman scriptures give details of Yagya. Main Brahman scriptures are Aitreya, Taittariya, and Satapath among others. Main Aranyak scriptures are Aitreya, Sankhayan, Brhdaranyaka, Taittariya and Tavalkar.

Vedant believes that the Brahm is everywhere. Brahm is the reality and ultimate truth. According to the **Vedant Sutra**, the Purush and Prakriti of the Sankhya are not independent substances, but modifications of a single reality. The world is unreal and appears so due to nescience. Brahm is the truth; the world is unreal (*Maya*); the individual soul (Jeev) is Brahm; no other (not different).The Vedant focuses on meditation, self-discipline and spiritual connectivity, more than traditional ritualism. Due to the rather cryptic and poetic nature of the Vedant Sutras, the school is separated into six sub-schools, each interpreting the texts in its own way and producing its own series of sub-commentaries which are explained a little later.

Same as the *Poorva Mimansa* tradition, the *Uttar Mimansa* School is concerned with explicating the contents of a particular portion of the Vedas. While the Poorva Mimansa concerns itself with the former portion of the Vedas, the *Uttar Mimansa* School concerned with the concluding part of the Vedas. Whereas the principal concern of the earlier portion of the Vedas is action and Dharma, the principal concern of the latter portion of the Vedas is knowledge and *Moksha*.

The great scholar Badarayan (?500-200 B.C), also known as Ved Vyas, tried to simplify the Upanishadic philosophy. He was the first scholar to take up the challenging task of systematizing the immensely vast philosophical doctrines of the Upanishads. The result of his efforts was one of the most illustrious works on Vedant. Badarayan's work is known as **Brahma Sutra or Vedant Sutra.** It is also referred to as **Uttar Mimansa Sutra**. The **Brahma Sutra** has 555 Sutras. Each of the five hundred and fifty-five Sutras (literally, 'threads') are extremely short and aphoristic, requiring a copious commentary to be understood. In explaining their meaning, various commentators presented Vedantic doctrines in different ways. Shankaracharya, the chief of the commentators and perhaps the greatest philosopher in the Indian tradition, espoused the *Advait*, non-dual, form of Vedant, the purest form of monism, which has never been excelled. But now Shankar's philosophy that the universe is a myth does not go well with the present day intelligentsia, as it is taken as a pessimistic philosophy.

Vedant was taught and practised by the sages of the Vedas and Upanishads and was handed over through a long line of sages. But Ved Vyas, who codified these teachings in the **Brahma Sutras,** is considered its founder. Several teachers or philosophers wrote commentaries on the **Brahma Sutra***s*, interpreting it in various ways and thus establishing various schools within the single system of Vedant. There are three famous commentaries (*Bhashyas*) on the **Brahma Sutra** that shine in the history of Hindu philosophy. These are the 8th century A. D. commentary of Shankaracharya (Advait), the 12th century A. D. commentary of Ramanujacharya (*Visishtadvait*) and the 13th century A. D. commentary by Madhavacharya (*Dvait*). These three are not the only commentaries. There appears to have been no less than twenty-one commentators on the *Brahma Sutra* prior to Madhav, and Madhav is by no means the last commentator on the *Brahma Sutra* either. Important names in the history of Indian theology are amongst the latter day commentators: Nimbark (13th cent. A. D.), Srikanth (15th cent. A. D.), Vallabh (16th cent. A. D.) and Baladev (18th cent. A. D.). However, the majority of the commentaries prior to Shankar have been lost to history. The philosophical positions expressed in the various commentaries fall into six major camps of *Vedant*: (1) *Advait* (non-dualistic which holds that the soul and the Brahm are one and the same), (2) *Dvait* (dualistic which espouses a belief in three separate realities: Vishnu, eternal soul and matter)), (3) Dvaitadvait (both dualistic and non-dualistic which holds that Brahm exists independently, while the soul and matter are dependent), (4) *Vishist Advait* (qualified non-dualism which teaches that the Supreme Being has a definite form, name (Vishnu) and attributes), (5) *Visuddh Advait* (pure non-dualism which believes that Krishna is the absolute form of Brahm) and (6) Achintya Bhedabhed (which combines monism and dualism by stating that the soul is both distinct and non-distinct from Krishna, or God). Among these, the commentaries of Shankaracharya, Ramnujacharya and Madhavacharya are regarded authentic and are held in very high esteem. They are regarded as the greatest scholars of Indian philosophy.

They principally differ on the metaphysics of individual selves and *Brahm*, though there are also some striking ethical differences between these schools as well. Shankar's *Advait Vedant* covers all the other systems. The main teachings of *Vedant* are that Self-realization is the actual goal of life, that the essence of the Self is the ever existent consciousness and bliss, the Self is free from all qualifications and limitations, that the self is essentially *Brahm*, supreme consciousness and this *Brahm* is the absolute, transcendent, attributeless reality but it eternally embodies within itself the capacity or power called *Maya*, which is the basis of mind and matter.

Vedant is one of the world's most ancient religious philosophies and perhaps the broadest of all. Based on the Vedas, *Vedant* affirms the oneness of existence, the divinity of the soul and the harmony of religions. *Vedant* is the philosophical foundation of Hinduism; but while Hinduism includes aspects of Indian culture, *Vedant* is universal in its application and is equally relevant to all countries, all cultures and all religions.

Vedant is the search for Self-knowledge as well as the search for God. What do we mean when we say God? According to Vedant, God is infinite existence, infinite consciousness and infinite bliss. The term for this impersonal, transcendent reality is Brahm, the divine ground of being. Yet Vedant also maintains that God can be personal as well, assuming human form in every age.

Most importantly, God dwells within our own hearts as the Divine Self or *Atman.* The *Atman* is never born nor will it ever die. Neither stained by our failings nor affected by the fluctuations of the body or mind, the *Atman* is not subject to our grief or despair or disease or ignorance. Pure, perfect, free from limitations, the *Atman*, Vedant declares, is one with Brahm. The greatest temple of God lies within the human heart. Vedant affirms that all religions teach the same basic truths about God, the world, and our relationship to one another. The world's religions offer varying approaches to God, each one true and valid, each religion offering the world a unique and irreplaceable path to God-realization. The conflicting messages we find among religions are due more to doctrine and dogma than to the reality of spiritual experience. While dissimilarities exist in the external observances of the world religions, the internals bear remarkable similarities.

The Vedant philosophy is focused on the *Jagat* (the universe), the *Jeev* (individual soul) and the Brahm (the Supreme Being). Brahm is the repository of all knowledge and power. *Jeevas* are trapped in the *Jagat*. Attached to the physical world and driven by passions and desires, they remain chained to ceaseless actions (Karma). As a result, they subject themselves to countless births in various forms. Their transmigration from this birth (life) to the next depends on the Karma (the quality of action). *Moksha* or *Mukti* (liberation) is the goal of life. This Vedantic philosophy, in general, is accepted by all the four sub-schools. Now let us understand the basic differences between the four sub-schools–*Advait, Dvait, Visishtadvait* and *Bhedabhed Vedant.*

I. *Advait Vedant* *(Non-dualism)—* *Advait* literally means 'not two, sole, unity'. It is a sub-school of Vedant, and asserts spiritual and universal non-dualism. Its metaphysics is a form of absolute monism, that is all ultimate reality stands for interconnected oneness. This is the oldest and most widely acknowledged Vedantic school. The foundational texts of this school are the **Brahma Sutras** and the early Upanishads from the 1st millennium BC. Its first great consolidator was the 8th century scholar Adi Shankar, who continued the line of thought of the Upanishadic teachers, and that of his teacher's teacher Gaudapada. He wrote extensive commentaries on the major Vedantic scriptures and is celebrated as one of the major Hindu philosophers from whose doctrines the main currents of modern Indian thought are derived.

The non-dualism of Adi Shankaracharya believes that the self/soul is the Brahm and the two are not different. Brahm is the only and ultimate truth and the universe is false. The world so appears due to super-imposition and nescience. The world is an appearance. It may in some way indicate towards reality but cannot be the reality. It is due to nescience that we see **Jeev** and the universe as things different from Brahm. The philosophy that world is an appearance is fiercely debated now, as it has generated enough fatalism and pessimism among the Hindus.

According to this sub-school of Vedant, all reality is Brahm, and there exists nothing whatsoever which is not Brahm. Its metaphysics includes the concept of *Maya* and Atman. *Maya* connotes "that which exists, but is constantly changing and thus is spiritually unreal". The empirical reality is considered as always changing and therefore 'transitory, incomplete, misleading and not what it appears to be'. The concept of Atman is of soul, self within each person, each living being. *Advait Vedantis* assert that *Atman* is same as Brahm, and this Brahm is within each human being and all life, all living beings are spiritually interconnected, and there is oneness in all of existence. They hold that dualities and misunderstanding of *Maya* as the spiritual reality that matters is caused by ignorance, and are the cause of sorrow, suffering.

The Advait philosophy is stated in a nutshell in the cardinal verse '*Brahm satyam jagan mithya Jeevo Brahmaiva naparah*' which means Brahm alone is real; this world is only an illusory appearance. The *Jeev* is verily Brahm and is not different from Him. The world has no separate existence apart from Brahm. The experiencing self (*Jeev*) and the transcendental self of the Universe (*Atman*) are in reality identical (both are Brahm), though the individual self seems different as space within a container seems different from space as such. Truly speaking, both Brahm and Atman are not different realities. They are identical. They are two different 'labels' for one and the same reality behind all the objects, all matter, all beings of the universe. The philosophy that the world is all Maya has made Hinduism a fatalistic and pessimistic religion. Most modern day philosophers do not subscribe Shankar's view of '*Jagan Mithya*'; rather, they contend the world may be dynamic and changing fast, but it is not a *Maya.* The world is a kind of reality. Sociologists outright discard the absurd philosophy Adi Shankar.

Plurality is experienced because of error in judgements (*Mithya*) and ignorance (*Avidya*). Knowledge of Brahm removes these errors and causes liberation from the cycle of transmigration and worldly bondage. This school deals with *Brahm, Atman, Vidya* (knowledge), *Avidya* (ignorance), *Maya* and *Moksha. Brahm* is *Sachchidanand,* i.e. *Satta-Chitta-Anand* (Pure Existence-Pure Consciousness-Pure Bliss). Brahm is eternal, immutable, inexpressible and unthinkable pure-existence, but it is not the cause or the creator of the universe.

Subsequent Vedantis debated whether the reality of Brahm was *Sagun* (with attributes) or *Nirgun* (without attributes). Belief in the concept of *Sagun Brahm* gave rise to a proliferation of devotional attitudes and more widespread worship of Vishnu and Shiva. But Advait Vedant is strictly grounded in a belief that the ultimate truth is Nirgun Brahm. The Visishtadvait and Dvait schools believed in *Sagun Brahm.*

The Advait Vedant focuses on the following basic concepts: *Brahm, Atman, Vidya* (knowledge), *Avidya* (ignorance), *Maya, Karma* and *moksha.*

(1) Brahm is the Ultimate, Supreme Reality. Brahm is eternal. Brahm is beyond words. It is beyond names and forms. Brahm cannot be perceived nor could it be described by words. It is beyond senses and intellect. It is indefinable. However, if at all it has to be described; Brahm can be considered as Pure Consciousness.

In the Vedantic philosophy, the *swaroop* of Brahm is referred to as Sachchidanand. Brahm is Sachchidananda, i.*e. Satta-Chitta-Anand* (Pure Existence-Pure Consciousness-Pure Bliss). Brahm is eternal, immutable, inexpressible and unthinkable pure-existence, but it is not the cause or the creator of the universe.

(2) *Atman* is the inmost Self or Spirit of man but different from the 'empirical ego'. *Atman* is the fundamental, ultimate, eternal, immutable pure consciousness. Thus, it appears that Brahm is the

ultimate reality behind all world-objects and *Atman* is pure spirit in all beings. Truly speaking, both Brahm and *Atman* are not different realities. They are identical. For practical purposes, they are referred to separately, which they are not. They are the eternal, all-pervading realities underlying all existence. They are two different 'labels' for one and the same reality behind all the objects, all matter, all beings of the universe.

(3) Maya is the unique power (*Shakti*) of Brahm. *Maya* is *trigunatmak*; it has three *Gunas* or attributes. But *Shuddha Brahm* is *Nirgun* and is free from attributes. *Shuddha Nirgun Brahm* alone is the Supreme Reality. When *Nirgun Brahm* comes to acquiesce Maya and acknowledges the *Gunas* of *Maya*, it is known as *Sagun Brahm. Sagun Brahm* is God, the creator, sustainer and destroyer of the world. *Sagun Brahm* is *Ishvar* or a 'personal god.' Man worships gods in different forms and names.

(4) Brahm manifests itself in the world with the help of Maya. The world and the world objects come into existence due to the power of *Maya. Maya* and its creation are termed illusory. It does not mean that the world is not real. Unreality and illusion are different. An illusion may not be an unreality for an illusion is grounded in reality. Reality is that which exists on its own. Maya is dependent on Brahm. *Maya* has created the world of appearances. So the world is illusion. But this does not mean at all that the world is non-existent. The Advait Vedant, with the help of the famous 'rope–snake' illustration, maintains that 'it is neither ultimately real, nor wholly unreal, illusory and non-existent.'

(5) *Avidya* (ignorance) has its seat in the human intellect. Avidya means not only absence of knowledge, but also erroneous knowledge. A man trapped in *Avidya* does not know what is real and thinks that the appearances are real. An individual identifies himself with empirical self. He equates his existence with the physical body. Under the influence of *Maya* and *Avidya*, he dissociates himself from the Ultimate Reality. When the man acquires knowledge, the duality of the self and Brahm disappears. He realizes that the self is really one with Brahm. This realization of the self puts an end to the ignorance (*Avidya*).

(6) *Moksha* is freedom from bondage of ignorance. Man suffers in the grip of incessant desires and ignorance. Upon realization of the

self, one becomes free from the shackles of desires, aspirations, passions, Karma and *Avidya*. This is *Moksha (Kaivalya)* or liberation. *Moksha* is to be attained here and now during this life-span only.

(7) Knowledge and truth are of two kinds: the lower one and the higher one. The lower, conventional knowledge and truth is referred to as *Vyavavahrik Satya*. It is a product of the senses and the intellect. The higher one is referred to the *Paramarthik Satya*. It is absolute. It is beyond words, thoughts, perception or conception. It is in no way, related to the senses and the intellect. It is non-perceptual and non-conceptual. It is a product of sublime intuition and 'divine vision'. The higher knowledge and truth brings about radical transformation in an individual so it is soteriological.

(8) Advait Vedant recognizes the six pramanas (sources and criteria of valid knowledge) on the basis of the Mimansa school of Kumaril Bhatt. They are as follows:

(1) Perception (*Pratyaksha*) (2) Inference (*Anuman*) (3) Testimony (*Shabda*) (4) Comparison (*Upaman*) (5) Postulation (*Arthapatti*) (6) Non-cognition *(Anupalabdi)*

II. Dvait (Dualism)— It refers to 'two'. Dvait School is based on the concept of dualism. Alternatively known as *Bhedvad, Tattvavad* and *Bimbapratibimbavad, Dvait Vedant* sub-school was founded by the 13th-century scholar Madhavacharya. He identified Brahm with Vishnu (Narayan) who is the independent Reality. *Prakriti* or matter, and the Jeevas or souls are entirely dependent on Him, although they are co-eval realities. His view of Reality was purely dualistic and is, therefore, called Dvait (dualistic).

The *Dvait Vedant* School believes that God (Vishnu, supreme soul) and the individual souls (*Jeevatma*) exist as independent realities, and they are distinct. According to *Dvait,* the *Jeevatma* is totally different from Brahm. Even though he is similar to Brahm, he is not identical. Madhavacharya emphasizes the distinction between God and individual soul (*Jeev*). In addition, the school differentiates God from matter as well as the soul from matter. The school maintains that the God, *Jeev* and the *Jagat* are three separate and everlasting entities. God governs the world and has control over the souls. The soul in its ignorance remains shackled in the world. By devotion and God's mercy, the soul can migrate to the Heaven above. It can obtain *Mukti* from the cycle of life and death and live with God forever in the Heaven.

Madhav propounds the theory of *Panchabheds* or five eternal differences between 1. *Brahm* and *Jeevas 2. Brahm* and *Prakriti 3. Jeevas* and *Prakriti 4. Jeev* and *Jeev* and 5.various objects of *Prakriti.* He categorizes Jeevas into three groups, viz 1. Those who are capable of attaining liberation 2. Those who are purely materialistic craving only for worldly pleasures, always going through the rounds of birth and death and 3. Sinners who degenerate into lower births and hell. *Jeevas* get liberation through devotion and the grace of Vishnu. In the state of liberation the *Jeevas* are not only free from suffering but enjoy positive bliss, while the differences among them persist.

Madhav stands for unqualified dualism. The three eternal entities, viz God, soul and the world are fundamentally different from one another. All these are eternal and real but the latter two are subordinate to God and dependent on Him. Independent (*Svatantra*) reality is the Brahm, the Absolute Creator of the world.

Concepts of Monism and Dualism— Let us dwell a bit more on 'monism' and 'dualism' to have a clearer understanding of these two terms. Monism deals with oneness whereas dualism deals with the concept of 'two'. Between these two terms, we can identify a number of differences. Both terms are used in philosophy and have got varied meanings. According to dualism, the individual soul is different from the Supreme soul. Hence dualism deals with two entities individual soul and supreme soul separately. Monism speaks of oneness of soul. Individual soul is a part of the Supreme soul and is as good as the Supreme soul. Let us examine the differences that exist between these two terms.

Monism accepts oneness of everything in the universe. It sees no difference in the diversification of the universe. All are, but one is the crux of monism. Dualism sees difference between things. Dualism does not accept the unity in diversity. Monism is one of the systems of the Indian philosophy. Brahm is the Supreme entity that manifested in this universe comprising of matter and space. All other concepts such as time, energy and being have sprung forth from the Supreme Brahm.

Just as a spider would create a web on its accord and withdraws it on its accord too, Brahm also would manifest itself in this universe comprising of nature and living beings and withdraws onto itself at the end of the epoch. The moment of withdrawal is called as deluge. Each and every soul is potentially divine according to monism. The divinity of man lies well within himself. He is as good as the Almighty and as powerful as Him too. Monism describes the appearance of the universe as an inexplicable phenomenon. It is called 'Maya' in the Indian philosophy of Advait. Universe is just illusory in its appearance. The Brahm alone is true, and everything else around us is false.

Dualism is exactly the opposite of monism in the sense that although it speaks of the existence of the Almighty, it does not approve of unity in diversity. It does not see the oneness in all the beings. Man cannot be as powerful and potential as the God. Man has his limitations. Only the Almighty is all-powerful and all-pervading. He is omnipotent and omnipresent. Man cannot be omnipotent and omnipresent as long as he is mortal. Man is man, and God is God. Dualism is as simple as that. Dualism gets the name 'Dvait' in the Indian philosophy. According the tenets expounded by the exponents of the Dvaita system of philosophy, *Atman* or the individual self can never become Brahm or the Supreme Self. The individual self is called the *'Jeev'*, and the Supreme Self is called the 'Brahm'. The *Jeev* cannot become one with the Brahm. Even at the time of liberation or '*Mukti*', the individual self would undergo and experience the 'real bliss', but it cannot be equated at any juncture with the Brahm. Brahm is also called as 'Parmatman'. Dualism does not approve of the belief system of Monism. It does not call the universe as an inexplicable phenomenon or untrue. It would call the universe as a separate true entity apart from all powerful Brahm, the second entity that is permanent too. This highlights the differences that exist between the two terms. Now let us summarize the difference in the following manner:

•Monism deals with the oneness of the existence. Dualism does not approve of the oneness of the existence.

•Individual self is as good and potential as the Supreme Self according to Monism. Dualism, on the contrary, identifies them as two separate entities.

•Monism accepts the individual self merging into the Supreme Self upon liberation. Dualism, on the contrary, does not accept the merging of the individual self into the Supreme Self upon liberation.

•Individual self becomes the all-powerful Brahm according to Monism. Dualism does not agree with the view of the monists that the individual self becomes one with the Supreme Self. According to them, the individual self experiences the 'real bliss' but cannot be equal to the Brahm.

III. *Visishtadvait Vedant* *(Qualified Non-dualism)*— The term '*Visishtadvait*' is often translated as 'Qualified Non-dualism.' An alternative, and more informative, translation is 'Non-duality of the qualified whole,' or perhaps 'Non-duality with qualifications.' The principal exponent of this sub-school of Vedant is Ramanuj. This sub-school of the Vedant school of Hindu philosophy grew out of the Vaishnav (worship of the God Vishnu or Narayan) movement prominent in South India from the 7th A.D. century onward. Jagadguru Ramanujacharya (1017-1137 B. C.) revealed the philosophy of *Visishtadvait Vedant* or qualified Non-dualism, which was opposite to Jagadguru Shankaracharya's (a philosopher of 8th A. D.) philosophy of *Advait Vedant*.

Ramanujacharya philosophy is called a special form of non-dualism or qualified non-dualism or the theism or Vishist-Advait. He believes that there are three elements, living, non-living and God. God is very special and different from the two. The God and Brahm are one and the same. These three, viz living, non-living and the God are collectively called Brahm. Though the world of matter and the individual souls have a real existence of their own, still neither of them is essentially the same as the Brahm.

There are three classes of self or *Jeev,* viz (i) eternal (*Nitya*) who dwell in heaven (*Vaikunth*), enjoying bliss and are free from *Karma* and *Prakriti*, (ii) the freed (*Mukta*) who achieve liberation through their wisdom, virtue and devotion, and (iii) the bound *(Baddha*) who are bound to the worldly affairs (*Sansar*) owing to their ignorance and selfishness. The souls wandering in '*Sansar'* are again distinguished into four classes, viz (a) celestial/super-human, (ii) human, (c) animal, and (d) stationary (*Sthavar*).

Ramanuj analyses the relation of the world to God. He argues that God is indeed real and independent but the souls of the world are also real though their reality is utterly dependent on that of God. The self *(Jeev)* is dependent on the God (*Isvara)* but is not different from the God. The universe is true (and not appearance only). Ramanuj vigorously protests against the doctrine of *Maya* and the phenomenality of the world. He believes in a spiritual principle as the basis of the world; the world is not an illusion, but is a reality.

Salvation, according to Ramanuj, is not the disappearance of the self but its release from the limitations. The released soul attains the nature of God, though it does not identify with Him. It desires nothing else, and so has no chance of returning to the world (*Sansar*). There is no *Jeevanmukti*. One attains the fellowship with God after exhausting all karma and throwing-off the physical body.

Ramanujacharya stresses that God alone exists. He says that Brahm is God. He is not formless. The Cosmos and the J*eevas* form his body. When the Jeev (soul) realizes that he is a part of *Parmatman* (God), the soul is liberated. On liberation, his soul enjoys infinite consciousness and infinite bliss of God. The soul is in communion with God, but it does not share the power of the creation or destruction.

Ramanuj taught that Ultimate Reality or *Brahm* had three aspects: *Ishwara* (Vishnu), *Chitta* (soul) and *Achitta* (matter). Vishnu is the only independent reality, while souls and matter are dependent on Him for their existence although they are also real. For him the relation between the infinite and the finite is like that between the soul and the body. Hence, non-duality is maintained, while differences can still be stated. Soul and matter are totally dependent on God for their existence, as is the body on the soul. According to Visishtadvait, the *Jeevatma* is a part of Brahm, and hence is similar, but not identical. This suggests a kind of duality

Because of this qualification of the Ultimate Reality, Ramanuj's system is known as Visishtadvait or qualified non-dualism, i.e. non-duality of Brahm, the Absolute, but *Vishista* or qualified by *Chitta* and *Achitta*. Brahm is similar to a tree with branches, leaves and fruits. Though the tree is 'one', it has several parts like roots, branches, etc. each of them differing from one another but the tree itself remaining as 'one'.

Shankaracharya's Advait philosophy says that Brahm is the ultimate truth, the world is an illusion, and there is no difference between the Brahm and individual self. Whereas Ramanuj's Visishtadvait philosophy says that Brahm is ultimate and He has numerous attributes. It is incorrect to say that Brahm is *Nirgun* (without attributes). Brahm, the ultimate truth, is different from individual self. At the same time Brahm is in every entity of this universe, which is His creation. Brahm is *Parmatman* (supreme soul) and individual self is *Jeevatma* (minute soul). They could be compared to an ocean and drop of water respectively. The ultimate goal of *Jeevatma* is to reach *Parmatman*, just like the destination of every rain drop is the ocean through complete surrender. Once *Jeevatma* reaches *Parmatman* it will continue to serve *Parmatman* in Paramapadama, the abode of Lord Narayana or *Mahapurush*.

According to Ramanuj, the world is real, absolutely real, but it is wanting in perfection. At the same time, it does not care for perfection. It has no destined goal. The world was created by God's inspiration, is sustained by His Concern and will be dissolved by His Will. The world is God's playground. He performs His *Lila*, 'drama' here. This eternal sport of His is His constant movement, His spontaneous expression in endless repetition. Man is real. But he has to depend on God. The world is real. But it has to depend on God. Without God, both man and the world are meaningless futility. But some difference between man and God will always remain. Man will remain eternally below God; hence he will always have to worship God. Ramanuj's path is mainly the path of devotion.

A soul is an infinitesimal fraction of God, just as a spark is a part of a fire. It remains at one place at a time, whereas God is omnipresent. The soul is ignorant, but God is omniscient and omnipotent. Being a fraction of God, the soul will always remain in existence. The soul could be considered equal to God only with respect to the experience of divine bliss. The only means for a soul to be liberated from Maya is selfless, whole-hearted devotion to God. The soul is an eternal servant of God. To refer to himself as God is a great sin.

Jagadguru Ramanujacharya gave special emphasis to selfless surrender to God. It is only through God's grace that a soul can attain ultimate divine happiness. He said that God resides in the heart of every soul as a witness. He is the supreme Divine personality. He alone is the Creator and Lord of the universe. Worldly happiness is an illusion in the same way that a rope may be mistaken for a snake. God is our Mother and Father, therefore, the duty of every child is to attain the grace of His Divine Mother and Father.

IV. *Bhedabhed Vedant* or ***Dvaitadvait***— *Bhedabhed Vedant* is one of the several traditions of Vedantic philosophy in India. '*Bhedabhed*' is a Sanskrit word meaning 'Difference and Non-Difference.' According to the *Bhedabhed* view, *Brahm* converts itself into the created, but yet maintains a distinct identity. Thus, the school holds that *Brahm* is both different (*bhed*) and not different (*abhed*) from creation and the individual *Jeev*.

Bhedabhed Vedantic ideas can be traced to some of the very oldest Vedantic texts, including quite possibly Badarayan's **Brahma Sutra** (app. 4th c. A.D.). *Bhedabhed* ideas also had an enormous influence on the devotional (*Bhakti*) schools of India's medieval period. Among the medieval Bhedabhed thinkers are Vallabh (1479-1531 A.D.), the founder of the Pustimarg devotional sect now centred in Nathdwar, Rajasthan and Chaitanya (1485-1533 A.D.) the founder of the Gaudiya Vaishnav sect based in the north-eastern Indian State of West Bengal.

Vallabhacharya believes that Brahm is one and the only element, which is non-dual. The whole world is real and subtly Brahm. The universe and the (living) self are the forms of pure Brahm and are not different from the Brahm. He admits that *Jeev, Kala* (time) and *Prakriti or Maya* are real and have eternal existences; these are being of Brahm and have no separate existence. Pure Brahm is the non-dual element. Brahm becomes whatever it wills by evolution (*Avirbhav*) and involution (*Tirobhav*) of its qualities such as bliss and consciousness.

According to this philosophy there are three categories of existence: Brahm, soul and matter. Soul and matter are different from Brahm in that they have attributes and capacities different from Brahm. Brahm exists independently, while soul and matter are dependent. Thus soul and matter have an existence that is separate yet dependent. Further, Brahm is a controller, the soul is the enjoyer, and matter, the thing enjoyed. Also, the highest object of worship is Krishna and his consort Radha, attended by thousands of Gopis of the Vrindavan and devotion consists in self-surrender.

The characteristic position of all the different *Bhedabhed Vedant* sub-schools is that the individual self (*Jeevatma*) is both different and not different from the ultimate reality known as Brahm. Each thinker within the *Bhedabhed Vedant* tradition has his own particular understanding of the precise meanings of the philosophical terms 'difference' and 'non-difference.' The real problem with this school is that philosophers of this school are themselves very confused about their views.

Prominent Unorthodox Schools

Jainism and Buddhism are the two main religions, which can be treated as separate from the Vedic base. Both these religions, and in particular Buddhism, have numerous followers. These do not recognise the existence of a creator God. Jainism believes that the universe has existed and will exist. The entities/substances of the universe, however, do undergo countless changes, but nothing is lost or destroyed. Everything is recycled in another form. Jainism has philosophical theories of non-absolutism or relative pluralism (*Anekantavad*) and modified scepticism. It teaches a path to liberation (*Moksha/Kaivalya*), which consists of the three jewels (trinity or *Ratna-traya*), viz right perception (*Samyak Darshan*), right knowledge (*Samyak* Gyan) and right conduct (*Samyak Charitrya*).

Jainism— Jainism is another school of thought that practices atheism and follows the teachings of Mahavir. The Jains consider the arguments about the existence of God as being fallacious. The universe has no beginning, so the question of a creator has no logical basis. Every one of us is a reservoir of positive energy. Divinity is not somewhere out there.

Though it is widely believed that Vardhaman Mahavir (? 599 B.C. – 527 B.C.?) founded Jainism, the Jain tradition maintains that he was the 24th Tirthankar of Jainism. Rishabhadev was the first Tirthankar. Parsvanath was the 23rd Tirthankar.

The two main sects of Jainism are: (1) *Digambar* (2) *Shwetambar*.

The *Digambaras* believe that a monk must give up all property including clothes and then only they get *moksha.* They also deny the right of women to *moksha.*

Jainism is both a philosophy and a religion. It is a heterodox philosophy in the sense that it does not uphold the authority of the Vedas. It is atheist and does not accept the existence of God. Jainism rejects the concept of a Supreme Being or the *Brahm* as the creator of the world. The Tirthankaras are the liberated souls. The followers offer prayers to the Tirthankaras.

A basic principle of Jain philosophy is based on *Anekantavad*, the idea that reality is perceived differently from different points of view, and that no single point of view is completely true (similar to the Western philosophical doctrine of Subjectivism). According to Jainism, only *Kevalis*, those who have infinite knowledge, can know the true answer, and that all others would only know a part of the answer. It stresses spiritual independence and the equality of all life, with particular emphasis on non-violence, and posits self-control as vital for attaining the realization of the soul's true nature.

Jainism believes that the universe is eternal and boundless (infinite). The Jains classify all the things into two groups: '*Jeev*' and '*a-Jeev'*. *Jeev* is what is known as the soul or the '*Atman*' or the '*Purush*' in other systems. *Jeev* can be considered as 'the composite unit of body and soul.' The soul manifests itself in a material body. Its essential character is consciousness. The *Jeevas* or the souls are innumerable and are divided into many grades or categories depending on the sense-organs they possess. The *Jeev* is not permanent. Its magnitude keeps on changing from body to body. The soul of an elephant is bigger than that of an insect.

While the Hindu philosophies maintain that the *Karma* is immaterial, Jainism advances the material form of *Karma*. According to Jainism, *Karma* is '*Paudgolik*'; it is constituted of subtle particles of matter.

Buddhism— Gautam Buddha (563 B.C.–483 B.C.) was the founder of Buddhism. It is a non-theistic system of beliefs based on the teachings of Siddhartha Gautam, a prince from present day Nepal, later known as Lord Buddha. The question of God is largely irrelevant in Buddhism, and it is mainly founded on the rejection of certain orthodox Hindu philosophical concepts (although it does share some philosophical views with Hinduism, such as belief in *Karma*).

Buddhism gives importance to the impermanence of existence and the sufferings associated with it. All existence, animate or inanimate, being in a state of flux, undergoes changes incessantly. Nothing is permanent. Existence is full of suffering, but ignorance is the cause of all suffering. The impermanence itself is the greatest *dukh*. Ignorance leads to sufferings and bondage. *Karma* is born out of ignorance. Karmic impressions are carried from this birth to the next birth. This means that the present conditions of life are the results of the past *Karma*. Every thought, word or action of the past existence has a bearing on the present existence.

The most 'striking' feature of Buddhism is the doctrine of non-self (*Anatta*). In a glaring and sharp contrast to the major philosophies, the Buddhism does not accept the permanent entity such as 'soul' or the 'Atman'. It maintains that there is no permanent and enduring entity in man. There is no distinct entity as the self or the soul. Buddhism advances the theory of *Nirvan*. Nirvan is a state of total freedom and no sufferings. With perfect knowledge, perfect peace and perfect wisdom, man is free from all bondage in a state of *Nirvan*.

Lord Buddha has presented four Noble Truths: (1) Existence is invariably associated with suffering. (2) Every suffering (*Dukh*) has a cause. (3) Suffering can be eliminated if the cause is eliminated. (4) There is a path to Nirvan which puts an end to all sufferings. Dr. S. Radhakrishnan has observed that these four noble truths of Buddhism correspond to the four truths of Sankhya Darshan.

The eight-fold path to *Nirvan* suggested by the Buddha is: (1) Right views; (2) Right resolve; (3) Right speech; (4) Right conduct; (5) Right livelihood; (6) Right effort; (7) Right mindfulness; and (8) Right concentration.

Buddhism is divided into two sects: Mahayan and Hinayan. Mahayan literature is written in Sanskrit and Hinayan literature is written in Pali. Buddha's argument is that if God is all-pervading, why is there so much evil all around? Like Charvak, the Buddha also rejected the concept of soul but he did argue in favour of continuity through life and successive lives. Atheism strengthens the divine in man and generates an inexplicable joy. Whoever denies God asserts his own divinity.

Charvakism

The Charvak School is one of the *Nastik* or 'heterodox' philosophies. *Charvakism* is materialism. It is believed to have stemmed in the post-Upanishadic era, but before the rise of *Buddhism*. A sage, Charvak, is believed to be the founder of this Indian system of materialism. It rejects supernaturalism, emphasizes materalism and philosophical scepticism, holding empiricism, perception and conditional inference as the proper source of knowledge. It holds that there is neither after life nor rebirth, all existence is mere combination of atoms and substances, feelings and mind are an epiphenomenon, and free will exists.

Brihaspati is sometimes referred to as propounder of atheism in Indian philosophy and this school is known as Charvak or Lokayat School. We also have annihilationists and naturalists, who did not believe in the existence of God. Much of the primary literature of Charvak, the Barhaspatya Sutras (ca. 600 BC), however, are missing or lost. Its theories and development have been compiled from historic secondary literature such as those found in the Shastras, Sutras and the Indian epic poetry as well as from the texts of Buddhism and from Jain literature.

Like other schools of philosophy, Charvakism explores the sources and validity of man's knowledge of reality. The Charvak materialists validate '*Pratyaksha*' (perception) as the sole source and criterion of knowledge. For the materialist, the sense perception (*Pratyaksha*) is the only acceptable source and hence they rule out 'inference' and 'testimony' as the source and criterion of knowledge. The materialists emphasize that what we perceive with our senses alone is true. They challenge the inference as the source or criterion of knowledge. They argue, 'The men you have encountered are mortal. Maybe, yes. But how can you say that all men in the past, present and future are mortal?' They contend that limited and perceived instances cannot lead to unrestricted universal generalizations.

Charvak believed only in four elements, namely earth, water, fire and air and did not believe in the element of sky, as it could not be proved. Only that exists which is present, could be seen and felt. He stated that out of the four, viz (i) passion (including sex) or desire (*Kama*), (ii) money or material well-being (*Artha*), (iii) religion or good deeds (*Dharma)*, and (iv) salvation (*Moksha*), the resultant pleasure is the essence of life. He also believed that death is the salvation.

He believed in the philosophy of 'eat, drink and be merry.' He stated that 'till you are alive, live with pleasure and even borrow for pleasure because once the body is turned to ashes after death, it will not come back again,' and you will not have a chance to enjoy. Charvak and his followers placed all of their attention on the aims of worldly pleasure. Like Epicureans, however, they also found that pleasure could be maximised and pain could be minimised by detachment. Immortality was found in the name and fame one leaves behind for noble deeds performed.

Believing in pleasure-seeking and rather unrestrained hedonistic philosophy, Charvak could not perceive the difference among various pleasures one may get. There could be different types of pleasures. The pleasure as meant to an animal, a scientist, a poet, a philosopher and a saint could be qualitatively different. He unwisely negated the religion, the duty, the values and ethics of life.

The materialists hold that matter is the only reality. They straight away reject gods and souls, as they are beyond perceptual experience. They also regard heaven and hell as non-existent as they are not perceivable. For the Charvakas, matter has always existed and will always exist. Matter is both the material and efficient cause of the universe. Hedonism seems to be a feature of Charvakism. However, not all followers seem to endorse them. Many of them acknowledge the importance of society, law and order. As a vital philosophical school, Charvakism appears to have died out some time in the 15th Century.

Neo-Vedant

Neo-Vedant, also called Hindu modernism, neo-Hinduism, Global Hinduism and Hindu Universalism, are terms to characterize interpretations of Hinduism that developed in the 19th century. The term 'Neo-Vedant' appears to have arisen in Bengal in the 19th century, where it was used by both Indians and Europeans. According to Halbfass, the term was introduced by a Bengali scholar, Brajendra Nath Seal (1864-1938), who used it to characterize the literary work of Bankim Chandra Chatterjee (1838-1894).

The terms like Global Hinduism and Hindu Universalism are also in use to characterize interpretations of Hinduism that developed in the 19th century. These modern interpretations incorporate Western ideas into traditional Indian religions, especially Advait Vedant, which is central or fundamental to Hindu culture. The development took place partly in response to the Western colonialism and orientalism, contributing to the Indian freedom struggle and the modern national and religious identity of Hindus in the Republic of India. This societal aspect is covered under the term of Hindu reform movements. Among the main proponents of such modern interpretations of Hinduism were Vivekananda, Aurobindo and Sarvepalli Radhakrishnan, who to some extent also contributed to the emergence of Neo-Hindu movements in the West.

Neo-Vedant has been influential in the perception of Hinduism, both in the West and in the educated classes of India. It has received appraisal for its 'solution of synthesis,' but has also been criticized for its Universalism. The terms 'Neo-Hindu' or 'Neo-Vedant' themselves have also been criticized for its polemical usage, the prefix 'Neo' then intended to imply that these modern interpretations of Hinduism are 'inauthentic' or in other ways problematic.

Integral Advaitism (Integral Dualism)— Sri Aurobindo (1872-1950) has propounded the theory of Integral Advaitism (Integral Dualism). The integral Advaitism of Sri Aurobindo believes that the Brahm is the Supreme element. The universe is the manifestation of the Brahm, the Absolute and is, therefore, true. The evolution is upward from non-living matter to life, from living to human beings and from human beings to super human-being. Thus, the evolution has four ascending planes of Matter, Life, Pure mind and Super mind. These planes are integral and non-dual.

OM TAT SAT

Chapter - 6

An Overview of the Srimad Bhagavad Geeta

The Srimad Bhagavad Geeta, basically a summary of the Upanishadic philosophy, is a sacred scripture written in Sanskrit and has been presented in the form of a dialogue between Lord Krishna, the Supreme Being, incarnated in human form and the warrior prince Arjun. It is set in the battlefield of Kurukshetra in the present State of Haryana. As we all know the Mahabharat is one of the two great epics of Hindus, the other being the Ramayan. They are considered to be the earliest epic of mankind.

The dictionary meaning of the word 'Geeta' is a song or poem containing an inspired doctrine and the word 'Bhagavad' means a blessed or adorable or venerable or divine One. Hence, the Srimad Bhagavad Geeta is variously called as 'The Song of God', 'The Divine Song', 'A Song of Fortune', 'The Lord's Song', 'The Holy Song of God', 'The Song of the Lord', *Gudarth Deepika, Geeta Rahasya, Gyaneshwari, Bhavaarthadipika, Sadhak Sanjeevani* and so on. The noted English poet, journalist and a Principal of the Government Sanskrit College at Pune, Sir Edwin Arnold (1832-1904) called his famous poetic version of the Srimad Bhagavad Geeta as 'The Song Celestial'. The Srimad Bhagavad Geeta's another title is '*Moksha Shastra*' or 'Scripture of Liberation'. However, it is more popularly known as 'The Geeta'. The Srimad Bhagavad Geeta is a sacred Hindu scripture, considered among the most important texts in the history of literature and philosophy. It represents the essence of Vedant for millions of Hindus.

As a Vedantic text, the Geeta is a splendid summary of the Upanishads. Traditional scholars include three texts of Vedant- Upanishads, Brahma Sutra and the Geeta- as a trilogy: foundational text. Lord Krishna is the divine milkman, the Upanishads are the cows and the Geeta is milk obtained for the sake of Arjun and all mankind, states a poem. The Upanishads and the Brahma Sutra are admittedly difficult texts to comprehend. The Geeta is much simpler and delightful to read and grasp. It is of later origin than the Upanishads, but perhaps precedes the Brahma Sutras. Hence, it can be stated that the Geeta is an improved version of the Upanishadic teachings. The Geeta is much more than a mere summary of the Upanishads. The Geeta is delightful and easy to read, as it takes the form of dialogue between Arjun and Lord Krishna. Dialogues exist in the Upanishads too, but they are very profound and complicated. Arjun has raised many everyday questions that tend to agitate the human mind.

Over 5,000 years ago Krishna instructed his confused friend Arjun on the philosophy of human life– its purpose, goal and its attainment. Known as the Bhagavad Geeta, the Song Celestial, it is accepted as the quintessence of all the Vedas. The Geeta is unique because, unlike any other religious scripture, it is spoken by God (Krishna) Himself. If there appear to be any contradictions and inconsistencies, they are only in the differing interpretations of the text.

Varying Interpretations

Unlike any other religious scripture, Srimad Bhagavad Geeta broadcasts its message in the centre of the battlefield. The choice of such an unholy ambience for the delivery of a philosophical discourse has been an enigma to many commentators. Several modern Indian writers have interpreted the battlefield setting as an allegory of 'the war within'.

Eknath Easwaran writes that the Geeta's subject is "the war within, the struggle for self-mastery that every human being must wage if he or she is to emerge from life victorious", and that "the language of battle is often found in the scriptures, for it conveys the strenuous, long, drawn-out campaign we must wage to free ourselves from the tyranny of the ego, the cause of all our suffering and sorrow." Swami Nikhilanand takes Arjun as an allegory of *Atman*, Krishna as an allegory of *Brahm*, Arjun's chariot as the body, and Dhritarashtra as the ignorance filled mind.

Mohandas Karamchand Gandhi, in his commentary on the Geeta, interprets the battle as 'an allegory in which the battlefield is the soul and Arjun, man's higher impulses struggling against evil'. Swami Vivekananda also emphasized that the first discourse in the Geeta related to the war could be taken allegorically. Vivekananda further remarked that this Kurukshetra War is only an allegory. When we sum up its esoteric significance, it means the war which is constantly going on within man between the tendencies of good and evil.

Such view about the Geeta is negation of the Mahabharat or Krishna as a historical reality. It is hard to subscribe the above view that the war of Mahabharat did not take place. No historian has described Mahabharat as a cock and bull story. The story of the Mahabharat might have contained some amount of exaggeration or somewhat distortion of facts or concoction in course of time, but archaeologists and historians have accepted the event of Mahabharat as a reality. There was no the necessity of telling things so figuratively or indirectly to a man in action in the battlefield. The occasion was not a class room lecture in the Department of Philosophy or Literature. It might be possible that an ordinary family feud was given a high sounding philosophical touch by later authors to convey their own views, but the argument that everything was imaginary cannot be easily accepted. Aurobindo has rightly rejected the interpretation that the Geeta, and the Mahabharat by extension, is 'an allegory of the inner life, and has nothing to do with our outward human life and actions'. The Geeta was composed in plain terms and professes to solve the great ethical and spiritual difficulties which the life of man raises, and it will not do to go behind this plain language and thought and wrest them to the service of our fancy.

Here in the Srimad Bhagavad Geeta, we find a practical handbook of instruction on how best we can re-organise our inner ways of thinking, feeling, and acting in our everyday life and draw from ourselves a larger gush of productivity to enrich the life around us, and to emblazon the subjective life within us.

The Bhagavad Geeta integrates various schools of thought, notably Vedant, Sankhya and Yog, and other theistic ideas. It remains a popular text for commentators belonging to various philosophical schools. The Geeta is one of the hardest books to interpret, which accounts for the numerous commentaries on it– each differing from the rest in one essential point or the other. Different translators and commentators have widely differing views on what multi-layered Sanskrit words and passages signify, and their presentation in English depending on the philosophical school they belong to. Commentators have either misinterpreted the verses or have gone beyond the tone and tenor of the authors of the Geeta or the messages conveyed by Sri Krishna Himself. Some have commented on the Geeta out of the context in which it was created or communicated to an ordinary mortal like Arjun. Some Indian scholars have offered unnecessarily mystical interpretation which has made the Geeta a book of clumsy and contradictory verses.

Being immensely impressed by the life and teachings of Lord Krishna as well as the Krishna Consciousness movement across the globe, I have tried to offer a brief and commonplace overview of the Geeta from the perspective of sociology of religion in an objective manner without opposing or supporting any religious or philosophical system of belief. Srimad Bhagavad Geeta should surely be read or viewed simply as it was presented before the common men and women of this country those days. It has got something for people of all faiths including non-believers or agnostics. The contemporary context is no less important, as the present should be viewed against the backdrop of past and the past should be viewed against the present. Present is never completely severed from the past and vice-versa.

As the great battle of Mahabharat arose out of family feud emanating from complete denial of share by the Kauravas to their cousins in the kingdom or land, sociological perspective assumes greater relevance than philosophical perspective. All the earlier commentaries on the Geeta so far appear to be a pure philosophically oriented. The commentators have treated Sri Krishna as great teacher of Hindu philosophy. Knowing the fact full well that Sri Krishna was not an ordinary human being, His teaching was definitely for ordinary men and women. It is indeed amazing that instead of explaining the general meaning of different verses to the wide-ranging readers, most commentators have tried to teach Krishna *Bhakti* to their reader which really hampers the objective presentation of the Geeta. In all fairness it should be left to readers to read between the lines of dialogues between Sri Krishna and Arjun. This is the usual expectation of any objective reader of the modern world.

Contents

The Srimad Bhagavad Geeta, literally means 'Song of the Lord', often referred to as the Geeta now. The Geeta is a poem of 700 verses, in fairly straightforward Sanskrit, known as *Bhishm Parva* of Mahabharat of which 574 are spoken by Sri Krishna and 84 by Arjun, and the rest by others. It opens with the blind King Dhritarashtra requesting his secretary and charioteer, Sanjay, to narrate the events of battle between his sons, the Kauravas, and their cousins, the Pandavas. The Geeta begins before the start of the climactic Kurukshetra War, where the Pandav prince Arjun is filled with doubt on the battlefield. Realizing that his enemies are his own relatives, friends, and revered teachers, Arjun turns to his charioteer and guide, God Incarnate Lord Shri Krishna, for His advice. Lord Krishna, the Supreme Personality of Godhead, out of affection for His devotee, the Pandav Prince Arjun, has agreed to drive his chariot in the battlefield. Responding to Arjun's confusion and moral dilemma, Krishna explains to Arjun his duties as a warrior and prince, elaborating on a variety of philosophical concepts. The Geeta is set in a narrative framework of a dialogue between Pandav Arjun and his charioteer Krishna. Facing the duty as a warrior to fight the *Dharma Yuddha* or righteous war between Pandavas and Kauravas, Arjun is counselled by Krishna to fulfil his Kshatriya (warrior) duty as a warrior and establishing Dharma. The Srimad Bhagavad Geeta was exposed to the world through Sanjay.

The Lord speaks the philosophy in the midst of the opposing armies of two closely related families ready to fight a fratricidal war. When Arjun is reluctant to fight against his kith and kin, whom he may have to kill, Krishna tells Arjun that he should not shirk from *svadharma* or ordained duty which, as a Kshatriya, is to fight. While most religions advocate compassion, mercy, forgiveness, and exhort to abjure war and killing, here God Himself urges Arjun to fight and kill.

Krishna convinces Arjun of where his duty lies, and the same Arjun who in the beginning refuses to fight now promises to Krishna's bidding. In no other scripture does God so unabashedly glorify Himself. To convince Arjun that He is the master and controller of all that be, Krishna recounts His innumerable *vibhutis* or glories, opulences and powers and shows His *virat-rup* or universal form in a brazen display of His majesty and powers. The Geeta jolts us into contemplation when it tells us that we are not the body and mind that we believe we are, and that, in fact, we are pure spirit soul or Atman, a tiny part (or *ansa*) of God, the Supreme Spirit, and we are eternal, indestructible and immutable. The realization of this basic truth is a pre-requisite to any spiritual progress.

The Geeta does not propose attainment of heaven and its sense pleasures as the goal of human life. Krishna warns that gratification of the senses cannot bring happiness. The Geeta describes the material world as *Dukhalayam*, a place full of misery, wherein birth and death take place in a continuous cycle (*Sansar*). It urges us to liberate ourselves from *sansar* and reunite with the Lord and thereby attain to His nature of *Satta-Chitta-Anand*, the state of being eternally existent– completely knowledgeable– full of bliss, which is the goal of human life and which alone can bring eternal peace and happiness.

To achieve that goal the Geeta elucidates four different paths: *Raj Yog* or meditation, *Karmayog* or work, *Gyanayog* or knowledge and *Bhaktiyog* or devotion– from which the aspirant may choose according to his temperament, capacity and inclination. In *Bhaktiyog*, the Geeta makes available to us an easy and effective means to reach Krishna. *Bhaktiyog* requires neither elaborate paraphernalia nor cumbersome rituals, for Krishna says: "If a *bhakta* offers Me with love and devotion, a leaf, a flower, a fruit or a little water, I will wholeheartedly accept it".

The essence of the Geeta is summed up in verses 65 and 66 of the concluding Discourse wherein Krishna asks Arjun to simply abandon all religious practices and pay homage to Him, adore Him, worship

Him and unconditionally surrender unto Him, after which Arjun need have no fear, for Krishna would absolve him of all his sins and take complete care of him.

The Song of God or the Bhagavad Geeta is unique because it is free from dogma. After explaining the most confidential spiritual knowledge, Lord Krishna tells Arjun that now you have heard everything, you are free to do what you think fit. In essence, the Geeta recognizes the individual's liberty and leaves the ultimate choice in the hands of the seeker. Liberal and without prejudice, the Bhagavad Geeta is Lord Krishna's gift to mankind, to help us deal with the turbulence of life in as rational a manner as is humanly possible.

The Bhagavad Geeta is a manual for life and living. The Geeta presents the laws and principles on which life works. Well before there was any concept of 'Hinduism', thousands of years ago, our ancestors called themselves the *Aryaputra* or noble race. Or Bharatas (*bha*– light and *rat*– revel), those revelling in the light of Consciousness. The result of this philosophy was prosperity, harmony and spiritual growth. The philosophy created a favourable environment for people to reflect on higher pursuits of life.

The Geeta deals with human problems in a human way. That is why it has a tremendous appeal. It has inspired the human mind in India for centuries and today it casts its spell on millions of people across the various parts of the world. It remains the most translated work in the world. The modern technology like the Internet has further increased its reputation by carrying its message to every nook and corner of the world. A mere click on the word 'Bhagavad Geeta' in the Google search engine throws about one million results. An incredible reach for any scripture! Among the great and extraordinary people who were inspired and found their outlook changed by the timeless wisdom of the Geeta are thinkers, writers, scientists and philosophers like Mahatma Gandhi, B.G Tilak, Sri Aurobindo Ghosh, Albert Einstein, Dr. Albert Schweitzer, Herman Hesse, Ralph Waldo Emerson, Aldous Huxley, Walt Whitman, Henry David Thoreau, Annie Besant, Robert Oppenheimer, Sir Edwin Arnold and Carlyle to name but a few.

In India it was left to Adi Shankar who lived in the 8th century A.D. to reveal the greatness of the Geeta to the world. He retrieved it from the mighty tomes of the epic, the Mahabharat, and wrote a brilliant commentary on it. It is this commentary which prevails as a classic text even today. Later great Acharyas like Ramanuj, Madhav, Vallabh and others came out with their own commentaries which are popular among their followers. In modern times Sant Gyaneshwar, B.G.Tilak, Aurobindo Ghosh contributed their original thinking on the text.

Despite this enormous popularity, Srimad Bhagavad Geeta remains a less understood but a better known text; people know more about it than what is it about. On the analogy of what Srimad Bhagavad Geeta says in Discourse 2, Verse 29 some look upon the book as marvellous, a scripture of extraordinary or mysterious value, some others speak of the book as wonderful. And still others though hearing its teachings do not comprehend its wonderful significance!

At Kurukshetra, when Arjun feels dejected that he is fighting against his kinsmen, he is overwhelmed with grief and he questions the propriety of fighting such a war. Arjun says to Sri Krishna, "My natural qualities to fight are engulfed by weakness of the mind. I do not know as to what my duty should be at this juncture. I am surrendering to you. Accept me as your disciple and instruct me properly about my duty."

The second discourse of the Geeta is the beginning of this great advice that reveals what Indians consider as the culmination of understanding Supreme Knowledge and the Supreme Being. Loss of the body does not bring about destruction of the soul, which it embeds. Just as a man abandons his worn-out clothes and wears a new one, the soul likewise abandons the worn-out body and takes a new one. Between life and death, the body passes through different phases such as adolescence, youth and old age. Ultimately death comes which is inevitable. Hence a wise man should not brood over it. Sri Krishna continues: Just as death is certain for those who are born, birth is also certain for those who die. While the former is common knowledge, the latter is incomprehensible.

Arjun is not convinced. Krishna then talks about action. Everybody should work, but without any desire for fruits. He emphasizes the need to rise above dualities of life, such as pleasure and pain, gain and loss, success and failure, heat and cold, and attraction and repulsion. He says that Sri Krishna takes birth again and again to preserve righteousness and order in the world. He prescribes duties for different categories of people and insists that one should always stick to *Swadharma* (one's own duty).

Sri Krishna reveals that he is the controller of everything, from matter to spirit. He pervades all space and time. He advises that as a member of the warrior clan Arjun's duty is to fight, irrespective of consequences. Fighting is his *Swadharma* and he would not incur any sin if he does his duty. Arjun is convinced; his conscience is now clear and he fights the war to establish *Dharma* and wipe out *Adharma*, as suggested by Sri Krishna.

Sri Krishna also says in the Geeta (7:3), "Among thousands of men, one by chance aspires for perfection; even among those successful aspirants only one by chance knows Me in essence." A question arises why such enlightened persons are so rare in our midst and why such an achievement is not within the reach of everyone.

Since the Vedant is a subjective science, one rarely tries to get rid of one's weaknesses and develop inner strength much less one tries to live up to the ideals propounded by it and bring about consequent re-adjustments in one's life. Very few feel this urge to evolve themselves and most of us do not even find the need for self improvement. We grope along by the voice of tradition, authority, herd-instinct and group-mentality. Of those who strive to see the truth and reach the goal, only a few succeed. Of those who gain the sight, not even one learns to live by the sight.

The Geeta was given to the skilled and noble Arjun when he became despondent on the battlefield at Kurukshetra, unable to withstand the challenge of having to fight his own relatives, teachers and friends. The gospel of the Geeta given by Krishna revived him despite the incapacitated state he was in.

The Geeta can be divided into three parts of six Discourses each. These three parts are said to represent the great Upanishadic aphorism, *Tat Tvam Asi,* You Are That.

The first part talks about '*tvam*', you, the individual. You meet challenges and are overwhelmed by them. You need to understand the purpose of life and conduct yourself accordingly. Doing that is your duty; it is *Karmayog,* path of action. *Karmayog* is working for a higher cause in the spirit of cooperative endeavour. When a person functions thus his worldly desires wane away and he is prepared for meditation. Through meditation he realizes his Self, the purpose of existence. The most famous verse in this section is probably *karmanyevadhikaraste* (2.47) – your right is to action and not to its fruit.

The second part talks of *'tat'*, that, the Supreme Reality, God. Krishna shows how Reality or God is in everything and everything is in God. He demonstrates this both by analyses and syntheses. He names individual things and says they are God and then puts it all together, synthesises them in the form of Vishwaroop, His cosmic form. In it, Arjun sees how everything is a part of Krishna or Reality, the good, the bad and the ugly. Whatever one sees is a manifestation of the Lord. With this vision one's mind expands in love and demonstrates the first quality of a *bhakta*, a devotee of God– *advesta sarva bhutanam, maitra, karuna eva cha*. That is, no hatred towards any being, and to be friendly, compassionate (12:13).

The third section talks about '*asi*', are, the relationship between the individual and God. He is the root and the world is the tree, the inverted *Ashvatha* tree. Like any family tree, the parent is shown on top and the descendants below. The world is made up of the three gunas– *Tamas*, ignorance; *Rajas*, activity; and *Sattva*, poise. They bind us in different ways and keep us from recognition of Reality. Beings in the world are all different– but different combinations of the three *gunas*. When one goes beyond the *Gunas* one finds one's true Self.

The text ends with Arjun overcoming the state of depression he was falling into and he is now ready to do his duty and fight a righteous war, Sanjay tells us that where there is the skill of Arjun and the Yog of Krishna– these are values they symbolise – there will be success, prosperity, victory and sound policy.

The Srimad Bhagavad Geeta is a universal scripture applicable to people of all temperaments the world over for all times. It is a book with sublime thoughts and practical instructions on Yog, devotion, Vedant and action. The Srimad Bhagavad Geeta has influenced so many great thinkers over the years. A careful perusal of the Geeta reveals that its philosophy is of the highest order of human thought. Its further improvement is humanly unattainable. No religious philosophy can ever match Geeta. The deeper we endeavour to go, the vaster it is. The essence of the Geeta is inherent in the following observations and self-posed questions:

Why do you worry without cause? Whom do you fear without reason? Who can kill you? The soul is neither born, nor does it die.

Whatever happened, happened for the good; whatever is happening, is happening for the good; whatever will happen, will also happen for the good only. You need not have any regrets for the past. You need not worry for the future. The present is happening...

What did you lose that you cry about? What did you bring with you, which you think you have lost? What did you produce, which you think got destroyed? You did not bring anything– whatever you have, you received from here. Whatever you have given, you have given only here. Whatever you took, you took from God. Whatever you gave, you gave to Him. You came empty handed, you will leave empty handed. What is yours today, belonged to someone else yesterday, and will belong to someone else the day after tomorrow. You are mistakenly enjoying the thought that this is yours. It is this false happiness that is the cause of your sorrows.

Change is the law of the universe. What you think of as death, is indeed life. In one instance you can be a millionaire, and in the other instance you can step into abject poverty. Yours and mine, big and small– remove these ideas from your mind. Then everything is yours and you belong to everyone.

This body is not yours, neither are you of the body. The body is made of fire, water, air, earth and ether, and will disappear into these elements. But the soul is permanent– so who are you?

Dedicate your being to God. He is the one to be ultimately relied upon. Those who know of his support are forever free from fear, worry and sorrow.

Whatever you do, do it as a dedication to God. This will bring you the tremendous experience of joy and life-freedom forever. When Arjun was in a state of deep despair just before the onset of actual war Krishna asked and suggested Arjun by saying, 'Never was there a time when I did not exist, nor you, nor all these rulers of men, nor shall any of us ever cease to exist in the future' (2:12). This is not a philosophy of this world. It is in no way human. It puts the Geeta on the top of the world.

The Srimad Bhagavad Geeta comprises 18 discourses: each Discourse has been levelled a *Yog*. Because of differences in recensions, the verses of the Geeta may be numbered in the full text of the Mahabharat as chapters 6:25-42. According to the recensions of the Geeta commented on by Adi Shankar, a prominent philosopher of the Vedant School, the number of verses is 700, but there is evidence to show that old manuscripts had 745 verses. The verses themselves, composed with similes and metaphors, are poetic in nature. The verses mostly employ the range and style of the Sanskrit *Anustubh* meter (*Chhandas*), and in a few expressive verses the *Tristubh* meter is used. Different discourses are highly imbalanced with respect to their size. Some discourse comprises merely 20 verses, while others comprise about 70 verses, possibly because of the variety of authors involved in compiling the Geeta or say the Mahabharat as a whole.

The Sanskrit edition of the Geeta names each Discourse as a particular form of Yog. However, these Discourse titles do not appear in the Sanskrit text of the Mahabharat. Swami Chidbhavanand explains that each of the eighteen Discourses is designated as a separate *Yog* because each Discourse, like *Yog*, 'trains the body and the mind'. He labels the first Discourse 'Arjun Vishad Yogam' or the 'Yog of Arjun's Dejection'. Sir Edwin Arnold translates this Discourse as 'The Distress of Arjun'. Yet another meaning of *Yog* is path and union (with the Supreme). Thus the word *yog* signifies both the method and the goal leading to spiritual liberation or salvation- freedom from rebirth and death. This overriding spiritual goal is also stated in the Upanishads, as the goal merging with the Supreme Being. Anyway, the eighteen Discourses are as follows:

1. Arjun-***Vishad Yog*** (Yog of the Despondency of Arjun contains 47 verses): Arjun has requested Krishna to move his chariot between the two opposing armies. His growing dejection is described as he fears losing friends and relatives as a consequence of war.

2. *Sankhya Yog* (Yog of Transcendental Knowledge contains 72 verses): After asking Krishna for his help, Arjun was given instructions or lessons on various subjects such as *Karmayog, Gyanayog,*

Sankhya Yog, Buddhiyog and the immortal nature of the soul. This discourse is often considered as the summary of the entire Bhagavad Geeta.

3. *Karmayog* (Yog of Action contains 43 verses): Krishna explains how Karmayog, i.e. performance of prescribed duties, but without attachment to results, is the appropriate course of action for Arjun.

4. *Gyan-Karma Yog* (Yog of Action and Knowledge contains 42 verses): Krishna reveals that he has lived through many births, always teaching Yog for the protection of the pious and the destruction of the impious and stresses the importance of accepting a *Guru.*

5. *Karma-Sannyas Yog* (Yog of Action and Renunciation contains 29 verses): Arjun asks Krishna if it is better to forgo action or to perform action ('renunciation or discipline of action'). Krishna answers that both are ways to the same goal, but that acting in Karmayog is superior.

6. *Dhyanyog* or *Atmasanyam Yog* (Yog of Meditation contains 47 verses): Krishna describes the *Ashtang Yog*. He further elucidates the difficulties of the mind and the techniques by which the mastery of mind might be gained.

7. *Gyan-Vigyanayog* (Yog of Knowledge and Wisdom contains 30 verses): Krishna describes the absolute reality and its illusory energy *Maya.*

8. *Akshar-Brahm Yog* (Yog of the Imperishable Brahm contains 28 verses): This Discourse contains eschatology of Srimad Bhagavad Geeta. Importance of the last thought before death, differences between material and spiritual worlds, and light and *dark* paths that a soul takes after death are described.

9. *Raj-Vidya Guhiya Yog* (*Yog of* Confidential Knowledge of the Ultimate Truth contains 34 verses): Krishna explains how His eternal energy pervades, creates, preserves and destroys the entire universe. According to theologian Christopher Southgate, verses of this Discourse of the Geeta are pantheistic, while German physicist and philosopher Max Bernhard Weinstein deems the work pandeistic.

10. *Vibhuti-Vistar-Yog* (Yog of the Divine Manifestations contains 42 verses): Krishna is described as the ultimate cause of all material and spiritual existence. Arjun accepts Krishna as the Supreme Being, quoting great sages who have also done so.

11. *Vishwaroop-Darshan Yog* (Yog of the Vision of the Universal Form contains 55 verses): On Arjun's request, Krishna displays his 'universal form' (*Vishwaroop*), a theophany of a being facing every way and emitting the radiance of a thousand suns, containing all other beings and material in existence.

12. *Bhaktiyog* (Yog of Devotion contains 20 verses): In this Discourse Krishna glorifies the path of devotion to God. Krishna describes the process of devotional service (*Bhaktiyog*). He also explains different forms of spiritual disciplines.

13. *Kshetra-Kshetragya Vibhag Yog* (Yog of Distinction between the Field and the Knower of the Field by Separation of Matter and Spirit contains 35 verses): The difference between transient, perishable physical body and the immutable eternal soul is described. The difference between individual consciousness and universal consciousness is also made clear.

14. *Gunatraya-Vibhag Yog* (Yog of the Division of the three Gunas contains 27 verses): Krishna explains the three modes (*Gunas*) of material nature pertaining to goodness, passion, and nascence. Their causes, characteristics, and influence on a living entity are also described.

15. *Purushottam Yog* (Yog of the Supreme Spirit contains 20 verses): Krishna identifies the transcendental characteristics of God such as omnipotence, omniscience, and omnipresence. Krishna also describes a symbolic tree (representing material existence), which has its roots in the heavens and its foliage on earth. Krishna explains that this tree should be felled with the 'axe of detachment', after which one can go beyond to his supreme abode.

16. *Daivasur-Sampad-Vibhag Yog* (Yog of Separateness of the Divine and Undivine contains 24 verses): Krishna identifies the human traits of the divine and the demonic natures. He counsels that to attain the supreme destination one must give up lust, anger, greed, and discern between right and wrong action by discernment through Buddhi and evidence from the scriptures.

17. *Shraddhatriya-Vibhag Yog* (Yog of the Threefold Division of the Faith contains 28 verses): Krishna qualifies the three divisions of faith, thoughts, deeds, and even eating habits corresponding to the three modes (*Gunas*).

18. *Moksha-Sannyas Yog* (Yog of Liberation and Renunciation contains 78 verses): In this Discourse, the conclusions of previous seventeen Discourses are summed up. Krishna asks Arjun to abandon all forms of Dharma and simply surrender unto him and describes this as the ultimate perfection of life.

The eighteen discourses of the Geeta can be classified into three broad sets of 6 discourses each explaining the Truth of the *Mahavakya* from *Samaved (Tat-Tvam-Asi),* which means 'You Are That'. This sentence summarizes the entire Vedic law and philosophy. The first 6 discourses of the Geeta explain the significance of the term 'You' (*Tvam*). The next 6 discourses from the 7th to 12th explain the term 'That' (*Tat*). The last 6 discourses give the meaning of the term '*Are*' (*Asi*) and explain the message of the entire *Mahavakya,* i.e. how the individual can blend with *Parabrahm* or attain liberation. This division does not mean any compartmentalization but implies a close relationship between the verses as also a logical thought flow from one discourse to another.

The following are the four *Mahavakyas* (Great Truths) taken out from each of the four Vedas all indicating the same truth.

Great Truths

Sr.No.	*Mahavakya*	Meaning
1.	*Pragyanam Brahm*	Consciousness is Brahm
2.	*Tat-Tvam-Asi*	That You Are
3.	*Ayam Atman Brahm*	This Atman is Brahm
4.	*Aham Brahm Smi*	I am Brahm

Madhusudan Saraswati has also classified the Geeta 's eighteen discourses into three broad sections of six discourses each, but he has done it for a different purpose of offering his own analysis of contents of the Geeta. Swami Gambhiranand characterizes Madhusudan Saraswati's system as a successive approach in which *Karmayog* leads to *Bhaktiyog*, which in turn leads to *Gyanayog:*

Discourses 1– 6 = *Karmayog* (action), the means to the final goal

Discourses 7–12 = *Bhaktiyog* (devotion)

Discourses 13–18 = *Gyanayog* (knowledge), the goal itself

While such divisions are very convenient as far as teaching or preaching of the Geeta is concerned, the various *Yogas* often get mixed up in several discourses. Many things have been said in a repetitive manner. Therefore, a clear-cut separation into three section or four is neither purposeful nor is it really a viable solution of anything.

Karmayog— As noted by various commentators, the Srimad Bhagavad Geeta offers a practical approach to liberation in the form of Karmayog. The path of Karmayog upholds the necessity of action. However, this action is to be undertaken without any attachment to the work or desire for results. Bhagavad Geeta terms this 'inaction in action and action in inaction (4:18)'. The concept of such detached action is also called *Nishkam Karma*, a term not used in the Geeta. Lord Krishna elaborates on the role performance, role performed without desire and attachment.

In simple terms the Geeta suggests that one should do one's duty and not worry or crave for results. One should always be ready to accept success and failures with equal calmness. You have only right to do your duty, you have no control over the results. Be detached from results, for they may bring name and fame one moment and disgrace or ignonimity on the other. The man of wisdom remains unmoved in prosperity or success as well as in adversity, unmindful of whether he is criticized or glorified. This is the seminal gospel of the Geeta. Those who believe in *Bhaktiyog*, they tend to underplay the *Karmayog* aspect of the Geeta. According to them *Bhaktiyog* alone is sufficient to attain liberation. The message of *Karmayog*, as rightly emphasized by Vivekananda, has got greater relevance in the modern world than *Bhaktiyog*.

Bhaktiyog— The introduction to discourse 7 of the Srimad Bhagavad Geeta explains *Bhakti* as a mode of worship which consists of unceasing and loving remembrance of God. Faith and total surrender to a chosen God (*Ishta-dev*) are considered to be important aspects of *Bhakti*. Theologian Catherine Cornille writes, 'The text [of the *Geeta*] offers a survey of the different possible disciplines for attaining liberation through knowledge (*Gyan*), action (*Karma*), and loving devotion to God (*Bhakti*), focusing on the latter as both the easiest and the highest path to salvation.' M. R. Sampatkumaran, a Bhagavad

Geeta scholar, explains in his overview of Ramanuj's commentary on the Geeta, 'The point is that mere knowledge of the scriptures cannot lead to final release. Devotion, meditation, and worship are essential.' Ramakrishna believed that the essential message of the Geeta could be obtained by repeating the word Geeta several times, 'Geeta, Geeta, Geeta', you begin, but then find yourself saying '*ta-Gi, ta-Gi, ta-Gi'*. *Tagi (pronounced as Taji)* means one who has renounced everything for God.' In the following verses, Krishna elucidates the importance of *Bhakti.*

The path of devotion has been continually stressed in the Geeta. Earlier the Vedas used to over-emphasize rituals and offerings to propitiate various Vedic gods, mostly for temporal or worldly gains. Taking the lead from the Upanishad or the later part of the Vedas, the Geeta emphasizes the supreme importance of devotion to a Supreme Being or Brahm. In fact, the Geeta goes one step further by suggesting devotion to God in personal form (i.e. God in human form) and in this case the Lord Krishna Himself. The Lord repeatedly talks about single minded devotion to Him alone. He has rejected the elaborate rituals and sacrifices of Vedic times. Such is the stirring message of the Geeta.

The Lord takes us to yet another height, the higher height. The easy path to that is the total surrender to the Lord. The Lord protects us in all circumstances and do away with our sins, shower grace on us and give liberation and freedom from future births and deaths. The Lord will give us inner peace and bliss; He will also give us knowledge of Brahm. Such is the gain of *Bhaktiyog.*

Gyanayog— *Gyan* (wisdom or knowledge) is considered the most difficult of the four main paths of Yog, requiring great strength of will and intellect. In *Gyanayog*, the mind is used to inquire into its own nature and to transcend the mind's identification with its thoughts and ego. The fundamental goal of *Gyanayog* is to become liberated from the illusionary world of *Maya* (thoughts and perceptions) and to achieve union of the inner Self *(Atman)* with the oneness of all life (Brahm). This is achieved by steadfastly practising the mental techniques of self-questioning, reflection and conscious illumination. The knowledge of the Self or the Atman is the central theme of *Gyan Marg*.

This path is often associated with the non-dualistic Vedantic belief of the identity of the *Atman* with the Brahm. For the followers of this path, the realization of the identity of *Atman* and Brahm is held as the key to liberation. When a sensible man ceases to see different identities due to different material bodies and he sees how beings are expanded everywhere, he attains to the Brahm conception (13:31). Those who see with eyes of knowledge the difference between the body and the knower of the body, and can also understand the process of liberation from bondage in material nature, attain to the supreme goal (13:35).

The Srimad Bhagavad Geeta presents a synthesis of the Brahmaical concept of Dharma, theistic *Bhakti,* the *yogic* ideals of *Moksha* through *Gyan, Bhakti, Karma,* and *Raj Yog* (spoken of in the 6th discourse) and Sankhya philosophy. Numerous commentaries have been written on the Srimad Bhagavad Geeta with widely differing views on the essentials. Vedant commentators read varying relations between Self and Brahm in the text: Advait Vedant sees the non-dualism of *Atman* (soul) and Brahm as its essence, whereas Bhedabhed and Visishtadvait see *Atman* and Brahm as both different and non-different, and Dvait sees them as different.

The Lord begins to tell us about the Self right from second chapter. He clearly says that it is the Self that gives life force *(Pran)* to all creatures, including the humans. The Self is present is non-living matter also as a lower form of consciousness. The Self is unborn and eternal. When a person dies, it is the body that dies, not the Self *(Atman)*. The Self discards the body and may take another body, just as one changes into new set of clothes after one gets frayed and tattered.

The Soul in the form of Brahm permeates the universe. Some analogies may again help here. Like the wind moving about the space, the Brahm pervades everything in the universe. Like the string that unites the pearls in a necklace, but is not seen as such, the Brahm connects all matters and activates them, but He remains invisible.

The Soul residing in the body is not different from the Brahm or *Parmatma.* The Soul is a small part of this Brahm, it activates the body, but the Brahm remains undiminished by forming innumerable creatures. The Lord is present in all of us, we are not present in the Lord, as waves depend on the sea and are parts of the sea but the sea does not depend on waves.

The Lord has lower form also, which is the action of the five senses and the mind and ego present in each of us. The higher form of the Lord is eternal, indestructible, imperishable Brahm or the Supreme Being. The lower form is perishable and constantly changing but not the higher form. This is the Supreme Knowledge.

It has been observed by some scholars the last six discourses are a later addition. It is apparent from the following words of Stephen Mitchell (**Bhagavad Gita**, 2002), "In Chapter 13 to 18 much of the material is dull and secondary at best; for long stretches the poem seems to be written by a scholastic philosopher bent on categorizing everything in the world according to three *Gunas*". As the Geeta deals with the philosophy of life, such additions have in a way enhanced the value of this holy book.

Methods of Studying the Geeta

The Srimad Bhagavad Geeta can be studied from different angles such as a historical document, a spiritual treatise, a scriptural text for daily chanting and prayer, a sublime poetry, an exposition of grammar and meter, or a management manual, depending on one's own outlook and purpose.

The objective here is to study it as a spiritual text and try to find out its main theme. Our ancient Rishis have given us a six-point test to determine the main theme of a text. This is called '*sadvidvidha tatparya nirnaya linga*'. In the light of this six-factor test let us look at the Geeta to discover its central theme.

The 1st point is called *upakrama* and *upasamhar*– the beginning and conclusion of a text. The crux of the subject in the text starts with Arjun's confusion, his acceptance of the delusion and surrender to the Lord as a disciple with a request to teach him what is the best for him. The text ends with his statement that all his doubts were cleared, his delusion is gone and he regained his memory of the Self. This kind of beginning and end of the text shows that the Srimad Bhagavad Geeta contains the Knowledge that removes the delusion and bestows the Supreme Good.

Even from the teacher's view point, the text starts from Sri Krishna telling Arjun that he is grieving for that which should not be grieved for thereby explaining how sorrow is borne of delusion. It ends by asking Arjun whether the delusion had gone. This makes it clear that the entire purpose of the dialogue between Krishna and Arjun was aimed at removing spiritual ignorance which is the cause of delusion. Thus the removal of sorrow and delusion (*shok moh nivritti*) is the main theme of the Geeta.

The 2nd point is called *Abhyas*– repetition and emphasis in the text. The 2nd discourse gives ample evidence to this aspect. Krishna frequently tells Arjun not to grieve and puts forward the reasons for that view from several angles like the true knowledge, duty, ignominy, etc. Similarly, the concept of *Sthitapragya* has been highlighted in several ways at various places. This shows imparting Self-Knowledge is the key note in the text.

The 3rd point is called *Apurvat*– the novelty or uniqueness of the theme. Sri Krishna calls this Self-Knowledge as a secret, *Guhyam,* because normal extroverted minds cannot grasp it and hence very few succeed in knowing it. Similarly, moderation in all walks of our lives has been stressed at many places. The teachings of the Geeta are thus unique.

The 4th point is *Phalam* or the fruit or the end result of the study of the text. Removal of sorrow and confusion and attainment of clear thinking and supreme knowledge- enlightenment- are the end result of the study of the text.

The 5th point is *Arthavad*–positive praise of the subject and negative condemnation of the opposite. We find many shlokas in the text extolling the supreme Self-Knowledge and condemning spiritual ignorance. Thus attaining the Supreme Knowledge is the goal of the Geeta.

The 6th and the last point is *Upapatti*– illustration and reasoning. We find in the text that Krishna has been giving a lot of logical explanations and reasoning to convince Arjun about his teachings. He uses profusely the word *'tasmat'* meaning 'therefore'. His arguments are given from many standpoints, the main goal of all His efforts being elimination of sorrow and delusion through Self-knowledge. The nature of Self is also revealed through examples and reasoning. These indicate the Supreme Knowledge (*Tattva gyanam*) as the main subject matter of the Geeta.

Therefore, Self-knowledge (*Atmagyan*) which eliminates our ignorance and the consequent problems created and bestows the ultimate good for all of us (*Shreyas*) is the core theme of the Geeta.

Some Select Principles of the Geeta

Purification of heart— The core summary of the principles of the Geeta is that a man should perform all his tasks and duties with a positive frame of mind with an attitude of detachment towards the rewards of his action. This attitude toward work will help him purify his inner being or heart. The only way to purify the heart is to perform work while removing the expectation of positive result from the psyche. Until and unless the heart is purified, man will not develop the intense desire to know the truth– and without this intense desire to know the truth, it is not possible to develop the desire for *Moksha* or liberation.

Develop true detachment— After the heart is purified, *Vivek* or inner knowledge arises in the man of truth. The development of *Vivek* simply means the ability to distinguish between the transitory (or variable) and the eternal (or Absolute). All the constituents of the world are transitory (or variable), and only the Atman, which is separate from these constituents, is eternal (or Absolute). When one can experience this truth, their *Vivek* gains immense strength. This strong sense of *Vivek* leads to the development of true detachment towards the world in the seeker's heart.

Path of renunciation— Man's progress towards the strengthening of true renunciation is not possible until he becomes detached towards the attainment of happiness and pleasure– in this world and beyond. Renunciation is the primary path to *Moksha* or liberation– and it is through renunciation that *sham-, dam-, titeeksha-* and *karma-* liberation is made possible. It is only after one is liberated from these four elements that the *Gyan* or knowledge which is necessary for attaining *Moksha* arises or dawns onto the seeker. It is impossible to reach the state of *Moksha* without obtaining this *Gyan* in its purest form.

The paths which lead to *Anitya* or impermanent results cannot lead one to the state of *Moksha*. One needs to assimilate the knowledge that man and the supreme Brahm are one and the same, before one can move towards *Moksha*. The complete understanding of this truthful knowledge is indeed the state of *Moksha*.

Doctrines of *Maya* and trurh— The apparent (false) distinction between man and Brahm is because of nature. The removal of this falsehood is only possible by the dawn of *Gyan* or knowledge. Those who believe otherwise remain trapped in the realm of *Maya* or ignorance. And that *Maya* is the cause of a lot of confusion and misery. It is neither the truth– nor is it the untruth– but it is the abode for *Dvait* or the philosophy which separates man from Brahm.

What we all know is not truth. That is why it has been deemed as unattainable. The truth is that *Maya* is also deception. Since untruth cannot be created from truth and truth and untruth can never meet– this means that untruth has no inherent strength. Hence the world is indeed imaginary and dream-like in nature.

Geeta leads to liberation— Adi Shankaracharya is the preacher of the path of liberation and *Nivritti*. He has prescribed that the Geeta is the primary path or means for obtaining *Nivritti*. According to him, it is not possible to obtain *Moksha* without committing to *Sannyas*. This is his repeated teaching. One must keep in mind that Shankaracharya preaches that the path of action or K*arma* is necessary for the purification of the heart and mind.

What is true *Sannyas*?— Adi Shankaracharya does not believe that everyone is deserving of or is entitled to the path of *Sannyas*. The true *Sannyas* is that in which one does not deliberately give up or relinquish his possessions; instead, just like a ripened fruit naturally falls from the tree, the man of *Sannyas* also becomes automatically detached from the world when his time is ripe. Does one need to wait for instructions on when to release a ball of golden hot metal from his hands?

Why to Study the Geeta?

The Srimad Bhagavad Geeta has been a source of inspiration and enlightenment for generations. The message of the Geeta is not merely a general spiritual philosophy or ethical doctrine but it has a bearing upon the practical aspects in the application of such principles in our day-to-day lives. It is indeed "An Users' Manual for the Practice of the Art of Right Living". Important thing about the Bhagavad Geeta is, it is not a religious book, it is a book about life, understanding who you are, why things happen and how to act in a situation of crisis. It applies to any timeframe right from the past to the current scenario and will be applicable in the future. It is a small example to show its validity in any timeframe.

The centuries old Bhagavad Geeta continues to be the most relevant beacon light for all of us today. The modern man, like Arjun, is at the crossroads where the focus is more on improving the Standard of Living rather than the Standard of Life, more on the Stock Exchange Index than on the Human Development Quotient, more on the Cost of Living than on the Quality of Life. This has resulted in his disorientation and imbalance in an environment of shifting values. While science aims to enhance the comfort of human life, spirituality teaches us how to be comfortable with what we have. That is the difference. In this scenario, the Geeta is the only source of strength for the development of an integrated personality, a complete man, within us.

The Geeta teaches how to achieve harmony with divinity in the midst of disharmony by subduing all outward energies and remaining in equanimity with pairs of opposites like pain and pleasure, aversion and attraction, success and failure, etc. The focus of the Geeta is moderation and its aim is the total surrender of man before the Supreme while continuing to perform his duties in the spirit of Yog.

The problem that is facing us today is that while the world is coming closer physically it is drifting apart mentally and emotionally. Hence we often see conflicts and violence, destruction and damage across the globe. The urgent need, therefore, is the reconciliation and reconditioning of the human mindset, to inculcate a global vision and bring about the universal brotherhood.

The Geeta is specially suited for the purpose, as it attempts to bring together varied and apparently antithetical forms of the consciousness and emphasizes the root conceptions of humanity which are neither ancient nor modern, belonging neither to the east nor the west, but eternal and universal.

Its beauty and sublimity lie in its everlasting relevance to the daily problems of human life, either occidental or oriental. It prescribes the methods which are within the reach of all. It has a message of solace, freedom, salvation, perfection and peace for all human beings. The more you study it with devotion and faith, the more you will acquire deep knowledge, penetrative insight and clear, right thinking. It is indeed a recipe for sane living for every man and woman across the world.

The Supreme Consciousness can be invoked through any means according to one's temperament and one can merge in and attain Supreme Happiness. Those who understand that sufferings arise because of the cycles of birth and death and realize that the Self is the Supreme Goal and culmination of all human pursuits and act with faith and wisdom attain Him. Such people do not have rebirth.

Bhagavad Geeta and Human Values

In the modern world a man tends to confront great inner and outer challenges every day. The inner challenges like self-esteem, concentration of mind and other factors keep an individual indecisive. In the process the higher values such as honesty, truthfulness, self-control and others, which are important aspects of a dynamic personality, take a back seat.

Being a book of practical wisdom, the Bhagavad Geeta has much to offer to all human beings to grow as balanced personalities. The Geeta gives the art of life management. The Geeta is the essence of all the Upanishads and is a concise guide to Hindu philosophy. The Geeta's message was given to Arjun by Lord Krishna when he declined to fight the Mahabharat war. The Geeta's message is extremely useful for all and for all times. Each discourse indicates to give a type of Yog. Yog is the science of individual consciousness attaining communion (intimate fellowship) with the Ultimate Consciousness. The Geeta explains five basic concepts: *Brahm* (the supreme controller), *Jeev* (living being/ the soul), *Prakriti* (matter), *Dharma* (duty) and *Kala* (time).

We can learn from the study of the Geeta about the ultimate truth, creation, birth and death, the results of actions, eternal-soul, purpose and goal of human life. It guides us in all directions, and helps us to lead a positive life while building a strong and pure personality by adopting noble human values. The three types of Yog– *Karmayog* (the way of selfless action), *Bhaktiyog* (the way of love to God) and *Gyanayog* (the way of wisdom) are a part of our life and are well explained in the Geeta for a joyful life. The different human values as mentioned in the Geeta are documented here briefly.

Values are the deeply held principles that guide our decisions and behaviours. They are those beliefs that are held in our heart. Values are our codes of internal conduct, the principles upon which we run our lives and make our decisions. Our first set of values is given to us by our parents. More get added by teachers and the society in which we live. Values also depend on our faith systems. There are some common values– Universal values, natural to all people, in all places, at any time. Truth (what we speak), Right Conduct (what we practice), Love (is what we live), Peace (is what we give) and Non-violence (is the fruit) are Five Common Human Universal Values.

Human values are eternal essences empowering, driving, charging and informing human activity which sustain and uplift both the individual and the society.

With the advancement of information and communication technologies the world has shrunk in space and time, but the human values have suffered a serious setback. This needs the development of responsive and ethical human beings through education. In four decades of my teaching and research experience, I have seen the rise of information and fall of real knowledge; rise in number of technical colleges and technical universities and fall in the thinking of teachers, administration and students about the set-standards for the students. Although the teachers and the students are aware of the human values to a good extent, these are implemented in a limited extent.

From the angle of modern world the following are important values which may be imbibed by one and all for the welfare of individual and society as a whole. Most of them were already emphasized in the Geeta: Assertiveness, Caring, Cleanliness, Commitment, Compassion, Confidence, Consideration, Cooperation, Courage, Courtesy, Creativity, Detachment, Determination, Diligence, Enthusiasm, Excellence, Flexibility, Forgiveness, Friendliness, Generosity, Gentleness, Helpfulness, Honesty, Honour, Humility, Idealism, Integrity, Joyfulness, Justice, Kindness, Love, Loyalty, Moderation, Orderliness, Patience, Peacefulness, Perseverance, Purposefulness, Reliability,

Respect, Responsibility, Self-discipline, Service, Tact, Thankfulness, Tolerance, Trust, Trustworthiness, Truthfulness, Understanding and Unity. The Geeta has something more to offer.

The Geeta tells us about life and how to manage it by acquiring the different values. Values are part of a different hymns of the Geeta and are building blocks of our life. In five discourses of the Geeta values are given in group form, following which one becomes a joyful and complete person. These are also mentioned in the Geeta in a scattered way. In group form these are given in Discourses 2, 4, 12, 13 and 16. The Geeta has propounded and recommended the virtue of being *Sthitapragya. Sthitapragya* is a noble man or perfect person described by the Geeta having all noble values. The values of a Sthitapragya may be noted thus:

He is free from all desires of mind and sorrows. For him pain and pleasure are the same. He is truthful, understands the soul, has the knowledge about the life cycle, and follows his *Swadharma*. He treats victory and defeat alike and is not moved by worldly desires. He follows the Upanishadic teachings. He acts not for the cause of fruits but for action only– in Yog spirit. He is free from passion, fear and anger. He is not attached to anything and has a stable mind. He is firmly established in God.

Discourse 16 of the Geeta teaches us about divine qualities. Divine qualities refer to twenty six values that one should acquire: Fearlessness (faith in God and His protection), wholesome purities of mind/heart (transparency to truth), steadfastness (in seeking wisdom and practising *Yog*), alms giving (charity), self-restraint (power to control senses), religious rites (as per Vedas and other great scriptures), right study (of great scriptures), self-discipline (*Tapas*, celibacy, practice by discrimination), straightforwardness (truthfulness, honesty), non-injury (*Ahinsa*), truthfulness, absence of wrath *(Akrosh*), abandonment (*Tyag*), peaceful (divine quality *Shanti*), absence of fault-finding, compassion (*Daya*), absence of greed, gentleness, modesty (feeling shame at any wrongdoing and willing to correct oneself), absence of restlessness (to avoid physical and mental roaming), radiance of character (*Tejas*, through meditation), forgiveness (*Kshama or 'Chhama'*), patience, cleanliness of body and purity of mind, non-hatred, lack of conceit (absence of excessive pride). The Bhagavad Geeta may be referred for different human values for peaceful and joyful living at any time under any circumstances. They are helpful for Self-realization and … Liberation.

Lessons to be Learnt from the Geeta

1. **Nothing is permanent**— Nothing is permanent in this universe and so is your body. Therefore, identifying yourself with your body is futile. Except your eternal soul, everything else is impermanent. There is no point in pinning your hopes on impermanent objects that would perish sooner or later. Attachment breeds misery.
2. **Inaction is foolishness**— A person who shuns his worldly duties and tries to escape responsibilities is deluded. True liberation is possible only when one renders his worldly duties without escaping.
3. **Work hard and don't worry about the result**— When you can put aside the worry about the results, you can work harder and stay happy irrespective of the nature of the result.
4. **Conquer desire**— A stable mind is the one which understands the nature and structure of desire and stays free from its control.
5. **Selfishness blinds your wisdom**— A mind clouded with selfishness is like a mirror covered with mist or dust. When selfishness is put aside, clarity of mind prevails.
6. **Avoid extremities-embrace moderation**— Too much or too little of anything can create imbalance in life. Whether it is sleep or food or physical pleasures, moderation is the key.
7. **Rage deludes you**— A fit of rage simply deludes you. Anger confuses you. All actions that are done in anger are futile. The mind loses logic and reason once a person is angry. Anger can be the sole reason for the downfall of even the greatest man.
8. **God is within you**— The supreme force is everywhere in the universe in every living and non-living thing. A human being is just a small piece of the whole and most of his circumstances are a play of the bigger forces or god. Therefore, fear of future is ridiculous.

OM TAT SAT

यदा यदा हि धर्मस्य ग्लानिर्भवती भारत।
अभ्युत्थानमधर्मस्य तदाऽऽत्मनं सृजाम्यहम ॥

PART- II

TEXT, TRANSLATION AND COMMENTS

Discourse - 1

Vishad Yog: Yog of the Despondency of Arjun

This Discourse introduces the scene, the setting, the circumstances and the characters involved in determining the reasons for Srimad Bhagavad Geeta's revelation. The setting is the great battle of Mahabharat which took place between the Pandavas and the Kauravas on the holy plains of Kurukshetra. This happened on the failure of Lord Krishna's peace mission, when he himself went to Hastinapur as an emissary of the Pandavas for their rightful share in the kingdom. The Pandavas were finally left with no alternative but to engage themselves in a fierce battle. The main characters were Lord Krishna and Arjun, but a host of other great warriors from both sides assembled to fight on the battlefield. Lord Krishna arrived on the scene in a magnificent chariot yoked with white horses. He was to act as the charioteer of Arjun, one of the Pandav princes. The din of hundreds of conches, blaring forth suddenly, declared the onset of the battle. As the two armies were arrayed, ready for battle, Arjun asked Krishna to place his chariot between them so that he could see or assess his opponents. He was bewildered by the scene before him, for he saw on the sides, fathers and grandfathers, teachers and uncles, father-in-laws, grandsons, kindred and comrades.

Having seen this Arjun had a deep sense of dejection against the war for fear of losing friends, kindred and family values as a consequence of the war. Serious confusions reigned in Arjun's mind–

should he participate in this terrible carnage? Was it proper to destroy one's relatives for the sake of a kingdom and some pleasures? Would it not be much better for him to surrender everything in favour of his enemies and retire in peace? As these thoughts rushed into his mind, a feeling of despondency overtook Arjun. He lost all enthusiasm to engage in the battle. Arjun was not prepared to incur consequent sins of his actions. Losing all interests in the kingdom and worldly pleasures, Arjun is ready for *Sannyas* and lead the life of a recluse. Letting his bow slip from his hands, Arjun could do nothing but turn to Lord Krishna for guidance and enlightenment. Arjun as a student, disciple or devout raised a volley of questions against the usefulness or relevance of war before Lord Krishna. The Lord as a friend, philosopher and guide listened Arjun carefully to answer all his questions, queries and misgivings in the subsequent Discourses.

It is said that the sage Vyas wanted to give the blind King (Dhritarashtra) the boon of eyesight so that the King could see the horrors of the war for which he too was accountable. But the King refused the offer. He did not have enough courage to see the dreadfulness of the war through naked eyes; but preferred to get the war report through his charioteer, Sanjay. Sage Vyas granted the power of clairvoyance and clairvision to Sanjay, as he was one of the disciples of the sage. With this power Sanjay could see, hear and recall the events of the past, present and future. He was able to give an instant replay of the eye-witness war report to the blind King sitting in his palace.

Those who do not admit the idea of bestowing the power of clairvoyance and clairvision to Sanjay by Vyas, they have considered the Geeta as a *post facto* creation. Same as in modern days, in ancient times also literature did not develop side by side the occurrence of events. As the Mahabharat in its present form passed through several hands in course of time, it was time and again revised and recast as per the taste and interests of story tellers and listeners. The complete Mahabharat, and so also the Geeta, is not a creation of a single author. Several persons named or designated as Vyas were involved in the final completion of the Srimad Bhagavad Geeta.

Dhritrashtra asked

धर्मक्षेत्रे कुरुक्षेत्रे समवेता युयुत्सवः।

मामकाः पाण्डवाश्चैव किमकुर्वत संजय ॥ 1.1 ॥

Shlok 1.1: O Sanjay, tell me in detail, what did they do when my troops and the sons of Pandu, eager to fight, were arrayed on the sacred plains of Kurukshetra?

Commentary: Here Kurukshetra simply refers to the 'region of Kurus' where both the parties belonging to the same Kuru scion assembled to fight a decisive battle. This region was described as *Dharmakshetra* (region or area of *Dharma*) possibly because both the intent and mode of war was pious. This region was also believed to be a pious one because Kurukshetra had been a seat of religious rites and rituals in the ancient days.

Since Lord Krishna was present on the side of Pandavas in the battlefield, the blind king Dhritrashtra was quite curious to know whether there was any chance of victory for his sons in the impending war. So he asked Sanjay (his charioteer) to narrate the course of events of war in detail. Despite a fair amount of uncertainty there might be some chance for victory as well, because the size of army of the Kaurav was much larger than that of the Pandav. That is why the king did not make any compromise to avoid war at the initiative of Lord Krishna. It seems the king was hopeful of success in the war as well. Well such a bewildering situation does arise in the day-to-day life of an individual.

Sanjay narrates the course of the war

Sanjay said:

दृष्ट्वा तु पाण्डवानीकं व्यूढं दुर्योधनस्तदा।

आचार्यमुपसंगम्य राजा वचनमब्रवीत्॥ 1.2 ॥

Shlok 1.2: Having seen the army of the Pandu sons, Prince Duryodhan approached his teacher Drone and spoke these words:

Commentary: Sanjay replied to the king saying that having seen the military forces of the Pandavas, Duryodhan immediately approached the Commander-in-Chief, Dronacharya, to inform him about the actual position of military strength.

Duryodhan addresses Drone

पश्यैतां पाण्डुपुत्राणामाचार्य महतीं चमूम् ।
व्यूढां द्रुपदपुत्रेण तव शिष्येण धीमता ॥ 1.3 ॥

Shlok 1.3: Look at this huge army of the Pandu sons, O teacher, arrayed for battle by the son of Drupad, that brilliant student of yours.

Commentary: Besides being a Commander-in-Chief, Dronacharya was also a teacher of Duryodhan and others taking part in the war on both the sides. Duryodhan tried to remind his teacher that the king Drupad, the father-in-law of Arjun, performed a great sacrifice to settle score with you and he received the benediction that Drupad's son Dhristdyumna, who is taking part in the war in favour of his brother-in-law Arjun, would kill you. Knowing this fact well in advance you taught him and other adversaries on the side of Pandavas about the strategy of warfare and knowledge of archery. How sad it is for all of us? Since Duryodhan was a crafty and wicked person, he has tried to provoke Dronacharya against the king Drupad.

अत्र शूरा महेष्वासा भीमार्जुनसमा युधि ।
युयुधानो विराटश्च द्रुपदश्च महारथः ॥ 1.4 ॥

Shlok 1.4: Here are heroes, mighty archers, equal in battle to Bhim and Arjun– Yuyudhan, Virat, and Drupad, the master of a chariot (*Maharath*).

Commentary: As the verse is easily comprehensible, it needs no specific explanation.

धृष्टकेतुश्चेकितानः काशिराजश्च वीर्यवान् ।
पुरुजित्कुन्तिभोजश्च शैब्यश्च नरपुंगवः ॥ 1.5 ॥

Shlok 1.5: There are also great heroic, powerful fighters like Dhristketu, Chekitan, the valiant king of Kasi– Purujit, Kunti-bhoj and eminent man Shaibya.

Commentary: As the verse is easily comprehensible, it needs no specific explanation.

युधामन्युश्च विक्रान्त उत्तमौजाश्च वीर्यवान् ।
सौभद्रो द्रौपदेयाश्च सर्व एव महारथाः ॥ 1.6 ॥

Shlok 1.6: The heroic Yudhamanyu, the brave Uttamauja, the son of Subhadra and the sons of Draupadi– all of them great warriors.

Commentary: As the verse is easily comprehensible, it needs no specific explanation.

अस्माकं तु विशिष्टा ये तान्निबोध द्विजोत्तम ।
नायका मम सैन्यस्य संज्ञार्थं तान्ब्रवीमि ते ॥ 1.7॥

Shlok 1.7: But, O noblest of the twice-born, hear about our superior men, the generals of my army. I will mention them by name.

Commentary: As the verse is easily comprehensible, it needs no specific explanation.

भवान्भीष्मश्च कर्णश्च कृपश्च समितिंजयः ।
अश्वत्थामा विकर्णश्च सौमदत्तिस्तथैव च ॥ 1.8 ॥

Shlok 1.8: There are personalities like you, Bhishma, Karn, Kripa, Ashvathama, Vikarn and also Jayadrath, the son of Somdatta called Bhurisarva, who are always victorious in battle.

Commentary (Shlokas 01.4-01.8): Furthermore, well Dhristdyumna might not be a potential barrier to success for the Kauravas in view of pre-eminent position of Dronacharya, but there are some formidable warriors like Bhim and Arjun on the side of Pandavas, who are a matter of concern for all of us. The name of those stalwarts on the side of the Kauravas can be seen in the aforesaid Shlokas.

It is also apparent from the above verses that persons of three-four generations from both the families of Kauravas and Pandavas were directly involved in the battle against each other. It was but natural because the battle arose out of a family feud.

(**Note:** It is hard to believe that the people belonging to four successive generations of a family were fighting collectively against each other. In fact, some were too old, while others were too young to take part in the battle of Kurukshetra.)

अन्ये च बहवः शूरा मदर्थे त्यक्तजीविताः ।
नानाशस्त्रप्रहरणाः सर्वे युद्धविशारदाः ॥ 1.9 ॥

Shlok 1.9: There are plenty of other heroes who have given up their lives for my sake. All of them are well equipped with various kinds of weaponry, and all of them are well versed in battle.

Commentary: All the great heroes who happened to be intimate friends of Duryodhan are ready to sacrifice their life for him. Duryodhan is quite confident of his victory due to the collective strength of his great friends and kinsmen like Jayadrath, Kritavarma, Salya, etc.

अपर्याप्तं तदस्माकं बलं भीष्माभिरक्षितम् ।
पर्याप्तं त्विदमेतेषां बलं भीमाभिरक्षितम् ॥ 1.10 ॥

Shlok 1.10: Our might is immeasurable, and we are very well protected by grandfather Bhishma, whereas the strength of Pandavas, carefully protected by Bhim, is limited.

Commentary: Duryodhan makes a comparative assessment of forces assembled both the sides. Possibly to satisfy himself about the preparations made for the war he feels that forces on his side are relatively superior because they are protected and guided by the most experienced commander like grandfather Bhishma, while the forces on the side of Pandavas are under the command of a much less experienced general. In view of this Duryodhan was confident of his victory in the war. Sadly enough, the Kauravas did not make out who Sri Krishna was.

अयनेषु च सर्वेषु यथाभागमवस्थिताः।
भीष्ममेवाभिरक्षन्तु भवन्तः सर्व एव हि ॥ 1.11 ॥

Shlok 1.11: Indeed, it is grandfather Bhishma you must all protect along all avenues of approach as you man your respective positions.

Commentary: Duryodhan further observes diplomatically that those around Bhishma are no less important in any respect. Though Bhishma is the greatest hero and most experienced General of the Army, he needs a high level of protection as he has grown quite old. Different heroes stationed at different strategic positions must not allow the enemy forces to break the flanx of army and reach near Bhishma and Guru Dronacharya. Duryodhan always feels that the success in this war is largely in the hands these two great warriors.

Both armies ready for battle

तस्य संजनयन्हर्षं कुरुवृद्धः पितामहः ।
सिंहनादं विनद्योच्चैः शङ्खं दध्मौ प्रतापवान् ॥ 1.12 ॥

Shlok 1.12: Then grandsire Bhishma, the eldest of the Kurus, blew his conch aloud, making a sound like the roar of a lion, for the purpose of cheering your son.

Commentary: The war was ultimately declared with the blowing of conch by Bhishma. This was necessary to commence the act of war in ancient times. It was also necessary to boost up the morale of the Kaurav's side and overawe the opposite party. The army assembled in the battlefield was, however, able to imagine the effectiveness of Krishna on the Pandav's side, though the Kaurav's side was numerically much larger in size in addition to possessing some experienced warriors.

ततः शङ्खाश्च भेर्यश्च पणवानकगोमुखाः ।
सहसैवाभ्यहन्यन्त स शब्दस्तुमुलोऽभवत् ॥ 1.13 ॥

Shlok 1.13: Then, all of a sudden, the conches, kettledrums, cymbals, big drums and horns were sounded: It was a tumultuous noise.

Commentary: As the verse is easily comprehensible, it needs no explanation.

ततः श्वेतैर्हयैर्युक्ते महति स्यंदने स्थितौ ।
माधवः पाण्डवश्चैव दिव्यौ शङ्खौ प्रदध्मतुः ॥ 1.14 ॥

Shlok 1.14: Then also, Madhav and Arjun, seated in their grand chariot yoked with white horses, blew their celestial conches with a terrific noise.

Commentary: As the verse is easily comprehensible, it needs no specific explanation.

पाञ्चजन्यं हृषीकेशो देवदत्तं धनञ्जयः ।
पौण्ड्रं दध्मौ महाशङ्खं भीमकर्मा वृकोदरः ॥ 1.15 ॥

Shlok 1.15: Hrishikesh (Krishna) blew the Panchjanya; Dhananjay (Arjun), the Devdatta; and Bhim, the glutton and the doer of remarkable deeds, blew his terrific large conch named Paundra.

Commentary: As the verse is easily comprehensible, it needs no specific explanation.

अनन्तविजयं राजा कुन्तीपुत्रो युधिष्ठिरः ।
नकुलः सहदेवश्च सुघोषमणिपुष्पकौ ॥ 1.16 ॥

Shlok 1.16: Prince Yudhisthir, the son of Kunti, blew the conch named Anantavijay, and Nakul and Sahdev, their Sughosh and Manipuspak;

Commentary: As the verse is easily comprehensible, it needs no specific explanation.

काश्यश्च परमेष्वासः शिखण्डी च महारथः।
धृष्टद्युम्नो विराटश्च सात्यकिश्चापराजितः ॥ 1.17 ॥

Shlok 1.17: The great archer, the king of Kashi, the great warrior Shikhandi, Dhristdyumna, Virat, the unconquered Satyaki;

द्रुपदो द्रौपदेयाश्च सर्वशः पृथिवीपते ।
सौभद्रश्च महाबाहुः शङ्खान्दध्मुः पृथक्पृथक् ॥ 1.18 ॥

Shlok 1.18: O Lord of Earth! Drupad and the sons of Draupadi, and the Mighty-armed son of Subhadra, all, also blew each of his respective conch.

स घोषो धार्तराष्ट्राणां हृदयानि व्यदारयत् ।
नभश्च पृथिवीं चैव तुमुलो व्यनुनादयन् ॥ 1.19 ॥

Shlok 1.19: The thundering sound resounding through the earth and sky tore the hearts of sons of Dhritrashtra.

Commentary (Shlokas 01.12-01.19): In response to blowing of conches by Bhishma and others on the Kaurav's side, Krishna and other warriors also blew their respective conch to accept their challenge and cheer up their side. Now both the sides are ready to meet challenges in the battlefield. Unlike the conches of Kauravas, Krishna's conch was transcendental. The hearts of sons of Dhritrashtra were shattered by the sounds and echoes of conches of the Pandav's party. This was enough indication of the fact that the goddess of fortune was on the side of Pandavas. There was no hope of victory of the other side.

Lord Krishna has been addressed as Hrishikesh in verse 15 because he is the complete controller of all senses. All the living beings are mere manifestation of his senses. Here on the battlefield the Lord directly controls the transcendental senses of Arjun and hence he is described as Hrishikesh. The Lord Krishna has different names according to his different activities such as Madhusudan, Govind, Vasudev, Parthsarthy, Janardan, etc.

Arjun's survey of the enemy

अथ व्यवस्थितान्दृष्ट्वा धार्तराष्ट्रान् कपिध्वजः ।
प्रवृत्ते शस्त्रसम्पाते धनुरुद्यम्य पाण्डवः ॥ 1.20 ॥
हृषीकेशं तदा वाक्यमिदमाह महीपते ।
सेनयोरुभयोर्मध्ये रथं स्थापय मेऽच्युत ॥ 1.21 ॥
यावदेतान्निरीक्षेऽहं योद्धुकामानवस्थितान् ।
कैर्मया सह योद्धव्यमस्मिन्रणसमुद्यमे ॥ 1.22 ॥

Shlokas 1.20-22: Then the ape-bannered son of Pandu, seeing the sons of Dhritarashtra lined up, lifted his bow as the clash of arms began and spoke these words to Hrishikesh, O Lord of the Earth: Achyut, station my chariot between the two armies, so that I may observe these men, standing eager for battle, with whom I must fight in this strenuous engagement.

Commentary (Shlokas 1.20-1.22): As all these verses are easily comprehensible, they need no specific explanation, except for the following note:

(**Note:** The emblem of ape or monkey on the flag of Arjun's chariot is a debatable fact. The verse seems to have been inserted later into the Geeta because ape or monkey was first seen in the battle against Ravan in the Valmiki's **Ramayan** which was a post-Mahabharat creation. Historians have contended that the epic Ramayan came into being sometime during 5th century BCE to first century BCE. The reference of ape or monkey on the flag has been done to glorify Hanuman as a very powerful deity, as he was said to have played a very decisive role in the victory of Ram over Ravan. It is a well known fact that the Mahabharat, historically speaking, was compiled or collated prior to **Ramayan** despite the fact that the Ramayan period preceded the Mahabharat period. Deification of Hanuman was done in course of series of events which formed the part of Ramayana's story. In fact, the glorification of Hanuman was further heightened with the rise in popularity of **Ramcharitmanas** of poet Tulsidas in the medieval period.

Let us throw some light on a very relevant anthropological fact concerning emblem on the flag here. Most primitive tribal groups even now tend to use some animal or natural object as their emblem because it is the totemic object. Such an object is revered by them as their founder. It was very much possible that monkey was the totemic object for the Pandavas. Totem was also used as a symbol of identity for each clan or family, nearly same as the national flag for each country in the modern days. Kauravas must be having the same emblem on their flag also because both belonged to the same family, but the Mahabharat is silent about the emblem of Kauravas or other groups of people collaborating with them.)

योत्स्यमानानवेक्षेऽहं य एतेऽत्र समागताः ।
धार्तराष्ट्रस्य दुर्बुद्धेर्युद्धे प्रियचिकीर्षवः ॥ 1.23 ॥

Shlok 1.23: I wish to see those who are assembled here for fight, wishing to please the evil-minded son of Dhritarashtra by taking his side on the battlefield.

Commentary: As the verse is easily comprehensible, it needs no specific explanation.

Sanjay said (to Dhritrashtra):

एवमुक्तो हृषीकेशो गुडाकेशेन भारत ।
सेनयोरुभयोर्मध्ये स्थापयित्वा रथोत्तमम् ॥ 1.24 ॥
भीष्मद्रोणप्रमुखतः सर्वेषां च महीक्षिताम् ।
उवाच पार्थ पश्यैतान् समवेतान्कुरूनिति ॥ 1.25 ॥

Shlokas 1.24-25: O Descendant of Bharat (Dhritrashtra), thus addressed by Gudakesh (Arjun), Hrishikesh (Krishna), having stationed the grandest of chariots in the middle of two armies; in the front of Bhism, Drone and all other rulers of the earth and spoke thus: 'O Parth, now look at all these Kurus assembled here.'

Commentary: As these verses are easily comprehensible, they need no specific explanation.

तत्रापश्यत्स्थितान्पार्थः पितृनथ पितामहान् ।
आचार्यान् मातुलान् भ्रातृन् पुत्रान् पौत्रान् सखींस्तथा ।।1.26 ।।
श्वशुरान् सुहृदश्चैव सेनयोरुभयोरपि ।
तान्समीक्ष्य स कौन्तेयः सर्वान् बन्धूनवस्थितान् ।। 1.27 ।।

Shlokas 1.26-27: Then the son of Pritha saw standing fathers and grandfathers as well as teachers, uncles, brothers, sons, grandsons and comrades, fathers-in-law and friends in both armies. When the son of Kunti (Arjun) saw all the kinsmen standing, he was overwhelmed with great compassion and sorrowfully spoke thus:

Commentary (Shlokas 1.20-1.27): With a view to having a closer view of the kind of people who are all set to fight and sacrifice their life in favour of his evil-minded cousins, Arjun requested Krishna to take the chariot between the two armies. Arjun was keen to see the army of opposite party to have a clearer understanding and assessment of the war scenario. Arjun wanted to make an estimate of the might of his adversaries which was always expected before the onset of traditional kind of warfare fought in a face-to-face situation. Conceding the request of Arjun, Lord Krishna positioned the chariot in the middle of two sets of forces possibly to see eagerly what Arjun was going to do there.

In verse 24 Arjun has been addressed as Gudakesh because he has conquered sleep or sluggishness. A person who is really eager to achieve anything in life must continually remain conscious of the goal of his life. Sleep or carelessness has no room in the life of committed people. One obviously cannot achieve anything without total commitment to one's goal. Arjun's confidence in success through Lord Krishna made him Gudakesh.

Standing between the row of armies on both sides, Krishna asked Arjun to observe the kind of people who are ready to fight against you. Arjun was amazed to see that even his close kinsmen, family friends, well-wishers and *Gurus* were present on the battlefield. Having seen all such intimate people on both sides in the battlefield, Arjun obviously got overwhelmed with compassion. The situation was really baffling for any ordinary human being.

Arjun's words of despondency

Arjun said:

कृपया परयाविष्टो विषीदन्निदमब्रवीत् ।
दृष्ट्वेमं स्वजनं कृष्ण युयुत्सुं समुपस्थितम् ॥ 1.28 ॥
सीदन्ति मम गात्राणि मुखं च परिशुष्यति ।
वेपथुश्च शरीरे मे रोमहर्षश्च जायते ॥ 1.29 ॥

Shlokas 1.28-29: O Krishna, seeing my kindred standing with a desire to fight, my limbs droop down and my mouth gets dry. My limbs shiver and my hairs stand on end.

गाण्डीवं स्रंसते हस्तात्त्वक्चैव परिदह्यते ।
न च शक्नोम्यवस्थातुं भ्रमतीव च मे मनः ॥ 1.30 ॥

Shlok 1.30: The Gandiv slips from my hands, and I fear my skin is intensely burning. I am also unable to stand and my mind is whirling round, as it were.

Commentary (1.28-1.30): Arjun could visualize the fate of his adversaries in the war. He was quite disturbed to see his kindred, friends and well-wishers ready to fight on the battlefield. Arjun had a deep sense of compassion for all such people. While Arjun was thinking of pros and cons of the war, his limbs were shivering and mouth became parched. This usually happens when a person is in a state of compassion for such near and dear ones who have freely chosen the path of their own destruction for no return. Arjun was very disturbed to see in his mind's eye the likely loss of life. A man like Arjun was pretty nervous to envision the scenario. His bow and arrows were slipping from his hands and shoulder. He was psychologically so upset that he had a burning sensation in his heart and skin. It is said that Arjun was under the influence of *Maya*.

निमित्तानि च पश्यामि विपरीतानि केशव ।
न च श्रेयोऽनुपश्यामि हत्वा स्वजनमाहवे ॥ 1.31 ॥

Shlok 1.31: And, O Keshav, I see evil omens and I do not see any good in the killing of my kindred in this battle.

न कांक्षे विजयं कृष्ण न च राज्यं सुखानि च ।
किं नो राज्येन गोविन्द किं भोगैर्जीवितेन वा ॥ 1.32 ॥

Shlok 1.32: I do not desire victory, O Krishna, nor kingdom, nor pleasure. Of what avail is dominion to us, O Govind? Of what avail are pleasures and even life?

Commentary (Shlokas 1.31-1.32): Because of a sense of attachment and affection for the people who are going to fight against him, Arjun was reluctant to stay on the battlefield for long. Irreparable loss of life and property caused by war weighed very heavily in the mind of Arjun. Success in war and consequent gain of the crown of Hastinapur was no compensation. Arjun thought that victory in the war would bring nothing but lamentation for him. Arjun thinks that by killing his friends and kinsmen, he would not secure happiness in life and therefore he was all against the war. In fact, he was contemplating to return forest and lead the life of a recluse. He lost all interests in kingdom or happiness, if it was to be secured through such a war. Such was the state of frustration for Arjun. He does not see any good in killing his own people in the battle. He desires for neither victory nor empire. He has no aspiration even for pleasure. The influence of *Maya* was so intense on the mind of Arjun that he was not all inclined to fight for his right. He was ready to forego everything for a peaceful living.

येषामर्थे कांक्षितं नो राज्यं भोगाः सुखानि च ।
त इमेऽवस्थिता युद्धे प्राणांस्त्यक्त्वा धनानि च ॥ 1.33 ॥
आचार्याः पितरः पुत्रास्तथैव च पितामहाः ।
मातुलाः श्वशुराः पौत्राः श्यालाः सम्बन्धिनस्तथा ॥ 1.34 ॥

Shlokas 1.33-34: Those, for whose sake we desire kingdom, enjoyments and pleasures are standing poised for battle and ready to give up their lives and wealth. The teachers, uncles, fathers, sons as well as grandfathers; maternal uncles, fathers-in-law, grandsons, brothers-in-law, and other relatives as well are there.

एतान्न हन्तुमिच्छामि घ्नतोऽपि मधुसूदन ।
अपि त्रैलोक्यराज्यस्य हेतोः किं नु महीकृते ॥ 1.35 ॥

Shlok 1.35: These, O slayer of Madhu, I do not wish to kill, though they kill me, even for the sake of the kingdom of the three worlds, and even less for the earth.

Commentary (Shlokas 1.33-1.35): Arjun reacts saying that Govind! I do not understand for whose sake I should kill my own people– pleasure, empire or fulfilment of certain desires. Arjun says that he does not need any of them. When all these intimate people such as grandfathers, maternal uncles, fathers-in-law, grandsons, brothers-in-law and other kinsmen have already renounced their life and property and assembled in the battlefield for decisive battle, I do not see any point in fighting against them. There is no rationale behind the war. Even for the sake of the kingdom of the three worlds, I do not want to kill my kinsmen.

Arjun's grief at the evils of war

निहत्य धार्तराष्ट्रान्नः का प्रीतिः स्याज्जनार्दन ।
पापमेवाश्रयेदस्मान् हत्वैतानाततायिनः ॥ 1.36 ॥

Shlok 1.36: O Janardan, what pleasure shall we find in killing our cousins? Upon killing these felons, we shall incur only sin.

Commentary: As the verse is easily comprehensible, it needs no specific explanation.

तस्मान्नार्हा वयं हन्तुं धार्तराष्ट्रान् स्वबांधवान् ।
स्वजनं हि कथं हत्वा सुखिनः स्याम माधव ॥ 1.37 ॥

Shlok 1.37: We had then better not slay our own kinsmen, the sons of Dhritarashtra; for, how can we be happy, O Madhav, after slaying our kinsmen?

Commentary: As the verse is easily comprehensible, it needs no specific explanation.

यद्यप्येते न पश्यन्ति लोभोपहतचेतसः ।
कुलक्षयकृतं दोषं मित्रद्रोहे च पातकम् ॥ 1.38 ॥
कथं न ज्ञेयमस्माभिः पापादस्मान्निवर्तितुम् ।
कुलक्षयकृतं दोषं प्रपश्यद्भिर्जनार्दन ॥ 1.39 ॥

Shlokas 1.38-39: Though they are seduced by greed and do not

see evil in the destruction of the family or sin in being treacherous to friends, why should not we, who clearly see evil in the destruction of the family, think about turning away from this sin, O Janardan?

Commentary (Shlokas 1.36-1.39): Sense of morality or the notion of sin weighed so heavily in the mind of Arjun that he did not want to fight for his right in view of the heavy loss of life of his own people. Arjun said to Krishna that even if the sons of Dhritrashtra were felons and there was absolutely no harm in killing such nasty people, the sin would definitely be incurred by him by slaying one's own kith and kin. Arjun is scared of committing such a sin because of high moral values of life, although there is no sin in slaying such evil-minded persons according to the Vedic precepts. Here Arjun seems to be a saintly person. It may be good to be saintly, but one should not be coward either. Arjun considered that rather than killing own kinsmen for political reasons, it would not be better to forgive them on the ground of religious morality and other familial considerations. Arjun did not consider such killings beneficial simply for the sake of temporary worldly pleasures in the form of empire. Disturbed Arjun made up his mind to forgo his material wealth and pleasure for the sake of his mental peace. Lord Krishna, however, never endorsed this view of Arjun, as Arjun has come to this world to serve a special purpose in life.

कुलक्षये प्रणश्यन्ति कुलधर्माः सनातनाः ।
धर्मे नष्टे कुलं कृत्स्नमधर्मोऽभिभवत्युत ॥ 1.40 ॥

Shlok 1.40: Eternal family traditions and codes of moral conduct are destroyed with the destruction of (the head of) the family in a war. And immorality prevails in the family due to the destruction of family traditions.

अधर्माभिभवात्कृष्ण प्रदुष्यन्ति कुलस्त्रियः ।
स्त्रीषु दुष्टासु वार्ष्णेय जायते वर्णसंकरः ॥ 1.41 ॥

Shlok 1.41: By the prevalence of impiety, O Krishna, the women of the family become corrupt. When the women become corrupt, there arises intermingling of castes (hybridization of castes), O Descendant of Vrishni.

Commentary: As the verse is easily comprehensible, it needs no specific explanation.

संकरो नरकायैव कुलघ्नानां कुलस्य च ।
पतन्ति पितरो ह्येषां लुप्तपिण्डोदकक्रियाः ॥ 1.42 ॥

Shlok 1.42: A rise in hybrid population surely causes hellish life both for the family and for those who destroy family values. The ancestors of such degraded families fall down to hell because the ritual of offering *pinda* (rice-ball) and water is completely stopped.

दोषैरेतैः कुलघ्नानां वर्णसंकरकारकैः ।
उत्साद्यन्ते जातिधर्माः कुलधर्माश्च शाश्वताः ॥ 1.43 ॥

Shlok 1.43: The everlasting qualities of social order and family traditions of those who destroy their family are ruined by the sinful act of illegitimacy.

Commentary (Shlokas 1.40-1.43): Dharma pertains to the duties and ceremonies practised by the family in accordance with scriptural injunctions. Arjun was not in favour of war also because the death of elderly people would not be good for the sustenance of family values and traditions (*Dharma*). Destruction of age-old values and traditions would tarnish the image of family and disturb the family line and posterity. Children and women of the family need special protection by elderly members of the family. Loss of male population in war would encourage adultery. Birth of unwanted or illegitimate children would create disorder, perversion and impiety both in family and society. The system of ancestor worship would also be adversely affected, as ancestors would be deprived of the offerings of rice-balls and water which are necessary for the roaming souls to rest in peace. The emphasis here is on the practice of rituals which seems to have been borrowed from the Rigvedic system of belief.

उत्सन्नकुलधर्माणां मनुष्याणां जनार्दन ।
नरकेऽनियतं वासो भवतीत्यनुशुश्रुम ॥ 1.44 ॥

Shlok 1.44: We have heard, O Janardan, that necessary is the dwelling in hell of the men whose family Dharmas are subverted.

अहो बत महत्पापं कर्तुं व्यवसिता वयम् ।
यद्राज्यसुखलोभेन हन्तुं स्वजनमुद्यताः ॥ 1.45 ॥

Shlok 1.45: Alas! We are ready to commit a great sin by striving to slay our relatives because of greed for the pleasures of the kingdom.

यदि मामप्रतीकारमशस्त्रं शस्त्रपाणयः ।
धार्तराष्ट्रा रणे हन्युस्तन्मे क्षेमतरं भवेत् ॥ 1.46 ॥

Shlok 1.46: It would be better for me, if the sons of Dhritarashtra, with arms in hand, should slay me while I am unarmed and unresisting in the battlefield.

Sanjay said to Dhritrashtra:
एवमुक्त्वार्जुनः संख्ये रथोपस्थ उपाविशत् ।
विसृज्य सशरं चापं शोकसंविग्नमानसः ॥ 1.47 ॥

Shlok 1.47: Having spoken this in the battlefield, Arjun, sad and dismayed, casting away his bow and arrow sank down on the seat of his chariot.

Commentary (Shlokas 1.44-1.47): Addressing Krishna, Arjun is talking about the bad consequences of war at the familial level (those days people thought of individual, family, scion, clan and finally God only. There was no thinking of society at large because the notion of community or state was not in existence). War creates situation for sinful activities at the familial level. Arjun favoured high moral situation for the welfare of family. Destruction of family values would lead us to hellish life. Arjun said that it was very sad that we would be involved in slaying our kindred out of greed for the kingdom.

Arjun strongly felt that he would prefer to be finished by the sons of Dhritrashtra while unarmed in the battlefield. In view of the likely outcome of the war Arjun reiterated that it would be better to be killed than to kill them (cousins and other kinsmen). While narrating the conversation between Krishna and Arjun to Dhritrashtra, Sanjay said that sorrow-stricken Arjun entered into such a state of depression that he surrendered his bow and arrows in the midst of the battle while sitting on the seat of chariot. Lord Krishna found Arjun very disturbed and upset over the situation arising out of the impending war.

(**Note:** In several other verses the practice of the Vedic rituals has been countered in the Geeta. Sri Krishna has merely emphasized total surrendering to Him with complete faith.)

OM TAT SAT

Discourse - 2

Sankhyayog: Yog of Transcendental Knowledge

In this discourse Sanjay explains how Arjun is so disturbed due to intense attachment for his kinsmen just before the onset of actual war. Lord Krishna teaches him against the state of his dejection and exhorts him to fight. After failing to convince Sri Krishna through his seemingly wise thoughts, Arjun realizes his helplessness and surrenders himself completely to the Lord, seeking His guidance to get over the conflict of his mind. Lord Krishna instructs him about the ways to get rid of his lamentation and grief, arising out of love and affection for his kindred.

One should bear in mind that Sankhya is a *Gyanayog*– route to salvation through knowledge only. Yog is a *dhyanayog*– meditation and asceticism. The Lord explains to Arjun that there is nothing to grieve worry or about the consequences of combat, as the *Atman* (soul) is imperishable. It has got no past, present and future. The *Atman* never dies; therefore, Arjun should not lament. It is unchanging and eternal. Death of his kinsmen and friends in the battle should not worry him at all. Krishna goes on to tell Arjun that if he refuses to fight and flees from the battle, people will be justified in condemning such action as unworthy of a warrior.

Having taught Arjun the immortal nature of the *Atman*, Lord Krishna turns to the performance of action without expectation of fruit.

A man should not worry about the consequences of the action, like gain and loss, victory and defeat. These are in the hands of the Lord. He should perform all his actions with a balanced mind, calmly enduring the pairs of opposites like heat and cold, pleasure and pain and gain and loss that inevitably manifest during action. Krishna advises Arjun to fight, free from desire for attaining kingdom like a person with stable mind (*Sthitapragya*). Arjun is eager to know the characteristics of a man who has got a stable mind. Such a person, Krishna tells him, will have no desires at all. Since he is content within, having realized the Self, he is entirely free from all desires. The consciousness of the *Atman* and abandonment of desires are simultaneous experiences. The various qualities of a *Sthitapragya* or a firm person are described by the Lord thus. He will not be affected by the adversity and will have no fear or anger. He will take things as they come, and will not have any likes and dislikes. He will neither embrace the world nor hate it. The man of stable mind will have perfect control over his senses. One should be able to withdraw the senses from objects same as the tortoise which tends to withdraw all its limbs within whenever necessary. Krishna asserts that the one who has the capacity to remain balanced in pleasure and pain alike is fit for immortality.

This Discourse is often described as a summary of the entire Bhagavad Geeta. Here many subjects are explained such as: *Karmayog, Gyanayog, Sankhyayog, Buddhiyog* and the *Atman.* But prominence has been given to the notion of immortal nature of the soul existing within all living creatures and this subject has been covered in a great detail.

(**Note:** Some scholars may have a doubt whther the thoughtful idea concerning soul and God was really taken up just before the onset of actual battle of Mahabharat. It was perhaps not the right moment to discuss such a serious subject in the battlefield. It seems that such a subject was appended and expanded by different spiritual thinkers and commentators as the Geeta grew over the years.

Let me also put across my reflection on the notion of *Sthitapragya.* To me, this notion appears to be quite hollow, an impractical or unrealistic state of mind. A human being in reality cannot be stable minded all the time in all the eventualities. Theoretically or philosophically one can only imagine of a person without any pain or pleasure, likes or dislikes in all circumstances, but in a real life situation it is not possible for a person to be *Sthitapragya* all the time. In fact, the lofty notion of *Sthitapragya* takes us to the state of mind of an inert person, when a person cannot be alive and dead at the same time. Being a member of a society he cannot be indifferent to everything around him. It is always easier said than done. In the entire Mahabharat no character, including Sri Krishna, appears to be a truly *Sthitapragya.* The war of Mahabharat would not have occurred, had Sri Krishna been truly *Sthitapragya* when the Pandavas were deprived of their share in the kingdom by the Kauravas.)

Arjun's weakness disapproved by the Lord

Sanjay said to Dhritrashtra:

तं तथा कृपयाविष्टमश्रुपूर्णाकुलेक्षणम् ।
विषीदन्तमिदं वाक्यमुवाच मधुसूदनः ॥ 2.1 ॥

Shlok 2.1: Seeing Arjun overwhelmed with pity and despair, eyes full of tears and mind depressed, Krishna or Madhusudan (the destroyer of Madhu), spoke these words.

Commentary: As the verse is easily comprehensible, it needs no specific explanation.

Sri Krishna said:

कुतस्त्वा कश्मलमिदं विषमे समुपस्थितम् ।
अनार्यजुष्टमस्वर्ग्यमकीर्तिकरमर्जुन ॥ 2.2 ॥

Shlok 2.2: My dear Arjun, how has the dejection come to you at this juncture? It is ignoble, it does not lead to heaven, and it is disgraceful for an Aryan.

Commentary: As the verse is easily comprehensible, it needs no specific explanation.

(**Note:** Here it appears that both Pandavas and Kauravas probably belonged to the Aryan race. So they must have been fair or white-complexioned people. Krishna's address to Arjun as an Aryan clearly suggests that Krishna belonged to the dark-skinned indigenous community of India, which is also obvious from the fact that in all the Hindu scriptures Krishna, along with Vishnu and Ram, has been invariably described as a dark-skinned person. The actual meaning of Krishna in Sanskrit is dark or black.)

क्लैब्यं मा स्म गमः पार्थ नैतत्त्वय्युपपद्यते ।
क्षुद्रं हृदयदौर्बल्यं त्यक्त्वोत्तिष्ठ परन्तप ॥ 2.3 ॥

Shlok 2.3: Son of Pritha! Do not become a coward because this is unworthy of you. Cast off this trivial weakness of your heart.

Stand up, Scorcher of Enemies!

Commentary (Shlokas 2.1-2.3): Sanjay is telling Dhritrashtra that according to Krishna tears or lamentation on the face of Arjun suggests his ignorance about the real nature of soul. He is so much engrossed in the worldly life that he is crying for those things in life which are mortal. Anyway such a conduct is not expected from Arjun. He lacks self-realization. A man who is able to understand what the real spirit is cannot lament. In the presence of such a personality as that of Lord Krishna Arjun's lamentation for the loss of friends and kinsmen is certainly unbecoming of Arjun and hence Krishna expressed surprise over the conduct of Arjun. Krishna advised Arjun not to behave like a coward. A warrior should behave like a warrior only.

The above instruction is in response to the state of depression of Arjun, who was overwhelmed with grief at the prospect of killing his kith and kin and respected teachers. This is the first practical lesson from the Geeta and is meant for the struggling humanity. The message is loud and clear– not to get disheartened in the face of any difficult situation. The right course is to face the crisis and cope with difficulties of life with courage, strength and manliness. There is no scope for weakness in the battle of life which takes place every moment in the mind of men. This battle for a moral struggle has to be fought with courage and determination. This is the first clear message for everybody– to deal with difficult situations with courage at all times.

Arjun seeks instructions from the Lord

Arjun asked:

कथं भीष्ममहं संख्ये द्रोणं च मधुसूदन ।

इषुभिः प्रति योत्स्यामि पूजार्हावरिसूदन ॥ 2.4 ॥

Shlok 2.4: O Madhusudan, how shall I strike my grandfather, my Guru, and all other relatives– who are worthy of my homage– with arrows in battle, O slayer of enemies?

Commentary: Arjun had a valid point here. In the Vedic culture, *Gurus*, the elderly and all other superiors were to be respected. One should not fight or even crack joke or speak sarcastically with them, even if one's sentiments are hurt. But the scriptures also say that anyone who is engaged in abominable activities or supports misdeeds against you or others, is no longer to be respected, but punished. Arjun says that respected persons like Bhishma, the grandfather, and Drone, the teachers, are not to be counter attacked, even if they attack him. Even when they are harsh with him, they are not supposed to be harshly treated in a revengeful manner.

गुरूनहत्वा हि महानुभावान् श्रेयो भोक्तुं भैक्ष्यमपीह लोके ।
हत्वार्थकामांस्तु गुरूनिहैव भुञ्जीय भोगान्रुधिरप्रदिग्धान् ॥ 2.5॥

Shlok 2.5: Better it is, indeed, in this world to live on alms than to slay the noblest teachers. But if I kill them, all my wealth and pleasures will be stained with their blood.

Commentary: As the verse is easily comprehensible, it needs no specific explanation.

न चैतद्विद्मः कतरन्नो गरीयो यद्वा जयेम यदि वा नो जयेयुः।
यानेव हत्वा न जिजीविषामस्तेऽवस्थिताः प्रमुखे धार्तराष्ट्राः ॥ 2.6 ॥

Shlok 2.6: We do not know which alternative– to fight or to quit– is better for us. Further, we do not know whether we will conquer them or they will con-quer us. Even the sons of Dhritarashtra, after slaying whom we do not wish to live, stand facing us.

Commentary: Arjun was unable to decide what to do. He was in a fix. He seems to have lost even his commonsense. Expert guidance of a *Guru* or the spiritual counsellor should certainly be sought during a moment of crisis or to overcome the perplexities of life. Arjun now requests Krishna for the guidance.

कार्पण्यदोषोपहतस्वभावः पृच्छामि त्वां धर्मसम्मूढचेताः ।
यच्छ्रेयः स्यान्निश्चितं ब्रूहि तन्मे शिष्यस्तेऽहं शाधि मां त्वां प्रपन्नम् ॥ 2.7 ॥

Shlok 2.7: I am confused about my duty (*Dharma*). I have lost the balance of my mind because my senses are overcome by weak sense of sympathy and pity. Please tell me decisively what is better for me. I am Your disciple, and I take refuge in You.

Commentary: The word '*Dharma*' has got multiple connotations. It may be defined as the eternal law governing, upholding and supporting creation and the world order. It is the eternal relationship between the Creator and His creatures. It also means the way of life, doctrine, principle, prescribed duty, righteousness, right action, integrity, ideal conduct, customary practices, virtue, nature, essential quality, commandments, moral principles, spiritual truth, spiritual values, and a function within the scriptural injunction or religion. But in the battlefield *Dharma* means duty of a person as a warrior.

न हि प्रपश्यामि ममापनुद्याद् यच्छोकमुच्छोषणमिन्द्रियाणाम् ।
अवाप्य भूमावसपत्नमृद्धं राज्यं सुराणामपि चाधिपत्यम् ॥ 2.8 ॥

Shlok 2.8: I do not see anything that will dispel this sorrow of mine which desiccates my senses, even if on earth I obtain unrivalled wealth, a kingdom, yes, even sovereignty over the gods!

Commentary: As the verse is easily comprehensible, it needs no specific explanation.

Sanjay said to Dhritrashtra:

एवमुक्त्वा हृषीकेशं गुडाकेशः परन्तप ।
न योत्स्य इति गोविन्दमुक्त्वा तूष्णीं बभूव ह ॥ 2.9 ॥

Shlok 2.9: Having thus addressed Hrishikesh (Lord of the senses), Gudakesh- Parantap (Arjun- the conqueror of sleep), the tormenter of foes, declared to Govind, 'I shall not fight,' and then fell silent.

Commentary: Arjun displayed grief and delusion which was caused by his attachment for, and the sense of separation from the elders, sons, friends, well-wishers, kinsmen, near and distant relations– all this arose from the notion that 'I am theirs and they are mine.' There is nothing unusual with attachments, as humans are by nature social beings. They have always led and pursued collective life characterized by conflict and cooperation.

तमुवाच हृषीकेशः प्रहसन्निव भारत ।
सेनयोरुभयोर्मध्ये विषीदन्तमिदं वचः ॥ 2.10 ॥

Shlok 2.10: O King, Lord Krishna, as if smiling, spoke these words to the distressed Arjun in the midst of the two armies:

Commentary: As the verse is easily comprehensible, it needs no specific explanation.

Self-knowledge alone eradicates despair

Lord Krishna said:

अशोच्यानन्वशोचस्त्वं प्रज्ञावादांश्च भाषसे ।

गतासूनगतासूंश्च नानुशोचन्ति पण्डिताः ॥ 2.11 ॥

Shlok 2.11: You grieve for those whom you should not grieve for and yet you speak like a wise man. Wise men do not grieve for the dead or for the living.

Commentary: The Geeta stresses the point that there should be no room for lamentation, either in the case of death or in other circumstances. The message of the Geeta is very loud and clear—why grieve over death of the perishable body when the real self in the soul, which is the master, does not die.

The principal character of life is the individual self or the soul which never dies. It is the external frame or the physical body which perishes. People meet and depart in this world same as two pieces of wood flowing down the river come together and after some time they get separated from each other. The wise, who know that the body is mortal and the soul is immortal, have nothing to moan about.

The soul (or *Atman*) is also called consciousness and is the source of life and the cosmic power behind the body-mind complex. Just as our body exists in space, similarly our thoughts, intellect, emotions and psyche exist in the soul, the space of consciousness. Soul cannot be perceived by our physical senses because soul is beyond the domain of the senses. The senses were designed to know physical objects only.

(**Note:** It may be pointed out here that the word '*Atman*' has been also used in varied senses in the 'Geeta' such as the lower self (body, mind, and senses), psyche, intellect, soul, spirit, subtle senses, oneself, ego, heart, human beings, Eternal Being (Brahm), Absolute Truth, individual soul, and the super-soul or the supreme Self, depending on the context.)

न त्वेवाहं जातु नासं न त्वं नेमे जनाधिपाः।

न चैव न भविष्यामः सर्वे वयमतः परम् ॥ 2.12 ॥

Shlok 2.12: Never was there a time when I did not exist, nor you, nor all these rulers of men, nor shall any of us ever cease to exist hereafter.

Commentary: The above verse corroborates that life is perpetual and eternal. Most of us do not know what life is all about? For an average person, life is the short span between birth and death. The first day of life starts with the birth and death brings the last day of life. This is only a short-sighted view of life and does not convey the whole reality. The Geeta tells us that there was life before birth and it also continues thereafter. It continues in different manners and forms and death in the present state of our existence is not the final destination.

Good and bad people would to be present in all ages. All sorts of people will come and go in a cyclical fashion. We are not here for the first time. We did exist in the past and we would definitely exist in future too. This is so because a soul never dies. Such an observation can be made only by a godly person. Ordinary human being cannot readily grasp it. We are replica of the past in a different form, but with respect to character we are largely the same. O Arjun, believe me nothing is permanent here, we need not unnecessarily worry to lose or miss anything. What seems to be ours is not really ours. All our worldly attachments are nothing but false and momentary.

देहिनोऽस्मिन्यथा देहे कौमारं यौवनं जरा ।
तथा देहान्तरप्राप्तिर्धीरस्तत्र न मुह्यति ॥ 2.13 ॥

Shlok 2.13: Just as the soul passes from childhood to youth, from youth to old age, similarly it passes from one body to another. A wise man is not confused about this.

Commentary: This verse simply suggests that soul is immortal. In this body, the embodied soul passes through childhood, youth and old age. In the same manner the soul goes from one body to another; therefore, the wise are never deluded regarding the soul. It is also suggested that death is merely another stage in the journey of soul through time. This is a normal and natural happening and one need not be perplexed when it happens.

मात्रास्पर्शास्तु कौन्तेय शीतोष्णसुखदुःखदाः ।
आगमापायिनोऽनित्यास्तांस्तितिक्षस्व भारत ॥ 2.14 ॥

Shlok 2.14: O son of Kunti, contacts with their objects give rise to cold and heat, pleasure and pain. They come and go and do not last forever, these learn to endure, O Descendant of Bharat!

Commentary: The contacts of the senses with sense objects give rise to the feelings of heat and cold, and pain and pleasure. They are transitory and impermanent. Therefore, one should learn to endure them bravely.

Our joys and sorrows, pleasant and unpleasant experiences arise out of our various activities in life. These activities take place when we come in contact with the external world either in thought or in action, at home or outside.

Thus, our life itself provides opportunities for pleasure and pain. So long as we live we have to face both these situations. Pleasure and pain are, therefore, unavoidable. The Geeta tells us how to deal with these happenings. The ultimate solution of this is in the last sentence which says, 'Learn to Endure'. There is no option but to endure. We must, therefore, learn how to face these situations with calm and composure and bear them with serenity of mind, knowing that these situations are bound to pass away.

यं हि न व्यथयन्त्येते पुरुषं पुरुषर्षभ ।
समदुःखसुखं धीरं सोऽमृतत्वाय कल्पते ॥ 2.15 ॥

Shlok 2.15: O Bull among Men, the man who remains the same in pain and pleasure, who is wise makes himself fit for eternal life.

Commentary: That person to whom pleasure and pain are alike– who neither exults in pleasure nor feels dejected in pain– who is a man of wisdom, whom heat and cold and other things such as those mentioned above do not affect in virtue of his vision of the eternal Self– that man, firm in his vision of the eternal Self and bearing calmly the pairs of opposites (such as heat and cold), is able to attain immortality (*Moksha*).

We should meet the situation of pleasure and pain with evenness of mind. In our moments of pleasure and happiness, we need not jump with abnormal ostentatious expressions of joy. Similarly in moments of pain and grief, one should not feel utterly miserable and aggrieved or disturbed. Equanimity must be maintained in both cases, which may not be easy in real life situations, a correct understanding and constant practice of endurance will be helpful.

Nothing can hurt one if the mind can be trained to withstand the impulse of the pairs of opposites– joys and sorrows, pains and pleasures, loss and gain. This world cannot exist without the pairs of opposites. Good and evil, pain and pleasure will always exist. The universe is a playground designed by God for the living entities. It takes two to play a game. The game cannot continue if the pairs of opposites are altogether eliminated. Before one can feel joy, one must know sorrow. Both negative and positive experiences are needed for our growth and spiritual development. Cessation of pain brings pleasure and cessation of pleasure results in pain. Thus, pain is born in the womb of pleasure.

Peace is born in the womb of war. Sorrow exists because the desire for happiness exists. When the desire for happiness disappears, so does the sorrow. Sorrow is only a prelude to happiness and vice versa. Even the joy of going to heaven is followed by the sorrow of coming back to the earth; therefore, worldly objects should not be the main goal of human life.

The soul is eternal, body is transitory

नासतो विद्यते भावो नाभावो विद्यते सतः ।
उभयोरपि दृष्टोऽन्तस्त्वनयोस्तत्त्वदर्शिभिः ॥ 2.16 ॥

Shlok 2.16: There is no becoming from the non-existent, nor any unbecoming from the existent. The boundary between these two has been perceived by those who see the basic principles.

Commentary: The unreal (*Asat*, body, creation) has a temporary (or *Mithya*) existence and the real (*Sat, Atman*) always exists. The reality of these two is indeed certainly seen by the seers of truth. What is changing must always be unreal. What is constant or permanent must always be real. The *Atman* or the eternal, all-pervading Self ever exists. It is the only Reality. This phenomenal world of names and forms is ever changing. Names and forms are subject to decay and death. Hence they are unreal or impermanent.

The soul exists everywhere and at all times– past, present, and future. The human body and the universe both have a temporary existence, but appear permanent at first sight. Our physical body is subject to birth, growth, maturity, reproduction, decay, and death; whereas the soul is eternal, indestructible, pure, unique, all knower, substratum, unchangeable, self-luminous, the cause of all causes, all pervading, unaffectable, immutable and inexplicable. The material body or the world is unreal and transitory; it undergoes changes, and the soul is real.

(**Note:** *Atman* is also called '*Jeevatma*' or '*Jeev*', which is the ultimate source of all individual selves. We have used the English words: Self, Spirit, spirit, soul, or individual soul interchangeably for different aspects of *Atman* (or *Sat*). Everything, except *Atman*, is considered second order of Reality, *Asat* (*Mithya*), changeable or unreal.)

अविनाशि तु तद्विद्धि येन सर्वमिदं ततम्।
विनाशमव्ययस्यास्य न कश्चित्कर्तुमर्हति ॥ 2.17 ॥

Shlok 2.17: Know That Spirit (Self) by which this entire body is pervaded is indeed indestructible. None can destroy the imperishable Spirit.

Commentary: It is stated that the Brahm is indestructible. Everything is pervaded by That. No one is ever able to destroy that Immutable. The Self pervades all objects like ether. Even if the pot is broken, the ether that is within and without it cannot be destroyed. Similarly, if the bodies and all other objects perish, the eternal Self that pervades them cannot be destroyed.

That, the Brahm, the '*Sat*' or the Real, pervades this entire world, including the *Akash*, same as pots and other objects are pervaded by the *Akash* or space. *Brahm* does not pass through any process of increase or decrease and is, therefore, inexhaustible. This *Brahm*, the '*Sat* ', is not exhausted in Itself; for, unlike the body, It has no parts. Nor does It diminish by anything belonging to It; for, nothing belongs to the Self. None can cause disappearance or destruction of the inexhaustible *Brahm*. Nobody– not even the *Ishvar* (God)– can destroy the Self because the Self is *Brahm* Itself. On the other hand, some philosophers have questioned the view that the Self or soul is a part of Brahm. They have argued that both appear to be the same or identical, but are not exactly the same. There are some who say there is nothing like a soul.

अन्तवन्त इमे देहा नित्यस्योक्ताः शरीरिणः ।
अनाशिनोऽप्रमेयस्य तस्माद्युध्यस्व भारत ॥ 2.18 ॥

Shlok 2.18: These bodies of the embodied (Soul), who is eternal, indestructible and unknowable, are said to have an end. Therefore, fight, O Descendant of Bharat (Arjun)!

Commentary: Lord Krishna says that since these bodies which are pervaded by of the Soul, who is eternal, indestructible and unknowable, would have an end like those seen in dreams. Human body has got very temporary existence. The things which are really indestructible are going to exist for ever. So you need not unnecessarily worry about the destruction which is inevitable. Hence, O Arjun, get ready to fight for the cause and do not hesitate.

य एनं वेत्ति हन्तारं यश्चैनं मन्यते हतम् ।
उभौ तौ न विजानीतो नायं हन्ति न हन्यते ॥ 2.19 ॥

Shlok 2.19: Mistaken are those who consider the *Atman* to be the slayer and also those who consider it to be slain. Neither does it kill nor is it ever killed.

Commentary: Those who think 'I slay' or 'I am slain' when the body is slain, and thus identify the Soul with the object of the consciousness of 'I,' the ego, they do not understand the real nature of the Soul. The Soul is neither the agent nor the object of the action of slaying.

The Soul is immutable

न जायते म्रियते वा कदाचिन्नायं भूत्वा भविता वा न भूयः ।
अजो नित्यः शाश्वतोऽयं पुराणो न हन्यते हन्यमाने शरीरे ॥ 2.20 ॥

Shlok 2.20: The self (soul) is neither born nor does it die. It did not originate from anything nor did anything originate from it. It is birthless, eternal, undecaying and ancient. It is not killed even when the body is killed.

Commentary: The soul is unborn, eternal, changeless, timeless (ancient). It is never destroyed even when the body is destroyed. This verse explains the difference between the body and the soul. Soul is the driving force of life. The Soul is immutable. It is so because He is never born, never dies, and so on. If the Soul has once existed, He does not cease to exist afterwards. In ordinary parlance He is said to die who, having once existed, afterwards ceases to be. Neither does the Soul come into existence, like the body, having not existed before. Not so is the Soul. He is unborn because He does not die. He is eternal. He is constant, not subject to change. Having no parts, He does not diminish in His own substance. As devoid of qualities, He does not diminish by loss of a quality. He is primeval, not subject to the change known as growth as opposed to decline. As devoid of parts, the Soul was as fresh in the past as He is now or will be in future. He is always the same. And He is not slain when the body is slain and He is not transformed when the body is transformed. The Soul is not subject to transformation. The passage, on the whole, suggests that the Soul is free from all sorts of change.

वेदाविनाशिनं नित्यं य एनमजमव्ययम् ।
कथं स पुरुषः पार्थ कं घातयति हन्ति कम् ॥ 2.21 ॥

Shlok 2.21: O Parth, how can a person– who knows that the soul is indestructible, changeless, unborn, and immutable– kill anyone or cause anyone to be killed?

Commentary: He who knows the Soul, as described in the preceding verse, is indestructible, i.e. devoid of birth, death and transformation, how does an enlightened man of this description do the act of slaying, or how does he cause another to slay? As a matter of fact, he slays nobody at all, nor does he at all cause another to slay. Birth and death of human beings do not mean birth and death of the Soul.

Death and migration of the soul

वासांसि जीर्णानि यथा विहाय नवानि गृह्णाति नरोऽपराणि ।
तथा शरीराणि विहाय जीर्णान्यन्यानि संयाति नवानि देही ॥ 2.22 ॥

Shlok 2.22: Just as we abandon our worn-out garments and put on new ones, so the spirit abandons an old body and enters a new one.

Commentary: The soul keeps on changing the body. As the body becomes worn out, the soul abandons it and moves into the new one without undergoing any change. Why is the soul quite changeless? Just as, in this world, a man casts off the clothes that have been worn-out and puts on others which are new, in the same manner, like the man (of the world), the embodied Self abandons old bodies, and, without undergoing any change, enters others which are new. The Lord says that death is the separation of the subtle body from the physical body. The living entity is a traveller. Death is not the end of the journey of the living entity. Death is like a rest area where the individual soul changes vehicles and the journey continues. Life is continuous and endless. Inevitable death is not the end of life; it is only an end of a perishable, physical body. Those who do not believe in rebirth are wrong, ignorant with very poor knowledge of spiritualism. Such thing cannot be taught to others with the help of logic and argument, as everybody cannot be made artists, scientists, saints and surgeons.

After death, the soul gets a new body. Thus death is only a transformation to another life which continues on and on. In the real life, this may not seem as simple and easy to understand but one must perceive and comprehend the real significance of death, as indicated in the Geeta. Life may be compared to a play in a theatre. An individual plays his role as assigned in life and then one day makes his exit from the worldly scene. Death becomes a doorway to another life, as the soul takes on another body.

नैनं छिन्दन्ति शस्त्राणि नैनं दहति पावकः ।
न चैनं क्लेदयन्त्यापो न शोषयति मारुतः ॥ 2.23 ॥

Shlok 2.23: No weapon can cut this *Atman*, no fire can burn it, no water can wet it, no air can dry it.

Commentary: The Self about whom we are talking about cannot be cut or pierced by any weapon such as sword. As He has no parts, there cannot be any division of Him into parts. Fire does not burn Him: even fire cannot reduce Him to ashes. Wind cannot dry him. It is infinite and extremely subtle. Because the destructive object like swords and the like cannot destroy the Self, therefore, He is everlasting.

Because being everlasting, He is all-pervading. Because all-pervading, He is stable like a pillar. Because stable, the Self is firm. Wherefore He is eternal, not produced out of any cause, not new. This gives some clue about the nature of Spirit or soul.

अच्छेद्योऽयमदाह्योऽयमक्लेद्योऽशोष्य एव च ।
नित्यः सर्वगतः स्थाणुरचलोऽयं सनातनः ॥ 2.24 ॥

Shlok 2.24: **It is uncleavable. It cannot be burnt and can neither he wetted or dried. It is eternal, all-pervading, unchanging and steadfast. It is eternal, all-pervading, unchanging and steadfast. It is the same forever.**

Commentary: This verse is largely repetition of what has already been stated before, that is, Soul is indestructible and unchangeable. Spirit or *Atman* is beyond time and space. The Spirit is said to be unexplainable, incomprehensible, and immutable. Knowing the Spirit as such, you should not grieve for the physical body. In the previous verses Sri Krishna asked Arjun not to worry about the indestructible spirit. A question may arise: Should one lament the death of (the destructible body of) our near and dear ones at all? The answer is in negative in the following verse:

अव्यक्तोऽयमचिन्त्योऽयमविकार्योऽयमुच्यते ।
तस्मादेवं विदित्वैनं नानुशोचितुमर्हसि ॥ 2.25 ॥

Shlok 2.25: **This Spirit is said to be unmanifested, unthinkable and unchangeable. Knowing the Spirit as such, you should not mourn it.**

Commentary: As the Self is inaccessible to any of the human sense, He is not manifest. Therefore, He is unthinkable. Only those things which are perceived by the senses can be an object of thought. The Self is unthinkable because He is inaccessible to the senses. The Self is quite unlike milk, which mixed with butter-milk, can be made to change its form. He is changeless also because He has no constituent part. A thing which has no part cannot undergo any change. Because the Self is changeless, He is unchangeable. In view of such nature of the Self, one should not grieve the death of a person.

अथ चैनं नित्यजातं नित्यं वा मन्यसे मृतम् ।
तथापि त्वं महाबाहो नैवं शोचितुमर्हसि ॥ 2.26 ॥

Shlok 2.26: Even if you regard it as eternally born or etrnally dead, you still should not grieve over it, Mighty-armed Prince.

जातस्य हि ध्रुवो मृत्युर्ध्रुवं जन्म मृतस्य च ।
तस्मादपरिहार्येऽर्थे न त्वं शोचितुमर्हसि ॥ 2.27 ॥

Shlok 2.27: Certain is the death of the born; and certain is the birth of the dead. Therefore, you should not lament over the unavoidable.

Commentary (Shlokas 2.26-27): Birth is inevitable to what is dead and death is inevitable to what is born. Since birth and death are unavoidable, one need not grieve regarding such an unavoidable thing. If death is natural to that which has had birth, and if birth is natural to that which has had death, the thing is unavoidable. Therefore, one should not lament the death of anybody at all. Lamentation is due to attachment, and attachment binds the individual soul to the wheel of transmigration. Therefore, the scriptures suggest that one should not mourn, but pray for several days after the person's death for salvation of the departed soul.

The inevitability of death and indestructibility of the soul, however, do not and cannot justify lawful but unnecessary killing of any creature, unjust war, or even suicide. The Vedic scriptures are very clear on this point with regard to the killing of human beings or any other living entity. The scripture says: One should not commit violence towards anyone. Unauthorised killing is punishable in all circumstances: A life for life. Lord Krishna is urging Arjun to fight– but not to kill wantonly– in order to establish peace and law and order on the earth as a matter of a warrior's duty.

Let us now examine the instances of grief on occasions other than death. One may grieve in other cases such as, disease, loss of wealth and property, failure and defeat, dishonour, personal jealousy and rivalry and bad behaviour faced in everyday life. Cases of this type may be multiplied. In short, grief happens due to unfavourable circumstances which had already taken place or are still in the process of happening or are likely to happen. In all these cases, one should try one's utmost to remove the obstacles, to the extent possible, and avoid the negative emotions of grief and dejections or depression. One must face the situation as it comes and act accordingly and not give in to despair and grief as these tendencies are unbecoming of a human being. One must face, observe, and analyse an adverse situation and act wisely and bravely. One must realize the fact that simply grieving will not help, so why grieve? Some soul searching and positive thinking are required to ward off grief in such cases. Firm faith in God and performance of one's duty without attachment are very helpful to keep grief at bay.

अव्यक्तादीनि भूतानि व्यक्तमध्यानि भारत ।
अव्यक्तनिधनान्येव तत्र का परिदेवना ॥ 2.28 ॥

Shlok 2.28: The beginning of all the creatures is hidden, the middle is manifested and unmanifested again is their end! O Bharat (Arjun). What reason is there to lament?

Commentary: All beings are unmanifest (or invisible to our physical eyes) before birth and after death. They manifest between birth and death only. The origin– prior to manifestation– of beings such as sons and friends, who are mere combinations of material elements correlated as causes and effects, is non-perception (*Avyakta*). And having come into existence, their middle state– previous to death– is perceived. Again their end is non-perception: after death, they become unperceived again. Thus it is said:

The physical body is a combination of the five elements. It is perceived by the physical eye only after the five elements have entered into such combination. After death the body disintegrates and all the five elements return to their original source. The body cannot be perceived then. It can be perceived only in the middle state. He who understands the nature of the body and human relationships based upon it will not grieve.

The indestructible spirit transcends mind and speech

आश्चर्यवत्पश्यति कश्चिदेनमाश्चर्यवद्वदति तथैव चान्यः ।
आश्चर्यवच्चैनमन्यः, शृणोति श्रुत्वाप्येनं वेद न चैव कश्चित् ॥ 2.29 ॥

Shlok 2.29: Some see the Spirit as a wonder, another speaks of

It as won-der-ful, and yet others hear of It as a wonder. Even after hearing about It, no one really knows It.

Commentary: It is hard to know the Soul. Though some see Him, hear Him and speak to Him and yet none realizes Him at all. The Soul is something like a wonder. He that speaks and he that hears of Him is only one among millions. One can readily recognize how difficult it is to understand the Spirit.

देही नित्यमवध्योऽयं देहे सर्वस्य भारत ।
तस्मात्सर्वाणि भूतानि न त्वं शोचितुमर्हसि ॥ 2.30 ॥

Shlok 2.30: O Arjun, the Spirit that dwells in the body of all beings is eternally indestructible. Therefore, you should not mourn for anybody.

Commentary: When the body of any creature whatsoever is killed, the Soul is not destroyed and therefore, you need not grieve for anybody whatsoever, no matter whether that person is Bhishma or somebody else.

A warrior should fight

स्वधर्ममपि चावेक्ष्य न विकम्पितुमर्हसि ।
धर्म्याद्धि युद्धाच्छ्रेयोऽन्यत्क्षत्रियस्य न विद्यते ॥ 2.31 ॥

Shlok 2.31: **Considering also your duty as a warrior, you should not hesitate because there is nothing higher for a Kshatriya than a righteous war.**

Commentary: Having regard also to the fact that fighting is a Kshatriya's duty, you ought not run away from this duty. Those days it was considered as a natural duty on the part of Kshatriya to fight for the righteous cause. Lord Krishna is persuading Arjun to get ready for the battle without any hesitation and confusion in mind, as the very cause of the war is righteous.

(**Note:** Here many commentators of the Geeta or the Mahabharat, not knowing much about the sociological aspect of the caste system, have offered caste-centric interpretation of this verse. Here Kshatriya refers to the duty of Arjun as a warrior, not as a member of the Kshatriya Varna. These days all Rajputs claim to be of the Kshatriya origin, but the Kshatriya Varna does not necessarily mean Rajput caste. All Rajputs neither belong to the Kshatriya Varna nor could all Kshatriyas become Rajput caste with the lapse of time. There is no correspondence or synchronization between the Varna system and the caste system, as the caste system has not evolved from the Varna system alone.

This and the subsequent verses, making reference of the Varna system and indirectly caste system also, have been inserted into the Geeta by Brahmins later on to underline the importance the *Varna* System and retain social superiority of the Brahmins and Kshatriya *Varna* or Rajput caste over others. They have used the name of Krishna for easy acceptance of their views by the people from the lower stratum of society. Krishna himself did not belong to the Kshatriya Varna.)

यदृच्छया चोपपन्नं स्वर्गद्वारमपावृतम् ।
सुखिनः क्षत्रियाः पार्थ लभन्ते युद्धमीदृशम् ॥ 2.32 ॥

Shlok 2.32: Happy are the Kshatriyas, O Arjun, who are called upon to fight in such a righteous war that comes of itself as an open door to heaven!

Commentary: The righteous war is not a religious war against the followers of other religions. The righteous war may be waged even against the evil-doers of the same kinship group. Life is a continuous battle between the forces of goodness and badness. A valiant person must fight with the spirit of a warrior– with a will and determination for victory– and without any compromise with the forces of evil and malice. God helps the valiant who adhere to morality. *Dharma* (righteousness) protects those who protect *Dharma* (morality, justice and righteousness).

It is better to die for a right cause and acquire the grace of sacrifice than to have an ordinary death. The gates of heaven are open wide for those who stand up to vindicate justice and righteousness (*Dharma*). Not to oppose an evil is to indirectly support it. Very similar ideas are expressed in other scriptures of the world. There is no sin in killing an aggressor. Whosoever helps and supports an aggressor is also an aggressor. Thus, all those who supported Kauravas were basically malevolent and deserved to be eliminated.

अथ चेत्त्वमिमं धर्म्यं संग्रामं न करिष्यसि ।
ततः स्वधर्मं कीर्तिं च हित्वा पापमवाप्स्यसि ॥ 2.33 ॥

Shlok 2.33: But you refuge to perform your righteous duty of

fighting, you will fail in your own duty, lose your honour as a warrior and incur sin (by not doing your duty).

अकीर्तिं चापि भूतानि कथयिष्यन्ति तेऽव्ययाम् ।
संभावितस्य चाकीर्तिर्मरणादतिरिच्यते ॥ 2.34 ॥

Shlok 2.34: People will ever talk about your disgrace; and to one who has been honoured, dishonour is worse than death.

भयाद्रणादुपरतं मंस्यन्ते त्वां महारथाः ।
येषां च त्वं बहुमतो भूत्वा यास्यसि लाघवम् ॥ 2.35 ॥

Shlok 2.35: The mighty warriors will assume that you have backed away from the battle out of fear. Those who held you in a high esteem would consider you insignificant.

अवाच्यवादांश्च बहून्वदिष्यन्ति तवाहिताः ।
निन्दन्तस्तव सामर्थ्यं ततो दुःखतरं नु किम् ॥ 2.36 ॥

Shlok 2.36: Your enemies will speak many unmentionable words and scorn your ability. What could be more painful to you than this?

हतो वा प्राप्स्यसि स्वर्गं जित्वा वा भोक्ष्यसे महीम् ।
तस्मादुत्तिष्ठ कौन्तेय युद्धाय कृतनिश्चयः ॥ 2.37 ॥

Shlok 2.37: Killed, then you will gain heaven; victorious, then you will enjoy the kingdom on the earth. Therefore, O son of Kunti, arise and get ready to fight.

Commentary (Shlokas 2.33-2.37): If you do not fight this battle which is enjoined on you as a duty, and which is not contrary to law either, you will, by neglecting this battle, have abandoned your duty and lost the name and fame that you have earned so far. In addition, you will also incur sin.

Even the common people, too, will speak about your bad name for a long time. To a person like you who has been admired as a hero and as a righteous man and as one possessing other such noble qualities, death is preferable to disrepute.

Duryodhan and others fighting the great war will think that you have withdrawn from the battle because you were afraid of warrior like Karna and others, but not because of compassion for the Kauravas. Having been thus considered, you will again become a very trivial person in their opinion. There is no pain more unbearable than that of disrepute thus incurred. Therefore, rise with the resolution, 'I will conquer the enemy or die.'

Arjun, you should get ready and fight now, as this war is in your favour both in case of victory and loss of life. If you succeed to win, you will rule the earth and if you lose your life, you will attain heaven. Thus your dithering attitude to war is not in your interests at all.

सुखदुःखे समे कृत्वा लाभालाभौ जयाजयौ ।
ततो युद्धाय युज्यस्व नैवं पापमवाप्स्यसि ॥ 2.38 ॥

Shlok 2.38: Treating pleasure and pain, gain and loss, victory and defeat as all alike, get ready for the battle of life. It is only in this way that you can avoid the hurdle to your becoming. By doing your duty this way, you shall not incur any sin.

Commentary: According to the Geeta, the battle of life has to be fought with equal-mindedness in all situations, without getting disturbed in emotional ups and downs. This is the *Yog* of equanimity or the doctrine of poise in action. If a person performs actions with the above mental attitude, he will not reap the fruits of such actions. Lord Krishna says here that even the violence done on the line of duty with a proper frame of mind, as discussed in the above verse, is sinless. This is the starting verse of the theory of *Karmayog*, the main theme of the Geeta.

Here 'the battle' would mean the battle of life: the trials and tribulations everyone has to face. A police officer may have to order his force to open fire to quell a rioting mob—no sin is attached to his actions. A hangman may have to execute a condemned murderer by hanging him. A teacher has to reprimand a student. Such actions should be performed without getting emotionally upset, since they are merely performance of proper duty.

The knowledge of *Karmayog*– the selfless service

एषा तेऽभिहिता सांख्ये बुद्धिर्योगे त्विमां शृणु ।
बुद्धया युक्तो यया पार्थ कर्मबंधं प्रहास्यसि ॥ 2.39 ॥

Shlok 2.39: Thus far I have imparted wisdom concerning

Sankhya to you, O Arjun. Now listen to wisdom concerning *Yog*. O son of Pritha, when you act in such knowledge you can free yourself from the bondage of works.

Commentary: The above verse mentions Sankhya (transcendental knowledge) and Yog. The earlier verses explain the reality of immortal soul, the perishable body, different stages through which the soul passes, the inevitable death and re-birth, grief, pleasure and pain, etc. This is the wisdom of *Sankhya darshan*. Having imparted the wisdom of Sankhya to Arjun, Lord Krishna then dwells on the wisdom of Yog. As indicated in the subsequent verses, Yog here means Karma Yog. It implies action with true understanding. It stands for the performance of one's duty with right understanding.

Yog, a safe course

नेहाभिक्रमनाशोऽस्ति प्रत्यवायो न विद्यते ।
स्वल्पमप्यस्य धर्मस्य त्रायते महतो भयात् ।। 2.40 ।।

Shlok 2.40: In this there is no loss of effort, nor is there any adverse effect. Even a little of this knowledge (even a little practice of this *Yog*) protects one from great fear of birth and death.

Commentary: The selfless action is also called *Seva, Karmayog*, sacrifice, science of proper action and yog of equanimity. A *Karmayogi* works with love for the Lord as a matter of duty without a desire for the fruits of work or attachment to the results, and becomes free from all fear. The word *Karma* also means duty, action, deeds, work, endeavour, or the results of past deeds. In *Karmayog* (selfless action) even a little effort brings immediate purification of the heart. Purification of the heart leads to fearlessness.

व्यवसायात्मिका बुद्धिरेकेह कुरुनन्दन ।
बहुशाखा ह्यनन्ताश्च बुद्धयोऽव्यवसायिनाम् ।। 2.41 ।।

Shlok 2.41: In this, O scion of Kuru, a *Karmayogi* has resolute determination for God-realization only, but the desires of one who works to enjoy the fruits of work are endless.

Commentary: Arjun, bear in mind that for a *Karmayogi* in this path to Bliss there is only one thought of a resolute nature, and it is opposed to all other kinds of thoughts. Other kinds of thoughts have got numerous branches and they are of no use for those who have a faith in Him. In fact they are endless and ever-spreading. But when, owing to discrimination produced by the right source of knowledge, these thoughts of endless variety cease to exist. Because of variety in each of their branches, the thoughts of the irresolute– of those who are not possessed of the discrimination produced by the right source of knowledge– are endless and such people are deviated from the path of Bliss.

The Vedas deal with material and ritual aspects of life

यामिमां पुष्पितां वाचं प्रवदन्त्यविपश्चितः ।
वेदवादरताः पार्थ नान्यदस्तीति वादिनः ॥ 2.42 ॥

Shlok 2.42: The ignorant ones who delight in chanting of the flowery words of the Vedas– without understanding the real purpose of the Vedas– think, O Parth, there is nothing else in the Vedas except the rituals for the sole purpose of obtaining heavenly enjoyment.

Commentary: The unwise, who lack discrimination or reason, lay a great stress on the *Karmakand* or ritualistic aspects of the *Vedas* which prescribe specific rules for specific actions for the attainment of specific fruit. They extol these actions and rewards unduly. The Vedic rites and rituals are no solution to your problem, exhorts Krishna. The *Vedas* are not the ultimate reality. In a way this suggests that the philosophy of the Geeta is much more pertinent and meaningful than the hymns of the Vedas, emphasizing ritual practices to obtain heavenly enjoyment. Ritual practices are no solution.

कामात्मानः स्वर्गपरा जन्मकर्मफलप्रदाम् ।
क्रियाविशेषबहुलां भोगैश्वर्यगतिं प्रति ॥ 2.43 ॥

Shlok 2.43: They are dominated by material desires and consider the attainment of heaven as the highest goal of life. They engage in specific rites for the sake of material prosperity and enjoyment. Rebirth is the result of their action.

भोगैश्वर्यप्रसक्तानां तयापहृतचेतसाम् ।
व्यवसायात्मिका बुद्धिः समाधौ न विधीयते ॥ 2.44 ॥

Shlok 2.44: The resolute determination for meditation and *Samadhi* (the state of Super-consciousness) is not possible for those ignorant ones who are attached to pleasure and power and whose judgement is obscured by ritualistic activities for attainment of pleasure and power, O son of Pritha.

Commentary: Self-realization is to know one's relationship with the Supreme Being and His true transcendental nature. The promise of material benefits of Vedic rituals is like the promise of candy to a child by the mother to induce him or her to take the medicine of detachment from the material life; it is necessary in most instances. Rituals must be changed with time and backed up by devotion and good deeds. People may pray and meditate anytime, anywhere, without any ritual. Rituals have played a great role in spiritual life, but they have been greatly abused also. Lord Krishna and Lord Buddha both disapproved the blind performance of Vedic rituals. Mere performance of rituals should not be the sole aim of life, as it does not lead us anywhere. Attainment of Bliss is not possible through religious practices.

त्रैगुण्यविषया वेदा निस्त्रैगुण्यो भवार्जुन ।
निर्द्वन्द्वो नित्यसत्त्वस्थो निर्योगक्षेम आत्मवान् ॥ 2.45 ॥

Shlokas 2.45: The Vedas deal with the subject of three modes (*gunas*- goodness, passion and ignorance) of material nature, O Arjun, rise above these three modes. Remain tranquil and unconcerned with the thoughts of acquisition and preservation of material objects.

Commentary: The Vedas treat of the triad of the *Gunas. Guna* means attribute or quality. It is substance as well as quality. Nature is made up of three *Gunas– Sattva* (purity, light, harmony), *Rajas* (passion, restlessness, motion), and *Tamas* (inertia, darkness). The worldly life is characterized by pairs of opposites such as pleasure and pain, heat and cold, gain and loss, victory and defeat, honour and dishonour, praise and censure.

Sri Krishna advises Arjun that he should try to be free from the triad of the *Gunas*. He should also be free from pairs of opposites (*Dwandwas*); in fact from all mutually opposed objects which are the causes of pleasure and pain. Be free from acquisition and preservation, ever remaining in the *Sattva* (Goodness) and self-possessed. Be without desires. Take your stand ever in the *Sattva:* practise purity. Be also self-possessed: be guarded. This is the advice you should follow when engaged in the performance of duty.

(**Note:** *Gunas* are the important subject of the *Sankhya Darshan*, as this philosophy deals with the dynamics of evolution with the help of the doctrines of *Purush* (cosmic male) and *Prakriti* (nature). Gunas are of three kinds and they are the intrinsic qualities of Nature. They characterize humans also because they too are made of nature. Nature is the cause of everything we see. Hence, the notion of Gunas is briefly explained here:

Sattva is the quality of balance, harmony, goodness, purity, universalizing, holistic, constructive, creative, building, positive, peaceful, and virtuous. A man whose nature is dominated by S*attva* will be clear thinking, radiant and truthful.

Rajas is the quality of passion, activity, neither good nor bad and sometimes either, self-centredness, egoistic, individualizing, driven, moving, dynamic. A man whose nature is dominated by *Rajas* will be passionate, quick to anger and greedy.

Tamas is the quality of imbalance, disorder, chaos, anxiety, impure, destructive, delusion, negative, dull or inactive, apathy, inertia or lethargy, violent, vicious, and ignorant. A man whose nature is dominated by *Tamas* will be stupid, lazy and stubborn.)

यावानर्थ उदपाने सर्वतः सम्प्लुतोदके।
तावान्सर्वेषु वेदेषु ब्राह्मणस्य विजानतः ॥ 2.46 ॥

Shlok 2.46: The Vedas are only as useful to an enlightened Brahm as is a tank in an area over-flooded with water all around.

Commentary: The verse suggests that a well is of little use to a person who has water all around; similarly, the Vedas are of little value to a person who has experienced the primordial reality. Scriptures become unnecessary after enlightenment of a person in much the same way as a reservoir of water has no use when there is floodwater everywhere. One who has realized the Supreme Being will not desire the attainment of heaven mentioned as the fruits of performing Vedic rituals. Scriptures, such as the Vedas, might be necessary means, but not the end.

Scriptures are meant to lead and guide us on the spiritual path. Once the goal is reached, they have served their purpose. This does not, however, mean that the *Vedas* are of no use. They are useful for neophytes or aspirants who have just started on the spiritual path.

Theory and practice of *Karmayog*

कर्मण्येवाधिकारस्ते मा फलेषु कदाचन ।
मा कर्मफलहेतुर्भूर्मा ते सङ्गोऽस्त्वकर्मणि ॥ 2.47 ॥

Shlok 2.47: On action alone let thy interest be fixed, never on its result; getting too much attached to the idea of the fruit will lead you to inaction.

Commentary: This well-known verse has been the credo of many ordinary people, both literate and illiterate, in India for generations– it is a clear instruction in Karma Yog. Several volumes of commentaries have been written on this single verse. This key verse contains the essential principle of disinterestedness or detachment. This verse of the Geeta has confused many people. They tend to interpret it to mean that one should work without expecting any result. No one can perform action without expecting some positive results. This verse simply means that we should not always expect only favourable results of our choice. If we keep on thinking of desired results all the time, it would disturb our concentration of mind at the time of performance of duty. So we should better try to do our best to concentrate on action alone while in action. Simultaneously we should also be prepared to face unfavourable results, if any.

When we do something, the act of doing is within our reach but the result is beyond our control as it also depends upon some extraneous factors as well, besides our efforts. Again the fruits of action may or may not be according to our expectations. However, it does not mean that we should not perform action or make no efforts on the plea that results are beyond us. The Geeta also lays stress on understanding (intelligence) while performing action. Thus action should be performed with understanding and renouncing their fruits, free from likes and dislikes and with the thought of God within.

The right outlook towards life develops when we fully understand that we have the ability to put our best effort into all endeavours, but we cannot choose the consequence of our work. We have absolutely no control over the results. The affairs of the world would not run if all were given the power to choose the consequences of their choice. One is given the power and the ability to do one's respective duty in life, but none is free to choose the desired results. Success in any endeavour becomes easier if one works hard without being bothered with the outcome, good or bad, of an action. The secret art of living a meaningful life is to be intensely active without any motive, as stated in the following verse.

(**Note:** The plain interpretation of this verse is indeed very risky. In the modern age the impacts of certain actions are so pervasive and devastating that the slightest of an error in the judgement can cause a colossal loss to the humanity. One can imagine the cost or consequences of such actions as World War II, Vietnam War, extremists' attacks on the innocent people. Now the science and technology is so advanced that a modern man must keep consequences of his action in mind before he initiates any action. The modern age is in no way comparable to the age of Mahabharat. There is no room for action without considering the consequences thereof.)

योगस्थः कुरु कर्माणि सङ्गं त्यक्त्वा धनंजय ।
सिद्ध्यसिद्ध्योः समो भूत्वा समत्वं योग उच्यते ॥ 2.48 ॥

Shlok 2.48: Do your duty to the best of your ability, O Dhananjay, abandoning all attachment to the results, and remaining calm in both success and failure, for evenness of mind is called *Yog*.

Commentary: This verse fortifies the earlier idea of performing action with even mind and adds the condition of non-attachment. One must perform actions, without attachment and without concern for fruits of actions. Sri Krishna advises Arjun to perform his duty in the best possible manner without keeping in mind any positive result like a *Karmayogi*. *Karmayog* is defined as doing one's duty while maintaining equanimity under all circumstances. Pain and pleasure, birth and death, loss and gain, union and separation are inevitable, being under the control of one's past deeds or Karma, like the coming of day and night. Fools rejoice in prosperity and mourn in adversity, but a *Karmayogi* remains tranquil under all circumstances. Evenness of mind in success and failure is called devotion (*Yog*).

If one cultivates even-mindedness, regarding success and failure in the same manner, without elation or getting depressed, one attains Yogic temperament. This verse is a singular message for our youngsters who get easily discouraged by apparent failures or setbacks. Do your actions well; the Lord will take care of the rewards. Don't lose your head with success; life is a never-ending struggle and a journey to greater heights.

दूरेण ह्यवरं कर्म बुद्धियोगाद्धनंजय ।
बुद्धौ शरणमन्विच्छ कृपणाः फलहेतवः ॥ 2.49 ॥

Shlok 2.49: Work done with selfish motive is by far inferior to selfless service. Therefore, be a selfless worker. O Dhananjay, seek refuge in wisdom (*Buddhi*). Pitiful are those who are motivated by rewards.

Commentary: Actions done with evenness of mind is the *Yog* of wisdom. Actions performed by one who expects positive results are far inferior to the *Yog* of wisdom wherein the seeker does not seek rewards. The former leads to bondage, and is the cause of birth and death. Miserable are those who are interested in action for favourable results. So do not always act with the expectation of favourable results only.

The discipline of intelligence requires discrimination of right and wrong. A person who has right understanding will perform right actions. The Geeta further mentions that the state of Yog (*Samadhi*) is achieved when intelligence becomes unshaken and stable. This verse indicates that perfection in Yog leads to the highest purity which comes from wisdom.

बुद्धियुक्तो जहातीह उभे सुकृतदुष्कृते ।
तस्माद्योगाय युज्यस्व योगः कर्मसु कौशलम् ॥ 2.50 ॥

Shlok 2.50: The man whose disposition is disciplined transcends both good and bad actions in this world. Therefore, prepare yourself for *Yog*. *Yog* means great strength in actions.

Commentary: A *Karmayogi* or the selfless person becomes free from both vice and virtue in this life itself. Therefore, strive for selfless service.

Working to the best of one's abili-ties without becoming attached to the rewards of work is called *Karmayog.* Here is another definition of yog—'*Yoga karmasu kausalam'*....skilfulness in action is Yog. The word 'skilfulness' means doing work with a balanced mind, for the outcome may be success or failure. One should not crave for rewards and should not detest work that may not be rewarding. If you feel that it is right to do a job, do it straightaway, whether it yields great rewards or earns you brickbats.

People should work for a noble cause with a spirit of detachment and should not expect any personal reward or recognition. Such persons enjoy the pleasure of selfless service that ultimately leads them to the bliss of salvation. *Karmayog* purifies the mind and is a very powerful and easy spiritual discipline that one can practice while living and working in society. There is no religion better than selfless service. The fruits of vice and virtue grow only on the tree of selfishness, not on the tree of selfless service. Dexterity or skilfulness in work lies in not getting bound by the bonds of one's *Karma* or worldly duty.

Contrary to the above, it is also stated that one works harder when one is deeply interested in, or attached to, the rewards of work. Therefore, *Karmayog* or selfless service may not be very conducive to the material progress of the individual or society.

कर्मजं बुद्धियुक्ता हि फलं त्यक्त्वा मनीषिणः ।
जन्मबंधविनिर्मुक्ताः पदं गच्छन्त्यनामयम् ॥ 2.51 ॥

Shlok 2.51: The wise who have freed themselves from the bonds of birth go to a condition free from all sorrows.

Commentary: Clinging to the rewards of actions is the cause of rebirth. A man interested in rewards of his work has to take another birth to enjoy them. The wise do not have to take rebirth because their actions are not reward oriented. If actions are done for the sake of God, without desire for the rewards, one is released from the bonds of birth and death and attains to immortal bliss.

यदा ते मोहकलिलं बुद्धिर्व्यतितरिष्यति।
तदा गन्तासि निर्वेदं श्रोतव्यस्य श्रुतस्य च ॥ 2.52 ॥

Shlok 2.52: When your mind crosses beyond the opacity of

illusion, you will become indifferent to both future and past revelations.

Commentary: Krishna tells Arjun that when the intellect becomes firmly grounded in the Divine, the individual develops inner intuition. He gets guidance from the Supreme-self, which helps him to go beyond the mire of delusion. The individual derives a sharp sense of discrimination between the real and unreal. This inner guidance disperses his confusion about the conflicting doctrines. The person becomes steady, he feels integrated and determined within. He feels confident and self-reliant. He himself experiences the presence of the higher power and becomes receptive to the guidance and instructions.

Scriptures become dispensable after enlightenment. According to Adi Shankar, this verse means one who has completely removed the veil of ignorance and realized the Truth, becomes indifferent to the Vedic texts that prescribe performance of elaborate rituals for the attainment of desired results. The Vedas become redundant for the enlightened persons.

श्रुतिविप्रतिपन्ना ते यदा स्थास्यति निश्चला ।
समाधावचला बुद्धिस्तदा योगमवाप्स्यसि ॥ 2.53 ॥

Shlok 2.53: When your mind, which is confused by hearing conflicting opinions and doctrines, shall stay steady and firm on the Supreme Being, then you shall become united with God in deep meditation.

Commentary: When your intuition (*Buddhi- antahkarna*) which has been perplexed by what you have heard about the multifarious ends and means in all their relations– concerning the life of activity and the life of retirement– shall stand firm, without distraction and doubt in the Self (*Samadhi*, i.e, the objective point of your meditation), then you will attain *Yog*, *Samadhi*, i.e. the knowledge which arises from discrimination.

Non-scriptural reading or reading of different philosophical writings is bound to create unnecessary confusion. One should learn from the scriptures that God alone is real and the world is illusory. One should know that only God is eternal and everything else is temporal. After Self-awareness, one finds God alone has become everything. Everything is His manifestation. He is sporting in various forms. In trance, or the super-conscious state of mind, the confusion arising from conflicting views ceases, and mental equilibrium is attained.

Arjun asked:

स्थितप्रज्ञस्य का भाषा समाधिस्थस्य केशव ।
स्थितधीः किं प्रभाषेत किमासीत व्रजेत किम् ॥ 2.54 ॥

Shlok 2.54: Keshav, how do we identify a person of settled enlightenment, a person steady in wisdom, a person steadfast in contemplation? How does such a person speak? How does he sit? How does he walk?

Commentary: As Arjun has got no idea of a man with steady knowledge (*Sthitapragya*), he has put these questions before Krishna: How does the man of steady knowledge himself speak? How does he sit? How does he move? In this verse Arjun asks in order to know the characteristic attributes of a man of steady knowledge. From verse no. 55 to the end of this Discourse, the characteristic attributes of a man of steady knowledge as well as the means of obtaining that knowledge are taught to him who, having from the very commencement renounced all works, has entered upon a course of devotion to knowledge (*Gyan-Yog-nishtha*), as well as to him who has reached that stage by means of devotion to works (*Karmayog*). For, everywhere in spiritual science (*adhyatmasastra*), the very characteristic attributes of the successful Yogis are taught as the means (of attaining that stage), since they are to be attained by effort. The Lord now points out those characteristic attributes which, as attainable by effort, constitute the means as well.

Qualities of a Self-realized person

(1) Satisfaction in the self

Lord Krishna said:

प्रजहाति यदा कामान्सर्वान्पार्थ मनोगतान् ।
आत्मन्येवात्मना तुष्टः स्थितप्रज्ञस्तदोच्यते ॥ 2.55 ॥

Shlok 2.55: O Parth, when a person is completely free from all desires of the mind and is satisfied with the bliss of knowing the Supreme Being, then one is called a man of steady wisdom.

Commentary: When a person does not have a longing for external possession or averse to everything else because of his acquisition of the immortal nectar, this is the state of realization of the Supreme Truth, then he is said to be a wise man. All the pleasures of the world are worthless to an illumined sage who is ever content in the immortal Soul. Desires for knowledge, devotion and salvation cannot be classed as desires because they are higher order desires. One should first replace the lower order desires with higher order desires and then renounce the highest desires also and become absolutely free. It is said that the highest freedom is the freedom from becoming free. If, on abandoning of all desires, nothing should be found to cause satisfaction while the cause of the embodied state still operates, it would follow that his behaviour would be like that of a mad man or a maniac. That is to say, he who has abandoned all desires connected with progeny, possessions and the world, who has renounced (all works), who delights in the Self and plays with the Self, he is the man whose knowledge is steady. A man without any kind of desire can never act like a normal human being. The idea of such a man is highly impractical in this world.

(2) Equanimity in pleasure and pain

दुःखेष्वनुद्विग्नमनाः सुखेषु विगतस्पृहः ।
वीतरागभयक्रोधः स्थितधीर्मुनिरुच्यते ॥ 2.56 ॥

Shlok 2.56: He whose mind is undisturbed in the midst of sorrows, whose cravings for pleasures are all over and from whom lust, fear and anger have passed away, is called a sage steady in wisdom.

Commentary: He whose mind is not agitated in calamities, who has no longing for pleasure, free from attachment, fear and anger, he is indeed a saint of steady wisdom. The heart of a steady man is not distressed in calamities. Unlike fire, which tends to increase when fuel is added, his longing for pleasures does not increase as more pleasures are attained. He is said to be a man of steady knowledge. He is called a sage, a *Sannyasin*, one who has renounced works. Attachment to people, places, and objects takes away the intellect, and one becomes myopic. People are helplessly tied with the rope of attachment. A sage or *Yogi* steady in wisdom is one who has been able to get himself fully detached and free from all sorts of attachments.

(3) Absence of attachment, delight and aversion

यः सर्वत्रानभिस्नेहस्तत्तत्प्राप्य शुभाशुभम् ।
नाभिनन्दति न द्वेष्टि तस्य प्रज्ञा प्रतिष्ठिता ॥ 2.57 ॥

Shlok 2.57: The mind and intellect become steady in a person who is not attached to anything (but Self), who is neither elated by get-ting desired results nor perturbed by undesired results.

Commentary: The true sage has no attachment even for the existence of his body. He does not exult in pleasure, nor is he averse to pain that may befall him. When he is thus free from delight and distress, his knowledge arising from discrimination becomes steady. True spiritualists have a peaceful and happy look on their faces under all circumstances.

(4) Complete withdrawal of senses from objects

यदा संहरते चायं कूर्मोऽङ्गानीव सर्वशः ।
इन्द्रियाणीन्द्रियार्थेभ्यस्तस्य प्रज्ञा प्रतिष्ठिता ॥ 2.58 ॥

Shlok 2.58: When someone draws his senses from outward objects, just as a tortoise draws its limbs from all sides, his understanding is stabilized.

Commentary: He, i.e. the devotee who strives on the path of knowledge (*Gyan-nishtha*), withdraws his senses from all objects as the tortoise withdraws its limbs from all sides out of fear. When a person learns to control or withdraw the senses from sense objects, as a tortoise retracts its limbs inside its shell in the time of danger and cannot be forced to extend its limbs again until the trouble is over, the lamp of Self-knowledge becomes lighted, and one perceives the self-effulgent Supreme Being within. A Self-realized person enjoys the beauty of the world, keeping the senses under complete control like a tortoise. The best way to purify the senses and control them perfectly like a tortoise is to engage them in the service of God all the time.

Control of one's five senses, thereby controlling one's mind, is repeatedly emphasized in almost all discourses. In many Vedic texts, the mind is also counted as one of the senses, that is, mind is taken as the sixth sense. Among the five senses, the sense of speech is most important and difficult to control. Therefore, Hindu and Buddhist scriptures often state that one should control body, speech and mind. Much of spiritual '*sadhana*' involves controlling one's speech and observing silence. The word 'silence', however, implies more than the control of speech. It means silencing one's mind or reducing the thoughts in the mind.

विषया विनिवर्तन्ते निराहारस्य देहिनः ।
रसवर्जं रसोऽप्यस्य परं दृष्ट्वा निवर्तते ॥ 2.59 ॥

Shlok 2.59: The desire for sensual pleasures fades away if one abstains from sense enjoyment, but the craving for sense enjoyment remains in a very subtle form. This subtle craving also completely disappears from one who knows the Supreme.

Commentary: The desire for sensual pleasure becomes dormant when one abstains from sense enjoyment, or experiences physical limitations imposed by disease or old age. But the craving remains as a subtle mental impression. But those who have tasted the nectar of unity with the Supreme Being no longer find enjoyment in the lower level sensual pleasures. Those who have realized the Supreme Self, they keep their senses under complete control. They do not have even subtle craving for anything.

Dangers of uncontrolled senses

यततो ह्यपि कौन्तेय पुरुषस्य विपश्चितः ।
इन्द्रियाणि प्रमाथीनि हरन्ति प्रसभं मनः ॥ 2.60 ॥

Shlok 2.60: The senses are so strong and impetuous, O son of Kunti, that they forcibly carry away the mind of even of a wise man who is striving to control them.

Commentary: The senses are dangerous. They agitate the mind of the man who is inclined to sensuous objects. Having thus agitated the mind, they carry it away by force, while the man is wide awake, though the mind is possessed of discriminative knowledge.

The wise always remain vigilant over the mind. The mind can never be fully trusted. It can mislead even a wise striving seeker. One has to be very alert and closely witness the wanderings of the mind. Never relax your vigilance until the final goal of God-realization is reached. It is the very nature of the mind to go to lower objects of enjoyment, just as it is the nature of water to flow downwards. The grace of God can make the mind go towards higher objects, just as the sun's rays lift the water to the sky.

The path of spiritual life is very slippery and has to be trodden very carefully to avoid falls. It is not a joyous ferryboat ride, but a very difficult path to tread like the sharp edge of a sword. Many obstacles, distractions, and failures come on the path to help the devotee become stronger and more advanced on the path, just like iron is turned into steel by alternate heating, cooling, and hammering. One should not get discouraged by failures, but carry on with determination.

(5) Devotion to the Lord

तानि सर्वाणि संयम्य युक्त आसीत मत्परः ।
वशे हि यस्येन्द्रियाणि तस्य प्रज्ञा प्रतिष्ठिता ॥ 2.61 ॥

Shlok 2.61: One should sit with mind firmly focused on Me as the Supreme goal after bringing the senses under control. One's intellect becomes steady when one's senses are under control.

Commentary: A wise man should bring the senses under control and sit calm and intent on Me (Vasudev) the Innermost Self of all, i. e. he should sit thinking 'I am no other than He.' The knowledge of that devotee becomes steady when he is able to bring his senses under control through practice.

Thought of sense-objects is the source of evil

ध्यायतो विषयान्पुंसः सङ्गस्तेषूपजायते ।
सङ्गात्संजायते कामः कामात्क्रोधोऽभिजायते ॥ 2.62 ॥

Shlok 2.62: When a man thinks of sense objects, attachment for them arises. From attachment arises desire; from desire arises anger.

Commentary: Attachment for objects arises when a man thinks of them in particular. When a person thinks of a sense object, again and again, he gets attached to that object. When we see an object and think about it constantly, attachment is produced. The intensity of attachment produces a desire to possess or enjoy or use that object in some way or the other. A desire is, therefore, a passionate feeling born out of attachment to a sense object. Desires, in some form or shape, are constantly being produced in the mind of an individual. If one desire of a person is satisfied, the urge to satisfy another crops up. This is how addictions to certain types of food, smoking, drinking and even drugs are produced and make life miserable. When a desire remains unfulfilled, anger is produced and the consequences of anger are indicated in the following verse:

क्रोधाद्भवति सम्मोहः सम्मोहात्स्मृतिविभ्रमः ।
स्मृतिभ्रंशाद् बुद्धिनाशो बुद्धिनाशात्प्रणश्यति ॥ 2.63 ॥

Shlok 2.63: From anger arises bewilderment, bewilderment causes loss of memory, from loss of memory comes the destruction of the capacity for taking intelligent decisions and because of the destruction of this capacity for intelligent decisions, a man perishes.

Commentary: It is, therefore, utmost essential to control the mind. The interplay of unending desires creates a world of illusion or *Mayajal* and this play of desires ends only with the end of life. It is generally observed that human desires are insatiable and satisfaction of one desire may give rise to another desire. In case some desires are not satisfied, one is likely to get angry and anger causes destruction of intelligence resulting in the loss of a sense of discrimination and when this happens the consequences are disastrous. Verily, when an angry man gets infatuated, he tends to insult even the *Guru* or the elderly. An angry person loses balance of mind and in such a situation, he does not listen to any advice. He loses sense of discrimination and in that state he does great harm to himself and others. A confused man is of no use even for himself. This is how anger can lead to havoc.

Sense-control leads to peace and happiness

रागद्वेषवियुक्तैस्तु विषयानिन्द्रियैश्चरन् ।
आत्मवश्यैर्विधेयात्मा प्रसादमधिगच्छति ॥ 2.64 ॥

Shlok 2.64: He who has disciplined his senses has freed himself from attraction and repulsion and has organized himself towards his becoming goes on to blissful tranquillity.

Commentary: The natural activity of the senses is characterized by love and hatred. He who aspires for deliverance resorts only to unavoidable objects with senses– hearing, seeing, etc. but devoid of love and hatred for objects through control over his inner sense (*Atma or Antahkaran*). Such a man attains peace, tranquillity, self possession. Real peace and happiness are achieved, not by sense gratification, but by sense control.

To attain mental peace one has to control the senses. But if one has achieved sense-control, one can move in the mundane world without cravings or dislike (*rag or dwesh*) for things of the world. In the initial stages, a great deal of sense-control is required for the seeker. After maturing in sense-control, he can move in this world without fear of temptations. Sri Ramakrishna had a useful analogy to bring out this truth: when a sapling is small and tender, it should be protected from the cattle by fencing. But after the sapling has grown into a big tree, even elephants can be tied to its trunk. Likewise, after a *yogi* has attained sense-control, he can move about in this world without having any fear of getting corrupt.

प्रसादे सर्वदुःखानां हानिरस्योपजायते ।
प्रसन्नचेतसो ह्याशु बुद्धिः पर्यवतिष्ठते ॥ 2.65 ॥

Shlok 2.65: All sorrows disappear on attaining tranquillity. The intellect of such a tranquil-minded person soon becomes completely steady and united with the Supreme.

Commentary: On the attainment of peace there is an end of all miseries concerning body and mind. Since the reason (*Buddhi*) of the pure-minded man soon becomes steady, pervading on all sides like the *Akash*; i. e, it remains steadfast in the form of the Self. The man whose heart is pure and whose mind is steady can achieve peace. When peace is attained all miseries are over.

नास्ति बुद्धिरयुक्तस्य न चायुक्तस्य भावना।
न चाभावयतः शान्तिरशान्तस्य कुतः सुखम् ॥ 2.66 ॥

Shlok 2.66: A person who is not attached to an Ideal is devoid of real wisdom and lacks a positive outlook in life. As such a person does not have a positive outlook, he is not at peace with himself; and as he is not at peace with himself, how can he ever be happy?

Commentary: To the unsteady or to the man who cannot fix the mind in meditation, there can be no wisdom (*Buddhi*), no knowledge of the true nature of the Self. To the unsteady, there can be no meditation, no intense devotion to Self-knowledge. So, to him who is not devoted to Self-knowledge there can be no peace, no tranquillity. To the disturbed man, how can there be happiness? Verily, happiness consists in the freedom of the senses from thirst for sensual enjoyment, not in the thirst (*Trishna*) for objects. This lust is mere misery indeed. While there is thirst, there can be no trace of happiness; we cannot so much as smell it.

Self-restraint necessary for steady knowledge

इन्द्रियाणां हि चरतां यन्मनोऽनुविधीयते ।
तदस्य हरति प्रज्ञां वायुर्नावमिवाम्भसि ॥ 2.67 ॥

Shlok 2.67: When the mind runs after the roving senses it carries away the understanding, as a wind carries away a boat on the water.

Commentary: Thus if the mind runs after the senses, the understanding is distorted and lost. When the mind gets attached to the objects of sense, a desire to possess or use that object is produced. If the desire is not satisfied, restlessness and anger arise. This can be understood in the following manner. As the wind carries away a ship from the intended course of the sailors and drives her astray, so the mind carries away the devotee's consciousness from the Self and turns it towards sense-objects. A person without control over the mind and senses drifts like a ship without its rudder, becomes a reactor instead of an actor, and develops negative *Karma*.

तस्माद्यस्य महाबाहो निगृहीतानि सर्वशः ।
इन्द्रियाणीन्द्रियार्थेभ्यस्तस्य प्रज्ञा प्रतिष्ठिता ॥ 2.68 ॥

Shlok 2.68: O Mighty-armed Prince, one's intellect becomes steady when the senses are completely withdrawn from sense objects.

Commentary: It has been shown that evil arises from the senses pursuing sense objects. Wherefore, that devotee's knowledge is steady whose senses have been restrained from sense-objects (such as sound) in all forms, subjective and objective.

(6) The universe, a mere dream to the sage

In the case of the man who possesses discriminative knowledge and whose knowledge has become steady, his experience of all matters, temporal and spiritual (*Laukik* and *Alaukik,* sensuous and super-sensuous), ceases on the cessation of nescience (*Avidya*); for, it is the effect of nescience; and nescience ceases because it is opposed to knowledge. To make this clear, the Lord proceeds:

या निशा सर्वभूतानां तस्यां जागर्ति संयमी ।
यस्यां जाग्रति भूतानि सा निशा पश्यतो मुनेः ॥ 2.69 ॥

Shlok 2.69: A *yogi*, the person of self-restraint, remains wakeful when it is night for all others. It is night for the *yogi* who sees when all others are wakeful.

Commentary: The sage lives in the Soul; this is day to him. He is unconscious of worldly phenomena; this is like night to him. The ordinary man is unconscious of his real nature. So life in the Soul is like night to him. He experiences sense-objects; this is day to him. Ascetics keep awake in the night of mundane existence of life because they are in quest of the highest truth. One is considered awake when one is free from worldly desires. A *yogi* is always aware of the Spirit about which others are unaware. A sage who sees is unaware of the experience of sense objects about which others are aware. The life of an ascetic is entirely different from the life of a materialist. What is considered real by a *yogi* is of no value for a worldly person. While most people sleep and make dream plans in the night of the illusory world, a yogi keeps awake because he or she is detached from the world while living in it.

All that one can see or hear or imagine are rooted in ignorance, nothing exists in reality. Just as in a dream a king becomes beggar, or a pauper becomes king of heaven, yet on waking one does not gain or losc anything, so must one look upon this world. But one's happiness or sorrow does not end till one wakes up. *Maya* comes in between Brahm and the world. Mind which is the other name of *Maya* creates this phenomenal world of illusion out of Brahm. Thus nothing is real in true sense in the creation. All are sleeping in the night of delusion and ignorance and while asleep they see all kinds of dreams and one does not even know that it is a dream world. Such is the delusive power of

Maya! Only right knowledge can remove this delusion.

(7) Subjugation of desire and personal self

आपूर्यमाणमचलप्रतिष्ठं समुद्रमापः प्रविशन्ति यद्वत् ।
तद्वत्कामा यं प्रविशन्ति सर्वे स शान्तिमाप्नोति न कामकामी ॥ 2.70 ॥

Shlok 2.70: He unto whom all desires enter as waters into the sea, which though ever being filled is ever motionless, attains to peace and not he who hugs his desires.

Commentary: The ocean is filled with water flowing from all sides. Its state remains unaltered, though water flows into it from all sides; it always remains within its bounds without any change. A person is a sage into whom desires of all sorts enter from all sides without affecting him, as water enters into the ocean. Such a person attains peace (*Moksha*), but not the other who has a longing for external objects. The tranquil mind of a *yogi* is like an ocean that takes in the rivers of desire without being disturbed by them because a *yogi* does not think about personal gain or loss. Human desires are endless. To satisfy a desire is like drinking water mixed with salt that will never quench thirst, but will increase it. It is like trying to extinguish a fire with fuel.

Krishna advises Arjun to create mental vastness like an ocean. He explains that an ocean remains unmoved and unperturbed when the river gushes into it because of its vastness. Similarly human beings should create a mental vastness so that worldly desires fail to create emotional agitations and we achieve a state of inner silence and peace. The Geeta recommends the practice of *Karma Sannyas*, an attitude of selfless, dedicated actions without desire for the fruits of these actions, which will eventually help the practitioner to achieve an expansive state of mind

विहाय कामान्यः सर्वान् पुमांश्चरति निःस्पृहः ।
निर्ममो निरहंकारः स शान्तिमधिगच्छति ॥ 2.71 ॥

Shlok 2.71: One who abandons all desires and becomes free from longing and the feeling of 'I' and 'my', he attains the peace.

Commentary: He who has freed himself from the constricting feeling of 'I' and 'mine' and has sublimated his ego goes towards peace and understanding. He who abandons all desires and acts free from longing, without any sense of meanness, he attains the peace. Thus desire which acts like enemy within must be abandoned and not nurtured. Freedom from all selfish desires leads to eternal peace. A person is a *Sannyasi* who abandons all desires. He remains happy with the bare necessities of life. In fact, he has no attachment even for those bare necessities of life which are needed for the mere bodily existence. Such a man of steady knowledge, that man who knows Brahm, attains peace. This marks the end of all the misery of mundane existence. In short, he becomes the very Brahm. The devotion to knowledge is extolled in the following verse:

Knowledge leads to divine felicity

एषा ब्राह्मी स्थितिः पार्थ नैनां प्राप्य विमुह्यति ।
स्थित्वास्यामन्तकालेऽपि ब्रह्मनिर्वाणमृच्छति ॥ 2.72 ॥

Shlok 2.72: O Arjun, this is the super-conscious state of mind. Attaining this state, one is no longer deluded. Gaining this state, even at the end of one's life, a person reaches the final emancipation.

Commentary: Being established in this knowledge even at the end of life, one attains Brahm (the Supreme Being). The Supreme Being is the ultimate reality and truth, knowledge and consciousness, and is limitless and blissful. The individual soul becomes blissful and filled with joy after knowing God. The giver of bliss is nothing but the Bliss Itself like the giver of wealth must have wealth. That from which the origin, sustenance, and dissolution of this universe are derived is called the Absolute. The Absolute is the substratum, or material as well as efficient cause of the universe. It is both the source and the sink of energy in one. It is also called the Unified Field, Supreme Spirit, Divine Person, and Total Consciousness that is responsible for the sense perceptions in all living beings by functioning through mind and intellect.

Here is a promise from the Lord. Even if a person leads a sinful life and contemplates on the Lord only at the end of his life, he will attain Brahm or be liberated. The familiar story of Ajamil in the **Bhagavatam** may be recalled. Ajamil led a sinful life. But at the time of his death, he called his son who was named 'Narayan'. Even this unmotivated and accidental utterance of the Lord's name was sufficient—the Lord gave him *moksha* or liberation.

(**Note:** Here the author intends to record a voice of disagreement with the above views and their further implications. It has been often exhorted by numerous saints, hermits, religious preachers and philosophers since time immemorial that the prime objective of life of a Hindu should be to attain oneness with God through righteous living. One should try to get rid of the bondage of birth and death. *Moksha* or *mukti* (complete emancipation from this mundane world) and attainment of ecstasy and happiness of heaven in the company of great God must be the only end of this worldly life. It is not good to take one birth after another on this earth, as this world is full of problems, ordeals, worry, agony, pain and miseries. Pleasure is very momentary. Everything is *Maya* and nothing is eternal here. Those who profess this philosophy, they have not realized the consequences of this viewpoint. They must realize that if everybody attains *Moksha*, the humanity would one day vanish from the earth in about a century or so. The process of birth and death would come to a halt.

The above view gives rise to a volley of genuine questions and queries for all of us and some of them may be put thus for serious consideration: where is the heaven by the way? Is it hanging like an earth in the universe? Who has created this heaven and what for? Where was the creator (possibly God) living when the heaven was created? If the earth is hell or hell alike, why was it created and how and why is it connected to heaven? Why do all gods and goddesses always live in heaven only? Are they so self-centred to seek and enjoy pleasures of life all the time? Who has seen the heaven and passed this secret information to the people on the earth that heaven is an ultimate place for living?

Subsequent to the above are another set of questions to be addressed. Why does God take *Avatar* or reincarnate on this hellish earth, leaving behind pleasureful heavenly abode? If God is omnipresent, he lives in both hell and heaven at the same time, suggesting that He lives in pain and pleasure simultaneously? If God is really almighty, he can set the wrong things right on the earth from the heaven itself. On the other hand, it is also evident from the idea of incarnation of God that He does not dislike or hate this earth. It seems to be a wonderful place to be. Everything is fine here for His living. Addressing Arjun Sri Krishna has Himself confessed in verse no 12, "Never was there a time when these monarchs, you, or I did not exist, nor shall we ever cease to exist in the future." This clearly suggests that God as well as human beings have to come here endlessly. It seems both are necessary for each other's well being. Good people must come to this earth again and again to help the people in distress or need. The great battle of the Mahabharat could not finish all the evils on the earth once for all. Bad people will always keep coming in a cyclical fashion to necessitate Sri Krishna's appearance to finish *Adharma* (lawlessness or unrighteousness). Selfish aspirations of people for attaining heaven or *Moksha* are not good for the well-being of humanity on the earth.)

Special messages

The second Discourse is considered as the epitome of all that stands for in the Geeta. Krishna's sermons are as follows:

1. The wise grieve neither for the living nor for the dead.
2. The Self within is eternal, indestructible.
3. The bodies enveloping the Self are ephemeral. They have a beginning and an end.
4. Death is certain for the born and birth for the dead.
5. Beings constantly pass through the repeated stages of unmanifest, manifest and again unmanifest. So why grieve over the inevitable?
6. The indwelling Self remains eternally the same.

OM TAT SAT

Discourse - 3

Karmayog: Yog of Action

Discourse three has tried to establish the fact that the performance of prescribed duties is obligatory for everyone. Here Lord Krishna explains in detail how it is the duty of each and every one in a society to carry out his function and responsibility in his respective stage of life according to the norms and expectations of the society to which he belongs. Further the Lord explains why such duties must be performed, what benefit is gained by performing them, what harm is caused by non-performance of the duties. Sri Krishna also explains what actions lead to bondage and what actions lead to salvation. All these points relating to duty have been explained in great detail here.

As Arjun had a high sense of attachment with the Kauravas, he was not inclined to fight for the sake of kingdom. Here Sri Krishna enlightened him by saying that people have a wrong notion about death. Death is for his body and not for *Atman* which embodies the body. The *Atman* is imperishable and the realization of which would grant him the freedom of the Eternal. A doubt, therefore, arises in Arjun's mind as to the necessity of engaging in action even after one has attained this state. Sri Krishna clears this doubt by telling him that although one has realized oneness with the Eternal, one has to perform action through the force of *Prakriti* or Nature. He emphasizes that perfection is attained not by ceasing to engage in action but by doing all actions as a divine offering, imbued with a spirit of non-attachment and sacrifice. Action is necessary not only for the one who has attained perfection but also for the one who is striving for perfection. Sri Krishna cites the example of Janak, the great sage-king of India, who continued to rule his kingdom even after attaining God-realization.

This discourse also deals with notion of *Prakriti* which is made up of the three qualities– *Rajas, Tamas* and *Sattva*. The *Atman* is said to be beyond these three qualities and their functions. Only when knowledge of this fact dawns in man, he is able to attain perfection. Sri Krishna tells Arjun that each one should do his duty according to his nature. Performance of duty suited to one's nature in the right spirit of detachment alone can lead to perfection. Arjun raises the question as to why a person commits such actions that cloud his mind and drag him downwards, by force, as it were. Sri Krishna answers that it is desire that impels man to lose his discrimination and understanding, and thus commit wrong actions. Desire is the root cause of all evil actions. If desire is done away with, then the divine power manifests in its full glory and one enjoys peace, bliss, light and freedom.

(**Note:** I have doubts whether Sri Krishna, who is believed to be Godhead, had felt any necessity of citing the example of Janak to persuade Arjun, as Janak was scarcely popular as a king those days. In fact, characters of the Valmiki Ramayan could be popular or become a household name only when **Ramcharitmanas** of Tulsidas came to light. Most likely the reference of Raja Janak was a later day insertion into the Geeta.)

Path of Selfless Service

Arjun asked Sri Krishna:

ज्यायसी चेत्कर्मणस्ते मता बुद्धिर्जनार्दन ।
तत्किं कर्मणि घोरे मां नियोजयसि केशव ॥ 3.1 ॥
व्यामिश्रेणेव वाक्येन बुद्धिं मोहयसीव मे।
तदेकं वद निश्चित्य येन श्रेयोऽहमाप्नुयाम् ॥ 3.2 ॥

Shlokas 3.1-02: If you think that knowledge is superior to action, O Janardan, why then do you ask me to engage in this terrible action, O Keshav? With these apparently conflicting words you confuse my understanding, as it were; therefore, tell me definitely that one thing by which I may attain bliss.

Commentary: As Arjun was in the state of confusion, he thought that Lord Krishna meant a contemplative life (*Buddhiyog*) was better than doing one's normal duty in life. Arjun requests Sri Krishna to teach him for certain either of the two– knowledge or action– is better to attain the highest good. The confusion is not real. It merely appears to be so. It is not the intention of the Lord to confuse Arjun, yet Arjun is confused. He explains thus:

Lord Krishna said:

लोकेऽस्मिन् द्विविधा निष्ठा पुरा प्रोक्ता मयानघ ।
ज्ञानयोगेन सांख्यानां कर्मयोगेन योगिनाम् ॥ 3.3 ॥

Shlok 3.3: In this world a two-fold way of life has been taught by Me, O blameless One (Arjun), the path of knowledge for men of contemplation and the path of work for men of action.

Commentary: As observed in the real world, human beings may be broadly classified into two types: (1)Those whose mental disposition is towards action or worldly pursuits and (2) Those who have a tendency to explore inner self. The two paths mentioned in the above verse are equally efficient means for liberation but are intended for two different types of individuals. However, the two categories of individuals mentioned here are not exclusive but complimentary. The dividing factor is the predominance of a particular tendency in any individual who may not be a wholly man of action or of knowledge. Thus, if in an individual, the tendency for action is stronger, he or she should follow the path of action or Karma Yog. The path of knowledge or Gyan Yog is suitable for those who are more inclined towards contemplations of inner self. However, it does not mean that these paths are opposed to each other. A man of knowledge cannot remain without action. Even modes like resting, thinking, sitting in silence, etc. are all actions.

At the very beginning of the creation, two types of people, those with contemplative and those with active temperaments, were in existence. Path of work refers to '*Seva*' or '*Karmayog*' which means sacrifice, selfless service, unselfish work, meritorious deeds, giving away something to others. Some people often get confused same as Arjun and think that leading a life devoted to scriptural study, contemplation, and acquiring transcendental knowledge is better for spiritual progress than doing one's worldly duty. It should be pointed out that both metaphysical knowledge and selfless service are means to attain the

Supreme Being. These two paths are not separate, but complementary. In this worldly life a combination of these two modes is considered the best.

What is actionless?

न कर्मणामनारम्भान्नैष्कर्म्यं पुरुषोऽश्नुते ।
न च संन्यसनादेव सिद्धिं समधिगच्छति ॥ 3.4 ॥
न हि कश्चित्क्षणमपि जातु तिष्ठत्यकर्मकृत् ।
कार्यते ह्यवशः कर्म सर्वः प्रकृतिजैर्गुणैः ॥ 3.5 ॥

Shlokas 3.4-05: By non-performance of work none reaches worklessness; by merely giving up action no one attains to perfection. Verily none can ever remain without performing action even for a moment. For everybody is made to act willy-nilly by the three properties *(Gunas)* produced by primordial nature (*Prakriti*).

Commentary: Even if a man abandons action, his mind may be active. One cannot reach perfection or freedom from action or knowledge of the Self merely by renouncing action. It is not possible for anybody to completely abandon action or work. Therefore, one should always be active in serving the Lord by various means of performing action. Performance of action till death with a desireless frame of mind is better than simply abandoning work and leading the life of an ascetic *(Sadhu),* because even an ascetic cannot escape the impulse of action. Mere desertion of action or running away from the normal life does not lead a person to perfection. What is needed is not desertion of work, but renunciation of selfish desires. Change from family life to saintly life is merely a change in style of living. So long as there is life, action is inevitable. Even thinking or living is also a kind of act. To be free from desire or from the illusion of personal interest is the true renunciation and not the physical abstention from activity.

These verses emphasize the role of action in life. Action is unavoidable in life. Although action leads to bondage, mere abstention from action or renunciation does not lead to emancipation. Our life is like a battlefield for action and Verse 38 of Chapter II tells us how to act in this battle.

कर्मेन्द्रियाणि संयम्य य आस्ते मनसा स्मरन् ।
इन्द्रियार्थान्विमूढात्मा मिथ्याचारः स उच्यते ॥ 3.6 ॥

Shlok 3.6: He, who restrains his organs of action but mentally thinks of sense pleasures, is called a hypocrite.

Commentary: One's growth comes from working selflessly rather than giving up work and practising sense-control before one is naturally ready for it. Bringing the mind under control is difficult, and spiritual life becomes a mockery without mastery over the senses. Desires may become dormant and rise again to give trouble, just as a sleeping person wakes up in due course of time.

Success in spiritual life does not come from prematurely wearing saffron clothes just to maintain an Ashram or livelihood without first conquering the six enemies– lust, anger, greed, pride, attachment and envy. It is said that such pretenders do a great disservice to society and themselves and become bereft of happiness in this world and the next. A pretending monk is considered sinful and a destroyer of the ascetic order of life. All societies are full of such people who pretend to be real priests, saint or ascetics. The five organs of action, the *Karmendriyas,* are the organs of speech, hands, feet, genitals and anus. Despite restraining these organs if one sits revolving in his mind the thoughts regarding the objects of these sense organs in order to give an impression that he is meditating on God, he is called a self-deluded hypocrite and a man of sinful conduct. True renunciation is not just the control of the organs of action or abstention from physical movement. It is the control of the mind and the organs of sensory experience. It is the absence of longing for the activity.

Why one should help others

यस्त्विन्द्रियाणि मनसा नियम्यारभतेऽर्जुन ।
कर्मेन्द्रियैः कर्मयोगमसक्तः स विशिष्यते ॥ 3.7 ॥

Shlok 3.7: But, O Arjun, he who restrains his senses with his mind and directs his organs of action to work, with no feeling of attachment, is indeed superior.

Commentary: He who controls the senses by the mind, follows without attachment the path of action, he is esteemed. Hence, our mind is to be controlled. This can happen only if we control the senses going after sense objects. Mind gets its inputs through five organs of perception which are also called sense-organs or organs of knowledge (*Gyan Indriyas*) from the outer world of sense objects. Mind perceives the sense objects by interacting with the sense organs and if that interaction is absent, perception of objects by the mind is not possible even though the objects might be within the range of the sense organs. This verse asks the seeker to control the sense organs by the mind. This implies substitution of sense objects by nobler and diviner alternatives for the mind to dwell upon. When the sense organs are thus controlled, a huge quantity of energy gets stored up which unless properly directed will disturb the inner equilibrium of an individual.

नियतं कुरु कर्म त्वं कर्म ज्यायो ह्यकर्मणः ।
शरीरयात्रापि च ते न प्रसिद्ध्येदकर्मणः ॥ 3.8 ॥

Shlok 3.8: Perform your obligatory duty, for action is superior to inaction. Even the bare maintenance of the body would not be possible if you remain inactive.

Commentary: In everyday life, one has to perform certain actions as obligatory duties, such as running of household, working for livelihood, maintenance of the body, etc. These actions need not be abandoned. Thus action has to be performed as a moral obligation or a physical necessity in order to contribute to the harmonious and smooth running of the cosmic mechanism.

A person who does not do so lives, in vain, as stated in Verse 3.16. The very fact of existence involves several natural and unavoidable actions which have to be performed by all. Even bodily existence in sustainable health is just not possible if someone prefers to live in a state of complete inertia and inaction.

Unselfish act does not create bondage

यज्ञार्थात्कर्मणोऽन्यत्र लोकोऽयं कर्मबन्धनः ।
तदर्थं कर्म कौन्तेय मुक्तसङ्गः समाचर ॥ 3.9 ॥

Shlok 3.9: Not by abstention of work does a man attain freedom from actions; nor by mere renunciation does he attain to his perfection. Therefore, O son of Kunti, give up attachment and

do your work as a sacrifice.

Commentary: All work is to be done in a spirit of sacrifice for the sake of the Divine. Yagya here means any unselfish action done with a pure motive. It is a self-sacrificing work undertaken in a spirit of self-dedication for the good of all. Such actions cannot be self-serving but self-liberating and do not bind the performer. An action which is not governed by the spirit of unselfishness binds one to worldliness despite being very glorious.

Help others is the first commandment of the Creator

सहयज्ञाः प्रजाः सृष्ट्वा पुरोवाच प्रजापतिः ।
अनेन प्रसविष्यध्वमेष वोऽस्त्विष्टकामधुक् ॥ 3.10 ॥

Shlok 3.10: When *Prajapati* in ancient times had brought forth creatures with sacrifice, he said: 'With this you shall procreate, this shall be the Cow of Plenty for your desires'.

Commentary (Shlokas 1.3-1.10): When the Universe was created by the Creator, *Prajapati*, He simultaneously created *Yagya* also, the spirit of self-dedicated activities which is seen everywhere. The shining of the sun and the moon, flowing of rivers, tolerance of the Earth, etc. are examples of such activities which stand for a kind of spirit of sacrifice without any selfish motive. The second part of the verse means that no achievement is impossible for a man who knows how to act in the spirit of self-effacement and self-sacrifice with the required amount of non-attachment. The Cow of Plenty here refers to the cow which yields all desires. Things can be achieved by sacrifice.

देवान्भावयतानेन ते देवा भावयन्तु वः ।
परस्परं भावयन्तः श्रेयः परमवाप्स्यथ ॥ 3.11 ॥
इष्टान्भोगान्हि वो देवा दास्यन्ते यज्ञभाविताः ।
तैर्दत्तानप्रदायैभ्यो यो भुंक्ते स्तेन एव सः ॥ 3.12 ॥

Shlok 3.11: Cherish the gods with this and may those gods cherish you, thus cherishing one another you shall attain the ultimate good.

Shlok 3.12: Gods, cherished by the sacrifice, will give you the desired objects. Indeed, he who enjoys gifts given by the gods

without sharing with others is, indeed, a thief.

Commentary (Shlokas 3.11-3.12): Helping others is the best deed one can do. The wise seek to serve themselves in the service of others while the ignorant serve themselves at the cost of others. To serve each other is the original or first commandment of the Creator that has been restated by Lord Krishna in the Geeta. We take birth to help each other and also to understand, care, love, give and forgive each other. Actually, we serve ourselves by serving others. Giving makes the world a better place for the entire humanity. 'Giving is Living'.

Whosoever enjoys– without offering to Them– Their gifts, he is verily a thief. Pleased with your sacrifices, the Gods shall bestow on you all enjoyments, including women, cattle, children, etc. He who enjoys what is given by Gods, i.e. he who gratifies the cravings of his own body and senses without discharging the debt due to the Gods, is a thief indeed, a robber of the property of the Gods.

One who makes no sacrifice, but grabs everything without helping others, is like a thief. It is said that celestials are pleased when people help each other. The capacity of the giver increases by the grace of God, fulfilling all desires to give. The spirit of cooperation– not competition or confrontation– between human beings, between nations, and between organizations seems to be hinted here by the Lord. All the necessities of life are produced by dedicated sacrificial services of other people. We are created to depend on each other. Nothing worthwhile can be achieved without cooperation and help from others. The world would have been a much better place if all inhabitants cooperated and helped each other, rather than fight or compete with each other. It is the selfish motive that prevents cooperation even between spiritual organizations. One who can truly say all organizations, temples, mosques, and churches are our own, is a true leader and a real saint.

यज्ञशिष्टाशिनः सन्तो मुच्यन्ते सर्वकिल्बिषैः ।
भुंजते ते त्वघं पापा ये पचन्त्यात्मकारणात् ॥ 3.13 ॥

Shlok 3.13: The righteous who eat the remnants of the sacrifice are freed from all sins; but those who cook food only for themselves, in fact, eat filth.

Commentary: The righteous, who eat the remnant of the sacrifice, are freed from all sins; but commit sin who cook for their own sakes. Those who, after performing sacrifices to the gods, eat the remains of the food are freed from all sins as well as from those sins which result from involuntary acts of injury and other causes.

Sins of the past are the cause for the present pains and the present sins are the cause for future sorrows. All the causes for the sorrows in social life can be removed if the members of the community find happiness in enjoying the results of their efforts performed in true *Yagya* spirit.

There is yet another interpretation of the verse is that 'those who cook for themselves only' means those who perform actions only with selfish motives are eating nothing but sin. By doing the work in *Yagya* spirit, the selfish life is transformed into an unselfish one and the individual becomes aware of the interdependence of all beings. One must learn to live for others.

अन्नाद्भवन्ति भूतानि पर्जन्यादन्नसम्भवः ।
यज्ञाद्भवति पर्जन्यो यज्ञः कर्मसमुद्भवः ॥ 3.14 ॥

Shlok 3.14: Beings spring from food, food springs from rain, rain springs from sacrifice, and sacrifice springs from action.

कर्म ब्रह्मोद्भवं विद्धि ब्रह्माक्षरसमुद्भवम् ।
तस्मात्सर्वगतं ब्रह्म नित्यं यज्ञे प्रतिष्ठितम् ॥ 3.15 ॥

Shlok 3.15: Know that action springs from Brahman, and that Brahman springs from the Imperishable.

Commentary: As both the verses are easily comprehensible, they need no specific explanation. The subsequent verse throws light on their meaning.

एवं प्रवर्तितं चक्रं नानुवर्तयतीह यः ।
अघायुरिन्द्रियारामो मोघं पार्थ स जीवति ॥ 3.16 ॥

Shlok 3.16: O son of Pritha, he who does not organize himself appropriately in view of this wheel's motion lives in vain.

Commentary: Of all the different paths of Yog described in the Geeta, Karma Yog, seems more suited to the householder, as every householder has to perform action in the form of obligatory duties on a regular basis. Karma Yog, which, in brief, is the path of right action, without attachment to its fruits, has greater role to play in the life of people. Action or duty is essential for every one of us because that keeps the wheel of nature moving. All actions are well connected and interdependent. So shirking of any action or duty is not proper. Saints, trees, rivers, and earth, for instance, are for the use of others. They all help each other. So people must learn to live for others. They should not confine their activities to their own interests only. Everyone should try to keep the wheel of society in motion for its continuity. Life of those who cannot do anything for others is useless.

यस्त्वात्मरतिरेव स्यादात्मतृप्तश्च मानवः ।
आत्मन्येव च संतुष्टस्तस्य कार्यं न विद्यते ॥ 3.17 ॥

Shlok 3.17: But for the person who delights only in the Self, who remains satisfied in the consciousness of Self and is contended in the Self alone; for him there is nothing to be done.

Commentary: That man, who is devoted to the Self, is satisfied with the Self, is content in the Self alone, for him there is nothing to do. This verse refers to the highest state of a person who has realised Self and is established and absorbed in the Self. Such a state is called '*Sahaj samadhi*'. Such a person has no action to perform. He may remain quiet or engage himself in daily chores without attachment. In recent times, Raman Maharshi (Tamil Nadu, India) was one such person. He used to engage himself in chopping vegetables and assist cooking in his *Ashram* kitchen.

नैव तस्य कृतेनार्थो नाकृतेनेह कश्चन ।
न चास्य सर्वभूतेषु कश्चिदर्थव्यपाश्रयः ॥ 3.18 ॥

Shlok 3.18: He has nothing at all to gain from actions performed or not performed, nor does he have any vested interest in anything.

Commentary: The man of perfection does not depend on external objects for his happiness. He finds his joy, bliss and contentment in his own Divine experience. When he has already achieved satisfaction and contentment, no more desires arise in him. Where there is no desire there is no action. Such a realized man is a person endowed with Self-Knowledge. He has no worldly duties to perform. He is the knower of Brahm.

An ordinary man is required to act for earning profit or avoiding loss. But for a man who discovered eternal satisfaction in his own Self and reached perfect contentment therein no purpose is served by engaging himself in any action because there is neither anticipation of gain nor fear of loss for him. Such a person depends upon nothing for his joy, neither on any being nor on any object. He has nothing to gain by what he does in this world, nor anything to lose by what he leaves undone; nor is there anyone (except God), among all beings, on whom he needs to depend for anything.

Leaders should set an example

तस्मादसक्तः सततं कार्यं कर्म समाचर ।
असक्तो ह्याचरन्कर्म परमाप्नोति पूरुषः ॥ 3.19 ॥

Shlok 3.19: Therefore, always perform your duty to the best of your abilities without any attachment to the results, because by performing action without attachment, one reaches the supreme goal of life.

Commentary: After explaining the wheel of action Sri Krishna reiterates by asking Arjun to perform actions which are obligatory on his part in his present status in life. The Lord warns him to keep his mind away from the pitfalls of attachments. It is suggested here that the work done without attachment is superior to the work done in a spirit of sacrifice which is itself higher than the work done with selfish aims. It takes us to perfection indirectly through the attainment of purity of mind. A work without attachment does not cause any disappointment or frustration in case of even negative result whatsoever.

कर्मणैव हि संसिद्धिमास्थिता जनकादयः ।
लोकसंग्रहमेवापि संपश्यन्कर्तुमर्हसि ॥ 3.20 ॥

Shlok 3.20: Through action alone Janak and others achieved perfection; even with a view to the guidance of mankind you must act.

Commentary: In olden times kings like Raja Janak and others attained perfection or liberation by the path of action, performing right actions in a spirit of detachment and self-dedication. They set an example to the world by their deeds and achievement. They attained purity of mind through the performance of duty and then realized Brahm. Sri Krishna suggests that being a man of princely class Arjun too should have the responsibility to protect his people, act diligently and perform his duties without running away from the battle of Kurukshetra.

यद्यदाचरति श्रेष्ठस्तत्तदेवेतरो जनः ।
स यत्प्रमाणं कुरुते लोकस्तदनुवर्तते ॥ 3.21 ॥

Shlok 3.21: Because whatever noble persons do, others follow. Whatever standard they set up, the world follows.

Commentary: People generally follow whatever eminent people do. A leader is obliged to set higher ethical and spiritual standards for the general population to follow. If the leader fails in this regard, the quality of the nation's life declines, and the progress of society is greatly hampered. Therefore, leaders have a great burden on their shoulders. The life of a true leader is the life of service and sacrifice.

Sri Krishna implies that if Arjun were to abandon his duty to act, then the entire community will follow the same low standard of retreating from action set up by him which will lead to general social decadence. The Lord cites Himself as an example for Arjun to act. Arjun is expected to set himself as an example for the common men. Running way from duty would set an ignoble precedence.

न मे पार्थास्ति कर्त्तव्यं त्रिषु लोकेषु किञ्चन।
नानवाप्तमवाप्तव्यं वर्त एव च कर्मणि ॥ 3.22 ॥

Shlok 3.22: There is nothing in the three worlds (heaven, earth, and the lower region- *Patal*), O Parth, that has to be done by Me, or is there anything unattained that should be attained by Me, yet I continue to engage Myself in work.

Commentary: Being a perfect man and a *Yogi*, Sri Krishna had nothing to gain in this world. His entire life is an example of a perfect life of complete detachment. Even though He had nothing that He did not gain nor had anything further to gain, He was engaging Himself constantly in activity. This verse lays stress on the significance of work in life. No one is free from action or Karma. Such is the role of action in life that it is not possible for anyone to abstain from it. Karma or action follows a person like a shadow. It is also not desirable to stop working. The Geeta teaches performance of action and does not support cessation of work.

यदि ह्यहं न वर्तेयं जातु कर्मण्यतन्द्रितः ।
मम वर्त्मानुवर्तन्ते मनुष्याः पार्थ सर्वशः ॥ 3.23 ॥
उत्सीदेयुरिमे लोका न कुर्यां कर्म चेदहम् ।
सङ्करस्य च कर्ता स्यामुपहन्यामिमाः प्रजाः ॥ 3.24 ॥

Shlokas 3.23-3.24: If I do not engage in action relentlessly, O son of Pritha, people would follow the same path in every way. The world would perish if I did not work, and I would be the cause of confusion and destruction.

Commentary: Although Sri Krishna has nothing to gain, he keeps on working relentlessly. If the Lord does not work it will be detrimental for the existence of the Universe. The Universe is not chaos but a cosmos in a perfect order. Nowhere chaotic conditions are seen in the working of the cosmic forces. Movement of planets, air, water, cloud, occurring of seasons, laws of the oceans, various social orders, disciplines, etc. always obey the law of nature. The Lord represents not only the law governing the outer world of things but also the law that governs the inner world of thoughts and emotions. In case the law governing the inner temperaments does not function there will be confusion in behaviour and instability in the character of people bringing about their own destruction.

What should the wise do to the ignorant?

सक्ताः कर्मण्यविद्वांसो यथा कुर्वन्ति भारत ।
कुर्याद्विद्वांस्तथासक्तश्चिकीर्षुर्लोकसंग्रहम् ॥ 3.25 ॥

Shlok 3.25: As the ignorant men act with attachment to work, O Bharat (Arjun), so should the wise act without attachment, wishing the welfare of the world.

Commentary: It is well known that every member of the society by and large always keeps himself busy throughout his life, performing actions in his chosen field. A man of self-realization also works in the world with the same enthusiasm and sincerity same as a common man of the society with the difference that the actions of the ignorant are motivated by attachments and anxieties for the fruits of actions, while the man of wisdom work without attachment and for the purpose of the welfare of the world at large. Here the advice to Arjun is that he must fight as a warrior who is called upon to protect the higher values of living unattached to his ego-centric conception of himself and his people. The idea is that as an ignorant person acts purely for his personal happiness, similarly a wise man should act, with the same zeal, for the welfare of others.

न बुद्धिभेदं जनयेदज्ञानां कर्मसङ्गिनाम् ।
जोषयेत्सर्वकर्माणि विद्वान्युक्तः समाचरन् ॥ 3.26 ॥

Shlok 3.26: Let no enlightened man unsettle the understanding of the ignorant who are attached to the fruits of work, but should inspire others by performing all works to the best of one's abilities (without attachment to results).

Commentary: This verse is a sort of precaution to the over-zealous persons giving advice to others. The unwise working in a particular way should not be suddenly asked by the wise to change their style of working. Rather they should fall in line with the common men and women and guide them through their actions in the right direction by setting their own example as a standard. The men of wisdom are warned not to go against the spirit of the times.

All works are the works of nature

प्रकृतेः क्रियमाणानि गुणैः कर्माणि सर्वशः ।
अहंकारविमूढात्मा कर्ताहमिति मन्यते ॥ 3.27 ॥

Shlok 3.27: All actions are performed by the *Gunas* of Nature. But he, whose mind is deluded by egoism, thinks 'I am the doer'.

Commentary: All actions are performed by the *Gunas* of Nature. Individuals have no role to play. They are merely instruments or agents of action. So no one should think that he or she is the doer of anything in the world. Arjun is not a doer of anything in the battle of Kurukshetra. Only a self-realized or wise person like Sri Krishna knows who the real doer is. A person is of deluded mind, if he thinks that he is the doer.

तत्त्ववित्तु महाबाहो गुणकर्मविभागयोः ।
गुणा गुणेषु वर्तन्त इति मत्वा न सज्जते ॥ 3.28 ॥

Shlok 3.28: O Mighty armed, one who knows the truth about the role of the forces of Nature (*Gunas*) in getting work done, does not become attached to work. Because such a person knows that it is *Gunas* that get their work done by using our organs as their instruments.

Commentary: He who is versed in the classification of the energies (*Gunas*) and their respective functions holds that the energies as sense-organs move amid the energies as sense-objects, but not the Self. One who knows that one has no role to play in the performance of certain acts, one does not get attached to the consequences of those acts. And only such people are called enlightened who are not attached to their work. Arjun is unnecessarily worried about the consequence of the war, because he is afraid of bad consequences of the impending war. Arjun must understand that he is merely an instrument in the hands of Super-Self to fight for justice. The agent can never be the doer.

प्रकृतेर्गुणसम्मूढाः सज्जन्ते गुणकर्मसु ।
तानकृत्स्नविदो मन्दान्कृत्स्नविन्न विचालयेत् ॥ 3.29 ॥

Shlok 3.29: The man of perfect knowledge should not disturb the mind of the ignorant whose knowledge is imperfect, who deluded by the *Gunas* of nature, attach themselves to the functions of the *Gunas*.

Commentary: The enlightened one should not try to dissuade others from performing their actions they are doing. Some people always remain deluded by the forces of Nature. All the three *Gunas* do not uniformly charactarize all the people. People tend to vary among themselves with respect to the degree of *Gunas* present in their personality. Some are more *Sattvic*, while others are more *Tamsic* and yet others are real *Rajsic* and the like. Working with attachment also has a place in the development of society and in the life of common people. The wise should mind their own business, showing little concern for what the imperfect people are doing.

मयि सर्वाणि कर्माणि संन्यस्याध्यात्मचेतसा ।
निराशीर्निर्ममो भूत्वा युध्यस्व विगतज्वरः ॥ 3.30 ॥

Shlok 3.30: Surrendering all actions to Me, and fixing the mind on the Self, devoid of hope and egoism, free from any fever of grief (dejection), fight your battle (of life).

Commentary: This verse is the core of this discourse conveying central theme. This verse sums up other Yog as well— that of *Dhyan* (fixing thy mind on the Self), that of *Bhakti* Yog (surrendering all actions to Me) along with *Karma Yog*. This verse gives complete instruction to a *Karma yogi,* to do one's duty without attachment, with thoughts focussed on the Supreme Self and offering the fruits of action to the Lord as a sacrifice.

Here the word 'me' means not Sri Krishna, the person but the Supreme Self, the Divine Being, the Supreme Lord, the Eternal and the Omniscient, the Self of all. The Lord asks Arjun to fight on surrendering all activities unto Him, with the mind always concentrated on the Self. Surrendering all actions does not mean inactivity but acting without attachment and the sense of possession for them. Actions performed with egocentric and selfish motives become a bondage. Actions performed without attachment and desires are not actions at all, inasmuch as they are not capable of producing any painful reactions. It also means giving up of wrong motives behind actions. Purification of motives is possible only when the mind is made to concentrate on the Self and the Divine glory. Actions performed with such mind cannot be ordinary actions but they will be activities performed for the sake of the Lord and are the expressions of the Supreme Will through an individual.

ये मे मतमिदं नित्यमनुतिष्ठन्ति मानवाः ।
श्रद्धावन्तोऽनसूयन्तो मुच्यन्ते तेऽपि कर्मभिः ॥ 3.31 ॥
ये त्वेतदभ्यसूयन्तो नानुतिष्ठन्ति मे मतम् ।
सर्वज्ञानविमूढांस्तान्विद्धि नष्टानचेतसः ॥ 3.32 ॥

Shlokas 3.31-3.32: Those who always practise this teaching of Mine– with faith and without finding fault– become free from the bondage of *Karma*. But those who find fault with this teaching

and do not practise it, should be considered ignorant, senseless, and confused.

Commentary: *Shraddha* (faith) is a mental attitude. It is faith in one's own Self and in the teachings of the spiritual preceptor. It is a combination of the higher emotions of reverence and humility. Sri Krishna advises that a *Karmayogi* should act having full faith in Him. Those who are adamant to find fault with His teachings without practising them are unwise and stupid. Such people are deluded and cannot have a proper understanding of right and wrong or moral and immoral. Arjun should fully trust Lord Krishna and act according to His advice having unflinching faith in him.

Action is driven by one's own nature

सदृशं चेष्टते स्वस्याः प्रकृतेर्ज्ञानवानपि ।

प्रकृतिं यान्ति भूतानि निग्रहः किं करिष्यति ॥ 3.33 ॥

Shlok 3.33: Even the wise act according to their own nature. All beings follow their nature– what will suppress them?

Commentary: Why do people not follow the teachings of the Lord and instead act on their own is answered in this verse: the reason is that their lower nature proves too strong for them. Everyone is conditioned by his thoughts which in turn are influenced by his nature (tendency) or *Prakriti*. Even a man of wisdom finds it difficult to practise the way of life shown by the Lord because of his own mental conditioning overwhelmed by his incapacity to pursue the path of action. *Prakriti* is the mental equipment with which one is born as the result of the past acts performed in a previous life. This nature is the mainspring of the man's action.

Barriers to the path of perfection

इन्द्रियस्येन्द्रियस्यार्थे रागद्वेषौ व्यवस्थितौ ।

तयोर्न वशमागच्छेत्तौ ह्यस्य परिपन्थिनौ ॥ 3.34 ॥

Shlok 3.34: Attachment and aversion are lurking in the object of every single sense. One should not come under the control of these two because they are, indeed, stumbling blocks (on one's path of perfection).

Commentary: 'Attachment' may be defined as a very strong desire to experience sensual pleasures again and again. 'Aversion' is the strong dislike for the unpleasant. The search for peace of mind, comfort, and happiness is the basis of all human endeavours, including the acquisition and propagation of knowledge.

Desire, like any other power given by the Lord, is not the problem. We can have desires with a proper frame of mind that gives us control over attachments and aversions. If we can manage our wants, most of the things we possess become dispensable rather than essential. With a right attitude, we can have mastery over all our attachments and aversions. The only necessity is to have a frame of mind that makes most items unnecessary. Those who have knowledge, detachment, and devotion have neither likes nor dislikes for any worldly object, person, place, or work. Personal likes and dislikes disturb the equanimity of mind and become a hindrance on the path of spiritual progress. Likes and dislikes are another form of fulfilled and unfulfilled desires respectively. Desires must be kept under proper control.

श्रेयान्स्वधर्मो विगुणः परधर्मात्स्वनुष्ठितात् ।
स्वधर्मे निधनं श्रेयः परधर्मो भयावहः ॥ 3.35 ॥

Shlok 3.35: Better is one's own duty, though imperfectly performed, than the duty of another well performed. Better is death in the doing of one's own duty; the duty of another is fraught with peril.

Commentary: The implication is that Arjun's thought of withdrawing from fight and going in for the peaceful life of an ascetic is prompted by man's natural desire to shun what is disagreeable and adopt what is momentarily agreeable to the senses. He should on no account yield to such weakness. It is indeed much better for a person to die while discharging his own duty, though it may not have any merit, than doing the duty of another, though it may be performed in a perfect manner, because the duty of another has many pitfalls.

Desire and anger as enemies

Arjun asked:

अर्थ केन प्रयुक्तोऽयं पापं चरति पूरुषः ।
अनिच्छन्नपि वार्ष्णेय बलादिव नियोजितः ॥ 3.36 ॥

Shlok 3.36: O son of Vrishni, what impels one to commit sin or selfish deeds as if unwillingly and forced against one's will?

Commentary: This question raised by Arjun is related to our daily life. Everybody knows what is right and what is not right, what is good and what is not good. Yet when it comes to action people are invariably tempted to commit the wrong. Arjun's query is why there is a divergence between one's ideology and one's own action. The Divine in us wants us to do great things but the devil in us wants us to do most terrible things many a time much against our will. We seem to be constrained by an outside force. Arjun wants to know the cause for this peculiar phenomenon.

Lord Krishna said:

काम एष क्रोध एष रजोगुणसमुद्भवः ।
महाशनो महापाप्मा विद्ध्येनमिह वैरिणम् ॥ 3.37 ॥

Shlok 3.37: It is the lust, born out of passion, which becomes anger (when unfulfilled). Lust is insatiable and is a great devil. Know this as the enemy.

Commentary: The cause of all sins and wrong actions in this world is desire. Anger is also a desire expressed in another form. When a man's desire is not fulfilled he becomes angry with those who stand as hindrances in the way of their fulfilment. When a desire arises the quality of Rajas in a man urges him to work for its satisfaction. The desire-anger-emotion combination of three-in-one is the root cause which forces a person to make compromise with higher values of life. Once the virus of desire enters the intellectual faculty the results are bound to be chaotic, blocking out the entire wisdom because desire is never satisfied by its gratification. One gets rid of desire only through the constant practice of detachment. Therefore, Sri Krishna says desire is the man's greatest enemy on the earth because a man commits sin only at the dictate of desire against his will and better judgement which lands him in terrible suffering in the form of repeated birth and death. Actually, mundane desire compels a person to engage in sinful activities. Control your wants because whatever you want, wants you too. Lord Buddha rightly observed: Desire is the root of all evils and misery.

How does desire affect man?

धूमेनाव्रियते वह्निर्यथादर्शो मलेन च ।
यथोल्बेनावृतो गर्भस्तथा तेनेदमावृतम् ॥ 3.38 ॥

Shlok 3.38: Just as fire is enveloped by smoke, a mirror is covered with dust, and the foetus in the womb is surrounded with a jelly-like substance, our wisdom is often covered with our never-ending desire to get more and more.

आवृतं ज्ञानमेतेन ज्ञानिनो नित्यवैरिणा।
कामरूपेण कौन्तेय दुष्पूरेणानलेन च ॥ 3.39 ॥

Shlok 3.39: O son of Kunti, wisdom is covered by never-ending lust, the eternal enemy of mankind. This never ending lust is like an insatiable flame.

Commentary (Shlokas 3.38-39): Here three different examples refer to the different degrees to which desire in the form of ignorance envelopes and obscures the inner Light in man and deceive our capacity to think rationally. Correct judgement is blocked by the sense of attachment in the mind for the worldly objects. Desires fall under three categories depending upon the nature of attachments– *Tamsic*– inert, *Rajsic*– active, and *Sattvic*– divine. Even *Sattvic* desires veil the correct judgement just as smoke envelopes fire where the rise of the slightest wind of discrimination can dispel the smoke of desire. The veiling is thin and hence it requires only a little effort to remove it.

Desires are insatiable. They are never satisfied by the enjoyments of the objects of the desires. Desire keeps on growing and changing in nature. They grow more and more as does the fire to which fuel is added. Desire screens off our capacity to discriminate right from the wrong, real from the unreal. The ignorant man considers desire as his friend because his senses are gratified. The wise man knows by experience that desire will bring nothing but suffering to him. Hence it is said to be the constant enemy of the wise but not of the ignorant.

Seat of desire

इन्द्रियाणि मनो बुद्धिरस्याधिष्ठानमुच्यते ।
एतैर्विमोहयत्येष ज्ञानमावृत्य देहिनम् ॥ 3.40 ॥

Shlok 3.40: The senses, the mind, and the intellect are said to

be the centre or the origin of desire. Through these, desire deludes a person by veiling Self-knowledge.

Commentary: If the enemy's hideouts are known, it is easy to capture him. Similarly Sri Krishna gives the clue to Arjun as to where the enemies of wisdom lurk so that he can locate and eliminate them. The Lord says the senses, the mind and the intellect, are seats of action for the desire to play havoc with the inner serenity and equipoise of a man. The sense organs transmit the stimuli received from the objects of enjoyment to the mind which working in close collaboration with the intellect starts living in the experience of sense enjoyments. To eliminate the inner enemy of desire at its source– sense organs, mind and intellect– is the crux of the problem.

तस्मात्त्वमिन्द्रियाण्यादौ नियम्य भरतर्षभ ।
पाप्मानं प्रजहि ह्येनं ज्ञानविज्ञाननाशनम् ॥ 3.41 ॥

Shlok 3.41: Therefore you should first control your senses, O Bull of the Bharatas, and slay this evil that destroys your knowledge and discrimination.

Commentary: Lust arises at three different levels: at the physical level in any one of the ten senses, at emotional level in the mind and at the thought level in the intellect. Therefore, one must carefully guard all three doors through which lust can enter and control our life. This mighty enemy enslaves the intellect by using the mind as its friend and senses and sense objects as its soldiers. These soldiers keep the individual soul deluded and obscure Absolute Truth as a part of the drama of life. The success or failure of our role in action depends on how we conduct ourselves and meet our destiny.

Sri Krishna states that the first step to kill desire is to control the senses. Desire is referred to here as a sinful thing posing a threat to both knowledge and wisdom. Desire is a sinful thing because it leads us to live a life of lowly nature. All desires cannot– and need not– be eliminated, but first selfish desires and motives must be eliminated for spiritual progress. All our actions by thought, word and deed, including desires, should be directed to glorify God and for the good of humanity.

How to control lust and attain the goal

इन्द्रियाणि पराण्याहुरिन्द्रियेभ्यः परं मनः ।
मनसस्तु परा बुद्धिर्यो बुद्धेः परतस्तु सः ॥ 3.42 ॥

Shlok 3.42: The senses are great, greater than the senses is the mind; greater than the mind is the intelligence but greater than the intelligence is He (the Self).

Commentary: In the human body, mind occupies a place above the senses but below the intelligence. There are five senses of knowledge and five senses of action. The mind acts as a coordinator between the two. Mind thinks, imagines, resolves and plans and thus plays a very vital role in the body set-up. Our worldly life is an interplay of senses, mind and intelligence. When the mind is under the sway of the senses, it is in bondage and gets deluded. But when it is united with intelligence, there is less bondage and more freedom. The highest freedom is attained when the mind is controlled by intelligence which is suffused by the light of the Supreme. The senses by their intrinsic nature run after sense objects. In this race, they develop a liking for the respective sense object. The eyes love to see beautiful objects, ears like to listen sweet words, songs and music, tongue relishes tasty food, nose would prefer pleasant smell. These feelings of love, liking or taste for their sense objects are created through the association or direction of the mind. Alone, senses cannot develop such feelings, as they act as mere channels or instruments of the mind. Having developed these likings, the mind follows the senses and makes them run after sense objects for more pleasure and satisfaction. The mind thus becomes enslaved through the senses because of the feelings of pleasure and enjoyment which it gets from sense objects.

When the mind becomes habitual to sense satisfaction, the intelligence also does not function properly. Consequently, the person gets trapped in the vicious circle of enjoyment of pleasure and lack of it, which results in pain as pleasure is always followed by pain because of it transient nature. The following verse of the Geeta is very relevant.

एवं बुद्धेः परं बुद्ध्वा संस्तभ्यात्मानमात्मना ।
जहि शत्रुं महाबाहो कामरूपं दुरासदम् ॥ 3.43 ॥

Shlok 3.43: Thus knowing Him who is superior to the intellect and restraining the self by the Self, O Mighty-armed Prince, destroy the enemy in the form of desire, no doubt hard indeed to conquer.

Commentary: This verse concludes discourse three of the Geeta, giving the seeker a technique to conquer desire, the inner enemy. In this verse, the Self or *Atman* is considered superior to the intellect. The modern man bases his decisions on his intellect. He is proud of his intellectual achievements. But the soul is superior to intellect and it provides intuitive perceptions that go beyond intellectual efforts. This verse also indicates how one controls senses by the mind, the mind by the intellect. Intellect is closest to the Self or *Atman*. By using one's intellect, that is, power of discrimination and judgement, one attains the wisdom of the Self. This theme is repeated several times in later verses.

The verse tells us about the hierarchy of levels of consciousness. The physical body is gross, external and limited. As compared to this the senses are superior because they are subtler and more internal and have a wider range of activity. Superior to the senses is the mind as it can direct the function of the senses (as it can undertake the work of the senses also). Superior to the mind is the intellect because it is endowed with the faculty of discrimination and finality; when the mind doubts, the intellect decides. But the Self is superior to even the intellect because the intellect draws its power to illuminate from the Self alone. The Self is the in-dweller in the body, the Witness of the activities of the body, senses, mind and intellect. Sri Krishna advises Arjun to conquer desire with this understanding of the superior power of the Self, though it is difficult to achieve. The Lord points out that a man of discrimination and dispassion will be able to achieve this by increasing his *Sattvic* quality and by appealing to the indwelling presence, the Self, through meditation. This controlling of the lower self, i.e. the mind with the knowledge of the higher Self is termed here as 'restraining the self by the Self'.

Restrain the lower self by the higher Self. Subdue the lower mind by the higher mind. It is difficult to conquer desire because it is of a highly complex and incomprehensible nature. But a man of discrimination and dispassion, who does constant and intense *Sadhana*, can conquer it quite easily. One must not spoil oneself by wrongful temporary pleasures of the senses. One who can control the senses can control the whole world and achieve success in all endeavours.

OM TAT SAT

Discourse - 4

Gyan-Karmayog: Yog of Action and Knowledge

In this Discourse Lord Krishna reveals how spiritual knowledge is received by disciples in a successive order and the reason and nature of His emergence in the material world. Lord Krishna declares that He is born in every age in order to raise man and take him to the Supreme Abode. Whenever there is a prevalence of lawlessness and the world is ruled by the forces of darkness, the Lord manifests Himself to destroy these adverse forces and to establish peace, order and harmony.

One who has true union with the Lord is not subject to rebirth. He attains immortality. Such a union can only be achieved when one is free from attachment, fear and anger, being thoroughly purified by right knowledge. The Lord accepts the devotion of all, whatever path they may use to approach Him. Various kinds of sacrifices are performed by those engaged in the path to God. Through the practice of these sacrifices the mind is purified and led Godward. Here also there must be the spirit of non-attachment to the fruits of actions.

Arjun is given the most heartening assurance that divine wisdom liberates even the most sinful. When knowledge of the Self dawns, all actions with their results are finished by the fire of that knowledge, just as fuel is finished by fire. When there is no idea of egoism, when there is no desire for the rewards of one's actions, actions are no actions. They lose their potency. In order to attain divine wisdom one must have supreme faith and devotion. Complete faith is, therefore, the most important pre-condition or qualification for a spiritual aspirant. The suspicious mind is deviated from the right path. Faith ultimately confers divine knowledge, which removes ignorance once and for all.

Mere intellectual knowledge does not lead to liberation. It cannot grant one supreme peace and freedom. When one has achieved complete self-mastery and self-control, when one has intense faith and devotion, then true knowledge dawns within and one attains liberation and freedom from all weaknesses and sins.

The Lord concludes by emphasizing that the soul that distrusts goes to destruction. Without faith in oneself, in the scriptures and in the words of the preceptor, one cannot make any headway on the spiritual path. It is distrust that prevents one from engaging in spiritual *Sadhna* and realizing the highest knowledge and bliss.

The Lord said:

इमं विवस्वते योगं प्रोक्तवानहमव्ययम् ।
विवस्वान् मनवे प्राह मनुरिक्ष्वाकवेऽब्रवीत् ॥ 4.1 ॥

Shlok 4.1: I expounded this imperishable *Yog* to Vaivasvat, Vaivasvat communicated this to Manu, and Manu to Ikshvaku.

Commentary: Vaivasvat is the Sun and Manu the law giver. *Yog* was first taught to Manu and Manu taught it to his son Ikshvaku, the first ruler, who was the illustrious ancestor of the Solar dynasty of the Kshatriyas. The Lord says that I taught to the Sun (Vaivasvat) at the initial stage of evolution in order to infuse strength into the Kshatriyas, the ruling class. It is only when possessed of the strength of this *Yog*, that they can protect the Brahmins, the priestly class. And when the spiritual and ruling classes are well maintained, it is possible to maintain the world. *Yog* is imperishable because of its imperishable results. Indccd, *Moksha,* the fruit of this *Yog* of complete devotion to right knowledge, never perishes.

(Note: There are several Manus in Hindu mythology. Here this Manu possibly refers to the 7th Manu named Vaivasvat and some other succeeding Manus. In the subsequent hymns there is a reference of the *Varna* system which forms a part of **Manusmriti** (it was not complied or wriiten the earliest Manu). Here the reference of Manu and also the *Varna* system in the subsequent verses has been made to re-establish the declining Hindu religion, Brahmanism in particular, after it received serious jolts from the rise and development of Buddhism in India. It is a well known fact that the Vedas, which formed the basis of Hindu religion, was countered by Lord Buddha during 6th Century BC and also during the subsequent period. He was dead against the Vedic rites and rituals and also the existence of God. Roots of Hindu religion was so shaken that the supporters of Brahminical ideology based Hinduism had to be re-established for its survival. As a part of strategy for rejuvenation of Hinduism they inserted the name of Manu and controversial philosophy of Manusmriti into the Geeta. But they did not realize that *Manusmriti* itself was very problematic. Modern scholarship suggests various manuscripts of *Manusmriti* and they are inconsistent with each other, and within themselves, raising concerns of its authenticity, insertions and interpolations made into the text in later times. It was compiled and codified by several sages covering the views of several Manus during 2nd century BC and 3rd century AD, shedding light on such topics as duties, rights, laws, conduct, virtues and others. This further suggests that the Geeta was not composed along with the Mahabharat, as the Mahabharat by far pre-dated the compilation of Manusmriti. Simultaneously it is also possible that numerous insertions and interpolations were done in the Geeta at later stages. Every effort was made to establish Sri Krishna as the real Almighty contrary to the Vedic Gods and goddesses. The Vedas do not mention Ram or Sri Krishna as God, but that does not undermine the significance of either Ram or Sri Krishna.)

एवं परम्पराप्राप्तमिमं राजर्षयो विदुः ।
स कालेनेह महता योगो नष्टः परन्तप ।। 4.2 ।।

Shlok 4.2: Thus, handed down in regular succession, this was learnt by the royal sages (*Rajarsis*). After a long time, this *Yog* dwindled away in this world, O Parantap (Scorcher of foes)!

स एवायं मया तेऽद्य योगः प्रोक्तः पुरातनः ।
भक्तोऽसि मे सखा चेति रहस्यं ह्येतदुत्तमम् ।। 4.3 ।।

Shlok 4.3: Today, I have described the same ancient *Yog* to you because you are my sincere devotee and friend, and this secret is profound indeed.

Commentary (Shlokas 4.2-4.3): The royal sages were kings who at the same time possessed divine knowledge. They learnt this *Yog*. This ancient *Yog* consists of profound and subtle teachings. Hence it is the supreme secret which the Lord reveals to Arjun. This *Yog* was gradually handed down in a regular succession among the Kshatriyas, the king-sages (men who were at once kings and sages). But the tradition of this *Yog* has now for a long time been broken here. Seeing that the *Yog* has been lost by falling into the hands of the weak who could not control their senses, the Lord is talking about the *Yog* to his trusted friend Arjun.

Divine incarnations

Arjun asked:

अपरं भवतो जन्म परं जन्म विवस्वतः ।
कथमेतद्विजानीयां त्वमादौ प्रोक्तवानिति ॥ 4.4 ॥

Shlok 4.4: You were born much later, but Vaivasvat was born in the beginning. How am I to understand that You told this science in the begin-ning of the creation?

Commentary: Arjun questions how Krishna, a contemporary of Arjun, could have taught this science of Karmayog to king Vaivasvat, who was born much long before Lord Krishna. The doctrine of Bhagavad Geeta came much later; it is relatively newer. Lord Krishna restated it in the Geeta for the benefit of humanity. All great masters come to rekindle the fire of forgotten Truth. Different people have said everything we hear or read at different times. Perhaps Arjun does know that Sri Krishna has come to this earth so many times.

Lord Krishna said:

बहूनि मे व्यतीतानि जन्मानि तव चार्जुन ।
तान्यहं वेद सर्वाणि न त्वं वेत्थ परंतप ॥ 4.5 ॥

Shlok 4.5: Many births of Mine have passed, as well as of thine, O Arjun! I know them all but thou knowest not, O Scorcher of foes!

अजोऽपि सन्नव्ययात्मा भूतानामीश्वरोऽपि सन् ।
प्रकृतिं स्वामधिष्ठाय संभवाम्यात्ममायया ॥ 4.6 ॥

Shlok 4.6: Though I am unborn and of perpetual nature, and though I am the Lord of all beings, yet, ruling over My own Nature, I come into being by My own *Maya (Yog-Maya)*.

Commentary: Explaining the circumstances Sri Krishna says that I am by nature eternal, pure, wise, and unbound and My power of vision is unobstructed. Sri Krishna does not come into being as others do, bound by Karma, under the subjugation of Nature. He is not tied by the fetters of the *Gunas,* because he is the Lord of *Maya.*

Sri Krishna says that my embodiment is only apparent and does not touch my true nature. *Yog-Maya* (Divine Light, *Brahm-jyoti, Noor*) is the creative power (*Anand-shakti*) of Lord Krishna. *Maha-Maya* is the fractional reflection of *Yog-Maya. Kal-Maya* is the reflection of *Maha-Maya*. And the illusory energy (*Maya*) is the supernatural, ex-traordinary, and mystic power of Eternal Being (Brahm). *Maha-Maya, Kal-Maya,* and *Maya* are also called *Adi Prakriti;* and *Prakriti*, the material Nature, is considered the reflection of *Maya. Thus Yog-Maya* is the origin of both *Maya* and *Prakriti*. The Eternal Light (*Brahmjyoti, Noor, Yog-Maya*) is the invisible potential energy; *Maya* is kinetic energy, the force of action of Brahm. *Maya* is also used as a metaphor to explain the visible world to common people.

यदा यदा हि धर्मस्य ग्लानिर्भवति भारत ।
अभ्युत्थानमधर्मस्य तदात्मानं सृजाम्यहम् ॥ 4.7 ॥
परित्राणाय साधूनां विनाशाय च दुष्कृताम् ।
धर्मसंस्थापनार्थाय सम्भवामि युगे युगे ॥ 4.8 ॥

Shlok 4.7: Whenever there is a decline of *Dharma* (righteousness) and a rise of *Adharma* (lawlessness), then I send forth Myself.

Shlok 4.8: For the protection of the good, for the destruction of the wicked and for the establishment of righteousness, I come into being from age to age.

Commentary (Shlokas 4.7-4.8): Let us understand the notions of *Dharma* and *Adharma* briefly. That which elevates a man and helps him to reach the goal of life and attain knowledge is Dharma (righteousness); that which drags him into worldliness is *Adharma* or lawlessness. That which helps a man to attain liberation is Dharma; that which makes him irreligious is lawlessness.

Whenever miscreants are born to destroy the world order (*Dharma)*, the Lord incarnates to put everything in a proper order.

His compassion is the main reason for Lord's incarnation. There are other reasons, besides the protection of righteousness (*Dharma*), for the Lord's incarnation. Though devoid of material attributes, unattached, and immutable, yet for the love of His devotees, the Lord assumes a form with attributes. The Supreme Being, which is beyond birth and death, incarnates in a human form through a great soul on the earth to satisfy the longings of devotees who want to see Him and be in His personal presence.

These verses indicate that God incarnates from age to age, for protecting the righteous and destroying the wicked and upholding the righteousness whenever it is in danger, or whenever the need arises. It is implied that the Supreme though unborn and imperishable, takes human from in order to destroy evil forces and to protect the good. Thus he assumes birth to re-establish righteousness. This gives rise to the theory of incarnation or avatars The greatest examples are Lord Ram and Lord Krishna who assumed human forms, fought with evil forces and destroyed them for the protection of the good and virtuous.

In Hindu theology, the cosmic cycle consists of four *yugas*. Lord Krishna appeared in *Dwapar yug*, and Lord Ram appeared in *Treta yug*. Each *yug* runs for several million calendar years. There are controversies on the duration of each *yug* and when they started. Though the Lord used the word *yug*, this verse could mean that the Lord incarnates in various periods when *Adharma* or wickedness increases beyond a critical point.

These verses indirectly establish that God is on the side of the righteous and the virtuous and ultimately destroys the wicked and evil. It, therefore, means that we humans should follow the path of righteousness in our lives.

जन्म कर्म च मे दिव्यमेवं यो वेत्ति तत्त्वतः ।
त्यक्त्वा देहं पुनर्जन्म नैति मामेति सोऽर्जुन ॥ 4.9 ॥

Shlok 4.9: Thus one who is truly conversant with the divine nature of my birth and actions is not born again, O Arjun. When he leaves his body, he comes to Me.

Commentary: He who knows in true light My divine birth and action, he is not born again after having abandoned the body. He becomes an inseparable part of the Supreme Being. Sri Krishna says that His birth is an illusion (*Maya*). It is divine, peculiar to *Ishvar,* not of ordinary nature (*Aprakriti*). All those who come to Me are liberated.

वीतरागभयक्रोधा मन्मया मामुपाश्रिताः ।
बहवो ज्ञानतपसा पूता मद्भावमागताः ॥ 4.10 ॥

Shlok 4.10: Many have become free from attachment, fear, anger, and at-tained salvation by taking refuge in Me, by becoming fully absorbed in My thoughts and by getting purified by the austerity of wisdom.

Commentary: The import is that the path of liberation here taught by Sri Krishna is not of recent origin, nor is it dependent upon His present manifestation, but has been handed down from time immemorial. Having attained to highest purity by means of this fire of austerity (*Tapas*), many have attained *Moksha.* Knowledge of Self or of the Supreme Being is enough for any human being for his or her liberation. The final aim seems to be to reach God. This verse has got a secular connotation in the sense that it applies to devotees of all faiths and belief.

Divine dispensation of worldly benefits and salvation

ये यथा मां प्रपद्यन्ते तांस्तथैव भजाम्यहम् ।
मम वर्त्मानुवर्तन्ते मनुष्याः पार्थ सर्वशः ॥ 4.11 ॥

Shlok 4.11: I accept people in whatever way they approach me. All the paths people follow are mine (paths leading to Me), O son of Pritha.

Commentary: I reward men by granting them the things they desire, just in accordance with the way in which they seek Me and the motive with which they seek Me; for they do not seek for *Moksha*. One cannot indeed pursue pleasure and at the same time seek for *Moksha*. Wherefore, I reward seekers of fruits by securing to them their selfish ends; I reward the unselfish, who do their prescribed duties and seek for *Moksha* by granting them knowledge. I reward men of knowledge who have renounced the world and seek for *Moksha* by granting them *Moksha*. Similarly I reward men in distress by relieving them from distress. Thus do I reward all, just in the way they seek Me. Lord's nature is to reciprocate our love for Him. God loves those who love Him. It is due to divine illusion (Maya) that most people seek temporary material gains, such as health, wealth, and success, and not Self-knowledge and devotion to His lotus feet.

काांक्षन्तः कर्मणां सिद्धिं यजन्त इह देवताः ।
क्षिप्रं हि मानुषे लोके सिद्धिर्भवति कर्मजा ॥ 4.12 ॥

Shlok 4.12: Those who long for success in actions in this world worship the gods. Success in work comes quickly in this hu-man world.

Commentary: No one, including all Devas and Brahma, has his or her own power. They all derive their powers from the Supreme Being, *Parabrahm.* In a prayer one asks the Lord's help in getting what one needs; in worship one adores, glorifies, and thanks Him for what one has. One should first be aware of and contemplate one's plight, feel helpless in getting out of the difficulty, then seek divine help– through prayer– in a state of helplessness with intense faith. Lord will take the first step if you know your plight and seek His help for transformation.

All prayers are answered, but prayers for the benefit of others are given first priority. Lord actually knows our needs all the times and is simply waiting to be asked for help due to our free will. Meditation is listening to God by stilling the mind and assuming a receptive posture in order to hear Lord's instructions, insights and revelations.

चातुर्वर्ण्यं मया सृष्टं गुणकर्मविभागशः ।
तस्य कर्तारमपि मां विद्ध्यकर्तारमव्ययम् ॥ 4.13 ॥

Shlok 4.13: I created the four divisions of human occupations based on thc ability of people (i.e. the Varna system). Though I am the author of this system of division of labour, one should know that I do nothing (directly), and I am eternal.

Commentary: This verse endorses the significance of the hierarchical four-fold divisions of Hindu society known as the Varna system. It is wrongly claimed to be the creation of the Supreme Being.

(**Note:** It is evidently clear that this verse has been inserted into the Geeta at a later stage to justify the existence of the hierarchical four-fold divisions of Hindu society based on the Varna system, as Sri Krishna need not say "I created the four divisions of human occupations based on the ability of people." This has originally come from the Rigved which incorporates the system of Varna. Since this is claimed to be God-ordained system, one may rightly pose a question here– if this Varna system was created by God Himself, then why has this system not existed elsewhere outside the Hindu society. Sri Krishna's name has been purposefully used because the Buddhists vehemently opposed the Vedic system. At the same time it has also been said in the same verse that such a system has not been directly created by God. This paradoxical assertion may be because of some guilt sense on the *part* of supporters of the Varna system. Furthermore, this verse dealing with the four-fold divisions of society appears to be irrelevant here, as this discourse primarily deals with *Gyanayog.)*

Action without attachment does not bind the soul

न मां कर्माणि लिम्पन्ति न मे कर्मफले स्पृहा ।
इति मां योऽभिजानाति कर्मभिर्न स बध्यते ॥ 4.14 ॥

Shlok 4.14: *Karma* (or action) does not bind Me because I have no desire for the rewards of that action. He who knows Me this way is also not bound by his *Karma*.

Commentary: Sri Krishna says for want of egoism (*Ahankar*), these actions do not pollute Me by necessitating incarnation; nor have I a desire for the fruit of these actions. On the other hand, it is but right that actions should pollute those men who are attached to their actions, thinking themselves to be the authors thereof, and longing for the rewards of such actions. As I have none of these (viz, desire and attachment), actions cannot pollute Me. Knowing that 'I am no agent, I have no longing for the fruits of actions.'

एवं ज्ञात्वा कृतं कर्म पूर्वैरपि मुमुक्षुभिः ।
कुरु कर्मैव तस्मात्त्वं पूर्वैः पूर्वतरं कृतम् ॥ 4.15 ॥

Shlok 4.15: The ancient seekers of salvation also performed their duties or actions without concern for the fruits. Therefore, you should do your duty as the ancients did in olden times.

Commentary: The ancient seekers of salvation also performed their duties or actions without concern for the fruits. Therefore, you should do your duty as the ancients did in olden times. As the ancients performed action, you should also perform your action; do not sit quiet, nor renounce action. If you are ignorant, you should perform action to purify the self. If you are wise and know the truth, you must perform action for the good of the masses. It was performed by the ancients such as king Janak in the olden time: it is not a recent institution.

Attached, detached and forbidden action

किं कर्म किमकर्मेति कवयोऽप्यत्र मोहिताः ।
तत्ते कर्म प्रवक्ष्यामि यज्ज्ञात्वा मोक्ष्यसेऽशुभात् ॥ 4.16 ॥

Shlok 4.16: Even the wise men are confused about what is action and what is inaction. Therefore, I shall clearly explain what action is, knowing which you shall be liberated from the evil.

Commentary: As the verse is easily comprehensible, it needs no specific explanation.

कर्मणो ह्यपि बोद्धव्यं बोद्धव्यं च विकर्मणः ।
अकर्मणश्च बोद्धव्यं गहना कर्मणो गतिः ॥ 4.17 ॥

Shlok 4.17: The true nature of action is very difficult to understand. Therefore, one should know the nature of attached action, the nature of detached action, and also the nature of forbidden (unlawful) action.

Commentary: Even the wise men are confused as to what is action and what is inaction. For that reason Sri Krishna explains to Arjun about the nature of action and inaction, knowing which he will be released from the evil of *Sansar*. Neither should he think that action means movement of the body, and inaction means absence of it, to sit quiet. What is there to be learnt about them? For that reason, the answer follows:

Attached action is selfish work, done in the mode of passion that produces Karmic bondage and leads to transmigration. Detached action is unselfish work, done in the mode of goodness that leads to salvation. Detached action is considered to be inaction because from the Karmic viewpoint, it is as if no action was performed. Action forbidden by the scriptures, done in the mode of ignorance, is harmful to both the doer and society. It creates misfortunes here and hereafter.

A *Karmayogi* is not subject to *Karmic* laws

कर्मण्यकर्म यः पश्येदकर्मणि च कर्म यः ।
स बुद्धिमान्मनुष्येषु स युक्तः कृत्स्नकर्मकृत् ॥ 4.18 ॥

Shlok 4.18: He who sees inaction in action, and action in inaction is wise among men; he is a Yogi and doer of all actions.

Commentary: Action means what is done, an act in general. Inaction can be seen in action, if a person has no attachment with action, that is, reward-free action. He who sees inaction in action and action in inaction, he is wise among men, he is a true devout. All acts are the acts of Eternal Being. The wise perceive the inac-tive, infinite, and invisible reservoir of potential energy of the Supreme as the ultimate source of all visible kinetic energy in the cosmos, just as invisible electricity runs a fan or air conditioner. The urge and power to do action come from the Supreme Being. Therefore, one should spiritualize all work by perceiving that one does nothing at all and everything is done by the energy of the Supreme Being, using us only as an instrument. A human being should merely consider himself as an agent of a given action; the real doer is the Supreme Being. Therefore, a sense of attachment for an action or expectation of reward for work is not proper. The simple essence of this verse is total surrendering to God, but different commentators have given different interpretations in a complex philosophical manner for the reason best known to them.

यस्य सर्वे समारम्भाः कामसंकल्पवर्जिताः ।
ज्ञानाग्निदग्धकर्माणं तमाहुः पण्डितं बुधाः ॥ 4.19 ॥

Shlok 4.19: Free in all his works from prickings of desire, burned clean in act by the white fire of truth, the wise call that man *Pundit.*

Commentary: The man whose works are free from desires and from selfish intention, he is considered a learned man even if he is engaged in a worldly action. He can set an example for the masses. If he has renounced worldly life, he performs deeds only for bodily maintenance, whose actions good or bad, are finished in the fire of wisdom which consists in the realization of inaction in action and vice-versa. Such a person is called a real learned man. In brief, Sri Krishna suggests that a man's worldly desires should not dictate or prevail over his action or *Dharma.*

त्यक्त्वा कर्मफलासंगं नित्यतृप्तो निराश्रयः ।
कर्मण्यभिप्रवृत्तोऽपि नैव किंचित् करोति सः ॥ 4.20 ॥

Shlok 4.20: One who has abandoned attachment to the fruits of work and remains ever content and independent, such a person, even when he is engaged in action, does nothing at all.

Commentary: He who has abandoned all concern for action and all attachment for its results, who is always content, no desire for sensory satisfaction; he who seeks nothing whereby to achieve any objective for want of any selfish end in view, though engaged in some action, really does nothing at all, since he is endued with knowledge of the actionless Self.

निराशीर्यतचित्तात्मा त्यक्तसर्वपरिग्रहः ।
शारीरं केवलं कर्म कुर्वन्नाप्नोति किल्बिषम् ॥ 4.21 ॥

Shlok 4.21: One who is free from desires, whose mind and senses are under control, and who has renounced all ownership, does not incur any sin by doing bodily action.

Commentary: He who has no desire, he who has controlled both mind and body, he who has disowned all property and does merely bodily action (action necessary for the bare existence of the body) without attachment, he incurs no sin which would produce evil effects. Even *Dharma* is a sin, if practised for liberation and hence it causes a kind of bondage. He is liberated from both (*Dharma* and *Adharma*); he is liberated from worldly life. It is desire which determines whether a particular action is sin or not. All actions without desire or personal interests are free from sin because all such actions are imbued with divine intensions.

यदृच्छालाभसंतुष्टो द्वन्द्वातीतो विमत्सरः ।
समः सिद्धावसिद्धौ च कृत्वापि न निबध्यते ॥ 4.22 ॥

Shlok 4.22: A *Karmayogi*– who is content with whatever gain comes naturally by His will, who is unaffected by pairs of opposites and free from envy, tranquil in success and failure– is not bound by *Karma*.

Commentary: He who is satisfied with whatever he may have, he who is not affected by the pairs of opposites (*Dwandwa*) as success and failure, he who has no feeling of envy and jealousy, he who is calm whether he obtains or not such things as might come to him without effort, such a devotee, feeling no pleasure or pain whether he obtains or not, food and other things necessary for the existence of the body, seeing action in inaction and vice-versa, is not bound by *Karma*. Though he performs the act of begging and the like required for the bare existence of the body, he is not bound, since action and its cause, which are the source of bondage, have been burnt in the fire of wisdom. This is only a replication of what has been already said in verses nos. 19 and 21.

गतङ्गस्य मुक्तस्य ज्ञानावस्थितचेतसः ।
यज्ञायाचरतः कर्म समग्रं प्रविलीयते ॥ 4.23 ॥

Shlok 4.23: To one who is free from attachment, who is liberated, whose mind is centred in knowledge, who works for the sake of sacrifice (for the sake of God), the whole *Karma* is dissolved.

Commentary: That man from whom all attachment is gone, from whom all cause of bondage, *Dharma* and *Adharma*, has dissipated, whose mind is ever fixed in wisdom alone, who acts with a view to the performance of a sacrifice, his action with its result is dissolved away, is reduced to nothing. Such is the characteristic of a liberated person.

ब्रह्मार्पणं ब्रह्म हविर्ब्रह्माग्नौ ब्रह्मणा हुतम् ।
ब्रह्मैव तेन गन्तव्यं ब्रह्मकर्मसमाधिना ॥ 4.24 ॥

Shlok 4.24: Brahm is the offering, Brahm the oblation; by Brahm is the oblation poured into the fire of Brahm; Brahm verily shall be reached by him who always sees Brahm in action.

Commentary: The man who has realized Brahm sees Brahm all around. He has no existence apart from that of the Self. What people look upon as the instrument of offering is nothing but Brahm. Brahm is the oblation, i. e. what is regarded as oblation is to him nothing but Brahm. So the fire wherein the oblation is offered is nothing but Brahm; and it is by Brahm that the offering is made, i.e. the agent is none other than Brahm. The act of offering is nothing but Brahm; and the result, the goal to be achieved by him who always sees Brahm in action, is nothing but Brahm. A stage comes in the life of a devotee when he sees only Brahm and nothing else.

Every action must be thought of as a holy sacrifice, a holy act. Everything may not be the Eternal Being (Brahm), but Brahm is the root or basis of everything. One attains salvation and becomes one with Brahm, without losing one's identity, when one per-ceives Brahm in every action, per-ceives the things one uses as a transformation of Brahm, and realizes that the very process of all action is also Brahm. Thus salvation or *Mukti* is not the destruction of individual soul (*Jeev*), but the realization of one's true nature that *Jeev* is like Brahm.

Different types of spiritual practices

दैवमेवापरे यज्ञं योगिनः पर्युपासते ।
ब्रह्माग्नावपरे यज्ञं यज्ञेनैवोपजुह्वति ॥ 4.25 ॥

Shlok 4.25: Some yogis offer sacrifice to the gods, others pour the sacrifice into the fire of Brahm by means of the sacrifice.

Commentary: Some *yogis*, devotees to action, perform only sacrificial rites in devotion to the gods, while others who know Brahm, the Absolute, sacrifice the Self by the Self in the fire of Brahm. The oblation (*Ahuti*) in this latter sacrifice is nothing but 'Atman'– who is in reality one with Brahm, but who is conditioned by the *Buddhi* with all their attributes superimposed upon Him. This oblation of the Self is poured by the Self into Brahm– here termed fire, the place into which that oblation is poured– as described in the following texts: 'Brahm is the Real, Consciousness, the Infinite.'

श्रोत्रादीनीन्द्रियाण्यन्ये संयमाग्निषु जुह्वति ।
शब्दादीन्विषयानन्य इन्द्रियाग्निषु जुह्वति ॥ 4.26 ॥

Shlok 4.26: Some offer their hearing and other senses into the fires of self-control; yet others offer sounds and other sense-objects into the fire of the senses.

Commentary: Some *Yogis* offer hearing and other senses into the fire of restraint (*Sanyam*); while others sacrifice the objects of senses into the fires of the several senses, i. e. they regard it as a sacrifice to direct their senses only to the unforbidden objects of senses.

सर्वाणीन्द्रियकर्माणि प्राणकर्माणि चापरे ।
आत्मसंयमयोगाग्नौ जुह्वति ज्ञानदीपिते ॥ 4.27 ॥

Shlok 4.27: Still others offer all sense actions, and actions of the vital breath, into the fire of self-control and the *Yog* kindled by knowledge.

Path of worship and prayers

द्रव्ययज्ञास्तपोयज्ञा योगयज्ञास्तथापरे ।
स्वाध्यायज्ञानयज्ञाश्च यतयः संशितव्रताः ॥ 4.28 ॥

Shlok 4.28: In the same manner, other devotees offer their wealth, their austerity and *yog* as sacrifice, while still others, of self-restraint and rigid vows, offer their Vedic study and knowledge.

Commentary (Shlokas 4.27-4.28): Of others, some sacrifice by way of giving away their wealth to the deserving; some by austerity; some by *Yog*, comprising such practices as *Pranayam* (restraint of vital airs) and *Pratyahar* (withdrawal of the mind from external objects); some by way of repeating Vedic texts such as the Rigved according to prescribed rules; some by way of studying the contents of the scriptures (*shastra*).

अपाने जुह्वति प्राणं प्राणेऽपानं तथापरे।
प्राणापानगती रुद्ध्वा प्राणायामपरायणाः ॥ 4.29 ॥

Shlok 4.29: There are others who are devoted to the control of breath; they discipline the movement of *Pran* (inhaled breath) and *Apan* (exhaled breath).

Commentary: This verse deals with various processes of breathing exercise as a part of meditation. Some do the breathing exercise by breathing in (*Pran*), then stopping the breath for a while (called in-*Kumbhak*) before breathing out (*Apan*) and then stopping the breath after breathing out (called out-*Kumbhak*) using yogic breathing techniques. Some *Yogis* practise inhalation, some practise exhalation, and some retention of breath. This is *Pranayam*.

अपरे नियताहाराः प्राणान्प्राणेषु जुह्वति ।
सर्वेऽप्येते यज्ञविदो यज्ञक्षपितकल्मषाः ॥ 4.30 ॥

Shlok 4.30: Others restrict their diet and reach the breathless state of trance by concentrating on the breath.

All these are knowers of sacrifice, whose moral stains are destroyed by sacrifice.

यज्ञशिष्टामृतभुजो यान्ति ब्रह्म सनातनम् ।
नायं लोकोऽस्त्ययज्ञस्य कुतोऽन्यः कुरुसत्तम ॥ 4.31 ॥

Shlok 4.31: Those who eat the remains of the sacrifice go to the eternal Brahm. This is not a world for those who do not sacrifice; how then any other world, O best of the Kurus?

Commentary: Performing the sacrifices mentioned above, they eat prescribed food in a prescribed manner. Food so eaten is called ambrosia, *Amrit* (immortal). If they wish for *Moksha*, they go to Brahm in course of time, not at once, as we should understand for consistency's sake. They go to the eternal Brahm after attaining knowledge of the Self through purification of the mind by performing the above sacrifices. He who does not like sacrifice or perform any of these is not fit even for this miserable world. How then can he hope to get a better world than this? This verse has laid stress on sacrifice to attain the bliss of the Supreme Being.

एवं बहुविधा यज्ञा वितता ब्रह्मणो मुखे ।
कर्मजान्विद्धि तान्सर्वानेवं ज्ञात्वा विमोक्ष्यसे ॥ 4.32 ॥

Shlok 4.32: Many types of sacrifices or *yagyas* are described in the Vedas. Know that all of them are the action of body, mind and senses prompted by the forces of Nature. Understanding this, one shall attain Nirvan or salvation.

Commentary: Thus various sacrifices, mentioned as above, are spread out in the mouth of Brahm, i.e. are known from the Vedas through such passages as the following: 'We sacrifice *Pran* in speech.' Keep in mind that all are not born of the Self, for the Self is actionless. If you realise that 'these are not my actions, I am actionless, I am unconcerned,' you will be released, by this right knowledge, from evil, from the bond of worldly life. In order to attain salvation, spiritual discipline or sacrifice should be performed as a duty without any attachment and with full understanding that oneself is not the doer.

A superior spiritual practice

श्रेयान्द्रव्यमयाद्यज्ञाज्ज्ञानयज्ञः परन्तप ।
सर्वं कर्माखिलं पार्थ ज्ञाने परिसमाप्यते ॥ 4.33 ॥

Shlok 4.33: Better than a sacrifice to the sacrifice of material wealth is a sacrifice of knowledge, O Scorcher of Enemies. All action without exception, O son of Pritha, culminates in knowledge.

Commentary: The wisdom-sacrifice is superior to the sacrifice of material wealth because Self-knowledge or devotion is the goal of all spiritual practices. The sacrifice performed with material objects produces material effects, whereas wisdom-sacrifice does not. For this reason wisdom-sacrifice is better than sacrifice of material wealth. For, wisdom, which is the means to *Moksha*, comprehends all action.

तद्विद्धि प्रणिपातेन परिप्रश्नेन सेवया ।
उपदेक्ष्यन्ति ते ज्ञानं ज्ञानिनस्तत्त्वदर्शिनः ॥ 4.34 ॥

Shlok 4.34: Therefore, know this that the sages who see the truth will show you the knowledge, due to your obeisance, inquiry and service.

Commentary: This is the only verse that emphasizes the need for a *Guru* and how one should approach a *Guru* with reverence and render service to him. One should question him to clarify one's doubts. In ancient India, questioning was widely encouraged. Many scriptures, the Geeta included, are in the form of questions and answers. The Upanishads are replete with examples of the question-answer format.

In the hoary Indian tradition, approaching a *Guru* with obedience, serving him in daily chores, most often living with him in an *ashram* (hermitage) are the steps necessary for the advancement of learning. In the controlled atmosphere of an *ashram*, not only is the disciple easily disciplined with regular habits, but the master also has an opportunity to carefully scrutinise the behaviour of the disciple and prescribe specific instructions. Such training is essential for *Chitta Shuddhi* and to cleanse bad habits and retrogressive thought-patterns. It should be noted that such training can be imparted to only a few at a time and therefore, modern ashrams with hundreds of disciples serve only to remind one of bureaucratised academic departments.

In this age too many bogus or the fake *Gurus* are available to teach or just give a *Mantra* for a price. These fake *Gurus* are nothing but merchants of *mantra*. They take money from disciples to fulfil their personal material needs without giving the true knowledge of the Supreme Being. A *Guru* is one who imparts true knowledge and complete understanding of the Absolute and the temporal. A Self-realized *Guru* is a Self-realized master mentioned in this verse here. A Self-realized *Guru* helps the devotee maintain God-consciousness all the time by his or her own intrinsic spiritual power. God is the Divine *Guru*.

When the mind and intellect are purified, Supreme Lord, the divine *Guru*, reflects Himself in the inner psyche of a devotee and sends a Guru or a realized Guru to him or her. A real *Guru* is a giver. He never asks any money or a fee from a disciple because he depends on God only. A real *Guru* would not ask anything from a disciple for personal or even for organization-al gain. However, a disciple is obliged to do the best he or she can to help the cause of the *Gurus*. It is said that one should not accept any fee from a pupil without giv-ing full instructions and understanding of the Absolute, divine kinetic energy (*Maya*), temporal material Nature, and the living entity.

यज्ज्ञात्वा न पुनर्मोहमेवं यास्यसि पाण्डव ।
येन भूतान्यशेषेण द्रक्ष्यस्यात्मन्यथो मयि ॥ 4.35 ॥

Shlok 4.35: After knowing the transcendental science, O son of Pandu, you shall not again become confused like this. With this eye of knowledge you shall see all in your own Self and thus within Me, the Supreme Self.

Commentary: Having obtained the wisdom imparted by them, you will not be again subject to confusion as you are at the moment. By this wisdom you will also immediately perceive all beings, from Brahm (the Creator) down to grass, in your own Self. You will then realize that 'these beings exist in Me.' You will also see them all in Me, Vasudev. The same life-force of the Supreme Being reflects in all living beings to support and activate them. Therefore, we are all part and parcel of the cosmic energy of Brahm, the Self, and connected with each other. At the dawn of enlightenment, one merges with the Absolute, and all diversities appear as nothing but the expansion of the higher Self.

अपि चेदसि पापेभ्यः सर्वेभ्यः पापकृत्तमः ।
सर्वं ज्ञानप्लवेनैव वृजिनं संतरिष्यसि ॥ 4.36 ॥

Shlok 4.36: Even if you are the greatest evil-doers of all sinners, you will cross over all wickedness simply by using the boat of knowledge.

यथैधांसि समिद्धोऽग्निर्भस्मसात्कुरुतेऽर्जुन ।
ज्ञानाग्निः सर्वकर्माणि भस्मसात्कुरुते तथा ॥ 4.37 ॥

Shlok 4.37: The fire of knowledge reduces all Karma to ashes, O Arjun, same as the blazing fire reduces wood to ashes.

Commentary (Shlokas 4.36-4.37): With the help of boat of this knowledge one can cross the ocean of sin. Just as a well-kindled fire reduces fuel to ashes, so does the fire of wisdom reduce all actions to ashes, i.e. it renders them impotent. The fire of wisdom cannot indeed literally reduce actions to ashes as fire reduces fuel to ashes. Accordingly we should understand that right knowledge is the cause which renders all actions impotent. Know the Truth, and Truth shall make you free from bondage. The fire of Self-knowledge burns all accumulated (*Sanchit*) *Karma* or the total Cosmic debt– the root cause of the soul's transmigration– just as fire instantly burns a huge pile of cotton.

Karma produces body, and body generates new Karma. Thus, the cycle of birth and death continues indefinitely. Only selfless service can break this cycle, and selfless service is not possible without Self-knowledge. Thus, transcendental knowledge breaks the bonds of Karma and leads to salvation. This knowledge does not manifest to a sinful person– or to any person whose time to receive the spiritual knowledge has not come. Loss and gain, life and death, fame and infamy lie in the hands of one's Karma. Fate is all-powerful. This being so, one should neither be angry nor blame anybody. People know virtue and vice, but one's choice is ordained by fate or Karmic footprints because the mind and intellect are con-trolled by fate. When success does not come in spite of best efforts, it may be concluded that fate precedes endeavour.

Self-knowledge is automatically revealed to a *Karmayogi*

न हि ज्ञानेन सदृशं पवित्रमिह विद्यते ।
तत्स्वयं योगसंसिद्धः कालेनात्मनि विन्दति ॥ 4.38 ॥

Shlok 4.38: There is nothing on earth equal in purity to wisdom. He who becomes perfected by Yog finds this of himself, in his self, in course of time.

Commentary: Verily, there exists no purifier equal to wisdom. The seeker of *Moksha* who has perfected and regenerated himself by Yog– by *Karmayog* and by *Samadhiyog*– will after a long practice, himself find spiritual wisdom in himself.

When knowledge is gained, all ignorance is removed and what was earlier obscure becomes clear. A person who has attained knowledge has complete control over his desires and his mind rests in God. There is nothing on the earth equal in purity to true knowledge. The intense fire of devotion to God burns all selfish *Karmas* and purifies and illuminates the mind and intellect just as sunlight illumines the earth. True knowledge of the Self is automatically reflected in a pure consciousness (*Chitta*). *Karmayog* cleanses the dirt of selfishness from the mind and prepares it to receive Self-knowledge. Selfless service (*Karmayog*) and Self-knowledge are thus the two wings to take one to salvation.

श्रद्धावाँल्लभते ज्ञानं तत्परः संयतेन्द्रियः ।
ज्ञानं लब्ध्वा परां शान्तिमचिरेणाधिगच्छति ॥ 4.39 ॥

Shlok 4.39: The man with *Shraddha*, the devoted, the master of one's senses attains (this) knowledge. Having gained this knowledge, one quickly attains the Supreme Peace.

Commentary: Here is a practical lesson for attaining wisdom and supreme peace. The man of unflinching faith, who has mastered his senses, attains wisdom. Having gained wisdom, he immediately attains the state of supreme peace. The Lord says that one should have faith in what is told by the Guru or master or the Lord in the Geeta. The Supreme peace leads to Supreme Joy—Bliss or Anand with further efforts.

Only a man of firm faith can obtain wisdom. But he may be slow because it is enjoined that he should ever be intently devoted to the means of obtaining wisdom, such as constant devotion to the teachers (*Gurus*). A man of faith and devotion may not have mastery over the senses; since it is also enjoined that he should withdraw his senses away from their engrossment in objects. Such a man of faith, devotion and self-control is sure to obtain wisdom.

अज्ञश्चाश्रद्दधानश्च संशयात्मा विनश्यति ।
नायं लोकोऽस्ति न परो न सुखं संशयात्मनः ॥ 4.40 ॥

Shlok 4.40: The ignorant, the man without *Shraddha*, and the disbeliever (atheist) go to destruction. The doubting self has neither this world, nor the next, nor happi-ness.

Commentary: The man who has no faith in the teachings and the words of his Guru, and the man whose mind is full of doubts are ruined. No doubt the ignorant and the faithless are ruined, but not to the same extent as a man of doubting mind. He is the most sinful of all. Even this world which is common to all men is not won by a sceptic, nor the other world, nor happiness.

Both transcendental knowledge and *Karmayog* are needed

योगसंन्यस्तकर्माणं ज्ञानसञ्छिन्नसंशयम् ।
आत्मवन्तं न कर्माणि निबध्नन्ति धनंजय ॥ 4.41 ॥

Shlok 4.41: O Dhananjay, works do not bind him who has renounced all works by Yog, who has destroyed all doubt by wisdom and who ever possesses his soul.

Commentary: The above verse implies that all bondage and all doubts are removed through *Yog*. He who sees the Supreme Being renounces all actions– *Dharma* and *Adharma*– by virtue of *Yog* or knowledge of the Supreme Being, he attains this stage when his doubt has been torn asunder by the realization of the oneness of the Self with the God. As he traces all actions to the interactions of the energies (*Gunas*), actions do not bind him; they do not produce any effects (good or bad) in the case of him who, in virtue of his *Yog*, has renounced all actions and is ever watchful over his self.

तस्मादज्ञानसंभूतं हृत्स्थं ज्ञानासिनात्मनः ।
छित्त्वैनं संशयं योगमातिष्ठोत्तिष्ठ भारत ॥ 4.42 ॥

Shlok 4.42: Therefore take up the sword of wisdom, O Arjun, and cleave asunder this self-doubt that has arisen out of ignorance and made its dwelling in the heart; be firm in *Yog* and arise, O descendant of Bharat.

Commentary: Doubt is most sinful. It is born of ignorance and lies in the *Buddhi*. Finish it by wisdom, by right knowledge of the Self. Arjun's doubt here is about the Self. If Arjun could ever think that one man's doubt is ever to be finished by another, then the Lord might say 'destroy your doubt' as opposed to other's doubt. Even if Arjun has been asked to finish the doubt concerning the Self, it implies also that the doubt is one which is cherished by Arjun. Knowledge is destructive of all evil, such as grief, folly, and the like. Having thus finished doubt, the cause of your ruin, applies yourself to *Karmayog*, the means of acquiring right knowledge. Now arise and fight, O Descendant of Bharat.

(**Note:** This Discourse has dealt with various forms of sacrifices or restraints relating to functions of different sensory organs (i.e. five bio-impulses). Sri Krishna's preaching to Arjun about the mechanism of surrendering to the Self by self is in fact humanly not possible. Such a quality in man is a kind of divine wisdom which was possessed by Sri Krishna alone. The whole exercise relating to restrain over usual sensory functions and get rid of attachments sounds very philosophical, weird and unworkable for a worldly man. It is highly impractical because a man who is living in this world cannot be absolutely free from the fetters of this world. To live in the human world and yet feel not living herein simply leads a person to a state of abnormality. Even in the Mahabharat not a single character can be described to have achieved this state of mind. Every character is known for some sort of human attributes, weaknesses or traits. Had there been any key character exercising full control over his senses on the side of Kauravas, there would not have occurred an all-out battle of Mahabharat.)

OM TAT SAT

Discourse - 5

Karma-Sannyas Yog: Yog of Action and Renunciation

In this Discourse Lord Krishna delineates the concepts of action with detachment and renunciation in action explaining that both are a means to the same goal. Here He explains how salvation is attained by the pursuance of these paths. Arjun wants to know conclusively which is superior, the path of action or the path of renunciation of action. The Lord says that both the paths lead to the highest goal of God-realization, but the path of Karmayog is superior. Actually there is no real difference between the two.

Krishna explains that perfection can be attained and one can be established in the *Atman* only after the mind has been purified through the performance of selfless action. The Karmayogi who is aware of the *Atman* and who is constantly engaged in action knows that although the intellect, mind and senses are active, he does not do anything. He is a spectator of everything. He dedicates all his actions to the Lord and thus abandons attachment, ever remaining pure and unaffected. He surrenders himself completely to the Divine Shakti. Having completely rooted out all desires, attachments and the ego, he is not born again.

The sage who has realized Brahm and is always absorbed in It does not have any rebirth. Such a sage sees Brahm within and without– within as the static and transcendent Brahm, and without as the entire universe. He sees the one Self in all beings and creatures– in a cow, an elephant, and even in a dog and an outcaste. He is ever free from joy and grief and enjoys eternal peace and happiness. He does not depend upon the senses for his satisfaction. On the other hand the enjoyments of the senses are generators of pain. Sri Krishna reminds Arjun that desire is the main cause of pain and suffering. It is the cause of anger. Therefore, the *Sannyasi* should try to get rid of his desire and anger if he is to reach the Supreme.

(**Note:** Lots of religious or spiritual people in India tend to unduly stress the exalted view of separation or isolation of individual from society and try to link up individual with God through the philosophical notions of soul and Brahm with respect to salvation. Persons with such an escapist view of life tend to lead the life of a *Sannyasi*, saint, recluse, beggar and pseudo god and goddess and prefer to reside in a make-shift hut, *Ashram*, temple, mountain cave, forest and huts on river banks, although such life is a kind of burden for others in society. Attainment of *Moksha*, the purpose or relevance of which is not really understandable to the most, is considered to be the highest goal of life in Hinduism.)

Arjun asked:

संन्यासं कर्मणां कृष्ण पुनर्योगं च शंससि ।
यच्छ्रेय एतयोरेकं तन्मे ब्रूहि सुनिश्चितम् ॥ 5.1 ॥

Shlok 5.1: O Krishna, You praise the path of transcendental knowledge, and also the path of selfless service (*Karmayog*). Tell me decisively which is the better one of these?

Commentary: In Discourse- 4 Sri Krishna has spoken of the desertion of all actions and He also exhorted Arjun to engage in the performance of action. Owing to the mutual contradiction between these two injunctions, action or renunciation, as they cannot be followed by the same individual at the same time. Hence Arjun asks Sri Krishna to indicate decisively as to which of the two is better, performance of (prescribed) actions or renunciation of those actions.

Renunciation means complete renouncement of doership, ownership, and motive behind an action, not the renunciation of work or worldly objects. Renunciation comes only after the dawn of Self-knowledge. Therefore, the words 'renunciation' and 'Self-knowledge' are used interchangeably in the Geeta. Renunciation is considered to be the goal of life. Selfless service *(Seva, Karmayog)* and Self-knowledge are the necessary means to achieve the goal. A true *Sannyasi* is one who surrenders all actions and possessions– including body, mind, and thought– to the service of the Supreme.

Karmayog suits the ignorant better than *Sannyas*

Lord Krishna said:

संन्यासः कर्मयोगश्च निःश्रेयसकरावुभौ ।
तयोस्तु कर्मसंन्यासात् कर्मयोगो विशिष्यते ॥ 5.2 ॥

Shlok 5.2: Both renunciation and the performance of action lead to freedom. Of these, performance of action is superior to the renunciation of action.

Commentary: The renunciation of action here involves renunciation of selfish action which leads to bondage. According to the Geeta, a true worker who works without attachment and desire for fruits of action is a true renouncer as he does his work in a detached spirit.

Sannyas and *Karmayog*, renunciation of actions and performance of actions, both lead to the liberation or the highest bliss. Yet of these, performance of action is better than renunciation of action without the knowledge of the Self. However, it will be seen later that renunciation of action with the knowledge of the Self is decidedly superior to performance of action without such knowledge.

Lord Krishna clearly states that one should perform actions but without attachment to the fruits of actions– in the spirit of *Karmayog. Sannyasis* or monks retiring into forests/caves may give up actions, but they should totally eschew worldly desires. If one holds desires in the mind but acts as renunciant while abstaining from performing actions, he is a hypocrite. Both *Karmayog* and *Tyag* (renunciation) lead to liberation. But for householders, the path of *Karmayog* is easier and should be followed.

ज्ञेयः स नित्यसंन्यासी यो न द्वेष्टि न काङ्क्षति ।
निर्द्वन्द्वो हि महाबाहो सुखं बन्धात्प्रमुच्यते ॥ 5.3॥

Shlok 5.3: Beyond dualities (conflicting aspects of personality), O strong-armed (Arjun), he (a real devotee, a true *Yogi*, an ideal-adhered person) is happily released from bondage.

Commentary: A person should be considered a true *Sannyasi,* who has neither attachment nor aversion for anything. Being free from the pairs of opposites, he is easily set free from bondage. The *Sannyasi* or *Karmayogi* who neither hates pain and the objects causing pain, nor desires pleasure and the objects causing pleasure, should be known as a perpetual renouncer (*Sannyasi),* though he is engaged in action. Likes and dislikes, gain and loss, honour and dishonour, praise and censure, success and failure, joy and sorrow and similar other pairs of opposites are the attitudes of mind by which it gains life's experiences. The *Karmayogi*, a true worker, is known as a *Nitya Sannyasi* or a true renouncer, for he does his work in a detached spirit without being influenced by the pairs of opposites. A man does not become a *Sannyasi* by merely giving up actions due to laziness, ignorance, some family quarrel or calamity or unemployment. A true *Sannyasi* is one who has neither attachment nor aversion to anything. Physical desertion of objects is no renunciation at all. What is needed is the desertion of egoism and desires.

Sankhya **and** ***Yog*** **lead to the same goal**

सांख्ययोगौ पृथग्बालाः प्रवदन्ति न पण्डिताः ।
एकमप्यास्थितः सम्यगुभयोर्विन्दते फलम् ॥ 5.4 ॥

Shlok 5.4: Children, not the wise, speak of *Sankhya* (knowledge) and performance of action, as distinct. He who is truly established in one, gains the fruits of both.

Commentary: This verse clarifies that there is no contradiction between the paths of *Sankhya* (knowledge) and performance of action. There are two ways of making an ordinary action into a divine action of dedication and worship, viz 1. By renouncing the idea of agency or doership in every action or 2. By performing actions without any worry for their fruits and maintaining equanimity in success and failure. The former is called *Sankhya* method and the latter is *Karmayog*. The Lord says that only the ignorant people (here referred to as children) who have no knowledge of the Self find a contradiction between the two methods. But the wise who have lived through either of the paths say that both the paths lead to the same goal, viz liberation or God consciousness.

यत्सांख्यैः प्राप्यते स्थानं तद्योगैरपि गम्यते ।
एकं सांख्यं च योगं च यः पश्यति स पश्यति ॥ 5.5 ॥

Shlok 5.5: The state (of liberation) reached by the *Sankhyas* (*Gyani*) is reached by the *Yogis* (*Karmayogis*) also. He truly 'sees', who 'sees' *Sankhya* (knowledge) and *Yog* (performance of action) as one.

Commentary: Sri Krishna emphasizes that Sankhyas are those who are devoted to knowledge and have renounced the world. They reach the state called *Moksha*. The same state is reached by Yogis also, but indirectly, through the attainment of true knowledge and renunciation, by those who perform their duties as a means of attaining knowledge, dedicating them to the Ishvar, and having no selfish end in view.

It is to be noted that Karmayogis perform actions, surrendering the result to God, attain purity of mind and thus qualify themselves for the path of knowledge i.e. Sankhya, the path of knowledge, through which the final experience of Bliss is achieved. Thus both ultimately produce the same result, viz liberation through Self-Knowledge. That man sees rightly who sees that Sankhya and Yog are one, as leading to an identical result.

Karmayog is a means to *Sannyas*

संन्यासस्तु महाबाहो दुःखमाप्तुमयोगतः ।
योगयुक्तो मुनिर्ब्रह्म नचिरेणाधिगच्छति ॥ 5.6 ॥

Shlok 5.6: But renunciation of action (the renunciation of doership and ownership), O Mighty-armed, is hard to attain to without performance of action; the man of meditation, purified by devotion to action, quickly goes to Brahm.

Commentary: The Lord says that the true renouncer is not the one who remains completely inactive but one whose work is done in a spirit of detachment. Renunciation is a mental attitude, the casting off all sorts of desire in work; true work is work without any desire. Selfless service (Karmayog) provides the preparation, discipline, and purification necessary for renunciation. Self-knowledge is the upper limit of Karmayog, and renunciation of doership and ownership is the upper limit of Self-knowledge. A person purified by the performance of selfless action attains Brahm. One who is engaged in selfless and unattached activities is called a Muni (sage). He who is actively attached to an Ideal goes soon towards the eternal.

A sage's actions do not affect him

योगयुक्तो विशुद्धात्मा विजितात्मा जितेन्द्रियः ।
सर्वभूतात्मभूतात्मा कुर्वन्नपि न लिप्यते ॥ 5.7 ॥

Shlok 5.7: With the mind purified by devotion to performance of action, and the body conquered, and senses subdued, one who realizes one's self, as the self in all beings, though acting, is not tainted.

Commentary: Sri Krishna states that one who is established in *Karmayog* gets his intellect purified which reduces mental disturbance or anxiety caused by desires from within. With the selfless action and no anxiety for the fruits, his intellect becomes immune from disturbances which are reflected in his mind.

When a man gains inward peace at mental level, it becomes easy for him to control his sense organs from his tendency to run after sense objects. A person who controls his body, mind and intellect in this manner is qualified for the highest meditation because all the stumbling blocks for purposeful meditation arise from worldly desires. This realization of the Self is complete and not partial. He sees the divinity of the Self as all pervading. He finds divinity everywhere all times.

When an individual after achieving the inner change comes to realize the Infinite Divinity and performs actions in the world, his actions cannot have any reactions on him because no sense of ego is left in him. This verse highlights that it is the desire-driven egocentric activities which create passions in the intellect which block the discriminative power to experience one's own essential nature of Eternal Divinity.

A sage's actions are really no actions

नैव किंचित्करोमीति युक्तो मन्येत तत्त्ववित् ।
पश्यञ्शृण्वन्स्पृशंजिघ्रन्नश्नन्गच्छन्स्वपन्श्वसन् ॥ 5.8 ॥
प्रलपन्विसृजन्गृह्णन्नुन्मिषन्निमिषन्नपि ॥
इन्द्रियाणीन्द्रियार्थेषु वर्तन्त इति धारयन् ॥ 5.9 ॥

Shlokas 5.8-5.9: 'I do nothing at all', thus should the knower of truth think, steadfast– though seeing, hearing, touching, smelling, eating, going, sleeping, breathing, speaking, letting go, holding, opening and closing the eyes– convinced that it is the

senses that move among these objects.

Commentary: A man of wisdom will not have any egoistic view about the general, natural or unavoidable activities of life such as eating, sleeping, breathing, speaking, closing and opening of eyes, etc. He remains as a witness to all the activities of the senses, endowed with the knowledge of the actionless Self, with an 'I do nothing at all' feeling. He identifies himself with the Self and sees inaction in action, for he realizes that in all works the senses occupy themselves with their objects and the Self remains inactive. He may be said to have renounced action, for he sees no action as performed by himself.

Senses need not be subdued if the activities of the senses are spiritualized by perceiving that all work, good or bad, is done by the powers of God. The liberated sage always remains only as a witness to the activities of the senses, as he identifies himself with the Self. This approach to life and activities, however, is very difficult and highly impractical in the real life. A human being cannot behave like a robot.

A *Karmayogi* works for God

ब्रह्मण्याधाय कर्माणि संगं त्यक्त्वा करोति यः ।
लिप्यते न स पापेन पद्मपत्रमिवाम्भसा ॥ 5.10 ॥

Shlok 5.10: Just as a lotus leaf remains unwetted and unsullied by the surrounding water, a person who dedicates his actions to Brahm and performs them without attachment is not smeared by sin.

Commentary: The Yogi lives in the world of objects with perfect detachment like the lotus leaf found in the water without getting itself wet. The sage lives in the world of objects detaching himself from his own perceptions of the world, likes and dislikes, etc. A Karmayogi does not work with selfish motives and therefore does not incur any sin. Selfless service is always sinless. Selfishness is the source of sin. One becomes happy, peaceful, purified, and enlightened by performing one's prescribed duties as an offering to God while remaining detached inwardly.

A life of detachment where one renounces the sense of doership is not easy to attain. One should be clear that total detachment is impossible for the human mind. So long as there is a mind it has to attach itself with something because that is its nature. The only practical way of achieving detachment, therefore, is to disassociate the mind from the unreal and attach it to the Real.

कायेन मनसा बुद्ध्या केवलैरिन्द्रियैरपि ।
योगिनः कर्म कुर्वन्ति सङ्गं त्यक्त्वात्मशुद्धये ॥ 5.11 ॥

Shlok 5.11: Devotees, on the path of work, perform actions, only with body, mind, senses and the senses and intellect, without attachment for the purification of the heart.

Commentary: The Karmayogis always utilize their organs of action, knowledge, mind and intellect renouncing all attachments. The sage remains as if he were a mere observer of all that is happening around him. The *Karmayogis* are those who are devoted to the path of action, free from egoism and selfishness, who work for the purification of their hearts without any attachment to the results of their actions and who dedicate all their actions to the Lord as their offering.

युक्तः कर्मफलं त्यक्त्वा शान्तिमाप्नोति नैष्ठिकीम् ।
अयुक्तः कामकारेण फले सक्तो निबध्यते ॥ 5.12 ॥

Shlok 5.12: A *Karmayogi* attains supreme peace by abandoning attachment to the fruits of work, while others who are attached to the fruits of work become bound by work with a personal motive.

Commentary: A Karmayogi is one who does actions for the sake of the Lord without any expectation of result and who considers all his actions as offerings to the Lord only without any intent of personal gains attains the peace called *Moksha*. Steadfastness is achieved through the following four stages of development, viz 1. purity of the mind; 2. attainment of knowledge; 3. renunciation of all actions; and 4. devotion to knowledge.

Peace is not a product of external origin but it is a mental condition in an individual when he is not agitated by any kind of disturbing thoughts. Peace is an unbroken feeling of joy and a symbol of an integrated personality. Sri Krishna says that this can be brought about through selfless actions undertaken in a spirit of Yagya. When a worker renounces his egocentric sense of agency and desire for the fruits of his actions he immediately becomes an integrated personality and experiences peace.

The one who is unbalanced or unharmonized, who is motivated by desire and attachment to the fruits of actions and who is full of egoism and sense of agency, gets himself bound and tortured by the reactions of his own actions.

The blissful embodied life of a sage

सर्वकर्माणि मनसा संन्यस्यास्ते सुखं वशी।
नवद्वारे पुरे देही नैव कुर्वन्न कारयन् ॥ 5.13 ॥

Shlok 5.13: The subduer (of the senses), having renounced all actions by discrimination rests happily in the city of nine gates, neither acting nor causing to act.

Commentary: *Sannyas* is not a physical escape from the real life situation, it is, in fact, a complete mental withdrawal from things which have got pure worldly significance. It is a state of mind and not an external behaviour. Therefore, the person who has brought all his sense cravings under perfect control and renounced all his egocentric desires is a real *Sannyasin.* Only then he comes to live in peace, joy and contentment in the city of nine gates. The human body has been called the City of Nine Gates (or openings) in the scriptures. The nine openings are: two openings each for the eyes, ears, and nose; and one each for the mouth, anus, and urethra. The Lord of all beings and the universe who resides in this city along with the individual soul or the living entity (*Jeev)* is called the Spiritual Being (*Purush*) performing and directing all actions. Sri Krishna says that such a *Sannyasi* remains unaffected, unattached and without any agitation. Hence, he neither acts nor causes others to act.

Nature is the source of activity

न कर्तृत्वं न कर्माणि लोकस्य सृजति प्रभुः ।
न कर्मफलसंयोगं स्वभावस्तु प्रवर्तते ॥ 5.14 ॥

Shlok 5.14: The Lord of the world does not act on our behalf, nor does He create actions or the conjunction of an action with its fruit; it is only the innate nature that operates.

Commentary: This verse gives some idea about the notion of God.

But the idea stated here is a description of the relationship between the Self and the not-Self, the *Atman* and the matter. The Supreme Self *(Prabhu)* neither creates any sense of agency nor does it initiate any action. He does not match every action with its corresponding fruit. The beneficiary of the fruits and the performer of actions in us is the ego and not the *Atman* or the Self. The Self becomes an actor performing all actions only when it gets conditioned by *'Swabhava'*-nature or the Divine *Maya* made up of the three *Gunas*. The Self comes under the control of *Maya* and regards itself as acting and enjoying the fruits of action. As long as the Self remains identified with *Maya* it is bound. But when it detaches itself from *Maya* it becomes free. They have no relevance from the standpoint of the Supreme Lord. It is the *Prakriti* or nature that does everything. Though God is the Supreme Authority, all beings always remain under the full control of *Maya* or the Nature. God is not to be held responsible for anything, good or bad, in the life of individual beings.

Wisdom and foolishness

नादत्ते कस्यचित्पापं न चैव सुकृतं विभुः ।
अज्ञानेनावृतं ज्ञानं तेन मुह्यन्ति जन्तवः ॥ 5.15 ॥

Shlok 5.15: The Omnipresent takes note of the merit or demerit of none. Knowledge is enveloped in ignorance, hence do beings get deluded.

Commentary: God does not punish or reward anybody. We ourselves do this by the misuse or the right use of our own power of reasoning and free will. Bad things happen to good people to make them better.

When the sun light passes through a plane glass it comes out clearly but if it passes through a prism it emerges as seven colours which are part and parcel of the same sun light. Similarly the Self passing through Knowledge emerges out as the Self which is all-pervading. But when the same Self passes through ignorance, i.e. body, mind and intellect it gets itself split up into the unending world of plurality. Through ignorance man separates himself from the Lord and comes under the spell of ego. Thus he thinks of himself as the agent of various works, good or evil and experiences pleasure and pain accordingly.

Where there is knowledge there is no place for ignorance and where there is ignorance knowledge cannot exist. So the statement that knowledge is enveloped by ignorance means that unveiling of truth is a process of removal of ignorance and not creation of knowledge and therefore it is only a re-discovery.

ज्ञानेन तु तदज्ञानं येषां नाशितमात्मनः ।
तेषामादित्यवज्ज्ञानं प्रकाशयति तत्परम् ॥ 5.16 ॥

Shlok 5.16: Transcendental knowledge destroys the ignorance of the Self and reveals the Supreme (Brahm), just as the sun reveals the beauty of objects of the world.

Commentary: Ignorance creates the egocentric conception which thrives in the body, mind and intellect and is the root cause of all sufferings. When this ignorance is wiped out by knowledge of the Self, the egocentricism ends and the Self becomes manifest just as the sun illuminates and reveals all the objects of the physical universe when the clouds surrounding it move away. Knowledge is the very faculty of knowing. So when the ego re-discovers the Self it becomes the Self. Therefore, the Self is awareness, consciousness or the Atman.

The sage has no rebirth

तद्बुद्धयस्तदात्मानस्तन्निष्ठास्तत्परायणाः ।
गच्छन्त्यपुनरावृत्तिं ज्ञाननिर्धूतकल्मषाः ॥ 5.17 ॥

Shlok 5.17: Persons whose intellect is fully absorbed in the Eternal Being, who are firmly devoted to the Supreme, who have God as their supreme goal and sole refuge, and whose impurities are destroyed by the knowledge of the Self, do not take rebirth.

Commentary: Persons merged in the Eternal Being fix their intellect on the Supreme Self. They feel and realize their identity with the Self. By constant meditation they get established in the Self. The whole world of names and forms cease to exist for them. They live in the Self alone. They rejoice in the Self alone. They are satisfied in the Self alone. Such men never return to this world as their sins or impurities (*Vasanas*) are removed by knowledge. The import of this verse is that Self-realization is the final experience in the process of evolution whereby the Soul of an illumined person does not return to this world to assume a physical body. He does not come again under the sway of *Maya.* In brief, those whose sins have been destroyed by wisdom go beyond the circularity of existence

The sage sees the one in all beings

विद्याविनयसम्पन्ने ब्राह्मणे गवि हस्तिनि ।

शुनि चैव श्वपाके च पंडिताः समदर्शिनः ॥ 5.18 ॥

Shlok 5.18: Wise men regard all beings as equal: a learned priest, a cow, an elephant, a rat, or a filthy, rat eating outcaste.

Commentary: The wise person looks upon a Brahman, endowed with learning and humility, a cow, an elephant, a rat, and a rat-eater with equal regard. In the society of those days, a learned priest belonging to the Brahmin caste was considered superior to others. A cow was always treated as a holy animal since it gives milk, which is converted into butter and ghee (clarified butter), which was used as a sacrificial offering in the fire during the Vedic rituals. An elephant was a means of attaining military superiority and maintained by the Kshatriyas or princely caste. A rat and an outcaste or untouchable who used to eat rat's meat were considered inferior beings. But for a wise person with Self-knowledge, all the four are equal. This equal-vision called *'samadrishti'* is indeed difficult to achieve for many seekers. But the Lord insists on this. This is a big lesson for all those modern days Hindus who practise casteism and sectarianism. There is no room for all such practices in the Geeta.

A Self-realized person does not consider any living entity different from all pervading Eternal Being. Such a person sees God everywhere, in everything, and in every being. After discovering the metaphysical truth, one looks at everything with reverence, compassion, and kindness because everything in the material world is a part and parcel of the cosmic body of Lord Krishna. The Self is not affected by any limiting factors as it is subtle, pure, formless and attributeless just as the sun's rays fall on the river Ganga, on the ocean and on the dirty drainage and yet the sun's purity and splendour are not spoilt by the quality of water on which its rays fall. The limiting adjuncts do not affect the Supreme Self just as the outer space is not affected by the pot, cloud, etc.

इहैव तैर्जितः सर्गो येषां साम्ये स्थितं मनः ।
निर्दोषं हि समं ब्रह्म तस्माद्ब्रह्मणि ते स्थिताः ॥ 5.19 ॥

Shlok 5.19: Everything has been accomplished in this very life by those, whose mind rests in evenness, since Brahm is even and is without imperfection: therefore, they indeed rest in Brahm.

Commentary: To have a feeling of equality for everybody is the greatest worship of God. Those who do not have such a feeling make discrimination. Therefore, the victims of injustice and discrimination should feel sorry for the discriminator and pray to the Lord for a change of the discriminator's heart rather than get upset, angry, or revengeful. The Lord says that a mortal who can maintain his equanimity under all conditions is indeed the one who rests in Brahm, i.e. aware of Brahm. Thus the Geeta is opposed to the system of inequality of all kinds.

Persons who have conquered their minds and live in perfect harmony in all conditions of life and its relationships are indeed aware of their identity with Brahm who is even, ever-perfect and uncontaminated though indwelling in all pure and impure bodies. Brahm is all pervading and homogeneous. Everything happens in it and nothing happens to it. Thus the Truth is changeless just as a river-bed remains motionless though water flowing on it is ever changing.

Characteristics of a man of perfection

न प्रहृष्येत्प्रियं प्राप्य नोद्विजेत्प्राप्य चाप्रियम् ।
स्थिरबुद्धिरसम्मूढो ब्रह्मविद् ब्रह्मणि स्थितः ॥ 5.20 ॥

Shlok 5.20: Whatever pleasures are born of worldly contact are sources of sorrow, they have a beginning and an end and no wise man delights in them.

Commentary: From this verse onwards Sri Krishna explains the characteristics of a man of perfection. A perfect man is characterized by a balanced intellect which refers to absence of egocentric influences. He is never deluded. He is one who has abandoned all actions as he rests in the Self. He is neither excited when he gets pleasant objects nor feels disappointed when he experiences unpleasant situation. This does not mean that he has no reactions at all. What he all means is that he remains balanced always with a sense of equipoise which cannot be shattered easily.

The sage's infinite joy

बाह्यस्पर्शेष्वसक्तात्मा विन्दत्यात्मनि यत्सुखम् ।
स ब्रह्मयोगयुक्तात्मा सुखमक्षयमश्नुते ॥ 5.21 ॥

Shlok 5.21: With the self unattached to external contacts, he finds the joy which is in the Self; with the Self engaged in the contemplation of Brahm he attains the endless happiness.

Commentary: He whose heart is unattached to external contact (with outside world) realises the happiness that is in the Self (Atman); being absorbed in Brahm by meditation, he attains to a state of eternal bliss. This conveys the Vedantic meaning of 'being absorbed in Brahm'– Imperishable Reality. This is the state for a *Gyani* to attain, as prescribed in the Upanishads. Brahm is often described as possessing three characteristics– *Satta, chitta and anada*. The happiness from the experiences of external objects is transitory, while the Bliss of Brahm is eternal. When the mind is not attached to the external objects of the senses, when one is deeply engrossed in the contemplation of the Self, one finds eternal peace within. Therefore, he who seeks for the endless joy of the Self should withdraw the senses from the momentary pleasure of external objects.

ये हि संस्पर्शजा भोगा दुःखयोनय एव ते ।
आद्यन्तवन्तः कौन्तेय न तेषु रमते बुधः ॥ 5.22 ॥

Shlok 5.22: O son of Kunti, whatever pleasures are born of worldly contact are sources of sorrow, they have a beginning and an end and no wise man delights in them.

Commentary: The wise constantly reflect on the futility of sensual pleasures that inevitably become the cause of misery; therefore, they do not become victims of sensual cravings. A human bcing always remains in search of happiness from the external objects. But he finds no permanent joy in them; rather, receives a lot of sorrows instead. The pleasures that are caused by contacts of the senses with sense-objects are only generators of pain, since those delights are caused by nescience (*Avidya*). One should, therefore, withdraw the senses from the sense objects which are not at all a source of permanent joy. One should fix the mind on the immortal, blissful Self within. The sense objects have a beginning and an end. The pleasure out of them is, therefore, momentary. One who has discrimination or knowledge of the Self will never rejoice in the objects of the senses.

The path of *Nirvan*

शक्नोतीहैव यः सोढुं प्राक्शरीरविमोक्षणात् ।
कामक्रोधोद्भवं वेगं स युक्तः स सुखी नरः ॥ 5.23 ॥

Shlok 5.23: One who is able to withstand the impulses arising from lust and anger before death is a *yogi* and a happy man.

Commentary: Desire (lust) and anger are powerful enemies of peace. It is extremely difficult to defeat them. One has to make strong efforts to demolish these enemies. He who has controlled desire and anger is the happiest man in the world. Desire is longing for a pleasant and agreeable object which gives pleasure when it is seen, heard or remembered. Anger is the feeling one gets when he finds obstacles in the way of getting the desired objects. The greater the desire for an object the greater will be the anger against any obstacle that comes between the desirer and the objects desired. Lust and anger create a disturbance in mind accompanied by appropriate physical symbols. A real Yogi is the one who controls the impulses of desire and anger, destroys likes and dislikes and attains equanimity of mind by resting in the Self. He is always happy because he is neither desire nor hatred against external object.

योऽन्तःसुखोऽन्तरारामस्तथान्तर्ज्योतिरेव यः ।
स योगी ब्रह्मनिर्वाणं ब्रह्मभूतोऽधिगच्छति ॥ 5.24 ॥

Shlok 5.24: He who is ever happy within, who rejoices within, who is illumined within, such a Yogi attains absolute freedom or Moksha, himself becoming Brahm.

Commentary: It is obvious from the above verse that he who finds his happiness within, his joy within and likewise his light within, that again becomes divine and attains to the beatitude of God. A man of perfection does not get joy in the ordinary sensual objects of the world. Renouncing all these he reaches a state of bliss where there is no place for desire or anger, love or hatred. The Lord says such a man alone can be said to be happy. Such an individual who lives in the Self is the one who has known Brahm. He becomes a *Jeevanmukta*. The subsequent verse clarifies that this state is not a state of destruction but the positive one full of knowledge and Self-possession.

लभन्ते ब्रह्मनिर्वाणमृषयः क्षीणकल्मषाः ।
छिन्नद्वैधा यतात्मानः सर्वभूतहिते रताः ॥ 5.25॥

Shlok 5.25: With imperfections exhausted, doubts dispelled, senses controlled, engaged in the good of all beings, the *Rishis* attain absolute freedom.

Commentary: The holy men whose sins are finished, whose doubts are torn asunder, whose minds are disciplined and who rejoice in good to all creatures, attain to the beatitude of God. When a man of perfection brings his senses under control, his sinful mental impressions are cleared which were blocking his vision of the Self behind several doubts about the Reality. Knowledge of his real nature comes to dawn on him and he comes to rediscover himself as the Self. Having thus reached the goal of all evolution his duties till he leaves his mortal body will be to engage himself in the good of all beings. Thus *Lokaseva* becomes his obsession. To overcome the world is not to become other-worldly. It is not to evade social responsibilities.

कामक्रोधवियुक्तानां यतीनां यतचेतसाम् ।
अभितो ब्रह्मनिर्वाणं वर्तते विदितात्मनाम् ॥ 5.26 ॥

Shlok 5.26: Those who are free from lust and anger, who have subdued the mind and senses, and who have realized the existence of the Self, easily attain *Nirvan*.

Commentary: The Lord emphasizes the control of senses, mind and intellect, for only then can one overcome lust, anger and fear. Here is a perfect example of direct, practical instruction from the Lord. When the seeker exercises complete control over his lust and anger and can face all the threats coming from within and without, he knows the Self and gains the Bliss of Perfection both here and hereafter. Those who, renouncing all actions, remain steady in right knowledge obtain instant liberation. It has often been and will be declared by the Lord that *Karmayog*, which is performed in complete devotion to the Lord and dedicated to Him, leads to *Moksha* step by step: first the purification of the mind, then knowledge, then renunciation of all actions and lastly *Moksha* (liberation).

Realization of the Lord by *Dhyan-Yog*

स्पर्शान्कृत्वा बहिर्बाह्यांश्चक्षुश्चैवान्तरे भ्रुवोः ।
प्राणापानौ समौ कृत्वा नासाभ्यन्तरचारिणौ ॥ 5.27 ॥
यतेन्द्रियमनोबुद्धिर्मुनिर्मोक्षपरायणः ।
विगतेच्छाभयक्रोधो यः सदा मुक्त एव सः ॥ 5.28 ॥

Shlokas 5.27-28: Shutting out all external objects, fixing the vision between the eyebrows, making even the inward and the outward breaths moving within the nostrils, the sage who has controlled the sense, mind and understanding, who is intent on liberation, who has cast away desire, fear and anger, he is ever freed.

Commentary (Shlokas 5.27-5.28): These verses briefly describe the method of meditation along with some conditions which are required to be fulfilled. Liberation is the goal of meditation. This technique of meditation is further supplemented in Verse 6.10.

The external world of objects by itself cannot bring any disturbances unless one remains in touch with them through body, mind or intellect. But if we shut out external objects– not physically– but through discreet intellectual detachment at the mental plane, we shall discover in ourselves the necessary tranquillity for starting meditation. Then the concentration should be fixed at a central place between the eye brows so that the eye balls remain steady. This is followed by rhythmical breathing which makes the mind quiet and perfect harmony is developed in the system. These instructions relate to physical adjustments.

The sound and other sense-objects enter the mind within through the respective organs. These objects which are external are kept outside when a man does not think of them. A sage (*Muni*) is one who is given to contemplation (*Manan*) and who renounces all actions. Keeping the body in the posture described, he should always look up to *Moksha* as his supreme goal. When the sage leads constantly this kind of life, renouncing all, he is no doubt liberated: he has nothing else to do for liberation.

(**Note:** The invisible astral channels of flow of energy in the human body are called *Nadis*. When the cosmic currents– flowing through Nadis in the astral spinal cord– are separated by the opening of the main Sushumna Nadi by the practice of yogic techniques, breath flows through both nostrils with equal pressure; the mind calms down; and the field is prepared for deep meditation leading to trance.)

भोक्तारं यज्ञतपसां सर्वलोकमहेश्वरम् ।
सुहृदं सर्वभूतानां ज्ञात्वा मां शान्तिमृच्छति ॥ 5.29 ॥

Shlok 5.29: On knowing Me as the dispenser of *yagyas* and asceticism, as the Great Lord of all worlds, as the Friend of all beings, he attains Peace.

Commentary: I am Narayan, the Lord of all sacrifices and austerities, both as their author and as their *Devata* (i.e. as the God whose grace is sought by their means). I am the Friend of all, doing good to them without expecting any return for it. Lying in the heart of all beings, I am the dispenser of the fruits of all actions and the witness of all cognitions. On knowing Me, they attain peace, the cessation of all worries of worldly life.

The gist of this verse is that spiritual experience is to realize that the Self is the one great ruler within, who presides over all the activities within the body-politic and before whom the ego surrenders. Knowing Him to be none other than Sri Krishna, the individual reaches the goal of peace, the eternal Perfection.

(**Note:** Ideas or thought conveyed through this Discourse is highly impractical and unviable for individuals living in the modern world. One must recognize certain hard truths of life, as no action can be performed without any interest or purpose. All actions or activities have got some sorts of inherent or obvious interests in them. All non-intuitive works or activities have got action-orientation. Some people may live like ascetics or escapists for some time outside the society, but that cannot be practised by one and all, as that would lead to extermination of humanity after some time. Human beings have to work to meet the basic necessities of their life and those of their dependents and participate in the reproduce process for the furtherance of humanity. Such acts may cause conflict of interests among the people. All actions are bound to have some consequences, reactions or repercussions and at times unpleasant too. Krishna, Arjun and their kinsmen along with numerous others did not engage themselves in the war of Kurukshetra without any interest or purpose. There is nothing like purposeless action in real life. All such philosophical ideas most probably developed outside the battlefield and were inserted into the Geeta at some subsequent stage.

Furthermore, the teachings of the Geeta do not match with the events of real life as described in the Ramayan and the Mahabharat. The war of Mahabharat itself was fought for claiming share in the kingdom. One can easily imagine the philosophy of life emanating from a series of real life events from the perusal of Valmiki Ramayan which dated back to the period prior to the Mahabharat. Engagement of Ram and his younger brother Lakshman in the battle against certain evil doers or devils at the behest of sage Vishwamitra or against Ravan for restoration of Sita from the clutches of Ravan and other such instances as depicted in the treatise was not without any interest, purpose or consequences. Sita, Ram and Lakshman have been described as incarnation of gods and goddesses, but they had themselves not exhibited the standard of conduct for a Karmayogi as set in the Geeta. Hence, ordinary humans can never imagine meeting even a part of the given standard set for the *Sannaysi* concerning action without attachments.)

OM TAT SAT

Discourse - 6

Dhyanyog or Atmasanyam Yog: Yog of Meditation

Sri Krishna reiterates once again that the *Yogi* or *Sannyasi* is one who has renounced the fruits of actions, not the actions themselves. The performance of actions without considering their fruits brings about the purification of mind. Only a purified mind, a mind free from desires, can engage itself in constant meditation on the *Atman*. Desire gives rise to imagination or *Sankalp*, which drives the soul into the field of action. Therefore, none can realize permanent freedom and tranquillity of mind without renouncing desires.

It has been suggested that the lower self must be controlled by the higher Self. All the lower impulses of the body, mind and senses must be controlled by the power of the higher Self. Then the higher Self becomes one's friend. He, who has perfect control of the body, mind and senses and is united with God, sees God in all objects and beings. He sees inwardly that there is no difference between gold and stone, between friends and enemies, between the righteous and the unrighteous. He is perfectly harmonised. Sri Krishna has given various practical hints concerning the practice of meditation. The aspirant should select a secluded spot where there is no likelihood of disturbance. He should arrange his meditation seat properly and sit in a comfortable posture, with the head, neck and spine erect but not tensed. He should fix his purified mind on the *Atman* by concentrating between the eyebrows or on the tip of the nose.

A *Yogi* is advised to practise moderation in his daily activities– in eating, sleeping, recreation, etc. Extremes are to be avoided as they hamper the practice of meditation. Living a life of such moderation, and gathering up all his forces and directing them towards meditation upon the *Atman,* the aspirant gradually transcends the senses and intellect and merges himself in the blissful *Atman.* He finds that the bliss of the *Atman* is incomparable, that there is no gain greater than the Self. Having thus attained perfect union with the Self, the *Yogi* no more descends into ignorance or delusion. He does not relish any more the pleasures of the senses. Lord Krishna again emphasizes that the concentration of the mind on the *Atman* should be like a steady flame in a windless place. This ultimately leads to the vision of the Lord in all beings and creatures. Arjun is doubtful whether it is at all possible to engage the mind steadily on the higher Self, as its very nature seems to be one of restlessness. Krishna assures him that the practice can succeed through *Vairagya* (dispassion) and constant effort.

Arjun wishes to know the fate of the aspirant who fails to realize the Supreme in spite of his faith and sincerity. Krishna tells him that the accumulated power of his *Yogic* practices will assure him a better birth in the future, with more favourable conditions for *Sadhna.* The aspirant will then be compelled to carry on his *Yogic* practices with greater vigour and faith and will finally achieve God-realization. Krishna states that the *Yogi*– one who has attained union with the Supreme Lord– is superior to the ascetics, to the men of bookish knowledge and the men of action, as the latter have not transcended ignorance and merged in the Self.

Renunciation in action

Lord Krishna said:

अनाश्रितः कर्मफलं कार्यं कर्म करोति यः ।
स संन्यासी च योगी च न निरग्निर्न चाक्रियः ॥ 6.1 ॥

Shlok 6.1: He who does something that he ought to do with no concern for the fruit of his action is a real ascetic (*Sannyasi*); an ascetic is not a person who lights no fires or does not perform any rituals.

Commentary: A *Sannyasi* is the one who engages himself in noble works, renouncing both his sense of doership and attachment to the fruits of his action. *Sannyas* or renunciation has little to do with outward works. It is an inward state of mind. It is mental purity and intellectual equipoise. Arjun thought *Sannyas* as mere abandonment of all activities, symbolised here by the word 'fire'. To become a *Sannyasi*, it is not necessary to give up the daily sacrificial fire and other rituals. Action without any expectation of fruitful or rewarding outcome is a real *Karma* and person attaining this state is a real *Sannyasi.* Prima facie, it is easier said than done, but in reality it is a very difficult state of mind.

यं संन्यासमिति प्राहुर्योगं तं विद्धि पाण्डव ।
न ह्यसंन्यस्तसंकल्पो योगी भवति कश्चन ॥ 6.2 ॥

Shlok 6.2: O Pandav, renunciation (*Sannyas*) is the same as *Karmayog* because no one becomes a *Yogi* who has not renounced selfish motives.

Commentary: No one can become a *Karmayogi* who plans future actions and expects the fruits of such actions. Only a devotee who renounced the thoughts of fruits of his actions can become a *Yogi* of steady mind because the thoughts of fruits of actions always cause mental disturbances. *Sannyas,* i.e. renunciation consists in the accomplishment of the necessary action without an inward striving for reward. This is true *Yog*, firm control over oneself, complete self-possession. This verse says that disciplined activity (*Yog*) is just as good as renunciation or *Sannyas*. *Karmayog* practised without regard to the fruit of actions forms a stepping stone and an external aid to Dhyanyog or meditation.

People are often seen amassing huge wealth for themselves or their posterity, renunciation can hardly be the choice of life in normal circumstances for common people in the modern world. Had renunciation been so easy to practise, there would not have occurred the war of Kurukshetra.

आरुरुक्षोर्मुनेर्योगं कर्म कारणमुच्यते ।
योगारूढस्य तस्यैव शमः कारणमुच्यते ॥ 6.3 ॥

Shlok 6.3: For a person who wishes to attain purification of heart leading to concentration, action is said to be the means; but for

the person who has already attained such concentration, inaction is said to be the means.

Commentary: For a devotee *(Muni)* who has given up the fruit of action, and who wishes to attain to *Yog*, i.e. who has not already risen to it, who is unable to remain steady in Dhyanyog, action (*Karma)* is said to be the means of attaining his end. For the same devotee, on the other hand, when he has attained to *Yog*, quiescence, i.e. the abstaining from all action, is said to be the means (of attaining his end).

When the required amount of concentration is achieved and his mind conquered, his agitations get well under control. In that state of mental growth his mind thoroughly gets fixed in the Self. These two means are not contradictory. Selfless work is necessary for a beginner; but an advanced seeker needs more calmness and self-withdrawal for deep meditation to realize the Self. All his actions are then performed with perfect equanimity.

Who is *Yogi?*

यदा हि नेन्द्रियार्थेषु न कर्मस्वनुषज्जते ।
सर्वसंकल्पसंन्यासी योगारूढस्तदोच्यते ॥ 6.4 ॥

Shlok 6.4: When a man is truly not attached to sense objects or to actions, having renounced all *Sankalpas*, then he is said to have attained concentration.

Commentary: Sri Krishna explains that when a *Yogi*, keeping the mind steadfast, feels no attachment for the objects of the senses such as sound, nor thinks that he has to do any action considering it useless for him; and when he has learned to habitually renounce all *Sankalpas* which give rise to desires for objects of this world and of the next, then he is said to have become a *Yogrudh*, to be one who has attained to *Yog*. An expression like renouncing all *Sankalpas* implies that all desires as well as all actions are renounced.

उद्धरेदात्मनात्मानं नात्मानमवसादयेत् ।
आत्मैव ह्यात्मनो बन्धुरात्मैव रिपुरात्मनः ॥ 6.5 ॥

Shlok 6.5: Let a man uplift himself by himself; let him not degrade himself. He himself is his friend and foe.

Commentary: There is no enemy other than an uncontrolled mind in this world. Hence the emphasis is on the fact that he alone is the friend of himself. And he alone is the enemy of himself. Therefore, one should first try to control and conquer this enemy by regular practice of meditation with a firm determination and effort. All spiritual practices are aimed towards the conquest of the mind. Firm control of the mind and senses is known as *Yog.* Control of the mind and senses is called austerity and *Yog*. The purpose of meditation is to control the mind so that one can focus on God and live according to His instructions and will. The mind of a *Yogi* is under control; a Yogi is never under the control of the mind. The above verse teaches the way of self development which lies in self- effort. If we exercise self-control, the self becomes a friend, otherwise foe. This thought is further developed in the following verse.

बन्धुरात्मात्मनस्तस्य येनात्मैवात्मना जितः ।
अनात्मनस्तु शत्रुत्वे वर्तेतात्मैव शत्रुवत् ॥ 6.6 ॥

Shlok 6.6: For him who has conquered his lower self by the higher self, his self is a friend but who has not done so, the self acts like an enemy.

Commentary: The mind, indeed, is the cause of bondage as well as liberation of the living entity. The mind becomes the cause of bondage when controlled by modes of material Nature, and the same mind, when attached to the Supreme, becomes the cause of salvation. The mind alone is the cause of salvation as well as bondage of human beings. The mind becomes the cause of bondage when controlled by sense objects, and it becomes the cause of salvation when controlled by the intellect. Absolute control over mind and senses is a prerequisite for any spiritual practice for Self-realization. One who has not become the master of the senses cannot progress towards the goal of Self-realization. Therefore, after establishing control over the activities of the mind, one should take the mind away from the enjoyment of sensual pleasures and fix it on God. The mind is the ruler of the other five senses. One who becomes master of the mind becomes master of all the senses.

जितात्मनः प्रशान्तस्य परमात्मा समाहितः ।
शीतोष्णसुखदुःखेषु तथा मानापमानयोः ॥ 6.7 ॥

Shlok 6.7: One who has control over the lower self– the mind and senses– is tranquil in heat and cold, in pleasure and pain, in honour and dishonour, and remains ever steadfast with the Supreme Self.

Commentary: This verse explains what exactly is achieved in the state of mental equipoise called '*Yogrudh*'. When the stage of *Yogrudh* or the state of mental equipoise is reached, the mind is held steadfast in the contemplation of the Supreme and the seeker is capable of maintaining consistency of meditation in all circumstances, favourable and unfavourable.

The man of serenity remains unruffled in all circumstances and in all conditions. One can realize God only when the mind becomes tranquil and completely free from desires and dualities, such as pain and pleasure. However, people are rarely completely free from desires and duality. But one can become free from the bonds of desire and duality if one uses the mind and senses in the service of the Lord. Those who master their mind, they get the spiritual wealth of knowledge and bliss. Self can only be realized when the lake of the mind becomes still, just as the reflection of the moon is seen in a lake when the water is still.

(**Note:** In the modern world indifference or apathy to all kinds of events, circumstances or conditions is very hard to attain in real life. It is not feasible for a man to remain insensitive to everything. One may even run the risk of life. Nothing is possible or nothing can be attained, when there is no life.)

ज्ञानविज्ञानतृप्तात्मा कूटस्थो विजितेन्द्रियः ।
युक्त इत्युच्यते योगी समलोष्टाश्मकाञ्चनः ॥ 6.8 ॥

Shlok 6.8: A true *yogi* is saturated in science and spirituality. He is unwavering in his approach to life. He has full control over his senses. His greed is so much in control that for him a handful of clay, a piece of stone and a lump of gold are all alike.

Commentary: Sri Krishna says that a person is called *Yogi* whose self is satisfied with knowledge and wisdom, who remains unshaken, who has conquered the senses, and to whom a lump of earth, a piece of stone and gold are equal. If a person is self-controlled and serene and contemplates constantly on the nature of the Self in all circumstances in life soon gets full divine satisfaction and becomes an unshakeable *Yogi*.

A *Yogi* who is contented with wisdom and direct perception of Truth, who has conquered his senses and is ever undisturbed, to whom a lump of clay, a piece of stone and gold pieces are the same, he is *Yukta* —a saint of steady wisdom. It is stated that material objects have no attraction for such a *Yogi*. He is one who had conquered the senses: the first step to realising the Self. *A Yogi remains* unperturbed by things and happenings of the world and is, therefore, said to be equal-minded to the events of this changing world. Such a saint remains tranquil with equal mental vision in all conditions of life. To him a clod of mud, a stone and gold are all the same. Thus equanimity of mind is the touchstone of spiritual development.

सुहृन्मित्रार्युदासीनमध्यस्थद्वेष्यबन्धुषु ।
साधुष्वपि च पापेषु समबुद्धिर्विशिष्यते ॥ 6.9 ॥

Shlok 6.9: He is esteemed, who is of the same mind to the well-wishers, friends, foes, the indifferent, the neutral, the hateful, relatives, saints and sinners.

Commentary: A person who has equal regard for well-wishers, friends, enemies, the indifferent, the neutral, the hateful, relatives, the righteous and the unrighteous, excels. The Lord says that such a man of excellence regards all relationships with equal love and consideration irrespective of whether they are friends or foes or the indifferent or the neutral or the hateful or the nearest relations. He does not make any distinction between the righteous and unrighteous, the good and the bad. In realizing the Self in him, he sees unity in all diversities and observes a rhythm in the world outside.

The method by which one can attain this highest goal with an assured result is called meditation which is explained exhaustively in the following verses.

Techniques of meditation

योगी युञ्जीत सततमात्मानं रहसि स्थितः ।
एकाकी यतचित्तात्मा निराशीरपरिग्रहः ॥ 6.10 ॥

Shlok 6.10: Let the *Yogi* try constantly to concentrate his mind

(on the Supreme Self), remaining in solitude, living alone with the mind and body controlled, free from desire and greed.

Commentary: The emphasis here is on concentration and control of mind, abandoning desires and greed. It is said that the place of meditation should have the serenity, solitude, and spiritual atmosphere of odour-free, noise-free, and light-free caves of the Himalayas. Massive, gorgeous buildings with exquisite marble figures of celestial controllers are not enough. These often come at the expense of spirituality and help religious business only. Keeping the general readers of this book in mind, here an effort is made to throw some light on how *Yog* is or should be practised to connect oneself with the Supreme Self

There are eight steps of meditation based on Patanjali's **Yog Sutras**: (1) Moral restraints, (2) Regulative principles, (3) Right posture and *Yogic* exercises, (4) *Yogic* breathing, (5) Sense withdrawal, (6) Concentration, (7) Meditation, and (8) Trance or super-conscious state of mind.

One must follow these eight steps, one by one, under proper guidance to make progress in meditation. Use of breathing and concentration techniques without necessary purification of the mind and without sublimation of feelings and desires by moral conduct and spiritual discipline may lead to a dangerous, neurotic state of mind. Patanjali says: The sitting posture for meditation should be stable, relaxed, and comfortable for the individual's physical body. Yogic breathing is not the forcible– and often harmful– retention of breath in the lungs as is commonly misunderstood and wrongly practised.

When the body is super-charged by the huge reservoir of omnipresent cosmic current flowing through the medulla oblongata, the need for breathing is reduced or eliminated and the Yogi reaches the breathless state of trance, the last milestone of the spiritual journey. One does not live by food, water, and air alone, but by the cosmic energy that comes from God. The cord of breath ties the living entity (soul) to the body-mind complex. A Yogi unties the soul from the body and ties it with the Super-soul during the breathless state of trance.

The withdrawal of the senses from the sense-objects is a major obstacle in the attainment of the goal of a Yogi. When sense withdrawal has been accomplished, concentration, meditation, and *Samadhi* become very easy to master. The mind should be controlled and trained to follow the intellect rather than let it be drawn towards and controlled by gross sense objects, such as hearing, touch, sight, taste, and smell. The mind is restless by nature. Watching the natural flow of breath coming in and going out, and alternate breathing help to make the mind steady.

The two most common techniques of sense withdrawal are thus: (1) Focus your full attention on the point between the eyebrows. Perceive and expand a sphere of white, rotating light there, (2) Mentally chant a *Mantra* or any holy name of the Lord as quickly as possible for a long time and let the mind get completely absorbed into the sound of mental chanting until you do not hear the ticking sound of a nearby clock. The speed and loudness of mental chanting should be increased with the restlessness of the mind, and vice versa. In meditation, one may tap the power of subconscious mind to achieve a noble desired goal in life.

It may be noted that concentration on a particular part of a deity, on the sound of a *Mantra,* on the flow of breath, on various energy centres in the body, on the mid-brows, on the tip of the nose, or on an imaginary white light of God inside the heart, stills the mind and stops it from wandering.

शुचौ देशे प्रतिष्ठाप्य स्थिरमासनमात्मनः ।
नात्युच्छ्रितं नातिनीचं चैलाजिनकुशोत्तरम् ॥ 6.11 ॥

Shlok 6.11: (He should find for himself) a steady seat at a well-cleaned spot, neither too high nor very low, with grass of *Kush* and a deer-skin thereon and on that a piece of cloth,

तत्रैकाग्रं मनः कृत्वा यतचित्तेन्द्रियक्रियः ।
उपविश्यासने युञ्ज्याद्योगमात्मविशुद्धये ॥ 6.12 ॥

Shlok 6.12: he should concentrate, with his whole mind, on a single object; if he practices in this way, his mind will soon become pure.

Commentary (Shlokas 6.11-12): Sri Krishna now gives a complete and exhaustive explanation of the technique of meditation. The seat for practice of meditation should be in a clean place, the external conditions have a direct bearing on the human mind.

The *Yogi* should sit steady in his seat without moving his body in any direction since physical movements upset the mental concentration and inner equipoise. In order to get established in a firm posture, it would be advisable to sit in any comfortable position with the vertebral column erect, fingers interlocked and hands thrown in front. The seat of meditation should not be too high or too low. Too high a seat causes a sense of insecurity and too low a seat may cause bodily pains. The mattress of *Kusa*-grass on the ground covered by a deer-skin and a piece of cloth on top of it protects one from dampness, cold and heat.

Sitting properly by itself is not *Yog*. While proper physical condition is necessary for inducing right mental attitude for spiritual practices, by itself it cannot assure any spiritual self development. One should make the mind single pointed by subduing the faculty of imagination and activities of the sense organs. Keeping the mind contemplating on the Ultimate Self constantly is the inner Yog suggested here.

The effect of such meditation is inner purification. A purified mind is the one wherein there is no agitation and when the mind becomes truly steady and pure, it discovers its own Real Nature just like one understands himself by looking at his own image in a mirror.

Short meditation with full concentration is better than long meditation without concentration. Fixing the mind on a single object of contemplation for twelve (12) seconds, two and a half (2.5) minute, and half an hour is respectively known as concentration, meditation and trance. Meditation and trance are the spontaneous result of concentration. Meditation occurs when the mind stops oscillating off the point of concentration.

In the lower stage of trance (*Savikalp Samadhi*), the mind becomes so centred on a particular part of the deity– such as the face or the feet– that it forgets everything. This is like a dream in a wakeful state where one remains aware of one's mind, thoughts, and the surroundings. In the highest stage of trance (*Nirvikalp Samadhi*), the body becomes still and motionless, and the mind experiences various aspects of the Truth. The mind permanently loses its individual identity, the ego, and becomes one with the cosmic mind.

The super-conscious state of mind is the highest stage of trance. In this state of mind, the normal human consciousness becomes connected to (or overpowered by) cosmic consciousness; one reaches a thoughtless, pulseless, and breathless state and does not feel anything except peace, joy and supreme bliss. In the highest state of trance, the energy centre (*Chakra*) on the top of the head opens up; the mind is merged into the infinite; and there is no mind or thought, but only the feeling of His transcendental existence, awareness and bliss. A person who reaches this state is a true sage or *Yogi*.

समं कायशिरोग्रीवं धारयन्नचलं स्थिरः ।
सम्प्रेक्ष्य नासिकाग्रं स्वं दिशश्चानवलोकयन् ॥ 6.13 ॥

Shlok 6.13: Keeping himself steady, holding the trunk, the neck and the head in a straight line and motionless, fixing his eye on the tip of his nose, and looking not around.

Commentary: The Lord tells that the *Yogi* should firmly hold his body in such a way that his vertebral column is completely erect– the head, neck and the spinal column should be in a vertical position. Holding the body firmly means that it should not be moved in any direction although it has to be kept relaxed. Patanjali points out that the posture should be steady and pleasing so as to aid concentration. A right posture gives serenity of body. The body must be kept clean if the living image of God is to be imagined in it.

One should keep attention pinpointed and penetrating four inches deep between the eyebrows near the master gland– the pituitary. Fixing the gaze on the nose tip is one of the gestures of *Kriyayog* recommended by Swami Shivananda to awaken the *Kundalini* power located at the base of the spine. After a little practice each day, the eyes will become accustomed and slightly convergent and see the two sides of the nose. As you gaze at the nose tip, concentrate on the movement of breath through the nostrils. After ten minutes, close your eyes and look into the dark space in front of your closed eyes. If you see a light, concentrate on it because this light can completely absorb your consciousness and lead you to trance according to Yogic scriptures. The beginner should first practice fixing the gaze at the mid-eyebrows or at the cerebrum before learning to fix the gaze on the tip of the nose. The help of a teacher and use of a *Mantra* is strongly recommended.

Celibacy helps to still the mind and awaken the dormant *Kundalini*.

Celibacy and certain breathing exercises cleanse the subtle body. The subtle body is nourished by seminal and ovarian energy, just as the gross body needs food for nourishment. Sarada Ma once warned her disciples not to be intimate with persons of the opposite sex even if God came in that form. The role of celibacy in spiritual life is overlooked in the West because it is not an easy task for most people. The individual should choose the right life partner for a successful spiritual journey if celibacy is not possible. It is very dangerous to force celibacy on oneself or disciples who are not ready for it.

प्रशान्तात्मा विगतभीर्ब्रह्मचारिव्रते स्थितः ।
मनः संयम्य मच्चित्तो युक्त आसीत मत्परः ॥ 6.14 ॥

Shlok 6.14: With the heart serene and fearless, firm in the vow of a *Brahmachari*, having controlled the mind, ever thinking of Me, let him sit (in Yog) having Me as his supreme goal.

Commentary: The word *'Prashant'* means inward peace. This is the inner joy in which the *Yogi* will find himself as a result of regular practice. Fear is the quality in a person who cannot believe that there is something beyond him which is the Supreme. The very process of turning towards the Supreme makes him afraid of nothingness. The seeker should, therefore, be fearless since it is the deadliest enemy for spiritual progress.

Even after the mind becomes peaceful and joyous and fearlessness achieved after a continuous practice of meditation and study of scriptures, no progress towards the goal is possible unless the seeker gets established himself in perfect *Brahmacharya. Brahmacharya* implies the observance of celibacy as well as the practice of self control in all fields of sense-stimulation and sense-gratification.

युञ्जन्नेवं सदात्मानं योगी नियतमानसः ।
शान्तिं निर्वाणपरमां मत्संस्थामधिगच्छति ॥ 6.15 ॥

Shlok 6.15: The *Yogi* of subdued mind, ever keeping himself harmonized, attains to peace, the supreme *Nirvan*, which abides in Me.

Commentary: When all the above stages of meditation have been gone through the seeker becomes an unwavering person in his physical and subtler existence. Such a person who constantly keeps his mind free from agitations surely reaches the Supreme. The word 'constantly' does not mean at the cost of his duty to his home and the society. It means a consistent inner silence during meditation. At the peak of meditation the mind becomes completely 'still' and comes to a 'halt'.

The individual comes to experience an infinite peace when his mind is calmed. This is the peace that always resides in the seeker. Thus when there is no mental, intellectual and bodily disturbance and agitation, the seeker attains the peace unknown to the outside world that ultimately ends in the Supreme Liberation. In brief, the *Yogi* awakens to his own status of Selfhood which is the attainment of the meditation.

नात्यश्नतस्तु योगोऽस्ति न चैकान्तमनश्नतः ।
न चाति स्वप्नशीलस्य जाग्रतो नैव चार्जुन ॥ 6.16 ॥

Shlok 6.16: (Success in) Yog is not possible, O Arjun, for him who eats too much or too little; nor for him who sleeps too much or too little.

Commentary: The central theme of His guidance is that moderation in all activities at all levels is a precondition for achieving success in meditation. Intemperateness in any field of behaviour and activity brings about mental agitation which is not conducive to the development of an integrated personality. Therefore, moderation in food, sleep and recreation is suggested.

Yog is not possible for those who eat too much nor for those who do not eat at all. Eating means not only the process of consuming food but includes enjoyments gained through all means of sense perceptions and inward experiences. Similarly, neither too much sleep which erodes the faculties nor lack of sleep which disturbs the body rhythm is advised for spiritual life. Everything in moderation is the golden rule of life.

युक्ताहारविहारस्य युक्तचेष्टस्य कर्मसु ।
युक्तस्वप्नावबोधस्य योगो भवति दुःखहा ॥ 6.17 ॥

Shlok 6.17: If a man harmonizes his eating and amusement, all his actions, even his sleep and waking with his attachment to the Ideal, his attachment leads to a cessation of all sorrows.

Commentary: He, who is moderate in eating and recreation, moderate in work, sleep and waking state, is a true practitioner of *Yog*. He destroys all his miseries. The Geeta teaches that extremes should be avoided at all costs in all spheres of life. Lord Buddha advocated moderation in habits; he did not advise self-mortification and torturing the body by denying it food and rest/sleep, as some yogis practiced. The same message of moderation in all things is stated in this verse. This is same as the Lord Buddha's philosophy of middle path or the noble path. A healthy mind and body are required for successful performance of any spiritual practice. Therefore, it is required that a Yogi should regulate his daily bodily functions, such as eating, sleeping, bathing, resting and recreation. Those who eat too much or too little may become sick or fragile. It is recommended to fill half of the stomach with food, one fourth with water, and leave the rest empty for air. If one sleeps more than six hours, one's lethargy, passion, and bile may increase. A Yogi should avoid extreme indulgence in uncontrolled desires as well as the opposite extreme of Yogic discipline– the torturing of the body and mind.

यदा विनियतं चित्तमात्मन्येवावतिष्ठते ।
निःस्पृहः सर्वकामेभ्यो युक्त इत्युच्यते तदा ॥ 6.18 ॥

Shlok 6.18: When the perfectly controlled mind rests in the Self alone, free from longing for the objects of desire, then is one called steadfast (in the Self).

Commentary: When the mind is completely under control it rests peacefully in the Self alone. Uncontrolled mind is the one which wanders around in search of sensory satisfaction. To make the mind withdraw from its wandering nature for contemplating continuously on the Self, which is the substratum that illumines all perceptions and experiences, one has to make it free from desires. While desires by themselves are not unhealthy, Geeta advises us to renounce our cravings for all objects of desires seen or unseen, belonging to this world or the next.

When the mind is withdrawn from sense objects, it becomes capable of contemplating on the Self as it is free from agitations. The finite and limited sense objects disturb the mind, while the unlimited and infinite Self brings peace and happiness to it. This condition of replacing sense oriented thoughts with contemplation on the Self is called steadfastness.

यथा दीपो निवातस्थो नेङ्गते सोपमा स्मृता ।
योगिनो यतचित्तस्य युञ्जतो योगमात्मनः ॥ 6.19 ॥

Shlok 6.19: As a lamp placed in a windless place does not flicker, such is the state of a *Yogi* with subdued mind, practicing union with the Self.

Commentary (Shlok 6.19): Just as a lamp does not flicker in a windless place, the mind of a yogi remains undisturbed. Here the Lord refers to a lamp with an open flame, like a candle or oil-wick lamp. The Yogi's mind is absorbed in the Self. This is a beautiful simile which *Yogis* often quote when they talk of concentration of mind. The sign of Yogic perfection is that the mind remains always undisturbed like the flame of a lamp in a windless place. But when the same mind is made to concentrate in the Self by the meditator its vacillations and wanderings are stopped. It becomes brilliant just as a flickering lamp when placed in a windless spot.

यत्रोपरमते चित्तं निरुद्धं योगसेवया ।
यत्र चैवात्मनात्मानं पश्यन्नात्मनि तुष्यति ॥ 6.20 ॥

Shlok 6.20: When the mind, restrained by the practice of Yog, attains quietude and when seeing the Self by the self, he is satisfied in his own self.

Commentary: The self is present in all living beings same as fire is present in wood. Friction makes the presence of fire in the wood visible to the eyes, similarly meditation makes the Self, residing in the body, perceivable. A psychophysical transformation (or the super-conscious state) of mind in trance is necessary for God-realization. Each of us has access to the super-conscious mind that is not limited by time and space.

Onc cannot comprehend the Infinite by reason. Reason is incapable to grasp the nature of the beginningless Absolute. The highest faculty is not reasoning but intuition, the comprehension of knowledge coming from the Self and not from the fallible senses or reasoning. Self can be perceived by the intuitive experience in the highest state of trance or by any other means. Yogananda has rightly observed that meditation can enlarge the magic cup of intuition to hold the ocean of infinite wisdom.

There is a famous anecdote relating to Sri Ramakrishna Paramhans: When someone asked him, 'When can I see God?', Sri Ramakrishna replied: 'When 'I' is not seen'.

सुखमात्यन्तिकं यत्तद्बुद्धिग्राह्यमतीन्द्रियम् ।
वेत्ति यत्र न चैवायं स्थितश्चलति तत्त्वतः ॥ 6.21 ॥

Shlok 6.21: When he (the Yogi) feels that Infinite bliss, transcending the senses, can be grasped by reason; when, steady (in the Self), he never moves from the Reality;

यं लब्ध्वा चापरं लाभं मन्यते नाधिकं ततः ।
यस्मिन्स्थितो न दुःखेन गुरुणापि विचाल्यते ॥ 6.22 ॥

Shlok 6.22: When, having obtained it, he thinks no other acquisition superior to it. When, therein established, he is not shaken even by the heaviest sorrow;

तं विद्याद्दुःखसंयोगवियोगं योगसञ्ज्ञितम् ।
स निश्चयेन योक्तव्यो योगोऽनिर्विण्णचेतसा ॥ 6.23 ॥

Shlok 6.23: Let that be known by the name of *Yog*, this disconnection from pain. This *Yog* should be practiced with determination, with heart undismayed.

Commentary ((Shlokas 6.21-23): The experience of the self is an enduring state from which there is no return. Sri Krishna says that having gained this Infinite Bliss, no one can come to the worldly sorrows and feel the urge to go after the worldly objects and pursuits. The Yogi who has attained the state of Supreme Truth will consider no other gain as equal to it and worth comparable. Thus Sri Krishna defines Yog as a state of 'disunion from every union with pain'.

The term Yog means contact. Man is always in contact with finite worldly objects through the instruments of body, mind and intellect and gets finite joy only. When this temporary joy ends on account of the cessation of the instrumentality of the senses, sorrow begins. Therefore, it is said that life through these worldly instruments is called the life of union-with-pain.

Detachment from this union is the process in which we disassociate ourselves from the fields of objects and their experiences. As mind cannot exist without any attachment, once it is detached from the unreal and pain giving world of objects, it has to get itself attached to the Real and Permanent Bliss, which is called meditation. In deep meditation, the senses do not function; they are resolved into their cause, i.e. the mind. And when the mind becomes steady and cognition alone functions, then the indescribable Self is realized.

Thus Yog may be described as the culmination of human spiritual endeavour. The Geeta describes Yog in different ways. It is the greatest gain; complete liberation from pain; state of complete rest and concentration, supreme happiness and infinite bliss. This is the supreme goal of life.

संकल्पप्रभवान्कामांस्त्यक्त्वा सर्वानशेषतः ।
मनसैवेन्द्रियग्रामं विनियम्य समन्ततः ॥ 6.24 ॥

Shlok 6.24: Abandoning without reserve all fancy-born desires, and completely restraining the whole group of senses from their objects in all directions;

शनैः शनैरुपरमेद्बुद्ध्या धृतिगृहीतया ।
आत्मसंस्थं मनः कृत्वा न किंचिदपि चिन्तयेत् ॥ 6.25 ॥

Shlok 6.25: little by little let him withdraw, by reason (*Buddhi*) held in firmness; keeping the mind established in the Self, let him not think of anything.

Commentary (Shlokas 6.24-25): The mind is so clever that it keeps certain desires in safe or reserve for its secret gratification. So one should completely abandon all desires without reservation. When the mind is freed with the help of spiritual practices from the impurities of lust and greed born out of the feeling of 'I, me and my', it remains tranquil in material happiness and distress.

He should make the mind constantly abide in the Self, bearing in mind that the Self is all in all and that nothing else exists. This is the highest form of Yog. The goal of Yog is to accomplish that state wherein the mind, through the practice of concentration, comes to get it absolutely restrained and achieves perfection or bliss. The way of attaining single pointedness of mind, what the single pointed mind should then do, how to approach and ultimately realize the Truth have all been dealt with here. The various stages to be undergone in this regard are: renounce all desires fully by controlling the mind and restrain all the sense organs from their fields of sense objects. This mind-quietening process cannot be achieved at one go. The mind should achieve quietude as a result of withdrawal from sense objects by degrees– slowly and slowly.

Thereafter, patiently, the mind should be made to contemplate on the Self with the aid of the intellect. A mind that continuously contemplates on the Self becomes still and gets pervaded by the divine tranquillity. This is the last stage of the journey that conscious and deliberate action any seeker can take any seeker. Sri Krishna cautions that the meditator after reaching the last stage of inner peace should not think of anything else. Undisturbed by any new thought waves he should maintain inner silence and come to live it more and more deeply.

यतो यतो निश्चरति मनश्चञ्चलमस्थिरम् ।
ततस्ततो नियम्यैतदात्मन्येव वशं नयेत् ॥ 6.26 ॥

Shlok 6.26: Whatsoever makes the wavering and unsteady mind wander away, let him restrain and bring it back to the control of the Self alone.

Commentary: The natural tendency of the mind is to wander. We know from personal experience that the mind is very difficult to control. To control the mind is an impossible task like controlling the wind. The human mind can be subdued by sincere spiritual practice such as meditation and detachment only. Most commentators, however, have stated that the mind should be restrained and brought back under the control of the Self when it starts to wander during meditation, but that is never easy. We know that restraining the mind is like restraining the wind.

Now let us throw some more light on the *Yogic* practices. The main aim of meditation, or any spiritual practice, is to get oneself out of the outer world and its activities, start the journey within, and become an introvert. Always keep in mind that you are not the body nor the mind nor the intellect, but Self (*Atman*) that is separate and superior to the body-mind-ego (BME) complex. Detach your Self from the BME and make the Self a witness during meditation. Withdraw your mind from the outside world and fix your gaze at any one centre of your choice (pituitary gland, the sixth Chakra, front portion of the nostrils, the heart centre, or the naval centre) where you feel most comfortable. Witness the activities of the mind without becoming judgemental– good or bad– about the thoughts coming to your mind. Just relax, take a joy ride in the back seat of the vehicle of mind, and watch the wanderings of mind in the thought-world. The mind will wander because this is its nature. It will not remain quiet in the beginning. Do not be in a hurry to slow down, pressure, control, or try to engage the mind in any other way, such as by chanting a *Mantra,* concentrating on any object or thought.

Detach yourself completely from your mind and watch the play, the mind. Do not forget that your job is to see your (lower) self, the mind, with the (higher) Self, the Atman. Do not get attached or carried away by the thought waves (*Vritti*) of the mind; just witness or follow it. After serious and sincere practice, the mind will start slowing down when it finds out that it is being constantly watched and followed. Do not add anything to the process of witnessing the inner world of thought process (*Chittavriti*). Slowly, your power of concentration will increase; the mind will join the inward journey as a friend; and a state of bliss will radiate all around you. You will go beyond thought to the thoughtless world of *Nirvikalp Samadhi*. Practice this for half an hour in the morning and evening or at any other convenient, but fixed, time of your choice. The progress will depend on several factors beyond your control, but just persist without procrastination. Always conclude the meditation process with the triple sound vibration of *Aum*, and thank God.

Who is Yogi?

प्रशान्तमनसं ह्येनं योगिनं सुखमुत्तमम् ।
उपैति शान्तरजसं ब्रह्मभूतमकल्मषम् ॥ 6.27 ॥

Shlok 6.27: Supreme happiness comes to the yogi whose mind is peaceful, whose passions are at rest, who is free from sin and has become on with God.

युञ्जन्नेवं सदात्मानं योगी विगतकल्मषः ।
सुखेन ब्रह्मसंस्पर्शमत्यन्तं सुखमश्नुते ॥ 6.28 ॥

Shlok 6.28: Such a sinless Yogi, who constantly engages his or her mind and intellect in Self-awareness, enjoys the eternal bliss of contact with Brahm (the Eternal).

Commentary (Shlokas 6.27-6.28): In these two verses the Lord describes the benefits of Yog. During meditation when the mind is withdrawn from the world of objects and is concentrated on the Self, it acquires quietude and the thought flow ceases. Where there is no thought flow, there is no mind.

Where the mind has ended, there the seeker experiences the Infinite nature of the Self and the meditator reaches to the Supreme Bliss by ending all his mental agitations. The ego discovers that it is none other than the Self and hence there is no dualism at this stage. Such a man of self-realization himself becomes Brahm. The meditator *(Upasak)* becomes one with the object of meditation *(Upasya)*.

A meditator slowly grows out of his own ignorance and imperfection represented by his ego and merges with the Supreme. He loses contact with the objects of the senses and comes into contact with the Self within- Brahm. This means that the seeker becomes Brahm and comes to experience the Infinite Bliss as against contact with the world of objects (not-Self) whose joy is always finite.

सर्वभूतस्थमात्मानं सर्वभूतानि चात्मनि ।
ईक्षते योगयुक्तात्मा सर्वत्र समदर्शनः ॥ 6.29 ॥

Shlok 6.29: He who is genuinely attached to an Ideal sees himself abiding in all beings and all beings in himself. Everywhere he sees the same.

Commentary: The Self abiding in all beings, and all beings (abiding) in the Self, sees he whose self has been made steadfast by Yog, who everywhere sees the same. Perception of oneness of the Self in every being is the highest spiritual perfection. Sage Yagyavalkya said: A wife does not love her husband because of his or her physical satisfaction. She loves her husband because she feels the oneness of her soul with his soul. She is merged in her husband and becomes one with him. Trying to develop any meaningful human relationship without a firm understanding of the spiritual basis of all relationships is like trying to water the leaves of a tree rather than the root.

When one perceives one's own higher Self in all people and all people in one's own higher Self, then one does not hate or injure anybody. Eternal peace belongs to those who perceive God existing within everybody as Spirit. One should love others, including the enemy, because all are your own self.

One who sees One in all and all in One, sees the One everywhere. To fully understand this and to experience the oneness of individual soul and the Super-soul, is the highest achievement and the only goal of human birth. In the fullness of one's spiritual development, one finds that the Lord, who resides in one's own heart, resides in the hearts of all others– the rich, the poor, the Hindus, the Muslims, the Christians, the persecuted, the persecutor, the saint and the sinner. Therefore, to hate a single person is to hate Him. This realization makes one a truly humble saint. One who realizes that the Super-soul is all-pervading and is none other than one's own individual self, bereft of all impurities collected over various incarnations, attains immortality and bliss.

यो मां पश्यति सर्वत्र सर्वं च मयि पश्यति ।
तस्याहं न प्रणश्यामि स च मे न प्रणश्यति ॥ 6.30 ॥

Shlok 6.30: I am not lost for him who sees Me in all things and sees everything in Me, nor is he lost for Me.

Commentary: One, who sees Me everywhere (and in everything) and sees everything as a part and parcel of Me, is not separated from Me, and I am not separated from him. This stage is one of the higher forms of *Bhakti*, when the devotee sees the Lord everywhere and is constantly aware of the Presence of the Lord. A Self-realized person sees Me in the entire universe and in oneself and sees the entire universe and oneself in Me. When one sees Me pervading everything, just as fire pervades wood, one is at once freed from delusion. One attains salvation when one sees oneself different from body, mind, and the modes of material Nature and non-different from Me. The wise see their own higher Self present in the entire universe and the entire universe present in their own higher Self. True devotees never fear any condition of life, such as rebirth, living in heaven or in hell, because they see God everywhere. If you want to see, remember, and be with God at all times, then you must practice and learn to see God in everything and everywhere.

सर्वभूतस्थितं यो मां भजत्येकत्वमास्थितः ।
सर्वथा वर्तमानोऽपि स योगी मयि वर्तते ॥ 6.31 ॥

Shlok 6.31: He who, being established in unity, worships Me who dwells in all beings– that Yogi dwells in Me, whatever may be his mode of living.

Commentary: The *Yogi* (someone having an active and ardent adherence to an Ideal) who, having perfect faith in the unity of existence, worships Me as abiding in all beings lives in Me, irrespective of where he lives. The *Yogi* who sees the Lord in all beings and worships Him through all beings has attained liberation. No matter how he lives and acts, he is always free. He is no longer under the control of scriptural injunctions. A real *Yogi* is the one who has completely surrendered to Sri Krishna. One should not consider oneself as the master of oneself.

आत्मौपम्येन सर्वत्र समं पश्यति योऽर्जुन ।
सुखं वा यदि वा दुःखं स योगी परमो मतः ॥ 6.32 ॥

Shlok 6.32: O Arjun, he who looks at everything and everyone as he looks at himself, in pleasure as in pain, is a true Yogi.

Commentary: He who sees with equality everything, in the image of his own self, whether in pleasure or in pain, he is deemed to be the highest *Yogi*. A *Yogi* sees that whatever is pleasant to him is pleasant to all creatures, and that whatever is painful to him is painful to all beings. Thus seeing that what is pleasure or pain to him is same as pleasure or pain to all beings, he causes pain to none. He is harmless. The true Yogi is one who feels the pains and joys of others as if they were his own. This is known as empathy in psychology and sociology. He feels the entire universe as his own form. Doing no harm, and devoted to right knowledge, he is regarded as the highest among all *Yogis*.

Practice and indifference as the means to *Yog*

Arjun said:

योऽयं योगस्त्वया प्रोक्तः साम्येन मधुसूदन ।
एतस्याहं न पश्यामि चञ्चलत्वात्स्थितिं स्थिराम् ॥ 6.33 ॥

Shlok 6.33: O slayer of Madhu, You have said that the *Yog* of meditation is characterized by equanimity of mind, but due to

restlessness of mind, I find it difficult to perceive it as steady.

Commentary: Perfect equanimity, a mind free from torpidity and restlessness, in all circumstances, conditions and challenges of life seemed an uphill task and impractical to Arjun. He says that achieving evenness of mind is day dreaming because the human mind, by its very nature, is restless in its own excitements.

चञ्चलं हि मनः कृष्ण प्रमाथि बलवद्दृढम् ।
तस्याहं निग्रहं मन्ये वायोरिव सुदुष्करम् ॥ 6.34 ॥

Shlok 6.34: The mind is restless, O Krishna, and unruly, overpowering and stubborn; controlling the mind is a difficult as controlling the wind.

Commentary: Arjun argues that the mind is fickle. It is impetuous, strong and obstinate and is as difficult to control it as the wind. The mind ever changes its point of concentration from one object to another. So it is always restless. It is not only restless but also turbulent and impetuous, strong and obstinate. It produces agitation in the body and in the senses. That is why the mind is even more difficult to control than to control the wind.

Mind is perceived as a continuous flow of thoughts. Reportedly an average of 80, 000 thoughts are generated in a day. These thoughts are related to our past experiences or future dreams. When we attach ourselves to a specific thought, we stay attached to it till we realise and become aware of the situation. This implies that person, who remains alert and observant of the thought processes, does not get easily attached to any thought. That is what Sri Krishna means when he says, be an observer of mind and remain always detached.

Lord Krishna said:

असंशयं महाबाहो मनो दुर्निग्रहं चलम् ।
अभ्यासेन तु कौन्तेय वैराग्येण च गृह्यते ॥ 6.35 ॥

Shlok 6.35: Indeed, O son of Kunti, the mind is restless and difficult to control, but it can be controlled, by constant practice and non-attachment.

Commentary: Sri Krishna agrees that mind is unsteady and restless and therefore difficult to control and that the goal cannot be easily reached. But through practice and detachment mind can be brought under control. Practice is the effort of the mind towards calmness. Detachment is freedom from thirst for any pleasure seen or heard of. It is acquired through a constant perception of evil in sensuous happiness, either of this life or hereafter. Our restless mind is compared to a drunken monkey bitten by a scorpion. Arjun has rightly posed a practical question: How to control the turbulent, restless mind which moves like the wind? The Lord gives two practical hints: one, relentless practice and two, dispassion. If a person practices dispassion, i.e devoid of cravings and aversions, his mind is not easily agitated. He is calm and serene, and thus he is able to control the restless mind.

Thus the Geeta shows the way to control the mind. The mind is restless, ever changing and extremely fast moving. However, constant practice and an attitude of non-attachment are the essential tools to control it. Both the mind and the senses have to be trained to exercise restraint vis-à-vis external influences. This is the process of *Yogic Sadhna.*

असंयतात्मना योगो दुष्प्राप इति मे मतिः ।
वश्यात्मना तु यतता शक्योऽवाप्तुमुपायतः ॥ 6.36 ॥

Shlok 6.36: *Yog* is difficult for one whose mind is not subdued. However, *Yog* is attainable by the person of subdued mind who strives through proper means.

Commentary: An uncontrolled mind cannot progress on spiritual path unless it discovers the Self. The discovery of the Self is possible by self-control achieved through the withdrawal of sense organs from their respective objects. *Yog* can be attained by striving hard to utilize the conserved energies for the Divine purposes.

Yog is the science of religion. The test of its validity lies in one's seeing results through actual experimentation. Hence the teachers of *Yog* emphasize self-control and other disciplines.

Destination of unsuccessful *Yogi*

Arjun asked:

अयतिः श्रद्धयोपेतो योगाच्चलितमानसः ।
अप्राप्य योगसंसिद्धिं कां गतिं कृष्ण गच्छति ॥ 6.37 ॥

Shlok 6.37: He who strives not, but who is possessed of faith, whose mind wanders away from *Yog*, having failed to attain perfection in *Yog*, what end, O Krishna, does he meet?

Commentary: This verse relates to a seeker who has faith in the efficacy of *Yog* but who is unable to control his sense and mind. Arjun asks what happens to such a person who has faith in the efficacy of *Yog* but does not strive on the path of *Yog*; and during the last moments of life his mind wanders away from *Yog*, with memory lost. Having failed to attain the fruition of *Yog*– namely, right knowledge– what end does such a man meet?

कच्चिन्नोभयविभ्रष्टश्छिन्नाभ्रमिव नश्यति ।
अप्रतिष्ठो महाबाहो विमूढो ब्रह्मणः पथि ॥ 6.38 ॥

Shlok 6.38: Do they not perish like a dispersing cloud, O Mighty-armed (Krishna), having lost both the heavenly and the worldly pleasures, supportless and deluded in the path of Brahm?

Commentary: Arjun wonders as to what will happen to the seeker who though full of faith but for want of mental restraint fails to achieve success having fallen from both. Fallen from both means achieving no success in the path of worldly success as also on the path of *Yog*. Rent cloud is that very small portion of the large cloud which gets detached from the latter on account of heavy winds and as a consequence moves about without any set direction hit by every passing breeze. Arjun inquires whether such unsuccessful seekers will meander about the universe as the rented clouds and get lost.

एतन्मे संशयं कृष्ण छेत्तुमर्हस्यशेषतः ।
त्वदन्यः संशयस्यास्य छेत्ता न ह्युपपद्यते ॥ 6.39 ॥

Shlok 6.39: O Krishna, only You are able to completely dispel this doubt of mine because there is none other than You who can dispel such a doubt.

Commentary: Arjun says that You should cut off completely this feeling of self-distrust in me. There is none other than you who can do this. There is no better teacher than the Lord Himself as He is omniscient and almighty. Arjun asked a very good question. Because the mind is very difficult to control, it may not be possible to achieve perfection during one's lifetime. Does all the effort get wasted? The answer comes:

Lord Krishna said:

पार्थ नैवेह नामुत्र विनाशस्तस्य विद्यते ।
न हि कल्याणकृत्कश्चिद्दुर्गतिं तात गच्छति ॥ 6.40 ॥

Shlok 6.40: Verily, O son of Pritha, neither in this world, nor in the next world is there destruction for him; none who does well, O my son, ever comes to grief!

Commentary: In the following five verses Sri Krishna elucidates the path of progress of a seeker whose spiritual endeavours have not been met with any success either on account of death or due to any other temptation. The Lord assures him that he who does not achieve perfection in Yog in this birth will not be destroyed either in this world or in the next. No destruction means that surely he will not take a birth lower than the present one in his next life. Doing good means striving for Self-realization.

The Geeta teaches that a person should not think of consequences when he is performing any action because he, as the performer of certain action, has got no control over its consequences. Correct approach is that one should surrender to God and be a steadfast in all circumstances. This definitely sounds great. But despite being present before the Lord Himself Arjun is curious to know about the fate of an unsuccessful Yogi in the next birth in this verse. Sri Krishna, surprisingly enough, assures him of good prospect after this birth even for unsuccessful *Yogi.*

The above reply suggests that an actor cannot detach himself from the consequences of his action. Action is obviously not an accident; it is often premeditated and result- oriented. Even the act of a *Yogi* too is very conscious and intentional, which simply suggests that detachment of consequences from action is impractical and unrealistic. Thus Sri Krishna's advice to Arjun to become a *Karmayogi* or *Sthitpragya* (steadfast) is problematic.

प्राप्य पुण्यकृतां लोकानुषित्वा शाश्वतीः समाः ।
शुचीनां श्रीमतां गेहे योगभ्रष्टोऽभिजायते ॥ 6.41 ॥

Shlok 6.41: Having attained to the worlds of the righteous and, having dwelt there for everlasting years, he who is fallen from *Yog* re-incarnates in the home of the pure and the prosperous.

Commentary: The Lord says that the one who was not able to attain perfection in *Yog* or the one who achieved some progress in *Yog* but had fallen due to lack of dispassion or on account of turbulent senses, attains the worlds inhabited by those pious souls who performed great religious sacrifices while living on this earth. Having lived there as long as the merit of his past spiritual life lasts he is born again in the house of prosperous persons whose conduct is governed by religion where he can continue his spiritual journey from the point where he had left in the previous birth. The future prospect of even unsuccessful *Yogis* seems to be so bright.

अथवा योगिनामेव कुले भवति धीमताम् ।
एतद्धि दुर्लभतरं लोके जन्म यदीदृशम् ॥ 6.42 ॥

Shlok 6.42: Or else he is born into a family of wise *Yogis* only; verily, a birth like this is very rare to obtain in this world.

Commentary: Sri Krishna says that those who are possessed of genuine dispassion but fail to achieve success in *Yog* are born in the family of enlightened *Yogis* poor in resources but rich in wisdom. A birth in such families is rare to obtain than the one mentioned in the preceding verse. It is rare because he is placed right from the beginning of his life in an environment which is conducive for the practice of *Yog* so that he could start his spiritual journey from a very early stage. Considering the greatness of the illumined souls, a birth in their families is stated to be very difficult to obtain.

तत्र तं बुद्धिसंयोगं लभते पौर्वदेहिकम् ।
यतते च ततो भूयः संसिद्धौ कुरुनन्दन ॥ 6.43 ॥

Shlok 6.43: The unsuccessful *Yogi* regains the knowledge acquired in the previous life and strives more than before for perfection from the point where he had left, O son of the Kurus.

Commentary: When he takes a human body again in this world, his previous efforts and practice of *Yog* does not go in vain. They bear fruit in this birth and hasten his moral and spiritual evolution. Our thoughts, actions and experiences are left in our subconscious mind in the form of subtle impressions. These impressions of the present and the past births will be re-energised in the next birth. The impressions of the *Yogic* tendencies will compel the seeker to work with greater vigour than in his former birth. Whatever progress a man makes on the path of *Yog* he retains. He again starts from there when the next opportunity arises.

पूर्वाभ्यासेन तेनैव ह्रियते ह्यवशोऽपि सः ।
जिज्ञासुरपि योगस्य शब्दब्रह्मातिवर्तते ॥ 6.44 ॥

Shlok 6.44: By that very previous practice alone, he is borne on, though unwilling. Even he who merely wishes to know of *Yog* rises superior to the word– Brahm.

Commentary: The man who has failed in *Yog* is carried forward to the goal, which he intended to reach in his previous birth, by the force of impressions of his past *Yogic* practices, though he may not be aware of it. If he had not done that many evil deeds as to overcome his *Yogic* tendencies, he will certainly continue his *Yogic* practices in this birth with great vigour by force of the impressions of the previous birth.

If the force of evil actions is very strong, the *Yogic* tendencies would be overpowered or suppressed by them temporarily. As soon as the fruits of evil actions are exhausted the *Yogic Vasnas* will again manifest themselves and he will eventually attain the final realization in the present or succeeding births. Sri Krishna says that no effort in the practice of *Yog* goes waste. Even the least effort bears some fruit either in this birth or in the next and there is no cause for any disappointment.

प्रयत्नाद्यतमानस्तु योगी संशुद्धकिल्बिषः ।
अनेकजन्मसंसिद्धस्ततो याति परां गतिम् ॥ 6.45 ॥

Shlok 6.45: Verily, a Yogi who strives with assiduity, purified from sins and perfected in the course of many births, then reaches the Supreme Goal.

Commentary: The *Y*ogi, who strives with assiduity cleansed of all sins, perfecting himself through many lives, then attains to the highest goal. Here the highest goal apparently means reaching God. One must be very careful in spiritual life, or there is a possibility of being carried away by the powerful wind of bad association created by *Maya*, and one may abandon the spiritual path. One should never get discouraged. The unsuccessful Yogi gets another chance by starting over from where he or she leaves off. The spiritual journey is long and slow, but no sincere effort is ever wasted. Normally it takes several births to reach the perfection of salvation. All living entities (souls) are eventually redeemed after they reach the zenith of spiritual evolution. In the course of many births he acquires facility in Yog little by little, and by the aggregate facility thus acquired in many births he is perfected. Then he obtains right knowledge and reaches the Supreme Goal. The Geeta gives us hopeful belief in the redemption of all.

Who is the best Yogi?

तपस्विभ्योऽधिको योगी ज्ञानिभ्योऽपि मतोऽधिकः ।
कर्मिभ्यश्चाधिको योगी तस्माद्योगी भवार्जुन ॥ 6.46 ॥

Shlok 6.46: The *Yogi* is thought to be superior to the ascetics and even superior to men of knowledge (obtained through the study of scriptures); he is also superior to the ritualists. Therefore, be a *Yogi*, O Arjun!

Commentary: Sri Krishna says that a *yogi* (a person actively attached to an Ideal) is greater than an ascetic; he is greater than even a man of learning; he is greater than a man of action. Therefore, Arjun, you should become a *yogi.* It is suggested here that meditation is more important than various other practices in the matter of spiritual development. He says that the meditator is nobler than the *Tapaswi*, the one who observes austerities of the body and physical self-denials. The meditator is nobler than the *Gyani* also who deeply studies the scriptures and acquires their knowledge. The meditator is nobler than Karmis who undertake actions like sacrifices and ritual practices. To be a *Yogi* is the best option in life.

योगिनामपि सर्वेषां मद्गतेनान्तरात्मना ।
श्रद्धावान्भजते यो मां स मे युक्ततमो मतः ॥ 6.47 ॥

Shlok 6.47: And among all the *Yogis,* he who, full of faith, worships Me with his inner self abiding in Me, he is deemed by Me as the most devout.

Commentary: Meditation or any other act becomes more powerful and efficient if it is done with knowledge, faith, and devotion to God. Meditation is a necessary condition but not a sufficient condition for spiritual progress. The mind should be kept ever absorbed in thoughts of God. The meditative mood is to be continued during other times through scriptural study, Self-analysis and selfless service. It is said that no single *Yog* alone is complete without the presence of other *Yogs*. Just as the right combination of all ingredients is essential for preparation of a good meal, similarly selfless service, chanting of Lord's name, meditation, and study of scriptures, contemplation, and devotional love are essential for reaching the supreme goal. The person who meditates with deep devotional love of God is called a *Yogi*-devotee and is considered to be the best of all *Yogis.*

(Remarks: It is strongly felt that this Discourse was developed and inserted much later into the corpus of the Geeta, definitely on the lapse of a long period of time, having realized the significance of *Yog* in life. The *Yog* related teaching did not seem to have formed a part of original conversation between Krishna and Arjun in the battlefield. The battlefield was obviously not the right place for discussing the relevance and methods of doing *Yogic* exercises. The subject is vast and intricate and requires a very peaceful state of mind to understand the notion of *Yog*. The above discussion incorporates ideas of *Yog* espoused by sage Patanjali who belonged to the post-Mahabharat period.

The period of Mahabharat was unquestionably older than that of sage Patanjali who is regarded as the earliest and the greatest expounder of *Yog*. He lived sometime between 500 and 200 B.C. The life of Patanjali is an enigma to historians, and almost nothing is known about this great master who epitomizes *Yog*. It is only with the help of legends that one can draw inferences about him.

Maharishi Patanjali is considered to be the compiler of the **Yog Sutras**, along with being the author of a commentary on Panini's **Ashtadhyayi**, known as **Mahabhasya**. He is also supposed to be the writer of a work on the ancient Indian medicine system, Ayurved. **Yog Sutras** is considered to serve as the basis of the Yogic techniques. Maharishi Patanjali, 'The Father of Yog', compiled 195 Sutras, which serve as a framework for integrating *Yog i*nto the daily routine and leading an ethical life. The exact date of the compilation of the **Yog Sutras** is not known. However, it is believed that they were collated somewhere around 200 BC. The core of Patanjali's teachings lies in the eightfold path of Yog, which have already been covered above. The path shows the way to Self-realization– an ultimate goal of life.

OM TAT SAT

Discourse - 7

Gyan-Vigyanyog: Yog of Knowledge and Wisdom

Arjun continues to have doubts as to how a man with limited intellect could ever understand the limitless or infinite with all its virtues and glory. Sri Krishna, therefore, clarifies this doubt in this Discourse by describing the nature of the Lord Himself, who is the point of concentration of the *Yogi*'s unwavering devotion. He tells Arjun that the Supreme Godhead has to be realized in both its transcendent and immanent forms. The *Yogi* who has reached this summit has nothing more to know. This complete union with the Lord is difficult to attain. Among countless human beings, very few aspire for this union, and even among those who aspire for it, few ever reach the pinnacle of spiritual realization. The Lord gives a clear description of the all-pervading, static and infinite state of His Being. He then proceeds to explain His manifestations as the universe and the power behind it.

He speaks of these manifestations as His lower and higher *Prakritis*. The lower *Prakriti* is made up of the five elements, mind, ego and intellect. The higher *Prakriti* is the life-element which upholds the universe, activates it and causes its appearance and final dissolution.

Krishna says that whatever exists is nothing but Him. He is the cause of the appearance of the universe and all things in it. Everything is strung on Him like clusters of gems on a string. He is the essence, substance and substratum of everything, whether visible or invisible. Although everything is in Him, yet He transcends everything as the actionless Self. *Prakriti* or Nature is made up of the three Gunas or qualities– *Sattva, Rajas* and *Tamas*. These three qualities delude the soul and make it forget its true nature, which is one with God. One can get rid of *Maya* only when a person fully surrenders to Sri Krishna.

Thus far Arjun has been taught the highest form of devotion, which leads to union with God in its static aspect as also with His dynamic Prakriti. Krishna tells him that there are also other forms of devotion which are inferior as they are performed with various motives. The distressed, the seeker of divine wisdom, and he who desires wealth, worship Him, as also the wise. Of these the Lord deems the wise as dearest to Him. Such a devotee loves the Lord for the sake of pure love only. Whatever form the devotee worships, the ultimate goal is the Lord Himself. The Lord accepts such worship, knowing that it is directed to Him alone.

Lord Krishna said:

मय्यासक्तमनाः पार्थ योगं युञ्जन्मदाश्रयः ।
असंशयं समग्रं मां यथा ज्ञास्यसि तच्छृणु ॥ 7.1 ॥

Shlok 7.1: O Parth, listen how you shall know Me fully without any doubt, with your mind attached to Me, taking refuge in Me and performing spiritual practices.

Commentary: Concentration on God is a precondition for developing attachment for Him. Music or prayer can be one of the ways to concentrate on God. If you sing the glories and praise attributes of the Lord, you will develop love for Him and then your mind will be ever fixed on Him. Intense love for the Lord is real devotion. With this you must surely get full knowledge of the Self.

Knowing the Lord in full implies knowing all His six attributes, viz infinite greatness, strength, power, grace, knowledge and detachment. As Arjun possesses the necessary qualifications, Sri Krishna assures that He will give him a complete or integral knowledge of the Divine, not merely the Pure Self but also its manifestations in the world.

Metaphysical knowledge as the ultimate knowledge

ज्ञानं तेऽहं सविज्ञानमिदं वक्ष्याम्यशेषतः ।
यज्ज्ञात्वा नेह भूयोऽन्यज्ज्ञातव्यमवशिष्यते ॥ 7.2 ॥

Shlok 7.2: I shall tell you in full both the transcendental knowledge and the transcendental experience or a vision, after knowing that nothing more remains to be known in this world.

Commentary: As the Lord is everything, when fully known, everything else is automatically known. The Lord as *Satta-Chitta-Anand* (existence-knowledge-bliss absolute) forms the real essence of all objects. Names and forms are mere illusory superimposition. The lord says that the message of wisdom that I am explaining to you in detail is a unified view integrating both science and spirituality.

Those who have transcendental experience become perfect. Everything becomes (as though) known when the Supreme Being is heard, reflected, meditated upon, seen, and known. The need to know all other things becomes irrelevant with the dawn of the knowledge of the Absolute, the Supreme Spirit. One who knows Lord Krishna as the Supreme Being (*Parabrahm*), is considered to have known all, but one who knows everything, but does not know Krishna, does not know anything. The purport of the above verse is that knowledge of all other subjects remains incomplete without one's understanding of who am I? He who knows Me in truth becomes omniscient. Thus the knowledge is productive of great results and is, therefore, very hard to obtain.

True seekers are rare

मनुष्याणां सहस्रेषु कश्चिद्यतति सिद्धये ।
यततामपि सिद्धानां कश्चिन्मां वेत्ति तत्त्वतः ॥ 7.3 ॥

Shlok 7.3: Among thousands of men, one perchance strives for perfection; even among those successful strivers only one perchance truly understands Me.

Commentary: The Self-realized masters are very rare, since such a realization is not within the reach of everyone. The Being of the Lord and His diverse manifestations are incomprehensible to the human mind. He is the Impersonal Reality, the Personal God, and in addition many other things as well. Of all living beings on the earth, man alone can inquire about his self and its relationship with the Lord. Among countless human beings, only a few develop a desire for such an inquiry. Among those who show such desire, only a few know the means of attaining knowledge and strive after it. Among those who strive, only a fortunate few succeed in acquiring the true knowledge of the Lord. Hence knowledge of God is rare on this earth.

Concept of spirit and matter

भूमिरापोऽनलो वायुः खं मनो बुद्धिरेव च ।
अहंकार इतीयं मे भिन्ना प्रकृतिरष्टधा ॥ 7.4 ॥

Shlok 7.4: Earth, water, fire, air, ether, thought *(Manas)* and reason *(Buddhi)*, egoism (*Ahankar*) are the eightfold divisions of My material Nature.

Commentary: 'Material Nature' is defined as the material object out of which everything is made. Earth, water, fire, air, ether, mind, reason and ego- such is the eightfold division of My nature. Material Nature is the original source of the material world, consisting of three modes of material Nature and eight basic elements out of which everything in the universe has evolved, according to the Sankhya doctrine. Material Nature is one of the transformations of divine power (*Maya*) and is the material cause of creation of the entire universe. Matter is thus a part of Lord's illusory energy, *Maya*. Material Nature is also referred to as perishable, body, matter, Nature, *Maya*, field, creation, and manifest state. That which creates diversity as well as the diversity itself, and all that can be seen or known, including the universal mind, is called material Nature. As a matter of fact, we find, from our ordinary experience, that egoism is the cause of the activity of every being.

अपरेयमितस्त्वन्यां प्रकृतिं विद्धि मे पराम् ।
जीवभूतां महाबाहो ययेदं धार्यते जगत् ॥ 7.5 ॥

Shlok 7.5: Material Nature or matter is My lower Nature. My other and higher Nature is the Soul by which this entire universe is upheld, O Mighty-armed.

Commentary: While the lower nature may be identified with the material field, the higher nature represents the conscious aspect which may be identified with the Soul. The higher nature is Pure Consciousness. It is the spiritual entity which enables the body, mind and intellect (which are all material) to function. It is this consciousness that awakens and sustains all activities in the material world. The higher nature of God is the Life Principle which sustains the entire world of experience.

The relationship between spirit and matter which is the source of creation is explained here. The Vedantic technical terms for these words are *'Purush'* for the indwelling spirit and *'Prakriti'* for the matter. Spirit is sentient and dynamic, while matter is inert and insentient. A combination of these two ingredients causes things to be born and function. (In modern Sanskrit *'Purush'* and *'Prakriti'* stand for male and nature respectively. *Purush* does not mean spirit any more outside the context of the Geeta.)

Prakriti is same as lower energy, material energy or material Nature. It creates the material world with the help of consciousness. The higher Nature is called the higher energy or the spiritual energy (*Purush*). This is derived from consciousness, the Supreme Spirit (or Spirit). *Purush* with the help of Prakriti creates and sustains the entire universe. Spirit is immutable; and material Nature, born of Spirit, is mutable. *Purush* (or spirit) observes, witnesses, enjoys as well as supervises material Nature. This *Prakriti* is inferior, impure, productive of evil, itself constituting the bondage of *sansar*; but the superior *Prakirti* is pure: it is My very Self, the *Kshetragaya*, that by which life is sustained, that which enters within the whole universe and sustains it.

The Supreme Spirit is the efficient cause of creation of the universe. The material Nature and Spirit are not two independent identities but the two aspects of the same Supreme Spirit. The Supreme Spirit, Spirit (*Purush*) and material Nature are the same, yet different as the sun and its light and heat are the same, but different.

Supreme spirit as the basis of everything

एतद्योनीनि भूतानि सर्वाणीत्युपधारय ।
अहं कृत्स्नस्य जगतः प्रभवः प्रलयस्तथा ॥ 7.6 ॥

Shlok 7.6: Know that everything originates from these natures. And I am the origin of this world and its dissolution also.

Commentary: The higher and the lower nature of God functioning in unison bring all the manifestations in the world. The world arises from God and at the time of dissolution is again withdrawn into Him. God constitutes everything and there is no other is nothing other than the ocean itself. The endless waves which rise ultimately fall into the ocean.

The entire creation of the universe is held together by the Supreme as the cluster of gems by the string. There is one and the same Supreme in all forms.

As the lower nature is activated by the higher, in the same way the material world manifests because of the spiritual factor. Thus the functioning of the entire universe takes place through the two natures of the Supreme which is the source of life and form of all beings and objects. It follows, therefore, that each individual has two aspects– conscious and unconscious and these represent the two natures of the Supreme. There is no other entity higher than this Supreme God who includes everything and affects all activities of the world.

If there is no matter, the latent dynamic energy of the Spirit will not have a field for its expression. The matter by itself is dormant and it cannot function unless the Spirit is there to activate it or to enliven it. An example of this principle is electricity and the bulb. The bulb is the inert matter and the electricity is the dynamic spirit. It is obvious that one is of no use without the other. When the spirit functions through the five layers of the matter it finds a place to express itself.

At the time of evolution, names, forms and life arise from *Prakriti* and at the time of dissolution they go back into it. But *Prakriti*, independent of the Lord (Consciousness or Brahm or Spirit) cannot generate anything. *Prakriti* is the Lord's instrument of creation, preservation and dissolution. Hence the Lord is the ultimate cause of the Universe. Brahm (the Lord) + Maya or Consciousness (Spirit) + Matter is the ultimate cause of the evolution and dissolution of the Universe or Creation or Manifestation.

मत्तः परतरं नान्यत्किंचिदस्ति धनंजय ।
मयि सर्वमिदं प्रोतं सूत्रे मणिगणा इव ॥ 7.7 ॥

Shlok 7.7: There exists nothing whatsoever higher than Me, O Dhananjay! All that is here is strung on Me like multitudes of gems on a string.

Commentary: All constituents of creation are manifestations of God and are held together by the force of God. There is no other cause of the universe but Me. Krishna alone is the cause of the universe. To show that the Self is one and the same in all created beings on the earth it is stated here that the Lord is the supporter of the Universe just as the string is of the gems on a garland. Without the string the gems will be scattered. The entire creation is permeated by Him. The Lord is the support of the universe, as the string is of the gems on a garland. Without the string the gems will lie scattered; without the Lord, the planets, the stars and all else will be dispersed. The Lord, manifesting Himself through the physical and moral laws, sustains the relative world. He is also the Unity that underlies the diversity of names and forms.

This well-known verse is widely quoted. When we look at a necklace, we see only the pearls; the string that holds the pearls together is not visible to us. Likewise, we see the phenomenal world– trees, mountains, ocean, sun, moon, stars and galaxies– but overlook the fact that is the Supreme Lord who supports and sustains the entire physical creation. We are captivated by the beauty of the physical world (which is part of *Maya*), but fail to see the One upholding it. A devout sees the Lord behind the physical Universe.

रसोऽहमप्सु कौन्तेय प्रभास्मि शशिसूर्ययोः ।
प्रणवः सर्ववेदेषु शब्दः खे पौरुषं नृषु ॥ 7.8 ॥
पुण्यो गन्धः पृथिव्यां च तेजश्चास्मि विभावसौ ।
जीवनं सर्वभूतेषु तपश्चास्मि तपस्विषु ॥ 7.9 ॥

Shlokas 7.8-09: O son of Kunti, I am the taste in water; I am the light in the moon and the sun, the sacred syllable 'OM' in all the Vedas, the sound in the ether, and potency in human beings. I am the purifying fragrance in the earth and the brightness in fire, the vitality in all beings, and the austerity in the ascetics.

Commentary: In these two verses the doubt as to what is the eternal factor which is common in all and yet not readily perceptible to anybody is cleared. That which remains always from beginning to end and without which the thing cannot be identified as such is declared to be its essence, its *Dharma*- the law of its being. All examples given here by the Lord like taste in water, radiance in the sun and the moon, syllable *OM* in the Vedas, the principle of sound in Space, manliness in man, brilliance in the fire, life in all beings, etc. indicate that the Lord is that factor or subtle principle which gives the individual units or objects different characteristics of their own. He is present in the entire creation both in tangible and intangible form. God cannot be separated from His creation, as brilliance cannot be separated from fire or austerity from ascetics.

बीजं मां सर्वभूतानां विद्धि पार्थ सनातनम् ।
बुद्धिर्बुद्धिमतामस्मि तेजस्तेजस्विनामहम् ॥ 7.10 ॥

Shlok 7.10: Know Me, O Parth, as the eternal seed of all beings; I am the intelligence of the intelligent, the bravery of the brave.

बलं बलवतां चाहं कामरागविवर्जितम् ।
धर्माविरुद्धो भूतेषु कामोऽस्मि भरतर्षभ ॥ 7.11 ॥

Shlok 7.11: I am the strength in the strong, but without desire and passion. I am the desire in beings, Bull of the Bharatas, but desire consistent with the law.

Commentary (Shlokas 7.10-11): These verses are repetition of what has already been said in the above. The Lord says that He is the source of everything we see or experience in the world. He continues to indicate the same truth by means of some more analogies. Sri Krishna tells that He is the strength among the strong but devoid of desire and attachment. Sri Krishna simply says whatever one sees or experiences in the world, I am behind all these. I am that energy which is necessary for the sustenance of the body, certainly not that which causes thirst and attachment (for sense-objects) in the case of worldly mortals.

Here the terms desire and attachment are not synonymous. Desire is for what is absent at present in the scheme of life and attachment or affection is for what one has already obtained. These two emotions are generally the cause of conflict between individuals, communities and countries assisted by their respective strength.

ये चैव सात्त्विका भावा राजसास्तामसाश्च ये ।
मत्त एवेति तान्विद्धि न त्वहं तेषु ते मयि ॥ 7.12 ॥

Shlok 7.12: And whatever beings are of Sattva or of Rajas or of Tamas (three modes of material Nature– goodness, passion, and ignorance) know them to emanate from Me: still, I am not in them, they are in me.

Commentary: This verse concludes the discussion started with the statement "All this is strung on Me, as a row of gems on a thread." All things (including the different states of mind) are in the Lord, but He is not in them just as all waves are in the ocean but the ocean is not in them. The universe is only an appearance superimposed by illusion (*Maya*) on the Lord. It is like a mirage in the desert. From the standpoint of the onlooker, the illusory water exists in the desert; but the desert does not depend upon or exist in the mirage. Likewise this universe, apparently superimposed on the Lord, exists in the Lord, but the Lord is not in the universe. None of the properties of the universe touches the Lord, just as the waters of the mirage cannot soak a single grain of the desert sand.

The *Gunas* constitute *Prakriti* or nature which is the lower manifestation of the Lord. Therefore the Lord is their ultimate cause. But the Lord is not, as in the case of worldly men, under the control of the *Gunas*. The *Gunas*, on the contrary, are subject to Him.

त्रिभिर्गुणमयैर्भावैरेभिः सर्वमिदं जगत् ।
मोहितं नाभिजानाति मामेभ्यः परमव्ययम् ।। 7.13 ।।

Shlok 7.13: Deluded by these three (sorts of) things composed of *Gunas*, this entire world knows not Me as distinct from them and immutable.

Commentary: The Lord now expresses that the people are so engrossed in the worldly life that they do not understand the Supreme Lord. He is by nature eternal, pure, intelligent and free; who is the Self of all beings, devoid of all attributes. All living beings are deluded by such things as love, hatred and attachment, which are all manifestation of *Gunas*.

The people of this world are deluded by the three gunas or qualities of nature. Affection, attachment and infatuated love, hatred are all the characteristics of the *Gunas*. On account of delusion created by these qualities they are not able to break worldly ties and turn their minds towards the Supreme Lord though the Lord is the inmost Self of all beings and the object of direct and immediate perception.

The Lord in His purest essence is untouched by the *Gunas* which belong only to His *Prakriti*. The Self is the essence which does not have the six modifications of the body, viz birth, growth, existence, old age, decay and death.

This verse answers the question as to why the ordinary mortals are not able to understand at least the presence of the great truth about the spirit and matter. The answer in short is that deluded by the modifications or attributes of the three *Gunas* the living beings become blind to the divine possibilities in themselves. So long as a ghost is seen in the post, the vision of the post will not be available to the perceiver. Thus deluded, the ego does not realize the Supreme as different from it.

How to overcome the delusive divine power (*Maya*)

दैवी ह्येषा गुणमयी मम माया दुरत्यया ।
मामेव ये प्रपद्यन्ते मायामेतां तरन्ति ते ॥ 7.14 ॥

Shlok 7.14: Verily this divine illusion of Mine called *Maya*, consisting of three modes of Nature (*Gunas*), is very difficult to overcome. Only those who surrender unto My Will, easily pass through the veil of *Maya* and know the Absolute Reality.

Commentary: *Maya* or illusion is divine because it is a part of the Lord's nature and inscrutable to human reason. The Lord makes it clear that due to *Prakriti* or Nature, which creates this illusory or mayic delusion of the phenomenal world, is a mirage. How does *Prakriti* operate in us? We are influenced by the three *Gunas– Sattva, Rajas and Tamas–* and through these *Gunas*, Nature binds us to this mayic or illusory world. There is little chance of overcoming this delusion, other than by taking refuge in the Lord. Sri Krishna Himself admits that it is not easy for any egocentric individual to transcend this illusion which is caused by His *Maya*. The Lord says that those who devote themselves to Him alone can overcome this obstacle which creates sorrows and imperfections in the objective world. When one fully dedicates one's life to the Supreme Power and depends on Him under all circumstances, just as a small child depends on his or her parents, then Lord personally takes charge of such a devotee. And when He takes charge of you, there is no need to be afraid of anything or to depend on anybody else for anything– spiritual or material– in life.

All those who abandon all formal religion (Dharma) and completely devote themselves to Me, their own Self, they cross over the Illusion which deludes all living beings: they are liberated from the bondage of worldly life.

The word '*Maya*' or illusion is frequently misinterpreted. *Maya* does not mean that the phenomenal world does not exist as such. This 'mayic' world is subject to change and is impermanent. It is as permanent as human life. When a person dreams a tiger following him, he flees from the tiger. This happens in the dream. Both the tiger and the person appear real in the dream. When a person awakens and recalls the dream, he knows for sure that he is real, but not the tiger. But in the state of dream, both he and the tiger appeared very real. In the same way, in the awakened state, only the *Atman* or Soul is real, the body, mind and intellect (BMI) that constitute our earthly existence are unreal, like the tiger in dream.

Who seeks God?

न मां दुष्कृतिनो मूढाः प्रपद्यन्ते नराधमाः ।
माययापहृतज्ञाना आसुरं भावमाश्रिताः ॥ 7.15 ॥

Shlok 7.15: The evil doers, the ignorant, the lowest of men who are attached to demonic nature and whose power of judgement has been taken away by divine illusive power (Maya), do not surrender to My Will.

Commentary: Sri Krishna says that the mean individuals, because of their delusion and indulgence in evil actions, follow the path of the devil (*Asur*) and get themselves deprived of their discrimination. The difference between man and animal is his rational intellect by which he can distinguish between the good and the evil, the high and the low, the moral and the immoral, etc. This rational discriminative capacity alone helps the man to cast off his imperfections and become aware of his essential nature of Absolute Divinity. The evil doers cannot attain to the Supreme, for their mind and will are not instruments of the Spirit but of the ego.

चतुर्विधा भजन्ते मां जनाः सुकृतिनोऽर्जुन ।
आर्तो जिज्ञासुरर्थार्थी ज्ञानी च भरतर्षभ ॥ 7.16 ॥

Shlok 7.16: O lord of the Bharatas, the virtuous ones who worship Me are of four kinds, the man in distress, the seeker of knowledge, the seeker of wealth and the man of wisdom.

Commentary: The Lord calls all the persons who offer prayers to

Him as virtuous and classifies them in the following four categories. The devotees of God are of four types: the man in distress, the seeker of knowledge, to seeker for wealth and the man of wisdom.

Most of the worshippers ask for something–wealth, material possessions, children, success in worldly pursuits, relief from sufferings and so on. The fourth kind of devotees is rare. They are single-minded devotees whose wisdom is concentrated on the Supreme. They seek nothing material, accept whatever comes to them and submit to the Divine will, whole-heartedly. They are without selfish desires and worship God with purity of heart and complete devotion. They are close to the Divine and are most dear to Him. Ultimately, such a devotee achieves the highest goal of life-may be in the present life or in the afterlife.

तेषां ज्ञानी नित्ययुक्त एकभक्तिर्विशिष्यते ।
प्रियो हि ज्ञानिनोऽत्यर्थमहं स च मम प्रियः ॥ 7.17 ॥

Shlok 7.17: Of these, the wise one, who is ever united with Me and whose devotion is exclusive, is the best. Because I am extremely dear to the wise and so is he to Me.

Commentary: Among the four types of devotees of God, the wise one who asks for nothing and is truly devoted to Him, is the best of all. Knowledge of God without devotion– the love for God– is a dry speculation, and devotion without knowledge of God is a blind faith. Gyani is the best of all *Yogis* or *Bhakta* in the above verse. Bhakti remains incomplete without *Gyan. Gyan* brings faith, without faith there can be no love for God, without love, devotion and detachment will not abide, any more than the fluidity of water.

In the case of a *Gyani* the spirit is invoked not for acquisition of any sensual enjoyments but for elimination of all the self-destructive desires. Therefore, Sri Krishna who is the personification of the Self says the wise are the best and the highest in the category of those who invoke Him. Such a *Gyani* because of his selfless love is dear to the Lord and in turn He is dear to him. The Lord is regarded as the very Self of the wise. The other three, noted as above, are not so dear to the Lord.

उदाराः सर्व एवैते ज्ञानी त्वात्मैव मे मतम् ।
आस्थितः स हि युक्तात्मा मामेवानुत्तमां गतिम् ॥ 7.18 ॥

Shlok 7.18: All these seekers are indeed noble, but I regard the enlightened devotee as My very Self (*Parabrahm*) because one who is mentally steadfast, he is established in Me alone, as the supreme goal.

Commentary: All devotees are noble because they are interested in the Self. But the wise is exceedingly dear to Him because he has a steady mind, with a single pointed concentration on Him. He does not desire any worldly objects except the Supreme Being. He seeks Him alone as the goal. He practices meditation on Him as the Self of all. He tries to realize that he is identical with the Supreme Self. So the Lord regards him as His very Self. While the first three types attempt to use God according to their ideas, the wise act according to the will of God. Therefore, they are the best among them all.

Everything is manifestation of God

बहूनां जन्मनामन्ते ज्ञानवान्मां प्रपद्यते ।
वासुदेवः सर्वमिति स महात्मा सुदुर्लभः ॥ 7.19 ॥

Shlok 7.19: At the end of many births the wise man takes refuge in Me, realizing that all this is Vasudeva. A sage who believes that God is (in) everything is difficult to find.

Commentary: This process of evolution takes place during several lives in different births. However, it does not mean those who strive hard in this birth have no chance of realizing the goal of life. At the end of many births occupied in spiritual regeneration as preparatory to the attainment of wisdom, the man of mature wisdom resorts to Me, Vasudeva, the innermost Self (*Pratyagatma*). He who thus comes to Me, Narayan, the Self of All, is a Mahatma, a man of high soul; there is no other either equal to him or superior to him. Extremely rare is a great soul who thinks that Vasudeva is everything.

(**Note:** Vasudeva means the Lord, the innermost Self of all beings, Sri Krishna. Vasudeva is Sri Krishna's father. It seems that it was a later day insertion by some other authors to establish the linkage of Sri Krishna with Vrindavan, Sri Krishna had no necessity to use the name of his father here. Such insertion creates unnecessary confusion, especially when Sri Krishna is described as

Supreme Being and Supreme Personality. He is eternal, without any origin and end.)

कामैस्तैस्तैर्हृतज्ञानाः प्रपद्यन्तेऽन्यदेवताः ।
तं तं नियममास्थाय प्रकृत्या नियताः स्वया ॥ 7.20 ॥

Shlok 7.20: Others again, those whose wisdom has been rent away by this or that desire, devote themselves to other gods, and practice of various religious rites led by their nature.

Commentary: There are people who possess varied kind of desires and in order to fulfil their desires they resort to worshipping of different kinds of gods (*Devatas*) and goddesses, other than *Vasudev*, the Self. They perform various kinds of rites and rituals to please their deities; they being constrained to do so by their own nature (*Prakriti*), by that peculiar tendency (*Sanskar*) which they had acquired in the previous births. This verse simply suggests that one should concentrate on only one God, i.e. Sri Krishna that alone would serve all purposes. It is implied that believe in only one God and do not try to roam around in vain to perform various religious rites with a view to achieving what we aspire for.

Worshipper of deity as worshipper of God

यो यो यां यां तनुं भक्तः श्रद्धयार्चितुमिच्छति ।
तस्य तस्याचलां श्रद्धां तामेव विदधाम्यहम् ॥ 7.21 ॥
स तया श्रद्धया युक्तस्तस्याराधनमीहते ।
लभते च ततः कामान्मयैव विहितान्हि तान् ॥ 7.22 ॥

Shlokas 7.21-22: Whosoever desires to worship whatever deity– using any name, form, and method– with *Shraddha* (faith), I make their *Shraddha* steady in that very deity. Endowed with steady faith, they worship that deity and attain their wishes through that deity. Those wishes are, indeed, granted by Me alone.

Commentary: Whatever forms of God (*Devata*) a man worships in devotion and faith, I confirm his faith in the worship of that same form. In Lord Krishna's time, just as they do today, people worshipped several divine forms or gods– Indra, Shiv, Brahma, Goddess Durga, Goddess Lakshmi, Ram and so on. Whatever the method or form people worship, the Lord supports all such devotional practices. All these different forms of worship reach Lord Krishna only. This suggests that people of all faiths, belief or cult are the same for God. Religious differences do not matter at all for Sri Krishna. He has got same love for everybody irrespective of varying faith.

The power in the deities comes from the Supreme Lord as the aroma in the wind comes from the flower. God is the bestower of fruits of work. God fulfils all desires of His worshippers. One should not look down upon any method of seeking God because all worships are the worship of same God. He fulfils all sincere and beneficial prayers of a devotee if He is worshipped with faith and love. The wise realize that all names and forms are His, whereas the ignorant play the game of holy war in the name of religion to seek personal gain at the cost of others. All deities are one; they are merely different aspects of the Absolute.

It is said that whatever deity a person may worship, all his or her obeisance and prayers reach the Supreme Being just as all water that falls as rain eventually reaches the ocean. Whatever name and form of divinity one adores is worship of the same Supreme Being, and one gets the reward of deity-worship performed with faith. Desired results of worship are given indirectly by the Lord through one's favourite deity. Human beings live in the darkness of the prison cells of pairs of opposites. Deities are like icons or a medium that can open the window through which the Supreme may be perceived.

अन्तवत्तु फलं तेषां तद्भवत्यल्पमेधसाम् ।
देवान्देवयजो यान्ति मद्भक्ता यान्ति मामपि ॥ 7.23 ॥

Shlok 7.23: But such material gains of these less intelligent human beings are temporary, worshippers of deities go to deities; My devotees come unto Me.

Commentary: There are people who worship lower level gods, goddesses or various kinds of deities to fulfil their desires. The statement 'worshippers of deities go to the deities' means that those who invoke a desired manifestation or aspect of the Supreme, gain only that particular result sought for and nothing else, for the Supreme accepts our prayers and answers them at the level we approach Him. No devotion goes in vain. Sri Krishna does not favour such kinds of worshipping. Lord

Krishna advises against such lower grades of worship and recommends worship of the one and only Supreme Lord.

God does not manifest to the ignorant

अव्यक्तं व्यक्तिमापन्नं मन्यन्ते मामबुद्धयः ।
परं भावमजानन्तो ममाव्ययमनुत्तमम् ॥ 7.24 ॥

Shlok 7.24: The unintelligent think of Me as the unmanifest being having become manifest, not knowing my highest state of being, which is imperishable and incomparable.

नाहं प्रकाशः सर्वस्य योगमायासमावृतः ।
मूढोऽयं नाभिजानाति लोको मामजमव्ययम् ॥ 7.25 ॥

Shlok 7.25: Clouded by the illusion of my magic power (*Yogmaya*), I am not visible to all. This deluded world does not recognize me as unborn and immutable.

Commentary (Shlokas 7.24-7.25): That which is available for the perception by the sense organs or for the feelings of the mind or for the understanding of the intellect is called the 'manifest'. That which is not available for any one of these instruments of cognition, feeling or understanding is considered as 'unmanifest'.

The ignorant think that the Lord, too, like an ordinary mortal, comes down from the unmanifested state and assumes a body, impelled by His past *Karma.* This belief is due to their ignorance of His real nature, which is unchanging and ever luminous. Thus disregarding the Lord, the foolish worship the minor deities for the fulfilment of their selfish desires.

The misunderstood men come to the conclusion that physical glory of an incarnation is all the eternal truth. Although the form of an incarnation can be the focus of concentration, it cannot by itself be the Truth. The forms we impose on the Formless are due to our limitations. We turn away from the contemplation of the Ultimate Reality to concentrate upon imaginative reconstructions.

All Gods except the One Unmanifest Eternal are forms imposed on Him. God is not one among many. He is the One behind the ever changing many, who stands beyond all forms, the immutable centre of mobility.

The Supreme Being is ever unmanifest, and, as such, He never becomes manifest. In a true sense, the Supreme Being or Absolute does not incarnate. He actually never leaves His Supreme Abode! It is the intellect of the Supreme Being that does the work of creation, maintenance, incarnation, and destruction by using His innumerable powers. People do not know the transcendental and imperishable nature of God and wrongly think that God also incarnates like an ordinary person. He does not incarnate, but manifests using His own divine potencies. His birth, activities and form are transcendental or out of this world.

The Transcendental Being is beyond the human conception of form and formless. Those who consider God formless are as wrong as those who say God has a form. The argument whether God is formless or has a form has nothing to do with our worship and spiritual practice. We can worship Him in any way or form that suits us. A name, form, and description of the imperceptible, all pervasive and indescribable Lord has been given by saints and sages for cultivating the love of God in the hearts of common devotees. A name and a form are absolutely necessary for the purpose of worship and to nurture devotion. God appears to a devotee in a form in order to make his or her faith firm if one believes in God with a form. He does not appear to those who believe only in a formless Brahm. It is necessary that one should respect all forms of God (or deity), but establish relationship and worship one form only.

वेदाहं समतीतानि वर्तमानानि चार्जुन ।
भविष्याणि च भूतानि मां तु वेद न कश्चन ॥ 7.26 ॥

Shlok 7.26: I know, O Arjun, the beings of the whole past, and the present, and the future, but no one really knows Me.

Commentary: Consciousness or the Self is the same everywhere which illumines the respective thoughts and ideas of the individual. Thus the Lord or the Self is omniscient, i.e. all-knowing. Hence He says that I know the beings of the whole past, of the present and of the future.

The concept of awareness is eternal because it illumined the objects before, is illumining now and will be doing so in future. It is beginningless and endless. Although the Self activates the mind and the intellect neither of them can perceive, feel or comprehend the Self. Hence the Lord says although He knows everything and everyone at all times and places, but none knows me, except that one who worships Me and seeks refuge in Me. Just for want of knowledge of My real nature, nobody worships Me. This is because of ignorance.

इच्छाद्वेषसमुत्थेन द्वन्द्वमोहेन भारत ।
सर्वभूतानि सम्मोहं सर्गे यान्ति परन्तप ॥ 7.27 ॥

Shlok 7.27: By the delusion of the pairs of opposites arising from desire and aversion, O Bharat, all beings are subject to delusion at birth, O Parantap!

Commentary: Every individual, due to the instinct of self-preservation, has desire for things that contribute to the existence and aversion for things that obstruct the attainment of such things desired. He suffers because of the conflict between desires and aversion and his mind and intellect are pre-occupied with chasing of objects desired as also running away from the objects of aversion. This agitation due to the pairs of opposites is that which veils the truth from being grasped by an individual. In these circumstances no knowledge of the Self can be possible.

Therefore, the only way we can discover our equipoise and tranquillity as the eternal Self is to strike at the root, i.e. to control the agitations. All spiritual practices in all religions are techniques- emotional, intellectual, and physical- that bring about mental poise at least for a moment. Such a moment of calmness is the moment of perfect mental illumination, fulfilment of re-union.

The Lord says that all beings fall into this delusion right at their very birth. To get out of this delusion and to gain right knowledge is the goal of life and the Geeta provides such knowledge to the erring souls guiding them to come out of confusions and reach Perfection.

येषां त्वन्तगतं पापं जनानां पुण्यकर्मणाम् ।
ते द्वन्द्वमोहनिर्मुक्ता भजन्ते मां दृढव्रताः ॥ 7.28 ॥

Shlok 7.28: Those mortals of pure deeds whose sin has come to an end, who are freed from the delusion of pairs, they worship Me with a firm resolve.

Commentary: The word ‘sin’ means an error of judgement in man which veils the Self from him. When the sins are renounced, when the ignorance is overcome, our life is spent in the service of the Lord, the One in all. In the process, devotion deepens and knowledge of God increases until it reaches the vision of the One Self everywhere. They are said to be free from delusion in the form of pairs of opposites who do not lose their balance of mind either in joy or sorrow. That is the life eternal, free from the cycle of birth and death.

जरामरणमोक्षाय मामाश्रित्य यतन्ति ये ।
ते ब्रह्म तद्विदुः कृत्स्नमध्यात्मं कर्म चाखिलम् ॥ 7.29 ॥

Shlok 7.29: Those who strive for freedom from the old age and death– by taking refuge in Me– they know Brahm (or Spirit, Eternal Being) and the whole of *Adhyatma* and *Karma* in its entirety.

Commentary: Most people develop a sense of fear of old age, sickness and death. One can overcome these fears by devotion to the Lord. Those who aim for purifying themselves from all negative tendencies for contemplating on the Self do so to gain the freedom from old age and death. This, however, does not mean physical continuity of existence in the world. Birth, growth, disease, decay and death are necessary modifications for all living creatures on the earth. What is implied here is that a spiritual seeker in his meditation on the Self is to get over all his identifications with change which is indicated by the terms 'old age and death.'

Such a meditator, concentrating on the Self, realizes his oneness with the Consciousness Principle or the Self in him. To realize the Self is to become Brahm, since Self in an individual is the One Self everywhere. This non-duality of the Truth is implied in the statement that those who meditate upon Me, the Self, come to know the Brahm. They realize in full the Reality underlying the Innermost individual Self (*Adhyatma*), and they know all about action (*Karm*).

Through this verse, we see a fusion of *Karma, Bhakti* and *Gyan Yogs*. They all lead to the same goal. Many philosophers have confused our minds due to adherence to a particular tradition or sect, by emphasizing only one of the Yogs to the exclusion of the others.

साधिभूताधिदैवं मां साधियज्ञं च ये विदुः ।
प्रयाणकालेऽपि च मां ते विदुर्युक्तचेतसः ॥ 7.30 ॥

Shlok 7.30: Those who realize Me in the *Adhibhut* (physical region), in the *Adhidaiv* (the divine region) and in the *Adhiyagya* (region of sacrifice), attain Me even at the time of death, steadfast in mind.

Commentary: Those who are steadfast in mind, those who have taken refuge in Me or those who know Me as knowledge of elements on the physical plane, they are not finished by death.Human beings cannot know God or Brahm. But those, who know God to be the governing principle of the whole creation and the underlying basis of all, are blessed ones. The creation is not done by Brahm, but creation is Brahm Itself. *Jeev* (individual soul), *Jagat* (the cosmos) and *Jagadish* or the God is not three separate entities, but One and the same. In other words, there is nothing other than *Atman* or God in the universe. Since *Atman* is invisible and creation is visible; human eyes cannot see the invisible connection between *Atman* and the creation. And our mind makes us believe that the creator is other than and separate from the creation.

Thus, creation appearing separate from the creator is just an illusion, similar to a dream, created by the mind. Actually *Jeev* and *Jagat* do not exist, only Brahm exists. We have to recondition our mind that *Atman* and physical bodies or creation are one and the same and nothing else but Brahm exists in all different forms. Creation– including our body, mind and ego– is just another form of Consciousness and part and parcel of God. All is nothing but Brahm. One should always practice to see Brahm in all with the firm understanding that all is Brahm. This is called constant remembrance of God and is much easier to practise than *Japa,* meditation or any other spiritual practice. The goal of any spiritual practice is to achieve this state of mind where there is no duality. This practice leads one from body consciousness to God consciousness and equanimity of mind. All human weaknesses such as likes and dislikes, attachment, etc. disappear, leading one to *Nirvan.*

The creation is not Brahm, but it is Brahm that exists in the form of creation. Creation is the visible part of the cosmic body of Brahm. Because we cannot see Brahm, the mind makes us believe that creation is separate and different from Brahm. Thus appearance of duality (or the world) is nothing but a creation of mind or *Maya*. This appearance of duality creates ego or ignorance due to which we think ourselves different and separate from *Atman* and other beings and go through the cycles of transmigration. Only Self-knowledge can break this cycle. A simple method of Self-realization is presented below:

One should always contemplate– I am neither this body, nor the mind or the intellect; but I have my body, mind and intellect. I am That all-pervading Brahm, because there is nothing other than Brahm in the universe. I, being the eternal *Atman*, have no birth and death and I am free. It's the physical body– the abode of *Atman*– that takes birth and dies. This is the gist of Vedantic teachings and Self-realization.

OM TAT SAT

Discourse - 8

Akshar-Brahm Yog: Yog of Imperishable Brahm

Arjun could not grasp the intricacies of certain terminology like *Adhyatma, Karma, Adhibhut, Adhidaiv* and *Adhiyagya* referred to him by Sri Krishna in the last two verses of the preceding Discourse. He wants to understand them along with the notion of Supreme Being. As this Discourse deals with the imperishable and absolute nature of God and the *Pranava Mantra 'OM'*, which symbolizes it, this Dscourse is entitled as *Akshar Brahm Yog* (*'Akshar'* means indestructible or imperishable).

Lord Krishna explains how those who attain Him do not have to come again and again into this world of pleasure and pain. All beings, including gods and goddesses, come again and again into this universe from the state of unmanifest being wherein they remained at the end of an age-cycle. But the Lord exists even beyond this unmanifest being. That radiant, imperishable Divine Reality is the highest goal to be attained. Single-minded devotion at heart is the means of attaining this highest blessed state.

Brahm is the Supreme Lord who has created the Universe. Sri Krishna says the day and night of Brahm each of which lasts for thousands of ages. Those who know the day and night of Brahm they really understand the notion of day and night. From the unmanifested all the manifested worlds proceed at the coming of the 'day' and at the coming of the 'night' they dissolve into that alone which is called the unmanifested.

But the Supreme Lord stands as a witness apart from this process of evolution and dissolution. Therefore, those who remember and meditate on the Supreme Being as the eternal witness, at the time of death, will never have rebirth in this world but will reach the Supreme itself, which is beyond space, time and causation.

Sri Krishna explains how *Yogis* realize the Supreme Self at the time of death. He mentions the two paths by which the souls of the *Yogis* travel. The realized *Yogis* following the path of Light will merge in the Supreme Being and thus will have no return. This is called liberation (*Moksha*). The others who have attachment for the material world will go through the path of darkness and will take birth in the world to go through the cycle of births and deaths.

A true *Yogi* knowing these two paths will not follow ritualistic practices expecting to enjoy their fruits because he understands that everything other than the Self is a source of pain and is transient. Hence he is always immersed in the awareness of Eternal Consciousness. He ultimately attains the Primeval Abode.

The secret of reaching the Divine Being and thus freeing oneself forever from birth and death and the pains and sufferings of this worldly life is to constantly practise complete devotion to the Lord all the time. If one practises such steady remembrance through regular meditation, then he will be rooted in His remembrance even at the time of his departure from this body. The soul thus separated would go beyond darkness and bondage and attain the state of eternal blessedness.

Arjun asked:

किं तद्ब्रह्म किमध्यात्मं किं कर्म पुरुषोत्तम ।
अधिभूतं च किं प्रोक्तमधिदैवं किमुच्यते ॥ 8.1 ॥
अधियज्ञः कथं कोऽत्र देहेऽस्मिन्मधुसूदन ।
प्रयाणकाले च कथं ज्ञेयोऽसि नियतात्मभिः ॥ 8.2 ॥

Shlokas 8.1-02: What is that Brahm? What is *Adhyatma* (the Individual Self)? What is Karma (action), O Purushottam? And what is called *Adhibhut* (the physical region), and what is *Adhidaiv* (the divine region)? Who, and in what ways, is Adhiyagya here in this body, O Madhusudan? How can You, the Supreme Being, be remembered at the time of death by the self-controlled?

Commentary: In the last two verses of the seventh discourse, Lord Krishna uses certain abstract terms. Arjun did not understand their meaning. These terms are *Brahm, Adhyatma, Karma, Adhibhut, Adhidaiv* and *Adhiyagya.* As Arjun did not understand them, he proceeds to pose questions before the Lord. The Lord proceeds to answer these questions in their respective order:

Definition of Supreme Self, Spirit and *Karm*

Sri Krishna answers:

अक्षरं ब्रह्म परमं स्वभावोऽध्यात्ममुच्यते ।
भूतभावोद्भवकरो विसर्गः कर्मसञ्ज्ञितः ॥ 8.3 ॥

Shlok 8.3: The Supreme Imperishable (*Akshar*) is the Brahm; Its essential nature is known as *Adhyatma.* The creative force which brings forth the existence of beings is called *Karma* (action).

Commentary: Brahm is the *Akshar* which means the Imperishable, i.e. the Supreme Self (*Paramatman*). And the epithet 'supreme' applies better to Brahm, the Imperishable, who transcends all. The same Supreme Brahm existing as the Ego, as the Innermost Self, as the *Pratyagatma*, in every individual body, is called *Adhyatma:* that which first shows itself as the Innermost Self in the body and turns out in the end to be identical with the Supreme Reality, the Brahm, is known by the term '*Adhyatma*'.

The sacrificial act which consists in offering cooked rice, cakes and the like to the Gods (*Devatas)*, and which causes the origin of all creatures, is known by the term '*Karma'*; for it forms the seed as it were of all beings; it is in virtue of this act that all beings, animate and inanimate, come into existence.

Spirit is also called Eternal Spirit, Spiritual Being, Eternal Being or God in English; and Brahm, or Eternal Brahm. Brahm is also spelled as Brahma, but Brahm is different from Brahma in Sanskrit). Spirit is the cause of all causes. The word 'God' is generally used for both Spirit and the Supreme Spirit (or the Supreme Being). We have used the word 'Eternal Being' for Spirit; and 'Supreme Being', 'Absolute', and 'Krishna' for the Supreme Spirit here and elsewhere.)

The subtle body consists of six sensory faculties, intellect, ego, and five vital forces called bio-impulses (life forces, *Pran*). The individual soul (*Jiv or Jeev*) is defined as the subtle body sustained by Spirit. The individual soul is enshrined in the physical body. The subtle body keeps the physical body active and alive by operating the organs of perception and action.

अधिभूतं क्षरो भावः पुरुषश्चाधिदैवतम् ।
अधियज्ञोऽहमेवात्र देहे देहभृतां वर ॥ 8.4 ॥

Shlok 8.4: *Adhibhut* pertains to My perishable nature; and the conscious principle *Purush* is the *Adhidaivata*. The entity concerned with sacrifice (*Adhiyagya*) is Myself, here in the body, O best of the embodied.

Commentary: *Adhibhut* is the perishable existence. It comprises all material objects, everything that comes into existence. It refers to the whole animated creation and is composed of the whole perishable existence, i. e. of everything which is possible through birth. A biological being is an example of *Adhibhut. Purush* is, literally, that by which everything is filled, or that which lies in the body. *Purush* is a cosmic male. A particular object of nature is alive because of its presence in that object.

Adhidaivata is that which underlies all the *Devatas*, the presiding deities of the sense organs, mind and intellect. Brahm or Sri Krishna is *Adhidaivata*.

Adhiyagya is the deity named Vishnu. He identifies himself with all acts of sacrifice. Vishnu is the deity concerned with all acts of sacrifice in the body. As an act of sacrifice (*Yagya*) has to be performed by the body, it is said to be inherent in it, and as such it may be said to rest in the body.

The implication of these definitions is that the Eternal Self alone is the real and all the rest is delusory and super-impositions upon It. Thus to know the Self is to know everything and having known It as one's own real nature one is free to act or not to act in any of the fields of Not-Self.

As the Inner Controller of the body– *Antaryamin*– Sri Krishna is the presiding deity directing the various physical functions which are described as acts of sacrifice. Though He rests in the body, He is not attached to it and is completely different from the senses.

Constant meditation of the divine

अन्तकाले च मामेव स्मरन्मुक्त्वा कलेवरम् ।
यः प्रयाति स मद्भावं याति नास्त्यत्र संशयः ॥ 8.5 ॥

Shlok 8.5: He who at the time of death thinking of Me alone leaves the body, he attains unto My Being. There is no doubt in this.

यं यं वापि स्मरन्भावं त्यजत्यन्ते कलेवरम् ।
तं तमेवैति कौन्तेय सदा तद्भावभावितः ॥ 8.6 ॥

Shlok 8.6: Whatever object one remembers as one leaves the body at the end of life, that alone is attained by him, O son of Kunti, (because) of his constant thought of that object.

Commentary (Shlokas 8.6-8.5): The most prominent thought of one's life occupies the mind at the time of death determines the nature of the body to be attained in the next birth. One's destiny is determined by the predominant thought at the time of death. The last thought of a dying person determines the quality of his next birth. The soul goes to that on which its mind is set during the last moments. What we think we become. Our past thoughts determine our present birth and our present ones will determine the future.

This belief that one attains what he thinks of at the time of death is ingrained in Hindu faith. The mind carries with it the last impression, which is actualised in the next birth. If one thinks of the Lord at the point of death, he reaches the Lord. We can think of God in the last moments only if we are devoted to Him. The Lord explains that whatever object one remembers while leaving the body, he reaches that alone because of his constant thought of that object. In Srimad Bhagavatam there is a famous mythological story of Jada Bharat, a saintly hermit who, at the time of death, thought of his deer that he had raished from the time it was a little fawn. In his next birth, Jada Bharat took the form of a deer. There is a similar belief in Mahayan Buddhism as well.

Method of realization of God

तस्मात्सर्वेषु कालेषु मामनुस्मर युध्य च ।
मय्यर्पितमनोबुद्धिर्मामेवैष्यस्यसंशयम् ॥ 8.7 ॥

Shlok 8.7: Therefore, at all times, constantly remember Me and fight. With mind and intellect absorbed in Me, you shall doubtless come to Me.

Commentary: The supreme purpose of life should be to remember Sri Krishna all the time; so that one can remember Him at the time of death. To remember the absolute or Supreme Being may not be possible for most human beings. Sri Krishna advises Arjun to constantly keep his mind fixed on Him and at the same time perform his *Swadharma* (to fight). The mind is purified when a man performs his own *Dharma*, considering himself as an instrument of God. Only a pure mind can constantly remember God.

अभ्यासयोगयुक्तेन चेतसा नान्यगामिना ।
परमं पुरुषं दिव्यं याति पार्थानुचिन्तयन् ॥ 8.8 ॥

Shlok 8.8: By contemplating Me with an unwavering mind that is disciplined by Yogic practice, one goes to the Supreme Purush, the Resplendent, O son of Pritha.

Commentary: One gets spiritual awakening and the vision of God by constantly thinking of God in meditation, silent repetition of the holy names of God and contemplation. The endeavour of our whole life shapes our destiny. Spiritual practices are meant to keep the mind absorbed in His thoughts and fixed at His lotus feet. Ramakrishna said that when you desire anything, pray to the Mother aspect of God in a lonely place, with tears of sincerity in your eyes, and your wishes shall be fulfilled. He also said that it might be possible to attain Self-realization within three days. The more intensely one practices spiritual disciplines, the more quickly one attains perfection. The intensity of conviction and belief, combined with deep yearning, restlessness, intense longing, and persistence determine the speed of spiritual progress. The real practice of Hath Yog is not only the Yogic exercises taught in modern Yog centres, but also the consistence, persistence, and insistence in one's search for the Supreme Truth.

Self-realization is not a simple act but a process of gradual spiritual growth, starting with resolve, proceeding gradually to vow, divine grace, faith, and finally realization of Truth. The Supreme Being is not realized through discourses, intellect, or learning. It is realized only when one sincerely strives for it with vigorous effort. Sincere effort brings divine grace that unveils the Supreme Being. God helps those who help themselves.

Resplendent Purush means the presiding deity of the solar system which is considered as the manifestation of the Absolute as the Cosmic Spirit. He is also known as *Sagun* Brahm. How to meditate on God at the time of death is described in the following verses:

Meditating and attaining *Purush*

कविं पुराणमनुशासितारमणोरणीयांसमनुस्मरेद्यः ।
सर्वस्य धातारमचिन्त्यरूपमादित्यवर्णं तमसः परस्तात् ॥ 8.9 ॥

Shlok 8.9: Whosoever meditates upon the Omniscient, the ancient, the ruler (of the whole universe), who is subtler than the subtle, the supporter of all, whose form is inconceivable, effulgent like the sun and beyond the darkness (of ignorance).

Commentary: In this verse Sri Krishna reflects upon the nature of Self. It is very difficult for anybody to conceive of His form though it exists. Like the Sun, He is glorious with the splendour of His Eternal Intelligence (*Nitya-Chaitanya*) which is beyond the darkness of delusion or nescience (*Agyan*). He says that humans have got limited knowledge, but the Self is the Supreme Knower who knows everything, i.e. Omniscient and without whom no knowledge is ever possible. The Self is considered as the most ancient because it is the Eternal Truth which was there before any creation could be possible. The Self is minuter than the atom. The smallest divisible particle of any element maintaining the properties of that element is called its atom. It indicates that the Self is the subtlest of the subtle. The more a thing is subtle the more is its pervasiveness. Water is subtler than the ice and hence water is said to be more pervasive than the ice and similarly steam is more pervasive than water. Although the Self is in the form inconceivable, It is not inexperienceable since an individual can apprehend It to be of his own real nature during the process of Divine awakening. Though Self is effulgent like the sun, it is inconceivable, inexperienceable and incomprehensible.

प्रयाणकाले मनसाचलेन, भक्त्या युक्तो योगबलेन चैव ।
भ्रुवोर्मध्ये प्राणमावेश्य सम्यक् स तं परं पुरुषमुपैति दिव्यम् ॥ 8.10 ॥

Shlok 8.10: At the time of death, with an unshaken mind full of devotion, by the power of 'Yog' fixing the whole '*pran*' (breath) between the two eyebrows, he (the seeker) reaches the Supreme, Resplendent '*Purush*.'

Commentary: Some of the authors have philosophised the meaning of this verse by saying that this verse is not concerned with 'the physical death' rather than with 'the death of the ego'. Let us proceed with the usual or commonplace meaning of the word 'death'. Those who are endowed with full devotion *(Bhakti)* and practice *yog* regularly, they develop inward strength that they can get themselves merged with the Self. They reach the resplendent Supreme person. Such persons can definitely remember God at the time of their death. Here Sri Krishna gives exhaustive guidance concerning the process of meditation by all. The meaning of the various terms used here is as follows.

यदक्षरं वेदविदो वदन्ति, विशन्ति यद्यतयो वीतरागाः ।
यदिच्छन्तो ब्रह्मचर्यं चरन्ति, तत्ते पदं संग्रहेण प्रवक्ष्ये ॥ 8.11 ॥

Shlok 8.11: That which the knowers of the Vedas call imperishable, that which the ascetics (*Sannyasi*) freed from passion enter and desiring which they practice *Brahmacharya* that goal I will describe to you in brief.

Commentary: Sri Krishna now talks about meditation upon the monosyllable 'OM' or the *Pran* which is the ultimate goal for man. Chanting of the syllable OM is advised in almost all the Upanishads as a prelude to the meditation for an easier concentration of the mind. OM is considered as an expression of the Supreme Self or Its symbol like an idol. 'Freed from attachment' means detachment from the world of objects or petty desires with full understanding of the goal of life. Men of least desires will have the maximum success on the path of knowledge. A *Brahmachari* is a religious student who takes the vow of continence and self restraint. Every moment of this life is based on asceticism and abstinence.

Mediation on Om at the time of death

सर्वद्वाराणि संयम्य मनो हृदि निरुध्य च ।
मूर्ध्न्याधायात्मनः प्राणमास्थितो योगधारणाम् ॥ 8.12 ॥

ओमित्येकाक्षरं ब्रह्म व्याहरन्मामनुस्मरन् ।
यः प्रयाति त्यजन्देहं स याति परमां गतिम् ॥ 8.13 ॥

Shlokas 8.12-8.13: Having closed all the senses, having confined mind in the heart, having fixed his life-breath (*Pran*) into the head, occupied in the practice of concentration, uttering the one-syllabled 'Om'– the Brahm, and mediating on Me– he who departs, leaving the body, attains the Supreme Goal.

Commentary: Realization of the true nature of mind leads to meditation. A simple or common technique of meditation is described here for the benefits of those who believe in the precepts of the Geeta. People of any religion can follow the following steps while retaining their own religious faith.

(1) Wash your face, eyes, hands, and feet and sit in a clean, quiet and dark place, using any comfortable posture, with head, neck and spine straight and vertical. No music or incense during meditation is recommended. The time and place of meditation should be same for everyday. Follow the good principles of living by thoughts, words, and deeds. Some Yogic exercises are necessary. Midnight, morning, and evening are the best times to meditate for 15 to 25 minutes every day.

(2) Remember any name or form of the personal god you believe in and ask His or Her blessings.

(3) Close your eyes, tilt head slightly upward, and take 5 to 10 very slow and deep breaths.

(4) Fix your gaze, mind, and feelings inside the chest centre, the seat of the causal heart, and breathe slowly. Mentally chant 'So' as you breathe in and 'Hum' as you breathe out. Think as if breath itself is making these sounds 'So' and 'Hum' (I am That Spirit). Mentally visualize the breath going in and coming out through the nostrils. Be alert, and feel the sensation created by the breath in the body as you watch the breath. Do not try to control or lead your breathing; just watch your natural breathing.

(5) Direct the will towards the thought of merging yourself into the infinite space of the air you are breathing.

(6) Be regular and persist without procrastination.

The sound of 'OM' or 'AUM' is a combination of three primary sounds: A, U, and M. It is the source of all sounds one can utter. Therefore, it is the fittest sound symbol of Spirit. It is also the primeval impulse that moves our five nerve centres that control bodily functions. Yognanda calls 'AUM' the sound of the vibration of the cosmic motor. In the beginning was the word of God (OM, Amen, and Allah) and the word was God. This cosmic sound vibration is heard by *Yogis* as a sound, or a mixture of sounds, of various frequencies.

The Omnic meditation, mentioned here by Lord Krishna, is a very powerful, sacred technique used by saints and sages of all religions. Briefly, the Omnic method entails getting the mind permeated by a continuous, reverberating sound of *OM*. When the mind gets absorbed in repeating this divine sound, the individual consciousness merges into the Cosmic Consciousness.

When a devotee closes all the avenues of his knowledge and concentrates on the lotus of the heart, he ascends by the *Nadi* which passes upwards from the heart, and then fixing life-breath in the head, he utters the syllable *'OM'* and meditates on me, his departure takes place by the Self leaving the body, not by the Self being destroyed.

अनन्यचेताः सततं यो मां स्मरति नित्यशः ।
तस्याहं सुलभः पार्थ नित्ययुक्तस्य योगिनः ॥ 8.14 ॥

Shlok 8.14: O son of Pritha, he who constantly meditates on Me and no one else, ever steadfast, reaches me easily.

Commentary: A simpler method of contemplation is given below by Lord Krishna for those who cannot follow the conventional path of meditation discussed above. Constantly remembering the Lord throughout one's life is the easiest way of attaining Him. He who thinks of Sri Krishna uninterruptedly throughout life and who is ever steadfast in thought, He is easily accessible. This being so, therefore, without thinking of another, one should ever dwell steadfast in Me.

As the moment of departure from the physical body is not known to anybody Sri Krishna advises Arjun that one should always keep the mind and intellect absorbed in Him when he will come to Him alone. Sri Krishna emphasizes the need to practise Yog at all times. If one practices meditation throughout one's life fixing the mind on God, God-consciousness will remain steady even at the time of death instead of on worldly objects.

मामुपेत्य पुनर्जन्म दुःखालयमशाश्वतम् ।
नाप्नुवन्ति महात्मानः संसिद्धिं परमां गताः ॥ 8.15 ॥

Shlok 8.15: After attaining Me, the great souls are not subject to rebirth in this miserable transitory world because they have attained the highest perfection.

Commentary: Those who have attained to Sri Krishna, they are not again subject to birth. Birth here is the seat of pain arising from the body. Having reached the highest stage called *moksha*, they do not take birth again. Those who do not attain to Me return again (to the earth). Human birth is full of suffering. Those who die without realizing the Lord come back again to the earth. Life on earth, in spite of many moments of happiness, is intrinsically painful. On account of the intense love of God, the devotees do not experience suffering on earth and after death they attain Him.

आब्रह्मभुवनाल्लोकाः पुनरावर्तिनोऽर्जुन ।
मामुपेत्य तु कौन्तेय पुनर्जन्म न विद्यते ॥ 8.16 ॥

Shlok 8.16: All the worlds, including the world of Brahma, are subject to return, O Arjun; but, after attaining Me, O son of Kunti, there is no rebirth.

Commentary: From the world of Brahma downwards, everything comes and goes in a circle. Complete liberation, attended by cessation of birth and death, is possible only for a man who has realized his identity with Brahm or the Eternal Being. All other worlds, whether sub-human or super-human, are places of transitory enjoyments, where men departing from earth, experience the fruit of their actions and after exhausting such fruits are re-born on this earth.

(**Note:** Here and elsewhere one should not try to interpret Brahm and Brahma in the same sense, as they are not synonymous. Brahma is the name of a Hindu god who is taken as the manifestation of Brahm, Eternal or Supreme Being)

The cycle of creation

सहस्त्रयुगपर्यन्तमहर्यद्ब्रह्मणो विदुः ।
रात्रिं युगसहस्त्रान्तां तेऽहोरात्रविदो जनाः ॥ 8.17 ॥

Shlok 8.17: Those who know that the day of Brahma lasts for a thousand *Kalpas* and that his night (too) lasts for a thousand ages, they are the ones who know that a day and a night mean (in this context).

Commentary: Brahma is the first manifestation of the Absolute, Brahm in time and space. Brahma is also known as the Prajapati. Those persons who know how to compute Time know that Brahma's day is a thousand *yugas* long, and that His night is of the same duration as His day. Because the worlds are thus limited by time, therefore they return again. Day means evolution or projection of the universe. It is the period of cosmic manifestation. Night means cosmic involution or dissolution of the universe. It is the period of non-manifestation. According to the Hindu philosophy time is the measurement of interval between two different experiences. In a given single experience there is no perception of time just as in case of one point there is no concept of distance. Distance can be measured only when there are two points in space.

The worlds are conditioned by time and hence they manifest again and again although the duration of their cycles vary and are very long– each cycle lasting for crores of years (in terms of our present understanding of 365 days). A thousand such cycles makes a day of Brahma and another such cycle is the night of Brahma. Those who can see and live through the day and night of Brahma can really know what a day is and what a night is meaning thereby that such *yogis* can visualize many Brahmas arising and disintegrating in the Ocean of great Cause. Thus they do not feel any attachment even to the happiness of the highest heaven, how much less to that of earth.

अव्यक्ताद्व्यक्तय: सर्वा: प्रभवन्त्यहरागमे ।
रात्र्यागमे प्रलीयन्ते तत्रैवाव्यक्तसञ्ज्ञके ॥ 8.18 ॥

Shlok 8.18: At dawn, all manifest creatures spring from the unmanifest and at the coming of night they all dissolve in the same unmanifest.

Commentary: The Lord says that from the Unmanifest all the manifestations proceed at the coming of the day; at the coming of the night they merge verily into that alone, which is called the Unmanifest. Coming of the 'day' is the commencement of creation. Coming of the 'night' is the commencement of dissolution. The Unmanifested (*Avyakta*) is the sleeping condition of the Prajapati (Brahma) who is asleep. Out of That, all manifestations (*vyaktas*, all creatures, unmoving and moving are manifested at the commencement of day, i. e. when Brahma awakes. So, at the commencement of night, i. e. when Brahma goes to sleep, all the manifestations dissolve there only, in what is called *Avyakta*, the one already spoken of.

It is believed that one complete creative cycle of Brahma lasts for 8.64 billion solar years. This consists of one day and one night of Brahma, the Creator. The duration of partial dissolution, during which all heavenly planets, the earth, and the lower planets are finished and rest within Brahma, is 4.32 billion years and is called Brahma's night or Kalp. Complete dissolution takes place at the end of Brahma's (or creative cycle's) full life-span of 100 solar years, or 8.64 billion years x 360 days/year x 100 years = just over 311 trillion solar years called one Mahakalp, according to Vedic astrology. At this time, the complete material creation, including the modes of material Nature, enters into one of the four main, partial manifestations of the Absolute– called *Avyakta Brahma* or *Adi Prakriti*, the source and sink of the total material energy– and is finished. During the complete dissolution at the end of a *Mahakalp*, everything is said to take rest in the abdomen of *Avyakta Akshar Brahma* until the beginning of the next cycle of creation. In the first phase of the cycle of creation, Lord's energies enter into the universe to create and support diversities. And in the next phase, the Absolute is diffused as the all-pervading super-soul in the universe and remains present within the atoms and every cell of everything– visible or invisible.

भूतग्रामः स एवायं भूत्वा भूत्वा प्रलीयते ।
रात्र्यागमेऽवशः पार्थ प्रभवत्यहरागमे ॥ 8.19 ॥

Shlok 8.19: O Parth, the multitudes of beings have their alternate existence and non-existence. They cease to exist helplessly at the coming of the (cosmic) night and emerge again at the dawn of the (cosmic) day.

Commentary: The same multitude of beings (that existed in the preceding of day Brahma), coming forth again and again, merge in spite of themselves at the approach of night and re-manifest themselves at the approach of day. This multitude of beings comprise those that move as well as those that do not– the same multitude that existed in the preceding *Kalp* or age, and no other– involuntarily comes into being at the beginning of day, and are dissolved again at the beginning of night, at the close of the day. Again, at the beginning of day, it involuntarily comes into existence.

How the Creator keeps Himself occupied during His day and night each of which is of long duration is explained. It is indicated that the Creator creates during His day and the entire creation ends during His night by merging itself in the unmanifested. Creation is the crystallization of the unmanifested dormant existence into the manifested existence with names, forms and qualities. In other words, creation is only the production of a name, form with some specific qualities, out of the raw material in which the same name, form and quality already exist in an unmanifested condition. When a pot is created out of the mud the potness is already prevalent in the mud because nothing other than a pot can be created out of mud.

In the cosmic process of creation and dissolution the Creator or the total mind during the waking hours of long ages project out the already existing *Vasanas* and at the night they merge into the unmanifested. The declaration that the very same beings are born again and again and merge in spite of themselves shows that Hinduism does not believe in a creation preceded by the condition of absolute non-existence.

परस्तस्मात्तु भावोऽन्योऽव्यक्तोऽव्यक्तात्सनातनः ।
यः स सर्वेषु भूतेषु नश्यत्सु न विनश्यति ॥ 8.20 ॥

Shlok 8.20: But beyond this unmanifest, there is yet another Unmanifest, Eternal Existence, who does not perish when all beings perish.

Commentary: Another unmanifest Eternal refers to *Parabrahm*, which is distinct from the unmanifest (primordial Nature), and which is of quite a different nature. It is superior to *Hiranyagarbh* (the creative Intelligence) and the unmanifest Nature because It is their cause. It is not destroyed when all beings from Brahma down to a blade of grass are destroyed. Another unmanifest eternal Being refers to the imperishable Brahm, which is imperceptible to senses and which is altogether of a different kind. It is supra-cosmic and beyond ignorance. It does not perish because it is beyond time, space and causality. 'All beings perish' implies that everything from Brahma downwards to all kinds of things tend to disappear. Nothing is *Akshar* except for Brahm.

अव्यक्तोऽक्षर इत्युक्तस्तमाहुः परमां गतिम् ।
यं प्राप्य न निवर्तन्ते तद्धाम परमं मम ॥ 8.21 ॥

Shlok 8.21: What has been called the Unmanifested and the Imperishable has been described as the Goal Supreme. That is My highest state, having attained which, there is no return.

Commentary: That *Avyakta* which is called Akshar, the Imperishable, the Unmanifested Beings. Having reached that state, none has returned to this *Sansar,* the mundane life. That is My Supreme Abode. The knower of such Imperishable, Eternal Brahm never again falls under the spell of Maya or ignorance (never comes back). The abode of Brahm is called Supreme because the relative universe is the inferior manifestation of Brahm.

पुरुषः स परः पार्थ भक्त्या लभ्यस्त्वनन्यया ।
यस्यान्तः स्थानि भूतानि येन सर्वमिदं ततम् ॥ 8.22 ॥

Shlok 8.22: That Supreme Purush, O Arjun, is attainable by unswerving devotion to Him alone within whom all beings dwell and by whom all this is pervaded.

Commentary: That which dwells in the body is *Purush*; the Consciousness principle is the presiding deity which rules the body and hence it is the *Purush.* Brahm is called *Purush* (Person) because He dwells in everybody or He is full (*Poornam*). None other than Him is higher. He is attained by exclusive devotion, i.e. by *Gyan* or knowledge of the Self. All the created beings abide within the *Purush;* for every effect rests within its cause; and by that *Purush* the whole world is pervaded.

The technique by which the Unmanifest, the Imperishable– the Supreme *Purush* is attainable is explained. Single pointed devotion with the total detachment from the world of body, mind and intellect is the means to achieve the Supreme *Purush.* The detachment from the false is achieved by the growing attachment with the Real. Total identification of oneself with the experience of the Self or the realization that nothing exists except the Lord, is pure devotion.

The two paths of departure

यत्र काले त्वनावृत्तिमावृत्तिं चैव योगिनः ।
प्रयाता यान्ति तं कालं वक्ष्यामि भरतर्षभ ॥ 8.23 ॥

Shlok 8.23: O Bull of the Bharatas, now I shall describe different time in which the *yogis* depart never to return and also the time in which they depart to return.

Commentary: Sri Krishna now tells about the paths adopted by the seekers to reach the two different destinations, viz the one from which there is a return and the other from which there is no return. The former is a Divine Mission seeking the Imperishable by ending the ego and re-discovering one's own Real Nature as none other than the Eternal Consciousness, the Changeless Substratum of the whole universe. The latter path is the life of satisfying the ego by gaining the experiences of joy among sense objects each of which ultimately brings forth sorrow.

These two situations differ from each other since the one leads to a return again and again to a finite embodiment for living a life of limitations and the other assures a goal, having reached which, there is no return and where one enjoys Absolute Bliss. Lord explains in verses 8.24-25 that there are two distinct goals of life which people to look for. These two goals are achieved through two different paths guiding the two types of seekers of their destinations. One is called the path of no return (verse 8.24), and the other is the path of return (verse 8.25). These two paths are renamed in verse 8.26 as the path of light and the path of darkness, the path of *Moksha* and path of coming and going, the path of the seekers of spirituality and seekers of materialism, path of the light of knowledge and of darkness and ignorance.

अग्निर्ज्योतिरहः शुक्लः षण्मासा उत्तरायणम् ।
तत्र प्रयाता गच्छन्ति ब्रह्म ब्रह्मविदो जनाः ॥ 8.24 ॥

Shlok 8.24: Fire, flame, day-time, the bright fortnight, the six months of the Northern passage of the sun– taking this path,

the knowers of Brahm go to Brahm.

Commentary: The path of no return is also called the path of gods (*Devayan*), the path of light of Self-knowledge, the northern path, the solar path, and the path of slow and gradual development (*Karm-mukti*), the ascending path of evolution. This path is blocked for the ignorant and persons devoid of necessary qualities like austerity, abstinence, faith and knowledge. Those who have above mentioned qualities will walk this path. It is also said that this path is closed during the six months of southern solstice of the sun as mentioned in verse 8.25.

Fire, light, day-time, the bright fortnight and the six months of the northern solstice of the sun indicate deities presided over by the Sun. It is said in the Upanishads that those who qualify for the northern path after death reach the celestial ruler of fire, light and from there to the celestial ruler of the day, from there to the celestial ruler of the bright fortnight, from there to the celestial ruler of the six months during which the sun travels northwards, from there to Sun, and from there to lightening. Then a Super-being, created from the mind of Brahma, comes and leads them to the world of Brahm. Becoming perfect at each stage, they stay in the world of Brahm till the end of the cycle of creation or a *Mahakalp*; at that time they merge in Brahm.

The northern path described above is open to those who know Brahm but are not completely Self-realized. Such persons have some trace of dormant desires (or *Vasana*) left. When all desires born of ego are completely eradicated by Self-knowledge, one instantly merges in Brahm in this very life after death. This is called *Jeevanmukti or Brahm Nirvan*. Time of death does not matter for such souls.

धूमो रात्रिस्तथा कृष्णः षण्मासा दक्षिणायनम् ।
तत्र चान्द्रमसं ज्योतिर्योगी प्राप्य निवर्तते ॥ 8.25 ॥

Shlok 8.25: Smoke, night-time, and the dark fortnight, the six months of Southern passage of the sun– taking this path, the righteous person (*Yogi*) attains heaven and comes back to the earth again.

Commentary: Fire, flame, day-time, the bright fortnight, the six months of the northern passage of the sun– all these indicate the path of the

Gods presided over by the sun while the path of the ancestors is described in the verse 25 which is presided over by the moon. The path of Gods is the path of illumination that leads to liberation from where there is no return for the departed souls. On the other hand the path of ancestors is the path of darkness which leads to rebirth.

This path is called the path of darkness, the path of return, the path of ignorance, the path of ancestors, lunar path and the path of materialism. This path is presided over by the Moon god, representing the world of matter and sense enjoyment. Those who qualify for this path, after death, reach the celestial ruler of smoke, from there to the celestial ruler of the night, from there to the celestial ruler of the dark fortnight, from there to the celestial ruler of the six months during which the sun travels southwards, and from there to heaven. Such *Yogis* return to the mortal world, after enjoying heavenly pleasures for a period of time, when the fruits of their virtuous deeds are exhausted.

शुक्लकृष्णे गती ह्येते जगतः शाश्वते मते ।
एकया यात्यनावृत्तिमन्ययावर्तते पुनः ॥ 8.26 ॥

Shlok 8.26: These bright and dark paths of the world are verily deemed eternal; by the one a man does not return, by the other he returns again.

Commentary: The bright path is the path to God taken by devotees. The dark path is taken by those who perform sacrifices or charitable acts with the expectation of rewards. The one is bright because it illumines knowledge; the other is dark because it is wanting in that light. The two paths are open to those only in the world who are engaged in action or devoted to knowledge; they are not open to the whole world.

Life is a conflict between light and darkness. The former makes for release and the latter for rebirth. The Lord here uses the ancient belief to illustrate the great spiritual truth that those who are lost in the darkness of ignorance go by the path of the ancestors and are subject to rebirth and those who live in the day of illumination and walk on the path of knowledge are free from rebirth. This attainment of liberation through Self-Knowledge, while living in a physical body, is the goal of human life. The other courses, paths, etc. are described in order to spur men to strive for Self-Knowledge and for attainment of liberation here on earth.

Unrighteous ones, who do not qualify for the two paths mentioned in verses 8.24 and 8.25, transmigrate into lower wombs, such as animals, birds, and insects. The immortal soul wanders endlessly through the ocean of transmigration, made up of 8.4 million different species of life on this planet. The good Lord, out of His sweet will known as 'The Law of Grace', bestows the precious gift of the human body that is like a raft to carry one across the ocean of transmigration. Consider what we are is God's gift to us, and what we become is our gift to God. It is also said that human birth, faith in God, and the help of a real Guru come only by His grace. Our present life provides the opportunity for preparation for the next life. According to the activities in this life, one can either get a promotion or salvation, a demotion or transmigration, or another chance for salvation by reincarnating as a human being.

Self-knowledge leads to salvation

नैते सृती पार्थ जानन्योगी मुह्यति कश्चन ।
तस्मात्सर्वेषु कालेषु योगयुक्तो भवार्जुन ॥ 8.27 ॥

Shlok 8.27: No *Yogi*, O son of Pritha, is deluded after knowing these two paths. Therefore, one should be resolute in attaining salvation– the goal of human birth– at all times.

Commentary: Knowing that one of the paths leads to this world and the other to *Moksha,* the *Yogi* takes up the one leading to illumination and rejects the other. Here *Yogi* is the one who has withdrawn himself from his false-identifications and entered into contemplation of the Self with single-pointed mind.

In short, this entire Discourse is Krishna's advice to Arjun that he should, even while acting in this world, strive constantly to be the one living in the awareness of the Divine, through selfless identification with the Eternal, the Imperishable *Purush*. The guiding principle is that whatever work one undertakes, he should not lose sight of the Eternal.

वेदेषु यज्ञेषु तपःसु चैव दानेषु यत्पुण्यफलं प्रदिष्टम् ।
अत्येति तत्सर्वमिदं विदित्वा योगी परं स्थानमुपैति चाद्यम् ॥ 8.28 ॥

Shlok 8.28: Having known all this, the *yogi* transcends the pious

gain accruing from (a study of) the Vedas, oblations, austerities, and acts of charity, and proceeds towards the supreme and primal abode.

Commentary: This verse states that whatever meritorious effect is declared (in the scriptures) to accrue from (the study of) the Vedas, (the performance of) *Yagyas*, (the practice of) austerities and gifts-above all rises the *Yogis*, having known to this, and attains to the Supreme, Primeval Abode. This *verse* has indirectly provided crutches to the philosophy of Vedas, while at several places the Vedas have been subjected to criticisms because the Vedas have vouched for the practice of elaborate rituals. The Geeta has always been opposed to *Yagya* and sacrifices, as justified by the Vedas. It is really very surprising to see the Vedas are being defended and supported here. This verse has been definitely added to the Geeta at a later stage by those who were in support of the Vedic ideals of life. Insertion or addition at the end of the Discourse is always very easy. There was hardly any necessity on the part of Sri Krishna, who is in the form of Supreme Being, to talk about the Vedas before Arjun in the battlefield.

A Summary of Concepts and Issues Discussed between Sri Krishna and Arjun

Sr. No.	Arjun's Questions (What is ....)	Sri Krishna's Answers
1.	Brahm	Brahm is that which is Supreme, Imperishable, Unchaning and all-pervading. It is the cause for all effects. It is causeless cause.
2.	Adhyatma	One's own individual Self or essential nature or individual consciousness is called Adhyatma. It is that part of Supreme Consciousness together with limiting ancillaries viz. time, space, name and form.
3.	Karma	It is the creative force which is the cause of existence, manifestation and sustenance of all beings.
4.	Adhibhut	It means all perishable things- the five elements of the Universe with all its objects, all things that have a beginning and an end, the intellect, mind, senses and body.
5.	Adhidaiv	The Universal Soul or the Divine Intelligence which is the controller of all. He is the vital energy or life-force behind all movable and immovable objects of the entire Universe.
6.	Adhiyagya	It is the presiding Deity of all sacrifices and the witnessing conciousness, i.e. who dwells in the body.
7.	How the Lord is to be known by the self-controlled one at the time of death?	He who dies with his last thought fixed on God will reach God alone.

OM TAT SAT

Discourse - 9

Raj-Vidya Guhya Yog: Confidential Knowledge of the Ultimate Truth

In Discourse nine Lord Krishna reveals knowledge relating to sovereign science and the sovereign secret. He explains how the entire material existence is created, pervaded, maintained and done away with by His external energy and now all beings come and go under His supervision. The subject matters covered are primarily concerned with devotional service and these subject matters are most confidential.

As Arjun was a qualified aspirant and endowed with faith, Krishna tells him about the sovereign knowledge and sovereign secret which is known by direct experience. Sri Krishna observes that without faith in this knowledge man fails to reach God and is born again to suffer.

Sri Krishna describes His nature as the eternal, all-comprehensive Truth. He is everything that is invisible and visible. He pervades everything that exists. He creates everything, sustains everything, and when final dissolution takes place, absorbs everything into Himself. He manifests them again when the next creation begins. All beings that are ignorant of this knowledge are caught helplessly in the cycle of birth and death. In the midst of this creation, preservation and dissolution of the universe, the Lord stands as a silent witness, unaffected and unattached. He is the sole director, sustainer and supervisor of His Cosmic *Prakriti.*

The ignorant are not able to recognise the Lord. Although the cruel beings assume a human form, their nature is that of demons. The

Mahatma, who has realized God, on the other hand, is a man of knowledge, and perceives Him indwelling all beings and creatures. He beholds the underlying unity of existence in all names and forms.

The Lord's divine protection is assured to all those who take refuge in Him. Whatever path a devotee follows, he ultimately reaches Him. He is the goal of various methods of spiritual practices. Devotion, Sri Krishna emphasizes, is the essence of all spiritual discipline. If this supreme element is present, then the devotee is freed from bondage. The Lord observes the motive and degree of devotion. Even the most sinful and diabolical man, if he takes a radical turn towards the path of righteousness and truth, reaches the Lord. Whatever vocation one follows, one can attain the Lord if one seeks earnestly and with loving devotion. The essential thing is to fix the mind on the Lord and dedicate everything unto Him– one's body, mind, actions, emotion and will. Complete surrender to Sri Krishna, without any expectation, is a real devotion to Him.

Lord Krishna said:

इदं तु ते गुह्यतमं प्रवक्ष्याम्यनसूयवे ।
ज्ञानं विज्ञानसहितं यज्ज्ञात्वा मोक्ष्यसेऽशुभात् ॥ 9.1 ॥

Shlok 9.1: Since you have faith in My words, I shall reveal to you the most profound, secret, transcendental knowledge together with transcendental experience. By virtue of this you will be released from all evils (of worldly existence).

Commentary: In this opening verse Sri Krishna assures Arjun that He will reveal the togetherness of science and spirituality. Such knowledge is the direct means of attaining liberation. This knowledge about the Self dwelling in the body, and about the identity of the individual self and the Supreme Self, is considered most profound mystery because it is realized through one's own experience or spiritual intuition. It cannot be expressed in words. Arjun is considered to be the most suitable person to know this deep mystery because he is free from jealousy and does not belong to the category of those who always find fault with others. Sri Krishna says that the one who receives this knowledge shall be free from problems of life and can rule over circumstances and face adversities with a smile. Krishna assures that by understanding that knowledge one will be released from the bondage of the world.

Knowledge of supreme is the highest mystery

राजविद्या राजगुह्यं पवित्रमिदमुत्तमम् ।
प्रत्यक्षावगमं धर्म्यं सुसुखं कर्तुमव्ययम् ॥ 9.2 ॥

Shlok 9.2: Of sciences, the highest; of profundities, the deepest; of purifiers, the supreme, is this; realizable by the direct perception, endowed with (immense) merit, very easy to perform, and of an imperishable nature.

Commentary: Sri Krishna is giving the knowledge to Arjun which is really a kind of science of all sciences and hence it is the highest kind of knowledge. It is the science of life which is sovereign in its import, deep in its substance and supreme in its purifying effects. It is clearly comprehensible since it can be verified by direct experience. It is knowledge by acquaintance and not by description. As a lamp, when lit in a room, instantly does away with deep darkness, so the knowledge of Brahm, when realized in the heart, reduces to ashes all the accumulated past karmas. Hence it is called supreme purifier. The Bliss arising out of the knowledge of Brahm, though easily acquired, is eternal.

अश्रद्दधानाः पुरुषा धर्मस्यास्य परन्तप ।
अप्राप्य मां निवर्तन्ते मृत्युसंसारवर्त्मनि ॥ 9.3 ॥

Shlok 9.3: O Scorcher of foes, those who have no faith in this knowledge do not attain Me and follow the cycles of birth and death.

Commentary: Everything is possible for the person who has faith in God. Faith in the Supreme power holds the key to unlock the gates of salvation. Those without faith mean those who regard the physical body as the self and do not believe in the indestructibility and immortality of the soul. Those who do not possess the knowledge about the Supreme Being, they keep coming and going endlessly. Salvation is not possible for such beings.

मया ततमिदं सर्वं जगदव्यक्तमूर्तिना ।
मत्स्थानि सर्वभूतानि न चाहं तेष्ववस्थितः ॥ 9.4 ॥

Shlok 9.4: All things in this universe are pervaded by Me in My unmanifest Form; all beings exist in Me, but I do not dwell in them.

Commentary: This entire universe is an expansion of, or pervaded by, My unmanifest aspect. All beings depend on Me as a gold chain depends on gold and milk products depend on milk. I do not depend on– or become affected by– them because I am the source of all. God does not dwell in any object of His creation. All the creations are perishable or destructible. God is above all these, as God is neither perishable nor destructible. God is always beyond His creation. Everything is the unmanifest form of God.

The above message is an esoteric one. Lord Krishna calls it Royal or Supreme secret message. Waves belong to the ocean, but the ocean does not belong to the waves. *Gyanis* and *Bhaktas* or devotees should strive to understand this concept. While the Lord pervades everything in subtle form, He does not dwell in them. Later, the Lord says that He dwells in the hearts of all– which means that he is in the consciousness of all beings.

न च मत्स्थानि भूतानि पश्य मे योगमैश्वरम् ।
भूतभृन्न च भूतस्थो ममात्मा भूतभावनः ॥ 9.5 ॥

Shlok 9.5: Nor do the beings exist in Me; behold My divine Yog! I Myself am the creator and sustainer of all beings, yet I do not dwell in them.

Commentary: This verse is very popular, but difficult for easy comprehension. It requires considerable reflection. One can understand the verse by way of an example. The wave is water, but the water is not wave. The water has become the vapour, the cloud, the rain, the ice as well as the bubble, the lake, the river, the wave, and the ocean. These are nothing but names of different forms (or transformations) of water. From a monistic viewpoint, there is no ocean, no wave, and no lake, but water only. The monoistic viewpoint does not dismiss the perception of duality, but dismisses only the reality of duality.

However, a wave is a wave as long as it does not realize its true nature– that it is not a wave but water. As soon as a wave decisively realizes that it is not a wave but water, the wave no longer remains a wave, but becomes water without delay. Similarly when one realizes that he or she is not this physical body– but the Eternal Being in the form of Spirit residing inside the physical body– one transcends physical body and immediately becomes one with the Spirit without undergoing any physical change. As a physical body, one is mortal, limited by a form, with colour, gender, and temperament. But as a part of the Spirit, one is free, immortal, and limitless. This is called *Nirvan,* or salvation.

Nothing can exist in this world unless the Lord, the Spirit, forms its substratum. Upanishads declare that the Lord, after creating the objects entered them as their indwelling consciousness to enliven them. Brahm, God, exists as the unmanifest Reality and pervades everywhere. Nothing exists other than Brahm. Yet because of delusion we see only the manifested world of beings and not it's underlying Reality. We superimpose the illusory world on the eternal Reality, Brahm. This is like a deluded person misunderstanding a post as a ghost in darkness. He is said to superimpose the figure of ghost on the post on account of his wrong perception. The post is the substratum of the ghost; the post pervades every part of the ghost; the ghost cannot exist unless there is the post but the post can survive in spite of the absence of the ghost. Similarly Brahm exists without the world, but the world's existence depends upon Brahm.

Hence Krishna declares that all things in this universe are pervaded by Him in His unmanifest aspect and that all beings exist in Him but He does not exist in them. This is just like saying that the ghost exists in the post but the post does not exist in the ghost. The post remains the source of the ghost. There can be no ghost without the post, but the post can remain without the ghost.

A thing devoid of inner reality cannot exist or be an object of experience. The Lord is the inner reality of everything. The reality of the Lord makes everything real in this world. But the reality of the Lord does not depend upon the world. He always exists whether the universe of names and forms exists or not. The Lord is incorporeal and therefore has no real contact with the material world. He cannot be contained in any object. He is self-existent and self-luminous. Only a fraction of His majesty illumines the sun, the moon and the universe. But He himself is transcendental. This is the nature of Sri Krishna. He should not be perceived in a human form despite the fact he existed or appeared in the human form in the battlefield of Kurukshetra.

The Lord, in reality, is neither the container nor the contained. In Him there is not the slightest trace of duality. In His purest essence He is above the law of cause and effect. In the final realization, the object and the subject become one; the whole universe merges in the Lord. In that state the Lord remains as One without a second, a homogeneous concentration of consciousness. The concepts of container and contained, cause and effect, apply to the realm of manifestation or Maya. Through Maya even though the Lord manifests in the tangible, relative universe, and appears to be its cause and support, yet He is always One without a second, transcendental, incorporeal and unattached. This is His eternal mystery- 'My Divine Mystery' as the Lord puts it in Verse 5.

यथाकाशस्थितो नित्यं वायुः सर्वत्रगो महान् ।
तथा सर्वाणि भूतानि मत्स्थानीत्युपधारय ॥ 9.6 ॥

Shlok 9.6: As the great wind, moving everywhere, ever abides in ethereal space (the Akash), so you know that all beings rest in Me.

Commentary: As objects like planets and stars appear hanging or stuck in the space without any visible connection at all, similarly the entire universe, including space itself, abides in the unified field called Consciousness. Time has no access to space; similarly Consciousness is everlasting, indivisible, and unaffected by everything going on in its field, just as clouds do not make the sky wet.

It is really difficult for the ordinary intellect to comprehend the idea that a substance which exists everywhere, allowing everything to exist in it, but at the same time it in itself does not get conditioned by the things existing in it. Although the wind moves everywhere in the space, exists in the space and is supported by the space yet the wind does not put any limitation on the space. Space holds them all but is touched by none. This illustrates the relationship between the Self and the not-Self. When the wind moves the space does not move. None of the qualities of the wind is the quality of the space. So also, the Real supports the unreal which seemingly lives in the Real and yet the unreal full of misery and sorrow can never condition the Real. On the same analogy, without affecting the Lord in any way, good and evil, pain and pleasure, and the other traits of this universe do not touch the Lord because from His point of view they are illusory. He can never be touched by anything happening in time and space. As a light cannot be affected by the good or evil deed done with its help, so the soul, which in its essence is one with the Lord, cannot be affected by the good and evil action of the body and mind.

Maya is the cause of creation and dissolution

सर्वभूतानि कौन्तेय प्रकृतिं यान्ति मामिकाम् ।
कल्पक्षये पुनस्तानि कल्पादौ विसृजाम्यहम् ॥ 9.7 ॥

Shlok 9.7: All beings, O Arjun, merge in me (at the end of the cosmic cycle). At the beginning of a new *Kalp* I send them forth again.

Commentary: As a spider spreads out the web from within, plays in it, and again draws the web into itself, similarly the Eternal Being (or Spirit) creates the material world from itself, plays in it as living entity, and takes it into itself during complete dissolution. All manifestations are born, sustained, and finally merge in Spirit as bubbles of water are born, sustained, and merge in water. Spirit manifests itself into the universe by using its own internal power without the help of any external agent. It is possible for one Spirit– by virtue of possessing diverse powers– to be transformed into multiplicity without any outside help. Spirit (or the Eternal Being) is thus both the efficient and the material cause of creation.

प्रकृतिं स्वामवष्टभ्य विसृजामि पुनः पुनः ।
भूतग्राममिमं कृत्स्नमवशं प्रकृतेर्वशात् ॥ 9.8 ॥

Shlok 9.8: I activate *Prakriti* and create this multitude of beings again and again. These beings are under the control of *Prakriti.*

Commentary: The whole process of creation, preservation and dissolution is due to the Lord's Maya, His lower *prakriti* or nature consisting of the three gunas in their undifferentiated state and yet He is unaffected by it. These three *gunas* are *Sattva* (goodness, constructive, harmonious), *Rajas* (passion, active, confused), and *Tamas* (darkness, destructive, chaotic). The three gunas are the most subtle qualities of Nature that underlie matter, life and mind. They are the energies through which not only the surface mind, but our deeper consciousness functions. They are the powers of the soul which hold the *karmas* and desires that propel us from birth to birth. The *gunas* adhere in Nature herself as her core potentials for diversification.

At the end of the time-cycle, the names and forms of the manifested universe go back into the seed state and remain merged in *Prakriti.* At this state the three *gunas* of *Prakriti* remain in equilibrium. When this balance is disturbed, again creation takes place. This process of creation and dissolution is without beginning. Thus the better terms to indicate creation and dissolution are manifestation or evolution and mergence or involution. The Lord, in His pure essence, remains unaffected by the activities of His *Maya*, though the insentient *Maya* is activated because of its proximity to the Lord. This verse says that the Lord with the help of *Prakriti* manifests the universe. Because of His very proximity, insentient Nature becomes active. *Maya or Prakriti* is under His control. But Jeev or the created being is under the control of *Maya*. Living beings come out of *Prakriti* which remains dormant at the end of the previous cycle. Dissolution or the state in which the three *gunas* remain at perfect balance is called the sleep (dormant state) of *Prakriti*.

The beings at the end of the previous cycle merged in *Prakriti* are still under the influence of Maya or ignorance. As *Prakriti* becomes active at the beginning of the next cycle, the beings also assume appropriate births according to their past karma.

न च मां तानि कर्माणि निबध्नन्ति धनंजय ।
उदासीनवदासीनमसक्तं तेषु कर्मसु ॥ 9.9 ॥

Shlok 9.9: These acts of creation do not bind Me, O Dhananjay, because I remain indifferent and unattached to those acts.

Commentary: Because the Lord is responsible for the manifestation of heterogeneous beings of unequal conditions, a question arises whether He is guilty of partiality as we normally think. This issue is answered here. The Lord says that He is unconcerned about fruit of His action relating to the creation of unequal and diverse beings.

It is attachment to the fruit that binds. He is unconcerned because He is totally devoid of the feeling of 'I do'. The creation belongs to the realm of Maya and the Lord is beyond Maya. There is no relationship between the Lord and creation just as there is no contact between the desert and the mirage. He is totally free from any desire, purpose, motive or agency so far as the creation is concerned.

The Self is neutral or indifferent to everything. It does nothing nor does It cause anything to be done. The Self has no attachment to the fruits of Its actions nor has It any egocentric feeling of agency or doership just as an Umpire is not interested in the results of the game he is umpiring. Therefore, the actions involved in creation and dissolution do not bind the Lord.

मयाध्यक्षेण प्रकृतिः सूयते सचराचरम् ।
हेतुनानेन कौन्तेय जगद्विपरिवर्तते ॥ 9.10 ॥

Shlok 9.10: O son of Kunti, with Me as the presiding deity, Prakriti (Nature) sends for the moving and non-moving entities. For this reason, the world (Universe) operates.

Commentary: The Lord presides over only as a witness; nature does everything. By reason of His proximity or presence, nature sends forth the moving and the unmoving. The prime cause of this creation is nature or *prakriti*. Although all actions are done with the help of the light of the sun, yet the sun cannot become the doer of all actions. Similarly, the Lord cannot become the doer of actions even though nature does all actions with the help of the light of the Lord. As the Self illumines ignorance or Maya, which is the material cause of this world, the Self is regarded as the cause of this world. The magnet is indifferent, although it makes the iron pieces move on account of its proximity. Similarly, The Lord remains indifferent although He makes the nature-Prakriti-create the world. He presides over the world which consists of moving and unmoving objects as a witness. By His presence the wheel of the manifested and unmanifested beings revolves round and round.

Devotion to the Supreme brings its great rewards

अवजानन्ति मां मूढा मानुषीं तनुमाश्रितम् ।
परं भावमजानन्तो मम भूतमहेश्वरम् ॥ 9.11 ॥

Shlok 9.11: The fool disregard me, dwelling in human form. They do not know my transcendental nature, as the great Lord of all beings.

Commentary: From time to time the Lord assumes a human form so that men may attain a godly nature. In that state the Lord acts outwardly like a human being though always remaining in full possession of the knowledge that He is unattached to anything material and that He is the very Self of all beings. The ignorant only see Him acting as a man and therefore take Him as an ordinary human being while the wise understand Him as the Supreme Self.

मोघाशा मोघकर्माणो मोघज्ञाना विचेतसः ।
राक्षसीमासुरीं चैव प्रकृतिं मोहिनीं श्रिताः ॥ 9.12 ॥

Shlok 9.12: Of vain hopes, of vain actions, of vain knowledge and senseless, they definitely are possessed of the delusive nature of Rakshasas and Asuras.

Commentary: Fools who do not have discrimination despise Me, dwelling in human form. I have taken this body in order to bless My devotees. These fools have no knowledge of My higher Being. I am the great Lord, the Supreme.

When Lord Krishna was here on this earth, in spite of accomplishing many transcendental and extraordinary feats, only a few people were able to recognize Him as an incarnation of the Supreme Being. Even a great soul like King Yudhishthir was quite amazed to learn from sage Narad that Krishna is the Supreme Being in human form. The moral is that the Supreme cannot be known without one's good Karma and His personal grace.

Here 'they' refers to those described in the previous verse. *Rakshasas* are those having *Tamsic* nature who indulge in acts of cruelty. *Asuras* are those having *Rajsic* nature with qualities of ambition, greed, and the like. They cling to the world of transient forms with the hope of finding peace and happiness and are victims of their own deceitful nature and disregard the Lord, who dwells in them as their underlying Reality.

महात्मानस्तु मां पार्थ दैवीं प्रकृतिमाश्रिताः ।
भजन्त्यनन्यमनसो ज्ञात्वा भूतादिमव्ययम् ॥ 9.13 ॥

Shlok 9.13: But the Mahatmas (great souls), O Parth, possessed of the Divine Prakriti, worship Me single-mindedly, knowing Me as the imperishable origin of all beings.

Commentary: The people of wisdom who possess divine or *sattvic* nature and are endowed with self-restraint, mercy, faith, purity, etc. know Him as the origin of all beings just as those who know the mud to be the origin of all earthen pots will see the mud in all pots. They worship Him with single minded devotion. Their whole life becomes a continuous adoration of the Supreme and hence they are Mahatmas.

सततं कीर्तयन्तो मां यतन्तश्च दृढव्रताः ॥
नमस्यन्तश्च मां भक्त्या नित्ययुक्ता उपासते ॥ 9.14 ॥

Shlok 9.14: Always singing My glory, striving with steadfast vows, bowing down to Me in devotion, they constantly worship Me!

Commentary: Singing the Lord's glory is called '*Sankirtan*'. One takes sacred vows like fasting on certain days, celibacy and so on. These vows vary in different traditions. The Lord emphasizes 'constant worship', that is, not to waste time in idle talk, discussion or gossip. The great souls always sing His glory, committed to lead a spiritual life. They always try by way of subjugating the senses, by way of cultivating the virtues of self-control, kindness, innocence, and the like. Firm in their vows, they worship Me in love. They prostrate before Him with total detachment and give up all false identifications. They worship Him with great faith and devotion, keeping in mind the nature of the Self as the substratum of the entire Universe and the essence of all beings.

ज्ञानयज्ञेन चाप्यन्ये यजन्तो मामुपासते ।
एकत्वेन पृथक्त्वेन बहुधा विश्वतोमुखम् ॥ 9.15 ॥

Shlok 9.15: Others, too, worship Me by acquiring and propagating Self-knowledge. Others worship the infinite as one in all (or non-dual), as the master of all (or dual), and in various other ways.

Commentary: Some worship with the knowledge of the real truth that the *Parabrahm* is one. Some worship with the knowledge that the Lord Vishnu Himself exists as different beings, as the sun, the moon and the like. Others worship Him, thinking that the one Lord exists in all the different forms, with his face on all sides. Some worship Him by making a distinction between the Lord and themselves which is the Dualistic view (Dvait). Some worship Him with the knowledge that He exists as the various Divinities like Brahma, Vishnu and Rudra, etc. (Visishtadvait). Thus there are so many ways to worship God, but they all worship the same God.

Everything is a manifestation of the Absolute

अहं क्रतुरहं यज्ञः स्वधाहमहमौषधम् ।
मन्त्रोऽहमहमेवाज्यमहमग्निरहं हुतम् ॥ 9.16 ॥

Shlok 9.16: I am the ritual, I am the sacrifice, I am the offering, I am the herb, I am the *mantra*, I am the clarified butter, I am the fire, and I am the oblation.

Commentary: This verse explains how all the different types of worship performed in variety of ways becomes the worship of the one Self. Arjun is told that all the methods of worship are nothing but the worship of the Self. Not only the different ritualistic prescriptions are presided over by the Self but all the vegetable, food and medicinal herbs used in the sacrifice, the ghee poured into the altar of fire, the oblations offered, the fire that is invoked, the *Mantras* chanted with which oblation is offered, the food offered to the ancestors and the Kratu- a kind of Vedic rite are all nothing but the Self expressed in different ways and through different fields. All the acts and stuff of worship are nothing but the Lord Himself.

पिताहमस्य जगतो माता धाता पितामहः ।
वेद्यं पवित्रमोंकार ऋक्साम यजुरेव च ॥ 9.17 ॥

Shlok 9.17: I am the Father of this world, the Mother, the Sustainer, the Grandfather; the Purifier, the (one) thing to be known, *Onkar,* and also the *Rig-,* the *Sam-* and *Yajur Vedas.*

Commentary: In order to show that the Self permeates everywhere Sri Krishna says that He is the father, the mother, the sustainer, the grandfather and the purifier of the universe. He is the one thing to be known because the Self is that which having known, everything becomes known. The Self, the substratum of the entire living universe, is symbolized by the Vedic *Mantra* called OM. Life, which is the flow of constant experiences, implies the sum-total of all experiences in each one of us during the waking, dreaming and deep-sleep states.

(**Note:** This verse seems to have been inserted at a later stage because it contains uncalled for reference of Vedas in a positive sense. The Vedas are equated with Sri Krishna, while the Vedic rituals have been criticized in the preceding discourses at several places. Sri Krishna was a man of very clear head. He did not have to pass conflicting views on the Vedas at different places, while giving discourse to Arjun.)

गतिर्भर्ता प्रभुः साक्षी निवासः शरणं सुहृत् ।
प्रभवः प्रलयः स्थानं निधानं बीजमव्ययम् ॥ 9.18 ॥

Shlok 9.18: I am the Goal, the Supporter, the Lord, the Witness, the Abode, the Refuge, the Friend, the Origin, the Dissolution, the Foundation, the Substratum, the Storehouse, the Seed immutable.

Commentary: The Lord continues to enumerate Brahm's various manifestations. He says that I am the goal, the fruit of action, I am the witness of what is done and what is not done by all living beings. I am the abode wherein all living beings dwell. I am the shelter for the distressed; I relieve those from distress who come to Me. I am the Friend: I do good without expecting any return, I am the source of the world. I am that in which it is dissolved, and that in which it stays. I am the treasure-house that which living beings shall enjoy in a future period. I am the imperishable seed, that which causes the growth of all things that germinate, and which endures as long as the world endures. Nothing indeed springs up without a seed; and since growth is constant, it is understood that continuity of the seed never fails. Now one can readily understand or imagine who Lord Krishna is.

Note that the Lord is the witness (*Sakshi*) for everything that happens. He is also the eternal seed from which all things have emanated.

तपाम्यहमहं वर्षं निगृह्णाम्युत्सृजामि च ।
अमृतं चैव मृत्युश्च सदसच्चाहमर्जुन ॥ 9.19 ॥

Shlok 9.19: (As the sun) I give heat; I withhold and send forth the rain; I am immortality and also death, existence and non-existence, O Arjun.

Commentary: This verse explains that the Self is the essence and the ruling factor behind all phenomenal objects and happenings in the universe. As Sri Krishna is a Super Being, He gives heat, sends forth rain or takes it back during eight months, and again sends it forth in the rainy season. He is the immortality of the gods (Devas) and the death of the mortals. He is manifested, the effect. He is both existence and the non-existence (the unmanifested, the cause) at the same time. Indeed the Lord can never be altogether non-existent; nor (can it be said) that the effect is existence and the cause is non-existent.

I am the Being and Non-Being: Sat (existence) and Asat (non-existence) are the terms used in Vedant to indicate cause and effect, the manifest and unmanifest. The Self being that Illuminating factor without which neither manifest nor unmanifest can be experienced, the Self is conceived of as the Essence in both the manifest and unmanifest. He is the being when manifested and non-being when the world is unmanifested.

Non-worshippers are caught in the wheel of births and deaths

त्रैविद्या मां सोमपाः पूतपापा यज्ञैरिष्ट्वा स्वर्गतिं प्रार्थयन्ते ।
ते पुण्यमासाद्य सुरेन्द्रलोक मश्नन्ति दिव्यान्दिवि देवभोगान् ॥ 9.20 ॥

Shlok 9.20: Those who know the three Vedas, the Soma drinkers whose sins have been cleansed, seek the way to heaven by making sacrifices to me. They reach the pure world of Indra and enjoy the divine pleasures of the gods in heaven.

Note: The verse containing reference of Vedas and Indra does not seem to be a part of the original Geeta. This is clearly evident from the fact that when Sri Krishna Himself states that He is the Supreme Being, He does not have to talk about the Lord of gods, that is, Indra. Indra is one of the Rigvedic gods who has been described as the head of heaven (see verses 9.25, 9.34, 10.2, 10.3 and 10.13). We also see reference of the use of Som drinks in the Ved. The insertion of this verse undermines the supremacy of Lord Krishna.

ते तं भुक्त्वा स्वर्गलोकं विशालं-क्षीणे पुण्ये मर्त्यलोकं विशन्ति ।
एवं त्रयीधर्ममनुप्रपन्ना-गतागतं कामकामा लभन्ते ॥ 9.21 ॥

Shlok 9.21: They having enjoyed the wide world of heaven, return to the world of mortals when their merits are exhausted; thus abiding by the injunctions of the three Vedas and desirous of

enjoyments, they are subject to birth and death.

Commentary: When their accumulated merits *(Punya)* are exhausted, they come to this world again. They have no independence. Those who perform Vedic rituals gain heavenly enjoyments after death, but such men are bound by the law of Karma as they are still lured by desire and they will return to this world again and again.

If we seek rewards in heaven, we will gain them but we return to mortal existence so long as we do not achieve the true aim of life. Human life is an opportunity to develop soul's divine nature from the imperfect material we are composed of. We operate from the ego-centred consciousness, whether we seek the pleasures of this world or a future paradise and therefore do not gain liberation from the ever running cycle of birth and death.

अनन्याश्चिन्तयन्तो मां ये जनाः पर्युपासते ।
तेषां नित्याभियुक्तानां योगक्षेमं वहाम्यहम् ॥ 9.22 ॥

Shlok 9.22: Persons who, mediating on Me as non-separate, worship Me in all beings, to them as thus ever zealously engaged, I carry what they lack and preserve and what they already have.

Commentary: Wealth and happiness automatically come to the righteous person, without having aspiration for it, as the river automatically goes to the ocean. Material wealth naturally comes to the virtuous person as river water naturally flows downstream. God always takes care of those who worship Him with unswerving devotion as a mother takes care of her child. One who always thinks of God is considered to be God-conscious, Krishna-conscious, or Self-realized. Lord personally takes charge of one who remembers Him single-mindedly. His nature is to reciprocate the love of His pure devotees by fulfilling their desires. The Source knows and gives all of what you need. Nothing is difficult to obtain when I am pleased, but a pure devotee whose mind is exclusively fixed upon Me does not ask anything from Me, including salvation, but the opportunity to serve Me life after life.

This verse can be interpreted to mean that the Lord takes up all the cares and burdens of His devotees. To become conscious of divine love, all other love must be abandoned. If we cast ourselves entirely on the mercy of God, He bears all our sorrows. We can depend on

His saving grace and energizing care. The Lord promises complete protection or final merger with His Immortal Being to those who love Him with all their body, heart and soul.

This verse conveys the central theme of the Geeta. It tells us about the promise made by Lord that a devotee need not be concerned about his material well-being or future needs. He or she is totally protected by the Lord. This does not mean that one should not lock the door or keep valuables in safety lockers. It means that one need not have to worry that certain unforeseen events would take place that would deprive him of his assets. Countless saints have lived unconcerned about their daily needs. The Lord had apparently protected them with loving care.

Worshipping of other Gods

येऽप्यन्यदेवता भक्ता यजन्ते श्रद्धयान्विताः ।
तेऽपि मामेव कौन्तेय यजन्त्यविधिपूर्वकम् ॥ 9.23 ॥

Shlok 9.23: Even those devotees who, endowed with faith, worship other gods, worship Me only, O Arjun, but by the wrong method.

Commentary: There is only one Absolute; the wise call Him and worship Him by various names. The worship of the divine as Mother is also found in the Vedas where the sage longs to be a child of the divine Mother. The Absolute has also manifested as celestial controllers– for sustaining creation– who is one with many names and forms. The Supreme Being is a woman, a man, a boy, a girl, and an old person. He exists in all forms. All deities, male or female, are representations of one divine. He is One in many and many in One. One should not worship material objects in creation, such as family, friends, and possessions; but one can worship the creator in material objects because God is in all rocks. The Vedic principle of celestial controllers does not diversify the Unity, but unifies the diversity. Deities are just different names and forms, or symbolic representations, of the energies of nature.

All different types of worship reach One and the same Lord as waters of all different rivers reach the same ocean. External worship with the help of an image or a symbolic representation of God is necessary for beginners. It is very helpful to develop a personal relationship with a deity of one's choice who can be consulted and counted upon for help during moments of crisis in life. Those who are against deity worship do not understand that all-pervading God can also exist within a deity. Such persons limit His supremacy.

अहं हि सर्वयज्ञानां भोक्ता च प्रभुरेव च ।
न तु मामभिजानन्ति तत्त्वेनातश्च्यवन्ति ते ॥ 9.24 ॥

Shlok 9.24: For I alone am the Enjoyer, and also the Lord of all sacrifices; but they do not know Me in essence (in reality), and hence they fall (return to this mortal world).

Commentary: This verse explains why these methods are wrong and why the pursuers of these wrong methods return to the mortal world when they have finished enjoying the joys of heaven which were the rewards for their merits (Punya) acquired through ritualism. These methods are wrong because only a limited potentiality of the Supreme is invoked and Its infinite glory is not realized. Hence they fall into the delusory mundane world again and again. The Lord alone is the enjoyer of all sacrifices and the lord of all sacrifices. As a result of their sacrifices they attain a higher plane to enjoy their merits.

यान्ति देवव्रता देवान् पितॄन्यान्ति पितृव्रताः ।
भूतानि यान्ति भूतेज्या यान्ति मद्याजिनोऽपि माम् ॥ 9.25 ॥

Shlok 9.25: The worshippers of the Devas or Gods go to the Devas; the worshippers of the ancestors go to the ancestors; and the worshippers of the ghosts go to the ghosts; but My devotees come to Me only, and are not born again.

Commentary: It is said that whatever one worships, one attains that destination only; or one achieves what one regularly thinks of. The votaries of the Gods, those whose devotion and vows are directed to the Gods, go to the Gods. The votaries of the ancestors or those engaged in performing *Shraddha* and other rites in devotion to the ancestors, go to the ancestors. While My worshippers come to Myself. Notwithstanding people do not worship Me alone because of their ignorance; rather, they worship multiple gods and deities. So they attain only small results.

Lord accepts offering of love and dedication

पत्रं पुष्पं फलं तोयं यो मे भक्त्या प्रयच्छति ।
तदहं भक्त्युपहृतमश्नामि प्रयतात्मनः ॥ 9.26 ॥

Shlok 9.26: I accept the devotional offering of a pious self even if it is only a leaf, a flower, a fruit or water.

Commentary: The Lord has great liking for love and the feeling of devotion. A dedicated heart, not complicated rituals, is needed to please God and attain His grace. One should consume food after offering it to God first. God accepts the food offered to Him to please His devotees. The mind becomes purified when one eats food after offering it first to the Lord. A gift, however small, is accepted by the Lord when it is offered with deep love and devotion. He is satisfied even with a leaf, a flower, a fruit or a little water when it is offered with single-minded devotion and pure heart. What is offered is not as important as how it is offered. Although all the objects of the world belong to Him only and not to the devotee, yet if they are offered to Him by a devotee they become the conveyors of the latter's love and dedication unto the Lord.

The Lord does not expect a costly sacrifice or worship by means of ostentatious offerings. What is of crucial importance is the pure heart of the devotee, always loving the Lord. It has become common practice in India to offer costly jewels to decorate the images of the Lord in the Hindu temples. Such offering do not necessarily endear the devotee to the Lord unless the devotee is pure hearted and does not indulge in corrupt, unlawful practices.

यत्करोषि यदश्नासि यज्जुहोषि ददासि यत् ।
यत्तपस्यसि कौन्तेय तत्कुरुष्व मदर्पणम् ॥ 9.27 ॥

Shlok 9.27: Whatever you do, whatever you eat, whatever you offer in sacrifice, whatever you give away, whatever you practice as austerity, O son of Kunti, do it as an offering to Me.

Commentary: It is neither necessary, nor sufficient that one should follow a certain routine, ritualistic offering of worship everyday to please God. Whatever one does as per one's nature by body, mind, senses, thought, intellect, action, and speech should be done with the thought that it is all for God only. People have achieved liberation by performing only one type of devotional service, such as chanting, hearing, remembering, serving, meditating, renouncing and surrendering.

शुभाशुभफलैरेवं मोक्ष्यसे कर्मबन्धनैः ।
संन्यासयोगयुक्तात्मा विमुक्तो मामुपैष्यसि ॥ 9.28 ॥

Shlok 9.28: You shall become free from the bondage, both good and bad, of Karma and come to Me by the *Yog* of renunciation.

Commentary: Sri Krishna continues the theme how by living the life in a spirit of surrendering the fruit of all actions to the Lord, an individual achieves the highest perfection. When actions are undertaken by an individual without ego, their reactions, good or bad, cannot bind him because the *Vasanas* in him were already eliminated due to egoless actions and absence of egocentric desires and the mind already got purified. The next stage is to lead a life of *Sannyasi* and *Yogi*. The word '*Sannyas*' does not mean physical rejection of the world. It is a renunciation of all egocentric activities and all cravings for fruits of actions. The offering of all works to the Lord constitutes the Yog of renunciation.

समोऽहं सर्वभूतेषु न मे द्वेष्योऽस्ति न प्रियः ।
ये भजन्ति तु मां भक्त्या मयि ते तेषु चाप्यहम् ॥ 9.29 ॥

Shlok 9.29: I am the same to all beings: to Me there is none-hateful or dear. But those who worship Me with devotion, are in me, and I too am in them.

Commentary: Lord Krishna says here that one should not be partial, but should treat a faithful or a helpful person better than others. Lord is neither merciless nor partial to anyone. Lord loves no one and hates no one, but does give special preference to His devotees. He said: My devotees do not know anything else but Me, and I do not know anyone else but them. To protect His devotee is His nature. Lord goes out of way to help and fulfil the desires of His sincere devotees. He also reciprocates by always thinking of those devotees who always think of Him and saves such devotees from all calamities and major problems. The best path of perfection– suitable to the individual's nature– is shown to His sincere devotees.

A father loves all his children equally, but the child who is devoted to the father is dearer although he or she may not be very rich, intelligent, or powerful. Similarly a devotee is very dear to the Lord. Lord does not give everything– such as both material and spiritual wealth– to everybody. One attains perfection– by the grace of God– through the practice of spiritual discipline. God chooses those who choose Him.

The grace of God, like rays of the sun, is equally available to all, but due to free will one must open the window of the heart to let the sunshine come in. It is said that divinity is our birthright; however, self-effort in the right direction is also necessary to remove hindrances brought about by our own past deeds. The grace of God comes expeditiously through our own effort. The grace of God is equally available to all of us, but one has to collect it by personal effort.

There is no unforgiveable sinner

अपि चेत् सुदुराचारो भजते मामनन्यभाक्।

साधुरेव स मन्तव्यः सम्यग्व्यवसितो हि सः ॥ 9.30 ॥

Shlok 9.30: If even the most sinful person resolves to worship Me with single-minded, loving devotion, such a person must be regarded as a saint because of making the right resolution.

Commentary: The Lord makes another very notable promise: He redeems even the worst sinner who has resolved to mend his ways. There is no unforgivable sin or sinner. The fire of sincere repentance burns all sins. A saint is the sinner who never gave up. Every saint had a past, and every sinner has a future. If a devotee keeps his or her mind focused on God, there will be no room for sinful desires to mature, and a sinful person soon becomes righteous if he resolves not to commit any sin again.

If a vicious sinner changes his evil thoughts his behavioural pattern gets transformed. If such a person worships the Lord with undivided devotion he is to be regarded as righteous and thoroughly rehabilitated. From the moment contemplation on the Supreme is taken up with devotion, the sinner becomes a saint because he has made a resolution to abandon the evil ways of his early life. He will soon grow out of himself into the spiritual glory. The evil of the past cannot be washed away except by his turning to God with undivided heart.

क्षिप्रं भवति धर्मात्मा शश्वच्छान्तिं निगच्छति ।
कौन्तेय प्रतिजानीहि न मे भक्तः प्रणश्यति ॥ 9.31 ॥

Shlok 9.31: Very soon, he becomes a righteous person and attains eternal peace. Know thou, Arjun that my devotee never perishes.

Commentary: What a promise of redemption from Lord Krishna! The effect of single-pointed devotion to the Lord is stated here. Sri Krishna says that such a person soon becomes righteous– he realizes the Divine *Atman* in himself. He attains eternal peace or inward peace which is beyond the tumults of the daily living. He lives in tranquillity free from agitations and excitements. He rediscovers in himself his own real nature which is Supreme Peace. Such a devotee never perishes or is destroyed. The seeker of the nobler values shall have no failures if his resolve is firm and his application is sincere.

Path of devotional is easier

मां हि पार्थ व्यपाश्रित्य येऽपि स्युः पापयोनयः ।
स्त्रियो वैश्यास्तथा शूद्रास्तेऽपि यान्ति परां गतिम् ॥ 9.32 ॥

Shlok 9.32: For, taking refuge in Me, they also O Parth, who might be of inferior birth– women, Vaishya and Shudras– attain the Supreme Goal.

Commentary: No one is disqualified due to caste, creed, gender or mental capacity to be a devotee. This verse casts off the discriminatory practice prevailing in society having religious sanctions. What is really important in life is devotion to the almighty. Most saints and sages consider the path of devotion the easiest and the best of all paths. A word of caution is needed here. The words such as persons of inferior birth- women, *Vaishya* and *Shudra*- should not be regarded as justifying the customs prevailing then debarring these segments of the society from Vedic study. Hinduism does not restrict salvation to any one group or section of society nor does it regard any kind of people as inferior by birth. More so, when the Geeta, the Universal Scripture, is addressed to the humanity in general without distinction of race, gender or caste. God does not believe in any kind of discrimination prevalent in the society. God is same for everybody irrespective of any dissimilarity in human attributes. Anybody can attain the Supreme Goal.

किं पुनर्ब्राह्मणाः पुण्या भक्ता राजर्षयस्तथा ।
अनित्यमसुखं लोकमिमं प्राप्य भजस्व माम् ॥ 9.33 ॥

Shlok 9.33: How much more easily then the holy Brahmins and devoted royal saints (attain the goal); having obtained this impermanent and unhappy world, do thou worship Me.

Commentary: The living entity, under the spell of illusory power of divine kinetic energy (Maya), goes through the repeated cycles of birth and death. Out of His grace the Lord gives to a living entity a human body that is very difficult to obtain. The human body, created in the image of God, is the jewel of creation and has the capacity to deliver the soul from the net of transmigration to higher levels of existence. All other forms of life on the earth, except human life, are devoid of higher intellect and reasoning.

As a tiger suddenly comes and takes away a lamb from the flock, similarly death takes away a person unexpectedly. Therefore, spiritual discipline and righteous deeds should be performed without waiting for a proper time to come. The goal and obligation of human birth are to seek Him. The search for God should not wait. One should continue this search together with other duties of life; otherwise, it may be too late.

मन्मना भव मद्भक्तो मद्याजी मां नमस्कुरु ।
मामेवैष्यसि युक्त्वैवमात्मानं मत्परायणः ॥ 9.34 ॥

Shlok 9.34: Always think of Me, be devoted to Me, worship Me, and bow down to Me. Thus, uniting yourself with Me by setting Me as the Supreme Goal, you shall certainly come to Me.

Commentary: The man should surrender to the Lord without reservation. Only then he will have the vision of God everywhere. All sorrows and pains will vanish. His mind will be one with Him. He will forever have his life and being in the Lord alone. This verse summarizes the ideas enunciated in the entire Discourse. The technique for self-development and self-perfection through right knowledge and meditation is 'contemplation on That, talking on That, discussing That, and to live on the bliss-concept of the Reality'. This is called the pursuit of Brahm or Brahm Vidya. This thought is expounded here by Sri Krishna. The Lord says 'with the mind ever filled with Me, My devotee makes all sacrifices and offers all salutations to Me at all times in whatever activity he is engaged in'.

It is not the personal Krishna to whom we have to give ourselves up utterly but the Unborn, Beginningless, Eternal who speaks through Krishna. The way to rise out of our ego-centred consciousness to the divine plane is through the focusing of all our energies, intellectual, emotional and volitional, on God. Then our whole being is transformed and lifted up into the unity and universality of spirit. Knowledge, love and power get fused in a supreme unification. Joy and peace are the result of self-oblivion, of utter abandonment, of absolute acceptance.

Sri Krishna suggests Arjun that taking Me as the supreme goal you shall come to Me. When one surrenders to the Lord without reservation, his whole life undergoes a wonderful transformation. His mind becomes one with the Divine Consciousness. Such a sage gets rid of ignorance and all limiting adjuncts through direct realization of the Self and becomes one with the *Parabrahm*. He attains *Jeevanmukti* or liberation in this very life.

Concepts and Issues

The Lord says that whosoever offers Him with love and devotion even water, a leaf, a flower or a fruit He accepts it. He is not concerned with the quality of the article offered to Him by the devotees, for He watches only their motive and devotion. Even if the worst sinners worship Him with exclusive devotion, they will be regarded as righteous, for they have taken a right step. In this discourse the Lord reveals the secret that nothing can exist apart from Him. He is both the Manifested and Unmanifested Reality of the Universe.

The fundamental principle is that Brahm is eternal and gets neither created nor destroyed. It temporarily manifests as physical creation. A human being does not exist before birth; then he gets born and comes into physical existence, lives for some time and then dies, disappearing from the physical world. So why should the temporary existence in between non-existence before life and again non-existence after physical life be taken seriously?

Let us understand this by way of an example. Before a movie show begins, the screen is blank. Then suddenly it comes alive and unfolds an interesting story with many characters. The audience gets involved in the story, identifying with the characters and their pains and pleasures. Then, when the movie ends, all those characters and the story vanish. They suddenly become irrelevant. Some members of the audience get emotionally affected, because they identify strongly with certain characters portrayed in the movie. But a rare few do not get affected because they never forget that the movie is an illusion and that their real identity is different and unaffected by the movie.

We should regard our life in this world like a movie show that our consciousness is watching and we should not identify with our physical body, nor get attached to the events in our life. The created world could be an illusion and so, may not really exist! So it has no beginning, no existence and no end. However, the illusion is nevertheless perceived by us and is felt as real. That illusion is as such quite powerful. The only way we can destroy this illusion is by developing *Vairagya*– disinterest /detachment– in the worldly life.

Some believe that there is a God, who has created this creation. However, God does not create anything. This creation is a natural manifestation of the Creator's *Prakriti*, inherent aspect. The Creator does not deliberately engage in any action to bring creation into existence– it just happens. So the Creator is not directly responsible for creation, though creation cannot come into existence without the Creator.

One way to understand this is to regard creation as the Creator's dream. A dream happens because the dreamer is sleeping and the dream is a natural phenomenon in sleep. The dreamer does not design the dream, nor does he control the dream, but it happens in a natural way that is inherent to the way the dreamer is. Like the dreamer is 'responsible' for the dream, the Creator may be said to be 'responsible' for creation, but only in a passive way. All the happenings in a dream are illusory with nothing actually happening in an external physical worldly sense.

OM TAT SAT

Discourse - 10

Vibhuti-Vistar Yog: Yog of the Divine Manifestations

Discourse ten reveals Lord Krishna's exalted position as the cause of all causes. He specifies His special manifestations and opulences. Arjun prays to the Lord to describe more of the opulences and the Lord describes those which are most prominent. Krishna tells Arjun that even the *Devas* and highly evolved souls fail to understand how He projects Himself as the universe and all its manifestations. He goes on to describe the various qualities that beings manifest according to their Karmas. All these qualities– wisdom, truth, contentment, etc– originate from Him. The true devotees of the Lord are wholly absorbed in Him. They completely surrender to Him and through single-minded devotion they are granted the power of discrimination, the discrimination that leads them from the unreal to the Real. Krishna emphatically declares that ignorance is shattered and knowledge gained through Divine Grace alone. Arjun accepts the descent of the Supreme in a human form, but wishes to know from the Lord Himself His Cosmic powers by means of which He controls the diverse forces of the universe. The Lord describes His Divine glories, bringing within the range of Arjun's comprehension His limitless manifestations, and how He upholds everything. In short, the Lord is the Almighty Power that creates, sustains and destroys everything.

(**Note:** This discourse is full of interpolations and insertions. Lot of absurd comparisons of Sri Krishna have been made with certain sages, animals, trees and inanimate objects to glorify their images in public. Such attempts, in fact, lower down the image of Sri Krishna, as Sri Krishna is the master of entire cosmic order.)

Lord Krishna said

भूय एव महाबाहो शृणु मे परमं वचः ।
यत्तेऽहं प्रीयमाणाय वक्ष्यामि हितकाम्यया ॥ 10.1 ॥

Shlok 10.1: Again, O Mighty-armed, listen once again to My supreme word that I shall speak to you, who are very dear to Me, for your well being.

Commentary: The all-compassionate Lord in His mercy wants to encourage Arjun and cheer him up, and so He Himself comes forward to give him instructions without any request having been made by Arjun. Encouraged by the keen interest shown by Arjun in the discourses so far and the resultant satisfaction visible in him, the Lord comes forward to repeat what He had told him in the previous discourses (Disc. 7 to 9) about His essential nature, manifestations and Divine glories. He does this because He desires Arjun's welfare who is also delighted to hear Him.

God as the origin of everything

न मे विदुः सुरगणाः प्रभवं न महर्षयः ।
अहमादिर्हि देवानां महर्षीणां च सर्वशः ॥ 10.2 ॥

Shlok 10.2: Neither the hosts of the Gods nor the Great *rishis* know my origin; for I am the source of all the Gods and the great *Rishis*.

Commentary: The Lord is without a cause. He is immutable. Yet He manifests His glories in the Universe in various ways. The mystery of these manifestations is not known even to the gods and sages much less to the ordinary mortals. Human reasoning cannot know His nature. He reveals Himself out of His infinite compassion in the pure hearts of His devotees. The Supreme is unborn and eternal and He is also the Lord of the universe. Though He has no birth, all existence derives from Him.

यो मामजमनादिं च वेत्ति लोकमहेश्वरम् ।
असम्मूढः स मर्त्येषु सर्वपापैः प्रमुच्यते ॥ 10.3 ॥

Shlok 10.3: One who knows Me as the unborn, the beginningless and the Supreme Lord of the universe, is considered wise among mortals and becomes liberated from all sins.

Commentary: As the Supreme Being is the cause of all the worlds, He is beginningless. As He is the source of all the gods and the great sages, so there is no source for His own existence. As He is beginningless, He is unborn. He is the great Lord of all the worlds. For instance, the Infinite cannot be born because It never expresses Itself in any finite manifestation. The ghost is born and hence it has to die; but the post which creates the illusion of ghost in the darkness cannot be said to have given birth to the ghost nor has the post taken birth from the ghost. The post was, is and shall always remain a post only. Similarly, the Self is eternal and therefore It is free from birth. Everything is born in the Self, exists in the Self and ends in the Self. Waves are born but ocean is without birth. Every wave– every manifestation– has a beginning and an end but the ocean has none. Hence the Self is beginningless.

बुद्धिर्ज्ञानमसम्मोहः क्षमा सत्यं दमः शमः ।
सुखं दुःखं भवोऽभावो भयं चाभयमेव च ॥ 10.4 ॥
अहिंसा समता तुष्टिस्तपो दानं यशोऽयशः ।
भवन्ति भावा भूतानां मत्त एव पृथग्विधाः ॥ 10.5 ॥

Shlokas 10.4-05: Intellect, knowledge, non-delusion, forgiveness, truthfulness, control over the mind and senses, calmness of heart, happiness, pain, birth, death, fear, fearlessness, nonviolence, equanimity, contentment, austerity, charity, fame, ill fame– these diverse qualities in human beings arise from Me alone.

Commentary: All sorts of human attributes originate in God. He happens to be the ultimate source of all. But on the other hand Sri Krishna has himself said that all *Jeevas* or the created beings are under the control of *Maya*. Living beings come out of *Prakriti*. Verse 9.10 says that by reason of My proximity, *Prakriti* produces all this, the moving and static, the world wheels round and round. The Lord merely presides over as a silent witness; nature does everything. By the reason of His proximity or presence, nature sends forth the moving and the unmoving. Thus the prime cause of this creation is nature or *Prakriti*. Somewhere the cause of everything is God Himself or somewhere it is *Prakriti* which is a kind of confusing description because of multiplicity of authors involved in the Geeta.

Continuing the idea that the Lord is the cause for the world of plurality within an individual and for the world outside, Sri Krishna enumerates the qualities of head and heart emanating from Him. The Lord alone is the cause and the basis of the universe and all its beings. Created beings are endowed with different attributes according to their *Karma*. The law of *Karma* functions in the relative world through the power of the Lord and thus the Divine is indirectly responsible for the pain and sufferings of the world. He is the lord of the world and guides it, though He is unaffected by its oppositions of duality.

महर्षयः सप्त पूर्वे चत्वारो मनवस्तथा।
मद्भावा मानसा जाता येषां लोक इमाः प्रजाः ॥ 10.6 ॥

Shlok 10.6: The seven great sages and also four ancient Manus possessed of powers like Me (due to their thoughts being fixed on Me), were born of My mind; from them are these creatures in the world.

Commentary: The seven great *Rishis* such as Bhirgu as well as the four Manus of the ancient times known as *Savarnas* had directed their thoughts to Me exclusively and were therefore endowed with the power of Vishnu. They were produced by Me by mind alone. Born in the creation of these Manus and of the Great *Rishis* are these creatures comprising the moving and the unmoving beings. The Lord is not only the material cause (*Prakriti*) of all, but, as the Omniscient Lord of all, He is also the Ruler of all, for He produced the Great *Rishis* and the Manus. The present denizens of this world are their creatures, by birth and by knowledge.

According to the theory of creation found in *Puranas,* Brahma in association with Maya created the universe. The first manifestation of Brahma in space and time is called *Hiranyagarbha* or *Pran* or *Sutratma* which pervades the universe as a thread runs through a garland. The process of creation further down the line is as under:

एतां विभूतिं योगं च मम यो वेत्ति तत्त्वतः ।
सोऽविकम्पेन योगेन युज्यते नात्र संशयः ।। 10.7 ।।

Shlok 10.7: He who in reality understands My manifestations and Yogic powers is united with Me by unswerving devotion. There is no doubt about it.

Commentary: He who in reality knows all pervasive power of the Lord, he gets united with Him in an unshakable manner. He has got total faith in the Supreme Being and he remains devoted to Him. The Yogi realizes that the Lord and his manifestations are one. The knowledge of the determinate Brahma (manifestations) is the way to the knowledge of the indeterminate (unmanifest Absolute) Brahm.

अहं सर्वस्य प्रभवो मत्तः सर्वं प्रवर्तते ।
इति मत्वा भजन्ते मां बुधा भावसमन्विताः ।। 10.8 ।।

Shlok 10.8: I am the origin of all. Everything evolves from Me. Knowing this, the wise worship Me with devotion and reverence.

Commentary: Knowing God as the cause of all creation, one should worship Him. Sri Krishna says that He is the source of the whole world. From Him alone evolves the whole universe in all its changes, including existence and disappearance, action, effect and enjoyment. Thus thinking, the wise who knows the Supreme Reality worship Me, ardently engaged in the contemplation of the Supreme Reality. God is the material and efficient cause of the world. Everything emanates from Me alone. He happens to be the ultimate source of everything.

मच्चित्ता मद्गतप्राणा बोधयन्तः परस्परम् ।
कथयन्तश्च मां नित्यं तुष्यन्ति च रमन्ति च ।। 10.9 ।।

Shlok 10.9: With their minds wholly in Me, with their senses absorbed in Me, enlightening one another, and always speaking of Me, they are satisfied and delighted.

Commentary: When the mind fully understands that the *Jeev* and the Self is one and the same, there is no disturbance in the mind. Humans fully concentrate on God and they always remain in the state of bliss and happiness. A true devotee is the one who remembers constantly the Consciousness principle. They ultimately lead him to be free from external circumstances and inner dissatisfactions. He experiences a sense of contentment and delight which provide an ideal backdrop for the spiritual progress.

Lord gives Self-knowledge to the devotees

तेषां सततयुक्तानां भजतां प्रीतिपूर्वकम् ।
ददामि बुद्धियोगं तं येन मामुपयान्ति ते ॥ 10.10 ॥

Shlok 10.10: I give to those who are constantly attached to Me and who worship Me with devotion the integrated understanding by which they come into Me.

Commentary: The Lord says that those who worship Him with consistent devotion and love, He grants them concentration of understanding by which they reach Him. Constant love and devotion to God are the means to reach Him. The Lord says that He gives *Buddhiyog* (the powers of analysis and reasoning to understand the metaphysical science) to those who are ever united with Him and lovingly contemplate Him by which they come to Him. To them who are ever devout, worshipping Him, not for any purpose of their own, but out of love for Him, to them He gives that devotion of right knowledge (*Buddhiyog*). *'Buddhiyog'* is the Yog of understanding by which they gain the wisdom which sees the One in all the forms which constantly change and pass.

तेषामेवानुकम्पार्थमहमज्ञानजं तमः ।
नाशयाम्यात्मभावस्थो ज्ञानदीपेन भास्वता ॥ 10.11 ॥

Shlok 10.11: I, who dwell within their inner psyche as consciousness, destroy the darkness born of ignorance by the shining lamp of wisdom out of mere compassion for them.

Commentary: I dwell in the *Antahkaran* of those who are engaged in thinking exclusively of Me and destroy their cover of ignorance, which is caused by the absence of discrimination and the lack of wisdom. The lamp of spiritual knowledge and God-realization can be easily ignited by the intense devotion to the Self, but never by intellect and logic alone.

Seekers who have established themselves in the constant awareness of the Supreme, with the aid of *Buddhiyog*, experience their real identity with the Self. This act of Self-revelation is performed by the Lord (the Self) who always abides in the hearts of the devotees out of the spirit of compassion. The Lord makes out how *Bhakti* or devotion leads to the destruction of ignorance and the rise of illumination. When ignorance is destroyed God stands revealed in the human spirit. When love and wisdom arise, the eternal is fulfilled in the individual. *Bhakti* is a means to *Gyan.* Through it we obtain Divine Grace and the power of understanding, *Buddhiyog*. Intellectual knowledge is rendered luminous and certain by the direct intuition of the *Buddhi*.

Arjun said

परं ब्रह्म परं धाम पवित्रं परमं भवान् ।
पुरुषं शाश्वतं दिव्यमादिदेवमजं विभुम् ॥ 10.12 ॥

Shlok 10.12: You are the Supreme Brahm, the Supreme Abode (or the Supreme Light), the Supreme Purifier, the Eternal, Divine Person, the Primal God, Unborn and Omnipresent.

आहुस्त्वामृषयः सर्वे देवर्षिर्नारदस्तथा ।
असितो देवलो व्यासः स्वयं चैव ब्रवीषि मे ॥ 10.13 ॥

Shlok 10.13: All the sages have thus declared of You, as also the celestial sage Narad, so also Asit, Devala and Vyas, and even You– Yourself are telling this to me.

Commentary: The Supreme Brahm is nothing but the Highest Self. The Primal God is One who existed before all other Gods. Arjun tells Sri Krishna that he was taught much earlier the same ideas as He has been telling him now such as Supreme Brahm, Supreme Abode, Supreme Purifier, Eternal, Self-luminous Purush, First Deva, Birthless and All Pervading. Here Arjun wonders how Sri Krishna who is standing before him be Himself the Infinite, the Supreme, the Birthless and the All pervading. Arjun has no doubt that Sri Krishna is Parabrahm. This has already been confirmed by saints and sages.

The real nature of reality is unknowable

सर्वमेतदृतं मन्ये यन्मां वदसि केशव ।
न हि ते भगवन्व्यक्तिं विदुर्देवा न दानवाः ॥ 10.14 ॥

Shlok 10.14: O Keshav, I believe all that You have told me to be

true. O Lord, neither the Devas nor the demons fully know Your manifestation.

Commentary: Arjun is convinced that Sri Krishna who is speaking to him is no other than the Supreme Godhead, the Absolute. He confirms by his own experience to the truth revealed by the seers who have seen It and become one with It. Arjun is fortunate to a first-hand experience of the Absolute. None, whether *Dev* and *Danav* (deity and demon) is able to understand Your manifestation.

स्वयमेवात्मनात्मानं वेत्थ त्वं पुरुषोत्तम ।
भूतभावन भूतेश देवदेव जगत्पते ॥ 10.15 ॥

Shlok 10.15: You alone know Your Self by Your Self– You, the Supreme Spirit, O the source and Lord of beings, O God of gods, O master of the universe!

Commentary: The Vedas left the final question of the origin of ultimate Reality unanswered by stating that nobody knows the ultimate source from where this creation has come. Sages went further by stating that perhaps even He Himself does not know. One who says that I know God does not know; one who knows the Truth says that I do not know. God is the unknown to a person of true knowledge; only the ignorant claim to know God. The ultimate source of cosmic energy is and will remain a big mystery. Any specific description of God, including a description of heaven and hell, is nothing but a mental speculation.

The Self cannot be understood as an object either by the best or the worst in us. The Self being itself Awareness or Knowledge no other knowledge is required to know It. Thus Arjun says 'You Yourself know Yourself by Yourself'.

वक्तुमर्हस्यशेषेण दिव्या ह्यात्मविभूतयः ।
याभिर्विभूतिभिर्लोकानिमांस्त्वं व्याप्य तिष्ठसि ॥ 10.16 ॥

Shlok 10.16: Therefore, only You are able to fully describe Your own divine glories or the manifestations by which You exist pervading the entire universe.

कथं विद्यामहं योगिंस्त्वां सदा परिचिन्तयन् ।
केषु केषु च भावेषु चिन्त्योऽसि भगवन्मया ॥ 10.17 ॥

Shlok 10.17: How shall I know You, O Lord, constantly contemplating on You? In what form of manifestation are You to be thought of by me, O Bhagwan?

विस्तरेणात्मनो योगं विभूतिं च जनार्दन ।
भूयः कथय तृप्तिर्हि शृण्वतो नास्ति मेऽमृतम् ॥ 10.18 ॥

Shlok 10.18: O Janardan, explain to me again, in detail, Your Yogic power and glory because I am not satiated in hearing the ambrosia (of your speech).

Commentary (Shlokas 10.16-10.18): Arjun tells Sri Krishna that Your nature or attributes are so vast and complex that he is not able to understand You. So he requests the Lord to describe Himself in His own words for a clear understanding of the Self. A human being is not capable in any respect to understand the true nature of the Absolute. It is same as a drop of water which tries to cover up the whole ocean. Addressing Sri Krishna Arjun says that he is not satisfied with His invigorating nectar-like words of discourses and requests Him to tell him in detail His Yogic power and eminent glory. This shows that Arjun has come to realize that the whole creation is nothing but the manifestation of the Lord's powers and no one but the Lord Himself knows the mystery. So he desires to learn about those powers from the Lord Himself.

Everything is a manifestation of the Absolute

Lord Krishna said

हन्त ते कथयिष्यामि दिव्या ह्यात्मविभूतयः ।
प्राधान्यतः कुरुश्रेष्ठ नास्त्यन्तो विस्तरस्य मे ॥ 10.19 ॥

Shlok 10.19: O Best of the Kurus, now I shall explain to you My divine attributes, according to their prominence; because there is no limit to my expansiveness.

Commentary: Now I will tell you of My heavenly glories, in their prominence, i. e. where they are severally the most prominent. It is not, indeed, possible even in a whole century to describe all of them, as there is no limit to the extent of My Glories. Sri Krishna in the rest of this Discourse explains exhaustively to Arjun the identity of the Self as individual being. The Lord makes it clear that without Him none of the constituent members of a community will have any organized existence. God is infinite and so His manifestation too is infinite. He manifests Himself in the universe through innumerable forms.

अहमात्मा गुडाकेश सर्वभूताशयस्थितः ।
अहमादिश्च मध्यं च भूतानामन्त एव च ॥ 10.20 ॥

Shlok 10.20: O Gudakesh, I am the Supreme Spirit (or Supersoul) abiding in the inner psyche of all beings as soul (*Atman*). I am the beginning, the middle, and also the end of all beings.

Commentary: O Arjun, I am the Self (unifying reality) that exists in the hearts of all beings. I am the beginning, the middle and also the end of beings. You should think of Me as the innermost Self, seated in the heart of all beings. 'Gudakesh' means either 'conqueror of sleep' or thick-haired. He who is unable to think of Me as the Self should think of Me in those things which are mentioned below; for I am the source and the end of all beings.

Spirit has no origin and is a property of the Supreme Being, just as sunlight is a property of the sun. Spirit supplies power and supports the senses, just as air burns and supports fire. Spirit is the basis and support behind every form of power, movement, intellect, and life in this universe. It is the power by which one sees, hears smells, thinks, loves, hates, and desires objects. The Lord tells Arjun, 'I am the Self that exists in the heart of all beings'. This general statement is the sum and substance of His entire talk in the Geeta. He specifically tells that He is the birth, life and death of all beings. The world is a living whole, a vast inter-connectedness, a cosmic harmony inspired and sustained by the One Supreme.

आदित्यानामहं विष्णुर्ज्योतिषां रविरंशुमान् ।
मरीचिर्मरुतामस्मि नक्षत्राणामहं शशी ॥ 10.21 ॥

Shlok 10.21: Of the *Adityas*, I am Vishnu of luminaries, the radiant Sun; of the winds I am Marchi; of the asterisms, the Moon (the moon among the stars).

Commentary: Adityas are Gods representing the twelve months of the year. Vishnu is considered the most important among them. Maruts are the gods controlling the winds. The twelve Adityas, luminaries like

Agni, Lightning, the Maruts, the Stars, etc. are the ordinary manifestations of the Lord. Vishnu, Marichi, the sun and the moon are his special manifestations and hence they have greater splendour in them. While the Supreme is in all things, He is more prominent in some than in others. There is an ascending order in the world. God is more revealed in life than in matter, in consciousness than in life and in saints and sages than in others. Within the same order, He is most revealed in the pre-eminent individuals. In all these verses of this Discourse Sri Krishna supplies the seekers with various items of thought (names and forms) over which the Lord can be superimposed for a deeper and highly focussed meditation.

वेदानां सामवेदोऽस्मि देवानामस्मि वासवः ।
इन्द्रियाणां मनश्चास्मि भूतानामस्मि चेतना ॥ 10.22 ॥

Shlok 10.22: Of the Vedas I am the Samaved, and of the gods I am Indra; among the senses I am the mind; and I am intelligence among living beings.

Commentary: Samaved– It is the essence of **Rigved** which is the most important of all the four Vedas. The **Samaved** has the additional characteristic of musical beauty with tunes, melody and rhythm. Sri Krishna is the Infinite Essence tuned to music as **Rigved** *mantras* are in the **Samaved.**

Vashav– The king of gods, Indra. The Self is as Indra among the Gods, ruling over the others, controlling, directing and organizing the lives.

Mind– Indra also means the king of sense organs, the latter being the Devas. Mind is the controller without which sense organs cannot have the power of functioning.

Intelligence– Of all the creations in the world intelligence is the mysterious power which is still beyond comprehension. It is that which illumines all from the intellect down to the grossest physical object.

रुद्राणां शंकरश्चास्मि वित्तेशो यक्षरक्षसाम् ।
वसूनां पावकश्चास्मि मेरुः शिखरिणामहम् ॥ 10.23 ॥

Shlok 10.23: Of the Rudras, I am Shankar; of the Yakshas and the Rakshasas, I am Kuber; of the Vasus, I am fire; of the

mountain peaks, I am Meru.

Commentary: Krishna says that among the Rudras He is Shankar; among the Yakshas and Rakshasas, the Lord of wealth (Kuber); among the Vasus He is Pavak (fire); and among the (seven) mountains He is the Meru.

Rudras– Deities of destruction. Destruction is a necessary precedent for construction just as the seed must perish to enable the plant to come out. Shankar is the deity for creative destruction.

Pavak– Vasus are the deities presiding over the seasons. The six external seasons get coloured by two internal seasons, viz joy and sorrow and all of these can be experienced only through Consciousness within.

Meru– A mythological mountain believed to be the centre of the Universe from which Ganga (Spiritual Knowledge) flows in all four directions to bless the humanity.

पुरोधसां च मुख्यं मां विद्धि पार्थ बृहस्पतिम् ।
सेनानीनामहं स्कन्दः सरसामस्मि सागरः ॥ 10.24 ॥

Shlok 10.24: And, among the household priests (of kings), O Arjun, know Me to be the chief, Brihaspati; among the army generals I am Skand; among lakes I am the ocean!

Commentary: Brihaspati– The spiritual teacher for the celestials. Skand– Son of Shiva the peacock rider and the wielder of the spear. Ocean– It is the source of all rivers because from it the evaporation of water takes place to flood the rivers. Similarly the sentient and insentient things and beings of the world cannot exist but for the Infinite Ocean of Truth, the Lord.

महर्षीणां भृगुरहं गिरामस्म्येकमक्षरम् ।
यज्ञानां जपयज्ञोऽस्मि स्थावराणां हिमालयः ॥ 10.25 ॥

Shlok 10.25: Among the great sages I am Bhrigu; among words I am the monosyllable Om; among sacrifices I am the sacrifice of silent repetition; among immovable things I am the Himalayas.

Commentary: Sri Krishna is saying figuratively that He is on the top of everything. This assertion is but natural, as he happens to be the Supreme Being. Sri Krishna does not have to compare himself with

Maharishi Bhrigu– a mind-born-son of Brahma, as He has himself described as Supreme Being in several verses. This is a pure interpolation by some disciples of Bhrigu.

A brief description of divine manifestations

अश्वत्थः सर्ववृक्षाणां देवर्षीणां च नारदः ।

गंधर्वाणां चित्ररथः सिद्धानां कपिलो मुनिः ॥ 10.26 ॥

Shlok 10.26: Among the trees (I am) the *Peepal*; among the divine sages I am Narad; among the Gandharvas, I am Chitrarath and of the achievers I am Kapil, the ascetic.

Commentary: *Peepal*– Both in magnitude and life span it is the largest and hence considered immortal. It has divinity attached to it and therefore worshipped. As per Upanishads and Geeta itself it represents pluralistic phenomenal world. Narad– He is a great devotee of Narayan. He is the greatest sage because he guides the deluded. He has the missionary zeal and enthusiasm. Gandharvas– Celestial beings famous for their art and music. Chitrarath is the most brilliant among them noted for his singing. *Siddhas*– Those who at their very birth attained virtue, wisdom and dispassion. They are great thinkers and perfected ones. Sage Kapil is the author of Sankhya philosophy and is the greatest thinker.

(**Note:** Sri Krishna does not need to make any absurd comparison with anyone in the cosmic world. He is the greatest of all without any doubt. References of certain mythological characters here are an indication of the fact that that they been incorporated into the Geeta at a later stage with a view to giving them special importance as well as to support the Brahminical philosophy, while the Geeta is a non-Brahminical literature. Sri Krishna does not need to make any reference of *Peepal* tree, Narad, Chitrarath or Kapil to describe His nature. Krishna is after all extra-ordinary personality. With a view to eulogising their master, this verse was seemed to have been inserted by the followers of sage Kapil who was the chief exponent of the Sankhya Darshan. Kapil himself did not believe in God, but his followers later on revised his philosophy in favour of a theistic ideology.)

उच्चैः श्रवसमश्वानां विद्धि माममृतोद्भवम् ।

ऐरावतं गजेन्द्राणां नराणां च नराधिपम् ॥ 10.27 ॥

Shlokas 10.27-28: Know Me as Ucchaisravas, born of nectar among horses; among lordly elephants (I am) the Airavat; and among men, the King.

आयुधानामहं वज्रं धेनूनामस्मि कामधुक् ।
प्रजनश्चास्मि कन्दर्पः सर्पाणामस्मि वासुकिः ॥ 10.28 ॥

Of weapons I am the thunderbolt; among cows I am the wish-fulfilling cow called Surabhi; I am the progenitor, the god of love; among serpents I am Vasuki.

(**Note:** Same as the above, this is a redundant verse. Krishna does not have to explain Himself through His comparison with animate and inanimate objects like horse, elephant, weapons, thunderbolts or serpents. This is a very low level of explanation, especially when Sri Krishna is none other than a Supreme Being. This is not the proper way of explaining the nature or notion of God. This verse was inserted into the Geeta later on by some unknown Geeta scholars.)

The splendour of the universal form

अनन्तश्चास्मि नागानां वरुणो यादसामहम् ।
पितृणामर्यमा चास्मि यमः संयमतामहम् ॥ 10.29 ॥

Shlok 10.29: I am Anant among the snakes; I am Varun among water-Deities; Aryaman among the ancesters I am; I am Yam among those who bind.

प्रह्लादश्चास्मि दैत्यानां कालः कलयतामहम् ।
मृगाणां च मृगेन्द्रोऽहं वैनतेयश्च पक्षिणाम् ॥ 10.30 ॥

Shlok 10.30: I am Prahlad among the demons; among the reckoners I am Time; among beasts I am the Lion; and Garuda among the birds.

(**Notes:** Same as the above, this too is a redundant verse. Such comparisons of Sri Krishna with mortal or destructible objects belittle the image of Sri Krishna as the Godhead. This verse was inserted into the Geeta later on by some unknown Geeta scholars.)

पवनः पवतामस्मि रामः शस्त्रभृतामहम् ।
झषाणां मकरश्चास्मि स्रोतसामस्मि जाह्नवी ॥ 10.31 ॥

Shlok 10.31: I am the wind among the purifiers and Ram among the warriors am I; among the fishes I am the shark; among the streams I am the Ganga.

Commentary: Same as the above, this too is a redundant verse. This belittles the image of Sri Krishna as the Godhead. This verse was inserted into the Geeta later on by some unknown reciters.

(**Note:** For obvious reasons Ram could be popular only after the treatise of Ramayan of Valmiki came into being. The historical evidence suggests that the Ramayan as piece of literature appeared much after the treatise of Mahabharat came into being, despite the fact that the incidence of Mahabharat belonged to much later period than the age of Ramayan. Krishna attained popularity prior to Ram because the story of Mahabharat became popular before Ramayan and hence it is assumed that the verse was inserted into the Geeta at a later stage. Historians have contended that the epic Ramayan came into being sometime during 5th century BCE to first century BCE.)

सर्गाणामादिरन्तश्च मध्यं चैवाहमर्जुन ।
अध्यात्मविद्या विद्यानां वादः प्रवदतामहम् ॥ 10.32 ॥

Shlok 10.32: Among creations I am the beginning, the middle and also the end, O Arjun! Among the sciences I am the science of the Self; and I am logic among controversialists.

Commentary: In verse 20 of this Discourse the Lord has stated that He is the beginning, middle and also the end of all individual beings (movable and immovable). Here He says that He is the essence of the entire creation. Here the word science refers to knowledge or experience relating to Self (the use of word 'knowledge' here and elsewhere has got very a special meaning). The science of Self is the way to salvation.

अक्षराणामकारोऽस्मि द्वन्द्वः सामासिकस्य च ।
अहमेवाक्षयः कालो धाताहं विश्वतोमुखः ॥ 10.33 ॥

Shlok 10.33: I am the letter 'A' among the alphabets. I am the dual compound among the compound words. I am verily the inexhaustible or everlasting time. I am the dispenser (of the fruits of actions), having faces in all directions.

Commentary: The letter 'A'– In Sanskrit the sound of the letter 'A' preponderates in every letter which makes the pronunciation of the words very sweet and rhythmical. This letter also occupies the first place among the alphabets in all languages.

As the Supreme Being is all pervading He is said to face all directions. In all perceptions whether physical, mental or intellectual there is the grace of Consciousness which is the Self and hence It is said to see in all directions.

मृत्युः सर्वहरश्चाहमुद्भवश्च भविष्यताम् ।
कीर्तिः श्रीर्वाक्च नारीणां स्मृतिर्मेधा धृतिः क्षमा ॥ 10.34 ॥

Shlok 10.34: And I am the all-devouring death, and prosperity of those who are to be prosperous; among feminine qualities (I am) Fame, Prosperity (or Beauty), Speech, Memory, Intelligence, Firmness and Forgiveness.

Commentary: Death is the supreme leveller. Separateness and individuality are maintained only during lifetime due to one's relationship with other than oneself. After death all individualities vanish and all beings wise and ignorant, rich and poor, noble and ignoble, strong and weak, etc. are reduced to the same state wherein no distinction can be made whatsoever.

The Lord is the source of all new creations that will have to come in future. In the scheme of life destruction is only a modification of the existing form into another new one to come in the future. Sri Krishna is both beginning and end of everything.

बृहत्साम तथा साम्नां गायत्री छन्दसामहम् ।
मासानां मार्गशीर्षोऽहमृतूनां कुसुमाकरः ॥ 10.35 ॥

Shlok 10.35: Of hymns I am Brihatsaman; of metrical forms, I am Gayatri; of months, I am Margasirsa; of seasons, I am the spring season full of flowers.

Commentary: Sri Krishna appears in so many forms in this world when manifest. He is always special of everything even when He is unmanifest. He is the best of all of everything. Sri Krishna says among the hymns He is the Brihatsaman; among metres He is Gayatri; among the months He is Margasirsa and among seasons He is the flowery season.

द्यूतं छलयतामस्मि तेजस्तेजस्विनामहम् ।
जयोऽस्मि व्यवसायोऽस्मि सत्त्वं सत्त्ववतामहम् ॥ 10.36 ॥

Shlok 10.36: I am gambling of the cheats, splendour of the splendid, victory of the victorious, resolution of the resolute, and goodness of the good.

Commentary: Gambling– Most deceptive game of that time on account of which Pandavas had to undergo extreme sufferings.

Splendour– It is the most satisfying experience. Victory, effort and goodness– Great qualities in an individual. Of the various methods of defrauding others, I am gambling, such as dice-play. Gambling is My manifestation. I am power in the powerful. I am victory in the victorious. I am effort in those who make that effort. Both good and bad are the product of divine power *(Maya). Maya* creates a multitude of merits and demerits that have no real existence. The wise do not attach too much importance to it.

वृष्णीनां वासुदेवोऽस्मि पाण्डवानां धनंजयः ।
मुनीनामप्यहं व्यासः कवीनामुशना कविः ॥ 10.37 ॥

Shlok 10.37: Among Vrishnis I am Vasudev; among the Pandavas I am Arjun; among sages I am Vyas; among poets I am Usan, the poet.

दण्डो दमयतामस्मि नीतिरस्मि जिगीषताम् ।
मौनं चैवास्मि गुह्यानां ज्ञानं ज्ञानवतामहम् ॥ 10.38 ॥

Shlok 10.38: Among the punishers I am the sceptre; among those who seek victory I am statesmanship; and also among secrets I am silence; knowledge among knowers I am.

(**Note:** I do not see any reason why Sri Krishna should recite this verse before Arjun, saying 'among Pandavas I am Arjun'. There is no justification behind such a description for Lord Krishna. There is no parallel between Sri Krishna and Arjun, though both are closely related through marriage. Such verse is unnecessary insertion. The next verse suggests that in all walks of life what is really special is nothing but Sri Krishna. Sri Krishna is special of everything manifest.)

यच्चापि सर्वभूतानां बीजं तदहमर्जुन ।
न तदस्ति विना यत्स्यान्मया भूतं चराचरम् ॥ 10.39 ॥

Shlok 10.39: Whatsoever is the seed of all beings, that also am I, O Arjun. There is no being, whether moving or unmoving, that has come out of any other source.

Commentary: A big tree with many branches, leaves, flowers, fruits, and seeds remains inside a tiny seed in unmanifest form and becomes manifest again and again into a tree. The tree again becomes unmanifest into the seed. Similarly all manifestations remain in the Absolute in unmanifest form and become manifest during creation and unmanifest during dissolution again and again. The fruit remains hidden in the seed and the seed in the fruit; similarly God is in human beings and human beings in God.

Self is the source of all creation just as the seed is the source of all trees. This idea is repeated in several ways. When the seed germinates it dies to become a tree. But this is not the case with the Self. Hence Sri Krishna says that He is the seed of the Universe and even after its germination and growth the tree (universe) is sustained by the seed (Self) just as all the waves during their appearance and disappearance are sustained by the ocean and without which waves cannot exist. Nothing can exist without the Self, which is the essence of everything like saying all cloth has come out of cotton and no cloth can exist without cotton.

Manifest creation is a small fraction of the Absolute

नान्तोऽस्ति मम दिव्यानां विभूतीनां परन्तप ।
एष तूद्देशतः प्रोक्तो विभूतेर्विस्तरो मया ॥ 10.40 ॥

Shlok 10.40: There is no end to my divine manifestations, O Parantap, but this is a brief statement by Me of the particulars of My divine glories.

Commentary: The variety in the universe, from the highest celestial controllers to the smallest insects and even the inert dust, is nothing but a manifestation of One and the same Absolute.

As the Lord is infinite so are His manifestations. Although there is no end to narrate all His glories the Lord has provided Arjun with some specific examples in order to teach him the Art of seeing the Unseen through the Seen.

The implication is that one should meditate upon these ideas or examples and try to discover the Infinite Resplendence of the Lord in every finite shape and name.

यद्यद्विभूतिमत्सत्त्वं श्रीमदूर्जितमेव वा ।
तत्तदेवावगच्छ त्वं मम तेजोंऽशसम्भवम् ॥ 10.41 ॥

Shlok 10.41: Whatever is endowed with glory, brilliance, and power– know that to be a manifestation of a very small fraction of My splendour.

Commentary: Through His cosmic sound vibration, God made all things; not one thing in creation was made without His cosmic energy. This cosmic manifestation is non-separate from the Absolute just as sunshine is not separate from the sun. The entire creation is a partial revelation and part and parcel of the Infinite. The divine manifests its glory through creation. The beauty and splendour of the visible universe are only a small fraction of His glory.

The above examples illustrate clearly that the Lord is present in all names and forms revealing Himself as the glorious or the great or the mighty aspect in all beings and things. Sri Krishna summarizes his discourse on His several glories by saying whatever that is great or glorious or mighty is nothing but the expression of a ray of His infinite splendour. Each one of the examples given by the Lord indicates as either the great one in the whole species or the noblest and the most glorious thing or happening or the mightiest among the powerful. This indication is useful to the seekers to perceive the play of the Infinite among the finite and ever changing world of names and forms.

अथवा बहुनैतेन किं ज्ञातेन तवार्जुन ।
विष्टभ्याहमिदं कृत्स्नमेकांशेन स्थितो जगत् ॥ 10.42 ॥

Shlok 10.42: What is the need for this detailed knowledge, O Arjun? I continually support the entire universe by a very small fraction of My divine power.

Commentary: Manifest creation is numerically a very small fraction of the Absolute. The universe reflects the divine splendour for human beings to see the invisible Lord. One should learn to perceive God, not only as a person or vision, but also through His splendour as manifested in the universe and through His laws that govern and control nature and life. He is existence, goodness, and beauty. Sri Krishna declares that the total world is supported and nourished by a fraction of Him or His glory. Not that the Divine glory is broken into fragments. This cosmos is but a partial revelation of the Infinite, and is illumined by one ray of His shining light. The transcendent light of the Supreme dwells beyond this entire cosmos, beyond time and space.

OM TAT SAT

Discourse - 11

Vishwaroop-Darshan Yog: Yog of the Vision of the Universal Form

In the previous Discourse the Lord explained His presence in all things and beings in His different manifestations indicating that the Self is the substratum for the world of multiplicities. In this Discourse He provides Arjun with a practical demonstration to show that everything exists in the Self. It is easier to see the Self in finite objects than to recognize the entire universe in the Self.

The concept of space divides the individual objects from one another. If there is no space in between them, all objects will come together so closely that they would form one single entity. In this mass of things there will certainly be different shapes and forms of all things at one and the same place and time. This is the picture of the Universal or Cosmic Man, the vision of the world viewed from a mind wherein there is no concept of time and space.

Sri Krishna removes the concept of space from Arjun's mind and assumes Himself the form of one universal structure to demonstrate that everything in the Universe is in Him. Having seen this form of the Lord, Arjun re-visits his faith and understanding. In this Discourse we see Arjun full of emotions of wonder, amazement, fear, reverence, devotion, etc. In its concept and description, this Discourse is considered as one of the highest philosophical poems in all the sacred books of the world.

A major part of this Discourse is solely devoted to a description of the Cosmic Body and praises offered by Arjun to the Lord manifested in that form; hence it has been given the title of *Vishwaroop Darshan Yog:* Yog of the Vision of the Universal Form.

On hearing the Lord's declaration that the entire universe is held in a mere fraction of His being, Arjun is desirous of seeing through his own eyes the form of the Lord that so sustains the world system. Therefore, extolling the Lord and His teachings, Arjun requests Him to grant him a direct vision of His Cosmic Body.

Seeing the Lord's cosmic form Arjun is struck with awe and wonder. He sees the entire universe in a single immeasurable form as also His destructive, all-devouring expression. Fraught with fear and overwhelmed with adoration, Arjun surrenders completely to that unimaginable colossal form. He bows, he prostrates and begs forgiveness for his lack of reverence towards Krishna in their day-to-day relationships.

Arjun is unable to bear the pressure of the sudden expansion of consciousness and is filled with fear. He begs the Lord to assume His usual form once more.

Krishna reiterates that this vision cannot be had through any amount of austerities, study, sacrifices or philanthropic acts. Supreme devotion is the only means by which one can have access to His grand vision. Discourse 11 is the climax of the Geeta wherein Krishna appears to Arjun in His supreme form. It is terrifying theophany, a glimpse into a level of reality that is more than the ordinary mind can bear.

Arjun's prayer for a vision of the Universal Form

Arjun said:

मदनुग्रहाय परमं गुह्यमध्यात्मसञ्ज्ञितम् ।
यत्त्वयोक्तं वचस्तेन मोहोऽयं विगतो मम ॥ 11.1 ॥

Shlok 11.1: My illusion is dispelled by the supremely profound words of wisdom You spoke out of compassion for me about the supreme secret of the Self.

Commentary: After hearing the glories of the Lord, Arjun has an intense desire to have the wonderful Cosmic Vision. Arjun expresses a word of gratitude to Sri Krishna for dispelling illusion from his mind. Now he understands what he is supposed to do on the advice of Sri Krishna.

भवाप्ययौ हि भूतानां श्रुतौ विस्तरशो मया ।
त्वत्तः कमलपत्राक्ष माहात्म्यमपि चाव्ययम् ॥ 11.2 ॥

Shlok 11.2: O lotus-eyed, I have heard from You in detail about the origin and dissolution of beings and Your inexhaustible glory.

Commentary: This needs no specific comment, as it is readily understandable.

Vision of God is the ultimate aim of a seeker

एवमेतद्यथात्थ त्वमात्मानं परमेश्वर ।
द्रष्टुमिच्छामि ते रूपमैश्वरं पुरुषोत्तम ॥ 11.3 ॥

Shlok 11.3: O Supreme Lord, You are same as You have said; yet I wish to see Your Ishvar form, O Supreme Purush.

Commentary: Ishvar is a Sanskrit word for God which stands for omnipotence, omnipresence, omniscience, infinite strength, infinite virtue and infinite splendour of the Supreme Being. These are the six qualities which characterize God. Arjun tells the Lord that he desires to see that Ishvar or Divine or Cosmic Form of His.

मन्यसे यदि तच्छक्यं मया द्रष्टुमिति प्रभो ।
योगेश्वर ततो मे त्वं दर्शयात्मानमव्ययम् ॥ 11.4 ॥

Shlok 11.4: O Lord, if You think I am capable of seeing Your universal form, then, O Lord of the Yogis, show me Your immutable form.

(**Notes:** There is no way to believe in God unless experienced. Faith in God rests on a shaky ground without a vision of the object of devotion. All our spiritual discipline is aimed at this vision. The vision is essential to dispel any lingering doubt in the mind of the seeker because, to a human mind, seeing is believing. Therefore, Arjun, like any other devotee, intends to see the transcendental form of the Lord.

It is one thing to know that the Eternal Spirit dwells in all things and another to have the vision of it. Arjun now wishes to see the Cosmic Form of the Lord, the visible embodiment of the Unseen Divine. The idea is that the abstract metaphysical truth should be given a visible reality.

Sri Krishna is a Lord of Yogis (Yogeshwar). A Yogeshwar is the Lord of Yogis. Yog is the identification of the individual soul with the Self.)

The revelation of the Lord

Lord Krishna said:

पश्य मे पार्थ रूपाणि शतशोऽथ सहस्रशः ।
नानाविधानि दिव्यानि नानावर्णाकृतीनि च ॥ 11.5 ॥

Shlok 11.5: Behold, O Parth, my various celestial forms, of different colours and shapes, by hundreds and by thousands.

Commentary: Sri Krishna helped Arjun to gain the necessary insight to enable him to perceive the Lord, who is already in front of him, in the form he desired. Sri Krishna did not transform Himself in the cosmic form but only bestowed His grace on Arjun to enable him to perceive the Divine form of the Lord and hence Sri Krishna says 'Behold'. The stupendous self-revelation of Divine power is manifested to Arjun who understands the true meaning of the cosmic process and destiny. The vision is not a myth or a legend but spiritual experience.

पश्यादित्यान्वसून्रुद्रानश्विनौ मरुतस्तथा ।
बहून्यदृष्टपूर्वाणि पश्याश्चर्याणि भारत ॥ 11.6 ॥

Shlok 11.6: Behold the Adityas, the Vasus, the Rudras, the (two) Ashwins and also the Maruts; behold many wonders never seen before, O Descendant of Bharat.

Commentary: The Lord enumerates the most important and striking factors to be seen in His Cosmic Form. Sri Krishna says that Arjun beholds the twelve Adityas, the eight Vasus, the eleven Rudras, the two Ashwins, the seven heptads of Maruts. Behold also many other marvels never seen before by you or anybody else in this world of humans. The various forms mentioned here were already explained in the previous Discourse.

इहैकस्थं जगत्कृत्स्नं पश्याद्य सचराचरम् ।
मम देहे गुडाकेश यच्चान्यद्द्रष्टुमिच्छसि ॥ 11.7 ॥

Shlok 11.7: Now behold today, O Gudakesh, the whole universe of the moving and the unmoving and whatever else you desire to see, all concentrated in My Body.

Commentary: The entire universe comprising of both moving and static objects and beings is being shown by Sri Krishna as compressed within the framework of His own physical structure. As explained earlier the concept of space as a divider between objects is being removed from Arjun's mind by the Lord leaving in him the concept of 'total space' which is equivalent to Sri Krishna's own physical dimensions. It is the vision of all in the One.

न तु मां शक्यसे द्रष्टुमनेनैव स्वचक्षुषा ।
दिव्यं ददामि ते चक्षुः पश्य मे योगमैश्वरम् ॥ 11.8 ॥

Shlok 11.8: But you are not able to see Me with your physical eye alone; therefore, I give you a divine eye to see My supreme power and glory.

Commentary: The Lord says that Arjun cannot see Him in the Cosmic Form with his own fleshy eyes *(Mamsa Chakshu)* and hence gives him the divine eye *(Divya Chakshu).* Human eyes can see only the outward form or tangible objects. They cannot perceive Cosmic object or Spirit.

No one can see Him with the physical eye. His transcendental form is beyond our field of vision. He is revealed through the faculty of intuition of the intellect that, residing within the inner psyche, controls the mind. Those who know Him become immortal. We, like colour blinds, are not able to see the full range of cosmic colour and light with human eyes. The divine vision, which is a gift of God, is needed to see the beauty and glory of the Supreme Personality of Godhead.

Manifestation of Lord's cosmic form

Sanjay said:

एवमुक्त्वा ततो राजन्महायोगेश्वरो हरिः ।
दर्शयामास पार्थाय परमं रूपमैश्वरम् ॥ 11.9 ॥

Shlok 11.9: Having thus spoken, O King, then, Hari, the great Lord of the mystic power of Yog, showed to the son of Pritha the Supreme Form as Ishvar.

Commentary: King: This verse is addressed to Dhritarashtra by Sanjay. Sri Krishna has been referred to as Hari which means God. Sanjay now starts describing the list of things that were visible within the framework of the Lord.

अनेकवक्त्रनयनमनेकाद्भुतदर्शनम् ।
अनेकदिव्याभरणं दिव्यानेकोद्यतायुधम् ॥ 11.10 ॥

Shlok 11.10: With innumerable mouths and eyes, faces too marvellous to stare at, dazzling ornaments, innumerable weapons uplifted, flaming—

दिव्यमाल्याम्बरधरं दिव्यगन्धानुलेपनम् ।
सर्वाश्चर्यमयं देवमनन्तं विश्वतोमुखम् ॥ 11.11 ॥

Shlok 11.11: crowned with fire, wrapped in pure light, with celestial fragrance, he stood forth as infinite God, composed of all wonders with faces on all sides.

Commentary (Shlokas 11.10-11): Total cosmos is not a subject matter that is amenable for easy mental comprehension. Sanjay, therefore, stumbles for words to give its description. He means to say that Arjun looked at this Cosmic Form in all its magnificence and saw the Lord everywhere, at all times and in everything indicating that He is beyond the three limitations of place, time and thing. The Self is everywhere as it is all pervading. It exists in the past, present and future. It dwells in all parts. It is, therefore, endless. With faces on all sides means He is the Self of all beings.

दिवि सूर्यसहस्रस्य भवेद्युगपदुत्थिता ।
यदि भाः सदृशी सा स्याद्भासस्तस्य महात्मनः ॥ 11.12 ॥

Shlok 11.12: If the splendour of thousands of suns were to blaze forth all at once in the sky, even that would not resemble the splendour of that mighty Being (great soul).

Commentary: The splendour of the Cosmic Form excels all others; it is indeed beyond comparison. In fact, not even a million suns could match The word 'thousand' is often used in Vedic scriptures to denote 'infinite'.

तत्रैकस्थं जगत् कृत्स्नं प्रविभक्तमनेकधा ।
अपश्यद् देवदेवस्य शरीरे पाण्डवस्तदा ॥ 11.13 ॥

Shlok 11.13: Arjun saw the entire universe unfolded, with its countless billions of life forms, gathered together in the body of the God of gods.

Commentary: In the Cosmic Form of the Lord, Arjun saw the entirety of the diversely fragmented universe gathered as one in the body of that God of gods. This does not mean that the Universe has shrunk into the physical structure of Sri Krishna. It means that Arjun could intellectually comprehend the sense of oneness in the world of matter. He could see many in the one and the One in the many. The vision is a revelation of the potential divinity of all earthly life. This is a very difficult aspect of Supreme Authority for many Western minds to understand and accept.

Arjun addresses the Lord

ततः स विस्मयाविष्टो हृष्टरोमा धनंजयः ।
प्रणम्य शिरसा देवं कृतांजलिरभाषत ॥ 11.14 ॥

Shlok 11.14: Trembling with awe, his body chilled, the hair standing up on his flesh, Dhananjay bowed his head to the Lord and prayed with folded hands.

Commentary: Sanjay tells the blind King about the strong emotions and humility passing through Arjun on seeing the Cosmic Form of the Lord. Arjun was struck with wonder causing his hairs to stand on end. He bent his head low and with folded hands spoke as under. This suggests that Arjun was not aware of the true identity of Sri Krishna before this moment.

Arjun said:

पश्यामि देवांस्तव देव देहे सर्वांस्तथा भूतविशेषसङ्घान् ।
ब्रह्माणमीशं कमलासनस्थमृषींश्च सर्वानुरगांश्च दिव्यान् ॥ 11.15 ॥

Shlok 11.15: O Lord, I see all gods in Your body and multitudes of beings, Brahma, the Lord, seated on the lotus throne, all other sages and the celestial serpents.

Commentary: These descriptions indicate not only the things of this world but also the Devas are represented in the Cosmic Form. Even the creator, Brahma; the annihilator, Shiv and the sustainer, Vishnu could be seen by Arjun. These names belong to 'Samashti' (Macrocosm). The things of microcosm (*Vyashti*) like serpents and sages also were seen.

The vision of God widens our horizon and takes us beyond the earthly tumults and sorrows which so easily obsess us. Sri Krishna is above all Gods and Goddesses.

अनेकबाहूदरवक्त्रनेत्रं पश्यामि त्वां सर्वतोऽनन्तरूपम् ।
नान्तं न मध्यं न पुनस्तवादिं पश्यामि विश्वेश्वर विश्वरूप ॥ 11.16 ॥

Shlok 11.16: O Lord of the universe, I see your endless form with numerous arms and bellies, mouths and eyes everywhere. Your infinite form, O limitless Lord, has no beginning, middle or end.

Commentary: The Self is omnipresent, all pervading, beginningless and endless. Various organs of the body mentioned here should not be taken literally. They only indicate the Truth from which all names and forms emanate, in which they exist and into which they merge back at the end of their temporary play on the earth. Everything in the universe is temporary or transitory, except for the Lord. God is free from birth and hence deathless.

किरीटिनं गदिनं चक्रिणं च तेजोराशिं सर्वतो दीप्तिमन्तम् ।
पश्यामि त्वां दुर्निरीक्ष्यं समन्ताद्दीप्तानलार्कद्युतिमप्रमेयम् ॥ 11.17 ॥

Shlok 11.17: I see You with Your crown, club, discus, and massive radiance, difficult to behold, shining all around like the immeasurable brilliance and blazing fire of the sun.

Commentary: Arjun is giving a detailed description of what he is seeing in that Cosmic Form. The items mentioned here are the symbolic insignia of Lord Vishnu. The reference to radiance shining everywhere like blazing sun and fire does not mean tremendous amount of light in its physical sense but it indicates the glory of Pure Awareness. Consciousness is the light through which we see our own thoughts and emotions. It is the light which illumines for us various objects, sound, etc. Hence Sri Krishna who Himself is Infinite Awareness is described as resplendent light immeasurable. Although the Universal Form is described here in an objective manner it is only a subjective experience and is not an object of human intellect.

त्वमक्षरं परमं वेदितव्यं त्वमस्य विश्वस्य परं निधानम् ।
त्वमव्ययः शाश्वतधर्मगोप्ता सनातनस्त्वं पुरुषो मतो मे ॥ 11.18 ॥

Shlok 11.18: I believe You are the Imperishable, the Supreme Being, the one thing to be known. You are the ultimate Refuge of the universe. You are the undying Guardian of the Eternal Dharma.

Commentary: Arjun is stating about Sri Krishna that he is the Supreme Being, Absolute. He is the eternal Truth and Supreme worthy to be known because He is the substratum from which the pluralistic world rises up, exists in and merges into. He is the sum total of experiences of every one at their physical, mental and intellectual levels. He is changeless.

Guardian of eternal *Dharma*: For Hindus the protector of *Dharma* is the Lord Himself and not any mortal. He is the guardian of the *sattvata Dharma.*

अनादिमध्यान्तमनन्तवीर्यमनन्तबाहुं शशिसूर्यनेत्रम् ।
पश्यामि त्वां दीप्तहुताशवक्त्रं स्वतेजसा विश्वमिदं तपन्तम् ॥ 11.19 ॥

Shlok 11.19: I see You with infinite power, without beginning, middle, or end; with many arms; with the sun and the moon as Your eyes; with Your mouth as a blazing fire, scorching the entire universe with Your radiance.

Commentary: This verse suggests that God is supremely glorious, as He is the Supreme Self. The Supreme Self is the one essential strength behind everything. Arjun says that he beholds Him as one without beginning, middle or end, of infinite power, of numberless arms, with the sun and the moon as His eyes and with His face as a mass of fire burning the whole universe with its radiance.

द्यावापृथिव्योरिदमन्तरं हि व्याप्तं त्वयैकेन दिशश्च सर्वाः ।
दृष्ट्वाद्भुतं रूपमुग्रं तवेदं लोकत्रयं प्रव्यथितं महात्मन् ॥ 11.20 ॥

Shlok 11.20: The entire space between heaven and earth in all directions is pervaded with you. Seeing Your marvellous and terrible Form, the three worlds are trembling with fear, O Great souled One.

Commentary: As the Lord is eternal and infinite He fills the whole universe with innumerable objects, animate and inanimate. The all-pervading, omnipresent Being penetrates and inter-penetrates the entire creation. As the Cosmic Form is of unusual nature Arjun says everybody is wonder-struck and trembling to look at it. Sri Krishna in cosmic form is entirely different from human being.

In order to remove the doubt entertained by Arjun as to his success, the Lord proceeds to show that victory for Pandavas is certain. Seeing Him, Arjun goes on:

अमी हि त्वां सुरसङ्घा विशन्ति केचिद्भीताः प्राञ्जलयो गृणन्ति ।
स्वस्तीत्युक्त्व महर्षिसिद्धसङ्घाः स्तुवन्ति त्वां स्तुतिभिः पुष्कलाभिः ॥ 11.21 ॥

Shlok 11.21: Hosts of supernatural rulers enter into You. Some with folded hands sing Your names and glories in fear. A multitude of great Rishis and Siddhas praise You with splendid hymns.

Commentary: So far Arjun described the Cosmic Form in Its static state. Now he describes it in its active state. He says some are entering and disappearing in His Form, some are praying with fear and some more praise Him singing hymns of His glory and lost in ecstatic worship. As a matter of fact, no word is appropriate to describe or understand the true nature of Sri Krishna.

The wonderfulness of the Universal Form

रुद्रादित्या वसवो ये च साध्या विश्वेऽश्विनौ मरुतश्चोष्मपाश्च ।
गन्धर्वयक्षासुरसिद्धसङ्घा वीक्षन्ते त्वां विस्मिताश्चैव सर्वे ॥ 11.22 ॥

Shlokas 11.22: The Rudras, Aditiyas, Vasus, and Sadhyas, Visvas and Ashwins, Maruts and Ushmapas, hosts of Gandharvas, Yakshas, Asuras, and Siddhas, they are all looking at Thee, all quite astonished.

रूपं महत्ते बहुवक्त्रनेत्रं महाबाहो बहुबाहूरुपादम् ।
बहूदरं बहुदंष्ट्राकरालं दृष्ट्वा लोकाः प्रव्यथितास्तथाहम् ॥ 11.23 ॥

Shlokas 11.23: Having seen your immeasurable Form, possessed, O Mighty Lord, of many mouths and eyes, of many arms and thighs and feet, and of many stomachs, and fearful with many tusks, the worlds are terrified, and I also.

Commentary (Shlokas 11.22-23): The terms used here were already explained in the previous Discourse. They are all of the Vedic origin. These terms of poetic description bring about the universality and omnipresence of Sri Krishna as the Supreme Being. The Universal form of the Lord reveals to Arjun the malevolent and benevolent aspects of the creation both of which are necessary to complete the picture and understand the whole containing the pairs of opposites. In brief,

God is great and too multifaceted to describe in any language.

Arjun is upset to see the Cosmic Form

नभःस्पृशं दीप्तमनेकवर्णं व्यात्ताननं दीप्तविशालनेत्रम् ।
दृष्ट्वा हि त्वां प्रव्यथितान्तरात्मा धृतिं न विन्दामि शमं च विष्णो ॥ 11.24 ॥

Shlok 11.24: I am frightened and find neither peace nor courage, O Krishna, after seeing Your effulgent and colourful form touching the sky and Your wide open mouth with large shining eyes.

Commentary: The vision experienced by Arjun here is not actually a physical appearance but a wide, all pervading manifestation of the Lord signifying the omnipotence of the Supreme. Arjun feels that His Universal Form has a definite shape and colour which is so uncommon and terrifying that he has no courage to face it. At the same time it is also true to say that the universal form of Sri Krishna has no definite shape and colour, as everything is the manifest form of Sri Krishna.

दंष्ट्राकरालानि च ते मुखानि दृष्ट्वैव कालानलसन्निभानि ।
दिशो न जाने न लभे च शर्म प्रसीद देवेश जगन्निवास ॥ 11.25 ॥

Shlok 11.25: I lose my sense of direction and find no comfort after seeing Your mouths with fearful tusks glowing like fires of cosmic dissolution. Have mercy on me, O Lord of the Devas, O Abode of the universe.

Commentary: Arjun was bewildered to see the cosmic form of Sri Krishna. He was confused and could not make out what to do under such a frightening situation not experienced before. It was not an experience of ordinary kind.

अमी च त्वां धृतराष्ट्रस्य पुत्राः सर्वे सहैवावनिपालसङ्घैः ।
भीष्मो द्रोणः सूतपुत्रस्तथासौ सहास्मदीयैरपि योधमुख्यैः ॥ 11.26 ॥
वक्त्राणि ते त्वरमाणा विशन्ति दंष्ट्राकरालानि भयानकानि ।
केचिद्विलग्ना दशनान्तरेषु सन्दृश्यन्ते चूर्णितैरुत्तमाङ्गैः ॥ 11.27 ॥

Shlokas 11.26-27: All the sons of Dhritarashtra and with them the crowd of kings, Bhishma, Drone and Karna, together with our chief warriors, are hastening into the fearful jaw of your terrible mouths. Some are seen with their heads crushed and caught in the gaps of your teeth.

Commentary: Arjun says that it is terrible to see them hastily rushing to the mouth having frightening teeth, some dead bodies being caught within the gaps between thy teeth, their heads being crushed to powder. As rivers impetuously rush hurling their water into an ocean's lap, in a like manner these mighty men, these lords of earth, fling themselves into thy flaming mouth. These strange descriptions of the Lord or the Cosmic Form are to reassure Arjun as to how the forces are entering into the inescapable mouth of time *(Kal)* and disappear. Destruction always precedes construction. Here the power of destruction of the Supreme as well as His dreadful and perilous forms is given.

Arjun thus observes Bhishm, Karn, etc. entering into the mouth of the principle of destruction as represented by the Cosmic Form. This sight not only frightens Arjun but generates in him self-confidence to face the impending scenario.

In the Universal Form of the Lord wherein He expresses Himself as the entire world of phenomena indicating the principle of oneness, the concepts of space and time disappear. Therefore, when the whole Universe is brought together at the same time and place Arjun could see the past, present and the future.

By now Arjun must have realized that the battle of Kurukshetra would be won by the grace of Sri Krishna alone.

यथा नदीनां बहवोऽम्बुवेगाः समुद्रमेवाभिमुखा द्रवन्ति ।
तथा तवामी नरलोकवीरा विशन्ति वक्त्राण्यभिविज्वलन्ति ॥ 11.28 ॥

Shlok 11.28: These warriors of the mortal world are entering Your blazing mouths as many torrents of rivers flow towards the ocean.

Commentary: Arjun sees all the warriors, whom he did not wish to kill, rushing to death. He knows now that the Lord has already destroyed them, so why should he worry about the life of their kinsmen and friends in the impending war. Arjun must admit now that he is not the real warrior. It is the Lord Himself who is present here and fighting the evil forces. Arjun is merely a means of Sri Krishna to finish the enemies.

यथा प्रदीप्तं ज्वलनं पतङ्गा विशन्ति नाशाय समृद्धवेगाः ।
तथैव नाशाय विशन्ति लोकास्तवापि वक्त्राणि समृद्धवेगाः ॥ 11.29 ॥

Shlok 11.29: All these people are rapidly rushing into Your mouths for destruction as moths rush with great speed into the blazing flame for destruction.

Commentary: The verse is same as the preceding one with respect to contents. It does not require any special comment. These two verses vividly illustrate how the assembled warriors rush to destruction, out of their own uncontrollable nature, with or without discrimination.

As the rivers flow towards the ocean, as the moths fly into the fire, so too all names and forms must, that too willingly, rush towards the unmanifest. If anyone realizes this, he can live without fear of death with the full understanding that life is nothing but a process of continuous change. One need not worry much about oneself. All those who are born are destined to die. Everything is mortal.

लेलिह्यसे ग्रसमानः समन्ताल्लोकान्समग्रान्वदनैर्ज्वलद्भिः ।
तेजोभिरापूर्य जगत्समग्रं भासस्तवोग्राः प्रतपन्ति विष्णो ॥ 11.30 ॥

Shlok 11.30: You are licking up all the worlds with Your flaming mouths, swallowing them from all sides. Your powerful radiance is filling the entire universe with effulgence and burning it, O Vishnu.

Commentary: The principle of destruction is never ending. Hence Arjun exclaims 'You are swallowing the entire world and licking Your lips in enjoyment'. This verse gives us an idea about the Trinity, viz Brahma, Vishnu and Maheshwar. Death, birth, sustenance and again death is the continuous process of existence which is revealed in the Cosmic Form. Arjun thus notices Its resplendence and wonders about the fiery radiance of the fierce rays of the Lord. Life is always temporary and death is always inevitable.

आख्याहि मे को भवानुग्ररूपो नमोऽस्तु ते देववर प्रसीद ।
विज्ञातुमिच्छामि भवन्तमाद्यं न हि प्रजानामि तव प्रवृत्तिम् ॥ 11.31 ॥

Shlok 11.31: Tell me, who are You in such a fierce form? My salutations to You, O Supreme Dev have mercy. I wish to know You, O primal Being, because I do not know Your purpose.

Commentary: Being terrified the disciple seeks to know the true identity of the Lord. Arjun, realizing the sanctity and divinity of the

Lord's power, bows down and humbly requests Him to tell him who He is. He refers to the Lord as Primeval One (Original Being). He asks Him His purpose or His mission in taking such a terrible form and presenting Himself before him exhibiting how the Kaurav forces are going in all hurry towards their destruction.

God as a judge

Lord Krishna said:

कालोऽस्मि लोकक्षयकृत्प्रवृद्धो लोकान्समाहर्तुमिह प्रवृत्तः ।
ऋतेऽपि त्वां न भविष्यन्ति सर्वे येऽवस्थिताः प्रत्यनीकेषु योधाः ॥ 11.32॥

Shlok 11.32: I am the mighty world destroying Time, here made manifest for the purpose of infolding the world. Even without your participation in the war, all the warriors standing arrayed in the opposing armies shall cease to exist.

Commentary: The power that is behind destruction and construction is that which rules over things and governs the lives of beings. Sri Krishna declares that this power is the all destroying *'Kal'*. *Kal* (Time) is the prime mover of the Universe. If God is thought of as time, then He is perpetually creating and destroying. Time is the streaming flux which moves unceasingly. Time absorbs in its womb of oblivion all names and forms. Sri Krishna says that He does not need any help to destroy the entire creation. In a way Arjun is a non-entity to finish the forces of Kaurav. Everything is done by the Supreme Being. Time is very crucial in matters of creation and destruction.

The Supreme Being takes up the responsibility for both creation and destruction. The doctrine that God is responsible for all that is good and Devil is responsible for all that is evil is a clumsy device. If God is responsible for mortal existence, then He is responsible for all that it includes— life and creation, anguish and death, pain and pleasure and so on. The Geeta teaches us to see Reality as a whole. God, the bountiful and prodigal Creator and Preserver are also the God, the Destroyer and Devourer.

We are all His instruments

तस्मात्त्वमुत्तिष्ठ यशो लभस्व जित्वा शत्रून्भुङ्क्ष्व राज्यं समृद्धम् ।
मयैवैते निहताः पूर्वमेव निमित्तमात्रं भव सव्यसाचिन् ॥ 11.33 ॥

Shlok 11.33: Therefore, get up and attain glory. Conquer your enemies, and enjoy the unrivalled dominion. I have already destroyed all these warriors. You are a mere instrument, O *Savyasachin.*

Commentary: Do your duty without attachment to results and consider yourself to be a mere instrument of God and not the doer. Sri Krishna says that this is My battle, not yours. I use you, O Arjun, only as an instrument. I do everything through your body. One must remember all the time that all battles are His, not of others. We are a mere divine instrument and not the doer, and He is in charge of all things. The will and power of God do everything. No one can do anything without His power and will.

द्रोणं च भीष्मं च जयद्रथं च कर्णं तथान्यानपि योधवीरान्।
मया हतांस्त्वं जहि मा व्यथिष्ठा युध्यस्व जेतासि रणे सपत्नान्॥ 11.34 ॥

Shlok 11.34: Drone, Bhishm, Jayadrath, Karn and all the other courageous warriors– these have already been slain by Me. Do not fear. You will certainly conquer the enemies in the battle; therefore, fight.

Commentary: Sri Krishna says whatever be the strength of the negative forces they have already been destroyed by the all powerful 'Time' and Arjun has only to act as an instrument in their ruin and claim victory to himself. In fact during all actions in our lives we are merely the instruments in the hands of the Lord. The concept of self-surrender for serving the world in the constant awareness of the Lord is the only way for claiming glory in our lives.

Every act is a symbol of something beyond itself. Sri Krishna specifically mentioned the names of the four great warriors because they were considered invincible and even then they were eliminated by the Principle of Destruction and therefore He advises Arjun not to be afraid of incurring sin by killing them and others, though they are venerable to him.

Arjun cannot take credit for his victory, as these four warriors have already been finished by Sri Krishna. Arjun has to merely enact a kind of farce to kill them in the battle to let the ordinary people see.

Arjun's prayers to the Cosmic Form

Sanjay said:

एतच्छ्रुत्वा वचनं केशवस्य कृतांजलिर्वेपमानः किरीटी ।
नमस्कृत्वा भूय एवाह कृष्णं सगद्‌गदं भीतभीतः प्रणम्य ॥ 11.35 ॥

Shlok 11.35: Having heard these words of Lord Krishna, the crowned Arjun, trembling with folded hands, prostrated with fear, spoke to Krishna in a choked voice.

Commentary: Arjun was extremely terrified on seeing the Cosmic Form and so he spoke in a choked and stammering voice. These words of Sanjay are very significant because he thought that at this late moment (after knowing full well the impending destruction of all in the Kaurav side) King Dhritarashtra would halt the war and call for peace to save at least his own sons from being killed. But the blind king was obstinate and did not consider Sanjay's indirect advice worthy.

Arjun's hymn of praise

Arjun said:

स्थाने हृषीकेश तव प्रकीर्त्या जगत्प्रहृष्यत्यनुरज्यते च ।
रक्षांसि भीतानि दिशो द्रवन्ति सर्वे नमस्यन्ति च सिद्धसङ्घाः ॥ 11.36 ॥

Shlok 11.36: Rightly, O Krishna, the world delights and rejoices in glorifying You. Terrified demons flee in all directions. The host of sages bow to You in adoration.

Commentary: In an ecstasy of adoration and anguish, Arjun praises the Lord. He sees not only the destructive power of Time but also the spiritual presence and law governing the cosmos. While the former produces terror, the latter gives a sense of peace.

कस्माच्च ते न नमेरन्महात्मन् गरीयसे ब्रह्मणोऽप्यादिकर्त्रे ।
अनन्त देवेश जगन्निवास त्वमक्षरं सदसत्तत्परं यत् ॥ 11.37 ॥

Shlok 11.37: Why should they not, O Great-souled one, bow to You– the original Creator– who is even greater than Brahma, the creator of material worlds? O infinite Lord, O God of the Devas, O Abode of the universe, You are both Eternal and Temporal, and the Supreme Being that is beyond Eternal and Temporal.

Commentary: The Lord is Supreme or Absolute. He is greater than all else. He is the imperishable, so He is the proper object of worship, love and delight.

त्वमादिदेवः पुरुषः पुराणस्त्वमस्य विश्वस्य परं निधानम् ।
वेत्तासि वेद्यं च परं च धाम त्वया ततं विश्वमनन्तरूप ॥ 11.38 ॥

Shlok 11.38: You are the Primal Dev, the most ancient *Purush*. You are the Supreme Refuge of the entire universe. You are the knower, the object of knowledge, and the Supreme Abode. O Lord of the infinite form, You pervade the entire universe.

Commentary: Just as the rope (the substratum for the superimposed snake) sustains the snake, so also the Self, through its nature of Existence, Knowledge and Bliss absolute, sustains this entire Universe. Everything in the universe is permeated with God, but He does not dwell in anything.

वायुर्यमोऽग्निर्वरुणः शशांकः प्रजापतिस्त्वं प्रपितामहश्च ।
नमो नमस्तेऽस्तु सहस्त्रकृत्वः पुनश्च भूयोऽपि नमो नमस्ते ॥ 11.39 ॥

Shlok 11.39: You are the fire, the wind, the water god, the moon god, the Creator (Brahma), as well as the father of the Creator (Brahma), and the controller of death. Salutations to You a thousand times, and again and again salutations to You.

Commentary: As the verse is easily comprehensible, it needs no specific explanation.

नमः पुरस्तादथ पृष्ठतस्ते नमोऽस्तु ते सर्वत एव सर्व ।
अनन्तवीर्यामितविक्रमस्त्वं सर्वं समाप्नोषि ततोऽसि सर्वः ॥ 11.40 ॥

Shlok 11.40: My salutations to You from front and from behind. O Lord, my obeisance to You from all sides. You are infinite valour and boundless might. You pervade everything, and, therefore, You are everywhere and in everything.

Commentary: The Supreme dwells everywhere within, without, above, below and around. There is no place where He is not. He is the all pervading essence like space in the Universe and also the source of all potentiality, power and capability. Since nothing can exist without Him, He is Pure Existence. Hence He is the All and He alone is the All.

सखेति मत्वा प्रसभं यदुक्तं हे कृष्ण हे यादव हे सखेति ।
अजानता महिमानं तवेदं मया प्रमादात्प्रणयेन वापि ॥ 11.41 ॥

Shlok 11.41: Considering You merely as a friend and not knowing Your greatness, I have inadvertently addressed You as O Krishna, O Yadav, and O friend merely out of affection or carelessness.

Commentary: As Arjun is begging before Sri Krishna for apology for using harsh or friendly expressions, treating Him as an ordinary human being. This was a natural conduct on the part of Arjun, as he did not know the true identity of Sri Krishna.

यच्चावहासार्थमसत्कृतोऽसि विहारशय्यासनभोजनेषु ।
एकोऽथवाप्यच्युत तत्समक्षं तत्क्षामये त्वामहमप्रमेयम् ॥ 11.42 ॥

Shlok 11.42: In whatever way I may have insulted You in jokes while playing, reposing in bed, sitting, or at meals; when alone or in front of others, O Achyut, the immeasurable One, I implore You for forgiveness.

Commentary: Arjun, beholding the Cosmic Form of the Lord, seeks forgiveness for his past friendly conduct with Him. He says he was treating Him with casualness and intimacy not knowing His greatness and glory. He asks the Lord for forgiveness for his misconception of His powers. So long, Arjun was thinking of Sri Krishna as a mere cowherd boy or cattle raiser with whom he, a prince, made patronizing friendship. But when he realized His true nature, Arjun bows down before Him in adoration and pleads for His mercy and forgiveness for whatever impropriety he might have committed either knowingly or unknowingly.

पितासि लोकस्य चराचरस्य त्वमस्य पूज्यश्च गुरुर्गरीयान् ।
न त्वत्समोऽस्त्यभ्यधिकः कुतोऽन्यो लोकत्रयेऽप्यप्रतिमप्रभाव ॥ 11.43 ॥

Shlok 11.43: You are the Father of this animate and inanimate world and the greatest Guru to be worshipped. No one is even equal to You in the three worlds; how can there be one greater than You, O Being of incomparable power.

Commentary: Arjun is stating that Sri Krishna is so great that He is not to be compared with anyone in the entire universe. After all, He is a Supreme Being, a true Almighty. It is altogether a different matter that He is present in an ordinary human form before him. It is not necessary that God should appear like God to everyone all the time.

तस्मात्प्रणम्य प्रणिधाय कायं, प्रसादये त्वामहमीशमीड्यम् ।
पितेव पुत्रस्य सखेव सख्युः प्रियः प्रियायार्हसि देव सोढुम् ॥ 11.44 ॥

Shlok 11.44: Therefore, O adorable Lord, I seek Your mercy by bowing down and prostrating my body before You. Bear with me as a father to his son, as a friend to a friend, and as a husband to his wife, O Dev.

Commentary: God as a father is a familiar conception in all religions. The Supreme is not to be regarded as a transcendent mystery but as close to us as a father to the son, a friend to the friend or as a lover to the beloved. These human relations find in God their fullest realization.

Arjun's prayer for the Lord's resumption of His usual form

अदृष्टपूर्वं हृषितोऽस्मि दृष्ट्वा भयेन च प्रव्यथितं मनो मे ।
तदेव मे दर्शय देवरूपं प्रसीद देवेश जगन्निवास ॥ 11.45 ॥

Shlok 11.45: Beholding that which has never been seen before delights me, and yet my mind is tormented with fear. Therefore, O Lord of Devas, the refuge of the universe, has mercy on me and show me your four-armed form.

Commentary: Even though Arjun experienced immense joy on seeing the Cosmic Form of the Lord yet the sudden expansion of consciousness caused in him great fear and distress. Hence he prays to Sri Krishna to resume His usual form and give up the terrifying aspects of the transcendental appearance.

One may see God in any form

किरीटिनं गदिनं चक्रहस्त-मिच्छामि त्वां द्रष्टुमहं तथैव ।
तेनैव रूपेण चतुर्भुजेन सहस्रबाहो भव विश्वमूर्ते ॥ 11.46 ॥

Shlok 11.46: I wish to see You with a crown, holding mace and discus in Your hand. Therefore, O Lord, with thousand arms and universal form, please appear in the four-armed form.

Commentary: This verse attempts to lay stress on the fact that Sri

Krishna is incarnation of Vishnu. That is why Arjun is requesting Him to return back in the form of Vishnu who possessed four hands. As Sri Krishna of the Mahabharat does not appear with four hands in the battlefield of the Kurukshetra, it is not understandable as to how Arjun requests Sri Krishna to 'appear in the four-armed form'. For those who are blessed with divine sight Sri Krishna was always present with multiple faces all around with numerous hands and bodies, as Sri Krishna was after all a Supreme Being. Almighty is at all times capable to appear in any form; otherwise, he is not almighty. This along with other such verses is later day insertion into the Geeta to establish Vishnu as Supreme Being in support of Puranic stories. In *Vaishnavism*, Narayan (Vishnu) is regarded as the Supreme God and it tells that it was He who produced Brahma and Shiva, but in *Shaivism* the Supreme God is Shiva. While the most Geeta scholars regard Sri Krishna alone as the Absolute Reality.

In short, Arjun wants the Lord to appear before him in a serene form with quiet attitude.

(**Note:** The composition date of Vishnu Puran is unknown and often contested, with estimates widely disagreeing. According to historian Vincent Smith the likely period is between 400 and 300 BCE, which means the present day Geeta was compiled or modified subsequent to this period. The **Vishnu Puran** was definitely not in existence at the time of Kurukshetra.)

The Lord resumes His usual form

Lord Krishna said:

मया प्रसन्नेन तवार्जुनेदं रूपं परं दर्शितमात्मयोगात् ।
तेजोमयं विश्वमनन्तमाद्यं यन्मे त्वदन्येन न दृष्टपूर्वम् ॥ 11.47 ॥

Shlok 11.47: O Arjun, being pleased with you I have shown you, through My own Yogic powers, My particular supreme, shining, universal, infinite, and primal form that has never been seen before by anyone other than you.

Commentary: The revelation of the Lord depends upon His grace alone. A man cannot see it by his own efforts. The Lord has shown His grace on Arjun because he is His beloved devotee. S. Radhakrishnan says: 'The vision is not the final goal of a seeker; in that case the Geeta would have ended here. Even trance or *Samadhi* is neither the end nor the essential element of spiritual life as some people think." However, the practice of meditation and *Jap* is recommended as a spiritual practice for the seeker. *Samadhi* is not the ultimate state of realization. The state of Self-realization or *Turiya* state is far beyond *Samadhi.*

न वेदयज्ञाध्ययनैर्न दानैर्न च क्रियाभिर्न तपोभिरुग्रैः ।
एवंरूपः शक्य अहं नृलोके, द्रष्टुं त्वदन्येन कुरुप्रवीर ॥ 11.48 ॥

Shlok 11.48: O great hero of Kurus, neither by study of the Vedas nor by sacrifice nor by charity nor by rituals nor by severe austerities can I be seen in this cosmic form by anyone other than you in this human world.

Commentary: God cannot be seen by one and all. Knowledge of Vedas, sacrifices or acts of charity cannot ensure revelation of God. Arjun is not known for any great knowledge of the Vedas, sacrifices and charity and yet he had an occasion to have a glimpse of the Supreme Being. This vision is granted only to the devotees who adore the Lord with single-minded, all-consuming, and unswerving love.

Lord shows His four-armed and the human form

मा ते व्यथा मा च विमूढभावो दृष्ट्वा रूपं घोरमीदृङ्ममेदम् ।
व्यपेतभीः प्रीतमनाः पुनस्त्वं तदेव मे रूपमिदं प्रपश्य ॥ 11.49 ॥

Shlok 11.49: Be neither afraid nor bewildered, having seen such a terrible form of Mine as this. With fearless and cheerful mind, now behold My four-armed form.

Commentary: The Lord saw Arjun in a state of distress and terror. Therefore, He withdrew the Cosmic Form and assumed once more His usual gentle form. He consoled Arjun and spoke to him with kindness. The microcosmic representation of Truth in the form of gentle and smiling Sri Krishna is macrocosmic Universal Form representing the essence in all forms and names.

(**Note:** This verse is a further attempt to prove that Sri Krishna was incarnation of Vishnu. When Sri Krishna is Almighty or Supreme Being, He is capable to take any form, why four-armed person.)

Sanjay said:

इत्यर्जुनं वासुदेवस्तथोक्त्वा स्वकं रूपं दर्शयामास भूयः ।
आश्वासयामास च भीतमेनं भूत्वा पुनः सौम्यवपुर्महात्मा ॥ 11.50 ॥

Shlok 11.50: So Vasudev, having thus spoken to Arjun, showed once again His four-armed form. And then assuming His pleasant human form, Lord Krishna, the Great-souled One, pacified Arjun, who was terrified.

Commentary: Sanjay confirms to Dhritarashtra that Sri Krishna came back to His usual form, i.e. the very form in which He was born in the house of Vasudev. This is the return to the state of finite from infinite. Such a drastic transformation of one's state is possible only in case of Super Being.

This verse negates the preceding verse because this verse suggests Sri Krishna was born as a two-armed person, which is the normal form for all sorts of people. Sri Krishna had a special appearance for special people endowed with the cosmic vision.

Arjun said:

दृष्ट्वेदं मानुषं रूपं तव सौम्यं जनार्दन ।
इदानीमस्मि संवृत्तः सचेताः प्रकृतिं गतः ॥ 11.51 ॥

Shlok 11.51: O Janardan, seeing this lovely human form of Yours, I have now become tranquil and I am back to my usual form.

Commentary: Arjun admits that when he sees the normal and gentle form of Sri Krishna he feels relieved from his inner tensions and agitations.

Devotion as the means to realization of the Universal Form

Lord Krishna said:

सुदुर्दर्शमिदं रूपं दृष्टवानसि यन्मम ।
देवा अप्यस्य रूपस्य नित्यं दर्शनकांक्षिणः ॥ 11.52 ॥

Shlok 11.52: This four-armed form of Mine that you have seen is very difficult, indeed, to see. Even the gods always yearn to see it.

Commentary: Sri Krishna says that even the Gods are eager to see the Universal Form but their wishes do not materialize even in their dreams. Such is the marvellous vision seen by Arjun so easily.

नाहं वेदैर्न तपसा न दानेन न चेज्यया ।
शक्य एवंविधो द्रष्टुं दृष्टवानसि मां यथा ॥ 11.53 ॥

Shlok 11.53: Not by a study of the Vedas, nor by penance, nor by acts of charity, nor by oblations can one ever see me in the form that you have seen.

Commentary: This is a repetition of verse 11.48 and hence there is no commentary. This has happened mainly because there was more than one person who compiled or prepared the Geeta in its present form at different points of time. This fact has already been pointed out in Chapter-1 of the book.

भक्त्या त्वनन्यया शक्य अहमेवंविधोऽर्जुन ।
ज्ञातुं द्रष्टुं च तत्त्वेन प्रवेष्टुं च परन्तप ॥ 11.54 ॥

Shlok 11.54: But by single-minded devotion, I can be seen in this form, can be known in essence, and also can be reached, O Arjun.

Commentary: The above verse tells us that the Supreme can be attained through devotion. There are other verses in the Geeta which emphasize the role of devotion for God-realisation. The reason why the Lord has shown the Cosmic Form to Arjun only and to none else is given here. Devotion is the sole means to the realization of the Cosmic Form. In unbroken devotion which seeks none but the Lord alone, nothing other than the Lord is experienced by the sense organs wherein egoism and dualism totally vanish. Such experience by means of direct and immediate perception is what is called seeing in reality.

The Lord emphasizes 'single-minded devotion', relegating rituals, study and other actions to a position of secondary importance. This is, indeed, the main message of the Geeta. This message, with its emphasis on devotion, is to be contrasted with the message of the Upanishads, which lay utmost importance on knowledge (*Gyan*) about the Self as the key to salvation. The Geeta, therefore, represents a definite shift from the Upanishadic emphasis on the acquisition of knowledge as the supreme function for attaining salvation. This has a much wider appeal to the unlettered masses, who are deprived of the means of acquiring knowledge— but who are certainly capable of *bhakti*.

मत्कर्मकृन्मत्परमो मद्भक्तः सङ्गवर्जितः ।
निर्वैरः सर्वभूतेषु यः स मामेति पाण्डव ॥ 11.55 ॥

Shlok 11.55: O Pandavas, one who performs all his actions for Me, who considers me as his goal and worships Me, free from attachment and without ill-will to all creatures, attains Me.

Commentary: This is the essence of the whole teaching of the *Geeta.* He who practises this teaching attains supreme bliss and immortality. Such a person realizes Him and enters into His Being, becoming completely one with Him. This verse contains the summary of the entire *Geeta* philosophy.

He who dedicates all works to the Lord, seeking no rewards for himself, who serves Him with all his heart and soul, who regards Him as his supreme goal, who lives for Him alone, who works for Him alone, who sees Him in everything, who sees the whole world as His Cosmic Form, cherishing no feeling of hatred or enmity towards anyone, who has no attachment to worldly objects, who seeks nothing but the Lord- such a person realizes Him and becomes completely one with Him. He enjoys eternal Bliss, peace and immortality.

Concepts and Issues

After hearing the secret of divine manifestation and its glory Arjun says his delusion has gone and expresses his eagerness to see the Lord's Cosmic Form. As the Cosmic Form cannot be seen by the ordinary physical eyes Sri Krishna bestows Arjun with divine vision to enable him to see such form.

It is an extraordinary form with myriads of faces, ornaments and weapons. Decorated with divine garlands and garments, the wondrous cosmic form is more brilliant than a million suns. The whole world of variegated forms constitutes only a small part of His being.

Excited by wonder and joy, Arjun starts praying to that Divinity. All beings– divine, human and subhuman– are found present in Him. He has several arms, stomachs and faces. He is extraordinarily brilliant. He has pervaded the whole space. All beings like gods, deities and sages, are praising Him with folded hands. The various heroes arrayed on the battlefield are entering into Him and getting destroyed like moths in the fire. Gripped with fear and wonder, Arjun prays to Him to disclose who He is.

The Lord replies that He is Time, the eternal destroyer. He has come to annihilate the warriors in the enemy armies. Since this task will be achieved by Him even without Arjun's involvement, the Lord advises Arjun to fight merely as an instrument and get victory, fame and kingdom.

Arjun once again prays to the Lord praising Him and asking for forgiveness for having treated Him lightly during the moments of their intimate friendship. He then requests Him to withdraw His Cosmic Form and reappear in His usual four-armed form with the crown, mace and discus. After doing so, Sri Krishna tells him that His Cosmic Form cannot be seen by the study of the scriptures or performance of sacrifices or even austerity, but only by single-minded devotion. The Lord adds that those who are free from attachment and hatred and who dedicate all their actions to Him with unswerving faith, knowing Him to be the supreme goal surely reach Him.

Whatever be our vocation and character, whether we are creative thinkers or contemplative poets or humble men and women with no special gifts, if we possess the one great gift of the love of God, we become God's tools, the channels of His love and purpose. When this vast world of living spirits becomes attuned to God and exists only to do His will, the purpose of life is achieved.

***Note*:** The verse such as 11.30 or similar other verses, comparing or equating Sri Krishna with Vishnu, suggesting Sri Krishna as incarnation of Vishnu, may not be a part of the original Geeta, as these verses downgrade or weaken the celestial status of Lord Krishna and so also the teachings of the Geeta. The message of the Geeta is that Sri Krishna is Parabrahm– Supreme Being. He is truly Absolute. It was He who created Brahma, Vishnu and Mahesh, as it is apparent from such verses as 10.6 and 11.37. Sri Krishna is unborn, immortal and eternal. He is almighty and omnipresent. Hence, he cannot be described as incarnation of Vishnu. Similarly in Hindu scriptures Ram, Buddha and Mahavir have also been described as incarnation of Vishnu. These are all imaginary stories concocted by Vaishnavite story-tellers. We do not know, except for the **Vishnu Puran**, who was the architect behind the propagation of such views relating to incarnation of Vishnu or some other God in the form of living being. The great Vedic Scholar like Maharishi Dayanand Sarswati has outright rejected the notion of incarnation of God. Most likely the earlier story-tellers or the later day scholars have inserted such verses to prove the supremacy of Vishnu over Sri Krishna. The Geeta is neither an extension of the Vedic view of Hindu Gods and Goddesses, nor does it endorse the Vedic ritualism. Verse 11.48 clearly states that God cannot be attained with the help of Vedic knowledge or practices. Such verses here and elsewhere are self contradictory. When God is one and a non-living being, how do these three Gods (Brahma, Vishnu and Mahesh) come up in Hindu scriptures? Additionally, they are stated to have been married and had progeny like normal human beings, while God is described as colourless, formless, attributeless and thus inexpressible. Reference of Vishnu in the Geeta creates unnecessary incongruity and misunderstanding. Such things have happened possibly under the influence of the Puranic literature, especially the **Vishnu Puran**.

OM TAT SAT

Discourse - 12

Bhaktiyog: Yog of Devotion

In the preceding Discourse Arjun had a rare opportunity to experience *Vishwaroop* or the universal form of Sri Krishna. So a doubt has naturally arisen in his mind as to which of the two forms is better to attain the spiritual realization– those who are worshipping the Lord in a manifest form or worshipping the Lord in the unmanifest form. Sri Krishna replies that those who worship Him with faith and devotion keeping their mind fixed on His manifest form are better. Those who control their senses and contemplate on the unmanifest Reality will certainly reach Him, but their path is relatively more difficult.

He advises Arjun to establish his mind and intellect in Him. Then he will live in Him. If he cannot do this, he should try to reach Him through repeated practice failing which he can try doing work for the sake of the Lord. If doing this also is not possible for him or any devotee, he can practise self control and offer the fruits of all his actions to Him.

The Lord says that knowledge is better than practice. Meditation is better than mere knowledge. Renunciation of the fruits of action is better than meditation. Sri Krishna says that by renunciation of desires one can attain Supreme Peace– Universal Consciousness.

Sri Krishna then describes the characteristics of a true devotee. A true devotee does not hate anyone. He is friendly to all and compassionate and free from egoism and possessiveness. He is well balanced in pain and pleasure, ever forgiving and contended. Having mastered his emotions he has dedicated his mind unto the Lord. He is never the cause of unrest for the world nor can the world upset him.

A true devotee is free from joy and anger, fear and anxiety. He is beyond pleasure and hatred, sorrow and desires and has abandoned all actions, good and bad. He has devotion and looks equally upon friend and foe and remain balanced in honour and dishonour. Ever contented, having no particular place as his home, he has steadiness of mind. Such a devotee is ever dear to the Lord. Those who follow this immortal *Dharma* with faith considering Him as the Supreme goal of life are exceedingly dear to Him.

Devotion and contemplation

Arjun asked:

एवं सततयुक्ता ये भक्तास्त्वां पर्युपासते ।
ये चाप्यक्षरमव्यक्तं तेषां के योगवित्तमाः ॥ 12.1 ॥

Shlok 12.1: Those devotees who, ever steadfast, thus worship You and those who worship the Imperishable and the Unmanifested– which of them have the greater knowledge of Yog?

Commentary: Arjun wants confirmation whether one should meditate upon the manifested form or upon the unmanifested form of the Supreme. Unmanifested is that which is not directly perceptible through the sense organs. The objects that can be perceived through the sense organs are the manifested. The Supreme Being has got two aspects: the 'Absolute or Brahm or the Unmanifest' and the 'Personal God or Ishvar or the Manifest'. Both these aspects of the Godhead have been described by Krishna in the Geeta, though with an emphasis on the Impersonal aspect in Discourses 2 through 10. The 11th Discourse deals with the Universal form of Godhead and ends with an exhortation to Arjun to worship It as the Lord of the universe. Now Arjun asks which of the two methods of worship is better; meditation on the Impersonal or worship of the Lord through work and love. Thus the answer is thus:

Lord Krishna said:

मय्यावेश्य मनो ये मां नित्ययुक्ता उपासते ।
श्रद्धया परयोपेतास्ते मे युक्ततमा मताः ॥ 12.2 ॥

Shlok 12.2: Those who, fixing their minds on Me, worship Me,

ever steadfast and endowed with supreme faith, they are the best Yogi in My opinion.

Commentary: The state of perfection of a yogi is again described here. Sri Krishna says that those, who fixing their minds on Me, worship Me ever earnest and possessed of supreme faith I consider them most perfect *Yogis*.

Devotion is defined as the highest love for God. Concentrate on God without any interest, showing intense love for God. Real devotion is seeking God's grace and serving with love to please Him. Thus, devotion is doing one's duty as service to the Lord with love of God in one's heart. A loving relationship with God is easily developed through a personal God. Some saints consider devotion superior to Self–knowledge. All spiritual practices are useless in the absence of devotion, the deep love of God. Ramanujacharya has said that those who worship the manifest reach their goal sooner and with less difficulty.

Earnestness and unflinching faith are the main ingredients of true devotion. The true devotee meditates on God with true love and all his actions are God-oriented. All his thoughts are fixed on Him. Devotion involves complete surrender to the Supreme. The path of devotion takes its stand upon the love and emotions of a person and turns these towards God. Individual ego is destroyed by the intensity of love of God. If does not take into account the reflection and reasoning of the mind and makes full use of love and adoration of the Divine. It is the yearning of the eager heart and seeks divine fulfilment of the emotional being of a person.

The worshippers of *Akshar*

ये त्वक्षरमनिर्देश्यमव्यक्तं पर्युपासते ।

सर्वत्रगमचिन्त्यं च कूटस्थमचलं ध्रुवम् ॥ 12.3 ॥

सन्नियम्येन्द्रियग्रामं सर्वत्र समबुद्धयः ।

ते प्राप्नुवन्ति मामेव सर्वभूतहिते रताः ॥ 12.4 ॥

Shlokas 12.3–04: Those who ever contemplate the Imperishable, the Indefinable, the Unmanifest, the Omnipresent and the Unthinkable, the Unchangeable, the Immutable, the Eternal– restraining all the senses, even–minded under all circumstances, engaged in the welfare of all creatures, they reach Myself.

Commentary: Because the Imperishable (*Akshar*) is unmanifest, He is not accessible to words and, therefore, cannot be defined. He is unmanifest which means not manifest to any of the organs of cognition. They contemplate the Imperishable everywhere all round. Contemplation (*Upasana*) consists in approaching the object of worship by way of meditating it according to the teaching of *Shastra* and dwelling for a long time steadily in the current of same thought like a thread of descending oil. The Imperishable is omnipresent, pervading all like the *Akash*. He is unthinkable, because He is unmanifest. Whatever is visible to the senses can be thought of by the mind also; but the *Akshar* is invisible to the senses and is therefore unthinkable. He is immutable and eternal. Devotees who contemplate the Imperishable, curbing all their senses, and always balanced whether they come by the desirable or the undesirable, they come to Me. Sri Krishna says that those who meditate on the unmanifest in the aforesaid manner, they too reach the same goal, the Supreme Self. But the Lord says that concentration on the unmanifest is difficult task for the worldly people.

Reasons for worshipping a personal form of God

क्लेशोऽधिकतरस्तेषामव्यक्तासक्तचेतसाम् ।
अव्यक्ता हि गतिर्दुःखं देहवद्भिरवाप्यते ॥ 12.5 ॥

Shlok 12.5: The difficulty of those whose thoughts are set on the unmanifest is greater for the goal of the unmanifest is hard to reach.

Commentary: Those who seek the Manifest Lord and those who seek the Unmanifest Lord reach the same goal, but the path taken up by the latter is arduous because the aspirant has to practise utmost self–control, renounce the worldly life, get rid of all human emotions and desires and fix the mind in the contemplation of the Absolute. It is also difficult to fix the restless mind on the formless and attributeless Self. Such a method of contemplation demands a sharp, highly focussed and subtle intellect.

For a majority of the seekers meditation upon the Lord as expressed in the Universe, a Personal God (manifested form) is easier because they have a tangible ideal of the Lord to whom they can direct their feelings, emotion, love, will, energies and knowledge.

The imperishable Self is very hard to reach for those who are attached to their bodies. Their restless mind will not be able to get fixed on the attributeless Self. One must be free from body–feeling and be established in feeling the existence of the Self alone if one wants to succeed in worship of formless Absolute. One becomes free from the bodily conception of life when one is fully purified and acts solely for the Supreme Lord. Attainment of such a state is not possible for the average human being, but only for advanced souls. Therefore, the natural course for the ordinary seeker is to worship God with a form. The method of worship really depends on the individual. One should find out for oneself which method suits one best. The path of Self–knowledge is difficult to comprehend, to explain and to follow. It is also very easy to fall down from the path of knowledge or retreat to the lower sensual plane of consciousness. In the next two verses, the Lord says that the path of devotion is not only easier, but also faster than the path of knowledge.

ये तु सर्वाणि कर्माणि मयि संन्यस्य मत्पराः ।
अनन्येनैव योगेन मां ध्यायन्त उपासते ॥ 12.6 ॥
तेषामहं समुद्धर्ता मृत्युसंसारसागरात् ।
भवामि नचिरात्पार्थ मय्यावेशितचेतसाम् ॥ 12.7 ॥

Shlokas 12.6-12.7: But to those who worship Me, renouncing all actions in Me, regarding Me as the supreme goal, meditate on Me with undivided devotion; whose minds are totally absorbed in Me, I become their saviour and liberate them from the ocean of death-bound existence, Oh! Arjun.

Commentary: Those who are engaged in contemplating Me exclusively, I (the Lord) will lift up from the ocean of mortal *Sansar,* since their thoughts are fixed on Me in the Universal Form. S*ansar* is just like an ocean, because it is very hard to cross beyond it.

People are born different. Anybody who prescribes one method for all is certainly deluded because there is no single method for one and all. A single method or system cannot meet the spiritual needs of all. Hinduism, with its many branches and sub–branches, offers a very wide range of choices of spiritual practices to suit persons. All paths lead to salvation because they all culminate in devotion to God.

Sri Krishna lays down certain conditions to be followed by those who want to meditate upon the form of the Lord and concludes that those who follow these instructions fully and sincerely will be saved from their mortal limitations by Himself on whose form they are contemplating. These conditions are as follows:

- •Renounce all actions in Him– renouncing one's individual ego and limitations and identifying oneself with Him by complete surrender to the Lord.
- •Regard Him as the supreme goal– directing one's energy and dealings for achieving the goal of self perfection symbolised in the form of the Lord.
- •Meditate on Him with unswerving devotion– Lifting the mind from agitation prone thoughts to a greater goal with single–pointed attention.

Devotion is the path of love which is neither merely physical attention nor intellectual appreciation. It is love at the level of the Supreme. It is not superficial and emanates from the heart. Devotion to God is the highest and the purest form of love. Love in the ordinary sense may be fascination or attraction for a person or an object. Such love is limited and temporary. We may call it attachment.

Devotion or Bhakti is spontaneous and for a higher cause. Simply going to a temple or a place of worship or performing some specific religious rites on certain occasions is not necessarily devotion. Devotion involves intense love and longing, unselfish love without asking for anything and without sensual enjoyment.

मय्येव मन आधत्स्व मयि बुद्धिं निवेशय ।
निवसिष्यसि मय्येव अत ऊर्ध्वं न संशयः ॥ 12.8 ॥

Shlok 12.8: Fix your mind on Me alone, place your intellect in Me; thereafter you shall, no doubt, live in Me alone.

Commentary: Fix thy mind (*Manas*), your purposes and thoughts in Me (the Lord in the Universal Form). Fix in Me your reason (*Buddhi*) also which resolves and determines. Then you will without fail abide in Me as Myself on the death of this body. You should not doubt it.

This is the path of meditation and contemplation on the Absolute for the contemplative mind. Thinking of God all the time is different from only worshipping a God with form, but both practices are the same in quality and effect. In other words, contemplation is also a form of worship. One should try to understand the following:

'Fix your mind on Me'– By meditation, mind can be made to concentrate on the form of the Lord giving up all thoughts relating to sensory objects.

'Place your intellect in Me'– The intellect, which discriminates and determines, should be made to focus itself on the Lord.

'Live in Me alone'– If the mind rests on the Lord and the intellect understands the Infinite, the individuality ends and one merges with the Infinite. There is no doubt about this, says Sri Krishna.

अथ चित्तं समाधातुं न शक्नोषि मयि स्थिरम् ।
अभ्यासयोगेन ततो मामिच्छाप्तुं धनंजय ॥ 12.9 ॥

Shlok 12.9: If you are unable to focus your mind steadily on Me, then by *Abhyas Yog* you seek to reach Me, O Dhananjay.

Commentary: If you cannot fix your thought on Me steadily in the manner I have mentioned, then you seek to reach Me in the Universal Form, by yog of constant practice (*Abhyasyog*). Practice (*Abhyas*) consists in withdrawing thought from all quarters and fixing it again and again on one particular object.

This is the path of performing rituals, prayer, and devotional worship recommended for people who are emotional, have more faith but less reasoning and intellect. Constantly contemplate and concentrate your mind on God, using symbols or mental pictures of a personal God as an aid to develop devotion. This verse lays special stress on constant practice or *dhyan* to attain the Supreme Being.

अभ्यासेऽप्यसमर्थोऽसि मत्कर्मपरमो भव ।
मदर्थमपि कर्माणि कुर्वन्सिद्धिमवाप्स्यसि ॥ 12.10 ॥

Shlok 12.10: If you are unable even to do any *Abhyas Yog*, then dedicate all your work to Me (or do your duty just for Me). You shall attain perfection by doing your prescribed duty for Me.

Commentary: If concentration on the Lord is found difficult on account of the outward tendencies of the mind or external circumstances, then do all actions for the sake of the Lord. One should keep on practising again and again. It has got no alternative. Lord Himself guides every endeavour of the person who works for the good of humanity, and success comes to a person who dedicates his or her life in the service of God. First try to attain purity of mind, then Yog or steadfastness, then knowledge, and then perfection (*Moksha*).

अथैतदप्यशक्तोऽसि कर्तुं मद्योगमाश्रितः ।
सर्वकर्मफलत्यागं ततः कुरु यतात्मवान् ॥ 12.11 ॥

Shlok 12.11: If you are unable to dedicate your work to Me, then taking refuse in Me and renounce (the attachment to and the anxiety for) the fruits of all action, being self controlled.

Commentary: If you cannot perform any action for My sake as you have just been told, then you perform actions renouncing them all in Me, and abandon the fruit of those actions. This is a very simple suggestion by Sri Krishna to Arjun. This is the path of Karmayog, the selfless service to humanity. Generally individuals waste their energies in worrying about the future results of their present actions. Sri Krishna urges here not to have such anxieties and not to worry about the consequences and then do the work without having any desire for positive result by surrendering all the fruits of actions to Him. This idea has already been conveyed in Discourse–3.

In the preceding four verses, the concentration of the mind on the Lord is enjoined first; in case of inability to do that, three alternatives have been put forward to achieve the same goal. They are:

- *Abhyas Yog*, constant practice to fix the mind.
- Performance of actions for the sake of the Lord alone.
- Giving up the fruits of actions to the Lord, i.e. the Yog of desireless action or *Nishkamakarm*.

Karmayog is the easiest way to begin with

श्रेयो हि ज्ञानमभ्यासाज्ज्ञानाद्ध्यानं विशिष्यते ।
ध्यानात्कर्मफलत्यागस्त्यागाच्छान्तिरनन्तरम् ॥ 12.12 ॥

Shlok 12.12: Knowledge of scriptures is better than blind practice; meditation with knowledge is better than mere knowledge; renunciation of (attachment to) the fruits of work is better than meditation because peace immediately follows

renunciation of all desires.

Commentary: Knowledge is better than blind practice; better than that knowledge is meditation (*Dhyan*) with knowledge; still better than meditation with knowledge is the abandonment of the fruits of actions. This can be understood more easily from the following explanations: Knowledge is better than practice– Spiritual practices mean listening to discourses on scriptures, performing rituals, etc. in a routine manner without understanding the significance behind them. Knowledge means acquiring discrimination and discipline at mental and intellectual levels.

Meditation is better than knowledge. More important is the meditation with the knowledge so acquired than the mere knowledge.

Renunciation of fruits of action is better than meditation. Meditation is an attempt by the intellect towards a better understanding of the knowledge acquired. Anxiety about the future causes mental tension. A tense mind is not suitable for meditation.

The attributes of a true devotee

अद्वेष्टा सर्वभूतानां मैत्रः करुण एव च ।
निर्ममो निरहंकारः समदुःखसुखः क्षमी ॥ 12.13 ॥
सन्तुष्टः सततं योगी यतात्मा दृढनिश्चयः ।
मय्यर्पितमनोबुद्धिर्यो मद्भक्तः स मे प्रियः ॥ 12.14 ॥

Shlokas 12.13–14: He who hates no creature, who is friendly and compassionate to all, who is free from attachment and egoism, balanced in pleasure and pain, and forgiving, ever content, steady in meditation, possessed of firm conviction, self–controlled, with mind and intellect dedicated to Me, he, My devotee, is dear to Me.

Commentary: He who hates nothing, not even that which causes him pain. He regards all beings as himself. He is friendly and compassionate. He is full of compassion for the distressed; has offered security of life to all beings, he is a real *Sannyasi*. He does not regard anything as 'mine' and is free from egoism, from the notion of 'I'. Pain and pleasure do not cause hatred and attachment in him. He remains unaffected when abused or beaten. He is always content without what he has got. He is also satisfied whether he comes by a good thing or not. He is a true yogi, always steadfast in thought. He has a firm conviction regarding the essential nature of the Self. This *Sannyasi* has directed to Me exclusively his *Manas*– purposes and thoughts– as well as his *Buddhi*– the faculty of determining. Such a devotee is dear to Me.

To attain oneness with God, one has to become perfect like Him by cultivating moral virtues. Virtues and discipline are two sure means of devotion. These two verses give 10 noble qualities of a true devotee, viz.

1. Hatred towards none
2. Friendly and compassionate to all
3. Freedom from attachment and egoism
4. Balanced in the pairs of opposites (*Sthitpragya*)
5. Forgiving nature
6. Remain content
7. Steadfast in meditation
8. Self–controlled
9. Firm in conviction and
10. Mind and intellect always focussed on the Lord.

यस्मान्नोद्विजते लोको लोकान्नोद्विजते च यः ।
हर्षामर्षभयोद्वेगैर्मुक्तो यः स च मे प्रियः ॥ 12.15 ॥

Shlok 12.15: He by whom the world is not agitated and who cannot be agitated by the world, who is freed from joy, anger, envy, fear and anxiety– he too is dear to Me.

Commentary: Human beings are usually confronted with six different hurdles on their way to realization of God. They are lust, anger, greed, pride, attachment, and envy. Only persons who are free from these are dear to Sri Krishna. In addition to earlier ten characteristics of a real devotee three more are added here.

1. He by whom the world is not agitated– where there is sun there can be no darkness; similarly where there is a man of equanimity and perfection an atmosphere of divinity, serenity, joy and peace prevails.

2. Who cannot be agitated by the world– not only serenity is spread around him but such a devotee cannot also be agitated or his inner equipoise disturbed by the chaotic conditions of the world around him.

3. He who is completely freed from joy, anger, envy, fear and anxiety which are all the causes for inner agitations.

Such a devotee, who is ever peaceful with himself and the world, is not a source of grief to any and none can make him grief-stricken.

There are other verses, too, which mention several other qualities. Thus in the path of devotion or Bhakti Yog, there is great emphasis on qualities rather than on mere performance of some religious rituals. Broadly speaking, these qualities are moral values, which include love, humility, mercy, gentleness, even-mindedness, self-restraint, contentment, firm determination; absence of egoism, anger, fear and attachment and some more. The service of humanity is also an essential aspect of devotion.

Constant remembrance of God with full faith, contemplation of his attributes, singing his praises, performing actions without attachment, in the spirit of service to God and practice of qualities mentioned above in real conduct and behaviour are part of discipline of devotion.

अनपेक्षः शुचिर्दक्ष उदासीनो गतव्यथः ।
सर्वारम्भपरित्यागी यो मद्भक्तः स मे प्रियः ॥ 12.16 ॥

Shlok 12.16: He who is free from expectation, pure, skilful in action, unconcerned and untroubled, renouncing all undertakings– he who is thus devoted to Me, is dear to Me.

Commentary: A true devotee is indifferent to the body, the senses, the sensory objects and their mutual connections. He is possessed of purity both internal and external. He is able to decide rightly on the spot in matters demanding prompt attention. He does not take the side of a friend and the like. He habitually renounces all actions calculated to secure objects of desire, whether of this world or of the next.

In this verse six more subtle qualities of a perfect devotee are added here. They are:

1. Free from expectation– A true devotee is independent of the world outside drawing equanimity from within himself.

2. Who is pure both externally and internally– External purity is cleanliness of physical body and things around. Internal purity is friendship, compassion, nobility and virtuous dealings with others.

3. Skilful– swiftness and enthusiasm in all actions and in decision making.

4. Unconcerned– It means not squandering away the mental energies by avoiding exaggeration of small difficulties in life and being impartial.

5. Untroubled– who never allows himself to be disturbed by agitations caused by desire.

6. Renouncing all undertakings– This does not mean abandoning all undertakings or productive efforts. It means renouncing the egoistic sense of self importance in undertaking any venture. All our undertakings are controlled by many external factors and our role is thus limited. Hence there is no place for self–importance in any work we undertake.

The devotee who has all these six qualities is dear to the Lord.

यो न हृष्यति न द्वेष्टि न शोचति न कांक्षति ।
शुभाशुभपरित्यागी भक्तिमान्यः स मे प्रियः ॥ 12.17 ॥

Shlok 12.17: He who neither rejoices nor hates, nor grieves, nor desires, and who has renounced good and evil, he who is thus devoted is dear to Me.

Commentary: A true devotee does not rejoice on attaining what is desirable. He does not fret on what is undesirable. He does not grieve on having to part with a beloved object. He does not aspire for what he does not possess. The ideas spelt out in verse 13 are dealt with in greater details here. A devotee is dear to me who does not:

1. Rejoice when he attains desirable objects,
2. Hate or fret and fume on getting undesirable objects,
3. Grieve over parting with beloved and cherished objects,
4. Who has a complete sense of fulfilment and has no desire for anything that he has not attained (he who has attained the Self, has really attained everything),
5. Renounces good and evil– none of the dualistic experiences can be of any consequence to him and
6. Who is of full devotion for the Supreme Being?

The import of this verse is that a true devotee does not rejoice when he attains desirable objects nor does he grieve when he parts with his cherished objects. Further, he does not aspire for the unattained.

समः शत्रौ च मित्रे च तथा मानापमानयोः ।
शीतोष्णसुखदुःखेषु समः संगविवर्जितः ॥ 12.18 ॥
तुल्यनिन्दास्तुतिर्मौनी संतुष्टो येन केनचित् ।
अनिकेतः स्थिरमतिर्भक्तिमान्मे प्रियो नरः ॥ 12.19 ॥

Shlokas 12.18-19: One who is the same to the friend and foe, in honour and disgrace, in heat and cold, in pleasure and pain; who is free from attachment; who is indifferent to censure and praise; who is quiet, and content with whatever one has, unattached to a place, a country, or a house; who is tranquil, and full of devotion– that person is dear to Me.

Commentary: A true devotee has no attachment for any object of any kind. He is content with the bare means of bodily sustenance. He is always content with his possession no matter what little he has got. He has no fixed abode; he is 'houseless'. His thought is fixed steadily on the Supreme Reality.

Who is really dear to Sri Krishna? The answer is as follows: That man who is

1. same for friend and foe,
2. same in honour and dishonour,
3. same in heat and cold,
4. same in pleasure and pain,
5. same in censure and praise (To a true devotee the worldly praise or censure has no meaning and significance.),
6. silent (He is a man of few words both physically and mentally.),
7. content with anything (The attitude of contentment is the only way to seek and achieve the divine goal of life.)
8. homeless (Home indicates a sense of possession and belonging. Homeless means the absence of such sense. As these souls exist not for any family or social group but live for mankind as a whole. They do not belong to one place or community. They are always free.)
9. steadfast in understanding of the goal and
10. fully devoted to the Lord.

In all of these situations a true devotee remains unagitated because he is free from attachment which is the cause of all the problems or sorrow in life. Sri Krishna has thus given the complete picture of a man of perfection, his relationship with the outside world, his psychological outlook and intellectual perspective of the world of beings and happenings. This verse lists the various moral and spiritual qualities of a true devotee.

(Note: In verses 13 to 19, Lord Krishna enumerates the qualities of a true devotee, which are summarised thus:

- He is friendly and compassionate and bears no ill-will.
- He is patient and even-minded in pleasure and pain.
- He is free from false pride and egoism.
- He is contented, self-controlled, firm in resolves and fully dedicated to God.
- He does not harm others.
- He is free from envy, fear and anxiety.
- He has no expectations and is free from dependence on the outside world.
- He is skilful in action, unconcerned and untroubled.
- He is pure-hearted and has renounced fruits of all his actions.
- He neither rejoices, nor hates, nor grieves, nor desires.
- He has same attitude towards friends and foes.
- He is free from attachment and remains undisturbed in heat and cold, pleasure and pain, success or failure.
- He is restrained in speech, unaffected by blame and praise and always content.
- He has no fixed abode and has a steady mind, devoted to God.

All such devotees are dear to God but a devotee who has complete faith in God and considers Him, his supreme goal is exceedingly dear to Him. Only a spiritually oriented person can make efforts and aspire to be so!).

One should strive to develop divine qualities

ये तु धर्म्यामृतमिदं यथोक्तं पर्युपासते ।
श्रद्दधाना मत्परमा भक्तास्तेऽतीव मे प्रियाः ॥ 12.20 ॥

Shlok 12.20: Those who have full faith in Me and holding me as their supreme aim, follow My immortal wisdom are exceedingly dear to Me.

Commentary: The Sanatan Dharma is summarised in the Verses 13 through 19 above. To realize the Self and live in that wisdom at all levels– physical, mental and intellectual– is the fulfilment of human existence. By following the ideal set in the above seven verses the devotee is freed forever from the cycle of birth and death and succeeds in realizing God who is immortality itself. It is in order to bring out this idea that the marks of a true devotee described above are spoken as '*Dharmamrit*' or the nectar of pious wisdom.

It is not enough that one gets the knowledge of Dharma (Law of Life) but such knowledge should be lived. He should be able to internalize it properly and become perfect in life. Therefore, Sri Krishna says he must be endowed with faith– the capacity to assimilate spiritual ideas through subjective personal experience. Such devotees are supremely dear to the Lord.

One may not have all the virtues, but a sincere effort to develop virtues is most appreciated by the Lord. Thus the striver is very dear to the Lord. The high-class devotees do not desire anything, including salvation from the Lord, except for one boon: devotion to the lotus feet of a personal God, birth after birth. Poor-class devotees use God as a servant to fulfil their material demands and desires. The development of unswerving love and devotion to the lotus feet of the Lord is the ultimate aim of all spiritual discipline and meritorious deeds, as well as the goal of human birth. A true devotee considers oneself the servant, the Lord as the master, and the entire creation as His body.

The path of devotion is a better path for most people, but devotion does not develop without a combination of personal effort, faith, and the grace of God. According to most saints and sages, the path of devotion is very simple and easy to perform. One can begin by simply chanting a personal *Mantra* or any holy name of God. There is no restriction on the correct time or place for chanting the holy name of God. The process of devotional service consists of one or more of the following practices: hearing discourses, chanting the holy name of God, remembering and contemplating God, worshipping and praying to Him. Five methods to attain Godhood are:

(1) Serving humanity (*Seva*, voluntary social services),

(2) Study of scriptures,

(3) any suitable spiritual practice,

(4) *Satsang*, and

(5) Surrendering to His will.

The four inter-connected paths of Yog discussed in the first twelve Discourses of the Geeta may be summarised as follows: The practice of Karmayog leads to purification of the mind from the stain of selfishness that paves the way for knowledge of God to be revealed. Knowledge develops into devotional love of God. Constantly thinking of God, the object of our love, due to devotion is called meditation and contemplation that eventually lead to enlightenment and salvation.

Lord Krishna has been talking about both manifest and unmanifest aspects of God in the previous Discourses. Arjun's question has been answered in great detail in this Discourse, but people still argue that one method of worship or certain religious practices are better than others. Such persons only understand half the truth. In our opinion, it is quite clear that the method of worship depends on the nature of the individual. What has worked for one may not work for all, so what makes you think your method is universal? There was no need for the Lord to discuss different paths of Yog if there was one path for all. If the chosen path of spiritual discipline does not give one peace or God–realization, then it must be understood that one is not practising correctly or the path is not right for the individual.

OM TAT SAT

Discourse - 13

Kshetra-Khetragya Vibhag Yog: Yog of Distinction between the Field and the Knower of the Field

This Discourse contains one of the most significant, most illuminating, most inspiring and mystical portions of the Bhagavad Geeta. The Lord gives us a highly revealing insight into the individual human being. It is the metaphysics of man, the unknown. Lord Krishna talks about the difference between the physical body and the immortal soul. He explains that the physical body is transitory and perishable, whereas the soul is immutable and eternal. The Lord also gives precise knowledge about the individual soul and the ultimate soul. The supreme transcendental Spirit, which is the eternal substratum beyond both, is also described in a wonderful manner.

Another important theme of this Discourse is the enumeration of twenty two qualities of a *Gyani* (enlightened person) on the lines of the listing of thirty five qualities of a *bhakta* in the previous Discourse. This Discourse concludes by showing the way towards realization of the Self and how with the Eye of Wisdom one can liberate himself.

In this Discourse Sri Krishna throws light on such notions as the *Kshetra* (Field) and the *Kshetragaya* (Knower of the Field) in a philosophic sense. The body is the Field and the Self or the Soul is the Knower of the Field. The *Kshetra,* the body and the *Kshetragaya*, the soul are entirely different from each other. It is due to ignorance that they are being identified as one and the same. In the present Discourse both these terms are differentiated for explanation and hence the title of this Discourse is *Kshetra Kshetragaya Vibhag Yog*: Yog of Distinction between the Field and the Knower of the Field.

In the ultimate analysis Sri Krishna is the Knower of the Field in all the Fields. Thus, Lord Krishna explains the mystery of the individual soul dwelling within this mortal body. This knowledge constitutes the main subject matter of all the scriptures and the highest philosophical works. The knower of the Supreme Reality is instantly liberated.

The five elements, the ego, the mind, intellect and the ten organs, desire and aversion and such factors constitute the Field. Next follows a superb summing-up of what constitutes true knowledge. Then follows the declaration of the Supreme Soul, the knowledge of which grants us immortality. That Supreme Reality is the one universal Essence present everywhere. It pervades all. It shines within the inmost chambers of our heart, it is everything, and it is the guide, sustainer, experiencer and Lord of all. One who knows this mystery is not bound by activity even in the midst of life. When we perceive this Supreme Self dwelling in all beings we cannot injure anyone. Krishna asks us to see and know the difference between the Field (body or *Prakriti*) and the Knower of the Field (Spirit or *Purush*), and thus reach the Self. This is the teaching and the message of this illuminating Discourse.

(**Note:** This Discourse is heavily based on the *Sankhya Darshan*, which was propounded by sage Kapil who himself did not believe in God. It is not known as to how all these verses have been placed through Sri Krishna. This shows that a fair amount of additions were made into the Geeta by the later day protagonists of Sankhya Darshan who amended their views in favour of the existence of God. It has been observed by some scholars that the last six Discourses are a later addition. In the words of Stephen Mitchell (**Bhagavad Gita**, 2002), "In Chapter 13 to 18 much of the material is dull and secondary at best; for long stretches the poem seems to be written by a scholastic philosopher bent on categorizing everything in the world according to three *Gunas*". It, however, does not matter much as to who has added what. In fact, one should focus on the relevance of teaching.)

Arjun asked:

प्रकृतिं पुरुषं चैव क्षेत्रं क्षेत्रज्ञमेव च।
एतद्वेदितुमिच्छामि ज्ञानं ज्ञेयं च केशव।।

O Keshav, I wish to learn about *Prakriti* (Nature or matter) and *Purush* (the Spirit or soul), *Kshetra* (the Field) and *Kshetragaya*

(the Knower) of the Field, knowledge and that which ought to be known.

(Note: *Prakriti* is matter, inert equipments. *Purush* is the Spirit, the vital sentient truth. *Prakriti* is unconscious activity and *Purush* is inactive consciousness. The spirit in itself has no expression except when it functions through matter. When *Purush* joins *Prakriti*, activity– good or bad– takes place. Electricity by itself is unmanifest but when it functions through different gadgets, it is manifested as light, heat or cold, etc.

Some editions of the Geeta omit the first verse of this Discourse containing Arjun's query seeking clarification on certain philosophic terms on the ground that it is a later interpolation in the text by some unknown Geeta experts. But its inclusion appears appropriate in view of the context of the question raised by Arjun.)

Theory of creation

Lord Krishna said:

इदं शरीरं कौन्तेय क्षेत्रमित्यभिधीयते ।
एतद्यो वेत्ति तं प्राहुः क्षेत्रज्ञ इति तद्विदः ॥ 13.1 ॥

Shlok 13.1: O son of Kunti, this physical body, the miniature universe, may be called the field (*Kshetra)* or creation. One who knows the creation is called the *Kshetragaya* (the Knower) of the Field or Creator (or the Spirit, *Atman,* God, *Ishvar*) by the seers of truth.

Commentary: *Kshetra* literally means field, but here it refers to the body because the fruits of action (*Karma)* are reaped in it as in a field. This physical body, the miniature universe, is a field or creation. One who knows the creation is called the Creator (or the Spirit or *Atman,* God or *Ishvar)* by the seers of truth. Whatever is here in the body is also there in the cosmos; whatever is there, the same is here too. The human body is in fact the microcosm or a replica of the universe (the macrocosm). The body is called the field of activities for the soul where one reaps what one sows as Karma– good and bad. The body or creation is different from the soul or the Creator. To understand this difference is a pure metaphysical knowledge.

The word *'Kshetragaya'* or knower of the field means the individual soul, which is, in reality one with the Supreme Soul who is the Subject. The entire range of objective reality, the *Prakriti*, the matter, which is open to knowledge through the equipments of mind, intellect and senses, are material in their constitution, perishable in their nature and mutable in their essence. *Kshetragaya* is the light of awareness, the Knower of all objects and He is neither the embodied mind nor an object in the world. He is the Supreme Lord, calm and eternal and does not need the use of the senses and the mind for His witnessing. In the Geeta, no distinction is made between the knower of the Field and the Supreme Lord, *Paramatman, Brahm.*

क्षेत्रज्ञं चापि मां विद्धि सर्वक्षेत्रेषु भारत ।
क्षेत्रक्षेत्रयोर्ज्ञानं यत्तज्ज्ञानं मतं मम ॥ 13.2 ॥

Shlok 13.2: O Descendant of Bharat, know Me as the knower of the field in all fields. I consider the true understanding of both the Kshetra and Kshetragaya to be true knowledge.

Commentary: The knowledge of the field (body) and its knower (spirit) is regarded as true knowledge as stated in the verse. Sri Krishna declares that only the knowledge of the perishable and inert matter and the nature of the Infinite and Imperishable Spirit is the true knowledge. Kshetra or the field is the matter consisting of equipments of perception and what is perceived by them. *Kshetragaya* is the knower of what is perceived through the instruments of perception.

The body (or creation) and Spirit (or the Creator) are distinct from one another. Yet, the ignorant are not able to distinguish between them. That knowledge is the true knowledge by which one is able to make a clear distinction between body and Spirit. Body is called the field (or the medium) of activities for the Spirit. The human body is the medium by which the individual soul enjoys the material world, gets entangled, and in the end attains liberation. The soul inside the body knows all the activities of its own body; it is, therefore, called the knower of the field of activities. The Super-soul knows all the bodies, whereas the individual soul knows only his own body. When one clearly understands the difference between the body, the individual soul inside the body, and the Super-soul, one is said to have true knowledge.

तत्क्षेत्रं यच्च यादृक्च यद्विकारि यतश्च यत् ।
स च यो यत्प्रभावश्च तत्समासेन मे शृणु ॥ 13.3 ॥

Shlok 13.3: What the Kshetra is, what its properties are, what its modifications are, what effects arise from what causes, and also who He is and what His powers are– hear all these from Me in brief.

Commentary: Sri Krishna says He is going to explain what constitutes the Field, its properties, its origin, its modifications, i.e. what its by-products are when it changes its form, what is the knowing principle in the Field and what are powers of perception, feeling and thought of the Knower of the Field?

ऋषिभिर्बहुधा गीतं छन्दोभिर्विविधैः पृथक् ।
ब्रह्मसूत्रपदैश्चैव हेतुमद्भिर्विनिश्चितैः ॥ 13.4 ॥

Shlok 13.4: All this has been sung by sages in many and different ways, in various distinctive hymns, and also in well reasoned and convincing passages indicative of Brahm.

Commentary: The Geeta supports other scriptures, dealing with the nature of Supreme Being. All scriptures as well as saints and sages of all religions draw the water of truth from the same ocean of Spirit. But they differ with respect to language of description and emphasis on a particular aspect of the Supreme Being.

Notions of field and the knower of field

महाभूतान्यहंकारो बुद्धिरव्यक्तमेव च ।
इन्द्रियाणि दशैकं च पञ्च चेन्द्रियगोचराः ॥ 13.5 ॥
इच्छा द्वेषः सुखं दुःखं सङ्घातश्चेतना धृतिः ।
एतत्क्षेत्रं समासेन सविकारमुदाहृतम् ॥ 13.6 ॥

Shlokas 13.5-06: The great elements, egoism, intellect and also unmanifest, the ten senses and the one (mind), and the five objects of the senses, desire, hatred, pleasure, pain, the physical body, consciousness, and willpower– the Kshetra has thus been briefly described with its transformations.

Commentary: From here onwards Sri Krishna starts explaining His promised themes one by one in great details. The above two verses explain various items constituting together as the Field which was earlier indicated as the physical body. The field consists of twenty four elements which are as follows:

•Five gross elements– earth, water, fire, air and ether.

•Four other factors are the mind, intellect, ego and the unmanifested– the latter includes mental impressions gathered as a result of previous interactions of sense-objects.

•The ten senses include five sense organs (eyes, ears, nose, tongue and skin) and five organs of action (hands, tongue, feet, and two organs of excretion).

•Five objects of the senses include sight, smell, taste, sound and touch.

These 24 items constitute *Kshetra*, the matter or the gross body or the Field. The material nature, as described above, is the Lower Nature of God. Besides this, there is Higher Nature of God.

Their modifications are enumerated now. They are desire, hatred, pleasure, pain, the assemblage of the body, intelligence, steadfastness, etc. In short, not only the gross body, mind and intellect but also the perceptions experienced through them, the world of objects, emotions and thoughts are included in the term 'Field'– this body. All the world of objects, which includes emotions and thoughts, are 'knowable' put together in a bunch. This is called the Field, the object. The Knowing Principle or the Knower is the subject. True knowledge consists in understanding the distinction between the object and the subject.

The following five verses enumerate the 22 qualities which together indicate the Knower of the Field.

Means of salvation

अमानित्वमदम्भित्वमहिंसा क्षान्तिरार्जवम् ।
आचार्योपासनं शौचं स्थैर्यमात्मविनिग्रहः ॥ 13.7 ॥
इन्द्रियार्थेषु वैराग्यमनहंकार एव च ।
जन्ममृत्युजराव्याधिदुःखदोषानुदर्शनम् ॥ 13.8 ॥

Shlokas 13.7-8: Humility, unpretentiousness, non-injury, forgiveness, uprightness, service to the teacher, purity, steadfastness, self-control, indifference to the objects of the senses, also absence of egoism, perception of evil of birth, death, old age, sickness and pain.

Commentary: Contemplation of suffering inherent in birth, old age, disease, and death are called the understanding of the Fourfold Noble

Truth in Buddhism. The fear of disease and death, etc. is due to body consciousness or ego and is removed when one becomes God conscious by Self-knowledge that I am not this body, but Atman. A Self-realized (or God conscious) person is not bothered by any adversity. A disgust and discontent for the meaninglessness and unreality of the world and its objects become a necessary prelude to the spiritual journey. As birds seek the shelter of a tree when tired, similarly human beings seek the divine shelter after discovering the frustrations and joylessness of material existence. The Lord has prescribed certain conditions necessary for understanding the Infinite Self. The following are necessary for making the spiritual journey:

1. Humility– absence of self-esteem.

2. Modesty– Unpretentiousness, not proclaiming one's own greatness.

3. Non-injury– not causing suffering to any other living being intentionally.

4. Forgiveness– forbearance and patience, capacity to put up with everything without getting disturbed.

5. Uprightness– straight forwardness in behaviour.

6. Service to the teacher– not merely physical but seeking mental and intellectual identity with the teacher's heart and intellect.

7. Purity– external: cleanliness of body and environment; internal: taintless thoughts, emotions, intentions and motives.

8. Steadfastness– firmness and consistency of purpose, concentration of all efforts in achieving the spiritual goal.

9. Self control– self-restraint practised in dealing with others.

10. Dispassion or absence of attachment to objects– does not mean running away from objects of the world but detaching oneself from becoming a slave to the sensuous objects.

11. Absence of egoism– absence of the sense of superiority in oneself.

12. Perception of evil in birth, death, old age and sickness– every physical body goes through these changes and at each stage of life encounters sorrows and troubles. Such facts should be thoroughly understood by a seeker.

13. Pain– birth, death, old age and sickness are full of miseries and all miseries are always painful which one should be conscious of. Pain is of three types, viz. those arising in one's own person, those produced by external agents and those produced by God, i.e. by circumstances beyond anybody's control. Birth, death, etc. are not miseries by themselves but they produce misery in their aftermath.

(**Note:** When the human life has always been so bad, painful or full of miseries, why has such a life been created by the Supreme Being. The humans cannot be held responsible, as they are not more powerful than the Supreme Being. Who is accountable for this state of affairs– *Purush or Prakriti*? How is *Purush* always helpless in this matter, especially when the *Purush* is defined as a Cosmic Male? These are very serious questions against the notion of *Gunas.* Are *Gunas* free from the control of the *Purush?)*

असक्तिरनभिष्वंगः पुत्रदारगृहादिषु ।
नित्यं च समचित्तत्वमिष्टानिष्टोपपत्तिषु ॥ 13.9 ॥
मयि चानन्ययोगेन भक्तिरव्यभिचारिणी ।
विविक्तदेशसेवित्वमरतिर्जनसंसदि ॥13.10 ॥
अध्यात्मज्ञाननित्यत्वं तत्त्वज्ञानार्थदर्शनम् ।
एतज्ज्ञानमिति प्रोक्तमज्ञानं यदतोऽन्यथा ॥ 13.11 ॥

Shlokas 13.9-11: Non-attachment, non-identification of the Self with son, wife, home and the rest, and constant even-mindedness on the attainment of the desirable and the undesirable, unswerving devotion unto Me by the Yog of non-separation, resort to solitary places, distaste for the society of men, constancy in Self-knowledge, perception of the end of true knowledge– this is declared to be (the means of) Self-knowledge. That which is contrary to this is ignorance.

Commentary: In continuation with the above, the following conditions or attributes are also necessary:

14. Non-attachment– When a man thinks that an object is his, the idea of 'Mine' ness is born in his mind. He identifies himself with that object, loves it and gets attached to it. Non-attachment is the absence of such identification with any object. Keeping the mind away from all attachments assures peaceful life.

15. Non-identification with kinsmen– Excessive love towards all

these is an intense form of attachment with them so much so one's own material happiness or otherwise is equated with the happiness or otherwise of the other.

16. Constant even-mindedness– Equanimity under all circumstances and conditions, desirable or undesirable, is a sign of knowledge.

17. Unswerving devotion to Me– Devotion to the Lord should be of single point concentration without any thought of other objects.

18. Yog of non-separation– Undivided attention and enthusiasm in the mind of the devotee.

19. Such an integrated mind and steady contemplation is not possible unless there is a conducive environment which is suggested in two ways, viz. (A) to resort to solitary places and (B) to develop distaste for the crowded social life.

20. Constancy in Self-knowledge– The knowledge of the Self is to be lived and not merely learnt. If the Self is everywhere and is real, then the seeker should try to live as the Self in his personality layers. This consistency of living the spiritual knowledge in all contacts with the world outside is one of the practices a seeker should always keep up. Knowledge includes practice of the moral virtues.

21. Understanding the end of True Knowledge– To keep the vision of the goal always before us adds enthusiasm in all our activities. Thus liberation from all our imperfections and limitations is the goal to be aspired for by all spiritual seekers.

22. All that is contrary to it is ignorance– Qualities such as pride, hypocrisy, cruelty, impatience, insincerity and the like are all ignorance and therefore should be avoided as tending to the perpetuation of *Sansar.*

These traits described as above are declared to be the true 'knowledge' because they are conducive to the realization of the Self. These qualities are said to be the 'knowledge' because once they have been fully developed the mind gets matured enough to reach the goal of Pure knowledge of the Self.

Cultivating the virtues described in verses 13.7-11 will enable one to perceive the body as different from the Self. Thus, one will attain Self-knowledge. Therefore, these virtues are called knowledge. Those who do not possess these virtues cannot get the true knowledge of the Self and will remain in the darkness of body-consciousness or ignorance.

When one becomes firmly convinced that God alone is everything– father, mother, brother, friend, enemy, sustainer, destroyer, and refuge– and there is nothing higher than Him to attain, and one has no thought of any other object, one is said to have developed unswerving devotion to the Lord through single-minded contemplation. In this state of mind, the seeker and the sought-after become qualitatively one and the same.

Description of Supreme Being

ज्ञेयं यत्तत्प्रवक्ष्यामि यज्ज्ञात्वामृतमश्नुते ।
अनादिमत्परं ब्रह्म न सत्तन्नासदुच्यते ॥ 13.12 ॥

Shlok 13.12: I shall fully describe the Supreme Being– the object of knowledge. By knowing this one attains immortality, the beginningless Supreme Being. It is called neither being nor non-being.

Commentary: The Lord says that He will declare now that is to be known, knowing which one attains immortality. The Supreme Brahm is beginningless: It is said to be neither *Sat* (real) nor *Asat* (unreal). This verse is similar to the verses in several Upanishads. Note that even the description Existence-Knowledge-Bliss (*Satta-Chitta-Anand)* is a limited description of Brahm. Brahm exists and does not exist. Brahm is beyond '*Sat'* and '*Asat*'. What can one say about Brahm? This is the highest teaching of the Upanishads or Vedant repeated in the Geeta.

The Rigved says that in the beginning there was neither Eternal Being (*Sat*, Brahm) nor temporal (*Asat*, Divine Beings, *Devas*)– no sky, no air, neither day nor night. There was nothing whatsoever other than the Absolute Supreme Being. It has been observed that the Absolute is beyond both Divine Beings (celestial controllers, *Devas*) and the Eternal Being (Spirit). Therefore, He is neither temporal nor eternal. The Supreme Being or the Absolute is also both temporal and eternal (Geeta 9.19) and beyond both temporal and eternal (Geeta 11.37 and 15.18) because He is everywhere, in everything, and also beyond everything. Therefore, the Absolute is all the three– neither temporal nor eternal, beyond both temporal and eternal, as well as both temporal and eternal– at the same time. Those who understand this reality, they attain immortality as this happens to be the only pure knowledge.

सर्वतःपाणिपादं तत्सर्वतोऽक्षिशिरोमुखम् ।
सर्वतःश्रुतिमल्लोके सर्वमावृत्य तिष्ठति ॥ 13.13 ॥

Shlok 13.13: The Supreme Being has His hands, feet, eyes, heads, mouths, and ears everywhere in the universe because He is all-pervading and omnipresent.

Commentary: Hands, feet, eyes, heads, mouths, and ears everywhere suggest the Principle of Consciousness functioning behind them all. The functioning of all the parts of the body in every human being is based on the Life Principle. The functions of perception, feeling and thinking are carried out only so long as there is life in the body. Life is said to be everywhere and hence the Principle of Consciousness exists pervading all. This Consciousness behind every living being, that which is common to all, is *Paramatman, Parabrahm*. As the one subject of all objects of experience, He is said to envelop all and have hands and feet, ears and eyes everywhere.

सर्वेन्द्रियगुणाभासं सर्वेन्द्रियविवर्जितम् ।
असक्तं सर्वभृच्चैव निर्गुणं गुणभोक्तृ च ॥ 13.14 ॥

Shlok 13.14: Shining by the functions of all the senses, yet without the senses; unattached, yet supporting all; devoid of *Gunas*, yet their experiencer,

Commentary: The Self in us functioning through the sense organs looks as though It possesses all sense organs. But the sense organs decay and perish while the Consciousness which functions through them and which provides each of them with its own individual faculty is Eternal and Changeless just as electricity is not the light in the bulb and yet when it functions through the bulb it looks as if it were light. The relationship of unattached support can be explained as follows. Waves are not the ocean but the ocean supports all the waves in as much as there can be no waves without the ocean.

The Supreme Being walks without legs, hears without ears, performs many actions without hands, smells without a nose, sees without eyes, speaks without a mouth, and enjoys all tastes without a tongue. All His actions are so marvellous that one finds His greatness utterly beyond description. The Supreme Being may be described only by parables and paradoxes and in no other way. Self expands Himself as the living entity to enjoy three modes of material Nature. God does not possess a body like an ordinary being. All His senses are transcendental, or out of this world. His potencies are multifarious. Any one of His senses can perform the action of any other sense. All His deeds are automatically performed as a natural consequence.

बहिरन्तश्च भूतानामचरं चरमेव च ।
सूक्ष्मत्वात्तदविज्ञेयं दूरस्थं चान्तिके च तत् ॥ 13.15 ॥

Shlok 13.15: It is outside all beings and still within every one of them; it is immovable and still moving; it cannot be perceived; it is so far and yet so near.

Commentary: He is inside as well as outside all beings, animate and inanimate. He is incomprehensible because of His subtlety. And because of His omnipresence, He is very near– residing in our inner psyche– as well as far away in the Supreme Abode. God is everywhere, but at the same time nowhere. This is simply extra-ordinary. This makes God different from all beings, and thus is not comprehensible by human mind.

Near and far: The concept of distance– nearness and farness– arises only in respect of conditioned things or those that which has limitations in terms of space or volume, etc. When a thing is all pervasive and exists everywhere the question of its being near or far does not arise; such things are both near and far. Consciousness is far because of its Absolute nature and yet it is near because of the existence of the living beings with shapes and forms through whom it functions.

अविभक्तं च भूतेषु विभक्तमिव च स्थितम् ।
भूतभर्तृ च तज्ज्ञेयं ग्रसिष्णु प्रभविष्णु च ॥ 13.16 ॥

Shlok 13.16: He is undivided, yet appears to exist as if divided in all beings. He is the object of knowledge and appears as the Creator, Sustainer, and Destroyer of all beings.

Commentary: Undivided yet divided: *Paramatman* is all pervading and yet it individualizes as special manifestation only at points where equipments are available just as electricity manifests as light only at the point of filament in the bulb. Although space is one entity it looks divided as room space, pot space, etc.

Creator, Sustainer, and Destroyer of all beings: The ocean is a sustainer of waves, waves are born in the ocean and yet the same ocean destroys all waves. The Truth or Self is the substratum on which the world of plurality is projected by the deluded mind and intellect and when we go beyond the mind and intellect the vision of *Sansar* gets swallowed up in the tranquillity of the Self.

One planet earth appears divided into so many countries; one country appears divided into several states; one state appears divided into several districts or counties, and so on; similarly one Reality appears as many. These are apparent divisions because they have the same order of reality. The term God is used for the Generator, Operator, and Destroyer aspects of Self. God is responsible for the creation or origin of the universe as well for complete destruction of the universe at the time of *Mahapralaya.*

ज्योतिषामपि तज्ज्योतिस्तमसः परमुच्यते ।
ज्ञानं ज्ञेयं ज्ञानगम्यं हृदि सर्वस्य विष्ठितम् ॥ 13.17 ॥

Shlok 13.17: The Supreme Being, the light of all lights, is said to be beyond darkness. As Knowledge, the object of knowledge, the goal of knowledge He is seated in the hearts of all.

Commentary: The Lord does not refer to Himself, but gives knowledge of Brahm referring to Brahm as 'It', 'That' and so on, in Upanishadic terms. It is the Light of Lights, and is said to be beyond darkness. It is Knowledge, One to be known and the Goal of Knowledge, dwelling in the hearts of all. One who knows the Almighty as much more radiant than the Sun and beyond the darkness of material reality transcends death. There is no other way. The Supreme is beyond the reach of senses and mind. It cannot be described or defined by words.

Since the Consciousness in us brings our various experiences within our understanding, it is compared to light. Consciousness is beyond the concept of darkness; it is the Light Absolute; where there is consciousness there cannot be any darkness or night. The Lord says that Consciousness, the Infinite, dwells in the hearts of all. Heart does not mean the blood supplying physical part of the body; rather, it means the mental area from where all noble thoughts emanate.

The Supreme can also be described, in a series of paradoxes, as follows:

•He is devoid of senses, yet sees, hears.
•He is unattached, yet supports everything.
•He is without gunas, yet enjoys them.
•He is without and within all beings.
•He is unmoving, yet moving also.
•He is far away, yet very near too.
•He is indivisible, yet seems to be divided among beings.

इति क्षेत्रं तथा ज्ञानं ज्ञेयं चोक्तं समासतः ।
मद्भक्त एतद्विज्ञाय मद्भावायोपपद्यते ॥ 13.18 ॥

Shlok 13.18: Thus the Kshetra as well as the knowledge and the object of knowledge have been briefly described. Understanding this, My devotee attains Me.

Commentary: Sri Krishna concludes the theme of His Discourse so far by saying those who seek the light through devotion to Him reach Him. Devotion here implies not only emotional surrender unto the Lord but intellectual apprehension of the Truth, the Self, through a correct understanding of the Field and the Knower of the Field. One who is able to recognize the one Sri Krishna as the vitalizing Consciousness Principle in all fields of matter envelopments, he is the true devotee who as the Lord says 'enters into His Being', attains liberation or release from birth and death.

Supreme Spirit, material nature and individual souls

प्रकृतिं पुरुषं चैव विद्ध्यनादी उभावपि ।
विकारांश्च गुणांश्चैव विद्धि प्रकृतिसम्भवान् ॥ 13.19 ॥

Shlok 13.19: Know thou that Prakirti and Purush are both beginningless; and know also that all forms and modes (called *Gunas*) are born of Prakirti.

Commentary: Matter (*Prakriti)* and Spirit (*Purush*) are both beginningless. They are the two aspects of *Ishvar*, the Lord. As the Lord is eternal so also is His two aspects– Matter and Spirit. The play of Matter and Spirit causes the origin, preservation and dissolution of the Universe.

Prakriti, matter or nature is inert. Matter is that out of which all forms (from intelligence down to the gross body) and *gunas* (qualities such as *Sattva, Rajas* and *Tamas,* which manifest themselves in the form of pleasure, pain, delusion and so on) come into existence. All changes or modifications are related to Matter. *Prakriti* is *Maya,* the *Shakti* or power of the Lord. It is the cause of the manifestation of the relative universe.

कार्यकरणकर्तृत्वे हेतुः प्रकृतिरुच्यते ।
पुरुषः सुखदुःखानां भोक्तृत्वे हेतुरुच्यते ॥ 13.20 ॥

Shlok 13.20: Prakirti is described as the cause in the creation of effects; Purush is described as the cause of the experience of pleasure and pain.

Commentary: Nature is the cause of the effect, the instrument and agency, while the soul is the cause of the experience of pleasure and pain. Nature is the material from which the body and the sense organs are produced. The five elements out of which the body is made and the five sense-objects are included inder the term 'body' or '*karya*' used in the verse. The sense organs are thirteen namely five organs of perception, five organs of action, the mind, intellect (*Buddhi*), and I-consciousness (*Ahankar*). Pleasure, pain, delusion and the rest, which are born of three *Gunas* of *Prakriti*, are included under the term organs or '*Karana*' since they cannot exist independently of the sense-organs.

Purush and *Prakriti* are stated to be the cause of *Sansar* or phenomenal existence. *Prakriti* transforms itself into body and senses, as also into pleasure, pain and so on and *Purush* experiences pleasure and pain. This union between *Purush and Prakriti* makes relative life possible. Even though the *Purush*, the Soul, identifies Himself with the body and appears to experience pleasure and pain, yet in reality He remains unchanging. It is this apparent experience which constitutes His illusory world or *sansar* and which makes Him a *sansari* or phenomenal being.

पुरुषः प्रकृतिस्थो हि भुंक्ते प्रकृतिजान्गुणान् ।
कारणं गुणसङ्गोऽस्य सदसद्योनिजन्मसु ॥ 13.21 ॥

Shlok 13.21: *Purush,* when seated in *Prakriti*, experiences the *Gunas* born of *Prakriti.* Attachment to the *Gunas* is the cause of his birth in good and evil wombs.

Commentary: The soul being amidst nature, enjoys the modes of nature, gets attached to them and due to this association, takes birth with these traits. This suggests that birth takes place in different forms of life on the basis of attachment of the soul to modes of nature. He experiences the qualities born of *Prakriti. Purush* identifies with the body and the senses which are the effects of *Prakriti* (Matter). Pleasure and pain, heat and cold, etc. arise out of Matter envelopments. The experiences of Matter become the experiences of the Spirit because of the latter's contact with the former. *Purush* not only experiences the sorrows and joys of life but develops attachment with them which is the cause of its birth in good or evil wombs.

Spirit is unaffected by *Prakriti* just as the sun's reflection in water is unaffected by the properties of water. Spirit, because of His nature, associates with the six sensory faculties and ego of material Nature and becomes attached, forgets His real nature, performs good and evil deeds, loses independence, and transmigrates as a living entity. The living entity does not know the divine illusory energy (*Maya*) as well as the supreme controller and its own real nature. The individual soul, figuratively speaking, is a reflection of the sun of Spirit in the water pot of human body.

Real nature of *Purush*

उपद्रष्टानुमन्ता च भर्ता भोक्ता महेश्वरः ।
परमात्मेति चाप्युक्तो देहेऽस्मिन् पुरुषः परः ॥ 13.22 ॥

Shlok 13.22: And the Supreme Purush in this body is also called the Witness, the Approver, the Supporter, the Experiencer, the Great Lord, and the Supreme Self.

Commentary: The Witness, the Approver or the Supreme Purush himself does not participate in the activities of the bodily organs, the mind and *Buddhi*, being quite apart from them, yet appears to be so engaged. And being a witness, He never stands in the way of the activities of *Prakriti* as manifested in the body. Indeed, all the consciousness or the intelligence that manifests itself in the activities of life is but the reflection of All-pervading, Absolute and Perfect Intelligence– the Supreme Spirit.

Prakriti with the help of *Purush* produces five bio-impulses (Life forces, *Pran*) and *Gunas*. Spirit, residing as the great Lord in the physical body that is a house with nine gates and made of twenty-four elements of material Nature, enjoys sense objects by associating with the modes of material Nature. Spirit forgets its real nature under the influence of divine illusory energy (*Maya*), feels pain and pleasure, does good and evil deeds, incurs the bondage of works done by free will due to ignorance, and seeks salvation. When the living entity renounces sense objects and rises above the modes of material Nature, it attains salvation.

Sri Krishna thus mentions here two *Purushas*, viz. the Lower one and the Higher one. The Lower *Purush* is the knower of the Field and the Higher one is Pure Consciousness unconditioned by the *Prakriti*. Both of these function in this body.

The Supreme Self, Pure Consciousness, is described as Spectator, a silent witness, *Upadrashta,* when it sees evil actions performed. When noble actions take place it is referred to as the Approver, *Anumantha*. When noble actions are done in a spirit of surrender to the Lord, the Supreme is referred to as the fulfiller. The individual in his Eternal Conscious state initiates all actions and reaps the fruit. Therefore, He is referred to as the Experiencer, *Bhokta*. Finally it is stated that the Higher Self, *Paramatman,* the Sovereign Lord is in this body itself.

Result of self experience

य एवं वेत्ति पुरुषं प्रकृतिं च गुणैः सह ।
सर्वथा वर्तमानोऽपि न स भूयोऽभिजायते ॥ 13.23 ॥

Shlok 13.23: He who knows the *Purush* and *Prakriti* together with *Gunas*, is not born again, regardless of their way of life.

Commentary: He who has realized in himself that which is the matter (*Prakriti)*

(a) that which is the Spirit (*Purush)* and who understands

(b) how the Supreme Spirit gets identified with matter and behaves as *Purush (*the knower of the Field)

(c) as also the mysteries of the *Gunas* under the influence of which the physical body functions is the one called 'Man of Wisdom'. Such a person frees himself from the cycle of birth and death regardless of his conduct.

ध्यानेनात्मनि पश्यन्ति केचिदात्मानमात्मना ।
अन्ये सांख्येन योगेन कर्मयोगेन चापरे ॥ 13.24 ॥

Shlok 13.24: Some perceive the self in the Self by the Self through meditation, other through the path of knowledge *(Gyanayog)* and still other by the path of action *(Karmayog)*.

Commentary: The above verse indicates the three paths of God-realisation. Realization of the Self is the goal of the spiritual seeker and many paths are prescribed for the purpose keeping in view the differences in the mental and intellectual capabilities of the seekers. The paths of meditation, knowledge and work are prescribed to cater to the temperaments of different types of people.

By meditation some may behold the Self. The second path, *Sankhyayog or Gyanayog*, is meant for those who do not have the steadiness of the mind and intellect is the study of the *Shastras*. The term 'Sankhya' means arriving at philosophical conclusions through logical thoughts. The third one, Karmayog, is for those who cannot even study and reflect on *Shastras* due to their inner limitations. Such a person surrenders his actions and their fruits to the Lord. This produces purity of mind which leads to the knowledge of the Self.

Faith and devotion can also lead to salvation

अन्ये त्वेवमजानन्तः श्रुत्वान्येभ्य उपासते ।
तेऽपि चातितरन्त्येव मृत्युं श्रुतिपरायणाः ॥ 13.25 ॥

Shlok 13.25: Others also, not knowing any one the above mentioned paths, worship, having heard of it from others; they, too, transcend death by performing any other spiritual practice with conviction.

Commentary: Three main paths– Yog of meditation, Yog of knowledge and Yog of action– were referred to in the previous verse. In this verse

Yog of worship is described. This path is shown to those who could not adopt any of the aforesaid three methods. Those who have not understood God, yet have belief in Him are very fortunate. If you believe, you will receive whatever you ask from God. It is not necessary to completely understand God to obtain His grace, to love Him, and to attain Him. Even an unlettered person can follow the path of devotion or Bhakti by listening to a preceptor and following some form of worship. One need not be a learned person or philosopher or a *Yogi.*

It is this *Bhakti Marg* (the path of devotion) that led to renaissance of the Hindu faith in the 10th to 14th centuries. Countless persons, unlettered and of very humble origins from lower strata of society attained sainthood in India. The formal Vedic religion, with emphasis on rituals and Sanskrit learning, became unimportant. Hymns and songs in local vernacular languages became the vehicle for devotion. Temple worship with devotion became the main plank for Hindu seekers. It was the Bhagavad Geeta that emphasized this form of religious practice.

यावत्संजायते किंचित्सत्त्वं स्थावरजङ्गमम् ।
क्षेत्रक्षेत्रज्ञसंयोगात्तद्विद्धि भरतर्षभ ॥ 13.26 ॥

Shlok 13.26: Whatever being is born– animate or inanimate– know them, O best of the Bharatas, know it to be the union of Kshetra and Kshetragaya.

Commentary: The union between the Field and the Knower of the Field is not of any physical kind or of any material nature but it is of mutual superimposition. It is illusory, confounding the one with the other. In every superimposition a delusion is recognized upon the substratum just like a ghost on the post. Not only all the characteristics of a ghost are projected upon the post but the post lends its existence to the non-existent ghost. As a result of their mutual union we find that the non-existent ghost comes into existence and the existing post gives place to non-existent ghost.

This trick of the human mind is called mutual superimposition which is known in Vedant as *Adhyasa*. This means false superimposition of one thing upon the other. This superimposition is due to *Maya* or absence of discrimination.

समं सर्वेषु भूतेषु तिष्ठन्तं परमेश्वरम् ।
विनश्यत्स्वविनश्यन्तं यः पश्यति स पश्यति ॥ 13.27 ॥

Shlok 13.27: He alone sees things in the right spirit who sees the supreme governing principle abiding in all beings, the indestructible underlying all destructible entities.

Commentary: The Supreme Lord abides in all beings equally; He is undying in the dying; He, who sees thus, sees Him truly. Birth is the root cause of the modifications of change, growth, decay and death. The other changes of state manifest after the birth of the body. But the Lord is changeless and He is birthless, decayless and deathless.

The substratum that supports all is the Supreme Lord remaining the same in all beings. Everything in this phenomenal world is subject to change and modifications– birth, growth, decay and death. The Changeless Consciousness that supports all changes is the Principle that illumines the changing world of plurality just as gold is the changeless factor in different types of ornaments which are always made and destroyed to make new ones of different types. The shape and size of ornaments change but the changeless factor in them all is gold. He who recognizes the harmony of Universal Spirit in all things, from the highest deity to the grain of sand, sees and becomes universal. The same divine spirit dwells in all. The difference between one object and another from the relative standpoint lies in the degree of manifestation of the Spirit in it. In a saint, the Spirit is highly manifested while in a lowly object the spirit is hidden.

समं पश्यन्हि सर्वत्र समवस्थितमीश्वरम् ।
न हिनस्त्यात्मनात्मानं ततो याति परां गतिम् ॥ 13.28 ॥

Shlok 13.28: Because he who sees the same Lord dwelling equally everywhere does not destroy the Self by the self, he attains the Supreme Abode.

Commentary: Finding the same supreme Lord in everything, a person does not destroy anything because he knows that destroying things would mean destroying himself. A person who develops this sense of identity with his environment elevates and exalts himself most speedily. Whenever the lower egocentric personality is not available for guidance by the higher wisdom, the lower becomes the enemy for the higher in us. Such an ignorant man destroys the Self by identifying himself with the body and the modifications of the mind and by not seeing the immortal Self in all beings.

In an individual who recognizes and experiences the one *Parameshwar* everywhere the lower cannot overshadow the higher. Such a sage does not destroy the Self by the self.

प्रकृत्यैव च कर्माणि क्रियमाणानि सर्वशः ।
यः पश्यति तथात्मानमकर्तारं स पश्यति ॥ 13.29 ॥

Shlok 13.29: One who sees that all actions are performed only by nature, and not by Self, he sees the real truth.

Commentary: The soul is not the doer but only the witness. Actions depend upon the quality of the matter. If the mind is evil, actions arising out of it cannot be good. The Self is perfect and there is no desire in it. Where there is no desire, there is no action. He who recognizes the Imperishable amidst the perishable is the right perceiver. He alone sees who sees. The true Self is not the doer but only the witness. It is the spectator, not the actor. Actions affect the mind and understanding and not the Self.

Attributes of the Spirit

यदा भूतपृथग्भावमेकस्थमनुपश्यति ।
तत एव च विस्तारं ब्रह्म सम्पद्यते तदा ॥ 13.30 ॥

Shlok 13.30: When he sees the diverse variety of separate existence as rooted in One and spreading out from That (One) alone, he then becomes Brahm.

Commentary: To know that the Self is the ultimate Truth behind names and forms is only half knowledge. It can become complete only when we understand how the multiplicity of names and forms arise from the Self and spread to become the Universe. When the variety of nature and its development are traced to the Eternal One, we assume eternity. He realizes the all pervading nature of the Self, because the cause of all limitation has been destroyed by the knowledge of unity with Brahm.

Attributes of Brahm

अनादित्वान्निर्गुणत्वात्परमात्मायमव्ययः ।
शरीरस्थोऽपि कौन्तेय न करोति न लिप्यते ॥ 13.31 ॥

Shlok 13.31: Because of being beginningless and devoid of *Gunas*, the Supreme Self, immutable, O son of Kunti, though dwelling in the body neither acts nor is affected.

Commentary: Because the Self is not the doer, therefore, He is not touched by the consequence of action. A man attains to unity with the Supreme when he knows or realizes through intuition that all these manifold forms are rooted in the One. Like waves in water, like rays in the sun, so also all forms are rooted in the One.

The eternal Super-soul is called attributeless because He does not have the three attributes of material Nature. The word 'attributeless' has been commonly misunderstood as formless. Attributeless refers only to the absence of material form and attributes known to the human mind. The Lord has an incomparable personality and transcendental qualities.

Spirit is present everywhere. It is present inside the body, outside the body, as well as all over the body. Actually, Spirit is inside and outside of everything that exists in creation.

A question arises here that if the Spirit dwelling in the body does not act and is not affected by the result of action, then, who is the performer or doer or agent of action and the reaper of its fruit? The answer to this riddle is that it is Prakriti that acts (Discourse 5.14). Through illusion arises the idea of the action, the doer, and the result of action. No action really exists in the Supreme Lord.

यथा सर्वगतं सौक्ष्म्यादाकाशं नोपलिप्यते ।
सर्वत्रावस्थितो देहे तथात्मा नोपलिप्यते ॥ 13.32 ॥

Shlok 13.32: Just as the all-pervading *Akash*, because of its subtlety, is not tainted, so the Self existent everywhere in the body, is not tainted.

Commentary: Akash means the concept of pure space. It is the subtlest of all gross elements and hence pervades everything that is grosser than it. Space being subtle, it allows everything to remain in it and yet nothing that it contains can contaminate it. The Supreme Self which is the cause of the very *Akash* and therefore is subtler than *Akash*. Hence It pervades all and nothing pervades It. It cannot be contaminated by anything that exists or is happening in the world of plurality. As the waters of the mirage cannot drench the desert, the world of plurality– the domain of matter and its activities– cannot contaminate the Eternal. The Self, though permeates and pervades the whole body, is not soiled by its virtuous or vicious actions just as space is not dirtied by the things accommodated under it.

यथा प्रकाशयत्येकः कृत्स्नं लोकमिमं रविः ।
क्षेत्रं क्षेत्री तथा कृत्स्नं प्रकाशयति भारत ॥ 13.33 ॥

Shlok 13.33: Just as the one sun illumines the whole world, so also the Lord of the Kshetra (the Supreme Self) illumines the whole Kshetra, O Descendant of Bharat.

Commentary: As one sun illumines all this world, similarly He who dwells in the body illumines all bodies... . The *Atman* residing in a *Jeev* is the same *Atman* residing in all living creatures. Lighting of the world by the sun is not an activity undertaken by it for achieving any purpose. Light itself is the very nature of the sun and in its light everything gets illumined. Similarly, the nature of Consciousness is awareness and in Its presence everything becomes known, i.e. illumined. The sun illumines everything, good and bad, beautiful and ugly, virtue and vice, etc. Similarly in our inner life, Consciousness functions through body equipments and illumines them but never gets affected by the actions of the body or by the emotions of the mind or by the thoughts of the intellect.

According to Adi Shankar, one sees the creation but not the Creator behind the creation due to ignorance, just as a person in the darkness of night sees the snake and not the rope that creates the false notion of a snake. If any object other than Spirit appears to exist, it is unreal like a mirage, a dream, or the existence of a snake in the rope. The absolute monism that negates all manifestation as a dream world is not the whole truth. According to the Vedas, God is both transcendent and immanent in one. The illustration of the world as a dream is a metaphor meant only to illustrate certain points and should not be stretched too far or taken literally. Vedant does not dismiss the perception of duality, but dismisses the reality of duality only. If the world is a dream, it is a very beautiful dream, indeed, of the cosmic dreamer who must also be extraordinarily beautiful.

क्षेत्रक्षेत्रज्ञयोरेवमन्तरं ज्ञानचक्षुषा ।
भूतप्रकृतिमोक्षं च ये विदुर्यान्ति ते परम् ॥ 13.34 ॥

Shlok 13.34: They who, through the eye of knowledge, perceive the distinction between the Field and its Knower, and also the liberation from the Nature of being, they go to the Supreme.

Commentary: They who know through the eye of intuition opened by meditation and the instructions of the Guru and the scriptures, that the Field is insentient, the doer, changing and finite, and that the Knower of the Field is pure Consciousness, the non-doer, unchanging and infinite, and who also perceive the non-existence of Nature, ignorance, the Unmanifested, the material cause of being– they attain the Supreme.

It was explained that the Spirit is the illuminator. It cannot be tainted by the qualities of the illumined. Sri Krishna now concludes that man's life is fulfilled only when he with his discrimination meditates upon and realizes the constitution of and relationship between the Field, the Knower of the Field and the Supreme Self in himself. This can be achieved through the eye of wisdom or intuition which is opened up by meditation, study of scriptures or teachings of the preceptors. One who realizes this is liberated and attains eternal freedom.

OM TAT SAT

Discourse - 14

Gunatraya Vibhag Yog: Yog of the Division of the Three Gunas

This Discourse explains why the same Spirit when expressed through matter manifests itself in different ways. Although the same water is poured in different bottles, it will look different not because of the water but because of the colour of the glass out of which the bottles were made. Similarly, the one Eternal Principle expresses itself differently in various matter equipments as different individuals even though the elements constituting matter are the same. This is due to *Gunas* born of *Prakriti.*

Gunas indicate not the properties of a material but the attitude with which the mind functions. These attitudes are three in number, viz. *Sattva*– unactivity, *Rajas*–Activity and *Tamas*– Inactivity. These three qualities influence the mind and intellect of every individual in different proportions at different times. Although all these three Gunas are always present in everybody their proportions differ from individual to individual. It is these diversities that differentiate one person from the other in character, conduct and behaviour, etc.

The three *Gunas– Sattva, Rajas* and *Tamas*– together constitute every human being. *Sattva* is stainless, pure and brilliant. When this predominates over the other two *Gunas*, a person's wisdom shines in his expression. *Rajas* is of the nature of passion which creates a craving for what you do not have and attachment to what you possess. When this Guna dominates over the other two, the person develops greed, becomes involved in endless activity and suffers from mental unrest.

Tamas arises out of ignorance which manifests as delusion, inertia and heedlessness. *Sattva* binds people through attachment to knowledge, and happiness. *Rajas* binds through attachment to action. Tamas binds through heedlessness, indolence and sleep.

This Discourse helps us to find out for ourselves the powerful tendencies that rule our minds (influences of *Gunas*) and take remedial measures wherever called for. A seeker who recognizes the influences under which he is forced to function at different times can take timely steps to arrest the wrong impulses, unethical urges and animal tendencies in order to keep himself fully under self-control and equanimous in all situations in life. The aspirant should know the symptoms and signs of their presence in his personality and acquire knowledge of their subtle workings. Only then he can maintain an unhampered and smooth progress in all activities of his life, both secular and spiritual. Lord Krishna teaches us this important subject in this Discourse from the ninth to the eighteenth verse. He declares that one who rises above all the three *Gunas* through spiritual practices, becomes free from birth, death, old age and sorrow, and enjoys immortality.

In reply to a question from Arjun, Sri Krishna describes the marks of one who has risen above the three *Gunas*. He states that if one constantly worships Him with exclusive devotion one will attain the highest divine experience and supreme peace and blessedness.

The highest knowledge

Lord Krishna said:

परं भूयः प्रवक्ष्यामि ज्ञानानां ज्ञानमुत्तमम् ।

यज्ज्ञात्वा मुनयः सर्वे परां सिद्धिमितो गताः ॥ 14.1 ॥

Shlok 14.1: I shall further explain to you that supreme knowledge which is above all knowledge; having known which all *Munis* have attained salvation.

Commentary: The subject matter of this Discourse is that supreme knowledge which is above all sorts of knowledge. It deals with the behaviour of man and the different influences that play on his subtle body in life. It is the highest knowledge inasmuch as without a correct understanding of this theme, self observation and analysis as also timely self-correction will be impossible on the spiritual path. On understanding this knowledge and learning about the real goal of life, men of reflection and contemplation have reached perfection. Reaching perfection indicates that with the aid of the exhaustive knowledge about the *Gunas,* men can foresee the obstacles and dangers on the way of spiritual attainment and prepare themselves to face them effectively.

इदं ज्ञानमुपाश्रित्य मम साधर्म्यमागताः ।
सर्गेऽपि नोपजायन्ते प्रलये न व्यथन्ति च ॥ 14.2 ॥

Shlok 14.2: They who, having taken refuge in this knowledge, attain to unity with Me, and are neither born at the time of creation, nor are they troubled at the time of dissolution.

Commentary: In this verse it is knowledge of the Supreme Self that is eulogised by the Lord. Sri Krishna says that he who has correctly understood the significance of this Discourse can reach the state of Perfection, i.e. 'Attain My Being'. Perfection is a state of awakening to a different level of Consciousness. When we go to sleep we become one with the sleeper leaving aside the waking personality. Similarly, on realizing the Self we cross over the body, mind and intellect and become one with the Spiritual Nature.

All beings are born from the Union of *Purush* and *Prakriti*

मम योनिर्महद्ब्रह्म तस्मिन्गर्भं दधाम्यहम् ।
सम्भवः सर्वभूतानां ततो भवति भारत ॥ 14.3 ॥

Shlok 14.3: O descendant of Bharat, the great Prakirti is the womb for me. I place the seed in that womb and that leads to the birth of all beings.

सर्वयोनिषु कौन्तेय मूर्तयः सम्भवन्ति याः ।
तासां ब्रह्म महद्योनिरहं बीजप्रदः पिता ॥ 14.4 ॥

Shlok 14.4: O son of Kunti, the great Prakirti is the real womb for all the forms produced in any womb and I am the seed-giving father.

Commentary (Shlok 14.3-4) *Prakriti* or material nature, a product of divine kinetic energy (Maya), is the origin of the entire universe. *Prakriti* creates living beings when the seed of Spirit is sown in it for germination. Sri Krishna, the Supreme Consciousness, is the Father of the entire Universe. A Field in itself has no existence without the Knower of the Field vitalizing it. Body, mind and intellect are mere inert matter till Consciousness enlivens them.

The Lord is the Father and the Mother of the universe. Matter and Spirit are His two aspects which are inherent in Him. As the Father or the Supreme Soul He casts the seed; as the Mother or nature, or matter or *Prakriti*, He receives the seed. From the embryo thus formed, which is termed as *Hiranyagarbha,* are produced all created beings.

This verse affirms that all existence is a manifestation of the Divine. He is the cosmic seed. With reference to this world, He becomes *Hiranyagarbha*, the cosmic egg. The world is the play of the Infinite on the Finite.

***Gunas* bind the soul to the body**

सत्त्वं रजस्तम इति गुणाः प्रकृतिसम्भवाः ।
निबध्नन्ति महाबाहो देहे देहिनमव्ययम् ॥ 14.5 ॥

Shlok 14.5: O Mahabahu, the three modes (*Gunas*)- goodness (*Sattva*), passion (*Rajas*) and dullness (*Tamas*), born of nature, bind down in the body, the imperishable dweller in the body (Soul).

Commentary: The three *Gunas* or tendencies of human nature influence the soul when the latter identifies itself with the former. In this way, the soul gets in bondage. In order to get out of bondage, the individual has to rise above the hold of *Gunas.* The three *Gunas– Sattva, Rajas* and *Tamas–* created by *Prakriti* bind the immutable embodied soul (*Atman*) in the body. All of these three *Gunas* are present in everyone and everything; it is the proportion that is different, according to the Hindu worldview. The interplay of these *gunas* defines the character of someone or something, of nature and determines the progress of life. *Gunas* are the primary constituents of the Prakriti and are the bases of all substances; they cannot, therefore, be said to be the attributes or qualities inherent in the substances as opposed to the substances. None is free from the operation of any one of the three qualities. They are not constant. Sometimes *Sattva* predominates and at others *Tamas* predominates. One should analyse and stand as a witness of these three qualities.

Gunas are not merely qualities but they are the primary constituents of nature. They are the base for all substances. They are the three different influences under which every human mind expresses itself in a variety of ways at different moments of changing environments.

If water in a vessel is stirred, the sun reflected in that water also appears to be agitated. So too, the pure Supreme Self appears to be bound by the three qualities of Nature through superimposition. In reality the Self is ever free and untainted and beyond them.

The *Gunas* depend for their existence on the Knower of the Field whom they bind very fast. The knowledge of *Gunas* is, therefore, necessary to come out of their clutches. These three *Gunas* are always present in all human beings and none is free from them. However, they are not always constant; every time any one of them will be predominant.

तत्र सत्त्वं निर्मलत्वात्प्रकाशकमनामयम् ।
सुखसङ्गेन बध्नाति ज्ञानसङ्गेन चानघ ॥ 14.6 ॥

Shlok 14.6: Of these, *Sattva* is illuminating and good because it is pure. The mode of goodness fetters the living entity by attachment to happiness and knowledge, O sinless Arjun.

Commentary: *Gunas* cannot be defined directly without explaining their symptoms and processes. In the following verses a description of the mind under the influence of each of the three *Gunas* is given by describing the type of emotions, thoughts and behaviour that emanate from the mind– intellect equipment.

Under the influence of *Sattva*, it being pure and hence luminous and without any blemish, the mind is steady and will constantly reflect on the Self. Though *Sattva* is thus the most Divine mental attitude, still it binds us and limits our spiritual nature.

When the mind is cleansed from all its agitations and evil thoughts the seeker achieves greater inward peace, happiness, better understanding and intellectual comprehension.

रजो रागात्मकं विद्धि तृष्णासङ्गसमुद्भवम् ।
तन्निबध्नाति कौन्तेय कर्मसङ्गेन देहिनम् ॥ 14.7 ॥

Shlok 14.7: O son of Kunti, know that *Rajas* (the mode of passion) is characterized by intense craving for sense gratification

and is the source of material desire and attachment. The mode of passion binds the living entity by attachment to the fruits of work.

Commentary: Now the characteristics of *Rajas* are described. When the influences of *Rajogun* predominate, the mind gets full of passions. Passion denotes urges, desires, emotions and feelings. These fall under two categories, viz. desires and attachments which are said to be the very sources of passion.

Thirst means insatiable desire. A human personality longs for the satisfaction of any desire that grows in him. Satisfaction of one kind of desire leads to attachment to the object desired. Desire is the mental relationship towards the objects that have not been possessed and attachment is the mental dependence on the objects so acquired.

When the Rajas predominates innumerable desires originate for things not acquired and deepest attachment sets in for things already possessed.

Actions emanate from passions and passions arise out of desires and attachments all of which are the symptoms of the predominance of *Rajogun* on the mind. If *Sattva Guna* binds one with anxieties for happiness and peace, wisdom and knowledge, *Rajogun* binds him to inexhaustible actions. Thus though the Self is not acting, *Rajas* makes him act with the idea that 'I am the doer'.

तमस्त्वज्ञानजं विद्धि मोहनं सर्वदेहिनाम् ।
प्रमादालस्यनिद्राभिस्तन्निबध्नाति भारत ॥ 14.8 ॥

Shlok 14.8: O Arjun, know that *Tamas* the mode of ignorance– the deluder of the living entity– is born of inertia. The mode of ignorance binds the living entity by carelessness, laziness, and excessive sleep.

Commentary: Now the discussion is about *Tamas*. Under the influence of *Tamogun* man's discriminatory capacity gets blunted and he gets deluded. The Lord says that *Tamas* in a human personality binds us to a lower nature with endless mis-comprehensions about the goal of life. In such a stupefied state one lives in indolence heedless of the higher purposes in life. Such a person practically lives in sleep; he has neither any goal in life nor any nobility in action.

So far the symptoms observable in the mind when it is influenced by these three *Gunas* have been described. They not only bring about different degrees of responses in an individual but also bind the Eternal Self to feel and act as if It were limited and conditioned by the matter envelopments.

सत्त्वं सुखे संजयति रजः कर्मणि भारत ।
ज्ञानमावृत्य तु तमः प्रमादे संजयत्युत ॥ 14.9 ॥

Shlok 14.9: Sattva attaches man to happiness, Rajas to action, O Arjun, while Tamas, shrouding knowledge, attaches him to heedlessness.

Commentary: The three modes are present in all individuals in different degrees. The prevailing mode has its consequences accordingly. *Sattva* makes us attached to the inward happiness arising from life fully lived. The mode of goodness keeps one away from sinful acts and leads one to Self-knowledge and happiness, but not to salvation. *Rajas* makes one passionate, thirsty of desires and deep attachments in fulfilling of which one perforce has to undertake endless actions. The mode of passion creates strong *Karmic* bonds and takes the individual further away from liberation. Such persons know right and wrong actions based on religious principles, but are unable to follow them because of strong impulses of lust. The mode of passion obscures true knowledge of Self and causes one to experience both the pain and pleasure of this worldly life. Such persons are very much attached to wealth, power, prestige, sensual pleasure, and are very selfish and greedy. *Tamas* conceals right judgement and knowledge of the Self in us. It results in indiscrimination and creates attachment to wrong comprehensions. In the mode of ignorance, one is unable to recognize the real goal of life, is unable to distinguish between right and wrong action, and remains attached to sinful and forbidden activities. Such a person is lazy, violent, lacks intellect, and has no interest in spiritual knowledge.

Nature has induced the three *gunas*, which bind the soul to the living body. *Sattva* (righteous, peace-loving), *Rajas* (passion, active) and *Tamas* (passive, deluded) are qualities to be found in different measures in different beings and things. Thus there are *sattvic* animals (deer, cow, and peacock), *Rajsic* animals (dogs, horses, elephant, lion, and tiger) and *Tamsic* ones (hippo, donkey). Each animal or living being, including humans, exhibits one of these gunas to a greater degree that the other two. When a person is kind and selfless in actions, he is *Sattvic*; when he is doing some work with passion or directing others, he is in *Rajsic* nature. When he is indifferent, insolent or sloppy, he is in *Tamsic* nature. People do change from *Guna* to another, but one of these always predominates.

According to the Geeta, one should overcome *Tamsic* tendencies by *Rajsic* actions. Then *Rajsic* tendencies are overcome by sattvic actions. A stage comes when a yogi realises that even sattvic tendencies bind him to this world, and that one has to give up *Sattvic* actions also– that is, one should go beyond the three gunas– or *Gunatitam*.

Features of three modes of nature (*Gunas*)

रजस्तमश्चाभिभूय सत्त्वं भवति भारत ।
रजः सत्त्वं तमश्चैव तमः सत्त्वं रजस्तथा ॥ 14.10 ॥

Shlok 14.10: Now *Sattva* prevails, O Descendant of Bharat, having overpowered *Rajas* and *Tamas;* now *Rajas*, having overpowered *Sattva* and *Tamas*; and now *Tamas*, having overpowered *Sattva* and *Rajas*.

Commentary: When one or the other of the *Gunas* asserts predominantly over the other two, it produces its own effect, *Sattva* produces knowledge and happiness; *Rajas,* action; and *Tamas,* veiling of discrimination, etc.

The question whether these three *Gunas* act on the mind all at a time or each separately at different points of time is answered here. The Lord says that these *Gunas* act at different times– each one of them becoming powerful at any onc point of time. At a given time human personality works under the influence of one predominant *Guna* when the other two *Gunas* get subdued but not totally absent.

Thus when *Sattva* predominates over *Rajas* and *Tamas* it produces on the mind its own nature of happiness and knowledge; when *Rajas* predominates over the other two it produces passions, desires, attachments and actions. When *Tamas* is prominent over *Sattva* and *Rajas* it shrouds discrimination and makes the mind unaware of its nobler duties.

सर्वद्वारेषु देहेऽस्मिन्प्रकाश उपजायते ।
ज्ञानं यदा तदा विद्याद्विवृद्धं सत्त्वमित्युत ॥ 14.11 ॥

Shlok 14.11: When through every gate (sense organ) in this body, the light of intelligence shines, then it may be known that goodness (*Sattva*) is predominant.

Commentary: The sense organs (nose, tongue, eye, skin, ear, mind, and intellect) are called the gateway to Self-knowledge in the body. The mind and intellect get into the mode of goodness and become receptive to Self-knowledge when senses are purified by selfless service, discipline, and spiritual practice. It is also said in verse 14.17 that the rise of Self-knowledge takes place when one's mind gets firmly established in the mode of goodness. As objects are seen very clearly in the light, similarly one perceives and thinks in the right perspective, and the senses shun whatever is improper. There is no attraction in the mind for sensual pleasures when the senses are illumined by the dawning of the light of Self-knowledge.

When Sattva predominates ears refuse to hear improper sounds, eyes will not see undesirable sights, tongue avoids anything not proper and mind is not attracted towards sensual objects. If there is increase of Sattva there is increase of knowledge.

लोभः प्रवृत्तिरारम्भः कर्मणामशमः स्पृहा ।
रजस्येतानि जायन्ते विवृद्धे भरतर्षभ ॥ 14.12 ॥

Shlok 14.12: Greed, activity, the undertaking of selfish actions, restlessness, excitement– these arise when *Rajas* is predominant, O Arjun.

Commentary: Sri Krishna enumerates the important qualities of the mind when *Rajas* dominates it.

- Greed– desire to appropriate the property of others.
- Activity– all activities motivated by selfish desires.
- Restlessness– lack of enjoyment and quietitude.

These three are inter-connected and one succeeds the other in their impact. Greed leads to selfish activity, activity leads to unrest over the results of such activities. When one is completely subjugated by *Rajas* he feels inexhaustible longing for objects.

अप्रकाशोऽप्रवृत्तिश्च प्रमादो मोह एव च ।
तमस्येतानि जायन्ते विवृद्धे कुरुनन्दन ॥ 14.13 ॥

Shlok 14.13: Darkness, inertness, heedlessness and delusion– these arise when Tamas is predominant, O Descendant of Kurus.

Commentary: The symptoms when Tamas predominates are given below:

- •Darkness– a condition in which intellect is not capable of arriving at any decision.
- •Inertness– sense of incapacity to undertake any endeavour and lack of enthusiasm to achieve anything in the world.
- •Mis- comprehension– Incapacity to respond to good or bad and miscalculation of one's relationship with others around.
- •Delusion– when such a person fails to understand the outside world he is always deluded.

Gunas as the vehicle of transmigration

यदा सत्त्वे प्रवृद्धे तु प्रलयं याति देहभृत् ।
तदोत्तमविदां लोकानमलान्प्रतिपद्यते ॥ 14.14 ॥

Shlok 14.14: One, who dies when goodness (*Sattva*) dominates, goes to spotless regions of the worshippers of the Highest.

Commentary: Sri Krishna now gives an idea as to the direction in which the mental equipment of the dead one would reach soon after death. There is always a continuity of thought in this life. Today's thoughts are an extension of yesterday's thinking and the thoughts of tomorrow will be conditioned by today's thinking. On the same analogy the type of thoughts entertained during one's life time will determine the type of thoughts that will follow after death also. So if the *Sattva Guna* is dominant at the time of death one attains the highest realm of abundant joy.

रजसि प्रलयं गत्वा कर्मसङ्गिषु जायते ।
तथा प्रलीनस्तमसि मूढयोनिषु जायते ॥ 14.15 ॥

Shlok 14.15: Meeting death in Rajas, he is reborn among those who are attached to action; and dying in Tamas, he is reborn in the womb of a lower creature.

Commentary: If the mind is under the influence of *Rajas* at the time it leaves the body, it takes the embodiment among those who are attached to action. It means that the mind will seek an appropriate field to exhaust the existing tendencies or Vasanas at the time of death. Similarly, when one dies when Tamas is dominant one reaches the realm of irrational beings such as animal or vegetable kingdom.

कर्मणः सुकृतस्याहुः सात्त्विकं निर्मलं फलम् ।
रजसस्तु फलं दुःखमज्ञानं तमसः फलम् ॥ 14.16 ॥

Shlok 14.16: The fruit of a Sattvic action is spotlessly clean, the fruit of a Rajasic action is pain; and the fruit of Tamas is ignorance.

Commentary: In this verse Sri Krishna summarizes what He told in the previous verses. The results obtained by living in the three *Gunas* are given here. The fruit of good action (*Sattva*) is said to be beneficial and pure; the fruit of passionate action (*Rajas*) is pain; and the fruit of ignorant action (*Tamas*) is laziness.

Sattva: If one lives a quiet and good life of service, devotion, of love and kindness, of mercy and compassion, it indicates the Sattvic nature of his mind. He achieves inward purity.

Rajas: Leading a life full of desires and continuous actions to satisfy them always results in sorrows and pain.

Tamas: Dullness in actions, lack of discriminating capacity and absence of understanding leading to ignorance is the fruit of *Tamas*.

सत्त्वात्संजायते ज्ञानं रजसो लोभ एव च ।
प्रमादमोहौ तमसो भवतोऽज्ञानमेव च ॥ 14.17 ॥

Shlok 14.17: Self-knowledge arises from *Sattva*; greed arises from *Rajas*; and negligence, delusion, and slowness of mind arise from *Tamas*.

Commentary: Wisdom is born of *Sattva*; greed of *Rajas*; false perceptions and ignorance arise from *Tamas*. When Sattva is predominant the intellect is enlightened and knowledge awakened. *Rajas* creates insatiable cravings, makes one to ignore the feelings of others and breeds selfish acquisitiveness. *Tamas* brings forth incapacity to perceive rightly the world outside and eliminates the power to right judgement.

ऊर्ध्वं गच्छन्ति सत्त्वस्था मध्ये तिष्ठन्ति राजसाः ।
जघन्यगुणवृत्तिस्था अधो गच्छन्ति तामसाः ॥ 14.18 ॥

Shlok 14.18: Those abiding in goodness (Sattva) go upwards, the passionate (those abiding in Rajas) stay midway, and the lazy (those abiding in Tamas) go downwards.

Commentary: Those who are established in goodness rise upwards, the passionate remain in the middle, and those who make a vile use of their energy sink downwards.

Go upwards– Those who are living a pure life of discrimination, clear thinking, right judgement and self– discipline cultivate more and more Sattva qualities in themselves. When the mind is thus quiet it evolves to a higher level.

Stay midway– Those of *Rajsic* nature, with all their desires and agitations, ambitions and achievements again and again manifest as human beings till they acquire the required purity.

Go downwards– Those of Tamsic nature that is full of misconceptions and deluded in their own lust and passions devolve themselves into the lower natures.

This verse repeats the ideas expressed in the verse which explained the continuity of existence even after death. It is made clear that all the three *Gunas* bind man to attachment; including Sattva which binds us to knowledge and happiness.

Three paths of departure after leaving this world are described above. The fourth path, the path of no return, is described in the subsequent verse. It refers to the path of liberation or the Moksha gained from the right judgement of the world.

नान्यं गुणेभ्यः कर्तारं यदा द्रष्टानुपश्यति ।
गुणेभ्यश्च परं वेत्ति मद्भावं सोऽधिगच्छति ॥ 14.19 ॥

Shlok 14.19: When visionaries perceive no doer other than the three modes of material Nature (*Gunas*) and know the Supreme, which is above and beyond these modes, they attain to My Being.

Commentary: The seer knows that the *Gunas* alone are responsible for all actions and He is distinct from them. The Lord has given only the faculties to act; He is not liable for one's actions. It is up to the individual to decide how to act. The decision is controlled by the modes of material Nature and is governed by one's past Karma. Those who understand this properly know how to act and do not blame God for their misfortunes or feel jealous of others' fortune.

गुणानेतानतीत्य त्रीन्देही देहसमुद्भवान् ।
जन्ममृत्युजरादुःखैर्विमुक्तोऽमृतमश्नुते ॥ 14.20 ॥

Shlok 14.20: When the soul transcends these three *Gunas* arising out of the body, it is liberated from birth, death, old age and pain and attains deathlessness.

Commentary: Thus after having become aware of three *Gunas*, a wise person shall surely try to inculcate *Sattvic Gunas* in his life. By means of Sattva, one can overcome ill effects of Rajas and Tamas. By developing the element of Sattva gradually through long practice, one has to try to get beyond all gunas and achieve the perfect stage of eternal life.

The man who is able to go beyond the three *Gunas* that arise from the body and is freed from the sorrows of birth, old age and death attains the Immortal.The man of realization not only experiences absence of sorrow but lives in perfection. This is nearly same as we forget our sorrows and pain in sleep. Sleep is a temporary relief against the worldly sorrows. But the Bliss experienced at the time of realization of the Self is not temporary cessation of tragedies of matter but a positive re-awakening of our changeless, infinite nature. Hence it is said that one experiences the state of immortality even in living in this body embodiment.

Arjun asked:

कैर्लिङ्गैस्त्रीन्गुणानेतानतीतो भवति प्रभो ।
किमाचारः कथं चैतांस्त्रीन्गुणानतिवर्तते ॥ 14.21 ॥

Shlok 14.21: What are the marks of those who have transcended the three *Gunas*, and what is their conduct? How does one pass beyond these three Gunas, O Lord Krishna?

Commentary: Arjun asks here three specific questions:

•What are the marks by which a man who has gone beyond the influences of these three Gunas can be recognized?

•In that state of perfection what would be his relationship with the world outside and his behaviour among those who are still under the influence of three Gunas?

•How does such a man of perfection conquer his inner confusions and entanglements and attains his spiritual glory?

The characteristics of perfection in whatever way it may be reached, are more or less the same as those of the *Sthitapragya* (2.55) or of the devotee (12.1).

Lord Krishna said:

प्रकाशं च प्रवृत्तिं च मोहमेव च पाण्डव ।
न द्वेष्टि संप्रवृत्तानि न निवृत्तानि काङ्क्षति ॥ 14.22 ॥
उदासीनवदासीनो गुणैर्यो न विचाल्यते ।
गुणा वर्तन्त इत्येव योऽवतिष्ठति नेङ्गते ॥ 14.23 ॥

Shlokas 14.22-23: One has transcended the three *Gunas* who neither hates the presence of enlightenment, activity, and delusion nor desires them when they are absent; who remains like a witness without being affected by the *Gunas*; who stays firmly attached to the Lord without wavering– thinking that only the *Gunas* are operating.

Commentary: In response to the questions Sri Krishna replies as follows:

The man of right understanding does not hate the effects of the three *Gunas* when they are clearly present in his inner life; nor does he long after these when they are absent. Equanimity in all circumstances is his hallmark and inner peace independent of all environments is his strength.

Just as we pull out a thorn by a thorn, so renouncing worldly things, we must renounce renunciation. By means of *Sattva* we overcome *Rajas* and *Tamas* and then we get beyond Sattva itself.

The real test of a perfect one is not in a secluded forest but in actual day to day life where he is faced with all sorts of temptations because the true nature of a man comes out only in adversities.

In all experiences in the world– good or bad– a man of steady wisdom will be as if he were unconcerned since he knows that all this is due to play of the mind and intellect. He is not agitated by anything that is happening around him. He understands that the changes in him are due to changes of the *Gunas* and the world outside changes according to one's own mental conditions. He is thus fully aware of the reasons behind the changes in himself and the world around him.

समदुःखसुखः स्वस्थः समलोष्टाश्मकांचनः ।
तुल्यप्रियाप्रियो धीरस्तुल्यनिन्दात्मसंस्तुतिः ॥ 14.24 ॥
मानापमानयोस्तुल्यस्तुल्यो मित्रारिपक्षयोः ।
सर्वारम्भपरित्यागी गुणातीतः स उच्यते ॥ 14.25 ॥

Shlokas 14.24-25: And one who depends on the Lord and is indifferent to pain and pleasure; to whom a clod of earth, a stone, and gold are alike and to whom the friend and the foe are alike; who is of firm mind; who is calm in censure and in praise and indifferent to honour and disgrace; who is impartial to friend and foe, abandoning all undertakings– he is said to have gone beyond the Gunas.

Commentary: He who is the same in pleasure and pain, self-possessed, regarding a lump of clay, of stone and gold alike; the same in praise and blame; the same to friend and foe, giving up all selfish actions, he is said to have crossed beyond the three *Gunas*. In this verse, the Lord repeats what he told earlier about equanimity. A *Yogi* who observes equanimity is one who has crossed the three *Gunas* or is freed from the clutches or weakness of human nature. He is not bound by actions– good or bad.

The Lord specifically says that a *Yogi* should treat all worldly possessions equally– here a stone could mean diamond or any gemstone. For a *Yogi*, a lump of clay, a precious stone or gold, all mean the same. He is indifferent to wealth of all kind. He lives in a world of his own. His mind does not react to the worldly situations. All possessions either full of value or completely valueless will have the same response. One of the clear signs of perfection is equanimity in honour and dishonour. Honour and dishonour are the evaluations of the intellect that change from time to time and place to place. To the one who has crossed over the ordinary plane of egoism and vanity, roses and thorns are the same. There is neither a friend nor an enemy to a man of wisdom. To him who has realized the oneness of the Spirit all others are not separate but they are also in him.

मां च योऽव्यभिचारेण भक्तियोगेन सेवते ।
स गुणान्समतीत्यैतान्ब्रह्मभूयाय कल्पते ॥ 14.26 ॥

Shlok 14.26: One who serves Me with love and unswerving devotion, rises above the three modes is fit for liberation.

Commentary: The way to rise above three modes lies in love and devotion for God. This answers Arjun's third question. Unswerving devotion is defined as the loving devotion in which one does not depend on any other person, but only God for everything.

The mode of goodness is the topmost rung of the ladder leading to the Truth, but it is not the Truth as such. The three modes of material Nature have to be transcended, step by step. First, one has to overcome the modes of ignorance and passion and become established in the mode of goodness by developing certain values and following certain disciplines. Then one becomes ready to surmount the dualities of good and bad, pain and pleasure, and to rise to the higher transcendental plane by going beyond the highest mode– the mode of goodness.

Sri Krishna advises a practical method of maintaining a thought for a longer period of time through a process of dedicated service. If all the work is undertaken in a spirit of dedication and service, then work becomes worship.

ब्रह्मणो हि प्रतिष्ठाहममृतस्याव्ययस्य च ।
शाश्वतस्य च धर्मस्य सुखस्यैकान्तिकस्य च ॥ 14.27 ॥

Shlok 14.27: Because I am the abode of the immortal Spirit (Brahm), of everlasting cosmic order (Dharma), and of the absolute bliss.

Commentary: Sri Krishna indicates in the last verse of this Discourse the nature of the state of God– consciousness; when a devotee enters this state he himself becomes the Brahm. The Lord declares that imperishable Brahm indicating that the latter is not different from Him, who is the God, possessed of attributes and that He is not different from Brahm. By realizing Brahm, man becomes immortal, i.e. freed from the cycle of birth and death. By referring to Himself as the ground of immortality, the Lord shows that He is none other than that immortality and that attaining immortality means realizing the Lord Himself.

Sri Krishna teaches the essential character of the three Gunas and how to get over from their clutches or how to become a *Gunatit*. He also explains that through undivided love for the Lord, meditation or selfless work one can transcend the Gunas and reach Supreme Consciousness and ultimately become one with that Brahm.

(Note: Those who really understand the meaning of this verse, they cannot argue that Sri Krishna was an incarnation of Vishnu. This verse clearly suggests that all gods (including Brahma, Vishnu and Mahesh), goddesses and all other deities reside within Sri Krishna who is the Supreme Godhead. The entire cosmic order is within Sri Krishna. Nothing exists beyond Him. The Supreme Being is the source or the basis of Spirit. Spirit is one of the expansions of the Supreme Being. It is Spirit (of the Supreme Being) that performs the entire cosmic drama and sustains everything.

It is very significant that Lord Krishna has used such words as 'worship the Supreme Being', 'worship Me, the Absolute or Atman' and 'the Absolute is the basis of everything.' In this verse and also elsewhere in the Geeta, Lord Krishna declares that He is the Supreme Being. Only a Self-realized master can say that I am the basis of everything. The word 'I' in this context does not mean one's body, but Atman. Krishna means different things to different people. Some commentators consider Krishna other than God; others call Him a 'Hindu God.' To some Krishna is a politician, a teacher, a divine lover, and a diplomat. To devotees, Krishna is the incarnation of the Absolute and the object of love and worship. Readers should merely try to understand and use Krishna's teachings in their daily lives without getting confused about the identity or greatness of Lord Krishna.)

OM TAT SAT

Discourse - 15

Purushottam Yog: Yog of the Supreme Person

In this Discourse Sri Krishna discusses the nature of the Spirit in all its implications and explains the Unknown from the known manifested objects of perception, emotion and thought. The Infinite is defined as the Imperishable (*Akshar*) with reference to the perishable (*Kshar*) equipments of matter. Speaking of the *Kshar Purush* (*Kshetra*), the *Akshar* Purush (*Kshetragaya)* and the Supreme Person *(Brahm*), it explains how Brahm is superior to both '*Kshar*' and '*Akshar*', why He is called the Supreme Person, what is the significance of knowing Him as the Supreme Person and how can He be realized. Hence this Chapter is entitled "*Purushottam Yog*" or the Yog of the Supreme Person or Supreme Spirit. The previous Chapter ended with a note that to worship the Lord with undeviating love leads to liberation. But such love is not possible without detachment from the world. So the Lord begins the present Discourse with a description of the World Tree in order to create in the aspirant an intense dispassion leading to love and knowledge of the Supreme Lord, *Brahm*.

In this Discourse Lord Krishna tells us about the ultimate source of this visible phenomenal universe from which all things have come into being, just like a great tree with all its roots, trunk, branches, twigs, leaves, flowers and fruits which spring forth from the earth, which itself supports the tree and in which it is rooted. Sri Krishna declares that the Supreme Being is the source of all existence, and refers allegorically to this universe is like an inverted tree whose roots are in *Parabrahm* and whose spreading branches and foliage constitute all the things and factors that go to make up this creation of variegated phenomena. This is a very mysterious 'Tree' which is very difficult to understand, being a product of His inscrutable power of *Maya*; and hence a marvellous, apparent appearance without having actual reality. One who fully understands the nature of this *Sansar* like a tree goes beyond Maya. To be attached to it is to be caught in it. The surest way of transcending this *Sansar* or worldly life is by wielding the excellent weapon of dispassion and non-attachment.

The Lord declares that it is a part of Himself that manifests here as the individual soul in each body. He is the effulgence inherent in the sun, moon and fire. He is like a nourishing element for the earth. He is the inner witness of all beings. He is the supreme Knower even beyond the Vedic knowledge. He is the resplendent Person who is beyond both this perishable phenomenal creation as well as the imperishable individual soul which is a part of His eternal essence. Thus, because He is beyond perishable matter and superior to the imperishable soul (enveloped in Maya), He is known in this world as well as in the *Vedas* as the Supreme Person.

The core message is that Sri Krishna (Brahm) alone exists in all names and forms, either movable or immovable objects of the universe. All the planets including the sun, the moon and the stars move and shine with a fraction of His energy. He alone exists as Consciousness in human beings in the physical, mental and intellectual levels. He who knows Him as the Supreme *Purush* is the knower of all and worships Him whole heartedly. He who understands this secret knowledge becomes wise; all his doubts and sufferings in the world come to an end spontaneously and he becomes the performer of all the duties.

Creation is like a tree created by *Maya*

Lord Krishna said:

ऊर्ध्वमूलमधःशाखमश्वत्थं प्राहुरव्ययम् ।
छन्दांसि यस्य पर्णानि यस्तं वेद स वेदवित् ॥ 15.1 ॥

Shlok 15.1: The sages talk about an indestructible *Peepal* tree, having its root above and branches below, whose leaves are the metres or hymns. One who truly understands this tree is a

knower of the Vedas.

Commentary: The creation is like an infinite tree that is ever changing but eternal. This tree has its root in the Supreme Being, the Eternal Being is the main stem. The Vedic hymns are just like the leaves of the tree. One who truly knows this marvellous tree, its origin, its nature and working, is wise in a true sense.

The phenomenal world is compared to the *Peepal* tree on account of its ever-changing nature. In an ordinary tree the roots extend downwards. But in the tree of the world the roots are stated to be above. This is just like an inverted tree. This is because the roots are Brahm with *Maya (Sagun Brahm*) since the Immortal Absolute (*Nirgun Brahm*) is beyond the category of causality and Brahm with *Maya* is very subtle and very great and is supreme over all things. The branches are the cosmic mind, egoism, five subtle elements and the other cosmic principles which are stated to extend downwards because as they go downward they become more and more gross.

अधश्चोर्ध्वं प्रसृतास्तस्य शाखा गुणप्रवृद्धा विषयप्रवालाः ।
अधश्च मूलान्यनुसन्ततानि कर्मानुबन्धीनि मनुष्यलोके ॥ 15.2 ॥

Shlok 15.2: Above and below its branches spread, blossoming because of the *Gunas* having sense-objects as their buds, deep down in the world are ramified its roots entangling men in the bondage of action.

Commentary: The human body, a microcosmic universe, has also been compared to a tree of human life and death (or transmigration) on earth. Karma is its seed; five basic elements are its main branches; and the ten organs of perception and action are its sub-branches. Right and wrong actions are its flowers and pain and pleasures are the fruits. Senses going towards sense objects produce worldly desires. Fulfilment of desires gives sense pleasures and creates attachment. Ignorance-born ego, worldly desires and attachment are the roots of Karmic bondage, causing cycles of transmigration.

How to slice the tree of life and attain salvation

न रूपमस्येह तथोपलभ्यते नान्तो न चादिर्न च सम्प्रतिष्ठा ।
अश्वत्थमेनं सुविरूढमूलमसङ्गशस्त्रेण दृढेन छित्त्वा ॥ 15.3 ॥

ततः पदं तत्परिमार्गितव्यं यस्मिन्गता न निवर्तन्ति भूयः ।
तमेव चाद्यं पुरुषं प्रपद्ये यतः प्रवृत्तिः प्रसृता पुराणी ॥ 15.4 ॥

Shlokas 15.3-04: Its form is not perceived here as such, neither its end nor its origin, nor its foundation nor resting place; having cut asunder this firmly-rooted *Peepal* tree with the strong axe of non-attachment. Then that goal should be sought after, whither having gone none returns again. Seek refuge in that primeval Purush from which comes forth the ancient activity or energy.

Commentary: Human life is also without beginning and end. It has no permanent existence or real form. One must sharpen the axe of metaphysical knowledge and detachment over the stone of spiritual practice, cut the feeling of separateness between the living entity and the Lord, cheerfully participate in the drama of life made up of passing shadows of joys and sorrows, and live in this world free from ego and worldly desires. When the attachments are severed, an attitude of sacred dispassion (*Vairagya*) takes place, which is the prerequisite for reaching the Supreme goal.

Then that goal should be sought from where having gone none returns again praying I seek refuge in that Primeval *Purush* from whom has come forth this cosmic process. In order to avoid misunderstanding about the tree, the Lord says that its form is not perceived here as such. The tree of life mentioned in the previous verses represents the entire field of manifested life. The experience of life is known through Consciousness. If the Consciousness is withdrawn from the body, mind and intellect, perception, emotion and thought necessarily end.

निर्मानमोहा जितसङ्गदोषा अध्यात्मनित्या विनिवृत्तकामाः ।
द्वन्द्वैर्विमुक्ताः सुखदुःखसञ्ज्ञैर्गच्छन्त्यमूढाः पदमव्ययं तत् ॥ 15.5 ॥

Shlok 15.5: The eternal goal is reached by the wise who are free from pride and delusion, who have conquered the evil of attachment, who are ever Self-conscious with all lust completely stilled, and who are free from dualities of pleasure and pain.

Commentary: Those who are constantly engaged in the contemplation of the Supreme Self and are free from dualities of life like pleasure and pain or loss and victory, they simply attain the Supreme Self. Such people are none other than *Sannyasi,* as they have no sense of attachment for anything. Eternal goal is easily reached by a true *Sannyasi*.

न तद्भासयते सूर्यो न शशाङ्को न पावकः ।
यद्गत्वा न निवर्तन्ते तद्धाम परमं मम ॥ 15.6 ॥

Shlok 15.6: The sun does not illumine My Supreme Abode, nor does the moon, nor the fire. Having reached there, people attain permanent liberation (*Moksha*) and do not come back to this temporal world.

Commentary: The Lord's abode, the Supreme Abode is beyond the common luminous things, the sun and the moon. It is the abode of Eternal Light. A similar verse occurs in **Mundak Upanishad**: "The sun does not shine there, nor the moon, nor the stars, nor do the lightnings shine there, much less this fire. He shines, everything shines because of Him; by His light all is lighted." It is implied that the Supreme Abode is beyond the phenomenal Universe perceived by us. It is self-luminous, not illumined by any other source. He illumines the sun and the moon as a luminous lamp illumines other objects. Transcendental light of Brahm (Divine Light, *Brahm Jyoti*) is the source of all light energy and is called the light of all lights in verse 13.17. The Supreme Being existed before the sun, moon and fire came into existence during creation, and it will exist even after everything gets dissolved into unmanifest Nature during complete dissolution.

The Lord as the life of the universe

ममैवांशो जीवलोके जीवभूतः सनातनः ।
मनः षष्ठानीन्द्रियाणि प्रकृतिस्थानि कर्षति ॥ 15.7 ॥

Shlok 15.7: The eternal individual soul (*Jeev, Jeevatma*) in the body of living beings is, indeed, My integral part. Abiding in material nature or the body, it activates the six senses, including the mind.

Commentary: The soul in the individual is a fraction of God. When it is in the body, it associates with the mind and the sense, which are born of nature. The soul draws the five senses and the mind (the sixth sense) which are part of Prakriti or Nature. Thus it is clearly stated that a small part of Him has become the soul in all beings. Once the soul manifests in a body, it operates through the senses and the mind. Therefore, our soul is part of the Supreme Being. This is in conformity with the views of Visishtadvaita of Ramanujacharya wherein the whole universe has been treated as the body of the Supreme Being. Thus Self is nothing but a part of the Super Self. It is similar to room space being a part of the unlimited space. The individual soul as well as the entire creation is a real but limited manifestation of the Absolute. Here is a description of how the subtle and causal bodies leave one physical body and acquire another.

शरीरं यदवाप्नोति यच्चाप्युत्क्रामतीश्वरः ।
गृहीत्वैतानि संयाति वायुर्गन्धानिवाशयात् ॥ 15.8 ॥

Shlok 15.8: When the Lord obtains a body and when He leaves it, He takes away the causal and subtle body from the physical body just as the wind carries away aroma from the flowers.

Commentary: The individual soul takes its subtle body– six sensory faculties of perception, intellect, ego, and five vital forces– from one physical body to another after death, as the wind takes dust from one place to another. The wind is neither affected nor remains unaffected by association with dust; similarly the individual soul is neither affected nor remains unaffected by association with the body. Physical bodies are limited in space and time, but invisible subtle bodies are unlimited and all pervading. The causal body stores individual's good and bad Karma. When all *Karmas* and trace of desires are wiped out from the causal body after the dawn of Self-knowledge, the physical body seems not to exist anymore and the conception of subtle body is firmed up in the mind. The astral or subtle body is an exact duplicate of the physical body. The beings in the astral world are more advanced in art, technology, and culture. They take up physical bodies to improve and enhance the physical world.

During a wakeful state, the physical body, mind, intellect, and ego are active. In a dream state, the individual soul temporarily creates a dream world and wanders in it with a dream body without leaving the physical body. In deep sleep, the individual soul completely rests in the Eternal Being (Spirit) without being bothered by mind and intellect.

Supreme Being, the Universal Consciousness, watches us as a witness during all the three states– wakeful, dream, and deep sleep. The living entity leaves one physical body and takes another body after death. The living entity becomes bound or lost, then tries to be liberated by discovering its real nature.

श्रोत्रं चक्षुः स्पर्शनं च रसनं घ्राणमेव च ।
अधिष्ठाय मनश्चायं विषयानुपसेवते ॥ 15.9 ॥

Shlok 15.9: Presiding over the ear, the eye, touch, taste and smell, as well as the mind, he enjoys the objects of the senses.

उत्क्रामन्तं स्थितं वापि भुंजानं वा गुणान्वितम् ।
विमूढा नानुपश्यन्ति पश्यन्ति ज्ञानचक्षुषः ॥ 15.10 ॥

Shlok15.10: The deluded do not see Him who departs, stays and enjoys; but they who possess the eye of knowledge behold Him.

Commentary (Shlokas 15.9-10): Presiding over the ear, the eye, touch, taste and smell, as well as the mind, He enjoys the objects of the senses. The *Jeev* enjoys the world of objects through sense organs and mind. Consciousness never directly illumines any object but when reflected upon mind and intellect It becomes Intelligence in which the sense objects become illumined. The *Jeev*, using the mind along with sense organs, enjoys the sense objects such as sound, touch, taste, smell, etc.

Senses lose their taste for material enjoyment when they develop a higher taste for spiritual bliss. The attainment of spiritual bliss is the real fulfilment of one's desire for sense gratification. A purified soul will refrain from doing wrong things that arise from *Vasana*, the residual, subtle desires for sensual pleasures.

The deluded do not see Him who departs, stays and enjoys, united with the Gunas; but they who possess the eye of knowledge behold Him. The Self is visible to the eye of knowledge only. Though the Self is the nearest and comes most easily within the range of their consciousness in a variety of functions, the ignorant and deluded do not see Him because of their complete subservience to the sense-objects. But those who are with intuitive vision could see the Self.

Those with the inner eye of knowledge behold the Self as entirely distinct from the body.

यतन्तो योगिनश्चैनं पश्यन्त्यात्मन्यवस्थितम् ।
यतन्तोऽप्यकृतात्मानो नैनं पश्यन्त्यचेतसः ॥ 15.11 ॥

Shlok 15.11: The Yogis, striving for perfection, behold Him dwelling in the Self; but the ignorant whose inner psyche is not pure, even though striving, cannot see Him.

Commentary: The *Yogis* striving for God-realization are able to see Atman abiding in their heart, but the ignorant, and whose intellect is not pure, do not perceive Him even with the help of great effort. The persons who want to behold Him dwelling in the self; two conditions should be met. Besides purity of mind his intellect should be tuned to have the correct understanding of the Self. If these two requirements are not met through devotion (*Bhakti*) and service (*Karma)*, all attempts at meditation in the Path of Knowledge will be futile. Those minds which are not purified despite sincere meditation have no chance of realizing the Divine because of attachment to sense objects.

Spirit is the essence of everything

यदादित्यगतं तेजो जगद्भासयतेऽखिलम् ।
यच्चन्द्रमसि यच्चाग्नौ तत्तेजो विद्धि मामकम् ॥ 15.12 ॥

Shlok 15.12: The light energy of the sun which illumines the entire world, which is in the moon and in the fire, knows that light to be Mine.

Commentary: Sri Krishna says that the very light emerging from the sun which illumines the whole world is the light that is emerging from Him, the Infinite Consciousness. Not only are this but even the light coming from the moon and the fire all expressions of the Infinite Reality expressing through the moon and the fire. The manifestations are different because the equipments are different just as the same electrical energy manifests in a bulb, in a fan and in a heater in different ways. Consciousness expressed through the sun is sun-light, through the moon is moon-light and through the fuel is fire. Yet all these manifestations are nothing but one Infinite Reality. The Infinite manifests itself in various forms in order to create conducive environment for the world to exist.

It is His light that is in wood, lamps, candles, and is the energy in all living beings. His light is behind all lights and the source of all energy in the universe. Without the power of the Supreme Being, fire is unable to burn a blade of grass. This light of the Supreme Being cannot be realized and seen unless one has completely stilled and strengthened the mind, purified the intellect, and developed the power of will and visualization. One must also be strong enough to bear the mental shock generated while experiencing the light of all lights in trance.

Just as the complete spectrum of sunlight is not visible to the human eye without a prism, similarly we cannot see the light of the Supreme Being without the grace of God and scriptural study. The Yogis who have tuned-in their consciousness with the supreme consciousness can see the eternal light in a trance. The entire universe is sustained by the energy of the Supreme Being and reflects His glory.

गामाविश्य च भूतानि धारयाम्यहमोजसा ।
पुष्णामि चौषधीः सर्वाः सोमो भूत्वा रसात्मकः ॥ 15.13 ॥

Shlok 15.13: Permeating the earth I support all beings by (My) energy; and, having become the watery moon, I nourish all herbs.

Commentary: The Lord says that the capacity in the earth to sustain life and nourish it are all His own vitality, meaning the same Consciousness expressing through the sun, the moon, the earth and the atmosphere which provide nourishment to all living beings. The energy of the Lord holds the entire universe together. The sun, the moon and the fire are the visible sources of energy in the world, but that which gives these phenomenal factors the capacity to give out energy from them is the Super Consciousness. The moon is considered to be the repository of all fluids neccessary for nourishing the living beings.

अहं वैश्वानरो भूत्वा प्राणिनां देहमाश्रितः ।
प्राणापानसमायुक्तः पचाम्यन्नं चतुर्विधम् ॥ 15.14 ॥

Shlok 15.14: Becoming the digestive fire, I remain in the body of all living beings. Uniting with vital breaths or bio-impulses, I digest all types of food.

Commentary: *Vaishvanar* is a kind of fire which abides in the body of all living beings. It helps in digestion of four-fold food. Fourfold food refers to the food which has to be eaten by mastication, that which has to be sucked out, the food which has to be eaten by devouring, and that which is eaten by licking. That Eternal Reality which is indicated as Life manifests as Digestive Fire (*Vaishvanar*) which assimilates food. The power in the digestive system is nothing but a manifestation of the Principle of Life. *Pran* and *Apan* are the physiological functions of perception and excretion that are present in all living creatures. It is the Lord that helps us to swallow the food, digest it and discard something as a wasteful material.

सर्वस्य चाहं हृदि संनिविष्टो मत्तः स्मृतिर्ज्ञानमपोहनं च ।
वेदैश्च सर्वैरहमेव वेद्यो वेदान्तकृद्वेदविदेव चाहम् ॥ 15.15 ॥
Shlok 15.15: I am seated in the heart of everything; from Me alone comes memory, perception and also their loss. I am That which is known in all the Vedas; I am the Author of Vedant and the Knower of the Vedas.

Commentary: In this verse, the Lord says clearly that I am that which is to be known in all the Vedas; I am the knower of the Vedas and the author of the Vedant. Here the term 'loss' refers to 'loss of memory of past lives'. From the Supreme Consciousness alone all memory, knowledge and forgetfulness come to us. Just as knowledge and memory occur in righteous persons as a result of their good deeds, so, as a result of their sins, loss of memory and knowledge occurs in the sinful. I, the Supreme Self, am to be known in all the Vedas. It is I who cause the teaching of the Vedant (Upanishads) to be handed down in regular succession, and It is I who know the Vedic teaching. The Supreme Being is the source of all scriptures.

What are the Supreme Spirit, spirit and the individual soul?
द्वाविमौ पुरुषौ लोके क्षरश्चाक्षर एव च ।
क्षरः सर्वाणि भूतानि कूटस्थोऽक्षर उच्यते ॥ 15.16 ॥
Shlok 15.16: There are two Purushas in this world, the perishable and the imperishable. All beings are the perishable, and the *Kootasth* is called the imperishable.

Commentary: God is unchanging and Imperishable, while the material objects are perishable. There are two aspects of *Purush*– Perishable and the Imperishable. Entire creation is *Kshar*, perishable or temporary. The unchanging is the Imperishable. With reference to this *Kshar Purush,* the Spirit is the Imperishable (*Akshar Purush).* With reference to the ever changing world of the matter, Consciousness is Imperishable and Changeless. This Consciousness Principle is referred to here as *Akshar* with reference to and contact with the *Kshar*. The Self in the midst of changes remains changeless and all changes can take place only in contact with It just as an anvil (*Kootasth*) remaining changeless and allows all the iron pieces kept and hammered on it to change their shapes. *Akshar Brahm* is the Divine person or the cause of all causes. *Parabrahm* is beyond *Kshar Purush* and *Akshar Purush* is referred to as *Akshratita Purush* or *Paramatman* or Lord Krishna in the following verses.

उत्तमः पुरुषस्त्वन्यः परमात्मेत्युदाहृतः ।
यो लोकत्रयमाविश्य बिभर्त्यव्यय ईश्वरः ॥ 15.17 ॥

Shlok 15.17: That Purush is verily something else. It is known as the Paramatman (the Absolute Self), that indestructible power that pervades and maintains the three spheres.

Commentary: But other than these is the *Supreme Purush* called the Highest Self, the Indestructible Lord who, pervading the three states (waking, dream and deep sleep), sustains them. The Imperishable is the quality attained by the Spirit with reference to the Field surrounding It. A man occupying a high position in an office acquires the dignity and the status of that position. Even if that position is removed the man never ceases to exist; he exists as an individual living being. When the Field of the matter is removed from the Knower of the Field what remains is the Knowing Principle, the Pure Knowledge. Similarly, when the perishable is transcended what remains is not the Imperishable but that which played as the Perishable and Imperishable Purushas. This is the Pure Spirit, the Supreme Self which sustains the three states or the three worlds of experiences, viz. waking, dreaming and deep sleep states of consciousness. The Self alone is the illuminator in all these three states of existence. Thus there are no three types of Purushas– Perishable, Imperishable or Supreme. If a pot is kept in a room we feel that there are three different types of space, one completely differing from the other– pot space, room space and the total space. But in fact there is only one space which can be understood if the factors conditioning or limiting the space are removed, i.e. if the pot is broken and the room is dismantled. The unconditioned pot space and room space are nothing but the total space itself. Thus the Consciousness is itself Perishable, Field in another form and as the knower of the Field the same Consciousness is the Imperishable Reality in the perishable conditionings. But when these conditionings are transcended the same Self is experienced as the Supreme Self– the *Paramatman, Purushottam*.

यस्मात्क्षरमतीतोऽहमक्षरादपि चोत्तमः ।
अतोऽस्मि लोके वेदे च प्रथितः पुरुषोत्तमः ॥ 15.18 ॥

Shlok 15.18: As I transcend the perishable and as I am higher even than the imperishable, I am, both in the Vedas and in the day-to-day language, known as Purushottam, the Absolute Self.

Commentary: As the Lord is beyond the Perishable and is above even the Imperishable, therefore in the World of Knowledge and in the Vedas He is known as the Supreme Being. Basically, there are two different aspects (or levels of existence)– Temporal Beings (also called Divine Souls, Divine Beings, temporal Divine Beings, Deva, celestial forces, guardian angels), and the Eternal Being (Spirit, Atman, *Brahm*)– of One and the same Absolute Reality known as the Supreme Being. The invisible, unchanging, and immutable entity is called Eternal Being. The temporal Divine Beings are the expansions of the Eternal Being in the material world. The entire creation is ever-changing and mutable and is also called temporal. Both Temporal and Eternal Being are expansions of the Supreme Being. The Supreme Being– the basis of both Temporal and Eternal– is the highest or the Absolute, who is referred to by various names. The personal aspect of the Absolute is called by names, such as Krishna, Mother, Father, and Allah. According to our scriptures, no one, except *Parabrahm Paramatman*, has their own power or consciousness. Everyone, including the Eternal Being (*Akshar Brahm*), receives power from the Absolute, Lord Krishna.

Sri Krishna says as I transcend the perishable and am higher than even the Imperishable, I am celebrated as the Supreme Person,

Purushottam, in the world and in the Vedas. The Lord explains here how He is the *Purushottam*, the Supreme Person. He says that Pure Consciousness is higher than both the Perishable and the Imperishable. The Perishable can continue the process of change only against the Imperishable Truth as no change is perceptible without reference to a changeless factor. If the changes in the matter– body, mind and intellect– have to be recognized there must be something which is steady that illumines these changes. This constant factor among the perishable is called the Imperishable. The illumining factor can be called Imperishable only when it is compared to the Perishable. Once the Perishable spheres are crossed over, the Imperishable Itself becomes the Pure Infinite which is *Purushottam*. Since the Truth, *Purushottam*, is experienced only after transcending both Perishable and Imperishable, the Absolute Truth is known as the Highest Spirit, *Purushottam*. This term is used to indicate the Supreme Spirit both in the Vedas and by the men of the world.

The Supreme Being (Lord Krishna) is beyond the perishable and the imperishable or Brahm. Thus the Supreme Being or Parabrahm (*Purushottam*) cannot be described as either perishable or imperishable, according to the Lord. This verse gives the highest Truth and must silence the endless arguments between the non-dualists (*Advaitins*) and dualists *(Dvaitins).* The Supreme Being cannot be contained in the labels of non-dualism (*Advaitam*) or dualism (*Dvaitam*).

Fruit of that knowledge

यो मामेवमसम्मूढो जानाति पुरुषोत्तमम् ।
स सर्वविद्भजति मां सर्वभावेन भारत ।। 15.19 ।।

Shlok 15.19: The wise, who truly understand Me as the Supreme Being, know everything and worship Me whole heartedly, O Descendant of Bharat.

Commentary: The Lord tells that the fruits gained by the one who realizes the Supreme Truth. Undeluded is the one who never looks upon the physical body as himself or as belonging to himself. To know means not only the intellectual comprehension but the subjective experience that he is the *Purushottam*. Sri Krishna declares that such a seeker is the greatest of the devotees because such knowledge leads to devotion. The Highest Spirit, *Purushottam*, being the Infinite Consciousness, is the all-knower because he knows that the principle of Consciousness is behind all perception, feeling and thought.

It is rightly said that without understanding His almighty power there can be no belief in God, without belief there can be no faith, without faith there can be no love, without love there can be no unshakable devotion to God. Thus to know is to love and to love is to know (Geeta10.10).

इति गुह्यतमं शास्त्रमिदमुक्तं मयानघ ।
एतद्बुद्ध्वा बुद्धिमान्स्यात्कृतकृत्यश्च भारत ॥ 15.20 ॥

Shlok 15.20: Thus, I have explained this most secret science of the Absolute. Having understood this, one becomes enlightened, one's all duties are accomplished, O Arjun.

Commentary: In this concluding verse the Lord praises the *Purushottam* theme which gives liberation from all sorrows and agitations. He says that He taught this most secret science; secret because It (the spiritual science, *Brahmavidya*) is a knowledge that cannot come to any one of its own accord unless one is initiated into it by the Knower of Reality. The secret is also that *Purushottam* is the substratum of everything. Sinless means the one with steady mind. The knowledge of the Self which gives emancipation from the cycle of births and deaths and freedom from the bonds of Karma is eulogized here. He who has realized the *Purushottam*– state of Consciousness becomes wise in as much as he cannot thereafter make any error of judgement in his life creating confusion and sorrows all around. The second benefit is the enjoyment of a complete sense of fulfilment, the joy of accomplishing what is expected of him (achieving the goal of life which is realization of Brahm). If this most profound teaching is understood it makes a man wise. After this there is nothing for him to learn or strive for. He has attained the goal of life and the aim of human existence. He has the complete knowledge of the Supreme Being and gets *Brahmagyan*. He becomes *Jeevanmukta,* who is beyond body-consciousness, three Gunas, three states of consciousness– waking, dream and deep sleep– pairs of opposites and the cycle of births and deaths. There is no rebirth for him. When a person has realized the

Self, he has discharged all the duties of his life. This Chapter is the essence of the Geeta, the Vedas and the Upanishads. It is generally recited before taking food as a mark of sacred offering to the Lord.

Concepts and Issues

Sri Krishna describes *Sansar* or the created world, comparing it to an inverted tree. Its root which is on the top is Brahm, the Absolute. The three Gunas are its branches, the Vedas its leaves and the Vedic rituals are its subsidiary roots. They have spread out below. However it is not seen as such. Neither its origin, nor its end, nor its middle can be discerned. One has to cut this tree by the weapon of detachment and search for that by reaching which, there is no return to mundane existence. One has to take refuge in that primeval person from which this tree of *Sansar* has emanated. Only those bereft of egoism, delusion and attachment, who are free from desires and pairs of opposites like pleasure and pain, who are devoted to the Lord, can attain that eternal abode. Neither the sun nor the moon nor the fire can light up that abode. After reaching it there is no return. The *Jeev* or the individual soul is a little part of the Supreme Lord and eternal. While being born here, he attracts to himself the mind and the five organs of knowledge. While leaving the body he takes them away with him even as wind carries away the smell. The *Jeev* enjoys the sense objects through these sense organs and the mind. He is too subtle to be perceived by the ignorant whereas the wise do perceive Him. The Yogis striving for perfection succeed in seeing Him. Sri Krishna says that He is the Lord, the Light of lights. It is He who supports the earth and He who sustains vegetation through the moon. It is again He that is responsible for the digestive process in the body, as the *Vaishvanar* fire. He is the spirit established in the hearts of all. He is the one sought by the Vedas. He is the creator of Vedant.

In this world there are two *Purushas* or beings– *Kshar,* the perishable and the *Akshar,* the imperishable. But He is the *Paramatman,* the Supreme Self, the *Purushottam*, the Being par excellence, different and distinct from them and pervading all the three worlds. Whoever realizes Him as such, becomes omniscient and worships Him in all respects.

OM TAT SAT

Discourse - 16

Daivasur-Sampad-Vibhag Yog: Yog of Separateness of the Divine and Undivine

In this Discourse the entire mankind has been classified into two categories– divine (good) and undivine or diabolical (bad or *Asur*). It deals with their respective traits and behaviour. Contrary to the scriptural injunctions, the demoniac always live in agitation, sorrow and bondage. Because of their endless desires they go through the cycles of birth and death, while the divine conquer their desires. They live in peace and harmony. The purpose of this discourse is that one may adopt the divine qualities and reject the demoniac qualities after fully understanding their nature in the journey towards God-realization. Listing two sets of qualities of opposite kinds, the Lord urges us to eradicate the latter and cultivate the divine qualities.

What kind of nature should one develop? What conduct must one follow? What way should one live and act, if one must attain God and obtain divine bliss? These questions are answered with perfect clarity here. The pure divine qualities are conducive to peace and liberation and the undivine qualities lead to bondage. Purity, good conduct and truth are indispensable to spiritual progress and even to an honourable life here.

Devoid of purity, good conduct and truth and lack of faith in God or a higher Reality beyond this visible world, a man degenerates into an animal life. Such a person becomes his own enemy and the destroyer of the happiness of others as well as his own. Caught in countless desires and cravings, a slave of sensual enjoyments and beset by a thousand cares, his life ultimately ends in misery and degradation. Haughtiness, arrogance and egoism lead to this dire fate. Therefore, a wise person, desiring success, must eradicate vice and cultivate virtue.

In this world there are three gates leading to so-called hell– the gates of passion, anger and greed. Released from these three problems one can succeed in attaining salvation and reaching the highest goal, namely God. Thus the sacred scriptures teach the right path of pure, virtuous living. One should, therefore, follow the injunctions of the sacred scripture like the Geeta where lies our real welfare and that teaches us noble things.

Traits of divine nature

Lord Krishna said:

अभयं सत्त्वसंशुद्धिर्ज्ञानयोगव्यवस्थितिः ।
दानं दमश्च यज्ञश्च स्वाध्यायस्तप आर्जवम् ॥ 16.1 ॥
अहिंसा सत्यमक्रोधस्त्यागः शान्तिरपैशुनम् ।
दया भूतेष्वलोलुप्त्वं मार्दवं ह्रीरचापलम् ॥ 16.2 ॥
तेजः क्षमा धृतिः शौचमद्रोहो नातिमानिता ।
भवन्ति सम्पदं दैवीमभिजातस्य भारत ॥ 16.3 ॥

Shlokas 16.1-03: Fearlessness, purity of heart, steadfastness in Yog and knowledge, alms-giving, control of the senses, sacrifice, study of scriptures, austerity and straightforwardness, harmlessness, truth, absence of anger, renunciation, peacefulness, absence of crookedness, compassion towards beings, uncovetousness, gentleness, modesty, absence of fickleness, vigour, forgiveness, fortitude, purity, absence of hatred, absence of pride– these are some of the qualities of those endowed with divine virtues, O Arjun.

Commentary (Shlokas 16.1-16.3): All these qualities described above give a complete picture of the man of Divine State. They serve as a guide to all those who are in search of a right way of living and endeavour to become perfect. They should be cultivated in life for peace, prosperity, happiness and God-realization. But the problem is that a man tends to suffer from various kinds of distresses. There are five distresses in human life according to Yogic scripture ***(Patanjali Yogsutra*, 2.3**):

1. *Agyan* (lack of Self-knowledge),
2. *Asmita* (or ego: considering oneself separate from Brahm),
3. *Abhinivesh* (fear of death and rebirth),
4. and 5. *Rag* and *Dvesh* (likes and dislikes for pair of opposites).

The fear of death is the greatest distress in human life. *Agyan* creates ego that causes fear of death, likes and dislikes, selfish desires and all other demonic qualities. Self-knowledge (*Gyan*) gives rise to divine qualities mentioned in verses 16.1-03. Lord abides in the heart of those with divine qualities as wealth abides in the heart of a greedy/ miser person. From the practice of virtue comes dispassion; from the practice of austerity, spiritual wisdom that bestows liberation.

It is also important to note that one must not condemn or commend anybody including oneself. We should treat others in the same manner as we would like ourselves to be treated. The dualities of friend and foe, joy and sorrow, good and bad, likes and dislikes, are but effects of Maya, not eternal reality. A person of demonic nature needs to be dealt with and controlled differently compared to a person of divine nature. No one is perfect. People do certain things because they don't know any better, so we should not censure them. We all pay the price for those who act out of ignorance. Speaking ill of others is the most heinous sin. Do not see others' faults; improve your own shortcomings until you yourself become enlightened.

One should not talk about, listen to, or even think about the faults and shortcomings of others. When we think about the defects of others, our own minds become polluted. Nothing is gained by finding fault with others; therefore, find your own faults and correct them. To love the unlovable, to be kind to the unkind, and to be gracious to the ungracious is really divine. It is said that we will have to account for how we treat others.

All kinds of people make up this world. You want to change others so that you can be free, but it never works that way. If you accept others totally and unconditionally, only then you are free. People are what they are because they have their own backgrounds, and they cannot be otherwise (Swami Dayananda Sarswati). You can love your spouse, unconditionally, and not like the way he or she acts. Your enemy might become your friend if you allow him or her to be who he or she is. If you want to make an enemy, try to change someone. People will change only when it becomes more difficult to suffer than to change. No one is in a position to disqualify another's way of life, thinking, or ideas.

Sri Krishna now starts the description of a man of demoniac (Asuric) nature in the following verses.

Demonic traits

दम्भो दर्पोऽभिमानश्च क्रोधः पारुष्यमेव च ।
अज्ञानं चाभिजातस्य पार्थ संपदमासुरीम् ॥ 16.4 ॥

Shlok 16.4: Hypocrisy, arrogance, self-conceit, anger and also harshness and ignorance, belong to one who is born in a demoniacal state, O Parth.

Commentary: Any of the following attributes such as hypocrisy, arrogance, self-conceit, anger, harshness and ignorance can be characteristic feature of persons with demonic nature.

Hypocrisy– Pretending to be righteous, but having an unrighteous way of life.

Arrogance– Pride in one's learning, wealth, social status or family connections thereby living in imagined self-importance. This leads to self-conceit.

Anger– When a person of self-conceit looks at the world and finds that its estimate of him is totally different from his own, he becomes angry over everything around him which leads to audacity.

All these qualities arise from one's own self-assessment out of self-delusion and ignorance about the scheme of life in the world around him. This ignorance of oneself and his relationship with the world around is the cause of his revolt against his environment and the resultant eccentric actions. These types of people are called demoniac or *Asuric* in contrast to the *Daivic* or Divine people described earlier. The effect of these two types is discussed now.

दैवी सम्पद्विमोक्षाय निबन्धायासुरी मता ।
मा शुचः सम्पदं दैवीमभिजातोऽसि पाण्डव ॥ 16.5 ॥

Shlok 16.5: The divine nature is conducive to salvation and the demonic to bondage. Do not grieve, O Pandav– you are born with divine qualities.

Commentary: On hearing the features of the Divine and Demoniac natures Arjun starts wondering about himself as to where he stands. Hence the Lord assures him that he is born with Divine qualities.

Habits of sinful activity are very difficult to get rid of; therefore, one should always avoid sinful acts and practice good deeds. Basic morality is the backbone of spiritual life. Self-knowledge without moral virtues is incomplete and is hypocrisy. The world seems good to the good and evil to the evil.

Types of human beings

द्वौ भूतसर्गौ लोकेऽस्मिन् दैव आसुर एव च ।
दैवो विस्तरशः प्रोक्त आसुरं पार्थ मे शृणु ॥ 16.6 ॥

Shlok 16.6: There are only two types of human beings in this world: The divine, or the wise; and the demonic, or the ignorant. The divine has been described at length; now hear from Me about the demonic, O Parth.

Commentary: Broadly speaking, all beings created in this world can be divided into two types– the good and the bad. They represent good and evil tendencies. According to the Geeta, those born with divine nature have following qualities:

•Fearlessness, purity of mind, knowledge and concentration, self-control, charity, austerity, sacrifice, study of scriptures and uprightness.

•Non-violence, truth, absence from anger, renunciation, tranquillity, compassion, absence of fault-finding, freedom from greed, humility, modesty and steadiness.

•Vigour, forgiveness, fortitude, purity, absence of malice and excessive pride.

Lord Krishna mentions above distinctive qualities of a perfect divine person. In actual life, all these qualities may not be fully present even in a learned or publically adored holy person, not to speak of an ordinary person. It seems Lord Krishna has standardized a set of good qualities for which an aspirant for divine perfection should make efforts. This is an ideal to be achieved. As human beings are expected to make sincere efforts to imbibe as many of these qualities as is possible for them, during the present span of their life. Our present life is a field of action for the practice of these divine qualities. Every effort made to acquire these qualities is a step towards achieving divine perfection. This should be the aim of a true aspirant of God-realisation.

The Geeta also mentions the evil tendencies which are summed up as follows:

•Hypocrisy, arrogance, excessive pride, anger and harshness, ignorance, ostentation, excessive desires, delusion and wrong beliefs.

•Lack of understanding, lack of purity and good conduct, falsehood, cruelty in deeds, lust for wealth and possessions, obstinacy.

The above tendencies represent evil. The highest aim of the demonic is the gratification of desires– which are insatiable. They believe in the materialistic doctrine– eat, drink and be merry till you live and there is nothing beyond death. Such people fall an easy prey to all sorts of temptations in life and they do not hesitate to use even foul and wicked means to achieve their selfish aims. They have no regard for ethics and practice of moral values. Our world is full of such people and that is why there is abundance of crime, unrest, injustice and corrupt practices in all walks of life.

(**Note:** There can be a third type of people who have got the characteristics of both divine and devil, depending upon the circumstances. Moderate people, who stand between the two extremes, are always found in all societies. For instance, all the people on the Pandavas side were not divine nor all the people on the Kauravas side demonic.)

Traits of demoniac people

प्रवृत्तिं च निवृत्तिं च जना न विदुरासुराः ।
न शौचं नापि चाचारो न सत्यं तेषु विद्यते ॥ 16.7 ॥

Shlok 16.7: Persons of demonic nature do not know what to do and what not to do. They have neither purity nor good conduct nor truthfulness.

असत्यमप्रतिष्ठं ते जगदाहुरनीश्वरम् ।
अपरस्परसंभूतं किमन्यत्कामहैतुकम् ॥ 16.8 ॥

Shlok 16.8: They say, the world is unreal, without a moral basis, without a God, and without an order. Sexual union of man and

woman alone and nothing else causes the world.

एतां दृष्टिमवष्टभ्य नष्टात्मानोऽल्पबुद्धयः ।
प्रभवन्त्युग्रकर्माणः क्षयाय जगतोऽहिताः ॥ 16.9 ॥

Shlok 16.9: Holding fast to this view, these degraded souls– with poor intellect and bad deeds– are born as enemies of the world.

काममाश्रित्य दुष्पूरं दम्भमानमदान्विताः ।
मोहाद् गृहीत्वासद्ग्राहान्प्रवर्तन्तेऽशुचिव्रताः ॥ 16.10 ॥

Shlok 16.10: Filled with insatiable desire, motivated by hypocrisy, vanity and arrogance; holding wrong views due to delusion, they act with impure motives.

चिंतामपरिमेयां च प्रलयान्तामुपाश्रिताः ।
कामोपभोगपरमा एतावदिति निश्चिताः ॥ 16.11 ॥
आशापाशशतैर्बद्धाः कामक्रोधपरायणाः ।
ईहन्ते कामभोगार्थमन्यायेनार्थसंचयान् ॥ 16.12 ॥

Shlokas 16.11-12: Obsessed with endless anxiety ending only with death, considering sensual pleasures as their highest goal of life, and convinced that sense pleasure is everything, bound by hundreds of ties of desire and enslaved by lust and anger, they strive to amass huge wealth by unjust means to fulfil sensual pleasures.

इदमद्य मया लब्धमिमं प्राप्स्ये मनोरथम् ।
इदमस्तीदमपि मे भविष्यति पुनर्धनम् ॥ 16.13 ॥

Shlok 16.13: This has been gained by me today; I shall fulfil this desire; I have this much wealth and shall have more wealth in future;

असौ मया हतः शत्रुर्हनिष्ये चापरानपि ।
ईश्वरोऽहमहं भोगी सिद्धोऽहं बलवान्सुखी ॥ 16.14 ॥

Shlok 16.14: That enemy has been destroyed by me, and I shall destroy others also. I am the Lord. I am the enjoyer. I am successful, powerful and very prosperous;

आढ्योऽभिजनवानस्मि कोऽन्योऽस्ति सदृशो मया ।
यक्ष्ये दास्यामि मोदिष्य इत्यज्ञानविमोहिताः ॥ 16.15 ॥

Shlok 16.15: I am rich and born in a noble family. Who else is equal to me? I shall perform sacrifice, I shall give charity, and I shall rejoice. Thus they are deluded by ignorance.

अनेकचित्तविभ्रान्ता मोहजालसमावृताः ।
प्रसक्ताः कामभोगेषु पतन्ति नरकेऽशुचौ ॥ 16.16 ॥

Shlok 16.16: Bewildered by many fancies, entangled in the net of delusion, addicted to the enjoyment of sensual pleasures; they fall into the foul hell.

आत्मसम्भाविताः स्तब्धा धनमानमदान्विताः ।
यजन्ते नामयज्ञैस्ते दम्भेनाविधिपूर्वकम् ॥ 16.17 ॥

Shlok 16.17: Self-conceited, stubborn, filled with pride and intoxication of wealth, they perform sacrifices only in name out of ostentation, not according to scriptural injunction.

अहंकारं बलं दर्पं कामं क्रोधं च संश्रिताः ।
मामात्मपरदेहेषु प्रद्विषन्तोऽभ्यसूयकाः ॥ 16.18 ॥

Shlok 16.18: These malicious people cling to egoism, power, arrogance, lust, and anger; and they deny My presence in their own body and in others' bodies.

Commentary (Shlokas 16.8-16.18): Sri Krishna has listed the above attributes of man with demonic qualities in all the verses from 16.8 to 16.18. All the attributes are so clearly specified that there is hardly any necessity of point-wise discussion here.

The demonic people carry out all sorts of licentious acts to the detriment of others ultimately leading to the destruction of society as a whole. They bring about a discordant note of disharmony in the society and help plunge the world into disaster. Such desperate men with all anxieties and cares lead a futile life. Struggling to achieve the desired goals and to be anxious for preserving what is acquired are all the cares of their lives. Gratification of lust is their highest goal. Their firm conviction is that there is nothing beyond this in life. They become restless and impatient with their surroundings and lose their sense of judgement. Irritated and constantly unhappy with their environment, they become angry over unfulfilled desires. They ceaselessly try to acquire more and more wealth to satisfy their sensual hunger losing sight of a diviner principle of existence. Such persons live in constant consciousness of what has been acquired and always exert to acquire more and more wealth. As their desires are insatiable, they remain in perpetual disappointment and thirst for unlimited possessions. They do not know what is peace, harmony and joy in life. Ultimately they end in miserable death, exhausted and disappointed.

They always raise the cry of success claiming themselves to be the lord and victor of all their enemies. They boast themselves to be perfect, powerful, healthy, wealthy and happy. They look down upon the world with conceit, vanity and contempt and entertain the hope of rejoicing in the world. Sri Krishna says that these people are deluded by their ignorance.

In short, such people fall into hell because of (a) their fanciful egocentric ideas, (b) their judgement and discrimination getting eclipsed by delusion and false values and (c) their addiction to sense gratification.

Suffering as the destiny of the ignorant

तानहं द्विषतः क्रूरान् संसारेषु नराधमान् ।

क्षिपाम्यजस्त्रमशुभानासुरीष्वेव योनिषु ॥ 16.19 ॥

Shlok 16.19: These malicious and cruel-evil doers, most degraded of men, I hurl perpetually into the wombs of *Asuras* only, in these worlds.

Commentary: Sri Krishna says I hurl these haters, these cruel, sinful and mean people into the cycles of death and birth in the womb of demons or degraded parents again and again, according to their Karm.

Such men continue to fall lower and lower each day. They are full of egoism, brute strength, arrogance, passion and anger. A person of this kind of attitude would ignore the sanctity of life, become malignant and because of egoism would hate even the Lord Himself or the Paramatman in his own body and those of the others. They will hate to seek the Self.

These people are considered the worst among the men in the world. They are malicious against the dignity of themselves and cruel to the people around. Hence Sri Krishna assuming the role of the Law of Action and Reaction orders such people again and again to be born in the *Asuric* environments till such time as they realize their follies.

आसुरीं योनिमापन्ना मूढा जन्मनि जन्मनि ।
मामप्राप्यैव कौन्तेय ततो यान्त्यधमां गतिम् ॥ 16.20 ॥

Shlok 16.20: Entering into demoniac wombs, the deluded ones, in birth after birth, without ever reaching Me, O son of Kunti, pass into a condition still lower than that.

Commentary: These deluded creatures are born, birth after birth, only in Tamsic wombs and pass into lower and lower states. Without ever reaching Me, the Ishvar, they fall into a condition which is still lower than they are in at present. Without reaching Me: Certainly there is no room whatever even for the supposition that they will ever reach Me. The meaning, therefore, is, 'without ever attaining to the right path taught by Me.'

Three gates to hell

त्रिविधं नरकस्येदं द्वारं नाशनमात्मनः ।
कामः क्रोधस्तथा लोभस्तस्मादेतत्त्रयं त्यजेत् ॥ 16.21 ॥

Shlok 16.21: Triple is the gate of this hell, destructive of the onward journey– lust, wrath and greed: therefore let man renounce these three.

Commentary: Lust, anger and greed were created to control the entry of human beings into heaven and to lead them to the gates of hell. Lust, anger and greed disappear from the mind only on discovering that there is no 'I' and 'my'.

Selfish desire or lust is the root of all evil. Mundane desires are also the origin of all demonic qualities. These demonic or negative qualities such as anger, greed, attachment, pride, jealousy, hatred and fraud are born out of desire and are also called sin. Desire, when fulfilled, brings more desires, thereby breeding greed. Unfulfilled desires cause anger. Anger is a temporary insanity. People do sinful acts when they are angry. They, who act in haste under the spell of anger, repent afterwards.

It may be pertinent to mention here that heaven and hell are not out of the world or imaginary places or destinations. These represent actual, real life good or miserable living situations in the existing world or the reincarnated world (i.e. life after death). The above three evils are the main causes of making life hell in the real world. One must, therefore, take full care to avoid these tendencies and make life heavenly on earth.

एतैर्विमुक्तः कौन्तेय तमोद्वारैस्त्रिभिर्नरः ।
आचरत्यात्मनः श्रेयस्ततो याति परां गतिम् ॥ 16.22 ॥

Shlok 16.22: A man liberated from these three gates of darkness, O son of Kunti, acquits himself in a way conducive to his journey and goes onward with maximum speed.

Commentary: Lust, anger and greed are the source of illusion (*Maya*) that must be defeated before salvation is possible. When these three gates to hell are abandoned, the path to salvation is cleared for the aspirant. He gets the company of sages, which leads to liberation. He receives spiritual instructions and practises them. He hears the scriptures, reflects, meditates and attains Self-realization.

The Lord advises how even the one who has fallen so hopelessly can improve his spiritual evolution. He says that the one who has abandoned these three gateways to darkness will steadily progress towards the life's real goal. He will be practising what is good for him; good in the sense that which not only brings happiness to the practitioner but also contributes much to the well being of the others around him. Progressing thus in the right direction such an individual goes to the Supreme, reaches the goal of life.

Scriptural injunctions

यः शास्त्रविधिमुत्सृज्य वर्तते कामकारतः ।
न स सिद्धिमवाप्नोति न सुखं न परां गतिम् ॥ 16.23 ॥

Shlok 16.23: One, who acts under the influence of desires, disobeying scriptural injunctions, neither attains perfection nor happiness, nor the Supreme Abode.

Commentary: The world becomes full of sweetness and beauty for those who live their life according to the laws of the scriptures. Scriptures need not mean the ritualistic ones but they mean the texts discussing the theory of Truth– *Brahm Vidya*. A seeker should renounce desire, anger and greed. Anger is the result when fulfilment of desire is obstructed and greed is the consequence of satisfaction of one desire.

One must not find fault or criticize any scripture because the scripture is the foundation stone of righteousness (Dharma) and social order. One can get name, fame, peace and salvation by just following the scriptures. The study of scriptures keeps the mind absorbed in high thoughts and is a spiritual discipline by itself. One is delivered by the practice of the truth of the scriptures and not by mere lip service.

(**Note:** This verse does not indicate the name of any particular scripture, while this is very necessary because Hindu religion has got numerous scriptures. Different scholars or sages have emphasized the importance of certain scriptures according to their own choice and preference. Diversity of views is clearly evident from the diversity of Hindu philosophies. This is also true that all the scriptures may not be equally useful for spiritual life. There are scriptures which have been created or compiled to support the age-old dogmas, rituals, caste system, Brahminism, fatalism and the like. Under the situation, the holy Geeta is undeniably the best choice for one and all.)

तस्माच्छास्त्रं प्रमाणं ते कार्याकार्यव्यवस्थितौ ।
ज्ञात्वा शास्त्रविधानोक्तं कर्म कर्तुमिहार्हसि ॥ 16.24 ॥

Shlok 16.24: So let the scripture is your guide in determining what should be done and what should not be done. You should perform your duty following the scriptural injunction.

Commentary: The seeker should, therefore, follow the authority of the scriptures in conducting his way of life as to what is to be pursued and what is to be avoided. Sri Krishna concludes with the command that having known the scriptural injunctions regarding the right way of living, one should act here and now without desire, anger or greed. The drive of desire must be displaced by the knowledge of right action, but when the supreme end of the freedom of spirit is attained, the individual acts not from instinct, not from law but from a deep insight into the spirit of all life.

The Ten Commandments of Hinduism according to sage Patanjali (PYS 2.30-2.32), which should be followed are thus: (1) Non-violence, (2) Truthfulness, (3) Non-stealing, (4) Celibacy or sense control, (5) Non-greed, (6) Purity of thought, word, and deed, (7) Contentment, (8) Austerity or renunciation, (9) Study of scriptures, and (10) Surrendering to God with faithful loving devotion. This has been adopted in Christianity, Buddhism, Islam and other minor religions with a little variation in language. Almost all religions have emphasized more or less similar teachings.

All great masters have given us Truth revealed by the Supreme. Krishna taught us to feel spiritual oneness by seeing divinity in each and everyone. Buddha taught us to purify ourselves and have compassion for all creatures. Christ asked us to love all beings as we love ourselves. Muhammad taught us to submit to the will of God and act like His instruments.

In some religions, however, only the members of one's own sect are considered favourites of God, and others are considered infidels. The Vedas teach not only mere religious tolerance but the acceptance of all other religions and prophets as analogous to one's own.

The Rigved (1.89.1) has observed 'Let noble thoughts come to us from everywhere'. The dignity and welfare of humanity lie in the unity of races and religion. True knowledge of religion breaks down all barriers, including the barriers between faiths. Any religion that creates walls of conflict and hatred among people in the name of God is not a religion, but selfish politics in disguise. Simply beware of all such pseudo-religions in the larger interests of peace and prosperity of mankind.

Concepts and Issues

Sri Krishna discusses those traits of character that make a person divine or demoniac, since the former leads to liberation whereas the latter leads to bondage. The list of divine traits comprises of 26 qualities, the chief ones being: fearlessness, purity of mind, self control, scriptural studies, austerity, non-violence and truth, spirit of renunciation, compassion, forgiveness and absence of pride.

The other list of demoniac traits consists of six vices: hypocrisy, vain glory, egoism, anger, harsh speech and ignorance of higher values.

Then the description of the demoniac persons and their way of life follows. They know neither the performance of good works nor the need to withdraw from the evil ones. They have neither purity nor truth. They consider lust as the sole cause of creation. Being addicted to it, they out of delusion, try to get unholy things. They boast about their wealth or works and take pleasure in destroying their adversaries.

They dislike the Lord who is the Self of all beings. Such persons are thrown by the Lord into abominable births.

The gateway to hell that ultimately causes self-destruction is threefold: lust, anger and greed. One who is free from these attains the highest abode. But, for this, one has to act according to the scriptures with *Shraddha* or faith.

Is the world we live in at present any different with all its multi-pronged fight against terrorism, scams, man-made disasters, trade wars, territorial aggressions, gross injustice, etc? The guidelines set forth in this Discourse will certainly help us to know where we are heading for and provide us tools to take corrective steps, if one cares to improve oneself.

OM TAT SAT

Discourse - 17

Shraddhatraya-Vibhag Yog: Yog of the Threefold Division of the Faith

In Discourse 17 Lord Krishna talks about three kinds of faith, revealing that it is these different qualities of faith in the Supreme that determine that character of living beings. These three types of faith determine one's consciousness in this world. The subject of this discourse arises out of the question asked by Arjun in *Shlok* 16.1with reference to the final and closing advice of Lord Krishna in the previous discourse, contained in the last two verses therein (Verses 23 and 24). Arjun asks, 'What about those who, even though setting aside scriptural injunctions yet perform worship with faith?'

This Discourse deals with the questions whether it is sufficient if one lives with faith for a life of good conduct or is it necessary that he must know the scriptures in order that his faith will be subservient to the injunctions laid down in the scriptures. In short, the question raised by Arjun is whether even without the knowledge of the *Shastras*, blind faith alone can take the seeker far.

Shraddha is that powerful force from within propelled by which all the faculties of a person act in their respective fields. It gives direction to a man's determination and endows him with character. The Lord has stated that the faith of such men who ignore the injunctions of the scriptures could be *Sattvic, Rajsic* or *Tamsic*. This would be in accordance with the basic nature of the person himself. And, conversely, as is the kind of faith, so develops the nature of the man.

Thus, in all things like sacrifice, worship, charity, penance, etc.

these qualities become expressed in accordance with the kind of faith in which the person concerned is based. They produce results in accordance with the quality of the doer's faith. These acts done with right faith lead to supreme blessedness. When done without any faith whatsoever, all these actions become barren and useless.

Arjun asked:

ये शास्त्रविधिमुत्सृज्य यजन्ते श्रद्धयान्विताः ।
तेषां निष्ठा तु का कृष्ण सत्त्वमाहो रजस्तमः ॥ 17.1 ॥

Shlok 17.1: What is the mode of devotion of those who perform spiritual practices with faith but without following the scriptural injunctions, O Krishna? Is it that of *Sattwa, Rajas* or *Tamas*?

Commentary: This discourse deals with the three kinds of faith, according to one's inherent nature– *Sattvic, Rajsic* or *Tamsic.* What Arjun wants to know is whether these selfless activities undertaken with detachment and faith by those who do not wilfully defy the rules of scriptures but are ignorant of them, come under the category of unactivity (*Sattva*) or of activity (*Rajas*) or of inactivity (*Tamas*). The answer given by the Lord is an exhaustive treatment of the three types of faith involved in all human endeavours.

Three types of faith

Lord Krishna said:

त्रिविधा भवति श्रद्धा देहिनां सा स्वभावजा ।
सात्त्विकी राजसी चैव तामसी चेति तां शृणु ॥ 17.2 ॥

Shlok 17.2: The *Shraddha* of the embodied is of three kinds: the Sattvic (pure), the *Rajsic* (passionate), and the *Tamsic* (dark). Now hear about these from Me.

Commentary: The nature of man consists of his latent tendencies created by his actions, good or bad, in his previous lives. The faith of each man takes the shape, colour, and quality given to it by his nature, *Svabhav*, the stuff of his being, his innate substance. Man acts according to his nature; he cannot easily change it. One can transform a worldly nature into a spiritual nature only with the help of insight gained through the study of the scriptures with an indomitable determination. This faith is of three types, viz. the *Sattvic,* the *Rajsic* and the *Tamsic.*

सत्त्वानुरूपा सर्वस्य श्रद्धा भवति भारत ।
श्रद्धामयोऽयं पुरुषो यो यच्छ्रद्धः स एव सः ॥ 17.3 ॥

Shlok 17.3: The *Shraddha* (faith) of each is according to his natural disposition, O Descendant of Bharat. The man consists of his *Shraddha;* he verily is what his *Shraddha* is.

Commentary: The Lord says that faith is of three kinds, viz. *Sattva*– the divine, the good, *Rajas*– the undivine, the passionate and *Tamas*– the diabolic, the dull. Faith is not acceptance of a belief. It is striving after self-realization by concentrating the powers of the mind on a given ideal. It governs our view of life which in turn conditions our desires, thoughts and actions. It is the pressure of the Spirit on humanity. It is the force that urges humanity towards what is better, not only in the order of knowledge but in the whole order of spiritual life.

One can attain success in any endeavour if one tries hard with firm determination. You do not fail until you give up. The doer of good acts becomes good, and the doer of evil becomes evil. One becomes virtuous by virtuous deeds and vicious by vicious acts. We all have the power to change. One becomes what one constantly and intensely thinks of, irrespective of reasons, such as reverence, fear, jealousy, love, or even hatred. You always get what you look for– consciously or unconsciously. The thought produces action; action soon becomes habits and habit leads to success in any endeavour when it becomes passion. Become passionate about what you want to achieve, and you will achieve it. Intense desire brings out the dormant forces.

We are the products of our own thoughts and desires that have accumulated over numerous lifetimes. Thoughts create our destiny. We become what we think. There is a tremendous power in our thoughts to draw on the negative or positive energies around us. Where there is a will, there is a way. We should harbour noble thoughts because thoughts precede deeds. Thoughts control our physical, mental, financial, as well as spiritual well-being. Never allow any negative thought or doubt to enter. We have such a great power at our disposal, yet the irony is that we fail to use it. If you do not have what you want, you are not committed to it one hundred percent.

यजन्ते सात्त्विका देवान्यक्षरक्षांसि राजसाः ।
प्रेतान् भूतगणांश्चान्ये यजन्ते तामसा जनाः ॥ 17.4 ॥

Shlok 17.4: Good men (*Sattvic*) worship God, the passionate (*Rajsic*) worship the demigods and the dull (*Tamsic*) worship the spirits and ghosts (forces of darkness).

Commentary: Influenced by three *Gunas* individuals conduct themselves accordingly. People worship different gods, goddesses or deities according to their inherent dispositions, as they tend to differ among them with respect to degree of predominance of three *Gunas* in their personality. As Hindu religion is not a monotheistic religion, Hindus have got wide ranging options of objects of worship. They have got too many gods, goddesses and deities since the Vedic time. With respect to objects of worship or the system of religious belief there are differences among the people within the monotheistic religion also, as the *Gunas* are the universal features of all beings– both animate and inanimate.

अशास्त्रविहितं घोरं तप्यन्ते ये तपो जनाः ।
दम्भाहंकारसंयुक्ताः कामरागबलान्विताः॥ 17.5 ॥
कर्शयन्तः शरीरस्थं भूतग्राममचेतसः ।
मां चैवान्तःशरीरस्थं तान्विद्ध्यासुरनिश्चयान् ॥ 17.6 ॥

Shlokas 17.5-06: Ignorant persons of demonic nature are those who practice severe austerities without following the prescription of the scriptures, who are full of hypocrisy and egotism, who are impelled by the force of desire and attachment, and who senselessly torture the elements in their body and also Me who dwells within the body.

Commentary: No spiritual enlightenment can be expected in wasting one's energy in wrong channels in the name of religion. Sri Krishna says that physical persecution of one's own body and self-denial would not constitute an austerity following which one would expect spiritual unfoldment and inner personality development. Some people undertake severe austerities merely as a show out of egoism and hypocrisy with a view to satisfy their lustful desires and attachment to worldly objects.

Even if such people gain anything out of such austerities, they will only misuse their new found strength for wrongful purposes and ultimately destroy themselves. These people belong to the Asuric type. Such unintelligent practices oppress the bodily elements and also the Self or the Divine Lord within. *Hattayog*, for instance, cannot lead one salvation.

Three types of food

आहारस्त्वपि सर्वस्य त्रिविधो भवति प्रियः ।
यज्ञस्तपस्तथा दानं तेषां भेदमिमं शृणु ॥ 17.7 ॥

Shlok 17.7: The food preferred by all of us is also of three types, and so are the sacrifice, austerity and charity. Now hear the distinction between them.

Commentary: The choice of food, friends, and types of emotions entertained and the view of life in general are all indicative of the type to which the seeker belongs. In the choice of one's food, in the type of sacrifices one will make, in the kind of *Tapas* one will indulge and in the quality of charity one will make, any one of the three types of faith can be discerned.

आयुः सत्त्वबलारोग्यसुखप्रीतिविवर्धनाः ।
रस्याः स्निग्धाः स्थिरा हृद्या आहाराः सात्त्विकप्रियाः ॥ 17.8 ॥

Shlok 17.8: The foods that promote longevity, virtue, strength, health, happiness, and joy are juicy, smooth, substantial and nutritious are liked by the Sattvic.

Commentary: One should eat good food for protecting and sustaining life as a patient takes medicine for protection from disease. Whatever a person eats, his or her personal deity eats the same. (Because) I am Thou, and Thou art I. The food we eat becomes divided into three constituents. Food is called the root of the body-tree. A healthy body and mind are the prerequisites for success in spiritual life. The mind will be healthy if the body is healthy. Sattvic persons like the food which increases vitality, supplies energy, enhances strength to resist temptations from the sense objects, provides health, augments joy and inward cheerfulness. Persons in the mode of goodness like vegetarian foods. One can also become a noble person by taking vegetarian food because one becomes what one eats.

कट्वम्ललवणात्युष्णतीक्ष्णरूक्षविदाहिनः ।
आहारा राजसस्येष्टा दुःखशोकामयप्रदाः ॥ 17.9 ॥

Shlok 17.9: The foods that are bitter, sour, saline, excessively hot, dry, pungent and burning, are liked by the Rajsic and are productive of pain, grief and disease.

Commentary: In order to fulfil their uncontrolled passions *Rajsic* men prefer food that has strong qualities like bitterness, sourness, hot, pungent, etc. Although such food produces good amount of energy ultimately, it leads to a life full of pain, grief and disease.

यातयामं गतरसं पूति पर्युषितं च यत् ।
उच्छिष्टमपि चामेध्यं भोजनं तामसप्रियम् ॥ 17.10 ॥

Shlok 17.10: That which is stale, tasteless, putrid, rotten and impure refuse (such as meat and alcohol), is the food liked by theTamsic.

Commentary: That which is stale, tasteless, putrid, rotten, refuse and impure is the food liked by the *Tamsic*. The kind of diet we take has its influence on our power of self control. Purity of mind comes from purity of food. Truth is revealed to a pure mind. One becomes free from all bondage after knowing the Truth. Gambling, intoxication, illicit sexual relationships and meat-eating are a natural, negative tendency of human beings, but abstaining from these four activities is really divine. One must avoid these four pillars of sin. It is believed that abstaining from meat-eating is equivalent to performing one hundred holy sacrifices. There are people and communities which are very violent or aggressive because their food habits are such. Jains and Buddhists, for instance, have a strong preference for vegetarian food and they are relatively much less aggressive than those who consume non-vegetarian food.

Three types of sacrifices

अफलाकांक्षिभिर्यज्ञो विधिदृष्टो य इज्यते ।
यष्टव्यमेवेति मनः समाधाय स सात्त्विकः ॥ 17.11 ॥

Shlok 17.11: Sacrifice, enjoined by the scriptures and performed without the desire for the fruit, with a firm belief and conviction that it is a duty, is in the mode of goodness *(Sattvic* or pure).

अभिसन्धाय तु फलं दम्भार्थमपि चैव यत् ।
इज्यते भरतश्रेष्ठ तं यज्ञं विद्धि राजसम् ॥ 17.12 ॥

Shlok 17.12: Sacrifice that is performed only for show or display and aiming for fruit, is in the mode of passion (*Rajsic*), O Arjun.

Commentary: In order to get some chosen result some people perform actions, while some others do so merely for show off and to satisfy their vanity. These acts do not constitute Divine act nor can they bring about inward cheer or peace. Such sacrifices are termed Rajsic.

विधिहीनमसृष्टान्नं मंत्रहीनमदक्षिणम् ।
श्रद्धाविरहितं यज्ञं तामसं परिचक्षते ॥ 17.13 ॥

Shlok 17.13: Sacrifice that is performed without following the scripture, in which no food is distributed, which is devoid of *mantra*, faith, and gift, is said to be in the mode of ignorance (*Tamsic*).

Commentary: Disregarding all the requirements laid down in the scriptures, acting against all Vedic injunctions, i.e. acts which are against all the principles of right living belong to the lowest type. These actions in which food is not distributed, i.e. where no sharing of wealth with others takes place, where rituals are conducted without *Mantras* and without *Dakshina* or distribution of reward are all *Tamsic*. The distribution of food and the payment of the fee are symbolic of help to others without which all work is self-centred.

Three kinds of penance

देवद्विजगुरुप्राज्ञपूजनं शौचमार्जवम् ।
ब्रह्मचर्यमहिंसा च शारीरं तप उच्यते ॥ 17.14 ॥

Shlok 17.14: The worship of celestial controllers (Devas), the twice-born, the Guru, and the wise; purity, honesty, celibacy, and non-violence– these are said to be the austerity of the body.

(Note: This verse was inserted by some unknown compilers or commentators of the Geeta. Sri Krishna had no interest or reason to advise Arjun to worship the twice-born– Brahmin. Mind it here Sri Krishna is in conversation with Arjun only, not with the people at large. Those who have inserted such a verse did not understand Discourse 9 and Verses 9.34 and 10.8 in particular. Sri Krishna has already disapproved worshipping of others or even deities. He has clearly advised Arjun that since He is the Supreme Power, He alone should be worshipped.)

अनुद्वेगकरं वाक्यं सत्यं प्रियहितं च यत् ।
स्वाध्यायाभ्यसनं चैव वाङ्मयं तप उच्यते ॥ 17.15 ॥

Shlok 17.15: Speech that is non-offensive, truthful, pleasant, beneficial, and is used for regular study of Vedas is called the austerity of the voice.

Commentary: Speech that causes no pain to others, is true as well as pleasant and beneficial, regular reading and chanting of the scriptures—these are called the austerity of speech. Truth is the divine path by which the sages, who are free from desires, ascend to the Supreme Abode. To be truthful is desirable. To speak what is beneficial is better than speaking truth. That which brings the greatest benefit to a person is the real truth. The real truth is that which produces the maximum benefit to people. That which harms a person in any way is untrue and wrong– although it may appear to be true at the first sight.

(**Note:** This as well as the preceding verse (Shlok 17.14) has been inserted by the Brahmin scholars. That is why they have recommended worship of twice-born persons and Vedas. Since Sri Krishna is Godhead, He has everywhere suggested that He alone should be worshipped. He cannot suggest anybody to worship human beings and religious scriptures like the Vedas. In fact, at several places He has criticized Vedas on the ground of emphasis on elaborate and expensive ritual practices as a part of worship.)

मनः प्रसादः सौम्यत्वं मौनमात्मविनिग्रहः ।
भावसंशुद्धिरित्येतत्तपो मानसमुच्यते ॥ 17.16 ॥

Shlok 17.16: Mental austerity includes serenity of mind, good heartedness, silence, self-control, and the purity of nature.

Commentary: Cheerfulness of mind, kindliness, silence, self-control, purity of heart—these are called the austerity of the mind. The five noble values of life mentioned in verse 16 constitute austerity of the mind. They are:

•Serenity of mind– this is the result of one's healthy relationship with the world outside.

•Kindness or good heartedness– a feeling of warmth towards all.

•Silence– this is not only non-speaking but an inward noiseless calm wherein no passions and desires are generated.

•Self control– controlling of lower nature within us.

•Purity of nature or honesty of motive– the motivating factor for any action should be noble and divine.

Three types of austerity

श्रद्धया परया तप्तं तपस्तत्त्रिविधं नरैः ।
अफलाकांक्षिभिर्युक्तैः सात्त्विकं परिचक्षते ॥ 17.17 ॥

Shlok 17.17: The above mentioned threefold austerity (of thought, word and deed) practised by Yogis with great *Shraddha*, without a desire for the fruit, is said to be *Sattvic*.

Commentary: As the verse is easily comprehensible, it needs no specific explanation.

सत्कारमानपूजार्थं तपो दम्भेन चैव यत् ।
क्रियते तदिह प्रोक्तं राजसं चलमध्रुवम् ॥ 17.18 ॥

Shlok 17.18: Austerity that is performed for gaining respect, honour, reverence, and for the sake of ostentation, yielding an uncertain and temporary result, is said to be *Rajsic.*

Commentary: As the verse is easily comprehensible, it needs no specific explanation.

मूढग्राहेणात्मनो यत्पीडया क्रियते तपः ।
परस्योत्सादनार्थं वा तत्तामसमुदाहृतम् ॥ 17.19 ॥

Shlok 17.19: Austerity performed with foolish stubbornness or with self-torture or for harming others, is said to be the *Tamsic*.

Commentary: As the verse is easily comprehensible, it needs no specific explanation. Yet something is added here to help understand the verse properly.

Austerities can be of three types, namely austerities relating to body, speech and mind. If practised by men of harmonious nature with no attachment for their rewards and with utmost faith and sincerity, they are called *Sattvic* type. If these austerities are practised with a view to gain respect, honour and reverence and with vanity and ostentation they are called *Rajsic.* Austerities resulting in unproductive and painful self denials are called *Tapas*. Austerities undertaken with a foolish obstinacy involving self torture and not knowing its aim and indulging in destroying others is of the lowest kind. These misconceived, wrongly practised austerities undertaken by anyone for bringing about sorrow and discomfort to others or to himself, are considered as Tamsic.

Three kinds of charity

दातव्यमिति यद्दानं दीयतेऽनुपकारिणे ।
देशे काले च पात्रे च तद्दानं सात्त्विकं स्मृतम् ॥ 17.20 ॥

Shlok 17.20: Charity given as a matter of duty, when and where help is needed, to a deserving person or organization, who does nothing in return, is considered to be *Sattvic*.

Commentary: Charity in the mode of goodness is the best purifying, beneficial, and righteous act. It equally benefits both the giver and the receiver. If you give a charity or gift, watch yourself closely for ulterior motives; don't look for anything in return. One never does anything for others, but for one's own benefit. Even charitable works done for others are really done for one's own good. It is the giver, not the receiver, who is blessed.

Charity taken unnecessarily– compelled by greed for name or fame– does great harm to the recipient. Improper charity harms both the giver and the taker. Give anything you can– love, knowledge, help, service, prayer, food, but look for no return. Love, the cheapest charity, holds the key to enter His Kingdom.

यत्तु प्रत्युपकारार्थं फलमुद्दिश्य वा पुनः ।
दीयते च परिक्लिष्टं तद्दानं राजसं स्मृतम् ॥ 17.21 ॥

Shlok 17.21: Charity that is given unwillingly or to get something in return or looking for some fruit, is said to be *Rajsic*.

Commentary: When you give something to a needy person, do not make a big show of it, but when you help a needy person, do it in such a way that nobody will not know about it. Secret charity is considered the best charity. To give charity to an unworthy person or cause and not to give to a worthy person, are both wrong and worse than giving no charity. Charity that is obtained without asking for it is the best; charity that is obtained upon asking is the second best; and charity given unwillingly should be avoided.

अदेशकाले यद्दानमपात्रेभ्यश्च दीयते ।
असत्कृतमवज्ञातं तत्तामसमुदाहृतम् ॥ 17.22 ॥

Shlok 17.22: Charity that is given at the wrong place and time to unworthy persons, without paying respect to the receiver and with contempt, is said to be in the mode of ignorance.

Commentary: At the wrong place and time– at a place which is not holy, where irreligious people and beggars assemble, where wealth acquired through illegal means such as gambling and theft, is distributed to gamblers, singers, fools, rogues, women of evil reputation; wealth that is distributed at an inauspicious time. This does not discourage the giving of alms to the poor.

Be considerate and compassionate to those less fortunate than you. Charity should be given without humiliating the receiver. Charity given by humiliating the receiver causes harms to the giver. One should always remember that God is both the giver and the receiver.

That gift which is given to someone out of conviction that it is an act that has to be done is the right kind of charity. Even if the recipient of the charity does no service in return, the giver of charity does not to make any discrimination among the recipients. The gift is to be made with a right faith, to the worthy person, in the right time and in the right place. Charity must come from within and out of one's heart. This is of *Sattvic* type.

That gift which is given with the hope of getting some benefit in return or looking forward to some reward or given with reluctance is Rajsic type.

Gifts which are made at the wrong place and time to an unworthy person with contempt and with no respect are said to be of *Tamsic* type.

Threefold aspects of God

ॐ तत्सदिति निर्देशो ब्रह्मणस्त्रिविधः स्मृतः ।
ब्राह्मणास्तेन वेदाश्च यज्ञाश्च विहिताः पुरा ॥ 17.23 ॥

Shlok 17.23: 'Om Tat Sat'—this is declared to be the triple name of Brahm, by which were made the (Vedic) scriptures.

Commentary: *Om Tat Sat* is a sentence of three words, each denoting one of the aspects of the Reality.

•'OM' is the *Pranava mantra* that led to cosmic creation. As 'OM', it signifies the aspects of creation, sustenance and dissolution of the Universe by the Supreme Being. OM is discussed at length in many Upanishads, especially in the **Mundak Upanishad**.

• *'Tat'* indicates the Eternal Goal, the Changeless and the Ever-perfect, that from which everything has come, in which everything exists and into which everything merges back in the end.

• *'Sat'* means existence, the principle functioning through all things.

Here the word 'scriptures' refers in particular to Vedic texts. Invoking this sentence purifies all our activities and motives behind them. When invoked in ritualism it removes all defects in the worship, it being the name for Brahm. The Eternal Reality indicated in the triple nomenclature of Brahm '*Om Tat Sat'* is the source from which all beings. All super-impositions arise from, exist on and disappear into that which is their own substratum, the Brahm.

तस्मादोमित्युदाहृत्य यज्ञदानतपः क्रियाः ।
प्रवर्तन्ते विधानोक्ताः सततं ब्रह्मवादिनाम् ॥ 17.24 ॥

Shlok 17.24: Therefore, with the utterance of *'Om'* are the acts of gift, sacrifice and austerity as enjoined in the scriptures, always be Guna by the followers of the Vedas.

Commentary: Acts of sacrifice, charity, and austerity prescribed in the scriptures are always commenced by uttering any one of the many names of God such as *OM, Amen,* or *Allah* by the knowers of the Supreme.

तदित्यनभिसन्धाय फलं यज्ञतपः क्रियाः ।
दानक्रियाश्च विविधाः क्रियन्ते मोक्षकांक्षिभिः ॥ 17.25 ॥

Shlok 17.25: The seekers of salvation perform various types of sacrifice, charity, and austerity by uttering: He is all or *'Tat'* without seeking a reward.

सद्भावे साधुभावे च सदित्येतत्प्रयुज्यते ।
प्रशस्ते कर्मणि तथा सच्छब्दः पार्थ युज्यते ॥ 17.26 ॥

Shlok 17.26: The word *'Sat'* or Truth' is used in the sense of reality and goodness. The word *'Sat'* is also used for an auspicious act, O Parth.

Commentary: The context in which the terms– *Om, Tat,* and *Sat*– have to be used is explained here. Sri Krishna says that when the acts of sacrifice, gift and austerity are undertaken by the seekers the term *OM* is to be uttered to cherish in the mind the divine awareness of the supremacy of the Infinite. This adds purpose and meaning to all our acts of sacrifice, charity and austerity by freeing the mind from the egocentric attachments.

With the utterance of '*Tat'* alone which indicates the universal truth of oneness of all living creatures all acts of sacrifice, penance and gifts are undertaken by the seekers of liberation without expecting any reward. The word 'Sat' means both reality and goodness. It is also used for all praiseworthy actions.

In our daily contact with the world of objects we more often believe that this world, as physically observed, is the reality although it is only relatively real in comparison to the unchanging substratum, the '*Sat*', the Absolute Reality.

यज्ञे तपसि दाने च स्थितिः सदिति चोच्यते ।
कर्म चैव तदर्थीयं सदित्येवाभिधीयते ॥ 17.27 ॥

Shlok 17.27: Faith in sacrifice, charity, and austerity is also called Truth. Selfless service for the sake of the Supreme is verily termed as '*Sat*'.

Commentary: The term 'Sat' is used to indicate man's faith and devotion in sacrifice, austerity and gift. It indicates steadfastness in *Yagya, Tapas* and *Dana*. If these activities are undertaken with faith and sincerity with the chanting of *OM*– the Supreme, *TAT*– the Universal and *SAT*– the Real (the Infinite Brahm), the seeker's mind gives up all its selfishness, arrogance and ego. The principle behind this advice is that actions will create reactions depending upon the motive and attitude of the performer while undertaking such actions.

अश्रद्धया हुतं दत्तं तपस्तप्तं कृतं च यत् ।
असदित्युच्यते पार्थ न च तत्प्रेत्य नो इह ॥ 17.28 ॥

Shlok 17.28: Whatever is sacrificed, given or performed, and whatever austerity is practised without faith, it is called *'Asat'*. O Parth, it has no value here or hereafter (after death).

Commentary: Whatever sacrifices, austerity or charity done without being dedicated to the Lord will be of no avail to the doer in this earthly life here or in the life beyond hereafter.

Sri Krishna in this concluding verse of this Discourse emphasizes that faith is man and even if anyone performs most glorious acts without faith they are of no use either here or hereafter. Actions create effects depending on the faith behind the actions. The Lord states that whatever sacrifice is made, whatever penance is performed or whatever charity is given it is called '*Asat*' if they are undertaken without faith; they are mere barren actions. Such faithless actions will produce no results.

The Lord thus indicates that the spirit of faith is unavoidable and that without faith no progress or evolution can ever take place. This is true in this life and the life after death. Both in the secular activities as well as in the sacred performances of the religion, the factor that determines the quality and quantity of the result is our faith in our own goodness and in the field of activity undertaken.

Concepts and Issues

Arjun raises an interesting question whether the *Shraddha* (faith) of the people who worship the various deities, but without following the injunctions of the scriptures, is *Sattvic or Rajsic* or *Tamsic.*

Sri Krishna replies that such *Shraddha* can be anyone of the three types depending upon the nature of such persons, their mental make-up. The *Sattvic* persons worship Gods, the *Rajsic* worship the demi-gods and the *Tamsic* worship the ghosts and the lower Spirits.

Like faith, food also is of three types; so also sacrifice, austerity and charity. Food conducive to health, strength and purity of mind and is pleasant is *Sattvic.* Food that is bitter, sour or saltish, pungent and which produces disease is *Rajsic*. Old and stale food that has lost its taste and flavour, petrified, spoiled and impure is *Tamsic.*

Sacrifice done as a duty and according to the injunctions of the scriptures is Sattvic. If it is done with show and pomp and for the fruits thereof, it is *Rajsic*. The *Tamsic* one is bereft of all the prescribed rules is done without faith and lacks in *Mantras* and *Dakshina*.

Tapas or austerity is of three kinds: *Sharir*– pertaining to the body, *Vangmaya*– pertaining to the speech and *Manas*– pertaining to the mind. Worship of Gods and *Gurus* as also observing purity and continence is *Tapas* of the body. Truthful and inoffensive speech as also study of one's branch of the Vedas is *Tapas* of the speech. Peace of mind, control of thoughts and speech and a pleasant demeanour is *Tapas* of the mind.

When this threefold *Tapas* is performed with faith and without desire for its rewards, it is *Sattvic*. If it is done in an ostentatious manner for name and fame it is *Rajsic*. If done without regard in one's capacity and for harming others it is *Tamsic*.

Dana or gifts given as a matter of duty to persons of the right type and in the right manner belong to the *Sattvic* kind. If given with the desire for future rewards and not very willingly, it becomes *Rajsic*. Gifts given in contempt to unworthy persons, violating the rules are *Tamsic*.

The Lord concludes that the three terms '*OM TAT SAT*' which form a threefold name for Brahm, act like a magic formula if uttered during *Yagya, Tapas and Dana* and while correcting the deficiencies therein, if any.

OM TAT SAT

Discourse - 18

Moksha-Sannyas Yog: Yog of Liberation and Renunciation

The eighteenth Discourse, which is the conclusion of the Discourse between Lord Krishna and Arjun, is in many ways a summary of the foregoing portions of the Geeta. It briefly covers numerous important points dealt with in the previous discourses. Here we find the ultimate result or effect of the Lord's discourse to Arjun. The drama of Arjun's utter despondency and breakdown is finally resolved in triumphant self-mastery, strength and bold resoluteness. Its central message emerges as an assurance that through the performance of one's respective duties in life one can qualify for the highest liberation, if one performs actions by renouncing egoism and attachment and surrendering all desire for selfish or personal gain. By regarding the performance of your duties as worship offered to God, you obtain the grace of the Lord and attain the eternal peace.

Significantly, this Discourse opens with a question by Arjun asking what is true *Sannyas* and true *Tyag* (abandonment). In reply to this important query, the blessed Lord makes it clear to us that real *Sannyas* or renunciation lies in renunciation of selfish actions, and even more in the renunciation of the desire for the fruits of any action. Very clearly we are told that selfless and virtuous actions and actions conducive to the welfare of others should not be abandoned. You must engage yourself in performing such action but renouncing attachment and greed. The true and proper renunciation is giving up of selfishness and attachment while performing one's legitimate duties. This is called *Sattvic Tyag*. We neither hate unpleasant action nor are we attached to pleasurable action. As it is not possible for you to renounce all action, the renunciation of egoism, selfishness and attachment in your activity is declared as true renunciation. *Karma* does not accumulate and bind one who is thus established in such inner renunciation.

It was explained that there are three types of personalities depending on their temperaments or *Gunas*. They are *Sattvic*– good, *Rajsic*– passionate and *Tamsic*– dull. This Discourse discusses how these *Gunas* create differences among individuals in their capacity to sacrifice, in their wisdom, in their actions, fortitude and happiness.

The teaching of the Geeta has been wound up in verse 66 of this Discourse with an exhortation to offer all actions to God who is the same as *Moksha*. It is for these reasons that this Discourse has been entitled '*Moksha Sannyas Yog'* or Yog of Liberation by Renunciation.

The divine injunction is that God must be made the sole object of one's life. This is the heart of the gospel of the Geeta. This is the central message in its teaching. This is the one way to your welfare here.

Now Sanjay concludes his narrative by declaring that where there is such obedience as that of Arjun, and such willing readiness to carry out the divine teachings, there surely prosperity, victory, glory and all blessedness will prevail.

(**Note**: Since this happens to be the last Discourse, massive amount of insertions have been done here. A lot of such auxiliary subjects have been adjoined which have either far-fetched relationships or have no bearing with the precepts of the Geeta. Verses relating to the Varna or caste system, fading of Vedic injunctions and Brahminical orthodoxy have been included here and there to give them a new lease of life. This chapter has got excessive coverage on the *Gunas* and *Sankhya Darshan*. They do not strictly fit into or match with the messages of the Geeta. Many of the ideas have been repeated and over stressed time and again. It is because of interpolation that this Discourse has become the most voluminous with the inclusion of disproportionately a large number of hymns (78 verses).

Arjun asked:

संन्यासस्य महाबाहो तत्त्वमिच्छामि वेदितुम् ।
त्यागस्य च हृषीकेश पृथक्केशिनिषूदन ॥ 18.1 ॥

Shlok 18.1: I desire to know separately, O Mighty-armed, the truth of renunciation (*Sannyas*), Hrishikesh, as also of relinquishment (*Tyag*), O Slayer of Keshin.

Commentary: This Chapter begins with Arjun's question seeking the precise meaning of *Sannyas (*renunciation) and *Tyag (*relinquishment). These terms are used at many places in different contexts in the Geeta with varying meanings. Sri Krishna replies this question exhaustively. The central theme of this Discourse revolves around the meanings of these two words.

Definition of renunciation and abandonment

Lord Krishna said:

काम्यानां कर्मणां न्यासं संन्यासं कवयो विदुः ।
सर्वकर्मफलत्यागं प्राहुस्त्यागं विचक्षणाः ॥ 18.2 ॥

Shlok 18.2: The wise understand *Sannyas* to be the renunciation of action with desire. The clear-sighted define sacrifice (*Tyag*) as giving up all the fruits of action.

Commentary: We have used the word 'renunciation' for *Sannyas*, and 'abandonment' or 'relinquishment' for *Tyag* in this rendering. Renunciation is not indifference to work, but indifference to the fruits of all kinds of work. Renunciation involves giving up of objects, abandoning of work, or action. A renunciant (*Sannyasi*) does not own anything. A true renunciant works for others and lives for others. *Sannyas* means complete renunciation of doership, ownership and personal motive behind an action, whereas *Tyag* means abandonment of attachment to the fruits of all work, or working just for God. Although both mean giving up of desire, *Sannyas* is giving up of desire-oriented action, while Tyag is giving up of desire for the fruits of actions. A person who does sacrificial service (*Seva*) to God is called *Tyagi* or a *Karmayogi*. Thus a *Tyagi* who thinks that he or she is doing all works just to please God will always remember Him. Therefore, it is mentioned in verse 12.12 that *Tyag* is the best spiritual practice.

The words '*Sannyas*' and '*Tyag*' have been used interchangeably in the Geeta because there is very little difference between the two (See verses 5.4, 5.5, 6.1, and 6.2). According to the Geeta, *Sannyas* does not mean living in the forest or any other secluded place outside society. *Sannyas* is a state of mind that is completely detached from the outcome or the fruits of work. In short, renunciation (*Sannyas*) means full understanding that I own nothing; everything belongs to God or Mother Nature, including my body, mind and senses. True *Sannyas* is the inner renunciation of ego and not outer renunciation of work, wealth, home or worldly life.

त्याज्यं दोषवदित्येके कर्म प्राहुर्मनीषिणः ।
यज्ञदानतपः कर्म न त्याज्यमिति चापरे ॥ 18.3 ॥

Shlok 18.3: Some wise men say that since all works are tainted, they should be given up; while others say that acts of sacrifice, charity, and austerity should not be relinquished.

Commentary: As against the principles of work stated in the previous verse, some philosophers (*Sankhyas*) declare that action itself should be abandoned as it is an evil because it produces *Vasanas* obstructing the realization of the Self, while some others say that acts of sacrifice (*Yagya*), charity (*Dana*) and austerity (*Tapas*) should never be given up. However, the imports of Sri Krishna's teachings in the Geeta is that only evil activities are to be renounced and that all the spiritual activities and one's own duties should be pursued in a spirit of dedicated selfless devotion and thus transform the work itself as a homage to the Supreme.

Three kinds of *Tyag* (relinquishment)

निश्चयं शृणु मे तत्र त्यागे भरतसत्तम ।
त्यागो हि पुरुषव्याघ्र त्रिविधः सम्प्रकीर्तितः ॥ 18.4 ॥

Shlok 18.4: Listen to My verdict on relinquishment, O best of the Bharatas; relinquishment is said to be of three kinds, you tiger among men.

Commentary: As the verse is easily comprehensible, it needs no specific explanation.

यज्ञदानतपः कर्म न त्याज्यं कार्यमेव तत् ।
यज्ञो दानं तपश्चैव पावनानि मनीषिणाम् ॥ 18.5 ॥

Shlok 18.5: Acts of sacrifice, charity and austerity should not be abandoned; to the contrary, they should be performed because

sacrifice, charity and austerity purify the wise.

Commentary: This verse reminds one that even a so-called *Sadhu* or monk should never give up actions. A monk should perform austere work. It is a cleansing mechanism for the mind. Monks may engage themselves in teaching, gardening and even in daily chores like drawing water. Indirectly, the Lord is admonishing those young men and women who take to monastic life to avoid work and to escape from worldly responsibilities.

एतान्यपि तु कर्माणि सङ्गं त्यक्त्वा फलानि च ।
कर्तव्यानीति मे पार्थ निश्चितं मतमुत्तमम् ॥ 18.6 ॥

Shlok 18.6: All dutiful actions ought to be performed giving up attachment and desire for fruits. This is My firm and definite opinion, O son of Pritha.

Commentary: The Geeta insists not on renunciation of actions but on performing duties with renunciation of desire for fruits of such actions. This is a summary of the doctrine of Karmayog already dealt with in preceding verses. The defect in *Karma* is not related to action itself; rather, in attachment and expectation of a reward for work done. Even the sacrifice (*Yagya*), charity (*Dana*) and austerity *(Tapas)* should be performed without any attachment, i.e. without any sense of egoism and desire for rewards. If any action is performed with attachment, the expectations of its fruits affect the efficiency in the action undertaken. To get rid of attachment and to be free from anxieties regarding the expected fruits of actions are the key doctrine of the Geeta.

नियतस्य तु संन्यासः कर्मणो नोपपद्यते ।
मोहात्तस्य परित्यागस्तामसः परिकीर्तितः ॥ 18.7 ॥

Shlok 18.7: Renunciation of a prescribed action is not right. The abandonment of such an action is caused by confusion, and is declared to be dominated by sluggishness.

Commentary: Relinquishment of obligatory duties is considered as the worst. Obligatory duties mean unavoidable duties such as daily worship and special duties such as certain rituals on special occasions both individually and from the view point of the society in which one lives. As the performance of these duties makes the aspirant's heart pure, giving up of such duties is considered as *Tamsic.*

दुःखमित्येव यत्कर्म कायक्लेशभयात्त्यजेत् ।
स कृत्वा राजसं त्यागं नैव त्यागफलं लभेत् ॥ 18.8 ॥

Shlok 18.8: If a man relinquishes certain action merely because it is difficult or because of fear of some bodily affliction, his relinquishment would be dominated by agitation, and would not bring him any fruit.

Commentary: If anyone gives up his obligatory duties because they are painful or on account of fear of bodily suffering such *Tyag* is considered as *Rajsic* because for a man of action to perform his duties only so long as they are not risky to his person is no heroism at all. Hence the Lord says that such a person shall not attain any fruit of his renunciation.

Kinds of *Tyag*

कार्यमित्येव यत्कर्म नियतं क्रियतेऽर्जुन ।
सङ्गं त्यक्त्वा फलं चैव स त्यागः सात्त्विको मतः ॥ 18.9 ॥

Shlok 18.9: O Arjun, obligatory work performed as duty, renouncing attachment to work and its fruit, is alone to be regarded as *Sattvic*.

Commentary: Renunciation of attachment to sensual pleasures is the real sacrifice (*Tyag*). The perfection of *Tyag* comes only after a person becomes free from the clutches of attachments and aversions. Selfish attachment to the fruit must be first given up before giving up all attachments. There is no eye better than the eye of Self-knowledge, no austerity better than truth, no pain greater than attachment, and no pleasure greater than *Tyag*. One cannot become happy without *Tyag*; one cannot become fearless without *Tyag*; and one cannot attain God without *Tyag*. The Geeta recommends renunciation while living in the world– not renunciation of the world as commonly believed.

Jesus Christ did not hesitate to sacrifice his own life for the noble teachings. Lord Ram gave up His kingdom and even His wife for the establishment of righteousness (Dharma). Give up attachment and attain perfection by renunciation is the message of the Vedas and the Upanishads. Selfless service or '*Tyag*' is the essence of the Geeta as given in this last Discourse. A person who is *Tyagi* cannot commit sin and is released from the cycles of transmigration. The nine types of renunciation leading to salvation, based on the teachings of the Geeta, are as follows:

(1) Renunciation of actions forbidden by the scriptures (16.23-24),

(2) Renunciation of lust, anger, greed, fear, likes and dislikes, and jealousy (3.34, 16.21);

(3) Spurning of procrastination in the search of Truth (12.9),

(4) Giving up feeling pride in one's knowledge, detachment, devotion, wealth, and charitable deeds (15.5, 16.1-04);

(5) Rejection of selfish motives and attachment to the fruits of all works (2.51, 3.9, 4.20, 6.10),

(6) Renunciation of the feeling of doership and ownership in all undertakings (12.13, 18.53),

(7) Giving up thoughts of using the Lord to fulfil material desires (2.43, 7.16);

(8) Spurning attachments to material objects, such as a house, wealth, position, and power (12.19, 13.9); and

(9) Sacrifice of wealth, prestige, and even life for a noble cause and protection of righteousness (Dharma) (2.32, 4.28).

न द्वेष्ट्यकुशलं कर्म कुशले नानुषज्जते ।
त्यागी सत्त्वसमाविष्टो मेधावी छिन्नसंशयः ॥ 18.10 ॥

Shlok 18.10: One who neither hates a disagreeable work, nor is attached to an agreeable work, is considered to be a wise relinquisher (*Tyagi*), imbued with the mode of goodness.

Commentary: A man of Sattvic relinquishment never hates any disagreeable work and environment nor gets attached to any agreeable fields of action and favourable scheme of things. He does his duties undcr all circumstances, agreeable or disagreeable, without getting elated when successful or dejected when faced with obstacles.

He is not overwhelmed by joy or sorrow; he is always equanimous. He is independent of the happenings around him. Even the low impulses like jealousy, anger, passion, greed, etc. do not influence his action. He does not become a victim of his worldly desires. Such a man is considered to be pervaded by purity. He is said to be educated, cultured and with clear vision of his goal without getting hampered by all sorts of doubts. He is termed a man of understanding, a *Medhavi.*

न हि देहभृता शक्यं त्यक्तुं कर्माण्यशेषतः ।
यस्तु कर्मफलत्यागी स त्यागीत्यभिधीयते ॥ 18.11 ॥

Shlok 18.11: For human beings it is not possible to relinquish action completely. Therefore, he who relinquishes the fruit of his action is the real relinquisher (*Tyagi*).

Commentary: The Lord says *Sannyasi* is not giving up work or action. It is a kind of disinterest in the fruits or results of action. Everyone has to perform some action. The true relinquisher (*Sannyasi*) has no desire for fruits of his actions. It does not matter whether one is involved in worldly matters or retires to a forest or monastery. What is important is detachment from the results, i.e. not hankering after rewards; many a social worker is hooked on the results, which is why he or she fails to work with a sense of service or sacrifice. If *Tyag* of *Sattva* type is not possible due to attachment to the world, relinquishment of attachment or anxiety to the fruits of actions which will materialize at a future time is advised by the Lord. A man who abandons his desire to enjoy the rewards for his action is called a *Tyagi*.

Three types of fruits of *Tyag*

अनिष्टमिष्टं मिश्रं च त्रिविधं कर्मणः फलम् ।
भवत्यत्यागिनां प्रेत्य न तु संन्यासिनां क्वचित् ॥ 18.12 ॥

Shlok 18.12: The threefold fruits of action– agreeable, disagreeable and mixed– accrue after death for those who have not relinquished, but there is none for those who have renounced.

Commentary: Earlier three types of *Tyag* were discussed. Now three types of fruits of *Tyag* are explained here. The fruits of action mean not only the results of actions accruing at a future date but also the changes that take place at the mental level or in the thought process itself. Such changes or reactions in the mind are of three types, viz. the disagreeable– those that are positively bad, the agreeable– those that are positively good and the mixed– those that include both good and bad.

The Lord explains that the person who is genuine renunciant, for him actions do not bear any reaction, so he remains free. It is indeed the attitude of selfless action that prepares the individual for total asceticism and renunciation. His action becomes liberating and does not create any bondage in the present life or in the life hereafter. The pleasant, unpleasant and mixed reactions– *Karmaphalam*– are applicable only to those who have an ego-centric identification with actions as well as their results. Relinquishment of the sense of ego and the anxiety for the results and serving the world as a service to the Lord is *Tyag*.

Five causes of any action

पञ्चैतानि महाबाहो कारणानि निबोध मे ।
सांख्ये कृतान्ते प्रोक्तानि सिद्धये सर्वकर्मणाम् ॥ 18.13 ॥
अधिष्ठानं तथा कर्ता करणं च पृथग्विधम् ।
विविधाश्च पृथक्चेष्टा दैवं चैवात्र पंचमम् ॥ 18.14 ॥

Shlok 18.13: Learn from Me, O Mighty-armed Prince, the five causes, as described in the *Sankhya* doctrine, for the performance of all actions.

Shlok 18.14: The seat of action (body or substrate of action), the doer (the agent), the manifold instruments (sense organs and mind) and different kinds of activities. The fifth factor is fate.

Commentary (Shlokas 18.13-18.14): Cause consists in a dynamic togetherness of the immediate and the larger context, the doer, the means, the several different operations, and the fifth and the last, the unseen. The five causes are thus: They are the physical body (the seat of *Karma*), the modes of material Nature (*Gunas*, the doer), the eleven organs of perception and action (the instruments), various life forces (*Pran*), and the fifth is the Karmic impressions (or *Sanskars*, fate).

(**Note:** Since Sri Krishna is the Ultimate Reality, He did not have to explain any philosophy of life using the word '*Sankhya* doctrine', as it is a lower order idea. In fact, the exponents of *Sankhya* doctrine, who inserted this verse here, should have said that such and such views of *Sankhya* doctrine get support from the Discourse of Lord Krishna. Sri Krishna did not take part in the Kurukshetra war to teach *Sankhya Darshan* to Arjun. This is a kind of verse which has found place in the Geeta through manoeuvring. The '*Sankhya* doctrine' developed subsequent to the great war of Mahabharat. In fact, it has already been noted that Discourses from 13 to 18 are later day additions by some philosophers).

शरीरवाङ्मनोभिर्यत् कर्म प्रारभते नरः ।
न्याय्यं वा विपरीतं वा पञ्चैते तस्य हेतवः ॥ 18.15 ॥

Shlok 18.15: The action that a man initiates with his body, voice, or mind, whether it is proper or improper, is caused by these five factors.

Commentary: Sri Krishna says that there are five aspects of action or five-fold division of work which are laid down in the Sankhya philosophy. The five components of action are thus:

1. The body– *Adhishthanam*– the gateway for the entrance and existence of stimuli
2. The ego– *Karta*– which seeks fulfilment of the action through the body
3. The organs of perception– *Karanam*– through which the inner personality comes into contact with the field of enjoyment and satisfaction
4. The organs of action and
5. The presiding deities of the organs of perception which make them work properly.

The deities represent an unseen power other than the human factors. Each of the sense organs is controlled by a reflection of Consciousness called Presiding deity.

It is this non-human factor that interferes and disposes of human effort. It is the wise, all-seeing will that is at work in the world. In all human actions, there is an unforseen element which is commonly called luck, destiny, fate or the force accumulated by the acts of one's past lives. It is called *Daiva* here.

तत्रैवं सति कर्तारमात्मानं केवलं तु यः ।
पश्यत्यकृतबुद्धित्वान्न स पश्यति दुर्मतिः ॥ 18.16 ॥

Shlok 18.16: Thus being the case, he who sees himself as the sole agent, because his intellect lacks training, is a fool and does not see all.

Commentary: The one who considers one's body or the Spirit (or soul) as the sole doer does not understand due to lack of training or foolishness. The Self is always actionless. It is always the silent witness.

But a man of poor understanding attributes the person as real the doer because of misconception of the facts. He equates the body with the Self because of his lack of knowledge of the pure, actionless Self.

यस्य नाहंकृतो भावो बुद्धिर्यस्य न लिप्यते ।
हत्वापि स इमाँल्लोकान्न हन्ति न निबध्यते ॥ 18.17 ॥

Shlok 18.17: He who is completely free from ego and whose mind is not sullied, even if he kills these people, he does not kill and is not bound by the act of killing.

Commentary: Those who are free from ego, likes and dislikes for their work, and detached from the fruits of work become free from Karmic bondage even for the act of killing.

There is no bondage or liberation for Atman. Ego is the cause of attachment and desires that become bondage. Desire to know and attain Brahm ends all other lower desires. Ignorance-born ego is the cause of bondage of individual soul and the absence of ego is *Moksha*. Bondage and liberation are both creation of mind and are not real. Mind creates an imaginary notion of bondage and tries to be liberated. Just like wind brings clouds and also removes it, similarly the power of imagination of mind creates bondage and also gets rid of it. Cloud created by the heat of the Sun covers the Sun; similarly ignorance created by the power (*Maya*) of Brahm covers Brahm. Jeev forgets the Source and considers itself independent and different from Brahm. *Moksha* is attained by the knowledge of unity between Jeev and Brahm.

Knowledge and action

ज्ञानं ज्ञेयं परिज्ञाता त्रिविधा कर्मचोदना ।
करणं कर्म कर्तेति त्रिविधः कर्मसंग्रहः ॥ 18.18 ॥

Shlok 18.18: Three factors incite action: knowledge, the known and the knower. Instruments, the action and the agent are three components of action.

Commentary: Knowledge or the subject, the object (of knowledge) and the knower are the threefold driving force to an action. The eleven organs, the action, and the actor or are three components of action.

The impulse to action is made up of knowledge *(Gyanam)*, the known *(Gyem)* and the knower *(Parigyat)*. They indicate the experience, the experienced and the experiencer respectively. No action is possible without these three constituents. From the experiencer the impulse for action comes out as a desire, from the experienced as a temptation and from the experience as a memory of enjoyment. The basis of action comprises the instruments of action in the form of organs of perception, mind and understanding. The object of action is that which is sought for and reached through action by the doer. The doer is in the form of ego that sets the organs going. Thus an activity consists of (i) an agent having a desire, (ii) who maintains in his mind a clear picture of the end or the goal and (iii) who possesses all the necessary instruments to act.

The performance of an action, either to obtain or to avoid a thing, is possible only when there is conjunction of these three; if any one of these items is absent no activity can take place. All actions inhere in these three: the instrument, the object and the doer; hence, they form the bases of action.

Three types of knowledge

ज्ञानं कर्म च कर्ता च त्रिधैव गुणभेदतः ।
प्रोच्यते गुणसंख्याने यथावच्छृणु तान्यपि ॥ 18.19 ॥

Shlok 18.19: Knowledge, action, and actor are said to be of three types according to their difference in properties. This is taught in the enumeration of properties (Sankhya doctrine). Hear duly about them.

Commentary: Knowledge, action and the actor or the doer fall under three categories because of differences in the temperaments or *Gunas* in an individual at any given time. These classifications are exhaustively discussed in the following verses. Since knowledge, action and the doer are characterized by the three *Gunas*, they fall into the nature of *Prakriti* or Nature or Matter. They have no connection with the Atman or the Self.

सर्वभूतेषु येनैकं भावमव्ययमीक्षते ।
अविभक्तं विभक्तेषु तज्ज्ञानं विद्धि सात्त्विकम् ॥ 18.20 ॥

Shlok 18.20: You should know that the knowledge by which one sees one and the same immutable, undivided divinity in all

beings– such knowledge is *Sattvic.*

पृथक्त्वेन तु यज्ज्ञानं नानाभावान् पृथग्विधान् ।
वेत्ति सर्वेषु भूतेषु तज्ज्ञानं विद्धि राजसम् ॥ 18.21 ॥

Shlok 18.21: The knowledge by which one sees each individual as different and separate from one another– such knowledge is dominated by agitation (*Rajsic).*

यत्तु कृत्स्नवदेकस्मिन् कार्ये सक्तमहैतुकम् ।
अतत्त्वार्थवदल्पं च तत्तामसमुदाहृतम् ॥ 18.22 ॥

Shlok 18.22: Know that the knowledge is said to be dominated by sluggishness which is attached to no object as though it were the whole for no good reason, contains no valid truth, and is trifling.

Commentary (Shlokas 18.20-18.22): That knowledge which can recognize the flux of things, which can feel the harmony underlying the unity in the diversity of forms and behaviours, which can live in the awareness of the same life that pulsates in every living being refers to the *Sattvic* intellect. Through this knowledge one Imperishable Being is seen in all existences. Though the body, mind and intellect equipments take different forms in different living creatures, the *Sattvic* knowledge recognizes all of them as the expressions of one and the same Non-dual Truth, Atman, which is the Essence in all of them.

That knowledge which looks upon other living entities as different from one another is Rajsic. An intellect to which the world is an assortment of various types, behaving under various moods differently, an intellect that recognizes the world as made up of an endless incomprehensible plurality has Rajsic knowledge. Finding creatures happy or unhappy, wise or ignorant, ugly or beautiful, a man endowed with Rajsic knowledge thinks that different souls dwell in different bodies.

That knowledge which regards without any reason and understanding a particular path or view as the sole end and sticks to that opinion with arrogance and egoism, that knowledge which considers the entire world of things and beings as meant for its owner and his pleasures alone and which does not recognize anything beyond its ego is Tamsic. The irrational, baseless, and worthless knowledge by which one clings to one single effect, such as the body, as if it is everything– such knowledge is *Tamsic.* This knowledge is of the lowest type of spiritual seekers which ignores totally the Divine Presence.

In brief, the knowledge of the *Sattvic* kind perceives oneness underlying the universe, that of the *Rajsic* recognizes the plurality of the world and that of the *Tamsic* is egoistic with a perverted view of the world.

Three kinds of action

नियतं सङ्गरहितमरागद्वेषतः कृतम् ।
अफलप्रेप्सुना कर्म यत्तत्सात्त्विकमुच्यते ॥ 18.23 ॥

Shlok 18.23: An action which is obligatory, which is performed without attachment, without love or hate by one undesirous of fruit that is said to be of goodness (*Sattvic*).

Commentary: The above verse indicates how good actions are performed. *Sattvic* actions are those that are one's own obligatory duties towards the society, performed without any attachment to the fruits thereof and that are not motivated by likes and dislikes. These duties are just performed spontaneously. Fulfilment and joy are sought in the very work itself. Such *Sattvic* actions are undertaken only by men who possess *Sattvic* knowledge. A *Sattvic* action produces peace and harmony in the field of activity. It is an obligatory action undertaken for its own sake in an attitude that work itself is worship. Such inspired activities are undertaken without any attachment and any anxiety for the rewards. They are not guided by likes or dislikes of the performer. Action itself is fulfilment.

यत्तु कामेप्सुना कर्म साहंकारेण वा पुनः ।
क्रियते बहुलायासं तद्राजसमुदाहृतम् ॥ 18.24 ॥

Shlok 18.24: An action performed with ego, with personal motive, and with too much effort, is in the mode of passion (*Rajsic*).

Commentary: *Rajsic* activities are those that are propelled by desires waiting for their fulfilment that are performed in a self-centred vainglorious attitude of 'I'ness and which are undertaken with great strain and labour on the part of the doer. They are undertaken by men of *Rajsic* knowledge. *Rajsic* action is undertaken to satisfy one's desire in a spirit of arrogance, egoism and vanity. Such actions involve considerable effort and strain.

The consciousness of suffering, the sense that we are doing something disagreeable, that we are passing through grim suffering and toil takes away value from the act. To feel consciously that we are doing something great, that we are sacrificing something vital is a failure of the sacrifice itself.

अनुबन्धं क्षयं हिंसामनवेक्ष्य च पौरुषम् ।
मोहादारभ्यते कर्म यत्तत्तामसमुच्यते ॥ 18.25 ॥

Shlok 18.25: An action that is undertaken because of delusion, disregarding consequences, loss, injury to others, as well as one's own ability, is in the mode of ignorance *(Tamsic).*

Commentary: *Tamsic* actions are those that are undertaken without any regard for the consequences thereof and that bring disaster and sorrow to all including the performer. They emanate in an individual out of his misconception about the goal of life. They are undertaken by men of *Tamsic* knowledge.

Three kinds of people

मुक्तसङ्गोऽनहंवादी धृत्युत्साहसमन्वितः ।
सिद्ध्यसिद्ध्योर्निर्विकारः कर्ता सात्त्विक उच्यते ॥ 18.26 ॥

Shlok 18.26: A Sattvic person is one who is liberated from obsessive attachment, who does not speak egoistically, is full of firmness and confidence, and is unmoved by success or failure.

Commentary: A doer who has no attachment to the field in which he is acting, who is not cgoistic, who is full of persistence and zeal unmindful of obstacles on the path, who is not perturbed by the results of his actions, be they success or failure, is considered a *Sattvic*. He is ever conscious of the power of the Infinite Light in all his activities at all times. A *Sattvic* person does everything gladly in utter unself-consciousness, with a smile on his face.

रागी कर्मफलप्रेप्सुर्लुब्धो हिंसात्मकोऽशुचिः ।
हर्षशोकान्वितः कर्ता राजसः परिकीर्तितः ॥ 18.27 ॥

Shlok 18.27: A Rajasic person is one who is swayed by passion, who is eager to obtain the fruit of his actions, who is greedy or harmful nature, impure, and is moved by joy and sorrow.

Commentary: A doer who yields to passions, desires and attachments, who eagerly seeks the fruits of his work, who is selfish, greedy and insatiable, whose acts cause harm to others, who is not pure in his means, who is tossed between joys and sorrows of life is considered to be a *Rajsic* actor.

अयुक्तः प्राकृतः स्तब्धः शठोऽनैष्कृतिकोऽलसः ।
विषादी दीर्घसूत्री च कर्ता तामस उच्यते ॥ 18.28 ॥

Shlok 18.28: A Tamasic person is one who is unattached to an Ideal, vulgar, obstinate, deceitful, malicious, indolent, despondent and procrastinating.

Commentary: A doer who has no control over his own base mental impulses and instincts, who is arrogant, vulgar and obstinate in his own wrong conclusions, who is unsteady, despondent, deceitful, indolent, procrastinating and malicious is considered to be a *Tamsic* actor.

Three kinds of intellect

बुद्धेर्भेदं धृतेश्चैव गुणतस्त्रिविधं शृणु ।
प्रोच्यमानमशेषेण पृथक्त्वेन धनंजय ॥ 18.29 ॥

Shlok 18.29: Now listen Me explain, fully and separately, the threefold division of intellect and resolution, based on modes of material Nature, O Dhananjay.

Commentary: Three types of intellect or understanding are explained here. Understanding or Buddhi means the intellectual capacity in the individual to grasp what is happening around.

प्रवृत्तिं च निवृत्तिं च कार्याकार्ये भयाभये ।
बन्धं मोक्षं च या वेत्ति बुद्धिः सा पार्थ सात्त्विकी ॥ 18.30 ॥

Shlok 18.30: O Parth, that intellect is in the mode of goodness (*Sattvic*) which understands the path of work and the path of renunciation, right and wrong action, fear and fearlessness, bondage and liberation.

Commentary: A doer who has no attachment to the field in which he is acting, who is not egoistic, who is full of persistence and zeal unmindful of obstacles on the path, who is not perturbed by the results of his actions, be they success or failure, is considered a *Sattvic-Karta*. He is ever conscious of the power of the Infinite Light in all his activities at all times.

यया धर्ममधर्मं च कार्यं चाकार्यमेव च ।
अयथावत्प्रजानाति बुद्धिः सा पार्थ राजसी ॥ 18.31 ॥

Shlok 18.31: That intellect is in the mode of passion (*Rajsic*) which cannot distinguish between righteousness (*Dharma*) and lawlessness (*Adharma*), and right and wrong action, O Parth.

Commentary: A doer who yields to passions, desires and attachments, who eagerly seeks the fruits of his work, who is selfish, greedy and insatiable, whose acts cause harm to others, who is not pure in his means, who is tossed between joys and sorrows of life is considered *Rajsic Karta*.

The *Rajsic* intellect is not able to distinguish between righteous and unrighteous actions. The understanding that erroneously judges both the right and the wrong that makes faulty conclusions about what should be done and what should not be done due to inaccurate egoistic pre-conceived notions is considered *Rajsic Buddhi*.

अधर्मं धर्ममिति या मन्यते तमसावृता ।
सर्वार्थान्विपरीतांश्च बुद्धिः सा पार्थ तामसी ॥ 18.32 ॥

Shlok 18.32: That intellect is in the mode of ignorance (*Tamsic*) which accepts lawlessness (*Adharma*) as righteousness (*Dharma*) and thinks that wrong is right and turns all matters upside down, O Parth.

Commentary: A doer who has no control over his own base mental impulses and instincts, who is arrogant, vulgar and obstinate in his own wrong conclusions, who is unsteady, despondent, deceitful, indolent, procrastinating and malicious is considered *Tamsic Karta.*

The understanding that deems the wrong as the right, reversing every value due to ignorance, sees all things in a perverted way, always against the truth is considered as the *Tamsic Buddhi*. In fact this is no understanding at all; it can only be a perpetual misunderstanding.

Types of resolve or will and goals of life

धृत्या यया धारयते मनःप्राणेन्द्रियक्रियाः ।
योगेनाव्यभिचारिण्या धृतिः सा पार्थ सात्त्विकी ॥ 18.33 ॥

Shlok 18.33: The resolution with which the actions of the mind, the life breath (*Pran*) and the senses are held by Yog, that will, O Parth, is dominated by *Sattvic* (clarity).

Commentary: Three types of understanding (*Buddhi*) are explained. Understanding or *Buddhi* means the intellectual capacity in the individual to grasp what is happening around. The understanding that can readily judge things that are to be done *(Pravirtti)* and things that are to be avoided *(Nivritti)*, that can readily discriminate the beings and situations in its field of activity, that can distinguish between the right field of pursuit and wrong field of false ideas, that understands fear and fearlessness is considered as the *Sattvic Buddhi,* an understanding of purity.

यया तु धर्मकामार्थान् धृत्या धारयतेऽर्जुन ।
प्रसङ्गेन फलाकाङ्क्षी धृतिः सा पार्थ राजसी ॥ 18.34 ॥

Shlok 18.34: O Parth, *Rajsic* will is attached to duty, sensual pleasures, power and wealth, with anxiety and a constant desire for results.

Commentary: The understanding that erroneously judges both the right and the wrong that makes faulty conclusions about what should be done and what should not be done due to inaccurate egoistic pre-conceived notions is considered *Rajsic Buddhi*.

यया स्वप्नं भयं शोकं विषादं मदमेव च ।
न विमुञ्चति दुर्मेधा धृतिः सा पार्थ तामसी ॥ 18.35 ॥

Shlok 18.35: O Parth, the will (resolution) by which a fool does not cast off dreaming, fear, grief, despondency, and arrogance, that resolution, Son of Pritha, is dominated by sluggishness.

Commentary: The resolution by which a fool does not give up sleep, fear, grief, despondency, and also excessive conceit, that resolution is called *Tamsic.* The understanding that deems the wrong as the right, reversing every value due to ignorance, sees all things in a perverted way, always against the truth is considered as the *Tamsic Buddhi*. In fact this is no understanding at all; it can only be a perpetual misunderstanding.

Types of pleasure

सुखं त्विदानीं त्रिविधं शृणु मे भरतर्षभ ।
अभ्यासाद्रमते यत्र दुःखान्तं च निगच्छति ॥ 18.36 ॥

Shlok 18.36: And now hear from Me, O Bull of the Bharatas, of the threefold pleasure, in which one delights by practice and surely comes to the end of his sorrows.

Commentary: Happiness is the universal aim of life. But the source of happiness varies from person to person depending on the *Gunas*. It is the Guna which really characterizes the human nature. If Tamas predominates in us, we are satisfied with violence and inertia, blindness and error. If *Rajas* prevails, wealth and power, pride and glory give us happiness. True happiness of human beings lies not in the possession of outward things but in the fulfilment of attainments, especially in the case of those who are of the Sattvic nature.

यत्तदग्रे विषमिव परिणामेऽमृतोपमम् ।
तत्सुखं सात्त्विकं प्रोक्तमात्मबुद्धिप्रसादजम् ॥ 18.37 ॥

Shlok 18.37: That happiness, which is like poison in the beginning and nectar at the end, born of the purity of one's own mind, is declared to be Sattvic,

Commentary: The above verse defines happiness for which one should aspire. The joy arising out of the inner self-control and consequent self-perfection which looks though painful and arduous in the beginning, is enduring in the long run, in contrast with the fleeting joys of sensual satisfaction. It is the result of inner discipline and contemplation. This brings about tranquillity in the intellect and from this tranquillity of the intellect emerges Sattvic happiness. This happiness that arises from consistent effort lasts long and yields greater sense of fulfilment which is the result of an individual's balanced and self-disciplined life of high ideals and divine values of life.

विषयेन्द्रियसंयोगाद्यत्तदग्रेऽमृतोपमम् ।
परिणामे विषमिव तत्सुखं राजसं स्मृतम् ॥ 18.38 ॥

Shlok 18.38: Rajsic happiness comes from contact between the senses and their objects, and is at first like nectar, but at last like poison.

Commentary: The happiness which springs from the contact of senses with sense objects, and which is like nectar in the beginning and poison in the end, is the characteristic features of the *Rajsic* personality. Worldly pleasure arises only when the sense-organs are directly in contact with the sense-objects. In the beginning it is alluring but it creates a sense of exhaustion and dissipation in the enjoyer in the long run. It is also vitiated by the anxiety about its diminution and ultimate loss. Therefore, the temporary happiness provided by the sense-objects is termed *Rajsic*.

There are two main paths of happiness in society– the long- term beneficial spiritual path and the short-term pleasant path of sensual pleasure. The wise (the *Sattvic*) choose the former while the ignorant chooses the latter. It is the natural

tendency of the senses to go easily towards the external sensual pleasures as water flows downstream. Regrets follow the fulfilment of all sensual and material desires. There is nothing as intoxicating as the desire for sexual pleasure, which has infatuated even the mind of saints and sages.

Worldly pleasure is like a mirage in the desert. Thirsty persons reckon it as water until they come to drink it and find nothing. Worldly happiness is temporary and flickering, whereas happiness derived from spiritual life is permanent and continuous. A person may be healthy and wealthy but still unhappy without a taste of spiritual pleasure. The ultimate goal of human birth lies in forsaking all sensual and worldly desires and develops knowledge of and love for the creator.

यदग्रे चानुबन्धे च सुखं मोहनमात्मनः ।
निद्रालस्यप्रमादोत्थं तत्तामसमुदाहृतम् ॥ 18.39 ॥

Shlok 18.39: Pleasure that befools a person from beginning to end as a result of sleep, laziness and carelessness is called *Tamsic.*

Commentary: This type of happiness arises from (1) sleep– not the physiological every day sleep but the non-apprehension of Reality and the incapacity to perceive the goal of life, (2) indolence– the incapacity of the intellect to think correctly about the problems that it faces to arrive at a correct judgement and (3) heedlessness– ignoring the values of higher ideals. Such people dominate crime world.

न तदस्ति पृथिव्यां वा दिवि देवेषु वा पुनः ।
सत्त्वं प्रकृतिजैर्मुक्तं यदेभिः स्यात्त्रिभिर्गुणैः ॥ 18.40 ॥

Shlok 18.40: There is no being on earth, or again in heaven, among the gods, who is totally free from the three qualities (modes) born of nature.

Commentary: This verse concludes the discussion so far made about the three *Gunas* influencing the personality and the behavioural pattern of the living organisms. Sri Krishna says that there is no creature either on the earth or among the Gods in the heaven who is free from the influences of these three Gunas. The play of these three *Gunas* is the very expression of *Prakriti.* Put together they are the manifestations of *Maya* which make the individuals differ from each other.

With these three measuring rods Sri Krishna classifies the entire humanity under four distinct types. The criterion of this classification of man is the quality of his inner equipments responsible for achievements in the field of his activities. The fourfold division of Hindu society is based on this principle. Certain well defined characteristics determine these four classes in the community. They are never determined by birth.

ब्राह्मणक्षत्रियविशां शूद्राणां च परंतप ।
कर्माणि प्रविभक्तानि स्वभावप्रभवैर्गुणैः ॥ 18.41 ॥

Shlok 18.41: The actions of Brahmins, Kshatriyas, Vaishyas and serfs, O Scorcher of enemies, are apportioned according to their own inborn qualities of nature.

Commentary: In the ancient Vedic system, activities of human beings were categorised into four social orders, based on the three modes of material Nature. These four orders are often mistaken for the caste system of modern times in India. The activities of Brahmins, the Kshatriyas, the Vaishyas and the Shudras have been divided in accordance with the qualities of their nature.

Individuals differ from one another, because of the presence of these three gunas in different proportions in them. Accordingly they have different types of character and behaviour. Based on the presence of these qualities in different individuals, the Geeta classifies the entire society into four types. This classification is not determined by their birth in a particular household. Colour or heredity is not the decisive factors either. This classification is based on individual characteristics and inherent attitudes by virtue of which they are fit to perform appropriate function in the society. It is emphasized that caste, based on birth in a particular family, is not at all the basis to categorise these classes, as has become the norm in the present day society. The existing classification of Brahmins, Kshatriya, Vaishya and Shudras has resulted from selfish manoeuvring by the people with vested interests. Such people did not want their progeny to lose the benefits accruing from their respective ascribed status. Unfortunately, it has resulted into the prevailing evils of caste system which has divided the Hindu community into high caste and low caste individuals. This obnoxious and unnatural division has become the bane of present day socio-political system. This is not at all recommended or sanctioned by the Geeta.

शमो दमस्तपः शौचं क्षान्तिरार्जवमेव च।
ज्ञानं विज्ञानमास्तिक्यं ब्रह्मकर्म स्वभावजम्॥ 18.42॥

Shlok 18.42: Serenity, self-restraint, austerity, purity, forgiveness, uprightness, a firm positive outlook, and faith in science and spirituality are characteristic features of people trying to realize Brahm.

Commentary: As the verse is easily comprehensible, it needs no specific explanation

शौर्यं तेजो धृतिर्दाक्ष्यं युद्धे चाप्यपलायनम्।
दानमीश्वरभावश्च क्षात्रं कर्म स्वभावजम्॥ 18.43॥

Shlok 18.43: Heroism, vigour, firmness, dexterity, steadfastness in battle, charity, and the exercise of power are all Kshatriyas' tasks, born of their nature.

Commentary: As the verse is easily comprehensible, it needs no specific explanation

कृषिगौरक्ष्यवाणिज्यं वैश्यकर्म स्वभावजम्।
परिचर्यात्मकं कर्म शूद्रस्यापि स्वभावजम्॥ 18.44॥

Shlok 18.44: Those who are good at cultivation, cattle rearing and business (including trade, finance, and industry) are known as business men (Vaishyas). Those who are very good in service and labour are classed as workers (Shudras).

Commentary: As the verse is easily comprehensible, it needs no specific explanation

स्वे स्वे कर्मण्यभिरतः संसिद्धिं लभते नरः ।
स्वकर्मनिरतः सिद्धिं यथा विन्दति तच्छृणु ॥ 18.45 ॥

Shlok 18.45: One can attain the highest perfection by devotion to one's natural work. Listen to Me how one attains perfection while engaged in one's natural work.

Commentary: As the verse is easily comprehensible, it needs no specific explanation

यतः प्रवृत्तिर्भूतानां येन सर्वमिदं ततम् ।
स्वकर्मणा तमभ्यर्च्य सिद्धिं विन्दति मानवः ॥ 18.46 ॥

Shlok 18.46: One attains perfection by worshipping the Supreme Being– from whom all beings originate and by whom all this universe is pervaded– through performance of one's natural duty dedicated to God.

Commentary: True worship of God lies in the true performance of one's duty and this is the means to attain perfection. As the verse is easily comprehensible, it needs no specific explanation

श्रेयान् स्वधर्मो विगुणः परधर्मात्स्वनुष्ठितात् ।
स्वभावनियतं कर्म कुर्वन्नाप्नोति किल्बिषम् ॥ 18.47 ॥

Shlok 18.47: One's defective, imperfectly performed, natural work is better than faultless, perfectly performed, unnatural work. One who does the work ordained by one's inherent nature incurs no sin or Karmic bondage.

Commentary: As the verse is easily comprehensible, it needs no specific explanation

सहजं कर्म कौन्तेय सदोषमपि न त्यजेत् ।
सर्वारम्भा हि दोषेण धूमेनाग्निरिवावृताः ॥ 18.48 ॥

Shlok 18.48: One's natural work, even though defective, should not be abandoned because all undertakings are enveloped by defects as fire is clouded by smoke, O son of Kunti.

Commentary (Shlokas 18.41-18.48): All the verses from 41 to 48 have been inserted by those crafty Brahmins who were strong votaries of the *Varna* system and so also the caste system. The name of Rigved or Krishna is often used or cited to justify or glorify this moribund caste system. In fact, this system is contrary to the essence of the Geeta. All these verses are pure absurdity here, as in a way this supports caste system and casteism prevalent in Hindu society. Buddhism, Islam, Sikhism and Christianity have always stood against the Hindu *Varna* system. Because of this age-old belief in the *Varna* System, the Shudras or so-called untouchable castes have been vehemently opposing Hindu religion and its holy books, even while staying within the Hindu fold and many of them preferred to convert themselves to Buddhism, Islam, Sikhism and Christianity in the past out of reaction against the discriminatory social practices. Hindus, especially Brahmins and their supporters, have been no less accountable than propagators of other religious faiths for massive conversion of Hindus into other religions.

These verses reveal one more interesting fact worth noting here. Lord Buddha was the first great opponent of the Vedic religion. He and his disciples opposed caste system, dominance of Brahminism, multiplicity of God and deities, elaborate religious practices, and so the Geeta was made to incorporate elements of Brahminical ideology and Vedic philosophy as a matter of defence mechanism. Hinduism could not tolerate threat from the rise of new religion in the form of Buddhism. It was the first great jolt to the orthodox Hindu Religion. Fresh emphasis on the Rigvedic ideology obviously suggests that the Geeta was revised over and over after the 6th century BC to reinforce as well as revive Hindu religion under the new wave of Jainism and Buddhism. Excessive Brahminical interventions over the years have caused a great damage to the cause of social solidarity of Hindus. The caste system has encouraged enough internal bickering among Hindus. This defeats the very purpose of the Geeta, for the Geeta does not vouch for social discrimination. The sole purpose the Geeta is to attain liberation regardless of caste, creed and class. All such discriminatory verses have been inserted to indirectly support the Rigvedic view of Hindu social order, which ultimately undermines the glorious philosophy of the Geeta.

The path to absolute perfection

असक्तबुद्धिः सर्वत्र जितात्मा विगतस्पृहः ।
नैष्कर्म्यसिद्धिं परमां संन्यासेनाधिगच्छति ॥ 18.49 ॥

Shlok 18.49: The person whose mind is always free from attachment, who has subdued the mind and senses, and who is free from desires, attains the supreme perfection of complete freedom from the notion of doership by right knowledge or renunciation.

Commentary: The Geeta is not tired of repeating that restraint and freedom from desire are essential to spiritual perfection. Attachments to objects, a sense of ego, are the characteristics of our lower nature. If we are to rise to knowledge of our true Self, we must conquer our lower nature with its ignorance and inertia, its love of worldly possessions, etc.

The state of actionlessness or transcending all work does not mean complete withdrawal from all work. Such a question is not possible so long as we live in the body. The Geeta insists on inner renunciation. As the ego and nature are akin, the liberated soul becoming Brahm, the Pure Self, described as silent, calm, and inactive, acts in the world of *Prakriti*, knowing what the latter is.

The highest state is here described, not positively as entering into the Lord but negatively as freedom from *Kama* (desire).

सिद्धिं प्राप्तो यथा ब्रह्म तथाप्नोति निबोध मे ।
समासेनैव कौन्तेय निष्ठा ज्ञानस्य या परा ॥ 18.50 ॥

Shlok 18.50: Hear from Me briefly, O son of Kunti, how one attains Brahm, which is the highest state of knowledge, when one has reached perfection.

Commentary: As the verse is easily comprehensible, it needs no specific explanation

बुद्ध्या विशुद्धया युक्तो धृत्यात्मानं नियम्य च ।
शब्दादीन्विषयांस्त्यक्त्वा रागद्वेषौ व्युदस्य च ॥ 18.51 ॥

विविक्तसेवी लघ्वाशी यतवाक्कायमानसः ।
ध्यानयोगपरो नित्यं वैराग्यं समुपाश्रितः ॥ 18.52 ॥
अहंकार बलं दर्पं कामं क्रोधं परिग्रहम् ।
विमुच्य निर्ममः शान्तो ब्रह्मभूयाय कल्पते ॥ 18.53 ॥

Shlokas 18.51-53: Endowed with a pure intellect, controlling the self with firmness, abandoning sound and other objects, and laying aside love and hatred; dwelling in solitude, eating little, with speech, body and mind subdued, always engaged in concentration and meditation, taking refuge in dispassion, having abandoned egotism, strength, arrogance, desire, enmity, property, free from the notion of 'mine', and peaceful, he is fit for becoming Brahm.

Commentary (Shlokas 18.51-18.53): Endowed with purified intellect; subduing the mind with firm resolve; turning away from sound and other objects of the senses; giving up likes and dislikes; living in solitude; eating lightly; controlling the mind, speech, and organs of action; ever absorbed in *Yog* of meditation; taking refuge in detachment; and relinquishing egotism, violence, pride, lust, anger, and proprietorship– one becomes peaceful, free from the notion of 'I, me, and my', and fit for attaining oneness with the Supreme Being.

Thus a true seeker of a higher life must seek solitude, live in temperance, subdue his body, mind and speech and must live in a spirit of dispassion. The qualities that are to be renounced for meditation are: strength, arrogance, desire, danger and covetousness. When the sense of agency and the endless chase of sense gratifications have been renounced, the seeker experiences a relative quietitude within him. These verses do not say that such an individual has reached perfection but it only says that he is worthy of becoming one with Brahm. Forsaking egoistic pride, power, lust, anger and greed, free from the notion of 'mine' and being peaceful, one is thus fit to become one with Brahm.

The highest devotional love

ब्रह्मभूतः प्रसन्नात्मा न शोचति न काङ्क्षति ।
समः सर्वेषु भूतेषु मद्भक्तिं लभते पराम् ॥ 18.54 ॥

Shlok 18.54: Being one with Brahm, he should be serene, neither grieve nor desire; alike to all beings, he thus attains Supreme Devotion to Me.

Commentary: After relinquishing egoism and its manifestations in the form of power, pride, lust, passion and sense of possession, the seeker experiences greater peace within himself as he becomes free from all false perceptions or conceptions about himself. Note that according to this verse, there is a state beyond being one with Brahm. This is the way a devotee, one following *Bhakti yog*, interprets his experiences. For non-dualistic philosophers, however, merging with the Brahm is the end of the journey.

भक्त्या मामभिजानाति यावान्यश्चास्मि तत्त्वतः ।
ततो मां तत्त्वतो ज्ञात्वा विशते तदनन्तरम् ॥ 18.55 ॥

Shlok 18.55: Through devotion he realizes My greatness and who truly I am, and when he has come to know Me truly, he forthwith enters into Me.

Commentary: There is no doubt God can be known only through faith and unswerving devotion. There are numerous spiritual practices– not just one– prescribed in the scriptures to get that faith and unswerving devotion. The investigation of the true nature of Reality is defined as Bhakti (devotion) by Adi Shankar. The knowledge that there is no other than Brahm in the universe is also called *Para Bhakti* or *Ananya Bhakti*. Thus, Bhakti and Gyan are not different but complementary to each other. Self-knowledge and devotion are one and the same like a seed and its tree. The process of spirituality gets started by the sparks of Self-knowledge and surrender that bring faith and devotion. The law of surrender and divine grace is beyond human comprehension. Divine grace has to be earned by Seva and surrender to His Will.

Delusion of Maya prevents people from knowing and seeing God. As one cannot see the ever-existing salt in ocean water with the eye, but can taste it by the tongue, similarly the Self can be realized only by faith and devotion, not by logic and reasoning. God may be realized not only by meditation and Self-knowledge, but also through ecstatic personal love and intense devotion to one's personal deity.

The moment one knows Him, one becomes one with Him. The knower of the Spirit becomes Spirit. Knowing is becoming. To know the Self is to become the Self. No one can realize God without first realizing its real identity that one is not this body, but Spirit behind the body. After realizing one's real identity, one at once becomes Brahm. To truly understand God is to love Him and become one with Him. Liberation or *Mukti* is a state of mind when one does not need anything and does not want to know anything.

सर्वकर्माण्यपि सदा कुर्वाणो मद्व्यपाश्रयः ।
मत्प्रसादादवाप्नोति शाश्वतं पदमव्ययम् ॥ 18.56 ॥

Shlok 18.56: He who makes Me his refuge attains, by My grace, the state of eternal imperishability.

Commentary: Performing all actions and taking refuge in Him mean rendering selfless service in society which should be without the sense of agency and with a sense of dedication to Him. An individual thus working in the field of activity reaches the Immortal State, the state of Perfection.

The above three verses indicate that the ultimate goal of the paths of knowledge, devotion and action is the realization of the seeker's oneness with the Supreme. This is the Integral *Sadhana* synthesizing the methods of Devotion, Work and Knowledge through disciplining body, mind and intellect.

Such actions will not bind him with further karma. He should take refuge in the Lord. Then the Lord's grace descends on him… Note that finally it is the grace of the Lord that seals his life, taking him to the Supreme Abode. This abode is referred to as Vaikunth for devotees of Vishnu. In this verse, the Lord reveals the first time, the fact of His divine Grace.

चेतसा सर्वकर्माणि मयि संन्यस्य मत्परः ।
बुद्धियोगमुपाश्रित्य मच्चित्तः सततं भव ॥ 18.57 ॥

Shlok 18.57: Resigning mentally all deeds to Me and set Me as the highest goal. Always reflect on Me by keeping the mind ever absorbed in My thoughts.

Commentary: The Lord advises Arjun to surrender to his thought to

Him and regard Him as the supreme of goal of life to obtain His Bliss. Here comes the final concept of '*Saranagati*' or surrender to the Lord. This action of surrender to receive the Lord's grace is embedded in all religions. Only the terminology differs. The word 'Islam' means surrender or submission in Arabic. From this verse onwards, in the final chapter, the Lord explains two aspects: surrender by the devotee and the Lord's bestowing of grace. One should surrender with faith in the Lord, and then wait for His Grace.

Everything we use or eat should be first offered to the Lord, the giver of all things, before we put it to our own use. This includes– but is not limited to– food, a new dress, a new car, a new house, a new baby and all our work. Offering everything to the Lord is the highest form of worship that one has to learn and practice every day.

मच्चित्तः सर्वदुर्गाणि मत्प्रसादात्तरिष्यसि ।
अथ चेत्त्वमहंकारान्न श्रोष्यसि विनङ्क्ष्यसि ॥ 18.58 ॥

Shlok 18.58: You shall overcome all difficulties by My grace when your mind becomes fixed on Me. But if you do not listen to Me due to ego, you will perish.

Commentary: The Lord says by fixing your thought on Me, you shall by My grace cross over all difficulties, but if from self-conceit, you do not listen, you shall perish. This is a stern warning from the Lord. In the light of above, all actions should be performed with full understanding and constant thought of God without any sense of egotism. People may fail to have faith in the Lord because of ego or the pride of free will. Then such a person takes to evil ways and perishes due to his own actions. The Lord earlier promised that his devotee would not perish. But if one misuses his free will, and fails to worship the Lord, there is no salvation for him.

Karmic bondage and the free will

यदहंकारमाश्रित्य न योत्स्य इति मन्यसे ।
मिथ्यैष व्यवसायस्ते प्रकृतिस्त्वां नियोक्ष्यति ॥ 18.59 ॥

Shlok 18.59: If due to ego you think: I shall not fight, your resolve is vain because your own nature will compel you to fight.

Commentary: As the verse is easily comprehensible, it needs no specific explanation.

स्वभावजेन कौन्तेय निबद्धः स्वेन कर्मणा ।
कर्तुं नेच्छसि यन्मोहात् करिष्यस्यवशोऽपि तत् ॥ 18.60 ॥

Shlok 18.60: O son of Kunti, you are bound by your own nature-born Karmic impressions (*Sanskar*). Therefore, you shall do– even against your will– what you do not wish to do out of delusion.

Commentary: The mind often knows right and wrong, but it runs after evil, reluctantly, by the force of Karmic footprints (*Sanskar*). The wise should always keep this in mind before finding fault with others. Sri Krishna tells Arjun that if he is under the impression that he would not fight due to self-importance, self-conceit and the temporary illusion of escapism, it would merely be an exercise in futility because being a Kshatriya, his Rajsic temperament will dominate and force him to fight. The Lord continues that in spite of his determination not to wage war Arjun will be compelled to fight by the power of his own nature ordered by his Karma or *Vasanas* existing in him at that moment. This is the law of life.

(**Note:** As the most commentators of the Geeta belong to the Brahmin or other upper caste category, here Arjun has been called Kshatriya by Krishna. This is a pure misrepresentation of fact. Nobody knew the actual caste of Arjun, as caste did not develop those days. Within the system of *Varna vyvastha* movement of an individual from one *Varna* to another was not prohibited. People were largely free to move from one social stratum to another. There was no rigid social order like the caste system those days. One of the wives of Arjun (Rukmini) was the sister of Sri Krishna who was a Yadav or Ahir. It is not proper to look at the Mahabharat's characters from any caste angle as the present day Indians tend to do.)

We become the puppets of our own freewill

ईश्वरः सर्वभूतानां हृद्देशेऽर्जुन तिष्ठति ।
भ्रामयन् सर्वभूतानि यंत्रारूढानि मायया ॥ 18.61 ॥

Shlok 18.61: The Lord dwells in the hearts of all beings, O Arjun, causing all beings to act by His illusive power as if they were mounted on a machine.

Commentary: The Supreme Lord (Ishvar) is the reflection of the

Supreme Spirit in the body. The Supreme Lord organizes controls, supervises, and directs everything in the universe. The indwelling Lord makes us spin around with desires, bodily activities, restless mind and feverish intellect. We are mere puppets in His hands– the Puppeteer. This verse should make us humble and surrender unto him

The Lord has made *Karmic* laws as the controller of all living beings. Therefore, one must learn to gladly endure all that fate imposes by taking refuge in Him and following the commandments. Vedas declare that the Lord, using *Karma*, makes us dance as a juggler would make his pet monkey dance. Without the laws of *Karma*, the scriptural injunctions, prohibitions, as well as self-effort, would have no value at all. *Karma* is the eternal justice and the eternal law. As a result of the working of eternal justice, there can be no escape from the consequences of our deeds.

People cannot escape from the consequences of their deeds, for as we sow, so we reap. Cause and effect cannot be separated because the effect exists in the cause as the fruit exists in the seed. Good and evil deeds follow us continually like our shadows.

One cannot take wealth, fame, and power from here to hereafter; but one can convert these into good or bad Karma and carry it to the next life. Even death cannot touch one's Karma. Those who have acted very piously in the past life achieve fame in this life without much endeavour.

तमेव शरणं गच्छ सर्वभावेन भारत ।
तत्प्रसादात्परां शान्तिं स्थानं प्राप्स्यसि शाश्वतम् ॥ 18.62 ॥

Shlok 18.62: Go to Him for refuge with all your being, O Bharat! With His grace you will reach supreme peace, the Eternal Abode.

Commentary: Arjun is advised to take refuge in the Supreme Lord alone, with loving devotion. His grace would help the people attain supreme peace and the eternal abode. This famous verse is the essential message to a devotee or *Bhakta*—one following *Bhakti Yog*. We must recognize Lord Krishna and then surrender to Him; and then wait for His Grace. When one reaches the eternal abode of the Lord, *Vaikunth*, there is no return, no more births. Vaikunth is taken as a place of eternal joy, the abode of the Lord; but in metaphysical terms, it is the state of cosmic consciousness.

इति ते ज्ञानमाख्यातं गुह्याद् गुह्यतरं मया ।
विमृश्यैतदशेषेण यथेच्छसि तथा कुरु ॥ 18.63 ॥

Shlok 18.63: Thus I have imparted you the most secret knowledge of all. After fully reflecting on this in its entirety, you can do what you like.

Commentary: This verse can be considered as the conclusion of the Lord's Discourses to Arjun in the battlefield of Kurukshetra. Sri Krishna says that he has declared to Arjun (through him to the entire humanity) all the essential features of the right way of living and its noble endeavours for which there is nothing more to add.

Sri Krishna advises Arjun to think and reflect over what all He had declared and thereafter take such decision as he thinks proper without blindly accepting what has been told to him. Teaching is not indoctrination. Thus the Lord leaves the decision to act and lead a higher life to Arjun's own free choice after considering all the points brought to his notice. Even after all this advice, Arjun retains the free will—he may or may not surrender to Krishna, he may still refuse to fight the righteous battle against his cousins. It is left to his will; the Lord respects the free will of Arjun!

There is no compulsion involved and free choice is the characteristic of Hinduism as the human personality cannot grow morally and ethically through coercion. The Supreme does not impose His command; we are free at any moment to reject or accept the Divine call. The integral surrender should be made with the fullest consent of the seeker. God does not do the climbing for us but supports us whenever we stumble, comfort us when we fall. He is prepared to wait till we turn to Him. Thus the Lord's approach is counselling but not commanding. The scriptures serve the purpose of telling man what he should do and what he should not. It is up to man himself to choose the right and to reject the wrong.

सर्वगुह्यतमं भूयः शृणु मे परमं वचः ।
इष्टोऽसि मे दृढमिति ततो वक्ष्यामि ते हितम् ॥ 18.64 ॥

Shlok 18.64: Listen once again My supreme word, the

profoundest of all because you are very dear to Me; therefore, I shall speak what is good to you.

Commentary: Although Arjun was given a free choice to make his independent decision he gave an impression that still some doubts and misgivings were lurking in his mind. Therefore, Sri Krishna tells Arjun that He will again confide in him the profoundest wisdom, the supreme secret because he is His dearest friend. This secret is revealed in the following two verses.

मन्मना भव मद्भक्तो मद्याजी मां नमस्कुरु ।
मामेवैष्यसि सत्यं ते प्रतिजाने प्रियोऽसि मे ॥ 18.65 ॥

Shlok 18.65: Fix your mind on Me; be devoted to Me; let your speech be a praise of My glories, prostrate yourself before Me, so you will come to me. I promise you because you are dear to Me.

Commentary: The Lord lays down four conditions for the success of a seeker. To the one in whom these are present an assurance of reaching Him is given. These conditions are:

- Fix the mind on the Lord, ever remembering Him.
- Regard Him as the sole refuge.
- Ever devotedly identify with Him through the process of performing selfless activities and
- Dedicate them to Him in an attitude of reverence and sacrifice.

Thought, worship, sacrifice and reverence, all must be directed to the Lord. We must surrender ourselves to God. Our spiritual life depends as much on our going to Him, as on His coming to us. It is not only our ascent to God but His descent to man. He is waiting only for our trustful appeal to Him.

The ultimate path to God

सर्वधर्मान्परित्यज्य मामेकं शरणं व्रज ।
अहं त्वा सर्वपापेभ्यो मोक्षयिष्यामि मा शुचः ॥ 18.66 ॥

Shlok 18.66: Abandoning all duties, come to Me alone for shelter. Be not grieved, for I shall release you from all evils.

Commentary: The above verses show the way to reach God through devotion and complete surrender to Him. This is the noblest of all the verses in the Geeta having brilliant import and yet this is the most controversial. Philosophers, translators, reviewers, critics and commentators have put forward several interpretations of this verse each maintaining their own point of view. To Sri Ramanuj, this is the final verse (*Charam-Shloka*) of the whole Geeta.

The stanza is important inasmuch as it is one of the most powerfully worded verses in the Geeta wherein the Lord undertakes to do something helpful for the seeker in case he is ready to obliterate his ego and put forth his best efforts. When we turn to Him and let Him fill our whole being, our responsibility ceases. He deals with us and leads us beyond all sorrow.

Surrendering to God does not involve leaving the world, but realizing that everything happens in accordance with His laws and by His direction and power. To fully recognize that everything is controlled and governed by a divine plan and order is to surrender to Him. Learn to accept all results as His Will. Soul is unable to get out of the trap of Maya without help from the Source. As birds seek the shelter of a tree when tired, similarly human beings should seek the divine shelter after long spiritual journey to attain union with Him.

Sri Krishna says, abandon all duties, take refuge in Me alone; I will liberate you from all sins. Hence you need not grieve. Setting aside all 'Dharmas' also means perform all duties (Dharmas) setting aside doership, attachment and ego or the false notion that an individual soul (*Jeev*) is separate, independent and different from Brahm. Ego stands on our way to God. It is not possible to progress on our spiritual journey without first renouncing ego, the origin of doership, ownership, and attachment to all works.

Surrendering is giving up confidence in our own effort and depending on God. Get rid of confidence in your self-effort and replace it with confidence in divine help. It is giving up sole reliance to one's effort alone to reach Him. God can be discovered by seeking His help in discovering Him and not by spiritual practices alone. Surrendering to Lord alone means turning only to Him for help. Give up individual will and accept the Will of God because the world is controlled by the laws or Will of God. One has to learn to abide by His Will. Be thankful in prosperity and resigned to His Will in adversity.

In this Verse, the Lord wants us to accomplish three distinct adjustments in our inner personality. They are: (1) Renounce all Dharmas through meditation; (2) surrender to My refuge alone; and while in the state of meditation, (3) stop all worries. And as a reward He promises: 'I shall release you from all sins'. This is a promise given to all mankind.

The concept of surrender to the Supreme Being as a means for liberation or final Beatitude is to be found in all religions—including Christianity and Islam. In the Bhagavad Geeta, especially in the last chapter, this method is expounded as the principal means for a devotee.

It may be concluded from what has been stated above that the same idea has been explained in several ways. Whether it is highest perfection, highest peace, freedom from all sorrows or evils, freedom from bondage, liberation of soul, purity of the spirit, reaching the Supreme the Absolute, the life eternal, the beatitude of God or some other similar state– all pointers lead to the same conclusion. The goal of life, therefore, may be summed up as God-realisation, which is the highest stage of spiritual attainment, beyond which there is nothing else to be attained.

इदं ते नातपस्काय नाभक्ताय कदाचन ।
न चाशुश्रूषवे वाच्यं न च मां योऽभ्यसूयति ॥ 18.67 ॥

Shlok 18.67: You must never mention this to one who is devoid of austerity, who is without devotion, who does not desire to listen, or one who bears a grudge against Me.

Commentary: Sri Krishna advises that this knowledge should not be spoken by you to one who is devoid of austerities, to one who is not devoted, nor to one who does not render service, nor who does not desire to listen, nor to one who speaks ill of Me. One should not force others to believe. The study of the Geeta is meant only for sincere persons. The recipient of knowledge must have spiritual inclination and sincerely seek it. Knowledge given without being asked for serves no purpose and should be avoided. There is a time for everything under the heaven. We cannot change the world; we can change only the lives of a few sincere souls whose time for a change has come.

Service to God and charity

य इदं परमं गुह्यं मद्भक्तेष्वभिधास्यति ।
भक्तिं मयि परां कृत्वा मामेवैष्यत्यसंशयः ॥ 18.68 ॥
न च तस्मान्मनुष्येषु कश्चिन्मे प्रियकृत्तमः ।
भविता न च मे तस्मादन्यः प्रियतरो भुवि ॥ 18.69 ॥

Shlokas 18.68-69: He, who with supreme devotion to Me will teach this supreme secret to My devotees, shall undoubtedly come to Me. And no one among men is a better friend to Me than he, nor will anyone else on the earth dearer to Me than he.

Commentary: Sri Krishna says that one who shall study and help propagate this supreme secret philosophy amongst My devotees shall be performing the highest devotional service (*Parabhakti*) to Me and shall certainly come to Me. He who hands down this *Geeta* to My devotees does immense service to Me. He is extremely dear to Me. In the present generation, there will be none dearer to Me in the world, nor shall there be in the future also. No other person shall do a more pleasing service to Me, and no one on the earth shall be dearer to Me. *Parabhakti*, Self-knowledge and *Moksha* to be obtained by spiritual practices as mentioned in verses 18.54-55 can be easily obtained by propagating the Supreme philosophy of the Geeta. The giving of the gift of knowledge is the best charity. It is equivalent to giving the whole world in charity. The best welfare is to help others discover their real nature that is the source of everlasting happiness rather than to provide material goods and comforts for temporary happiness. Happiness is not attained through wealth and sense gratification, but through fidelity to a worthy cause.

Grace of the Geeta

अध्येष्यते च य इमं धर्म्यं संवादमावयोः ।
ज्ञानयज्ञेन तेनाहमिष्टः स्यामिति मे मतिः ॥ 18.70 ॥

Shlok 18.70: I believe that I will be loved by him who recites this, our dialogue which is faithful to the law, as a sacrifice of knowledge.

Commentary: Those who study our sacred dialogue shall be performing a holy act of propagation and acquisition of Self-knowledge;

such is My conviction. God and His words are one and the same. The study of the Geeta is equivalent to worship of God. Life in modern society is all work and no spirituality. In verses 18.68-70 Lord Krishna declares that studying, teaching, and propagating the spiritual knowledge of the Geeta in any way to be the highest form of *Karmayog, Bhaktiyog* and *Gyanayog* combined in one. This alone can take a seeker to enlightenment.

श्रद्धावाननसूयश्च शृणुयादपि यो नरः ।
सोऽपि मुक्तः शुभाँल्लोकान्प्राप्नुयात्पुण्यकर्मणाम् ॥ 18.71 ॥

Shlok 18.71: Whoever even listens this sacred dialogue, with *Shraddha* (faith) and free from malice, he, too, is liberated and shall attain to the happy worlds of those of righteous deeds.

Commentary: A summary of the glory of the Geeta as elaborated in the scriptures is given below. Reading this glory of the Geeta generates faith and devotion in the heart that is essential for reaping the benefits of the study of the Geeta.

The goal of human birth is to master the mind and senses and reach one's destiny. A regular study of the Geeta is sure to help achieve this noble goal. One who is regular in the study of the Geeta becomes happy, peaceful, prosperous, and free from the bondage of *Karma*, though engaged in the performance of worldly duties. Sins do not taint those who regularly study the Geeta, just as water does not stain a lotus leaf. The Geeta is the best abode of Lord Krishna. The spiritual potency of the Lord abides in every verse of the Geeta. The Bhagavad Geeta is the storehouse of spiritual knowledge. The Lord Himself spoke this supreme science of the Absolute containing the essence of all the scriptures for the benefit of humanity. To reiterate, all the Upanishads are the cows; Arjun is the calf; Krishna is the milkman; the nectar of the Geeta is the milk; and persons of purified intellects are the drinkers. One need not study any other scripture if one seriously studies the Geeta, contemplates the meaning of the verses, and practices its teachings in one's daily life. The Geeta is the ripe fruit of the tree of Vedic knowledge given to us by Lord Krishna for the welfare of humanity.

The Geeta is like a ship by which one can easily cross the ocean of transmigration and attain liberation. It is said that wherever the Geeta is chanted or read with love and devotion, Lord makes Himself present there to listen and enjoy the company of His devotees. Going to a place where Geeta is regularly chanted or taught is like going to a holy place of pilgrimage. One who regularly reads, recites to others, hears, and follows the sacred knowledge contained in the Geeta is sure to attain liberation from the bondage of *Karma* and attain *Nirvan*.

Though engaged in the performance of worldly duties, one who is regular in the study of the Geeta becomes happy and free from *Karmic* bondage. All the sacred centres of pilgrimage, gods, sages, and great souls dwell in the place where the Geeta is kept and read. Help during troubles comes quickly where the Geeta is recited, and the Lord dwells where it is read, heard, taught, and contemplated. By repeated reading of the Geeta, one attains bliss and liberation. One who contemplates the teachings of the Geeta at the time of death becomes free from sin and attains salvation. Lord Krishna personally comes to take such a person to His Supreme Abode– the highest transcendental plane of existence.

The interest in a serious study of the Geeta is not available to all but only to those with good *Karma*. One should be very earnest in the study of the Geeta. The Geeta is the heart, the soul, the breath, and the voice of the Lord. No austerity, penance, sacrifice, charity, pilgrimage, vow, fasting, or continence equals the study of the Geeta.

कच्चिदेतच्छ्रुतं पार्थ त्वयैकाग्रेण चेतसा ।
कच्चिदज्ञानसम्मोहः प्रनष्टस्ते धनंजय ॥ 18.72 ॥

Shlok 18.72: O Parth, did you listen to this with single-minded attention? Has the confusion caused by your ignorance been dispelled, Dhananjay?

Commentary: Sri Krishna wants to ascertain Arjun whether Arjun has understood what has been explained by Him all along and whether his distraction of thought, caused by false values and judgement of affairs, has been dispelled. The implication is to hear from Arjun to what extent these Discourses benefited him.

Arjun said:

नष्टो मोहः स्मृतिर्लब्धा त्वत्प्रसादान्मयाच्युत ।
स्थितोऽस्मि गतसन्देहः करिष्ये वचनं तव ॥ 18.73 ॥

Shlok 18.73: O Achut, by Your grace my delusion is dispelled; I have gained Self-knowledge. I stand here free from doubts. I shall act on Your words.

Commentary: Arjun conveys that his confusions have ended as if he were woken up from a state of unconsciousness. This statement of Arjun is not a mere meek acceptance of the arguments of Sri Krishna. It is an affirmation of re-gaining and re-cognizing his own real nature on account of the awakening of the hero in him as well as his confirmation that the neurosis which conquered his mental make-up temporarily has vanished. The awakening of wisdom is the end of ignorance. In this state all vacillations of the mind, doubts and despairs, dejections and hesitations, fears and weaknesses disappear.

With such a rejuvenated mind Arjun declares that he will do according to the word of the Lord who is nothing but Pure Existence. This is the surrendering of oneself to one's own inner personality. To surrender oneself and declare that he would do the Lord's bidding is the beginning and the end of all spiritual life. There is no more sense of separate existence for the declarer apart from the Godhead. This evolution means shedding of all pretences and evasions.

Sanjay said:

इत्यहं वासुदेवस्य पार्थस्य च महात्मनः ।
संवादमिममश्रौषमद्भुतं रोमहर्षणम् ॥ 18.74 ॥

Shlok 18.74: Thus, I heard this wonderful dialogue between Vasudev and great-souled Parth, causing my hair to stand on end.

Commentary: Thus have I heard this wonderful dialogue between Vasudeva and the high-souled Parth causing my hair to stand on end. Earlier, Arjun proclaimed that he will not fight and became despondent. It is the same Arjun now entirely revived who declared that all his doubts were cleared and he shall abide by 'His Will'. Sanjay concludes his running commentary in the last five verses of the Geeta. They contain his expressions of the glory of the Geeta, the revival of Arjun, his own reaction as he listened to the dialogue between the Lord and Arjun and the affirmation of his faith in the true culture of the Hindus.

The conversation between Vasudev and Arjun is a dialogue between the 'Higher' and the 'Lower' in man. It is between the Spirit and the Matter. Vasudev is a symbolism that stands for the Consciousness that illumines the concept of time projected by the intellect of man. Vasudev is the Atman, the Self. Parth represents the matter. The act of understanding oneself as the matter vesture is the art of unveiling the Infinite through the finite, the technique of which is the theme of the Geeta.

Sanjay describes the philosophy of the Geeta so far heard by him as marvellous and wonderful because it revealed the real personality of Arjun. Arjun is referred as high souled because of his great achievement in understanding the philosophy of the Geeta and shedding all his confusions which is something worthy of appreciation. This is also a warning to Dhritarashtra about the consequences of war with the rejuvenated Arjun.

व्यासप्रसादाच्छ्रुतवानेतद् गुह्यमहं परम् ।
योगं योगेश्वरात्कृष्णात् साक्षात्कथयतः स्वयम् ॥ 18.75 ॥

Shlok 18.75: By the grace of sage Vyas, I heard this supreme and most secret Yog directly from Krishna, the Lord of Yog, Himself speaking to Arjun.

Commentary: In this verse Sanjay expresses his gratitude to sage Vyas who had given him the special faculty to see and hear from a distance all that transpired in the battlefield of Kurukshetra so that he might report the events to the blind king, Dhritarashtra.

He terms what had been heard by him from Sri Krishna as the supreme and the most profound Yog. His joy is more due to his hearing the philosophy of the Geeta directly from the Lord than listening to the Discourse itself and hence Sri Krishna is referred to as the Lord of all Yogs. This is also an indirect reminder to the blind king about the futility of war with Pandavas.

राजन्संस्मृत्य संस्मृत्य संवादमिममद्भुतम् ।
केशवार्जुनयोः पुण्यं हृष्यामि च मुहुर्मुहुः ॥ 18.76 ॥

Shlok 18.76: O King, whenever I remember this marvellous and auspicious dialogues between Keshav and Arjun, I am thrilled again and again.

Commentary: Sanjay describes the deep impression created in his mind by listening to the Geeta philosophy. He says the Discourse between Sri Krishna and Arjun– between God and Man, between the Perfect and the Imperfect, between the Higher and the Lower– is at once wonderful and holy. The response in Sanjay is so powerful that he says it had given him the utmost thrill of joy again and again. The implication is that the Geeta should be studied and reflected upon continuously until we are re-educated in the way of life as expounded in It. The reward for such a study is to know the very purpose of our existence and to activate the power in us to tackle intelligently the chaotic happenings around us.

तच्च संस्मृत्य संस्मृत्य रूपमत्यद्भुतं हरेः ।
विस्मयो मे महान् राजन् हृष्यामि च पुनः पुनः ॥ 18.77 ॥

Shlok 18.77: And whenever I recollect miraculous form of *Hari* (God), I am greatly amazed, and I rejoice over and over again.

Commentary: Sanjay confesses that he had been enchanted not only by the philosophy of the Geeta but also even by the memory of the Lord's magnificent form as the total manifested Universe.

The dialogue of Sri Krishna and Arjun and the fact of God are not philosophical propositions but are spiritual facts. We do not learn their meaning by simply recounting them but by dwelling upon them in a spirit of prayer and meditation.

Necessity of Self knowledge and duty

यत्र योगेश्वरः कृष्णो यत्र पार्थो धनुर्धरः ।
तत्र श्रीर्विजयो भूतिर्ध्रुवा नीतिर्मतिर्मम ॥ 18.78 ॥

Shlok 18.78: Wherever there is Krishna, the lord of Yog, and wherever there is Parth as well, there is always a blessed victory. This is not only my own view. This is a truism validated by time and experience.

Commentary: Where there is *Dharma* (righteous duty), there is the grace of Lord Krishna; where there is the grace of Lord Krishna, there will be peace and victory. Everlasting peace and prosperity in the family are possible only by performing one's duty with full metaphysical knowledge of the Absolute. Peace and prosperity of a nation depend on mastering both the knowledge of scriptures and the knowledge of the use of weapons of protection, as well as science and technology. It is said that science and technology without spirituality are blind, and spirituality without technology is lame. In this concluding verse of the Song Celestial Sanjay summarizes the assessment of his total experience of hearing the conversation between Sri Krishna and Arjun.

Sri Krishna, the Lord of *Yog*– All through the Geeta Sri Krishna represented the Self, the Atman, the substratum upon which everything happens. He can be invoked within us by means of any one of the techniques of *Yog* taught in the Geeta.

Arjun, ready with the bow– Parth represents in the Geeta a confused, limited, ordinary mortal with all his weaknesses, agitations, fears and pairs of opposites. When he has thrown out his instruments of action, i.e. bow and arrows, there can be no hope of success or prosperity for him. But when he is ready with his bow he is prepared and willing to use his faculties to face the challenges of life.

Taken these two together– Sri Krishna, the *Yogeshwar* and Arjun, the *Dhanurdhar*– they symbolize a way of life wherein man, with the spiritual understanding, gets ready to face the battle of life. For him success is assured.

The teaching of the Geeta is *Yog* and the teacher is ***Yogeshwar***. When the human soul becomes enlightened and united with the divine, fortune and victory, welfare and morality are assured. Sanjay expresses his great joy for having heard this wonderful Discourse directly from Sri Krishna and seen His Cosmic Form. He declared that wherever there is Sri Krishna, the *Yogeshwar*, the Lord of the *Yog* and Arjun, the *Dhanurdhar*, the wielder of the bow, success, wealth and eternal good will accrue.

OM TAT SAT

PART- III

APPENDICES, REFERENCES AND GLOSSARY

1

The Essence of Bhagavad Geeta

The summary or the essence of the Bhagavad Geeta cannot be really presented in few lines, pages or even a book. A true essence of the Bhagavad Geeta can hardly be summarized by a human being, not even by an enlightened one. Right from the beginning of the cosmos, when the Supreme Being exploded Self with a big bang, to the stage of dissolution of cosmos (termed *Pralaya*), all is explained in the Bhagavad Geeta quite explicitly. The basic doctrine of the Bhagavad Geeta evolved during the battle of Mahabharata between Pandavas and Kauravas. When Arjun refused to fight his kinsmen who happened to be his arch enemies, the sermon of the Bhagavad Geeta was delivered by Lord Krishna to Arjun. The essence of the Geeta can only be fathomed by contemplating on knowledge or wisdom as contained in the Bhagavad Geeta. Hence the summary of the Geeta need not be deduced literally. The sacred wisdom contained in the Bhagavad Geeta demands reading in between the lines. A cursory glance or wishful reading carries no meaning in the spiritual world. In the domain of Supreme Being there is no place for ifs and buts. One can never reach God via the path of religion or the path of rituals. The teachings of the Bhagavad Geeta doctrine given to the mankind by Lord Krishna have no parallel in human history. The messages contained in 700 verses form the summum bonum of spirituality, epitome of spiritual pursuit. On the path of pure spirituality, other than assimilating the gist of the Bhagavad Geeta, there is nothing further to be achieved by human beings.

The Bhagavad Geeta is not about praising or worshipping God. God truly does not reside in temples, churches or mosques. Supreme Being already exists in every human being in a miniscule form as our soul, the spirit within. Reaching our soul, the spirit within, is reaching Supreme Being in all its glory. The doctrine of the Bhagavad Geeta is not like a religious tale of an epic to be told repeatedly until one learns the wisdom contained therein. The teachings of the Bhagavad Geeta contain A to Z of spirituality following which one could easily gain enlightenment in the present life. One can never reach God by following the path of religion. For reaching God the spiritual path is an absolute necessity. No human being in the world has ever reached the stage of enlightenment via any religion other than Hinduism, so was ordained by the Supreme Being in the entire history of mankind till date.

The essence of the Bhagavad Geeta can only be realized by taking the spiritual path uncharted by the path of spirituality that takes one directly to the abode of Supreme Being. Indulgence in the Bhagavad Geeta is necessitated for the travellers of the spiritual path never for those following religion or the path of rituals. The biggest hurdle Hindus tend to face in following the Bhagavad Geeta is its contents that can never be devoured literally. It demands reading in between the lines. As many readings of the Bhagavad Geeta so many different meanings are derived. For removing inner darkness, veil of ignorance, we have no other alternative than to study the Bhagavad Geeta through the path of contemplation.

No matter how many times a Hindu reads the Bhagavad Geeta its contents can never be fully realized by one. It has rightly been said as many human beings so many different paths to Supreme Being can there be. A spiritual preceptor, a spiritual master can become our guide in the journey of life but even a spiritual preceptor cannot make one fully understand the gist of the Bhagavad Geeta. For establishing absolute control over five senses and mind, for taking the path of complete celibacy (Brahmacharya Vrat), for full awakening of *Kundalini shakti* (the coiled serpentine energy lying dormant in base of spine) wisdom contained in the Bhagavad Geeta is necessitated. Other than teachings of the Bhagavad Geeta there is nothing required to be learnt further in the field of religion and spiritualism.

Assimilating knowledge and wisdom contained in the Bhagavad Geeta, any human being belonging to any religion, faith or belief can finally reach the portals of the Supreme Being in this very life. Why cling to ephemeral riches when nothing is carried to the next life after the death of present body. What is ultimately transferred to the next manifestation are virtues earned in the present life. As revealed in the Bhagavad Geeta, the Supreme Being is the only absolute reality. As summarized in the Bhagavad Geeta nothing other than Supreme Being exists in the cosmic system. According to the doctrine of Maya (veil of illusion) deduced and propagated by Adi Shankaracharya every human being is but a cluster of atoms and molecules the basic building block of cosmic system. The Bhagavad Geeta is not only good reading material but also forms the core of life. By patiently establishing control over five senses human beings ultimately establish absolute control over their mind. One immediately reaches the stage of *Nirvikalp Samadhi* (a stage of absolute nothingness) when not a single thought enters our brain uninvoked.

The Bhagavad Geeta is not limited to Hindus alone; it has got universal appeal. Hinduism primarily comprises many faiths and beliefs. Hinduism is never termed as a religion; it is always treated a way of life. The teachings of the Bhagavad Geeta can be followed by any human being the world over belonging to any religion, faith or belief. Hinduism is a truly universal religion not bound by limitations set by human beings. For assimilating wisdom contained in the Bhagavad Geeta one need not convert to Hinduism ever. For Hindus, for followers or believers of Hinduism, the Bhagavad Geeta is the most sacrosanct scripture existing in the world. Knowing the Bhagavad Geeta any human being can reach the stage of enlightenment (*Moksha*) in this very life.

The abstract teachings of the Bhagavad Geeta are not easily fathomed. This is the reason why people prefer taking the path of rituals, not the path of spirituality. In the present materialistic world dominated by a bloated ego (*Aham*), most human beings prefer material riches rather than taking the path of pure spirituality that takes one directly to the Supreme Being. As per the Bhagavad Geeta, of the total of 8.4 million manifestations by our soul the initial 7.3 million manifestations occurred in the forms of insects, plants and animal life. In the remaining

1.1 million manifestations in the human form one is expected to reach the stage of enlightenment and finally liberation. One of the most fundamental aspects of the Bhagavad Geeta is that we are primarily a soul on its cosmic journey of 8.4 million manifestations, an earthly life cycle of 96.4 million years. The human form is the highest manifest stage in the cosmic life cycle. It is only in a human form that our soul becomes a finally liberated self from the cycle of birth and death forever.

It is the Bhagavad Geeta that tells us for the first time that the journey of life always belongs to our soul or the spirit within and never the manifest human form. As revealed in the Bhagavad Geeta our soul or the spirit within is absolute master and controller of human body and not vice versa. It is not within the capability of human body to manifest a soul. The Bhagavad Geeta makes absolutely clear the relationship between Supreme Being, souls and all other lower forms of life. As per the Bhagavad Geeta the initial 7.3 million manifestations by our soul occurred in insect, plant and animal form. In the remaining 1.1 million manifestations in human form one is expected to reach the stage of enlightenment (*Moksha*). To cleanse self of dross impurities within to work out its karma starts cosmic life cycle of every soul. In the life of a soul the human form is but a temporary sojourn, a means to an end. Human form is the highest manifest stage in cosmic life cycle. It is only in human form that a soul finally regains its lost original pure prime pristine primordial form. Travel in human form is the most pleasant experience for a soul. Human beings taking spiritual path are truly noble. Reaching the stage of enlightenment (*Moksha*) is the ultimate goal of life for human beings. Enlightenment is also termed self-realization or god-realization. Realizing our true inner self or reaching God all means the same.

The gist of the Bhagavad Geeta is not difficult to understand. We only need to follow the path of absolute truthfulness always and ever. Unless we follow the path of absolute truth none can follow the path of pure spirituality that leads directly to the Supreme Being. Remaining truthful in life is a very important pre-condition of spiritual path, but most human beings never realize in life. The Supreme Being can never be reached via the path of religion or the path of rituals. No human being in the world, who visits temples, churches or mosques, has ever gained anything in life. Such travellers of religious path always remain immersed in the ephemeral pursuits of life never realizing that essentials of life always lay in taking the spiritual path, not the path of religion.

Sri Ramakrishna Paramhansa and Maharishi Ramana started their spiritual journey via the path of *Bhakti Yog,* the path of religion. But finally both switched to the path of *Gyan Yog* (path of absolute wisdom) as revealed in the sacred Bhagavad Geeta. The path of *Gyan Yog* can only be taken by following the dictates contained in the sacred Bhagavad Geeta. The absolute control over five senses and mind is necessitated for reaching God. The path to establish absolute control over five senses and mind is clearly revealed in the Bhagavad Geeta.

The Bhagavad Geeta also makes it clear that the Supreme Being is the only truth of life. Apart from the Supreme Being nothing exists in whole cosmos. The Supreme Being the cluster of all pure souls in cosmos was the only reality of life. When seen from senses' point of view things appeared solid otherwise all is gaseous formation as per the Bhagavad Geeta.

Maharishi Ramana advocated the path of *Neti* (not this, not this) as means to reach God in present life. Indulgence in *Neti* lying in *Shavasna* pose of Yog is a sure method of gaining enlightenment *(Moksha)* in present life. Maharishi Ramana was a free practitioner and staunch advocate of the path of *Neti* something he practised all his life until gaining enlightenment.

Virtues can be gained only by taking the spiritual path, never the path of religion or the path of rituals. No matter how many dips we took in the sacred Ganges River we cannot wash away sins of present life that way. *Karma* can only be negated by indulgence in positive *karma* or good *karma* all the time. Those who pursued materialistic goals of life never gained anything on spiritual path.

Understanding the Bhagavad Geeta becomes easy when we take the path of absolute truthfulness. Comprehending knowledge and wisdom contained in the Bhagavad Geeta was not as difficult as most human beings the world over projected. Values of life always lay in small affairs of life. By leading a simple life, by remaining truthful to self and Supreme Being one could easily gain enlightenment. In the last about 150 years amongst 7 billion people existing all over the world only Sri Ramakrishna Paramhansa and Maharishi Ramana finally succeeded in gaining enlightenment (*Moksha*). Why not follow the path of these enlightened ones and reach God early. Both Sri Ramakrishna Paramhansa and Maharishi Ramana were down to earth persons. Having burnt their ego in totality having dissolved their ego forever both these spiritual stalwarts initially started their search for God via the path of *Bhakti*, the *Yog* path of rituals, the path of religion. But finally both switched to the path of *Gyan Yog* (path of absolute wisdom) as revealed in the sacred Bhagavad Geeta.

Stage of enlightenment cannot not be reached in the absence of teachings of the Bhagavad Geeta. The Bhagavad Geeta forms summum bonum of spirituality, epitome of spiritual pursuit. Any human being the world over desirous of reaching God in the present life must follow the dictates of the Bhagavad Geeta without fail. In the absence of the Bhagavad Geeta none can reach God. Enlightenment cannot be gained via the path of Christianity, Buddhism, Islamic Dharma or any other religion of the world other than Hinduism, Buddhism and Jainism. Lord Krishna who was an *Avatar* of his era (God manifest in a human form) belonged to India and so did Mahavir and Gautama Buddha. Both Jesus Christ and Prophet Mohammed owed their spiritual knowledge to wisdom of the Bhagavad Geeta. In the entire history of mankind not a single human being reached God in the absence of teachings contained in the Bhagavad Geeta. The 700 shlokas (verses) contained in the Bhagavad Geeta can be easily understood by following the path of absolute truthfulness all throughout.

Most Hindus or even most Indians consider the Bhagavad Geeta sacrosanct. As detailed in Hindu mythology the follower of the Bhagavad Geeta finally becomes recluse breaking all relationships with those who formed a part of family, relatives and friends included. This is an absolute misnomer. In the present scientific age one need not go to Himalayas for contemplation on Supreme Being.

It is only through the path of contemplation, the path of self inquiry human beings can finally unveil sacred teachings of life hidden in the Bhagavad Geeta. Understanding the Bhagavad Geeta is simple but human beings have made it complicated. We just cannot have two goals of life at the same time. We can never be religious and also spiritual.

The path of pure spirituality or the teachings of the Bhagavad Geeta are not based on ifs and buts. Whims and fancies carry no meaning in spiritual world. Most human beings as of today pretend as if taking spiritual path all the time. The spiritual path is never taken that way. We have to negate *karma* in totality for reaching the Supreme Being in the present life.

In addition to the above here are a few more noteworthy lessons we have enumerated from the illustrious life of Lord Krishna:

1. Be calm and composed (steadfast)

After birth Lord Krishna was carted off from his birth place to a safer place in a small village called Gokul in present Uttar Pradesh to secure his safety from the evil king Kansa. Here Krishna lived a simple life with no luxuries as his foster mother Yashoda took care of him. Later in his childhood he went to Mathura and was offered highly luxurious life. But he never took those materialistic things seriously. Whether he lived a simple or princely life, he was always neutral or steadfast.

From this we too must try to be neutral or steadfast. Nothing is permanent in life. If we are enjoying many riches presently that doesn't mean our future will reciprocate the same. Rather learn to be contented with whatever we have and accept everything as God's blessings.

2. Never give up what you love

Lord Krishna, with a country to rule, a war to fight, demons to conquer and through various other commitments, still managed to inculcate the music he loved in his life. He never let his passion for music take a back seat on account of his commitments. He enjoyed playing his flute, mesmerizing those around him with lively tunes. Music is a part of life, enjoy it.

But, unfortunately in the modern era, with our many commitments, we tend to lose sight of our hobbies. The lesson is, no matter how much busy you are with your commitments, don't ever give up on your hobbies.

3. Be a true friend

In this contemporary world of intense competition, relationships tend to take a backseat. Friendships begin to fade into oblivion. This story of Lord Krishna on how he valued his friendships and treated his friends, rich and poor, with a lot of love and genuine affection gives us some lessons about the value of human relationships.

Once Lord Krishna's childhood friend, Sudama visited him hoping to ask for some assistance. Sudama, unlike Krishna, was a poor man, whose family could hardly make both ends meet. While visiting his friend, Sudama wished to give a beautiful present to Krishna but he did not have money to buy. Hence, he gifted him a handful of rice, he had at that time. Despite being opulent, Lord Krishna happily accepted the handful of rice with so much joy as it was a gift from his childhood friend. But once after being there, Sudama couldn't impose his problems on his friend Krishna. On returning home Sudama was astonished to see his home as it was transformed into gold and there were all kinds of precious stones and wealth. Lord Krishna being the genuine friend, he understood Sudama's plight even without Sudama uttering a word. That is the true meaning of friendship.

4. Be humble and generous

Lord Krishna ruled over the splendid Dwarka, a king no less. This Supreme Being during the Kurukshetra war preferred the role of a humble charioteer. Lord Krishna was the embodiment of simplicity and his role as a charioteer is a testament to that. Similarly, we too must try to be humble in our life. It helps us cultivate genuine relationships with genuine people.

Remember that when a person does something good to us, try to do as much as we can to return the favour. Be generous enough to give people more reasons to be happy in their life.

5. Always try to help the helpless

You must stand up and revolt whenever you see the weakest are victimised. Remember how Krishna stood for Draupadi when the Kauravas tried to be immodest with her?

Draupadi was stripped off her clothes and humiliated in front of the entire court. Her own husbands thought of her as a property they have lost in a game and didn't move a muscle to protest. It was Krishna who stepped into the scene and presented her with a *sari*.

The lesson is it was not that Sri Krishna wanted to impress Draupadi, but he acted so as to defend a woman's dignity. He was acknowledged for his active involvement in defending women's rights and that's probably why he continues to reside in the hearts of women till date.

6. Duty to parents

Krishna, as a baby was carted off from his birth parents to a safer place in a small village, Gokul, to secure his safety from the evil king Kansa. His parents underwent torture under the hands of Kansa; their lives were steeped in misery. Once Krishna reached manhood and came to know about his parents, he gave up his carefree life as a cowherd; risking his own life, he defeated Kansa and liberated his parents from his clutches. Lord Krishna did his duty for his parents.

Unfortunately the familial values system has changed quite considerably. Children digress from their duties towards their aged parents. Many fail to realize the love that parents have towards their children and only acknowledge them as a source of burden. Maybe society needs to take a cue from Lord Krishna's life and preachings.

Select Messages of the Geeta

The Bhagavad Geeta is one of the greatest religious books of the Hindus. The Bhagavad Geeta reveals the path to the lost, provides clarity to the confused and wisdom to all. Here are some of the most popular and important teachings from the greatest spiritual book the world has ever known… .

1. 'Surrender the fruits of your actions'.

When we work keeping the fruits of our labour in mind, we can never really give our best. It's because we are overly obsessed with the possible rewards. We always remain worried about the positive result. We may also feel disheartened if our task or action does not yield good outputs. Therefore, just doing our work without really thinking about its result should be our motive. Find contentment in the journey you are on, regardless of the outcome!

2. 'Life is a battlefield: Fight boldly'.

Even when the walls are crumbling around you and the earth is cracking beneath your feet, do not expect or fear anything. Expectations and fears limit our possibilities.

3. 'Our soul never dies'.
Our soul never dies. Even after our death, it continues to exist. It is immortal. It just changes bodies after the death of a person. Moreover, our body is made up of 'Agni' (fire), 'Jal' (water), 'Vayu'(wind), 'Prithvi' (earth) and it combines with them after death.

4. 'Accept the dualities of life'.
Imagine your most disgraceful moment and then imagine yourself at ease in it, sitting quietly while the leaves of worry float away in the breeze. Feeling sad about your losses will only way you down. Accept your desire without coveting or needing that which you want.

5. 'We all have to die one day'.
This world is not immortal. One who takes birth, has to die one day. That is the ultimate truth of this world. Nothing exists permanently. One has to leave this world, even though he wishes not to. No magic can actually help a person to stay forever. Everyone has their set life periods.

6. 'Accept the equanimity of life'.
When you see all beings as equal in suffering and in joy, when you are rooted in the oneness of all beings, you cannot love or hate anyone because it is all part of the same thing. In other words, love your enemy as yourself. Refuse to speak badly about those who hurt you or your enemies.

7. 'Progress and development are the rules of this Universe'.
Things may not be the same, the way they used to be. Things and circumstances change. We should neither expect people, nor surroundings, not even society, to be the same. They all change with time. We move ahead. The Universe forgets old things and moves forwards, so do we. We should not stick to one place. That will make our existence much more problematic in this world.

8. 'Every action and deed of ours should be dedicated to Krishna'.
Whatever we do in the course of our lifetime should be dedicated to the supreme personality of Godhead. This will always result in giving us peace and satisfaction. One should remember Krishna during every action of ours. This makes us feel God's presence with us all the time, making all our actions turn out to be positive.

9. 'Krishna is always there for you'.

Krishna is the ultimate support of any human being. Our fellow humans may not care for us or support as or may even leave us in our bad times, but Krishna is always there for us. The person who knows this truth is never really troubled by sadness or grief.

10. 'Krishna is the Supreme'.

Krishna is the supreme personality of Godhead. He is the original cause of all causes. He starts everything and ends everything too. He is there everywhere. He is omnipresent and omnipotent. We are just puppets whom he controls. He is divine and transcendental.

11. 'Desires come and go'.

Desires come and go, but one should remain a dispassionate witness, simply watching and enjoying the show. Everyone experiences desires but one should not be moved by them. They should not bother a person. People sometimes undertake really evil actions because of their desires. One should simply not get caught in the chains of desire.

12. 'A mind obsessed with money cannot meditate'.

The Bhagavad Geeta talks a lot about meditation and its importance. Meditation is considered extremely helpful for inner peace and '*Sadhna*'. Moreover, a person who thinks about making money all the time cannot really engage in meditation. When a person's mind is not stable and he or she imagines only about money, then meditation would be a failed effort for such a person.

OM TAT SAT

2

Select Myths About Hindu Religion

In order to understand and appreciate the rise and development of Hindu religion and philosophy or Santan Dharma with special emphasis on the Geeta it seems necessary to throw some light on the following topics or subjects:

Being an ancient religion, Hinduism now is plagued with many wrong and false ideas about it. These probably arose over time because people did not always adhere to the proper sources of knowledge. Moreover, most books available on Hinduism in bookshops today are written by non-Hindu Westerners who, intentionally or unintentionally, failed to capture its real essence. Interpretations and re-interpretations have given birth to a bundle of confusions and misconceptions.

It is natural to unknowingly approach Hinduism with foreign notions of God, soul, heaven, hell and sin in mind. We translate Brahm as God, Atman as soul, *Pap* as sin, *Dharma* as religion. But Brahm is not the same as God; Atman is not equivalent to the soul, Pap is not sin and Dharma is much more than mere religion. To obtain a true understanding of sacred writings, such as the Upanishads, one must read them on their own terms and not from any other perspective.

Myth 1: Hinduism is a religion

Hinduism is unlike all the major religions of the world. The most obvious misconception about Hinduism is that most people tend to see it as a religious faith. To be precise, Hinduism is a way of life. Hinduism was not founded by any prophet or messenger of God on a particular date. It developed slowly over a long period of time. It does not have a core doctrine, there is no central authority, it does not require followers to accept any one idea, and no one can agree on when or even where it began.

The word Hinduism itself is not to be found in any of the scriptures. It was named after the people of Sindh, who settled between the rivers Indus and Sindh in what is now a part of Pakistan. The Persians named people of Sindh 'Hindus.' Hinduism is essentially a conglomeration of diverse religious, philosophical, and cultural ideas, beliefs and traditions. It is characterized by the belief in rebirth, one absolute being, the law of *Karma*, a path of righteousness and liberation from the cycle of births and deaths.

Myth 2: There are 33 crore Gods and Goddesses in Hinduism

This misconception is based on distorted interpretation of Hindu scriptures. The Vedas do not refer to millions of deities but 33 supreme deities. As a matter of fact, 33 divinities are mentioned in the *Yajur Ved, Atharva Ved, Satapath Brahman*, and in several other Vedic and later texts. The number thirty-three occurs with reference to divinities in the Parsi scriptures of *Avesta* as well. The word *'Koti'* in *Trayastrimsati Koti* does not mean the number 'thirty-three crore'. Here *Koti* means 'supreme', pre-eminent, excellent, that is, the 33 'supreme' divinities. The word *Koti* has the same meaning as '*Uchha Koti'* or higher class.

It was a problem even in AD 725 when Subhakarasimha and his Chinese colleague I-hsing translated the *Mahavairochana-Sutra* into Chinese. They rendered the compound *Sapta-Koti-Buddha* as *Shichi (Sapta) Kotei (koti) Butsu (Buddh*) in which they did not translate the word Koti that transliterated its pronunciation as kotei. The Buddhas were not 'seven crore', but only 'Seven Supreme Buddhas': six predecessors and the historic Buddh.

In the *Vrihadaranyak Upanishad*, Discourse 3, Yagyavalkya has said that in reality there are only 33 gods and goddesses. Of these 8 are Vasus, 11 Rudras, 12 Adityas, and Indra and Prajapati. 8Vasus + 11Rudras+ 12Adityas+ 2Heaven and Earth (8+11+12+2= 33).

Myth 3: Hinduism is an 'open-source' religion

Hinduism is fairly relaxed and tolerant, but that doesn't mean we are a free for all. The Vedas are called *Shruti*– meaning that no kind of alteration is permitted. When we are initiated into the religious practice during *Upanayanam*, we have to exactly recite the mantras as they are.

Myth 4: Hinduism has atheism within it

It incorporates both *Astik* and *Nastik* ideology. There were a few '*Nastik* schools' of philosophy in ancient India. But, that doesn't mean they form a part of the Hindu canon that is followed in practice today. Hindu philosophy is a subset of all ideas that originated in India. All the mainstream religion texts are all theistic with explicit reference to God. Vedas speak of God, in Bhagavad Geeta Krishna leaves no room for doubt when it comes to God, Adi Shankar leaves no room for further doubt in *Bhaj Govindam*.

Myth 5: A Hindu is a member of the *Sanatan Dharma*

A Hindu is one who lives around and beyond, south-east of the Indus river. Basically, Indians are 'Hindus'. *Sanatan Dharma* is followed only if one believes in all the different Gods and Goddesses– these are not even the conventional Gods and Goddesses that the religions of the world talk about. These are *Devatas*, which represent natural elements, human emotions, desires, actions, among other things.

Myth 6: Hindus are idol worshippers

Idols are merely medium of worshipping almighty God. Under the Yog and Bhakti system no idol is necessary to worship God. In reality, Hindus worship a reminder of God. No Hindu will say he or she is worshipping an idol. Instead, Hindus believe a physical representation of God– in the form of an idol– helps them focus on an aspect of prayer or meditation. For instance, a person who has just opened up a new business may worship Ganesh, the elephant god who represents success. The images of Gods and Goddesses, or *Murtis*, are used as focal points to help aid in meditation and prayer.

Myth 7: Hindus worship cows

In reality, Hindus have developed special regard for the cows. There are several other creatures too for which Hindus have regard and hence they do not kill them. All creations are considered sacred. Hindus believe every living thing has a soul. It is true, however, that cows hold a special place in Hindu society. That's why Hindus refrain from eating beef. Cows are seen as gentle, maternal figures that are providers of milk and other forms of sustenance. They are honoured for their value.

Myth 8: Hinduism supports a discriminatory caste system

The caste system is a perverted form of old Varna System. Hindus are opposed to this age-old evil practice. In actuality, caste discrimination is rooted not in religion but culture. Caste was an ancient system of occupational class delineated in Hindu texts that over the years developed into a rigid social hierarchy. The lowest castes, or untouchables, were marginalized and faced persecution. But many modern Hindus have argued that caste-based discrimination is not intrinsic to Hinduism and should not be thought of as religiously sanctioned.

Myth 9: Srimad Bhagavad Geeta is like the Bible

This is not really true. There is not one central, authoritative book in Hinduism. But Hinduism is rich in scripture with a vast collection of ancient religious writings. Hindus believe God revealed truths to wise men who passed them on for thousands of years through a rich oral tradition. The scriptures include the **Vedas,** the **Upanishads,** the **Puranas** and **Srimad Bhagavad Geeta, Ramayan.** Part of the epic tale, **Mahabharat,** Geeta is the world's longest poem and captures the core beliefs of Hinduism but not all Hindus read the Geeta.

Myth 10: Karma is philosophical

Everyone has the ability to choose life's actions. This is the theory behind *Karma*: for every action a person sets in motion, there is a corresponding reaction. Hindus believe they have to face the consequences of past actions. Each person creates his or her destiny with deeds. The ultimate goal is to have *Karma* that will free a soul and gain moksha, or liberation from the cycle of rebirth.

Myth 11: Hindu texts are about spirituality

Writings we now categorise as Hindu scriptures include not just books relating to spirituality but also secular pursuits like science, medicine and engineering. This is another reason why it defies classification as a religion. Further, it cannot be claimed to be essentially a school of metaphysics. Nor can it be described as 'other worldly'. In fact, one can almost identify Hinduism with a civilization that is flourishing even now.

Myth 12: Hindus are allowed to eat meat

Hinduism does not mandate that its followers be vegetarian. Many adherents of Hinduism are not vegetarian, although a vegetarian diet is encouraged in accordance with principles such as *Ahinsa* (non-violence) extended to animals.

Myth 13: Woman's place in Hinduism is not equal to males

The ancient society was in fact quite considerate and respectful to those (both men and women) engaged in various vocations, and people were free to make choices or changes in their careers or skills if the opportunity existed. Vedic prayers also indicate that the women had considerable say in selecting their marriage partners, and were espoused to live in monogamous relationships while enjoying same rights as their husbands. Furthermore, in the Vedas there is little evidence of child marriages, dowry system and the practice of Sati.

Similarly, there is no indication of any stigma relating to widowhood or the remarriage of a widow. There is also no religious restriction against women cremating or lighting the funeral pyre of their departed kin. Note also that the well-educated, scholarly and charismatic women of yore, who also participated in many philosophical debates with men, included Gargi (the daughter of Vachaknu— from the Vrihadaranyak Upanishad).

Myth 14: Manusmriti is an important social and religious text

It is a great misunderstanding to consider the *Manusmriti* (or Manu's proclamation) as being an important part of the Hindu *Varna-ashram Dharma*. This confusion persists even in spite of the fact that *Manusmriti* as a *Smriti* often contradicts the *Shruti* (or Veda) on several important points relating to the caste system and women. *Manusmriti* was never popular among the Hindus. Moreover, they never used it as a religious or social text.

Myth 15: Hinduism advocates being anti-materialistic

What Hinduism says is that materialistic pursuits or running behind sensual pleasures is not going to fetch you everlasting happiness. It only says that behind any unbridled searching for enjoyment, there is always a pain lurking behind. Hinduism advises one to practise moderation, to be watchful, and not to get carried away. Hinduism does place liberation– '*Moksha*' as the ultimate goal of life and for the majority, the path of progress towards the goal (*Moksha*) includes *Dharma* (righteousness), *Artha* (materialism) and *Kam* (sensual enjoyments).

OM TAT SAT

3

Names, Nicknames and Glossary of the Geeta

The following is the list of select Sanskrit words, names and nicknames used in this book. Most of the Sanskrit words have got multiple meanings. Knowing this well, various commentators of Srimad Bhagavad Geeta have skilfully used them to give their own interpretation. This has made room for much ambiguity in the interpretation of the *Shlokas*. The readers should try to familiarise themselves with these words and names of important characters to have a proper understanding of this book. They are thus:

Abhimanyu: A powerful warrior. Son of Arjun.

Acharya: Religious teacher.

Achyut: Krishna, means 'unfallen, firm.' Used as a name for Krishna in the Geeta, but also used for others in the Mahabharat.

Aditya: The sun.

Adityas: A class of gods who are the sons of Aditi and Kashyap. There are twelve of them, of whom Vishnu is the most important.

Advait: Non-duality; a school of Vedant philosophy teaching the oneness of God, soul, and universe, whose chief exponent was Shankaracharya.

Agamas: The Vedas.

Agni: The god of fire or the fire itself.

***Agnihotra*:** A Vedic sacrifice in which oblations are offered to Agni.

Agyan: A term of Vedant philosophy meaning ignorance, individual or cosmic. According to Non-dualistic Vedant it is Agyan that is responsible for the perception of multiplicity in the relative world, and also for man's bondage and suffering.

Ahankar: Egoism. This, according to Brahmanism, causes one to become ignorant of his duty as designated by his Guna (inherent quality).

Airavat: Indra's elephant.

***Akash*:** The first of the five material elements that constitute the universe; often translated as "space" and "ether". The four other elements are vayu (air), Agni (fire), AP (water), and Prithvi (earth).

***Anandam*:** Bliss.

Anant: One of the three kings of the serpents; the other two are Vasuki and Takshak. Means 'the infinite.' Also known as Shesha.

Anantavijay: Yudhishthir's conch.

Antahkaran: It stands for the inner organ; the mind. Its essential constituents are 1. *Manas*– the lower mind; 2. *Buddhi*– the intellect; 3.*Chitta*– the subconscious mind and 4. *Ahankar*– the empirical ego.

***Apan*:** A modification of the vital breath, by the action of which the un-assimilated food and drink go downward and are ultimately ejected; the movement of the out-going breath.

Aranyak: One of the sections of the Vedas.

Aryaman: The sun god.

Ashvathama: The son of Drone and Kripi. An elephant of the same name was killed during the battle to make Drone believe that his son had been killed.

Ashvattha: The holy fig tree; also called the bo or pipal tree.

Ashvins: Ancient India's divine twins. They are the surgeons to the gods. Because of their beauty, they are often used in comparisons.

Asita Devala: A seer. Also known as just Asita or Devala.

Ashram: Hermitage; also any one of the four stages of life: the celibate student stage (*brahmacharya*), the married householder stage (*garhasthya*) the stage of retirement and contemplation (vanaprastha), and the stage of religious mendicancy (*sannyas*).

Asvamedh: The Horse-sacrifice, performed in ancient India by kings and emperors to demonstrate their sovereignty over other princes.

Atharvaved: One of the four Vedas.

Atman: The Self, or Soul; denotes both the Supreme Soul and (with small a) the individual soul, which, according to Non-dualistic Vedant, are ultimately identical.

Aum: The same as Om.

Avidya: Lack of knowledge of Atman due to the mind's attachment to sense objects induced by the force of the gunas. Avidya causes grief.

Badrayan: The author of the Brahma Sutras and other philosophical works; also known as Vyas.

Best of the Kurus: Arjun. Although primarily a Pandav, he is also a Kaurav.

Bhagavads: Followers of the cult centred on Lord Krishna, also known as Vasudevas.

Bhagavan: (Lit., One endowed with the six attributes, namely, infinite prosperity, strength, glory, splendour, knowledge, and renunciation.) An epithet of the Godhead; also the Personal God of the devotee.

Bhagavat: A well-known scripture dealing mostly with the life of Sri Krishna.

Bhakti movement: It refers to the spiritual devotional trend that emerged in old-fashioned Hinduism in medieval India.

Bhakti: Worshipping of Lord Krishna with single-minded devotion. Now it is more than worshipping Krishna.

Bhaktiyog: This consists of two elements: Bhakti of the Bhagavads and Yog of the Upanishads. Yog here stands for single-minded effort to achieve a specific goal. In the Geeta it consists of two elements: Sannyas and Tyag. Bhaktiyog means worshipping of Lord Krishna or God with single-minded devotion in the spirit of Yog.

Bharat: In the Geeta, Arjun and Dhritarashtra. In the plural, the Descendants of Bharat.

Bhima: One of the five Pandu brothers also called Bhimasen. He is the son of Kunti and the reputed son of Pandu, but really the son of Vayu.

Bhishma: The son of Shantnu and the river Ganges. He is a master of statecraft, and a great warrior fighting for the Kauravas.

Bhrigu: A seer or sage.

Bhuh: Earth.

Bhuvah: The space between earth and heaven; the atmosphere.

Brahm: Ultimate Reality. The primordial principle or shapeless substance of which the universe is made, and to which it returns. This is the all-pervading Universal Spirit, which is to be found everywhere and in everything. The part of Brahm residing in the heart of man as his divine essence is known as Atman. Brahm is without any Nature-born Qualities, known as the Gunas, hence it is known as Nirgun (devoid of Guna). Brahm is beyond the perception of senses. Hence it is said to be 'Not this; not this! (Naeti, Naeti). In the Vedas, Brahm was known as a mysterious force. This entity became the main focus of the Upanishads.

Brahm Sutras: An authoritative treatise on Vedant Philosophy ascribed to Vyas. One of the three central texts of Vedantic philosophy, the other two being the Upanishads and the Geeta itself.

Brahma: The Vedic god, also known as Prajapati, the originator of all beings; the First Person of the Hindu Trinity, the other two being Vishnu and Shiva.

Brahmacharin: A celibate student who lives with his teacher and devotes himself to the practice of spiritual discipline.

Brahmacharya**:** The first of the four stages of life; the life of an unmarried student.

Brahmalok**:** The Plane of Brahma, roughly corresponding to the highest heaven of the dualistic religions, where fortunate souls repair after death and enjoy spiritual communion with the Personal god.

Brahmana: One of the two main sections of the Vedas, which also includes the Aranyaks and the Upanishads.

Brahmarandhra: The aperture at the top of the head through which the soul of an illumined person leaves the body at death.

Brahmavidya**:** The Knowledge of Brahm.

Brahmic: Brahm-related, sacred, or holy.

Brahminism: This was the instrument of law and social order in the ancient Indian society. It is also known as Orthodox Vedic Dharma. It controlled the society by means of a hierarchical class system known as Varnashram system. The Brahminic Dharma rested on the bedrock of the doctrines of the Gunas and Karma. The four pillars on which its super-structure stood were: sanctity of the Vedas; sacrificial rites known as Karma or Yagyas; class system known as Varnashram Dharma which stood for supremacy of Brahmins over the other three varnas.

Brahmins: The priestly class/caste that dominated the Hindu society. They were the most learned of the four varnas, and they monopolised all ancient religious scriptures and performance of rites and rituals to serve their interests best.

Brahmism: All sacrifices were dedicated to them. Lord Krishna absorbs them all into His person in Srimad Bhagavad Geeta. It is not to be confused with Brahminism which means dominance of the Brahmin caste over others, jeopardizing the interests of other castes.

Brihaspati: The priest (Purohit) of the gods, and also the planet Jupiter.

Buddhiyog: It is the method by which one's mind is steadied by yoking it with Buddhi (wisdom). When the mind controls its senses (desires for sense objects), it becomes connected with Buddhi. The mind then operates as per the dictates of Buddhi. The mind thus steadied by yoking with Buddhi is known as *Buddhiyukta* mind. A person who has achieved this is known as the Buddh, the Enlightened. Opposite of *Buddhiyukta* is Dwandwa (unsteadiness of mind). *Buddhiyog* counters Dwandwa of mind. All actions performed in the spirit of *Buddhiyog* earn neither good nor bad Karmaphal (fruit of deed). A person of *Buddhiyukta* mind always does the right thing.

Buddhi: Intellect or wisdom. It is that part of mind which stands for discriminatory powers, judgement, reasoning, insight, moral values, noble virtues, memory, knowledge, etc.

Bull among Men: In the Geeta, Arjun and Shaibya.

Bull of the Bharatas: Arjun.

***Chandralok*:** The Plane of the Moon, where souls repair after death to enjoy the fruit of their meritorious deed done with a selfish motive. Afterwards these souls are reborn on earth.

Chekitan: The valiant king of Kasi belonging to the Vrishni tribe.

***Chitta*:** Consciousness.

Chitrarath: The king of the Gandharvas.

Cow of Plenty: A cow that belongs to the sage Vasishtha. She was produced by the churning of the Milk Ocean and is supposed to grant all wishes. Also the mother of all cows and a symbol of fertility.

***Cycle*:** A world period, representing the duration of the universe between its manifestation and its return to the unmanifested state.

Devadatta: Arjun's conch.

***Devalok*:** The Plane of the Deities.

Devas: Vedic gods and goddesses representing the forces of Nature:

Indra, Varun, Vayu, Agni, Varun, Ashwins, etc. They were the principal deities of Hindus.

Devatas: Same as devas.

Dhananjay: Arjun. Means 'winner of wealth.'

Dharma: The literal meaning is 'that which holds.' In practice it stands for righteousness, religion, law, system, duty, order, what ought to be done, and the right thing to do. Opposite of Dharma is *Adharma* (irreligion). *Para-Dharma* stands for alien or heterodox Dharma.

Dhristketu: The king of Chedi.

Dhritrashtra: The brother of Pandu and Vidur. Born blind, he is the husband of Gandhari and the father of one hundred sons, the Kauravas. His eldest son is Duryodhan, whom the Pandavas fight against.

Draupadi: The wife of five Pandav brothers.

Drishtadyumna: A warrior and the son of Drupad. Killed by Ashvathama.

Drone: The military teacher of both the Pandavas and the Kauravas, and the general of the Kauravas.

Drupad: The king of Panchal and the father of Draupadi.

Dualism (Dvait): It is the idea or theory that something (an object, an idea or the whole world) is split into two parts. These parts are separate from each other, and the thing cannot be divided up in any other way.

Duryodhan: The eldest son of Dhritarashtra and the leader of the Kauravas.

Dvija: (Lit., twice-born.) An epithet applied to members of the three upper castes after their investiture with the sacred thread, which is their second, or spiritual birth. The first birth is the physical birth from their mother's womb.

Dwandwa: Pairs of opposites the mind experiences when it comes into contact with sense objects: likes and dislikes; pleasure and pain; gain and loss; honour and dishonour; virtue and vice, and the like. It also means stress, unsteadiness of mind, fickleness of mind, ambivalence, doubt, restlessness, mood swings, unsteadiness, confusion, mental conflict, obsession and loss of focus and loss of discrimination. The practical meaning of Dwandwa is loss of wisdom or discriminating faculty. Opposite of Dwandwa-ridden mind is Buddhiyukta (steady) mind.

Enemy Slayer: Krishna.

Gandharvas: Celestial musicians and singers in Indra's abode or heaven.

Gandiv: Arjun's bow.

Ganges: The holiest river flowing in northern India.

Garuda: A mythical bird and the mount of Vishnu.

Gayatri Mantra: A sacred verse of the Vedas, recited daily by Hindus of the three upper castes after their investiture with the sacred thread.

Gayatri: A poetic meter. It is also a specific verse in the Rigved which every orthodox Brahmin must repeat at his morning and evening prayers.

Govind: Krishna. Means 'protector of cows.'

Gudakesh: Arjun is called Gudakesh because he has conquered sleep or sluggishness.

Guna: According to Sankhya philosophy, prakriti (nature or matter) consists of three gunas- usually translated as 'qualities'- known as *Sattva, Rajas,* and *Tamas*. *Tamas* stands for dullness or inertia; rajas, for restlessness or activity; Sattva, for balance or righteousness. They are the three strands forming the twisted rope of nature, by which a man is bound to the relative world. The Gunas express themselves by means of senses (desires) and organs of action (*Karmendriyas*) such as hands, legs, mouth and genitals.

Gyan: Knowledge. In the Geeta this term refers to knowledge of

Atman.

Gyanayog: This is the art and science of Yog by which one renounces his desire for, attachment to and possessiveness of sense objects and progressively attains the knowledge of Atman. This is how realization of God takes place.

Gyanendriyas: It refers to the five sense organs: 1. Ghraan– nose; 2. *Rasana*– tongue; 3. Chaksu– eye; 4. *Tvak*– skin and 5. *Shrotra*– ear.

Gyani: One who follows the path of reasoning and discrimination to realize Ultimate Truth; generally used to denote a non-dualist.

Hari: Vishnu.

Hastinapur: Located in Uttar Pradesh was the kingdom of the Kuru clan.

Hero of the Kurus: Arjun. Although primarily a Pandav, he is also a Kauravas.

Himalayas: The world's highest mountains, located in regions covering India, Nepal and Tibet. Means 'place of snow.'

Hinduism: Hinduism is a complex religion and a way of life, with a diversity of ideas on spirituality and traditions. It has no ecclesiastical order, no unquestionable religious authority, no governing body, no prophet(s) nor any binding holy book; Hindus can choose to be polytheistic, pantheistic, monotheistic, monistic, agnostic, atheistic or humanist.

Hiranyagarbha: (Lit., the Golden Egg.) The first manifestation of Sagun Brahm in the relative universe.

Hotri Priest: A priest conducting a sacrifice; especially one who recites the prayer of the Rig-Ved at the sacrifice.

Hrishikesh: Krishna. Lord of the senses.

Ikshvaku: A son of Manu Vaivasvat, he was the first king of the solar dynasty of Ayodhya.

Indra: The king of the gods.

Indriyani: It refers to senses. The senses not only represent the functions of five senses, but also the raw impulse or drive (desire) to obtain sense objects. They also stand for attachment and possessiveness. They represent the Id in modern psychology.

Ishwar: The Lord. Parameshwar: The Supreme Lord.

Jagat: The relative universe.

Jahnu: An ancient king and sage. When the Ganges was brought down from heaven, it was forced to flow over the earth to the ocean and thence descended to the netherworld. In its course, it inundated the sacrificial ground of Jahnu, who drank up its waters but consented to discharge them from his ears. Hence the river Ganges is regarded as his daughter and called Jahnavi.

***Janak*:** One of the ideal kings in Hindu mythology, who combined Yog with enjoyment of the world. A king of Videh or Mithila in present Bihar

Janakanda: The part of the Vedas that teaches philosophical wisdom.

Janardan: Krishna.

Jayadrath: A king fighting on the Kauravas' side.

Jeev: (Lit., living being.) The individual soul, which is essence, is one with the Universal Soul.

Jeevnmukta: One enjoying Liberation while living in the body.

Joy of the Kurus: Arjun. Although primarily a Pandav, he is also a Kaurav.

Kamya Karma: This refers to desire-oriented action. In Srimad Bhagavad Geeta it refers to sacrificial rites performed to gain wealth and heaven or to fulfil other desires of life.

Kanad: A sage who was the founder of the Vaisheshik philosophy.

Kandarpa: The god of love, also known as Kama or Kamadev.

Kapil: The well-known founder of the Sankhya philosophy.

Karma Sannyas: An attitude of selfless, dedicated actions without desire for the fruits of these actions.

Karma: Action; a sacrificial ritual ('the works'); obligatory duty designated by one's social class; fruit of one's action known as Karmaphal.

***Karmakand*:** The part of the Vedas that deals with rituals and sacrifices.

Karmaphal: Fruit of one's action. The Brahminic theory said that all actions lead to earning Karmaphal. The fruits of our actions accumulate. When one dies, he would go to hell or heaven depending upon the consequences of his deeds. After exhausting his merit or demerit, he would be reborn on earth in a higher or lower class of people. This cycle of birth, death, and rebirth is known as Sansar. This theory motivated people to do virtuous works in life. It also explained to them the cause of their current misery in life.

Karmayog: This is the Yog of selfless action. This was taught by Krishna to Arjun in the Geeta to replace Kamya Karma. Krishna is opposed to Kamya Karma.

Karmendriyas: It represents the physical organs of action and the corresponding subtle organs. They are related to the active solar energy of the *manas tattva.* The following are the five *Karmendriyas: 1. Paayu*– the excretory organ. It is the organ of excretion. Associated with the *mooladhar chakra* and the earth element. *2. Upastha*– the sexual organs. This is the generative organ. *3. Paada*– the locomotion organ. Legs are the locomotory organs. 4. *Paani*– the organ of apprehension. Hands are the most complex organ of action as they can express, feel and touch. *5. Vaak*– the speech organ

Karna: The king of Anga and the elder brother on his mother's side of the Pandu princes. He was the son of the sun god Surya by Kunti before her marriage to Pandu. Afraid of the censure of her relatives, Kunti abandoned the child in a river, where he was found by a charioteer named Adhirath and nurtured by his wife Radha. Hence, Karna is sometimes called Sutaputra or Sutaja (son of a charioteer).

Kashi: The holiest city of India, located on the bank of the Ganges in modern Uttar Pradesh. Also called Banaras or Varanasi.

Kauravas: Descendants of Kuru. The term primarily refers to the sons of Dhritarashtra, who are the enemies of the Pandavas. However, the Pandavas are also, strictly speaking, Kauravas, since they all descend from Kuru.

Keshav: Krishna.

Keshin: A demon killed by Krishna.

Kripa: A son of Sharadvat, reared by Shantnu.

Kshatriyas: The warrior class. They were second in hierarchy in the four-tier Varnashram system. Upanishadic philosophy was mostly their creation. In fact, the attempt to overthrow Brahminism in Srimad Bhagavad Geeta was led by them.

Kunti: The first of Pandu's two wives. Kunti was the daughter of a Yadav prince who let the childless Kuntibhoj adopt her. After receiving a charm from a sage, which enabled her to have children by any god she chose, her sons Yudhishthir, Bhim, and Arjun were fathered by the gods Dharma, Vayu, and Indra respectively.

Kuntibhoj: A Yadav prince who adopted Kunti.

Kuru: The ancestor of the Kurus, a tribe. Also the name of their country, and the field on which the great battle is fought. Both the Kauravas proper and the Pandavas descend from Kuru. Technically, they are all Kauravas, but the term is only used for the hundred sons of Dhritarashtra, whereas the others are referred to as Pandavas. Lord of the Earth Dhritarashtra. This is a general term for a king, but it is used twice for Dhritarashtra in the Gccta.

Kurukshetra: It is a place of great historical and religious importance in the State of Haryana. It is also known as Dharmakshetra, as the Kurukshetra War, also known as the Mahabharat War, was believed to have taken place here.

Lord of Yog: Krishna.

Lotus Eyed: Krishna.

Madhav: Krishna.

Madhusudan: Krishna. Means 'destroyer of (the demon) Madhu.'

Madhvacharya: The chief exponent of Dualistic Vedant (A.D. 1199-1296).

Madri: Second wife of Pandu. Mother of Nakul and Sahadev.

Mahah: The fourth of the seven upper planes in the relative universe; it is an intermediary region between the three planes constituting *Brahmalok* and the three planes known as Bhuh, Bhuvah and Svah

Maheshvar: (Lit., the Great Lord.) The Lord of all the Isvaras, or Governors, of the innumerable Brahmandas, or world systems; an epithet of Sagun Brahm.

Manas: The Mind, the middle of three components of the mental apparatus. Its three functions are thinking, feeling and acting. Dwandwa is experienced in this part. Manas is superior to the senses (Indriyani) and inferior to the Buddhi (Intellect).

Manipushpak: The conch of Sahadeva, one of the five Pandavas.

Mantra: Holy Sanskrit text; also (with capital M) one of the two main sections of the Vedas, which describes the hymns used in the sacrifices.

Manu: In the Vedas, man par excellence, the representative man, and the father of the human race. In later mythology, the name Manu is especially applied to fourteen successive mythical progenitors and sovereigns of the earth, the seventh of which is Manu Vaivasvat, mentioned in verse 4.1. In verse 32.6, the four Manus are related to the four yugas, or ages of the world.

Margashirsha: In the Hindu calendar, the month in which the full moon enters the constellation Mrigashiras. It corresponds to November-December in the Western calendar.

Marichi: A seer.

Maruts: The storm gods, who are companions of Indra.

Math: Monastery.

Maya: A term of Vedant philosophy denoting ignorance obscuring the vision of Reality; the cosmic illusion on account of which the One appears as many, the Absolute as the relative world.

Meru: A mythical mountain abounding in gold and precious stones. The abode of Brahma, the Creator, and a meeting-place for the gods, demigods, rishis and other supernatural beings, Meru is regarded as the axis around which the planets revolve.

Mighty-armed Prince: Arjun. A generic epithet for warriors.

Mimansakas: The followers of the Poorva-mimansa philosophy, a system based upon the ritualistic portion of the Vedas, whose chief exponent was Jaimini.

Moksha: The Bhagavad concept of liberation of Atman from Sansar, the cycle of birth, death and rebirth, resulting in union with the Supreme Lord.

Nakul: The twin brother of Sahadeva and half-brother of Arjun, Bhim and Yudhishthir. He is the fourth of the Pandu princes and the son of Madri, Pandu's second wife, and reputedly Pandu, but actually was the son of the Ashvins. Narad, a seer. In later mythology, he is a friend of Krishna and regarded as the inventor of the veena, or lute. In epic poetry, he is a Gandharva.

Narayan: The Lord of all. Supreme Being.

Nastik: Atheist. Such persons do not accept the authority of religious scriptures or God. One of the Indian philosophical schools is known as Nastik philosophy.

Nyaya: Indian Logic, one of the six systems of orthodox Hindu philosophy, founded by Gautama.

Nirgun Brahm: (Lit., Brahm without attributes.) A term used to describe the Absolute.

Nirvan: Final absorption in Brahm, or All-pervading Reality, through the annihilation of the individual ego. An Upanishadic concept of liberation from sansar and the final merger of Atman with Brahm

Nitya Karma: Daily obligatory work, such as worship of God, by the performance of which sins accumulated in past lives are gradually destroyed and the propensity to new sins is checked.

Non-dualism: A school of Vedant philosophy teaching the oneness of God, soul and universe. See Advait.

Om: The most sacred word of the Vedas; also written Aum. It is a symbol both of the Personal God and of the Absolute.

Panchamahabhoothas: It refers to five elements. They are as follows:
(a) *Prithvi* (earth) corresponds to the *mooladhar chakra*
(b) *Apas or Jala* (water) corresponds to the *svadhistan chakra*
(c) *Agni* (fire) corresponds to the *manipur chakra*
(d) *Vayu* (air) corresponds to the *anahat chakra*
(e) *Akasha* (ether) corresponds to the *vishuddh chakra.*

Panch pranas. It suggests that five major or vital energies form the pranic body. They are: 1. *Pran*—it is the upward moving force of the chest region mainly connected with the function of respiration. It corresponds to the *Anahat chakra* and is denoted by yellow colour; 2. *Apan*—is the downward moving energy of the sacral region connected with the functions of excretion and reproduction. It corresponds to the *Mooladhar chakra* and is orange– red in colour; 3. *Saman*– is the laterally moving energy of the navel region helping in digestive functions. It corresponds to the *Manipur chakra* and is denoted green; 4. *Udan*– is the energy that compress. It is situated mainly at the throat region. It causes deglutition and also separates physical body from astral. Corresponds to the *Vishuddh chakra* and is violet– blue; 5. *Vyan*– is the energy moving in circles in the entire body. It is connected with the circulatory system. Corresponding to the *svadhistan chakra* it is denoted rose in colour. There are five minor *pranas*: 1. *Naga; 2. Kurma; 3. Krikkara; 4. Devadatta and 5. Dhananjay*

Panchjanya: Krishna's conch.

Pandavas: The sons of Pandu. They are Yudhishthir, Arjun, Bhima, Nakul and Sahadeva. Pandu A son of Vyas and one of the widows of Vichitravirya, he is the brother of Dhritarashtra and

Vidur. He is ostensibly the father of the five Pandavas, although in reality they are the sons of various gods.

Parthsarthy: Krishna

Patanjali: The author of the Yog system, one of the six systems of orthodox Hindu philosophy, which deals with concentration and its methods, control of the mind, Samadhi and similar matters.

Paundra: Bhim's conch.

Pitriyana: The Southern Path or Way of the Manes, by which departing souls attain to Chandralok, or the Plane of the Moon.

Parabrahm: Supreme Being or Lord Krishna

Prahlad: The king of the titans, who are not unlike the titans of Greek mythology.

Prajapati: The creator. The Vedic Lord of beings; also known as Brahma, means 'lord of creatures.' In later times, the name was also applied to Vishnu, Shiva, Time personified, the sun, fire, etc. as well as to lesser mythological figures.

Prakriti: Primordial nature; the material substratum of the creation, consisting of Sattva, rajas and tamas.

Pran: The vital breath, which sustains life in a physical body; the primal energy or force, of which other physical forces are manifestation. In the books of Yog, Pran is described as having five modifications, according to its five different functions. These are: *Pran* (the vital energy that controls the breath), *Apan* (the vital energy that carries downward unassimilated food and drink, *Vyan* (the vital energy the pervades the entire body), *Udan* (the vital energy by which the contents of the stomach are ejected through the mouth and the soul is conducted from the body at death), and *Saman* (the vital energy that carries nutrition all through the body). The word *Pran* is also a name of the Cosmic Soul, as endowed with activity.

Pranayama: Control of the breath; one of the disciplines of Yog.

Prarabdha Karma: Action performed in a past life, the fruit of which is being reaped in the present life.

Prayag: Confluence of two or more rivers. It is considered as a holy place, especially when one of the rivers is Ganga.

Pritha: Kunti.

Puranas: Books of Hindu mythology.

Purujit: The brother of Kuntibhoj. Fights on the side of the Pandavas.

Purush: (Lit., person.) A term of Sankhya philosophy denoting Spirit, or the Conscious Principal. The universe evolves from the union of prakriti (nature) and Purush. In Vedant the word also denotes the Soul and the Absolute.

Poorva-Mimansa: One of the six systems of orthodox Hindu philosophy, whose chief exponent was Jaimini. It is based upon the ritualistic portion of the Vedas.

Qualified Non-dualism: A school of Vedant founded by Ramanuj, according to which the soul and nature are modes of Brahm and the individual soul is a part of Brahm.

Rajas: The principle of restlessness or activity in nature.

Rajyog: A system of Yog ascribed to Patanjali, dealing with concentration and its methods, control of the mind, Samadhi and similar matters.

Rakshasas: Member of a class of demigods; monsters.

Ram: This name is shared by many figures in Hindu mythology. The most famous are Parashuram (Ram with the axe, the sixth incarnation of Vishnu), Ramachandra (the seventh incarnation of Vishnu, who killed the demon Ravan), and Balaam (the strong Ram, regarded as the eighth incarnation of Vishnu).

Ramakrishna: A great saint of Bengal, regarded as a Divine Incarnation (A.D. 1836-1886).

Ramanujacharya: A great saint of southern India, the founder of the school of Qualified Non-dualistic Vedant (Ad. 1017-1137).

Rechak: Exhalation of the breath.

Rig: A verse of the Rigved.

Rigved: The earliest Ved, consisting mostly of hymns in praise to the gods.

Rik: Same as Rig.

Rishi: A seer of Truth to whom the wisdom of the Vedas was revealed; a general name for saint or ascetic.

Rudra: Shiva. Means 'roarer, howler.' In the Vedas, he is the god of tempests and the father and ruler of the Rudras and Maruts. It became a name for Shiva in classical Hinduism.

Sachchidananda: (Lit., Existence-Knowledge-Bliss Absolute.) A name of Brahm or Ultimate Reality.

Sadhyas: A class of celestial beings.

Sagun Brahm: (Lit., Brahm with attributes.) The Absolute conceived of as the Creator, Preserver and Destroyer of the universe; corresponds to Isvara, or the Personal God.

Sahadev: The youngest of the five Pandu princes. He is the son of Madri and the reputed son of Pandu, but really the son of the Ashvins. The twin brother of Nakul.

Shaivas: The worshipper of Shiva.

Shakti: Power, generally the Creative Power of Brahm; a name of the Divine Mother in the Hindu religion.

Samadhi: It is the ultimate goal of Yog. It is a mystical experience in which one attains absolute bliss of Atman by means of the mind's merger with Atman.

Saman: A modification of the vital breath, by the action of which nutrition is carried all through the body.

Samaved: The third Ved, consisting of hymns for chanting during rituals. Most of the verses are taken from the Rigved.

Samhita: A section of the Vedas containing the collection of hymns used in the sacrifices; same as Mantra.

Sankhya: One of the six systems of orthodox Hindu philosophy, which teaches that the universe evolves as the result of the union of prakriti (nature) and Purush (consciousness). According to this system, which is attributed to Kapil, there are as many Purushas or units of consciousness, as there are living beings.

Sansar: The relative world; the unceasing round of births and deaths.

Sanjay: A bard and charioteer. He is the narrator of the Bhagavad Geeta.

Shankar: Short for Shankaracharya.

Shankaracharya: One of the greatest saints and philosopher of India, the foremost exponent of Advait Vedant (A.D. 788-820).

Sannyas: The monastic life; the last of the four stages of life. See Ashram.

Sannyasin: A Hindu monk, who renounces the world in order to realize God.

Sat: Reality, Existence.

Sattva: The principle of balance or righteousness. See *Guna.*

Satyaki: Yuyudhan.

Satyalok: The highest world in the universe; the abode of Brahma.

Scorcher of Enemies: A general epithet, used in the Geeta for Arjun and Dhritarashtra.

Shaibya: The king of the Shibis.

Shakuni: Maternal uncle of Duryodhan.

Shankar: Shiva. See also Vishnu. Shankaracharya is also called Shankar.

Shikhandi: A son of Drupad, he was born as a female, but was changed into a male by a Yaksha. In the great war between the Pandavas and the Kauravas, he was instrumental in the killing of Bhishma, but afterwards was himself killed by Ashvathama.

Shishya: An Upanishadic disciple.

Shokum: Grief one experiences when one loses someone he is attached to. This happens because one's attachment to people leads to loss of knowledge that Atman is deathless.

Shruti: Ancient 'revealed' scriptures. Literal meaning is 'that

Turiya: (Lit., the Fourth) A name of the Transcendental Brahm, which both transcends and pervades the three states of waking, drama and deep sleep.

Tyag: Renouncing the fruit of one's action, the second of two pillars of Yog.

Ucchaisravas: Indra's horse. Produced by the churning of the Milk Ocean, and regarded as the archetype and king of horses.

Udan: A modification of the vital breath, by the action of which the contents of the stomach are ejected through the mouth and the soul is conducted from the body at death.

Udgatri Priest: One of the officiating priests in a Vedic sacrifice; his duty was to recite from the Samaved.

Ugrasrava: One of disciples of Vyas who assisted him in compiling the Mahabharat.

Upadhi: A term of Vedant philosophy denoting a limitation imposed upon the Self or upon Brahm through ignorance.

Upanishads: These are also 'revealed' scriptures which are basically opposed to Brahmnism. However, they were incorporated into the Vedic literature as Vedant, the end of the Vedas.

Upasana: Ritualistic worship with meditation.

Ushanas: An ancient sage, in later times identified with Shukra, the teacher of the Asuras (demons).

Uttamauja: One of the warriors in the Mahabharat.

Vaisheshik: One of the six systems of orthodox Hindu philosophy, it was founded by Kanad.

Vaishyas: Vaishya is one of the four varnas of the Hindu social order, whose profession was business and cattle-raising. Krishna belonged to this category of the then social order.

Vaishwanar: Consciousness functioning through the collective gross body in the waking state.

Vajna: Sacrifice, either in the form of an oblation offered to God or of an action performed with a spiritual motive.

Varnashram Dharma: This is the hierarchical class system by which the Brahminic society was divided into four categories arranged in the following order: Brahmins, Kshatriyas, Vaishyas and Shudras. Then there were outcastes, who were outside the pale of the society. They were the *Chandals* called untouchables.

Varun: An Aditya. Varun is one of the oldest of the Vedic gods. He is often regarded as the supreme deity, being styled 'king of the gods' or 'king of both gods and men' or 'king of the universe.'

Vasav: Indra as chief of the Vasus.

Vasudev: Krishna.

Vasuki: One of the three kings of the serpents. See also Ananta.

Vasus: A particular class of gods whose chief was Indra, then later Agni and Vishnu. They are eight Vasus.

Vayu: A epithet of the Cosmic Soul; same as Hiranyagarbha, Pran and Sutratma. Also the god of wind or only wind.

Vedant: (Lit., the essence or the concluding portion of the Vedas.) A system of philosophy ascribed to Vyas, discussed mainly in the Upanishads, the Bhagavad Geeta and the Brahma Sutras. It is one of the six darshanas (perspectives), or schools of Indic philosophy.

Vedantasar: An authoritative treatise on Vedant, ascribed to Sadanand.

Vedas: 'Revealed' ancient scriptures. The collection of sacred hymns and ritual texts that are the earliest scriptures of Hinduism. There four Vedas: Rigved; Yajurved; Samaved, and Atharvaved. Also known as Shrutis, that which were heard.

Vidur: He was the prime minister of Hastinapur and also the uncle of Pandavas and Kauravas.

Vidya: Knowledge; (with capital V) Knowledge leading to Liberation, i.e. to the Ultimate Reality.

Vikarn: A son of Dhritarashtra.

Vinita: One of Kashyap's wives, and the mother of Suparna, Arun, and Garud.

Viraj: An epithet of Sagun Brahm conceived as the aggregate of all physical bodies.

Virat: Consciousness limited or conditioned by the upadhi of the aggregate of gross bodies; an epithet of the Cosmic Soul. An ancient king. The Pandavas, forced to conceal themselves during the thirteenth year of their exile, journeyed to his court and entered his service in various disguises.

Vishayan: Sense objects such as money, wealth, people, power, etc.

Vishnu: One of the principal deities of classical Hinduism, he is regarded as 'the preserver.' Along with Brahma 'the creator' and Shiva 'the destroyer', they constitute the Trimurti, or triad. Although Vishnu comes second in the triad, he is identified with the supreme deity by his worshippers, and was later accorded the foremost place among the Adityas. He allows a portion of his essence to become incarnate on ten principal occasions in order to save the world from various great dangers.

Vishvedevas: A class of gods. Means 'the all-gods.'

Visishtadvait: Qualified Non-dualistic Vedant, as expounded by Ramanujacharya.

***Visva*:** Consciousness functioning through the waking state.

Visve-devas: The name of a particular class of gods.

Vivasvat: The sun. In epic poetry, regarded as the father of Manu Vaivasvat.

Vrishnis: Krishna's tribe (also known as the Yadavas).

Vyan: A modification of the vital breath, by the action of which the vital energy pervades the entire body. See prana.

Vyas: A celebrated mythological sage and author. Often called Vedavyas and regarded as the original compiler and arranger of the Vedas, he is also called Vadarayan, Badarayan, and Dvaipayan. When grown, he retired to the wilderness to lead the life of a hermit, but at his mother's request returned to become the husband of Vichitravirya's two childless widows, with whom he was the father of Dhritarashtra and Pandu. He was also the supposed compiler of the Mahabharat (yet also appears as a character within the epic), the Puranas, and other portions of Hindu sacred literature. But the name Vyas, meaning 'arranger, compiler,' seems to have been given to any great editor or author.

Wolf Belly: Bhima.

Yadav: Krishna, so called because he belonged to the Yadav tribe (also known as the Vrishnis). Also simply a Descendant of Yadu.

Yadu: An ancient hero. Also the name of a country west of the Yamuna River in present Uttar Pradesh.

Yajurved: One of the four Vedas.

Yajus: Same as Yajurved.

Yakshas: A class of supernatural beings, or spirits. Usually regarded as benevolent, but sometimes as malignant.

Yama: The god of death, a Vedic deity.

Yog: This word stems from the word 'yoke.' It means harnessing oneself to a specific task with single-minded concentration. Yog in the Bhagavad Geeta refers to the skill of union with the ultimate reality or the Absolute. Also one of the six *darshanas* (perspectives), or schools of Indic philosophy. The Yog system of philosophy, ascribed to Patanjali, deals with the realization of Truth through concentration of the mind.

Yogi: In the Geeta, most often means 'a master of mental discipline.'

Yogin: One who practices Yog.

Yudhamanyu: A warrior on the side of the Pandavas.

Yudhishthir: The eldest of the five reputed sons of Pandu, but really the child of Kunti by the god Dharma, so he is often called Dharmaputra or Dharmaraj. He ultimately succeeded Pandu as king, first reigning over Indraprastha, and afterwards, when the Kuru princes were defeated, over Hastinapur.

***Yuyudhan**:* A son of Satyak, he is a warrior who fights for the Pandavas.

OM TAT SAT

4

Some Quotes from Eminent Personalities on the Bhagavad Geeta

Albert Einstein— "When I read the Bhagavad-Geeta and reflect about how God created this universe everything else seems so superfluous."

Aldous Huxley— "The Bhagavad-Geeta is the most systematic statement of spiritual evolution of endowing value to mankind. It is one of the clearest and most comprehensive summaries of perennial philosophy ever to have been done; hence its enduring value is subject not only to India but to all of humanity.

Mahatma Gandhi—"When doubts haunt me, when disappointments stare me in the face, and I see not one ray of hope on the horizon, I turn to Bhagavad-Geeta and find a verse to comfort me; and I immediately begin to smile in the midst of overwhelming sorrow. Those who meditate on the Geeta will derive fresh joy and new meanings from it every day."

Henry David Thoreau— "In the morning I bathe my intellect in the stupendous and cosmogonal philosophy of Bhagavat Geeta; since whose composition years of the gods have elapsed, and in comparison with which our modern world and its literature seem puny and trivial."

Dr. Albert Schweitzer— "The Bhagavad-Geeta has a profound influence on the spirit of mankind by its devotion to God which is manifested by actions."

Sri Aurobindo—The Bhagavad-Geeta is a true scripture of the human race a living creation rather than a book, with a new message for every age and a new meaning for every civilization."

Herman Hesse— "The marvel of the Bhagavad-Geeta is its truly beautiful revelation of life's wisdom which enables philosophy to blossom into religion."

Ralph Waldo Emerson— "I owed a magnificent day to the Bhagavad-Geeta. It was the first of books; it was as if an empire spake to us, nothing small or unworthy but large, serene, consistent, the voice of an old intelligence in which in another age and climate had pondered and thus disposed of the questions which exercise us."

Swami Vivekananda— "The Geeta is a bouquet composed of the beautiful flowers of spiritual truths collected from the Upanishads".

Wilhelm von Humboldt—"The most beautiful, perhaps the only true philosophical song existing in any known tongue ... perhaps the deepest and loftiest thing the world has to show."

OM TAT SAT